Also by Lewis L. Gould

Wyoming: A Political History, 1868–1896

Progressives and Prohibitionists: Texas Democrats in the Wilson Era

The Presidency of William McKinley

Lady Bird Johnson and the Environment

The Presidency of Theodore Roosevelt

1968: The Election That Changed America

Reform and Regulation: American Politics from Roosevelt to Wilson

Lady Bird Johnson: Our Environmental First Lady

America in the Progressive Era, 1890–1914

The Modern American Presidency

GRAND
OLD
PARTY

A memorial plaque in Jackson, Michigan, circa 1910, reflects the nationalism and antislavery origins of the party. Both Jackson and Ripon, Wisconsin, claim credit as the location where the Republicans were launched.

GRAND
OLD
PARTY

A History of the Republicans

Lewis L. Gould

Random House • New York

RANDOM HOUSE and colophon are registered trademarks
of Random House, Inc.

Library of Congress Cataloging-in-Publication Data

Gould, Lewis L.
Grand Old Party: a history of the Republicans / Lewis L. Gould.
p. cm.
Includes index.
ISBN 0-375-50741-8
1. Republican Party (U.S.: 1854–)—History. I. Title.

JK2356.G68 2003
324.2734'09—dc21   2003046604

Random House website address: www.atrandom.com
Printed in the United States of America on acid-free paper

2 4 6 8 9 7 5 3 1

First Edition

BOOK DESIGN BY MERCEDES EVERETT

Frontispiece photograph: From the author's collection

To the memory of Herbert F. Margulies

PREFACE AND ACKNOWLEDGMENTS

In 2001, Random House invited me to write a history of the Republican Party from its founding in 1854 through the presidential election of 2000. The prospect of such a book was an intriguing one because my professional involvement with the Grand Old Party as a historical subject extends back to the 1960s when I wrote a dissertation on a Supreme Court justice named Willis Van Devanter, a Republican appointee of William Howard Taft. That project led to a book on the early political history of Wyoming as a territory and state that focused on the career of the state's Republican senator, Francis E. Warren. Subsequent articles explored the role of the Republicans in the late nineteenth and early twentieth centuries.

After a second book on the history of Texas Democrats during the era of Woodrow Wilson, I returned to the Republicans with books on the presidencies of William McKinley (1980) and Theodore Roosevelt (1991), and a study of the presidential election of 1968 (1993) that culminated in the administration of Richard Nixon. Understanding the historical development of the GOP and its evolution into the modern form of the party has thus been one of the central concerns of my scholarly work.

Since I am not a Republican in my personal political views, my interest in the party as a historian may seem odd. Although the inner workings of parties and public policy are not in favor among historians, I came to the profession at a time when the study of this subject was still considered legitimate and appropriate. I was fascinated by politicians and their activities, and that interest has not flagged four decades later. I also believe that it is possible for scholars to write fairly about all aspects of American politics, and I have sought to approach the Republicans in that spirit.

In the case of politicians of any party, it is most fruitful to assume a basic sincerity of their views, to believe that they meant what they said about policy issues, and to judge them by their actions and outcomes, rather than by their assumed motives. Naturally, Republicans and Democrats often fall short of their ideals, but working on the premise that they identified with their stated positions is the most revealing and informative way to proceed.

The narrative that follows takes the Republicans from their antislavery origins in the 1850s through the election of George W. Bush to the presidency in 2000. The story is not a simple one because, like the Democrats, the Republicans have undergone dramatic changes in their stated philosophy as a party during the 150 years of their history. Abraham Lincoln, for example, believed that the United States existed as a nation prior to the creation of the states, and his vigorous nationalism, exemplified during the Civil War, reflected the views of the generation of politicians that abolished slavery and saved the Union. By the 1980s, however, Ronald Reagan was contending that the states pre-dated the federal government, and the proper role of the national government was to cede power back to the states.

The course of Republican history has thus moved from a party of national power to restrict slavery, preserve the Union, and promote business enterprise in the nineteenth century to an organization that, while still pursuing the interests of the business community, favors small government, a greater role for the states, and a suspicion of efforts to use federal power on behalf of African Americans and other minority groups. In the years after 1912, when Theodore Roosevelt's bid for the party's nomination was defeated, the Republicans began to stand against the idea that government should endeavor to regulate the excesses of an industrial society and provide a safety net for all citizens. Creating such institutions to provide minimal social benefits to the population fell to the Democrats during the era of Franklin D. Roosevelt and the New Deal. From that point onward until the 1960s the Republicans were reactive against the rise of labor unions, the expansion of welfare programs, and greater regulation of business.

As the Democrats pressed forward in the 1960s under Lyndon Johnson with the Great Society (involving a war on poverty, Medicare, and expanded civil rights) amid a period of racial turmoil and a foreign war, Republican conservatism found a greater degree of popular favor. The election of Ronald Reagan in 1980 grew out of voter unhappiness with the high taxes and intrusive governmental programs of the Democrats in and out of Congress. Once in office, however, the Republicans found that the electorate resisted efforts to dismantle the New Deal and such popular programs as Social Security. With cuts in taxes now the key doctrine of the Grand Old Party, the Republicans could reduce the revenue stream feeding government programs; they could not remove the causes for the spending itself.

In foreign policy, the Republicans have been by turns imperialistic at the beginning of the twentieth century, isolationist in the 1930s and 1940s, and anti-Communist from the 1950s through the collapse of the Soviet Union in the 1990s. The suspicion of foreign involvement has animated a significant portion of the GOP coalition. Other Republicans want to thrust American power overseas. The tension between these two points of view has remained a key aspect of the party's history since 1900.

A political party that exists for a century and a half as one of the two primary policy alternatives in the nation meets deeply felt needs among the American people. This book attempts to understand what choices the Republicans have offered to the voters, the sources of support for their positions, and the ways in which their leaders have endeavored to put Republican ideas into practice over the years. Criticism of Republican policies and the leaders who pursued them is offered when appropriate, but these comments do not reflect the partisan stance of the adversaries of the GOP at the time or later. Few Democratic voices will be heard throughout the narrative to indict what the Republicans were doing at any point. Simply rehashing the partisan struggles of prior days would not promote informed understanding of what the Republican Party has provided to the long sweep of American politics.

The title of the book reflects the nickname that the Republicans acquired during the 1870s when editorial writers and party advocates first referred to themselves as members of the "Grand Old Party." The phrase was shortened over time to GOP, and it has remained shorthand for the party throughout the twentieth century. By 2002, however, at least one major newspaper, *The Wall Street Journal*, decided to abandon use of GOP because not all of its readers knew what the letters meant. Despite this development, Republicans, commentators, and scholars continue to use the phrase, and it is so identified with the party as to be an indelible part of its legacy.[1]

The symbol of the elephant as the mascot of the party originated from the work of cartoonist Thomas Nast at the same time as the "Grand Old Party" tag. He created the Democratic donkey and the Republican pachyderm for *Harper's Weekly* during the mid-1870s, and subsequent cartoonists found the pairing irresistible. Several cartoons in this book reflect the many ways that artists have used the elephant image to comment on the changing fortunes of the Republicans.[2]

Many individuals contributed to the making of this book, and it is a pleasure to recognize their kindness and support. I first learned about American political history in depth from John Morton Blum and Howard R. Lamar at Yale University during the early 1960s. They were great teachers and excellent scholarly examples. Later, at the University of Texas at Austin, the generous assistance of Clarence G. Lasby and Robert A. Divine helped me extend my interest in the workings of the two major parties. Productive conversations with H. Wayne Morgan enabled me to understand with more precision the role of the Republicans during the Gilded Age.

Throughout my career, R. Hal Williams has shared with unfailing generosity his knowledge of the life and times of James G. Blaine. He also read many chapters of this book and provided timely and thoughtful criticisms. William G. Shade read the opening chapter and gave me the insights based on his deep knowledge of the formative years of the Grand Old Party.

I owe thanks as well to my agent, Jim Hornfischer, for bringing my name to the attention of Random House and for his tireless efforts on my behalf. Don E. Carleton played a vital role in suggesting me as a possible author. Jules Witcover, my colleague in this project of writing modern histories of the Republicans and Democrats, read the chapters on recent GOP history and gave me the benefit of his expertise and insight. Charles Calhoun has been very generous with information from his own extensive research into the thought and actions of Gilded Age Republicans.

The book is dedicated to the memory of a good friend, Herbert F. Margulies of the University of Hawaii. Herb and I had an extensive correspondence about Republicans and their fortunes for almost three decades. In his scholarly work about such progressive Republicans as Robert La Follette and Irvine Lenroot, and in his private letters, he maintained the energy and commitment to gradual change that animated the reformist Republicans he wrote about with such skill and insight.

Richard Buck, whom I met through eBay, allowed me to look at some of the papers of his father, Sheldon Buck, and to use them for part of the conclusion. Michael Bayes of the Republican National Committee facilitated my research through his kindness in providing copies of the proceedings of the party's most recent national conventions.

A number of former students, now pursuing their own teaching careers, provided valuable information and inspiration to my research and writing. Martin Ansell, Thomas Clarkin, Stacy Cordery, Debbie Cottrell, Patrick Cox, Byron Hulsey, Jonathan Lee, Craig Roell, Mark Young, and Nancy Beck Young were indispensable colleagues. I owe thanks as well to Kate Adams, the late John A. Andrew III, Ralph Elder, and Bob Lester.

Patricia Schaub conducted some of the important research for this book and also read large portions of the manuscript to check quotations and citations back to the sources. Her dedication and patience were important elements in the completion of the book.

At Random House, Katie Hall guided me through the initial stages of writing the book. Matt Thornton was a wise and thoughtful editorial presence as the narrative took shape.

Acquiring illustrations for the text led me to call on a number of librarians and archivists for assistance. Dewey Mosby and Diane Butler of the Picker Art Gallery at Colgate University generously shared cartoons in their collections. Jim Detlefsen at the Herbert Hoover Presidential Library, Bonnie Burlbaw at the George Bush Presidential Library, and the staffs at the Library of Congress, the Dwight D. Eisenhower Presidential Library, the Ohio Historical Society, and the Ronald Reagan Library made photographs from their holdings available. The Department of State kindly furnished the photograph of Colin Powell. Michael Gillette at the Center for Legislative Archives at the National Archives, and his associates Matt Fulgham and Jessie Kratz, facilitated my use of the Clifford Berryman cartoons in their collections. Russell James of the Washington Post Writers Group kindly granted permission to use the Berryman cartoons as well. Marilyn Suggett of the Universal Press Syndicate helped me obtain permission to use the Pat Oliphant cartoon. H. Wayne Morgan generously provided photographs that he had used in his own work. Leah Linney and the excellent staff at Kwik-Kopy Printing on Medical Parkway in Austin helped a novice through the process of having images scanned onto disks and CDs.

Dr. Larry Breedlove, Madeline Brock, Christi Eubank, Dr. David Ferguson, Claire Hyder, Ellen Smith, and Dr. Martin Stocker helped me withstand the rigors of writing this book. Dr. Karen Gould read the whole manuscript with great editorial care, listened to comments about Republicans, and encouraged me to keep working on the project at times of her own stress and concern.

Despite the sustained support of all these helpful individuals, I am responsible for any errors of fact or interpretation in this book. Also, the opinions that are expressed are mine, and no one who helped me should be regarded as sharing the conclusions or judgments I have reached. Readers with corrections are encouraged to write me through the publisher, and if a revised, updated edition becomes a reality, their changes will be incorporated in that text.

Lewis L. Gould
Austin, Texas
April 2003

CONTENTS

GRAND
OLD
PARTY

In this Republican cartoon from 1860, Abraham Lincoln, dressed in the military uniform of the Republican "Wide Awake" clubs, approaches the White House as the Constitutional Union candidate, John Bell, warns Stephen A. Douglas, the nominee of the northern Democrats, to open the door to the White House quickly. On the right, President James Buchanan tries to pull in John C. Breckinridge, the candidate of the southern Democrats, as "Breck" warns him of possible disunion.

Chapter 1

THE PARTY OF LINCOLN,
1854–1865

CHICAGO HAD NEVER seen anything like it. Ten thousand Republicans had crammed themselves into a pine-board frame building called the Wigwam to nominate a candidate for president in mid-May 1860. After two days of deliberations about the platform, the enthusiastic delegates turned to the key business of nominations on Friday, May 18. Everyone knew who the front-runners were: William H. Seward of New York and Abraham Lincoln of Illinois. Two or three dark horses were also in the mix. The Illinois crowd clamored for Lincoln; some timely printing of bogus tickets helped inflate the crowd with supporters of "Honest Abe." After Lincoln's name was placed in nomination, the arena exploded with noise. "No language can describe it," said one observer. "A thousand steam whistles, ten acres of hotel gongs, a tribe of Comanches, headed by a choice vanguard from pandemonium, might have mingled in the scene unnoticed."[1]

In the balloting that followed, Seward led Lincoln on the first tally, but neither had the 233 votes needed for nomination. The second ballot produced a big gain for Lincoln; Seward's lead was a scant 3 votes. When it became evident on the third ballot that Seward could not win, Lincoln moved steadily toward a majority as the other contenders fell away. When he reached 231½ votes, four Ohio delegates switched their votes, and Lincoln was then the nominee of the Republican Party. Another tumultuous celebration ensued, while back in Lincoln's hometown of Springfield the new Republican leader was flooded with congratulatory telegrams. The Republicans had become the party of Lincoln.

What made the moment surprising was the rapid rise of both the nominee and his party to political prominence. Six and a half years earlier, in January 1854, the Republican Party did not exist, and Abraham Lincoln was a successful but politically obscure attorney in Springfield. If anyone in Illinois that winter seemed likely to become president, it was the state's Democratic senator, Stephen A. Douglas. Yet with a speed that in retrospect seems incredible and almost preordained, the new party became one of the two major political organizations in the United States.

To Americans in the 1850s the chain of events that led to the rise of the Republicans and the Lincoln presidency was fueled by the crisis over human slavery that convulsed the nation. Twists and turns, unexpected episodes, and some plain historical luck enabled the Republicans to survive the turbulent circumstances of their early years and put Lincoln in the White House in 1860. Once in power, the party that had begun as an effort to restrict the further expansion of slavery found itself involved in a major war that required an unprecedented expansion of governmental power for victory. At the same time, the struggle with the South posed the problem of how to structure a multiracial society after the fighting ended. That dilemma would divide the country and shape the destiny of the Republicans for the next century and a half.

AMERICA IN 1854

> The dispersion of the old parties was one thing, but the organization of their fragments into a new one on a just basis was quite a different thing.
>
> —George W. Julian[2]

The Republican Party came into being in a United States that was still an agricultural and rural nation. Census takers counted 23 million people in 1850; the figure rose to 26 million four years later. There were thirty-one states, with California on the West Coast as the most recent addition. The bulk of the population lived east of the Mississippi River, and most Americans still made their living off the land through farming or raising livestock. Industrialization and urbanization had made beginnings in the North, and these forces accelerated during the 1850s. In Lincoln's Illinois, for example, the 110 miles of railroad track in the early 1850s expanded to nearly 2,900 miles by the end of the decade.

Economic times were good. The discovery of gold in California in 1848 and an influx of British investment into the United States fueled a robust economic expansion. Railroad building surged as money poured into the new industry. With immigration climbing as well, the country had a growing, hardworking labor force in the North. So dramatic was this rise in prosperity that some commentators predicted an end to the partisan issues that had shaped national politics for two decades: the wisdom of having a national bank, the merits of a protective tariff, and the constitutionality of internal improvements such as canals, wagon roads, and railroads. As a Maryland capitalist wrote about the Democrats and the Whigs that had battled since the 1830s, "The great dividing lines between the two old parties are fast melting away—and such changes are taking place in the world, that, issues formerly momentous are now of comparatively trifling importance."[3]

Yet Americans knew that beneath the surface the United

States was a troubled land. The tide of immigration in the 1850s exacerbated social tensions. In 1853, 369,000 people arrived from overseas. Almost half were newcomers from Ireland; another 141,000 were of German origin. Immigration peaked in 1854 with 427,000 individuals entering the country. The Irish, because of their Roman Catholic faith, and many of the Germans, also Catholics, aroused fears among native-born Protestants who remembered the Reformation, disapproved of the elaborate rituals, and worried about the fealty of devout Catholics to the papacy. These new Americans usually aligned themselves with the Democrats, who were seen as more culturally tolerant than their major rivals, the Whigs.

In the 1850s, religious beliefs and national origin often shaped voting decisions as much as economic class and social status. These ethnocultural pressures showed themselves in the reaction against the tide of immigrants. So large had been the arrival of newcomers and so powerful had been their impact on local and state politics in New York, Pennsylvania, and Massachusetts, for example, that native voters reacted against the immigrant presence with laws to mandate the teaching of English in public schools, the closing of saloons on Sundays, and the prohibition of alcohol. The vehicle for these antiforeign impulses became a new political party that emphasized secrecy in its opposition to both immigrant and Catholic influence. When asked about their organization, members were told to say, "I know nothing," a phrase that gave the movement its name. Know-Nothings, or the Native Americans, as they were sometimes called, picked up followers during the first half of the 1850s at a rate that stunned politicians. "At the bottom of all this," remarked a Pennsylvania Democrat, "is a deep-seated religious question—prejudice if you please, which nothing can withstand." Many public figures hoped or feared that the Know-Nothings might replace the embattled Whigs as the primary alternative to the Democrats.[4]

THE PECULIAR INSTITUTION

> Commerce and political power, as well as military strength, can never permanently reside, on this continent, in a community where slavery exists.
>
> —William H. Seward[5]

Even more troubling to many people in the North was the presence of human slavery in the South. There were 3.2 million men, women, and children in bondage in the South in 1850, and the "peculiar institution," as the South referred to slavery, dominated every aspect of life in the fifteen slave states that stretched across the South from Maryland and Delaware to Texas. Law, custom, and the Constitution meant that slavery also wove its way through American government and daily life. Northerners understood that by law they must help return fugitive slaves to their owners in the South and that slavery could not be eliminated without changing the Constitution. Though the issue had quieted since the approval of the Compromise of 1850, feelings remained volatile. Harriet Beecher Stowe's novel, *Uncle Tom's Cabin,* became an instant best-seller in 1852 in the North for its depiction of the cruelties of slavery and their impact on a mother and her family.

The South saw slavery not as a moral burden on the nation or an evil to be expunged, but more and more as a positive good for both master and slave. The southern states, said a Texas editor in 1861, "have for centuries fostered the institution of slavery, which has resulted in the Christianizing of that portion of the African race and in making them useful members of society, in restraining them in the only position that is congenial to their natures and for which they are fitted intellectually and morally." As a result, many leading southerners believed that they should have the right to take their human property wherever they wished. Efforts to restrict slavery or limit its expansion, said many southerners, would justify secession from the Union.[6]

The North was more divided. Slavery had receded from the

region by 1853, but northerners did not have a coherent view of the institution's future. Radical abolitionists, a definite minority, opposed slavery on moral grounds. Others disliked slavery because its spread might bring blacks into the North and West as competitive cheap labor. In 1848, northern opponents of slavery established a Free-Soil Party that sought to block the spread of slavery in the West. Still others, driven by racist impulses, wanted African Americans to stay in the South or be returned to Africa. Whatever their attitudes toward slavery, residents of the North often resented the South's political power and regarded the land below the Mason-Dixon line as backward, out of step with progressive currents of the nineteenth century. An uneasy sectional peace, based on the Missouri Compromise of 1820 and the Compromise of 1850, existed as 1854 began.

These two historic sectional bargains defined the way in which Americans viewed the politics of slavery as the 1850s began. In 1820, Congress had decided, after heated debates, to admit the new state of Missouri as one where slavery existed, and Maine as one where it did not. In the rest of the territory gained from the Louisiana Purchase of 1803, slavery would be barred north of a line running along 36 degrees, 30 minutes of latitude. Conscious of themselves as sections divided by slavery, North and South accepted this arrangement for three decades. But in the wake of the Mexican War, another crisis threatened over the fate of the western land obtained from that victorious conflict. Lawmakers decided to let California enter the Union as a free state, to leave the fate of slavery in the rest of the new territories in limbo for the time being, and to strengthen the right of the South to capture and return fugitive slaves from the North. Neither side was really mollified by the settlement, but most moderate Americans agreed that the Compromise of 1850 maintained the sectional balance and extended the principles of the Missouri Compromise. Undoing these compromises would plunge the nation into renewed turmoil.

THE POLITICAL SYSTEM

> Under our system of government there will always be parties of some kind and the interests of the people will be better subserved, and their rights more securely maintained with the checks and balances afforded by two great permanent opposing parties, than by the substitution of numberless smaller factions.
>
> —*Kennebec Journal*
> Augusta, Maine[7]

American politics responded to these conflicting pressures. At the time and for much of the rest of the nineteenth century, partisan warfare occupied much more of the nation's attention than would be true a century and a half later. Frequent elections kept voters attuned to the fortunes of their party. Allegiance to a party defined the lives of most male voters; independents represented only a small portion of the electorate. Participation in elections occurred at rates that would be unthinkable now. Turnouts of eligible voters in the North regularly exceeded seventy percent. Parties were not scorned as corrupt institutions but valued for their role in democracy. "Party is the great engine of human progress," said one northern Democrat in 1852. Loyalty to a party was essential and, as a result, "to forsake a party is regarded as an act of greatest dishonour."[8]

Interest in elections and press coverage of politics was intense. Newspapers did not pretend to be objective dispensers of information. Owned by partisans, they slanted reporting and editorials to advance party fortunes. Yet overall coverage of conventions, rallies, and speeches was far more detailed and elaborate than at present. In effect, there were hundreds of partisan newspapers, the C-SPANS of their day, keeping voters up to date on the latest successes or failures of the party.

Meanwhile, voters and their families attended "mass meetings" and political rallies where speakers might go on for an hour or two. Such events often lasted all day and into the night, with meal breaks. Audiences were well informed on the issues and expected a sophisticated treatment of contemporary concerns. Orators had to have the complexities of their subject at their command, whether it was slavery in the territories, the merits of a protective tariff, or the constitutionality of a national bank. No one used speechwriters, and an orator's thoughts on the stump were very much his own. "What the theatre is to the French, or the bull-fight or fandango to the Spanish, the hustings and the ballot-box are to our people. We are all politicians, men, women, and children."[9]

On the surface, the United States had a working two-party system in 1854 with the Democrats in power and the Whigs as their main opposition. The Democrats in the mid–nineteenth century were the party of small, limited government and of white supremacy. They did not believe that the national government should be in the business of sponsoring economic growth through canal construction, road building, or railroad promotion. Accordingly, their platform in 1852 opposed "a general system of internal improvements," promised "the most rigid economy in conducting our public affairs," and asserted that Congress had no power to interfere with slavery in the South. Well established in the North and strong in the South, the Democrats (or the "Democracy," as they were sometimes called) had the stronger national base of the two parties. However, sectional divisions within the Democracy over slavery meant that there were in the North potential recruits for an antislavery party among unhappy Democrats. The Democrats were more fragile than they seemed even after the landslide election of Franklin Pierce in 1852.[10]

The Whigs, meanwhile, had fallen into disarray after 1852. The party had originated during the turbulent politics of the Jacksonian era when opponents of Andrew Jackson adopted the term "Whig" to evoke memories of the antimonarchical party in England. "King Andrew" united many men against his strong presidential leadership between 1829 and 1837. Democrats applauded what Jackson had done with his authority to prevent government excesses. As a result, suspicion of executive power was one Whig tradition that carried over to the Republicans.

So, too, were the Whig economic policies associated with "The American System" of Henry Clay of Kentucky. That program advocated the use of government power to promote the growth of enterprise through a protective tariff, a national bank, sale of public lands, and internal improvements. Whigs stressed the common interests of society and contended that their policies helped all classes. Yet the identification of the Whigs with business and commercial interests led the Democrats to accuse them of being the party of the rich. But throughout the 1830s and 1840s the Whigs were credible rivals to the Democrats in both the North and the South.

As the slavery issue came more to the fore, the Whigs found themselves more and more divided between their northern and southern wings. Their platform labeled slavery a dangerous issue in 1852 but said little more than that the sectional compromises should be maintained. The decisive defeat of the Whig nominee in 1852 raised serious doubts about whether the Whigs could survive. That candidate had been Winfield Scott, a Mexican War hero, but unlike William Henry Harrison in 1840 and Zachary Taylor in 1848, he had suffered a stunning defeat in the electoral vote of 254 for Pierce to 42 for Scott. Although the Whig candidate's popular vote total trailed Pierce's by only 200,000 ballots, the party's fortunes were declining.

Partisan allegiances were still strong in the early 1850s, but the old party system was fractured and its responsiveness to national concerns questionable. Local issues of prohibition of alcohol and nativist sentiments against immigrants shaped politics in individual northern states. Meanwhile, the policy questions and, more important, key Whig platform ideas that had dominated the 1830s and 1840s seemed antiquated. As industry grew, the need for a protective tariff ebbed. With money abundant, the national bank became a dead issue. "Without any present questions of political importance to preserve the old lines of parties," said a Pennsylvania editor in 1853, "parties yet preserve the old

names which prove convenient vehicles to convey certain individuals to places of trust and distinction and emolument."[11]

The Kansas-Nebraska Act

> The Nebraska bill is but the first . . . step in this compre-
> hensive plan of Africanizing the whole of the American
> hemisphere, and establishing Slavery upon what its ad-
> vocates regard as an impregnable basis.
>
> —*New York Tribune*[12]

On January 4, 1854, however, American politics took a dramatic
turn that eradicated the Whig Party, split the Democrats, and
enabled the Republicans to come into being. The clamor over
the Kansas-Nebraska Act thrust the slavery question to the forefront of the national debate. Senator Stephen A. Douglas, an Illinois Democrat, reported out of his committee a bill in Congress
to organize the western territory of Nebraska. The measure
soon became legislation to create the territories of Kansas and
Nebraska. What made it so explosive was the attitude of the legislature and Douglas toward the future of slavery in the area and
therefore in the nation as a whole.

The Missouri Compromise of 1820 specified that slavery
would be outlawed north of the line of 36 degrees, 30 minutes.
Although Missouri was admitted to the Union as a slave state,
the territory west and north of its southern border was closed to
bondage. The firm dividing line between slave and nonslave territory that the Compromise established was popular in the
North. As time passed, more and more southerners regarded
the restriction of slavery on the basis of a geographic line as an
unfair limit on their ability to take their property wherever slavery might prosper.

The Compromise of 1850, in addition to admitting California as a free state and toughening the law on the return of fugitive slaves, dealt with the question of how the area acquired from
Mexico after that war should be organized into territories and

states. The Compromise legislation stated "that, when admitted as a State, the said Territory, or any portion of the same, shall be received into the Union with or without slavery, as their Constitution may prescribe at the time of their admission." Since most of the Mexican cession lay below the Missouri Compromise line in areas where the growth of plantation slavery seemed difficult, this approach did not unduly rile northern feelings. In addition, because of Mexican law, the territory did not have slavery.[13]

But in the case of Kansas and Nebraska, the situation was entirely different. The proposed territories were above the Missouri Compromise line, and when Douglas used the language of the Compromise of 1850 in his legislation, he was in effect abrogating the 1820 settlement and opening these areas to slavery. To make his point explicit, Douglas was forced to add wording which stated that the Missouri Compromise restriction "is hereby declared null and void." As a northern Democrat who believed that climate made slavery ill-suited for the western plains, Douglas saw the bill as a way to conciliate the South without giving up anything of real substance. The people of the new territories themselves would decide whether to have slavery or not, a doctrine that was known as "popular sovereignty." Douglas did not like slavery as such, but he saw no moral issue involved since in his mind African Americans were a lesser order of human beings with few of the rights of their white counterparts.[14]

Because it subverted the Missouri Compromise that many in the North regarded as a solemn sectional bargain and a way of confining slavery to the South, the Kansas-Nebraska Act ignited a firestorm of criticism in the North during the first half of 1854. By the time the southern Democrats and allies of Douglas enacted the Kansas-Nebraska Act into law on May 30, 1854, protest meetings and political upheaval convulsed the North.

THE REPUBLICAN PARTY IS LAUNCHED

> That in view of the necessity of battling for the first prin-
> ciples of republican government, and against the
> schemes of aristocracy the most revolting and oppressive
> with which the earth was ever cursed, we will co-operate
> and be known as Republicans until the contest is termi-
> nated.
>
> —Platform of the Michigan Republicans, 1854[15]

In two states, protesting citizens from both the Democratic and
Whig Parties, outraged at the implications of what Douglas was
proposing about slavery in the territories, began to shape a new
political party almost at once. Antislavery sentiment was strong
in Wisconsin and Michigan while nativist sentiments were not
as powerful. At Ripon, Wisconsin, on February 28, a coalition
of dissident Democrats, Whigs, and members of the Free-Soil
Party vowed to create a new "Republican" Party if the Kansas-
Nebraska Act became law. This action represented one of the
earliest uses of the name Republican for a political organization.
Their second meeting on March 20, 1854, is often called the
birth of the Republican Party. Michigan's claims to primacy as
the Republican birthplace rest on a state convention in Jackson,
Michigan, that gathered on July 6, 1854, nominated candidates
for state office, and wrote a platform for the campaign.[16]

Why did the name "Republican" gain such favor? Simply as
a title, it connected voters with the original political organization
of Thomas Jefferson in the 1790s, the Democratic-Republican
Party. Tying the new party to the framer of the Declaration of Independence underlined the commitment of northerners to doctrines of political equality and expanding economic opportunity.
In a broader context, "Republicanism" tapped into a rich historical tradition dating back to the Italian renaissance and the
English revolution that saw republics as embodying public-
spirited citizens acting in the political sphere to preserve civic
virtue and the welfare of all. There was a strong ethical strain in

Republicanism that accorded well with attacks on slavery as both unjust and menacing to free labor in the North.

The problem for antislavery northerners in 1854 and 1855 was not how to create a new party in an institutional sense. Most men knew from their own experience as Democrats or Whigs how a party was organized. The key was the system of conventions at all levels where white male voters took part in elections. In a precinct or election district, partisans assembled in a convenient meeting place where they picked candidates, created platforms, and debated issues. Their most important function was choosing delegates to a convention at the next level of the congressional or judicial district. At the top was the state convention that set policy for the party until the next election or the next convention.

Every four years the process culminated in a national convention to select a presidential candidate. These gatherings did not simply ratify a selection already made in preferential primaries (which did not exist as such in the 1850s) but selected a nominee for the party after a series of multiple ballots. Convention strategies evolved based on what convention delegates from around the nation would do on a second, third, or fourth ballot. Republicans wisely never adopted the Democratic rule that a winning candidate had to receive the ballots of two-thirds of the delegates.

Putting a party organization together was easily done once a sufficient number of like-minded men agreed to act in concert. The problem for those who wanted a northern party devoted to curbing slavery in 1854–55 was the Know-Nothings. They provided an alluring alternative for voters who were unhappy with the Democrats and their policies, and they attracted voters that the new Republicans needed to become a viable national party. The Know-Nothings (or the Americans, as they now called themselves) contended that the menace of immigrant voters loyal to the Roman Catholic Church and antagonistic to American values posed a greater danger to the nation than slavery or southern aggression. Before the Republicans could become a vi-

able rival to the Democrats, they had to extinguish the hopes of
the Know-Nothings.

The Republicans accomplished this feat in 1855–56, thanks
in part to Know-Nothing divisions over slavery and better leadership that outfought their adversaries in key northern states.
Nonetheless, the success of the new party was not preordained.
The fragility of the Republicans was one reason that a man such
as Abraham Lincoln did not enlist immediately in their ranks in
1854. Other antislavery parties had flourished briefly and then
died. Until Lincoln and men like him were sure that the Whigs
were indeed doomed, they kept their political options open.

The political tide in 1854 ran strong against the Democrats.
Lincoln spoke out against Douglas and the Kansas-Nebraska Act
on October 16, 1854, at Peoria, Illinois. He objected to the new
law "because it assumes that there *can* be *moral right* in the en-
slaving of one man by another." Lincoln conceded that public
opinion and his own views would not allow for freeing the slaves
and making them, "politically and socially, our equals." But he
believed that what Douglas had done contradicted the promise
of the Declaration of Independence. "Our republican robe is
soiled, and trailed in the dust," he concluded. "Let us repurify
it. Let us turn and wash it white, in the spirit, if not the blood of
the Revolution."[17]

The elections showed that the Whigs were essentially dead.
Their candidates failed, and the Republicans received much of
the antislavery protest vote. But it was not yet clear that the
Republicans could surpass the Know-Nothings in the North.
Indeed, events in 1855 seemed to indicate that the Know-
Nothings would have an edge over the Republicans in the contest for voter support. Although Republicans joined with the
Know-Nothings in Ohio to achieve a victory, elsewhere, running
on their own, the Republicans suffered defeats. As one disgruntled Massachusetts Republican remarked in November 1855,
anti-Irish and anti-Catholic voters in his state "want a Paddy
hunt & on a Paddy hunt they will go."[18]

These comments attested to the problem that the Republicans faced in overcoming the desire of many northerners to pursue ethnic tensions rather than antislavery ends. The animus against Irish immigrants permeated a society where Protestant values seemed threatened by social and economic change. Many nativists saw these newcomers as unwilling to adapt to American political customs. "It is the prevailing and besetting sin of Irishmen that when they come to America they will not become *Americans*, but persist in remaining *Irishmen*, with all the crotchets and absurdities which their national education has given them," said the *Chicago Tribune*, an opponent of Irish immigration. The ease with which immigrants could vote raised the specter of undue influence at the polling place as well. The Catholic Church appeared to large numbers of voters as a menace at least as potent as the South and slavery.[19]

THE PRESIDENTIAL ELECTION OF 1856

> By great odds the most effective deliverance made by any man to advance the Republican party was made by the bludgeon of Preston S. Brooks.
>
> —Alexander K. McClure[20]

Republican fortunes improved during the first half of 1856. They elected Nathaniel Banks, a former Know-Nothing, as Speaker of the House of Representatives by combining with the Know-Nothings in Congress and thus established their first national base. In May, incidents in widely separated parts of the country further boosted the Republicans. On May 21, a proslavery mob attacked the town of Lawrence, Kansas, a center of sentiment to make Kansas a free state, in what the Republicans called the "sack of Lawrence." The next day a more celebrated episode occurred in the United States Senate. Charles Sumner, a Massachusetts Republican and a passionate foe of slavery, had denounced, in personal terms, a senator from South Carolina during debate. A relative of the southern solon, Congressman Preston Brooks, attacked Sumner with a heavy rubberlike cane and beat him into submission. The episode outraged moderate northern opinion as an example of southern aggression. "*Brooks* has knocked the scales from the eyes of the blind, and they now *see!*" observed a Vermont Republican.[21]

Coming only a month before the Republicans held their first national convention in Philadelphia, these traumatic events offered encouragement to the young party about potential victory in the fall. The Republicans nominated the popular western explorer John C. Fremont as their presidential candidate and hoped to ride his celebrity into the White House. Their platform was explicit about their efforts to curb slavery. The delegates denied the right of Congress to sanction slavery in the territories. Instead, it was the "imperative duty" of Congress to "prohibit in the Territories those twin relics of barbarism—Polygamy and Slavery." The Mormons in Utah practiced multiple marriages to the dismay of Republicans. The main thrust of the convention was indicated in the party's new slogan: "Free Speech, Free Press, Free Men, Free Labor, Free Territory, and Fremont."[22]

To win the contest the Republicans now confronted a problem about electoral votes that recurred over the next century. With 296 electoral votes in contention, the Democrats had a virtual lock on the slave South and could thus rely on 112 electoral votes before any ballots were tallied. The Republicans had to find their majority of the electoral college from the remaining 184 votes among northern states. A state such as Pennsylvania, with 27 electoral votes, thus became a key battleground between the Republicans and Democrats. Fremont and his party did well in 1856, but the Democratic nominee, James Buchanan, and his party carried Pennsylvania, New Jersey, and several other northern states, to amass 174 electoral votes to 114 for Fremont. Millard Fillmore, a former president and candidate of the Know-Nothings, won Maryland's 8 electoral votes. The Know-Nothing Party faded from the national scene as a political force after 1856, although the voters it had enlisted remained important in Republican calculations. They had lost the presidency, but the Republicans were pleased with their strong showing in the North. They looked forward to 1860 with anticipation. As one Maine Republican commented: "We are beaten, but we have frightened the rascals awfully."[23]

The Republicans now faced the question of how to win the next presidential election. Opposition to slavery had built a strong base for their new organization, but would it be enough to win the next election? Republican efforts to broaden their base to attract more votes in the North had aroused some of the most intense historical criticism of any aspect of the Republican record. In attempting to secure support through economic appeals such as the protective tariff, for example, were the Republicans demonstrating that they were really more interested in political power than the moral issues that had brought the party into being? The question of Republican attitudes toward race and their capacity to measure up to standards of justice and equity has been a point of contention since the late 1850s.

REPUBLICANS AND RACE

> We do not say that the black man is, or shall be, the equal of the white man; or that he shall vote or hold office, however just such a position may be; but we assert that he who murders a black man shall be hanged; that he who robs a black man of his liberty or property shall be punished like other criminals.
>
> —Joshua Giddings[24]

The underlying problem of Republican sincerity and morality on racial issues goes deeper. Democrats at the time and historians since then have questioned whether the Republicans in the 1850s were sincere opponents of slavery, whether their underlying motives were genuine and based on an honest belief in equality, and whether the Civil War that broke out in 1861 was worth the blood and sacrifice that ensued. The even larger question turns on the issue of race, a problem that runs through the record of the major political parties for all of their history. In the case of the Republicans, the test has been whether their opposition to human bondage looked forward to the racial egalitarianism of the twentieth century. A fair answer must be "Yes and no," depending on which Republicans are examined for the 1850s and 1860s. While even in the nineteenth century it was correct to call the Republicans "the party of freedom," the label requires some clearer definition in light of the racial attitudes of that period.

The United States in the 1850s was a nation where color and ethnic prejudices ran deep. Belief in the concept of the common humanity of all people did not yet exist. Instead, white Americans thought that they were naturally superior to blacks, Native Americans, Mexicans, and Orientals. Racial stereotypes, crude jokes, and insulting images pervaded the culture. Those who dared to think that all human beings ought to have political and legal rights were a small minority in the North.

As a result, expressions of racial prejudice show up in the private and public statements of Republicans. "I want to have nothing to do with the free negro or the slave negro," contended Lyman Trumbull. Another party leader said in 1858 that "it is certainly the wish of every patriot that all within the limits of our Union should be homogeneous in race and of our own blood." The most famous such statement, of course, was that of Abraham Lincoln in his fourth debate with Stephen A. Douglas on September 18, 1858: "I am not nor ever have been in favor of making voters or jurors of negroes, nor of qualifying them to hold office, nor to intermarry with white people; and I will say in addition to this that there is a physical difference between the white and black races which I believe will for ever forbid the two races living together on terms of social and political equality."[25]

Southerners and Democrats in the 1850s, and many historians since, have used such statements either to indict the Republicans for insincerity and hypocrisy or to accuse them of having other motives for their opposition to slavery. These goals allegedly include a desire to keep blacks in the South as slaves or wage laborers and thus advance capitalism. More powerful has been the charge that simple antisouthernism fueled the Republican dislike for slavery. The new party is said to have exploited conspiracy fears in the North and thus transformed the South into a pro-slavery monolith that never existed. The Republicans could then evoke the menace of an internal threat to American liberties for their own political purposes. The Slave Power, wrote *The New York Times*, "will stop at no extremity of violence in order to subdue the people of the Free States and force them into a tame subservience to its own domination."[26]

To judge Republican attitudes on race without including the views of either northern Democrats or southerners leaves the misleading impression that if only Republicans had adopted egalitarian positions and been less prejudiced their political success would have been secure. The opposite is in fact the case. One constant that Republicans confronted was the intensity of northern prejudice against blacks that Democrats exploited endlessly. Stephen A. Douglas said in 1858, for example: "I do not question Mr. Lincoln's conscientious belief that the negro was made his equal and hence is his brother, but for my own part, I do not regard the negro as my equal and positively deny that he is my brother or any kin to me whatever." No Democrat ever received a rebuke from his party leaders for going too far in bigotry, and the South was even less restrained.[27]

The Republicans were opposing majority opinion in the North when they asserted that slavery needed to be restricted and that the fate of slaves affected the nature of the Union. When a leader such as Lincoln made the case that free Negroes in the North were human beings who were entitled to the opportunities of the Declaration of Independence, his opinions represented a significant advance in what society would do for African Americans in terms of legal rights. Republicans still contended that blacks should not be allowed to vote or hold office, but in the exercise of other political and legal rights they should be treated as all other citizens were. Such a stance might seem modest in light of the more enlightened racial views of the twenty-first century, but in the context of the mid–nineteenth century it represented a significant change in the nation's racial practices.

Two other issues have clouded the reputation of Republicans during this period of their history. If slavery was on the decline as an unprofitable institution and would have disappeared in due course, then Republican attempts to restrict it were not needed and made the situation worse, or so runs the argument. To the contrary, Republicans believed that slavery was dynamic and expanding, and much modern scholarship bears out their claim. While hypothetical scenarios are unprovable, there is strong evidence from the economic behavior of slaveholders that if the Civil War had not intervened, bondage could have prospered and been adapted to industrial conditions that would have kept it going for many decades.

The second problem relates to Republican fears about the "Slave Power" in the South and whether southern politicians were as determined to protect slavery and imperil the Union as many northerners believed. That there was not a vast web of conspiracy across the South is, of course, correct. But there was a consensus among southern political leaders and their constituents that slavery deserved the right to become a nationwide institution. Accordingly, southern leaders acted in concerted ways, both in and out of Congress, to ensure that the peculiar institution was protected by law and custom. When this regional agenda was pursued after 1854, the North saw in operation an attitude from the South that insisted on northern deference to the right of slavery to exist, expand, and in the end become established everywhere in the United States. As Abraham Lincoln said of the South in 1860, "Holding, as they do, that slavery is morally right, and socially elevating, they cannot cease to demand a full national recognition of it, as a legal right, and a social blessing."[28]

A judgment on Republican ideology on the slavery question turns in the end on whether the Civil War was justified as a means of preserving the Union and abolishing slavery. It is easy to assert that some way of ending slavery and avoiding disunion

without the death of 600,000 men in combat should have occurred. Critics of the Republicans in this regard do not face the
question of why black Americans should have been asked to endure more decades of bondage and its cruelties as their contri-
bution to the preservation of the Union in 1860–65. On this
issue, for all their lapses into racial prejudice, political equivocation, and poor judgment on specific aspects of the sectional crisis, the Republican Party was on the right side of the historical
argument in the 1850s, and its opponents were not. Modern Republicans who find appeal in the neo-Confederate arguments
for states' rights and limited government separate themselves
from the founding traditions and moral high ground of their
party.

During 1857 a series of striking events boosted Republican
fortunes. The Supreme Court on March 6, 1857, decided in the
Dred Scott case that Congress lacked the power to keep slavery
out of the territories. The ruling intensified Republican fears
that the "Slave Power" might, through a court ruling, validate
slavery nationwide. The ongoing struggle over Kansas as a free
or slave state split the Democrats between the forces of Douglas
and President Buchanan. The new administration generally favored the claims of southerners to take their slaves into Kansas
and establish the institution there. Moreover, Republicans saw in
the tactics of the Buchanan administration and the South to
make Kansas a slave state further evidence of the existence of a
conspiracy to nationalize bondage. When a severe economic
downturn began in October 1857, the depression that it triggered lasted for four years and added to the woes of the Democrats.

As a result, Republicans looked forward to the 1858 congressional elections with confidence. To capitalize on the discontent from hard times, the new party advocated a protective tariff
and homestead legislation to encourage western settlement.
With the tide of events running their way, the Republicans made
important gains. They did well in Pennsylvania, an important
state in the 1860 contest, and also won victories in such crucial

states as New York and Ohio. Overall, the party was attracting conservative voters in the North to their cause.

The Rise of Abraham Lincoln

> The great battle of the next Presidential election is now being fought in Illinois.
>
> —*Richmond Enquirer,* August 10, 1858[29]

The election of 1858 produced one of its most important results in Illinois where Abraham Lincoln ran against Stephen A. Douglas for the United States Senate. The seven debates that the two men conducted have become legendary in American political history. For the Republicans, the confrontation was decisive because it thrust their greatest leader and most potent political symbol onto the national stage and on his way to the presidency in 1860.

Abraham Lincoln was forty-nine in 1858, and at the beginning of the year would have seemed an improbable presidential candidate. After an impoverished youth, he had made his way as a lawyer in Springfield, Illinois, and gained a reputation as a dedicated member of the Whig Party in the 1830s and 1840s. Following a single congressional term in 1847–49, he had returned to Springfield where he prospered and, with his wife, Mary Todd Lincoln, raised their three sons. Lincoln had sought a United States Senate seat in 1855 but had lost in the balloting of the Illinois legislature.

Though his record as an officeholder was sparse, Lincoln became recognized during the mid-1850s as an articulate champion of the policy of restricting slavery in the territories. He hated slavery as an institution but accepted that Congress lacked the power to abolish its existence in the South. Believing that slavery contradicted the promises of the Declaration of Independence, Lincoln contended that both North and South should agree to place it "in the course of ultimate extinction." To that end, Lincoln favored schemes to colonize former slaves in

Africa. At this stage of his life, Lincoln did not see a viable future for blacks in the United States, but neither did he have any practical answers for their situation when and if slavery ended.[30]

For the moment, Lincoln's goal was his own political future and the defeat of Senator Douglas. As the Illinois senator broke with President Buchanan over Kansas, some eastern Republicans, such as the editor of the *New York Tribune,* Horace Greeley, looked to a possible alliance with Douglas and a union of Republicans and antislavery Democrats. In Lincoln's mind, Douglas's moral indifference to the evils of slavery disqualified him for such a political partnership. During the debates, Lincoln sought to draw a bright line between himself and Douglas over the issue of restricting slavery. His famous "house divided" speech of June 16, 1858, kicked off his Senate campaign with the statement that " 'a house divided against itself cannot stand.' I believe that this government cannot endure permanently half *slave* and half *free.*" Either slavery would be put on the road to extinction "or its *advocates* will push it forward, till it shall become lawful in *all* the States, old as well as *new—North* as well as South."[31]

Lincoln pressed the argument during the seven debates that slavery presented a moral issue for the United States that could not be evaded. If the institution was not restricted, it would expand. As the primary social evil in the nation, it must be confined and eventually eliminated. When Douglas labeled him an advocate of social and political equality with blacks, Lincoln responded with the language his critics have so often identified as racist. Yet, had Lincoln espoused broader rights for African Americans in the United States of 1858, he would have had no political future. The difference between Lincoln and Douglas was that the Republican senatorial candidate did not rule out that black people should have the opportunity to better themselves through their own efforts. "I agree with Judge Douglas he [a black man] is not my equal in many respects—certainly not in color, perhaps not in moral or intellectual endowment. But in the right to the bread, without leave of anybody else, which his

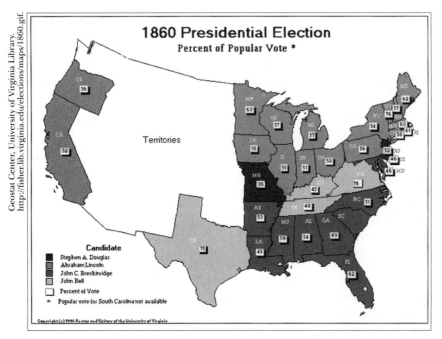

This 1860 electoral map shows the sectional split when Lincoln was elected.

own hand earns, *he is my equal and the equal of Judge Douglas and the equal of every living man.*"[32]

THE 1860 PRESIDENTIAL ELECTION

> Upon no organization, except the republican party, can the country rely for successful resistance to these monstrous propositions, and for the correction of the gross abuses which have characterized the present national administration.
>
> —Republican circular, 1859[33]

Although Lincoln lost the senatorial election to Douglas, his performance in the debates fueled talk of a presidential candidacy throughout 1859. The apparent front-runner for the nomination was William H. Seward of New York, a party leader identified with the antislavery cause in the popular mind. In a famous speech, Seward had predicted an "irrepressible conflict" between North and South. Yet Seward was weak where Lincoln was strong. The New Yorker had denounced nativism, which did not sit well with former Know-Nothings. Republicans grumbled that Seward could not win in the five northern states that had gone for Buchanan and the Democrats in 1856 and were essential for Republican victory in 1860.[34]

Lincoln, on the other hand, while opposed to the Know-Nothings, had not said much to alienate them. He could carry Illinois and perhaps Pennsylvania where Seward could not. Lincoln appeared sound on slavery without the appearance of radicalism that plagued Seward. By the spring of 1860, the Republicans were looking for a candidate with broad appeal. In the wake of John Brown's unsuccessful raid on Harper's Ferry, Virginia, in late 1859 to trigger a slave insurrection, antislavery passions had been muted. Since the Democrats had split at their convention and the northern wing of the party had nominated Douglas, Lincoln more and more seemed the best choice to carry the Republicans to victory against Douglas, John Bell of the Constitutional Union Party, and John C. Breckinridge, the candidate of the southern Democrats.

The convention that nominated Lincoln at Chicago in May 1860 also adopted a platform that took account of popular fears about the new party taking control of the White House. The delegates affirmed that slavery in the South would not be harmed, and they denounced "the lawless invasion by armed force" of any state or territory as John Brown had done. But the Republicans also asserted that "the normal condition of all the territory of the United States is that of freedom," and they criticized southern calls to reopen the slave trade and any idea that slavery in the territories might be legal.[35]

At the end of the platform, the delegates called for a protective tariff, a homestead law, internal improvements, and construction of a Pacific railroad. By these planks the Republicans were endeavoring to assemble a majority coalition to win a presidential contest and thus went beyond an appeal grounded only on their opposition to slavery. For the party to follow such a course was hardly surprising. Political parties in the United States grow by winning elections rather than suffering defeats based on a perceived moral purity. Yet in 1860 and in historical accounts, the Republicans were criticized both for risking the Union because of their antislavery position and for hypocrisy when they muted their opposition to slavery to attract potential voters.

With victory assured if the Democratic split persisted, the Republicans in 1860 concentrated on keeping enthusiasm high and getting their voters out to the polls. Their style of campaigning, which featured marching units of "Wide Awake Societies," became a characteristic trademark of subsequent campaigns for more than three decades. Meanwhile, Lincoln remained in Illinois and said almost nothing in public. By long-standing tradition, presidential candidates did not make a personal appeal for votes.

When the votes were tallied, Lincoln was a sectional and minority president with less than forty percent of the popular vote. He won all the northern states except New Jersey, which he split with Douglas. As a result, Lincoln had 180 electoral votes to the combined total of 123 votes for his three opponents. Even if the votes of Douglas and Bell in the North had been lumped together, Lincoln would still have won. The Republicans were very conscious, however, that they had not received a popular majority and feared what would happen if the Democrats, North and South, ever reunited.

THE REPUBLICANS AND THE CIVIL WAR

> This war has been the means of developing resources and capabilities such as you never before dreamed that you possessed.
>
> —Godlove S. Orth[36]

The election of Lincoln was followed by the secession of the South, the formation of the Confederate States of America, and the Civil War. For the Republicans the experience of the conflict transformed their party. During the four years from 1861 to 1865, they achieved the destruction of slavery and the preservation of the Union in which the power of the South was much reduced. The war and Reconstruction that followed also created real political rights for African Americans in the United States for the first time. By 1865 the antislavery agenda of the Republicans had been realized in full.

In winning the war, however, the Republicans expanded the power of the national government in the economic sphere. They established a national banking system, imposed an income tax, created a system for dispersing public land in the West, and started a transcontinental railroad. The role of the national government in promoting economic growth went beyond even what the Whigs had contemplated. A corollary was an increasing identification of the Republicans with the ambitions and power of the business community in the North and Middle West. A party that began as an attack on the existing political order became an organization that believed in an identity of the interests of capitalists, workers, and farmers. Over time, the commitment to business outweighed the concern for other elements in the economy.

These accomplishments occurred despite the continuation of the partisan struggle with the Democrats throughout the conflict. While many loyal Democrats in the North supported the war and the preservation of the Union, there was less agreement on how the South should be subdued and, more important, on how black Americans should be treated during and after the fighting. The Democratic identification with white supremacy had wide appeal in sections of the North, and Republicans remained a minority party in a significant number of states. In the congressional elections of 1862, the Democrats made gains in the House and Senate. Even in the 1864 presidential election where Lincoln defeated George B. McClellan as the Union military triumphs crested, the Democrats still polled forty-five percent of the popular vote.

The war shaped a distinctive Republican view of the Democrats that cast a long shadow into the future. While the majority of the northern Democrats supported the war effort and, with somewhat less enthusiasm, the Lincoln administration, a substantial minority of the opposition wanted a negotiated peace with the Confederacy even at the price of perpetuating slavery. At the fringes of the party, some Democrats, notably Clement Vallandigham of Ohio, did more to give aid and comfort to the South. Fairly or unfairly, the Democrats gained in the minds of Republicans a reputation as a party that had trifled with treason. In the presidential election of 1864, the party's speakers and newspapers assailed the Democrats for their alleged disloyalty. The opposition was, said the *New York Tribune,* "ready to barter the integrity of the Union for the sake of political power." The term "copperhead," meaning a southern sympathizer, became identified with the peace wing of the Democrats.[37]

At some instinctive level, Republicans were convinced that their political opposition was less patriotic, even less American, than Republicans were in the nation's greatest crisis. As a result, while they did not openly question the right of Democrats to hold power, over the years in the minds of Republicans a Democratic president lacked legitimacy, especially if the chief executive had come to office with less than a majority of the popular vote. These attitudes originated during the Civil War when, as one writer noted in 1864, the Democratic Party gained "the taint of disloyalty, which whether true or false will cling to it, like the poisoned shirt of Nessus, for a century."[38]

THE REPUBLICANS AND GOVERNMENT

> This is our country. Let it have one national Government—one destiny.
>
> —Elbridge G. Spaulding[39]

The requirements of winning the Civil War led the Republicans to champion the largest expansion of the government's role in the economy up to that point in the nation's history. Since the Republicans were, until the terrorist attacks of September 11, 2001, the perceived advocates of limited government in the twentieth century, their image as the party of expanded government in the nineteenth century may seem improbable. The evidence shows them to be the supporters of a large federal role in the wartime emergency, including a strong commitment to income taxes. As one Republican leader in the Senate, John Sherman of Ohio, put it in 1863, "All private interests, all local interests, all banking interests, the interests of individuals, everything, should be subordinate now to the interest of the government."[40]

The measures enacted from 1861 to 1863 in the Thirty-seventh Congress included the issuance and sale through popular subscription of bonds to finance the Union cause. The government also issued paper money ("greenbacks" because of the color of the paper) to pay for the cost of armies and their supplies. The government's debt rose dramatically because of these moves, but Republican editors contended that there was little risk to such a financial policy. Better a national debt owed to Americans than to foreign bondholders. *"What is owed to our own people is no loss,* the nation is no poorer for it."[41]

In 1863, Congress created the National Banking System. Since Andrew Jackson had destroyed the Second Bank of the United States in the 1830s, the country had not had any kind of organized banking structure. The National Banking System established a kind of national currency supported by government bonds that enabled banknotes to circulate. In the process, a market for government bonds was initiated. The measure reduced the power of state banks and concentrated financial power toward Washington. The bill was passed in February 1863, and President Lincoln quickly signed it. An amended law passed a year later, and Congress subsequently imposed a tax on state banknotes to reduce the power of these state institutions. John Sherman captured the centralizing philosophy of wartime Republicans: "The power of taxation cannot be more wisely exercised than in harmonizing and nationalizing and placing on the secure basis of national credit all the money of the country."[42]

Financing the war effort required that the Republican Congress impose higher tariff duties and an income tax. In the case of the Morrill Tariff law of 1861, Congress imposed duties on more than just manufactures. It sought to protect from foreign competition a wide range of agricultural items and useful minerals. Republicans contended that such policies would help farmers and free laborers as well as business owners. The new law became the basis for Republican tariff legislation during the late nineteenth century.

But even higher tariffs did not bring in enough revenue to sustain the Union cause. The desperate need to find more funds led to the adoption of an income tax. The Republicans adopted versions of the income levy in the various revenue laws enacted to pay for the war in 1861, 1862, and 1864. During the congressional debates, Republicans contended that "a tax properly levied, upon incomes . . . is an equitable and just tax." Some party members favored making the tax system graduated so that the burden fell more on the wealthy. After much discussion, Congress accepted such a proposal in the tax bill of 1864. Individuals with incomes over $10,000 would pay ten percent in taxes. The *Chicago Tribune*, writing in 1862, said that "the rich should be taxed more than the poor." Although one Republican probably exaggerated in 1864 when he said, "The universal cry of this people is to be taxed," the citizens of the North tolerated most of the revenue legislation as a necessary war measure for ultimate victory. After the war, in 1872, the income tax lapsed. Nonetheless, the Democrats labeled the Republicans the party of high taxes and big government for decades.[43]

Efforts to promote agricultural settlement on the western plains also embodied the Republican commitment to governmental activism during the Civil War. The party's ideology favored the free laborer, providing him access to land to pursue farming. The Homestead Act of 1862–63 granted 160 acres of land from the public domain to actual settlers. As the proponents of the measure argued, the establishment of a prosperous nation of independent farmers was a worthy goal. "What is beneficial to the people cannot be detrimental to the Government; for in this country the interests of both are identical," said a Republican congressman.

A similar spirit lay behind the creation of a Department of Agriculture and the establishment of a system of land-grant colleges to diffuse education among the children of farmers. A key element in Republican thinking, adopted from the Whigs, was the belief in an identity of interests among all the producing elements of society. Accordingly, the federal government should encourage and promote the diverse classes of the economy, and all would profit together.[44]

A railroad to the Pacific Coast would further knit the nation together and hold California and the Pacific Coast within the Union. The presence of cheap, efficient transportation would also stimulate the development of the agricultural sector. The advocates of the railroad project believed that honest businessmen, acting in the national interest, would build a rail line at a reasonable profit for themselves. As it turned out, the increasing complexity of an industrializing economy brought into the project capitalists who pursued profit over efficiency. The resulting scandals in the 1870s involving the Crédit Mobilier company suggested that the Republican faith in a congruence of private and public interest was less certain than many party members believed. The Republicans did not want government regulation of the economy, preferring to allow the workings of the marketplace to correct inequities. Promotion without regulation was viable in the 1860s and helped win the Civil War. How it would fare in peacetime in an industrial nation remained an issue for the future.

The war proved a powerful engine of economic prosperity for the North. Even though there were several hundred thousand Union dead and many more wounded, the population expanded as immigrants came to fight and to work. Such industries as railroading, clothing, and meatpacking expanded to meet wartime demands. Young capitalists—such as Andrew Carnegie and John D. Rockefeller—laid the foundations for their businesses and fortunes. Many unskilled workers did not share in the good times as inflation rose and real wages declined, but skilled workers did well. Overall, the perception that Republican economic policies had promoted prosperity even in the midst of a bloody and devastating Civil War created an association between the party and the nation's economic health that lasted until the Great Depression of the 1930s.

The Republicans and President Lincoln wielded the power of government in other ways during the war. The right of habeas corpus was suspended. A draft was adopted to raise an army after volunteering ebbed. Press censorship of dissenting newspapers occurred, and some instances of political arrests took place as well. Despite Democratic protests and the opposition of parts of the judiciary, the federal government sought to punish disloyalty and prevent the undermining of the Union cause with its greatly expanded powers. On the other hand, relatively few dissidents were punished. Amid all this turmoil, the political battles continued during the war and elections were held on schedule.

THE REPUBLICANS AND RECONSTRUCTION

> We can't undertake to run State governments in all these Southern states. Their people must do that, though I reckon at first some of them may do it badly.
>
> —Abraham Lincoln, April 14, 1865[45]

Although the Republicans remained generally united against the Democrats, internal divisions marked their history during the first half of the 1860s. The main point of contention turned on the issue of race and the party's position on the future of black Americans. Those Republicans who favored the expansion of rights for black Americans and a stringent policy toward the South became known as "Radicals." A middle ground of the party styled themselves "Moderates," while those who wanted to win the war but not do much for freed slaves became known as "Conservatives." Lincoln generally acted as a middleman among these divergent parts of the party. The size and strength of these factions shifted with specific issues and problems as Republican policy toward slavery and then Reconstruction emerged.

Among the Radicals, the most famous leaders in Congress in historical terms were Charles Sumner, the Massachusetts senator, and Thaddeus Stevens, a House member from Pennsylvania. While both men had influence, neither of them dominated his colleagues in Congress in the manner that Democratic critics alleged. Radicalism was a more wide-ranging movement within Republican ranks. The motivation, purposes, and achievements of these Republicans are still being debated.

In the first half of the twentieth century, the Radicals came under fire as militants who sought to impose racial egalitarianism on the South despite evidence that white southerners did not want such a social change, and convincing proof, at least in the minds of those who assailed the Radicals, that African Americans had not been ready for self-government during Reconstruction. This critique of the Radicals, racist in its essential elements, held sway until the end of World War II.

After 1945 and with rising intensity during the civil rights movement of the 1960s, the Radicals were rehabilitated. In a time such as the 1860s when racism dominated the United States, the Radicals seemed at least a "vanguard" for a more just and equitable nation. Yet the Radicals did not always embody modern ideals, and their performance often fell short of their proclaimed goals. Historians suggested that the Radicals had not been militant enough. Instead of seeking social change in race relations with vigor, they had settled for half a loaf. As a result, when Reconstruction faltered and the white South regained control of blacks in the 1870s, segregation closed in and the Radical program became a dead letter. After generations of criticism for having done too much, the Radicals now are indicted for having done too little for African Americans.

From 1861 to 1865, in the midst of the Civil War, the Republican Party wrestled with the issue of what the political role of black Americans should be and what legislative and constitutional means could best achieve these aims. The debate about the Republicans and blacks during the war has centered on President Abraham Lincoln. His assassination in April 1865 left forever unsolved the mystery of what he would have done with the defeated South. Historians have gone over and over his record in the White House searching for clues. Was Lincoln close to the Radicals or distant from their program? Was he moving toward the idea of votes for some blacks when he was killed? How would he have dealt with the southern states once the fighting stopped? Everyone knows what happened when Andrew Johnson became president. Was he carrying on Lincoln's plan (as he said he was), or did Johnson's accession mark a major change in policy toward the South and African Americans? These questions have dogged debate about the nature of the Republican Party during the 1860s.

Black Americans and the Civil War

> The two terms, slavery and rebellion, are now synonymous, the one will live as long as the other, and both will expire together.
>
> —*Philadelphia Inquirer*[46]

What is most notable about the Republicans during the Civil War is the changes in the status of black Americans that they had agreed upon during the fighting. At the start of the conflict, President Lincoln recognized the strategic importance of the border states, Maryland, Kentucky, Delaware, and Missouri, to the Union cause. If those states joined the Confederacy, defeating the rebellion would become almost impossible. Accordingly, the president resisted efforts in 1861 and 1862 to make emancipation of the slaves Union policy. As the corrosive effects of the war on slavery as an institution became more apparent, Lincoln concluded that freeing the slaves would strengthen the Union with European nations that might otherwise be tempted, for economic or diplomatic reasons, to recognize the Confederacy as an independent state. Freeing the slaves also undermined the economic base of the South as those released from bondage by the Union advance left their homes.

The Emancipation Proclamation of 1862–63 was not in itself an inspiring document. It did not free any slaves beyond Union control. But it did put the North on a course of changing the situation of African Americans in the United States that would be difficult to reverse. A return to slavery was manifestly impossible. The next step was calling on black males to join the Union Army to provide vital manpower for the North. As blacks performed well in combat and supplied resources to defeat the Confederacy, it became harder to contend that they were not human beings entitled to some degree of political rights.

Abraham Lincoln pushed northern war aims a step further toward a broader affirmation of political liberty in the Gettysburg Address of November 19, 1863. When he spoke of "these honored dead" who had fought for "a new birth of freedom," he indicated that the larger purpose of the conflict was to achieve freedom for all Americans, black and white. The leader of the Republican Party thus identified himself with the aspirations of African Americans to a better life after the fighting ended, but he did so within the limits of a nation where currents of racism persisted.[47]

In 1864–65, Republicans looked more and more to a constitutional amendment outlawing slavery as a means of putting the issue beyond the reach of a temporary majority should the South rejoin the Union or the Democrats regain power in the presidential election of 1864. The strongly Republican Senate easily passed the measure. The amendment did not obtain the necessary two-thirds vote in the House of Representatives when on June 15, 1864, the Republicans united in its favor and the Democrats stood almost solidly against it. Once the National Union Party (as the Republicans styled themselves in 1864) had

won the election and Lincoln received a second term, the House
voted to approve the antislavery amendment on January 31,
1865. Lincoln himself signed the amendment, though he did
not have to do so.

What to do with the South once the war was over competed
for attention during the fighting with the issue of African Americans in the United States. Although Reconstruction seemed to
have commenced once the war was over, Lincoln and his administration had been grappling with the problem for several
years. The president had hoped to use the possibility of amnesty
and leniency to pull southerners away from the Confederacy.
Like many in the North, Lincoln was convinced that loyal southerners, their pro-Union views repressed by the Confederates,
were ready, with the proper inducements, to support the Union
cause. In December 1863, Lincoln put forward a plan that allowed southern men who had taken the oath of loyalty to the
Union to create state governments in the South based on as little as ten percent of the white population. Freed slaves would
not be allowed to vote. The plan did not attract many southerners, but it did seem inadequate and much too lenient to Radical
Republicans.

Their answer was embodied in the bill that Republicans
Benjamin F. Wade of Ohio and Henry Winter Davis of Maryland
introduced in 1864. This measure imposed much more stringent requirements on the South. Confederate veterans would be
barred from holding office, and a majority of white male citizens
in each southern state would have to endorse a constitutional
convention to establish a new state government. The Wade-Davis
Bill looked to reshape southern society to ensure black freedom
and to give the Republicans a chance to be competitive in the region. Although the Wade-Davis Bill passed both houses, Lincoln
used a pocket veto to prevent it from becoming law. The president did not want Congress to tie his hands in reconstructing the
South.

In the 1864 presidential election, the Republicans nominated Lincoln for a second term at Baltimore in June. The dele-

gates adopted the name of the National Union Party in an effort to make it easier for pro-war Democrats to support Lincoln. Some Republicans believed that the party had achieved so many of its goals from the 1850s that it was time to break with the abolitionist past of Republicans and find a label more appealing to a broad spectrum of voters. For all their success, the Republicans were still mindful that they had not yet become the majority party in the North. In any case, the "National Union" appeal seemed reasonable at a time when the military fortunes of the North were still stalemated in the bitter fighting between Ulysses S. Grant and his Army of the Potomac and the Confederates under Robert E. Lee.

The effort to present a broad front against the Democrats and their probable candidate, General George B. McClellan, led to one fateful decision at the convention. Lincoln's vice president was Hannibal Hamlin of Maine, a state the party was sure to carry. In the historic tradition of balancing the ticket, the delegates dumped Hamlin and selected Andrew Johnson from Tennessee to run with Lincoln. Johnson was a war Democrat who had served as military governor of his state. As American politicians have always done, the Republicans assumed that Johnson would perform the routine duties of the vice presidency and stay out of Lincoln's way. No one inquired about Johnson's views of African Americans, his possible style as president, or his character as a politician.

The National Union strategy worked in the short run. Lincoln benefited from Union Army victories during the fall of 1864, the support of the soldiers who voted for him in large numbers, and the ineptitude of the Democrats. While Lincoln won all but three states, he received just fifty-five percent of the popular vote, attesting to the residual strength of anti-Republican sentiment. The Republicans understood that Democratic assaults on them as champions of black equality struck a strong response among a sizable minority of the northern electorate.

Union victory arrived in April 1865 when Lee surrendered

at Appomattox. Victory made the Civil War a struggle that the Republican Party had fought and won despite all the internal disagreements and temporary setbacks of those painful four years. The preservation of the Union and the end of slavery imparted a sense that the Republicans and the United States were identical entities. Republicans had won the war and now promised to make their country a more prosperous and just society. Much remained to be done with the defeated South in mid-April 1865, but with the wise, war-tested Lincoln in the White House, all things seemed possible for a party that had not even existed a dozen years earlier.

The last thing America expected after four bitter years of war was that the president would be assassinated. Angry over Lincoln's commitment to black rights and determined to avenge the defeat of the South, John Wilkes Booth murdered Lincoln on the evening of April 14, 1865, in Ford's Theater. The nation plunged into mourning. A president who had been the subject of vicious attacks just months earlier became a martyred hero to a grieving nation. As Lincoln was almost deified, the party he had led embraced him as their transcendent political symbol. Republicans boasted that they were "the party of Lincoln."

They had reason to be proud of their fallen leader. In the crisis of the Civil War, Lincoln had shown himself to be a masterful wartime president and an eloquent spokesman of the Union cause. Although he never adopted the agenda of the Radical wing of his party, Lincoln had come a long way from the views of blacks that he had expressed in his debates with Stephen A. Douglas. In his own person, he had little of the color prejudice that so many white Americans displayed. By the end of his life, Lincoln endorsed a limited form of suffrage for blacks. Whether he would have gone further with the Republicans toward the Fourteenth Amendment is unknowable. It seems improbable that Lincoln would have moved toward the Democrats and away from his own party as he implemented Reconstruction.

But Lincoln was now dead, and a southern Democrat, Andrew Johnson, sat in the White House. The new president clearly hated the Confederacy and its leaders, and spoke in harsh terms about those who had waged the rebellion. Yet he really did not oppose slavery as such. Perhaps Johnson would prove to be a wise choice for vice president. As April 1865 brought the first peacetime spring in Washington in four years, Republicans waited to see where President Johnson would lead them.

Chapter 2

REPUBLICANS AND RECONSTRUCTION, 1865–1877

The permanent pacification of the Southern section of the Union and the complete protection of all its citizens in the free enjoyment of all their rights, are duties to which the Republican party is sacredly pledged.

—Republican platform, 1876[1]

THE LINES OF marching men stretched for miles down Pennsylvania Avenue. On May 23 and 24, 1865, the Union veterans strode for three miles from the Capitol to the White House in review. Crowds cheered and waved handkerchiefs, and the bands played "The Battle Hymn of the Republic" and "Marching Through Georgia" as the armies paraded one last time before the grateful residents of the nation's capital. The conflict that defined several generations of American history and shaped national politics for decades was over. The leadership of the country had already turned to the vexing issues of Reconstruction—the return of the South to the Union and the place of newly freed African Americans in postwar society.

A burst of exuberant nationalism followed. The population soared from nearly 36 million people in 1865 to over 46 million eleven years later on the nation's centennial. New states, Nebraska in 1867 and Colorado in 1876, swelled the total to thirty-six. In 1868, the purchase of Alaska from Russia added another vast expanse to the continental territory. Railroads penetrated the West as a transcontinental line was completed in 1869. On the frontier, the new territory of Wyoming instituted woman suffrage as a way of attracting immigrants to its arid spaces. Above all there was a strong sense that the Civil War had marked a turning point in American history. The older society had been remade in the crucible of the bloody conflict. A historian concluded in 1869 that a "great gulf" existed "between what happened before it in our century and what has happened since, or what is likely to happen hereafter. It does not seem to me as if I were living in the country in which I was born."[2]

Although the Republicans came out of the war with the luster of victory and an indelible link to the memory of the martyred Abraham Lincoln, the dozen years from 1865 to 1877 proved fateful for the party. Their policies on Reconstruction left permanent changes in the Constitution as the Fourteenth and Fifteenth Amendments joined the Thirteenth in defining the rights of former slaves under the law. However, the effort to create a viable Republican Party in the South, despite some initial successes, proved to be a transitory one. By 1877 the white Democratic South was on its way toward dominance in the region and the establishment of a one-party structure that would remain in place for seventy-five years.

The other development that affected the historical reputation of the Republican Party stemmed from its increasing identification with the business community and burgeoning industrial growth. In the wake of the war, ethical standards were often compromised; a series of scandals in the federal government touched many Republican officials and imparted a sense of pervasive corruption to the period. The labels of the misdeeds tell the story: the Gold Corner, the Whiskey Ring, the Crédit Mobilier, and the Salary Grab. As a result, the Republicans in power found themselves the object of popular derision. In fact, neither party had a monopoly on virtue, but the Republicans sometimes had acted as though they did. The 1870s showed the error of that presumption.

Reconstruction became intertwined with scandal. Democrats used examples of malfeasance to undercut the racial policies of their opponents. As the pressures of war receded, moreover, the traditional American suspicion of government resurfaced along with white society's. Since they were perceived as the party of black rights and stronger government, the Republicans suffered the most in electoral terms as these forces operated. By 1877 the natural partisan balances of American politics had reasserted themselves. Any hope that the Republicans could become the nation's majority party seemed illusory. Perhaps the Civil War had not transformed American politics after all.

Andrew Johnson and Reconstruction

> This is a country for white men, and by God, as long as I am President, it shall be a government by white men.
>
> —Andrew Johnson[3]

The murder of Abraham Lincoln and the accession of Andrew Johnson to the presidency proved a permanent disruption for Republican policy on Reconstruction. While Lincoln's policies before his death were ambiguous as to how the South would be brought back into its proper political relationship with the rest of the Union, the slain president had recognized that freed slaves would have to play some part in the governance of the South. In his last speech on April 11, 1865, Lincoln said about black suffrage that "I myself would prefer that it were now conferred on the very intelligent, and on those who serve our cause as soldiers."[4] At the very least that would have meant enfranchising several hundred thousand black men. The president had earlier endorsed the Bureau of Refugees, Freedmen, and Abandoned Lands that Congress had created on March 3, 1865, to assist the transition from slavery to freedom.

Having been a member of the Republican Party since 1855 and then its first president, Lincoln saw his political future in his second term as linked to the party. While he was not a Radical by any means, neither was it likely that, if confronted with an intransigent South after the war, Lincoln would have moved toward the Democrats. Whatever his differences with men such as

Charles Sumner and Thaddeus Stevens, they all spoke the same partisan language and saw the world in the same terms.

This was not the case with President Andrew Johnson. The nominal leader of the Republicans was born in 1808 and had risen to prominence in Tennessee as a Democrat. He had stayed with the Union when the war began, and Lincoln rewarded his loyalty with an appointment as military governor in Tennessee in 1862. His strong performance in that role led in turn to his nomination for the vice presidency on the Union ticket. During the war and before he became president, Johnson denounced the white leadership of the South for secession and advocated harsh treatment for their "treason." When Johnson was inaugurated on March 4, 1865, he had taken some brandy for a cold, made a slurred and rambling speech, and embarrassed himself in the process. But politicians hoped that Johnson would be sympathetic to the Republican view of how the South should be handled.[5]

Once the South had been defeated, though, Johnson's belief in white supremacy and his personal racism conflicted with mainstream Republican thought. The president believed in the easy readmission of the southern states to the Union and expected white southerners to resume their historic dominance over blacks. After all, in his mind, African Americans were an inferior race and not fit to govern themselves.

So in May 1865, Johnson set in motion a process that provided a swift amnesty for most whites in the South. He did ask the political leaders of the region to ratify the Thirteenth Amendment, repudiate the secession ordinances of 1860–61, and agree that their states would not seek payment for the debts of the Confederacy. But he ignored any provision for black suffrage, even along the lines that Lincoln had indicated.

The question of blacks voting was a divisive one in the victorious North. Voters in Connecticut defeated an amendment to the state's constitution that would have given the two thousand African Americans residing there the right to vote. Two other northern states rejected similar proposals during the fall of 1865. Johnson calculated that northern prejudices would trump wartime idealism and produce a political alliance of northern and southern Democrats, along with conservative Republicans from the north, that could pave the way for Johnson to win the presidency in his own right in 1868.

During the second half of 1865, the intransigent position of the defeated South emerged. Though they had lost the conflict on the battlefield, southerners were confident in their antiblack ideology in the long term. A Texas newspaper on June 30, 1865, proclaimed that "the only hope of permanent free government is to be found in the maintenance of the principles of State rights and the view that has hitherto prevailed as to the status of the negro."[6] If the North expected contrition and regret for the war from their beaten enemies, they were to be disappointed.

And the posture of Andrew Johnson encouraged the South to believe that lenient treatment and a quick return to normal would occur. No real change in the status of black southerners would be required as the constitutional conventions set about writing new fundamental documents. Often the delegates said nothing about Confederate debts or secession. To recapture the privileges of slavery, these conventions and state legislatures enacted "Black Codes" that limited in severe ways the economic rights of African Americans. While many Republicans had gone along with Johnson's program, they did so on the assumption that the South had accepted its defeat, would show a submissive spirit, and would provide some economic and political future for former slaves.

But as Republicans looked on with dismay, the southern states seemed anything but contrite. In Louisiana and other states, blacks and Unionists found themselves under political assault and even the threat of renewed violence. A Republican editor wrote of the South: "We conclude (from every source of information within our reach) that public sentiment is still as bitter and unloyal as in 1861."[7] When they elected senators and representatives to return to Congress, southern white voters sent former Confederate officers who were disqualified to take an oath of allegiance to the United States. The South seemed to be pretending that the war had never happened. Republicans wondered if their recent victory had been real or just a passing illusion.

With the president casting his lot with the South, Republicans looked to the session of Congress that assembled in December 1865 to straighten out the confusion and show the former Confederates their real position. The Republican majority decided not to seat the newly elected members from the South. Had they done so, the future of any Reconstruction policy would have been compromised by the presence of southern lawmakers. In the winter of 1866, Republican lawmakers sought to frame laws that would protect the freed slaves and give their party a chance to gain a foothold in the South.

Three measures defined the emerging struggle between the Republican Congress and Andrew Johnson. The Freedmen's Bureau, which Congress had established in early 1865, before Lincoln's death, was by modern standards a small federal agency. It deployed some nine hundred agents across the South, and they set about creating procedures for contracts and rules between white landowners and their black workers. Scheduled to exist for only one year after the war, the Bureau was up for renewal in January 1866, and the bill went through quickly. It was not a revolutionary measure, but it did make white discrimination against blacks more difficult. The Republicans thought the president would endorse it.

President Johnson vetoed the Freedmen's Bureau Bill on February 19, 1866, on the grounds that Congress lacked the power to enact such a law once the war had ended. In addition, the South was not represented in Congress and therefore should not be subject to such legislation. A day later, Johnson lashed out at his enemies in an intemperate speech. Despite unhappiness in Congress with Johnson's position, enough Republicans in Congress still supported Johnson so that his veto was sustained.

The Republican majority pressed forward with a bill to safeguard the rights of freed slaves. It declared that African Ameri-

cans were citizens of the United States and entitled to all the
rights and privileges of that status. The bill did not provide voting rights to black men, and the political rights accorded to the
freed slaves were minimal. Nonetheless, Johnson vetoed the
civil rights measure on the grounds that it moved "toward centralization and the concentration of all legislative power in the
National Government." The president also argued that the bill
could allow Congress to void state laws prohibiting racial intermarriage. These contentions irritated congressional Republicans.[8]

The Republicans overrode Johnson's veto and made the
Civil Rights Act of 1866 law. It was clear, however, that a future
Democratic Congress could repeal the legislation and would do
so if the Democrats triumphed in the fall elections. As a result,
the majority party coalesced around a new principle: there must
be a separate amendment to the Constitution that wrote the
principles of the civil rights legislation into the fundamental law
of the nation. In what became, in effect, the peace terms of the
Civil War, the amendment established the concept of national
citizenship for everyone born or naturalized in the United
States. It became illegal for any state to deprive any person "of
life, liberty, or property, without due process of law."[9] The
amendment did not mandate black suffrage, but included language penalizing the southern states if they excluded African
Americans from political life.

The Fourteenth Amendment has sparked many interpre-
tations since 1866, but it remains one of the most important
historical legacies of the Republican Party. The Fourteenth
Amendment could only have been approved in the postwar context and as a result of the obstructive behavior of President
Johnson. Later, the amendment's language served other purposes. In the years after it was adopted, corporation lawyers and
the United States Supreme Court used the "due process" clause
to block state regulation of business. During the twentieth century, the amendment became a means of extending the rights
of citizens beyond even what its framers had envisioned. Few

amendments to the Constitution after the first ten have had the enduring impact of the Fourteenth.

President Johnson denounced the amendment and urged the southern states to oppose ratification, which they did. Johnson hoped to unite the South, northern Democrats, and Conservative Republicans into a political coalition that would keep him in the White House. His plan included a meeting of Unionists in August 1866 that supported his program. He also allocated federal patronage to line up supporters in each state. The midterm elections in 1866 provided a key test of Johnson's approach to Reconstruction.

But Johnson had misread northern sentiment. While the Republicans disagreed among themselves on a number of economic issues, such as the protective tariff, the proper amount of currency in circulation, and the role of banks, they shared a common distaste for the South and a suspicion of what would happen to freed slaves if white southerners regained power. When Johnson made an issue of the Reconstruction question, he identified a subject on which most Republicans agreed.

Then the president took an unprecedented political step; he launched a personal campaign to sway voters to his position. For a president to make a speaking tour, or a "Swing Around the Circle," as it became known, on behalf of congressional candidates was regarded as undignified. As with most presidential innovations, the trip would have won praise had it been successful. The president was out of touch with northern attitudes. He castigated Radicals in speech after speech, comparing himself to the martyred Lincoln, and asked if his opponents wanted his blood, too. As the president's rhetoric became more ill-tempered and coarse, audiences booed him. The president yelled back at the hecklers. By the time the election day neared, it was clear that Johnson's initiative had flopped. He had once said, "I care not for dignity."[10] To most northern Republicans, Johnson's disastrous tour underlined the accuracy of this remark.

Adding to the Republican indignation was southern brutality toward black Americans. Race riots in Memphis in May and in New Orleans in late July confirmed southern intransigence. The Republicans contended that only the election of a Congress with enough opponents of Johnson to make a veto-proof majority would safeguard northern rights. Voters gave the Republicans the mandate that they sought. In both houses of Congress, the party now had enough members to override a Johnson veto. "The people expect a bold and independent course with regard to the President," said Senator Benjamin F. Wade, one of the leading Radicals.[11]

RADICAL RECONSTRUCTION

> The whole fabric of southern society *must* be changed, and never can it be done if this opportunity is lost. Without this, this Government can never be, as it has never been, a true republic.
>
> —Thaddeus Stevens[12]

The Republicans and President Johnson continued their struggle in the short session of Congress that ended on March 4, 1867. The majority in Congress decided that some form of military rule was necessary for the unrepentant South. The Reconstruction Act, passed on March 2, 1867, divided the South into five military districts and provided a process by which the southern states could regain power. They must convene constitutional conventions to write new fundamental documents. These bodies in turn must approve the Fourteenth Amendment and allow all men to vote. Once the new constitutions had been written, a majority of the citizens of the state and Congress must approve them. Only after all these steps had been followed would the individual southern states be readmitted to the Union. This process would secure ratification of the Fourteenth Amendment and place the civil rights of blacks beyond the reach of any temporary Democratic majority in Congress.

Passing this act produced the results that the Republicans wanted. One by one the southern states approved the Fourteenth Amendment. The coercive nature of the process made the Republicans vulnerable to later charges that they had imposed "Radical Reconstruction" on the South, and so they had, as victors in civil wars usually do to their defeated adversaries. Southerners who had been eager to leave the Constitution behind in 1861 now assailed the Republicans for amending it.

Reconstruction in the South that followed received negative historical evaluations until the 1960s when the emergence of the civil rights movement caused scholars to reexamine the effort to reshape the South between 1867 and 1877. Previous historians had criticized Republicans for going too far in their approach to the South; now the conclusion became that the party, flawed by its own racist views, had done too little to ensure the rights of black Americans. The allegation had some merit, but it also overlooked the forces working against progress both in southern race relations and in the nation at large.

The way in which the Republican Congress had shaped Reconstruction policy laid rough hands on the states of the former Confederacy, but there was no inclination to abolish these states within the Union and start anew. Nor was there among a majority of Republicans in the North a disposition to overturn property rights in the South by redistributing land to the freed slaves. That would have demanded an expansion of government power beyond what had been contemplated during the war and would also have been an implicit threat to property rights in the North.

Remaking the South was therefore to be left to an alliance of newly enfranchised African Americans and whites who supported Republican policies. During the early years of Reconstruction, there was also the threat of military force from the Army. Both of these elements proved to be more fragile than Republicans had anticipated. Black voters were intimidated by such terrorist groups as the Ku Klux Klan. Whites who endorsed the Republicans faced economic and cultural pressure to remain in the Democratic column. As the size of the postwar Army dwindled with time, its ability to support Republican parties in the South waned. The idea of using the military to sustain unpopular governments became an increasingly hard case to make, especially as northern interest in changing the South eroded in the 1870s.

The Reconstruction experiment did produce positive results during its brief existence. Blacks voted and held office in the South, though the number of elected African Americans did not equal their proportion of the population. White and black Republicans, using the power of state governments, addressed long-deferred issues such as public education and economic development. The governments that Republicans formed had some corrupt elements, to be sure, but so did the Democratic administrations that "redeemed" the South when white Democratic rule triumphed. Southern Republicans were not saints, but their days in power represented a better chance for the region than the ideology of the Democratic Party at that time. Because southern Democrats wrote the history of Reconstruction, Republicans of both races were usually maligned in the accounts of Reconstruction that appeared between 1877 and 1965. In many parts of the South these stereotypes about corruption and black dominance persist, and the constructive achievements of the Republicans in Dixie have been forgotten.

Another challenge that the Republicans faced nationally in the late 1860s was the effort to drive Andrew Johnson from office through impeachment and conviction. Until the possible impeachment of Richard Nixon in 1973–74 revived interest in the earlier episode, the impeachment and trial of Johnson was depicted as a vindictive step of Radical Republicans to complete their takeover of the government.

The reappraisal of Johnson as a racist who frustrated Republican endeavors to accord blacks political rights caused historians in the 1970s to look again at this first case of presidential impeachment. While scholars did not find that Johnson had committed indictable offenses such as the ones alleged against Richard M. Nixon, they did decide that the president had used all the powers at his command to block the Reconstruction policies of the Republican Congress in 1867–68. This continuing resistance to legislative initiatives finally led to the effort to remove Johnson from office.

Obstructionism by Johnson took many forms. He removed Army generals in the South who were sympathetic to Congress and its policies. Despite the Tenure of Office Act, which required Senate approval for the ouster of Cabinet officers, Johnson removed Secretary of War Edwin M. Stanton early in 1868. For these and other violations of the edicts of Congress, the House voted to impeach Johnson on February 24, 1868. His trial began on March 30 and ran for more than five weeks. As the proceedings went on, Johnson bent in his opposition to Reconstruction in order to stave off conviction. In the end, Johnson was acquitted when the Senate fell one vote short of the two-thirds needed for conviction.

A number of elements produced this result. The case against the president was political, not criminal, and even on that score the evidence was ambiguous. Ousting Johnson would have made the president *pro tem* of the Senate, Benjamin F. Wade, the next president, and he was too radical for most members of Congress since he favored woman suffrage. The biggest point in favor of leaving Johnson in office was that his term would end in only nine more months. The senators who voted to acquit, while not profiles in courage, did not think it was worth disturbing the constitutional system to remove Johnson. Neither were those Republicans who voted to acquit Johnson driven out of the party or forced into political oblivion. They supported Grant in the fall election.

Andrew Johnson was a major disruptive force in the history of the Republican Party. As president he made the least of the historic opportunity afforded to him, and his racism has tainted his reputation. For the Republicans, the need to fight Johnson and his obstructive policies prevented them from forming a consistent and clear policy toward the South in 1865 that might have gained acceptance from the defeated rebels. Johnson encouraged the South to believe that it could escape the consequences of the war. In so doing, the president made the task of

Reconstruction divisive and bitter. The nation and the Republican Party would long feel the effects of the decision to put Andrew Johnson on the party's ticket in 1864.

THE 1868 PRESIDENTIAL ELECTION

> General, I have come to tell you that you have been nominated by the Republican party for President of the United States.
>
> —Edwin M. Stanton[13]

By the summer of 1868, the Republicans thought that they had a presidential candidate who could lead them to victory in the fall and, more important, end all the wrangling with Congress over the proper policy to pursue toward the South. The hero of the Union, Ulysses S. Grant, was the unanimous choice when the Republicans gathered in convention on May 20, 1868, just four days after Johnson was acquitted. There were no candidates other than Grant, and the Speaker of the House, Schuyler Colfax, became his running mate. The sentiment of the party was, said John Sherman of Ohio, "that our candidate should be so independent of party politics as to be a guarantee of peace and quiet."[14]

The election of 1868 is usually described using the phrase with which Grant closed his formal letter accepting the Republican nomination: "Let us have peace." In fact, the presidential contest that year illustrated the extent to which the race issue affected American politics after the Civil War and emphasized the perilous political and electoral positions of the Republicans with regard to the voters. There had been strong signs in 1867 that northern voters did not endorse Republican efforts to achieve suffrage for blacks in the South and the full extent of the legislative aspects of Radical Reconstruction. The Democrats won state elections in Connecticut in April 1867 because Republicans there had pushed for black voting. Similar results occurred in September in Maine and California. A month later, Democrats carried Pennsylvania, and a suffrage amendment went down in a stinging defeat in Ohio. In the Buckeye State, a Democrat said that Ohio must be spared "the thralldom of niggerism." Overall, the Democrats bounced back dramatically from their 1866 defeats. The lesson that many Republicans took from the election results was that racial issues must be played down. "The Negro will be less prominent for some time to come," said one Ohio operative. These events formed the political setting in which Grant sought the White House.[15]

The Republican presidential candidate did not campaign and only issued a public letter or two on specific questions in dispute during the contest. This posture was in accord with the tradition that presidential candidates did not actively seek the highest office. However, other Republicans had to meet the spirited challenge from resurgent Democrats who played the race card for all that it was worth in a manner that was vicious even by nineteenth-century standards. They promised to rid the nation of "an irresponsible oligarchy upheld by a standing army and negro votes."[16]

To oppose Grant, the Democrats nominated Horatio Seymour, the former governor of New York, and Frank Blair of

This Thomas Nast cartoon from *Harper's Weekly* shows the Democratic vice presidential candidate, Frank Blair, as a little dog "War" snapping at the dignified watchdog of "Peace," the Republican candidate for president, Ulysses S. Grant. Pro-Republican newspapers made much of Grant's war record and standing as a national hero during the campaign.

Missouri. Their platform pledged to abolish the Freedmen's Bureau "and all political instrumentalities designed to secure negro supremacy." Meanwhile, they accused the Republicans of subjecting the southern states, "in time of profound peace, to military despotism and negro supremacy." In the campaign the Democrats proclaimed that they were the defenders of Stephen A. Douglas, who had proclaimed "ten years ago, a government by white men, of white men, for white men."[17]

The Republicans countered with charges that their opponents wanted a return of the South's power and a reversal of the outcome of the war. Their platform endorsed the principle of "equal suffrage to all loyal men at the South" but added that "the question of suffrage in all the loyal States properly belongs to the people of those States." Backing away from an endorsement of black suffrage nationwide defused Democratic attempts to capitalize on racial prejudice in the North, but it also undercut some of the Republicans' moral standing. By 1868 the postwar zeal of the North to remake the South had waned.[18]

Reviving the lingering animosity about southern loyalty remained a winning tactic for the Republicans. On one occasion a party orator held up a bloodstained tunic of a Union veteran and urged the crowd to vote the way they had shot in the war. The moment was immortalized in the phrase "waving the bloody shirt," which became a coded slogan for Republican emphasis on the passion of the war over more reasoned and presumably important issues.

Examples of "bloody shirt" oratory abound. One of the most succinct expressions of the device came in a speech by Oliver P. Morton of Indiana in 1866:[19]

Every man who labored for the rebellion in the field, who murdered Union prisoners by cruelty and starvation, who conspired to bring about civil war in the loyal states, who invented dangerous compounds to burn steamboats and Northern cities, who contrived hellish schemes to introduce into Northern cities the wasting pestilence of yel-

low fever, calls himself a Democrat. Every dishonest con-
tractor who has been convicted of defrauding the government, every dishonest paymaster or disbursing officer
who has been convicted of squandering the public money
at the gaming table or in gold gambling operations, every
officer in the army who was dismissed for cowardice or
disloyalty, calls himself a Democrat. Every wolf in sheep's
clothing, who pretends to preach the gospel but pro-
claims the righteousness of man-selling and slavery; every
one who shoots down negroes in the streets; burns negro
school-houses and meeting-houses, and murders women
and children by the light of their own flaming dwellings
calls himself a Democrat.

Morton then ended his tirade with a flourish:

In short, the Democratic party may be described as a
common sewer and loathsome receptacle, into which is
emptied every element of treason North and South, and
every element of inhumanity and barbarism which has
dishonored the age.

That Republicans such as Morton used the Civil War for partisan purposes is clear. But critics of the party rarely add that the
Democrats in the South used memories of the war, too. Some
were still invoking the luster of the Confederacy as late as 1920.
    Grant defeated Seymour and the Democrats in 1868, but
the results fell well short of a popular landslide. Grant and the
Republicans won twenty-five states with 214 electoral votes to
eight for the Democrats with 80 electoral votes. Grant received
just under fifty-three percent of the popular vote, while Seymour garnered just over forty-seven percent of the ballots. In
the South, where the Republicans had readmitted seven states
during 1867–68, Grant won 41 electoral votes in six states that
were more likely to be Democratic in future elections. Three
other states, Texas, Virginia, and Mississippi, were not yet back

in the Union, and they, too, would be Democratic in future contests.

From the Republican point of view the most telling result was that Seymour and Blair won a majority of the white vote nationally. New black votes put Grant over the top and enabled him to do well in southern states where former Confederates were still barred from voting. Nonetheless, southern Republicans and blacks faced political terror tactics in the 1868 contest. To many Republicans the outcome underlined the dangers of pressing forward with more vigorous Reconstruction policies in the South. The problem of changing the southern states, said the *Chicago Evening Journal,* "can never again be brought into the area of popular politics as a vital issue."[20]

Before Grant was inaugurated, the Republicans in Congress adopted another constitutional amendment, on February 26, 1869. The Fifteenth Amendment guaranteed universal manhood suffrage for all races (but did not include Indians). Such a change in the Constitution would finesse the problem of a lack of white support for unlimited male suffrage in the North and would also build a Republican base in the South. President Grant endorsed the amendment in his inaugural address. A year later the amendment had been adopted. The Republicans believed that they had ensured political rights for the freed slaves with the Fourteenth and Fifteenth Amendments. They were mistaken, as southern ingenuity in thwarting these documents would soon prove.

When Grant was elected, the *New York Tribune* announced that the nation "may now look forward to a long era of peace and prosperity." In the history of the Republicans, few predictions have proved more inaccurate. A great general in the Civil War, Grant has come down in American history as a weak president who tolerated corruption in his administration. Along with Warren G. Harding, Grant usually ranks among the presidential failures, and a recent history of the party says that the president "found politicians intimidating and so surrounded himself with army buddies and nobodies whom he thought he could control."[21]

Grant was far from a great president, and corruption did stain his administration. Nonetheless, he faced a daunting set of circumstances in the South as Democratic resistance to blacks in politics hardened during the 1870s. By modern standards, Grant's policies fell well short of protecting African Americans from Democratic terror tactics and consistent intimidation in the South. There was only so much that the president and the remaining Radicals in Congress could do to stem the shift of national attention away from the issues of Reconstruction and toward the emerging questions of an industrial society.

The new president was a month and a half short of his forty-seventh birthday when he took the oath of office on March 4, 1869. Nine years earlier, as the Civil War neared, Grant was an obscure former West Pointer who had left the army in the 1850s and, after a string of failures, was working for his father in the tanning business in 1860. The outbreak of war brought Grant back into the Army, and from there his prowess as a commander led him to victory, national fame, and, ultimately, the presidency. A wartime observer said of Grant that he was "in appearance a very ordinary looking man, one who would attract attention neither in one way or the other." But, as his Confederate enemies had discovered, the president was a determined individual who would approach his White House duties with a similarly strong sense of personal resolve and purpose.[22]

But the Republican Party that he now led was far from a united and cohesive political organization. Within each state, competing factions sought advantage. Beyond that customary state of affairs, some party members, many of them younger Republicans, hoped to address newer issues of economic development through the protective tariff and government subsidies for business enterprise. In the East, advocates of deflation endorsed a currency policy that saw every dollar in circulation backed by an equal amount of gold. Western party members were less certain of the benefits of higher tariffs, and, as representatives of a developing area, they hoped for easier credit that put more money in circulation.

While suspicion of the South and dislike of the Democrats

united Republicans, the question of what to do about the future of black Americans produced different answers in 1869. By now all but three southern states were back in the Union and entitled to conduct their own political affairs. The dilemma for Republicans was acute. If the federal government left southern Republicans to fend for themselves, these fragile organizations would be vulnerable to Democratic pressure, intimidation, and violence. Yet if the Army was sent in to preserve order and repress terror tactics, the Republicans would be admitting that their southern colleagues lacked genuine popular backing. Reliance on the military in peacetime also conflicted with the principles of the Constitution.

These and other problems taxed Grant's modest political skills from the outset. Not a strong partisan at the beginning of his administration, he hoped to govern without undue deference to Republican leaders in Congress. Yet the experience of congressional Republicans in resisting Andrew Johnson made them skeptical about the exertion of presidential power even from a chief executive of their own party. The ingrained Republican belief that Congress was the preeminent branch of government shaped the party's internal history during the Grant years.

The new president got off to a shaky start over his Cabinet. He did not give much heed to party leaders and selected men whom he had known before or who impressed him as cautious and efficient. In the case of his Secretary of the Treasury nominee, Alexander T. Stewart of New York City, Grant ran afoul of the law that had created the Treasury Department in 1789. That statute barred those involved in trade from holding the post. The Senate refused to make an exception for the new president, and Grant suffered an embarrassing moment.

Other problems plagued Grant's first year. In the summer, two New York speculators, Jay Gould and James Fisk, sought high profits by manipulating the market in gold to achieve a "corner" (a monopoly of the available supply). The price of gold rose, and by September 24, 1869, investors who had agreed to sell their gold at lower prices faced ruin. The administration broke the scheme by selling some of its gold from government vaults. The furor over the episode embarrassed the White House when it was revealed that members of Grant's family had aided Gould and Fisk. The president was in no way involved, but this scandal was the first of many that would mar his presidency.

The administration also embarked on an ill-fated venture to annex Santo Domingo. The diplomatic initiative was handled in a way that aroused suspicion in the Senate, particularly from Charles Sumner of Massachusetts, who remained committed to the idea of prewar abolitionism. The debate over the treaty to achieve annexation led to a break between the Massachusetts Radical and the president. The pact itself was defeated during the summer of 1870. The episode contributed to a popular impression of a president in over his head and an administration in disarray.

Reconstruction policy provided Grant with his biggest challenge. In his first year, the president saw Republicans lose ground in the South as Democrats intimidated both blacks and white Republicans. The following year a new phenomenon surfaced. Republicans who sought an end to Reconstruction aligned themselves with Democrats in what were called Liberal Republican alliances in states such as West Virginia and Missouri.

THE LIBERAL REPUBLICAN CHALLENGE TO GRANT

> We demand the immediate and absolute removal of all disabilities imposed on account of the Rebellion, which was finally subdued seven years ago, believing that universal amnesty will result in complete pacification in all sections of the country.
>
> —Liberal Republican platform, 1872[23]

One hundred and thirty years later the words "liberal" and "Republican" would not coexist in the same sentence, but during the 1870s, "liberal" connoted a set of political values entirely different from what it does now. At the start of the Grant presidency, the term meant a dislike of the growth in the size of government, disapproval of the protective tariff, and opposition to the continuation of Reconstruction. Another reform that Liberals endorsed passionately was the introduction of a nonpartisan civil service to staff the government. At a time when political patronage determined who got jobs in the federal service, civil service reform hit at the strength of politicians and promised an objective, nonpartisan standard for government employment. Among the leaders of the Liberal Republicans were Carl Schurz, a German American from Missouri; Charles Francis Adams of Massachusetts; and Horace Greeley, editor of the *New York Tribune*.

Some of the Liberal Republicans' attacks on the excesses of politicians had merit. However, they had a large blind spot when it came to race, and their gripes with their party often reflected a troubling amount of bigotry. The prospect of blacks' involvement in politics disturbed them almost as much as the sight of immigrants voting in the large cities where many of the Liberals lived. Liberals led the way toward the Republican abandonment of civil rights in the South and eventually pulled the rest of the party along with them.

President Grant was determined not to give in to the pleas of his Liberal critics. The Democrats could always placate dissidents more than he could, and wavering would only alienate his base with the regulars among the Republicans. So the president turned to those in his party who offered loyalty to the White House. One leading exponent of the president's faction was the colorful and controversial Senator Roscoe Conkling of New York.

Conkling was forty years old when Grant took office. He had served six years in the House from Utica, New York, before his election to the Senate in 1867. In the upper house, Conkling cut quite a figure. His dress often included green trousers and yellow shoes. Well groomed with a prominent "Hyperion curl" that fell just above his handsome face, Conkling dazzled women in

Washington and was rumored to have a long-running affair with Kate Chase Sprague, wife of the senator from Rhode Island. Conkling had built a political organization to control the faction-ridden New York Republicans, and party regularity was the guiding principle of his career. Real and fancied slights aroused instant resentment. As one observer put it, he "seemed to consider all men who differed with him as enemies of the human race."[24]

One enemy whom Conkling never forgave was a magnetic fellow Republican from Maine, James G. Blaine. The two men disliked each other from the start. During a debate in the House in 1866, Blaine twitted his colleague about his "haughty disdain, his grandiloquent swell, his majestic, super-eminent, over-powering, turkey-gobbler strut." Blaine was ready to apologize and let the incident pass as one of those moments that occur among politicians. Conkling nursed his resentment and determined to have his revenge in the future.[25]

The emergence of an individual such as Conkling among Republicans reflected the shift in the party that was occurring in the late 1860s. The earlier generation that had opposed slavery and fought the Civil War was giving way to professional politicians who approached their calling with less concern for ideology and more for their continued electoral survival. Economic issues such as the currency and the protective tariff meant more to these men than did the fate of African Americans in the South. As long as voters in the North responded to Civil War issues, the regulars would endorse protection for blacks, but it was not a high priority. Their interests and those of the Grant administration ran together in the early 1870s since neither group wanted to see the Liberal Republicans gain power with the co-operation of the Democrats.

The 1870 congressional elections were a setback for Grant and his party. With the South now fully restored to national politics, the Democrats picked up forty-one seats in the House and narrowed the Republican majority to thirty seats. The Democrats added another six Senate seats as well. Many Republicans contended that the results confirmed the need to abandon harsh Reconstruction policies and be more conciliatory toward the South. After all, the party had freed the slaves and given them a chance. That was all that black Americans could expect. As a Boston newspaper with leanings toward the Radicals observed in 1870, "A party cannot be maintained on past traditions. It must move on to new conquests."[26]

Before the party turned to these newer issues, however, it faced one more challenge from the white South that could not be ignored. During the 1870 elections and afterward, reports of violence against blacks in the South multiplied. The Ku Klux Klan, founded in 1866 as a paramilitary terror organization, depended on intimidation and murder to keep African Americans from voting. Blacks who ran for office were told, as one Republican in Tennessee put it after the Klan beat him, "that they didn't dispute I was a very good fellow . . . but they did not intend any nigger to hold office in the United States." Republican campaign rallies were often broken up. The outright killing of blacks became known as a "negro chase." A North Carolina Republican leader warned President Grant: "An organized conspiracy is in existence in every County in the State, and its aim is to control the government."[27]

While not all Republicans believed that the threat of the Klan demanded action, most did in 1870–71. "If the Federal Government cannot pass the laws to protect the rights, liberty, and lives of the citizens of the United States in the States," asked Benjamin Butler of Massachusetts, "why were guarantees of those fundamental rights put in the Constitution at all?" Congress enacted laws to counter fraud and coercion in state elections. The lawmakers went even further in the Ku Klux Klan Act of 1871. That measure made it a crime to deprive voters of their civil rights and to prevent qualified citizens from holding office. The government was given greater power to use district attorneys and military force to curb the Klan. The Democrats denounced these measures as unconstitutional, but Republicans responded: "Tell me nothing of a constitution which fails to shelter beneath its rightful power the people of a country."[28]

Under the leadership of Attorney General Amos T. Akerman

and the new Department of Justice created in 1870, the government went after the Klan in 1871, resulting in hundreds of trials and the conviction of some of the key leaders in states such as North Carolina and South Carolina. This kind of federal resolve drove the Klan back into the shadows of southern society and helped restore the political morale of Republicans in the region. The need to subdue the Klan, according to Akerman, "revealed a perversion of moral sentiment among the Southern whites which bodes ill to that part of the country for this generation." The suppression of the Klan was one of the notable achievements of Grant's presidency.[29]

As the 1872 election approached, Grant's popularity with the average Republican voter remained high despite some of the more awkward episodes of his administration. Grant was correctly perceived as the strongest candidate the party could nominate. But for the Liberal Republicans another term for the president would be intolerable. They recoiled from the perceived failures of Reconstruction and the increase in governmental power that had accompanied it. The alleged corruption of southern Republican governments and their reliance on the votes of poorly educated African Americans offended the aristocratic sensibility of these upper-class reformers. They wanted to leave issues of the Civil War behind as well as those who benefited as a result of that conflict. "Reconstruction and slavery we have done with," wrote the editor of the *Nation*, a periodical friendly to the Liberal cause, "for administration and revenue reform we are eager."[30]

Choosing a popular and likely candidate to run against Grant on the Liberal Republican ticket was another matter. Most of the disaffected Republicans in the Liberal camp were disappointed candidates or losers in factional struggles with men such as Roscoe Conkling, Simon Cameron in Pennsylvania, or Zachariah Chandler in Michigan. None of them seemed much like presidential timber, although that did not stop seven or eight of them from dreaming of the prize. His birth in Germany disqualified Carl Schurz, and a lack of real popular appeal stalled the aspirations of Charles Francis Adams, son of former

President John Quincy Adams. These Republican rebels gathered in convention in Cincinnati in May 1872 to unite on a single candidate, and out of their tangled deliberations came an odd choice in the person of the editor of the *New York Tribune*, Horace Greeley. In his long career as a journalist, he had opposed most of the issues that had brought the Liberals together in the first place. They supported lower tariffs; Greeley was a protectionist. Civil service reform was a large issue to the Liberals but a matter of indifference to a New Yorker. Moreover, Greeley had endorsed prohibition, vegetarianism, spiritualism, and the use of human manure to improve agriculture. Mainline politicians found Greeley's views odd. "No two men could look each other in the face and say 'Greeley' without laughing." The one place on which the Liberals and Greeley concurred was leniency toward the South and an end to efforts to help black Americans.[31]

The Democrats saw Greeley as their best chance to defeat Grant, and they, too, nominated him as their candidate. Both parties adopted identical platforms that asked "for the Nation a return to the methods of peace and the constitutional limitations of power." But the journalist proved to be an inept candidate who made a speaking tour in defiance of the conventional approach that an aspirant for the presidency let others make an appeal for him. If Greeley had been a compelling speaker, the innovation might have worked, but his appearances produced few converts. "That Grant is an Ass no man can deny," concluded a Liberal Republican in Ohio, "but better an Ass than a mischievous Idiot."[32]

To counter the Liberal Republican–Democratic campaign and keep potential defectors in the party, the Republican Congress reduced tariff duties and extended amnesty to those former rebels who had not yet had their political rights restored. Grant did not campaign, but the Republican leadership turned out for him. The prospect of a Democratic victory galvanized African-American voters. Frederick Douglass, the most famous black politician of the day, summed up the views of most African Americans two years later: "The Republican party is the ship and all else is the sea." That view largely prevailed for the six decades that followed.[33]

The collapse of Greeley's chances resulted in a decisive victory for Grant and the Republicans. It was the last such solid triumph for more than twenty years in presidential contests. Greeley carried only six states, three in the South plus Kentucky, Tennessee, and Missouri. Everywhere else Grant prevailed with fifty-six percent of the vote and a margin of three-quarters of a million ballots. The Liberal Republican vote fizzled out, and the Democrats also seemed repudiated. The elections in the South had been relatively fair, featuring fewer acts of violence, which enabled the Republicans to rebound in the region.

But these results proved only temporary. While the Liberal Republicans and the Democrats lost the electoral war in 1872, they won the battle of ideas. The Liberal critique of Reconstruction as costly and corrupt impressed many in the North who nevertheless voted for Grant and his party. Civil service reform and the attacks on politicians it engendered resonated with voters who read about Democratic leader William M. Tweed's corrupt political machine in New York City in their daily newspapers. In the future, Democrats played down their overt identification with racist ideas and pro-southern policies. They assailed the Republicans for their ties to business, their spending of government funds, and their activism on social issues involving religion and alcohol. Because of these changes in tone, the Democrats were well positioned when the economy faltered in late 1873.

The End of Reconstruction

> The North is *tired* of the Southern question, and wants a settlement, no matter what.
>
> —Daniel Chamberlain[34]

As the Civil War faded into patriotic memory, the Republican commitment to changing the South and assisting the freed slaves also waned. The South seemed of less concern than the economic depression and social unrest that emerged in the mid-1870s. As a northern Republican newspaper noted after the election, "The President will recognize all the South as no longer disturbed and threatening, but as part and parcel of a purified Union controlled by patriotic purposes and loyal principles." In this setting, black Republicans were more and more on their own. Northerners read partisan tracts about wrongdoing in southern state governments and concluded that African-American incapacity explained the failures of Republicanism in the region. Meanwhile, the powerful forces of racism within both major parties reasserted themselves after the brief heyday of egalitarianism during Reconstruction.[35]

A flurry of political scandals enhanced the impression that corruption had stained American politics. Just before the 1872 election, the Crédit Mobilier scandal came to light, cresting at the start of 1873. The firm, named for a French business, had been set up by investors in the Union Pacific and provided with government contracts to build the transcontinental rail line during the 1860s. Shares in the company were given to key members of Congress who voted on the subsidies for the rail construction. Their votes increased the value of the securities that they owned. The public discovery of this scheme compromised the reputations of Schuyler Colfax, Grant's first vice president; Henry Wilson, Grant's running mate in 1872; and other notable congressional figures, including the future president, James A. Garfield.

While the Crédit Mobilier issue was becoming public, Congress voted itself a forty percent retroactive pay raise as the lame-duck session of Congress wound down in early March 1873. The press dubbed the measure "The Salary Grab Act," and criticism pelted the lawmakers for their covert greed. While the Democrats had been part of the legislation, the onus for the move fell on the majority Republican Party.

Not since 1857 had the nation experienced a severe economic downturn. The Panic of 1873, which began with the failure of the banking firm of Jay Cooke and Company on September 18, scrambled American politics for the remainder of the decade. As other banks failed and businesses laid off workers, the economy collapsed. Overexpansion of railroad construction following the Civil War led to a boom in the stock market premised on the idea of ever-greater returns from the profitable transportation sector. When the traffic from these new rail lines did not sustain profits, the bubble burst, the lines went bankrupt, and investors lost large amounts in the ensuing collapse.

The 1870s produced a transformation in the American economy. Increased production from industrialization drove down prices and began a period of sustained deflation that lasted for over twenty years. Businesses in such key areas as steel and oil consolidated under the leadership of Andrew Carnegie (steel) and John D. Rockefeller (oil). Reliance on machinery and relentless cost-cutting produced greater profits and efficiency, but also led to unemployment for many skilled workers. As a result, strikes and labor unrest spread.

Republicans had preached and believed in a harmony of workers and capitalists in a society of small farmers and businesses of modest size. Through tariffs and other subsidies, the government could encourage all segments of the nation to prosper together. But as Republican policies promoted economic growth during the 1860s, they replaced this version of an interdependent society with an economic order where division between capital and labor widened and social conflict became more of a fact of life. It wasn't that the party and its defenders had forsaken their original ideology, but that their identification with American business strengthened as the late nineteenth century unfolded.

In the short run, the Republicans, as the party in power, suffered the political repercussions from the events of 1873. This kind of periodic crisis was called a "panic" because of the hysteria it evoked. The twentieth century would replace that loaded term with the ostensibly more reassuring label of "depression." When Congress assembled in December 1873, the question for Republican leaders was what, if anything, should be done about

the spreading hard times that produced increasingly irate voters. The Democrats were ready to ride the issue into the 1874
congressional elections.

Economic orthodoxy in the nineteenth century provided
few options for the government in the face of a slump in the
business cycle. Neither the Republicans nor the Democrats envisioned any kind of large-scale government intervention to lessen
the direct effects of hard times. Grant floated the idea of the national government generating jobs through public works, but
his congressional advisers and Cabinet members told him, in the
words of one of them, "it is no part of the business of government to find employment for people." When middle western
Republicans supported a bill to increase the amount of money in
circulation as a way of easing the crisis, the president, following
the advice of counselors who favored hard money and deflation,
vetoed the measure. Divisions over currency policy among Republicans would persist for two decades.[36]

The congressional elections of 1874 were a strong political
rebuke to the Republicans. They lost eighty-five seats in the
House as the Democrats regained control for the first time since
before the Civil War. The Democrats also gained ten seats in the
Senate. In New York, Samuel J. Tilden led the state Democratic
Party to a triumph that endangered Republican prospects of
carrying that crucial state in 1876. With Grant not able to run
again because of the two-term tradition, Republican chances of
holding the White House now seemed in doubt.

In the wake of their electoral defeat, the lame-duck Republican Congress enacted one more civil rights measure in early
1875 that provided rights of public accommodation for blacks
in theaters, on railroads, and in hotels. The statute did not provide any enforcement mechanism beyond suits by individuals
against discrimination that they had experienced. In 1883, the
Supreme Court declared the law unconstitutional as an infringement on the rights of the states. No other civil rights law
would pass Congress for eighty-two years.

During 1875, the Republicans moved away from Reconstruction and toward an emphasis on issues of finance and trade. President Grant used the Army to avert a Democratic threat to the Republican state government in Louisiana, a move that attracted criticism from even northern Republicans. Democrats regained control of state politics in Mississippi when the administration and congressional Republicans concluded that they could no longer sustain their southern counterparts with military intervention.

More scandals plagued the Grant White House in 1875. The president's secretary, Orville E. Babcock, was linked to the infamous Whiskey Ring in which officials received kickbacks when they did not collect the federal excise tax on the beverage. Babcock was ultimately acquitted, but his difficulties embarrassed the White House. The Secretary of War, W. W. Belknap, had taken cash gifts from a man who sold supplies to Indian tribes. Belknap resigned rather than face impeachment. Though none of these and other episodes ever touched Grant himself, the Republicans faced a record of misdeeds on which the Democrats intended to capitalize. By 1876 the party sought ways to escape further connection with Grant's political baggage.

As the election neared, the Democrats united around Governor Tilden, who was dubbed "Whispering Sammy" for his soft-voiced approach to politics and "The Great Forecloser" because of his stern approach to business affairs. He had gained a reputation as a reformer when he supported the campaign that overthrew Boss Tweed in New York City. The Democratic platform denounced "the rapacity of carpet-bag tyrannies" in the South and charged that the Republicans had "infected States and municipalities with the contagion of misrule, and locked fast the prosperity of an industrious people in the paralysis of hard times." Promising reform, denouncing corruption, and playing down their racial views, the Democrats thought that Tilden could lead them back to the White House.[37]

The Republicans seemed to have one leading contender in the person of James G. Blaine, a popular orator and former Speaker of the House of Representatives. Blaine had cemented his standing among Republicans when he led the fight to prevent the Democratic majority in the House from providing amnesty to Jefferson Davis and other high-ranking Confederates earlier in 1876. "The Man from Maine" appeared to be on the verge of leading the Republicans. But days before the Republican National Convention opened in Cincinnati, questions about Blaine's financial relations with an Arkansas railroad surfaced in newspapers. Blaine responded with a vigorous, if somewhat misleading, rebuttal to the charges in the House. Six days later he suffered an apparent physical collapse. With controversy swirling around him, Blaine remained the front-runner, but many in the party hoped to select an unblemished candidate as an alternative.

The national convention well illustrated some of the unique features of the Republican Party in the late nineteenth century. While religious piety underlay much of the appeal of the party, the Republicans also had room for unorthodox opinions. Robert G. Ingersoll placed James G. Blaine's name in nomination. One of the most famous Republican orators of the period, Ingersoll was also noted for his passionate belief in atheism, a commitment that did not bar him from addressing the party faithful. He gave one of the great speeches of the era that had the delegates enthralled. In his peroration, he alluded to Blaine's opposition to Democratic attempts to provide amnesty for Jefferson Davis and other Confederate leaders: "Like an armed warrior, liked a plumed knight, James G. Blaine marched down the halls of the American Congress and threw his shining lance full and fair against the brazen foreheads of the defamers of his country and the maligners of his honor."[38]

It was a superb piece of oratory that provided indelible imagery about Blaine for the rest of his career. But as good as Ingersoll was, he could not overcome Blaine's liabilities. Nominating him would hand the Democrats the issue of ethics and make the party defend its nominee's misdeeds. After six ballots the anti-Blaine Republicans united behind Governor Rutherford B. Hayes of Ohio. A Civil War veteran and former member of Congress with no hint of scandal in his record, Hayes could carry his home state and would not alienate former Liberal Republicans as Blaine would have done. Although he favored temperance and respected the religious beliefs of others, Hayes did not belong to a church himself. Such a stance was not a bar to the presidency in this period. Hayes stood for civil service reform and, most of all, would be conciliatory toward the South. The convention then selected William A. Wheeler of New York to balance the ticket with someone from the East who could help in Tilden's home state.

The platform asserted that "the United States is a nation, not a league," and the Democratic Party was "the same in character and spirit as when it sympathized with treason." In their control of the House of Representatives, the Democrats were also guilty of "reasserting and applauding in the national capitol the sentiments of unrepentant rebellion." Republicans promised to protect all citizens in the South "in the free enjoyment of all their rights," endorsed the civil service, and approved "the substantial advances recently made toward the establishment of equal rights for women."[39]

The Republicans knew that they were in for a hard battle to get Hayes elected. If Tilden carried New York, New Jersey, and Indiana, and swept the South, he would be over the 185 electoral votes needed to win. The Republicans had an outside chance in a few southern states if the black vote was not suppressed, but the odds seemed to favor Tilden and his resurgent party. The Republicans premised their campaign on the issue of the war but did not stress black rights in their appeal to northern voters. Money was tight during the depression, and the Republican National Committee concentrated their limited funds on the states that Hayes had to carry. The candidate himself observed the custom of not campaigning. In the South, the Democrats kept black votes well below the levels of 1872 through a combination of coercion and violence.

For the northern electorate, military-style campaigning was the order of the day as "the Boys in Blue" marched through the streets of cities and towns. These Republican clubs and marching societies staged flag and banner raisings to stir partisan enthusiasm. Campaign songs based on familiar melodies filled the night air with pledges that "we will not vote for Tilden." The crowds listened to men such as Robert Ingersoll denounce the Democrats: "Soldiers, every scar you have on your bodies was given to you by a Democrat." Hayes endorsed the bloody shirt strategy because "it leads people away from hard times, which is our deadliest foe."[40]

On election night the early returns forecast an apparent Tilden triumph. The Democrat had carried Indiana, Connecticut, New Jersey, and New York with their 75 electoral votes and was running well in the South. His popular vote total was running ahead of Hayes's. As the night wore on, Tilden had 184 electoral votes from sixteen states in his column and was one short of victory. Hayes had 165 electoral votes from the eighteen states he carried. The Republican managers noted that Hayes could still win. If he triumphed in the remaining southern states of Florida, Louisiana, and South Carolina, their electoral votes would give him the White House.

The Republicans had a tenuous hold on the governments of these three states, and the directors of the Hayes effort on the Republican National Committee fired off telegrams to local officials asking them to "hold your state." The chairman of the committee, Senator Zachariah Chandler of Michigan, told reporters the next day that "Hayes has 185 electoral votes and is elected." Soon the state election boards in the three states declared Hayes entitled to their electoral votes. The Democrats countered with their own returns from the three states and dispatched their electoral results to Washington for Tilden. Lawmakers were now confronted with two sets of votes from the three states in dispute. It would be up to Congress to decide who was the winner of the 1876 election.[41]

The Constitution did not provide a clear road map of how to resolve such a dispute. If a challenge was made to a state's electoral vote when the Congress tabulated the returns, then a stalemate would likely occur because the Senate was Republican and the House was Democratic. Neither house could settle the crisis without the endorsement of the other. To bring the disputed election to a conclusion, Congress created an electoral commission with fifteen members, ten from Congress and five from the Supreme Court. The panel was to be evenly divided politically and have one independent member, Supreme Court justice David Davis of Illinois. It was presumed that Davis would cast an unbiased vote to break ties. Then Davis was elected to the United States Senate when Democrats in the Illinois legislature gave him their votes to oust the Republican incumbent senator. Davis left the commission, and a Republican justice took his place. In a series of eight-to-seven votes, the commission accepted the Republican electors from the three southern states, and Hayes was declared the winner with 185 electoral votes to 184 for Tilden.

Who, in fact, did win the election of 1876? Tilden led in the popular vote with a majority of 264,000, and he had gained a majority of the white vote in South Carolina, Louisiana, and Florida. In those states, however, black voters had been terrorized. As a black from South Carolina reported, "They have killed col'd men in every precinct." What an honest vote in these states would have shown can never be determined, but on the merits, the Republicans had as good a claim to these electoral votes as the Democrats did.[42]

The decision of the electoral commission still had to receive congressional approval, especially from the House Democrats. They began a filibuster to pressure negotiators for the two parties. As the inauguration date of March 4, 1877, approached, intense bargaining ensued as southern Democrats sought railroad subsidies and other economic concessions in return for accepting Hayes as president. But both parties realized that the larger issue was the end of Reconstruction. Hayes made it clear that he would not continue to support Republican regimes in the South with military power. A Kansas Republican summed up the situation tersely: "I think the policy of the new administration will be to conciliate the White men of the South, Carpetbaggers to the rear, and niggers take care of yourselves."[43]

These words proved accurate. The House Democrats gave

up their filibuster, and Hayes became president on March 4, 1877. Once in office, the new chief executive took federal troops out of politics in Louisiana and South Carolina (but not out of the states themselves), indicating that Reconstruction was over. Black Americans were now on their own, and commentators predicted that their fate would cease to be an element in national politics.

On a basic level, the Republicans simply refused to concede during the crisis of 1876–77. From the night of the election onward, they maintained that Hayes had been elected and was entitled to the presidency. Tilden and the Democrats had a failure of nerve. They seemed to have decided from the outset of the controversy that they could not win the White House, and the best they could do was force some concessions from the Republicans. They also hoped that anger over the election tactics of the Republicans would provide a campaign issue for 1880. When the Democrats investigated the disputed vote after 1877, it turned out that they had been as opportunistic and underhanded in the South as their opponents. In this election, the Republicans' assumption that they were the more legitimate of the two parties worked in their favor.

Although the outcome in 1877 did not signify complete Republican abandonment of black Americans, it did mark an important turning point in the nation's approach to race. Over the next quarter of a century, the South became less Republican and more segregated. Civil rights would not return to the region for seventy-five years. In the America of 1877, there was probably little that Republicans could have done to avert this result. After a generation of trying to build a freer and more open society for all its citizens, the United States lapsed back into the customs and prejudices of old.

Nevertheless, the Republicans had reason to be proud of what they had done during the Civil War and Reconstruction. The Thirteenth, Fourteenth, and Fifteenth Amendments were building blocks on which racial justice could later rest. Republicans had done their best between 1865 and 1877 to make

Reconstruction achieve its purposes in the face of intense Democratic opposition. But when all justifiable historical reasons for the Republican abandonment of black Americans have been recalled, there remains the hard truth that a party committed in its origins to human freedom came up short on that issue at a crucial moment in its history.

Chapter 3

REPUBLICANS IN THE GILDED AGE,
1877–1893

ELECTION DAY, NOVEMBER 4, 1884, was the climax of a long and bitter presidential campaign between Republican candidate James G. Blaine and his Democratic rival Grover Cleveland. For months the nation was regaled with the personal scandals over moral depravity of each candidate. Had Cleveland fathered a child out of wedlock? Was Blaine's marriage legitimate? Was the Republican nominee a lackey of big business and anti-Catholic as well? Had Cleveland failed the test of patriotism when he hired a substitute to serve for him during the Civil War? Were these two candidates the best the nation could offer in its political leadership?

Bands of marching men, clad in gaudy uniforms and moving with military precision, sounded these issues as they tramped through the streets of cities and towns large and small throughout the autumn. The Democratic supporters chanted:

> *Blaine, Blaine, James G. Blaine*
> *Continental liar from the State of Maine!*
> *Burn this letter!*

Republicans countered with marchers who pushed baby carriages, symbolizing Cleveland's alleged illegitimate child, and asking:

Ma, Ma, where's my pa?[1]

In the militarized ballyhoo and spectacular hoopla that marked the politics of the late nineteenth century, the election of 1884 had it all: controversial candidates, sizable doses of scandal, and a close contest. A mere thousand votes swung the key state of New York to Cleveland's column to provide enough electoral votes for him to win the presidency. Commentators argued about the reasons large and small that won the election for Cleveland and brought the Democrats back into national power after twenty-four years in the minority. Everyone understood that the 1884 race would live in memory. After all, so much was at stake and the outcome was so close. No one would ever forget all that excitement.

More than a century later, the 1884 election and the intense politics of that gaslight era before electricity became widespread seem remote and antiquated. Did groups of marching men fill the streets for their candidate? How quaint. Did newspapers print column after column filled with speeches pro and con about the protective tariff? How distant from an era of sound bites and photo opportunities. Did those Americans who were eligible go to the polls at much higher rates than now? How odd and how partisan. When thinking about late-nineteenth-century politics at all, modern observers pigeonhole both the Republicans and the Democrats as irrelevant to the real needs of the society that was experiencing industrialism, labor unrest, and constant change. Many historians say the British commentator who wrote at the end of the 1880s, James Bryce, had it right at that time when he observed that "neither party has any principles, any distinctive tenets." His conclusion remains part of the conventional wisdom about political parties in this period. "All has been lost, except office or the hope of it."[2]

STRANGER THINGS HAVE HAPPENED.
HOLD ON, AND YOU MAY WALK OVER THE SLUGGISH ANIMAL UP THERE YET.

This Thomas Nast cartoon is the first to show the Republican elephant and the Democratic donkey together. Senator Thomas F. Bayard of Delaware tries to save the Democratic donkey from tumbling into the pit of financial chaos while Senator John Sherman, an Ohio Republican, stands over the prostrate Republican pachyderm.

The Republicans have suffered the most in historical terms from this negative interpretation of the late nineteenth century. Up until 1877, the Grand Old Party, as it now called itself, at least stood in theory for the rights of black Americans against the racist Democrats. But with the Compromise of 1877 and the end of Reconstruction, the Republicans are said to have revealed their true colors. As the party of big business, special privilege, and corporate America, they forfeited most of their claims to historical respect. This harsh verdict, though undermined by several generations of research, has proven long-lasting and powerful. The real story of Republicanism during the last quarter of the nineteenth century is more complex and more interesting than these historical clichés suggest.

Mark Twain and Charles Dudley Warner gave this period an enduring label when they titled their 1873 novel *The Gilded Age.* Its main character, Colonel Beriah Sellers, became a symbol of the expansive, often fraudulent, style of boosterism and pretense that was associated with the economy's explosive growth. The words themselves suggested an era when surface opulence hid the true depths of economic inequality, business avarice, and corporate power. An unregulated economy had little room for the rights of the needy and less powerful.

The late nineteenth century had all these problems and more. Yet it was also a time when Americans struggled to make sense of a dizzying pace of change. Inventions crowded in to transform daily life: the telephone, the phonograph, the motion picture, and, at the end of the period, the automobile. Cities exploded in size, railroads crisscrossed the landscape, and laboring men and women stirred with resentment and aspiration as big business grew. The Indian wars sputtered to an end after three centuries, and the frontier no longer existed as a recognizable line of settlement by the 1890 census. While many Americans cursed the changes that industrialism brought, others found the quickened pace of life exhilarating.

Politics in an Age of Industrialism

> Altogether, I concluded, the United States, politically
> and socially, are a country living prosperously in a nat-
> ural modern condition, and conscious of living prosper-
> ously in such a condition.
>
> —Matthew Arnold[3]

In 1870, the national income stood at $7 billion. When the cen-
tury closed, the figure had reached $17 billion. The spread of
railroads, the rise of oil and steel as major industries, the creation of a national market—these developments put telephones
in 1 million homes and four thousand automobiles on the road
by 1900. Big business and its bureaucratic style of management
shaped the working experience of more and more Americans.
The entrepreneurs who made this happen—Andrew Carnegie,
John D. Rockefeller, James J. Hill—became national celebrities
as symbols of the rapid growth of large enterprises. Some called
them "robber barons." They preferred to see themselves as industrial statesmen bringing new products and services to millions. How their behavior should be controlled, if at all, was one
of the nascent concerns of the late nineteenth century. Neither
the Republicans nor the Democrats had ever faced the problem
of government power in quite this way in the past.

The dilemma of how to deal with the upsurge of industrialism arose because the growth of big business had not occurred
on a wave of national prosperity and steady economic growth.
Instead, a long period of deflation followed the Panic of 1873
and lasted until the late 1890s. Cost-cutting in major industries,
combined with the productivity of American workers, brought
prices down and fueled industrial expansion. The burden of
falling prices weighed on farmers, whose income diminished.
Unskilled workers, whose incomes often receded in the periodic
recessions of the 1880s and the depression of the 1890s, suffered
in the knowledge that their employers might terminate them at
will without cause.

Adding to the economic turbulence of the period was the upsurge in immigration that marked the postwar era. During the two decades after 1870, nearly seven and a half million immigrants swelled the national population. "New Immigrants" from southern and eastern Europe settled in the large cities of the East Coast and the Middle West. The lifestyles of Poles, Italians, Hungarians, Russian Jews, and Czechs mixed uneasily with the already established cultural patterns of earlier immigrants and native-born Americans. Often the Democrats proved more adept at recruiting these newcomers. The Protestant moralism of many Republicans, who emphasized temperance in the consumption of alcohol, insisted on the use of English in public schools, and faithfully observed the Sabbath, did not sit well with many Catholic and Jewish immigrants. If a newly emigrated workingman wanted to watch baseball with his children on a Sunday afternoon, have a beer in the park, or go to a dance, why should the local Republican government tell him he could not because of a Sunday closing law?

In a volatile economic and cultural climate, the underlying political issue for both parties became how best to spur the growth of the industrial sector while addressing the plight of farmers, workers, and small business. The idea that the national government might regulate the economy to lessen the impact of industrialism was advanced only on the fringes of the political spectrum in the 1870s and into the 1880s. But primarily the parties did not anticipate modern alignments in the role of government. Despite their subsequent position in the twentieth century, the Democrats in this period contended that government should play as small a role as possible, with limited taxation, frugal government expenditures, and a reliance on states' rights. The last principle dominated in the southern base of the Democrats because greater governmental power might mean more rights for African Americans.

The Republicans, on the other hand, were the party of governmental activism and economic nationalism. As they did during the Civil War, Republicans continued to insist that the broad powers of the national government should be used to distribute public lands, promote the expansion of railroads and other enterprises, and encourage the growth of industry through high customs duties on goods imported from overseas. "Protecting" American capitalists from foreign competition seemed a wise use of national power. The party envisioned the national economy as "a vast cooperative productive enterprise, in which the social or the public economic interest was promoted by energetic and promiscuous stimulation of productive agencies in private hands."[4] This sense of innate social harmony as the central fact of American political and economic life remains a key element in Republican thought and is revealed in their frequent criticism of the Democrats for relying on "class warfare."

Since the Republicans controlled the presidency for all but four years between 1876 and 1892, they should have been well positioned to enact their philosophy into public law, but politics in the Gilded Age was not that simple. What might appear at first glance a period of Republican supremacy was anything but. A closer look at the electoral situation reveals not Republican dominance but sixteen years of political stalemate. The Republicans took the White House by narrow margins time after time. Although the Compromise of 1877 put him into office, Rutherford B. Hayes lost the popular vote to Samuel J. Tilden in 1876. Four years later, James A. Garfield had a plurality over his Democratic rival of just 39,000 votes. In 1888, Benjamin Harrison also lost the popular vote to Grover Cleveland by more than 89,000 ballots but triumphed in the electoral college. When the Democrats won in 1884, Cleveland outpolled James G. Blaine by just under 30,000 votes. Only in 1892, in his second race against Harrison, did Cleveland achieve a 372,000-vote plurality over his Republican opponent. Landslides and big swings of voter sentiment from one party to another were nonexistent during the Gilded Age.

The balance of political power in Congress presented a similar picture. The Republicans controlled both houses of Congress in 1881–83 and again from 1889 to 1891. The Democrats enjoyed one brief period of control of both houses, from 1879 to 1881. Otherwise, the Democrats usually won the House of Representatives, in part because of their strength in the South. The Republicans kept a majority in the Senate, whose members were still chosen by state legislatures, because of their strength in many northern states. In this closely balanced setting, getting any legislation through Congress was a real accomplishment.

During this period when every vote counted, most white male voters belonged to one of the two major parties. Independents made up at most about five percent of the electorate. Belonging to a political party was a civic duty. Voting was expected, and so voters in the northern states would regularly turn out for elections at rates of seventy to eighty percent, twenty to thirty points above what was common in the late twentieth century. As an upcoming young Iowa Republican, Jonathan P. Dolliver (later a United States senator), put it in 1884: "The man who, having the right to vote, is too lazy or high-toned to mingle with his fellow citizens at the polls, is the merest ape and echo of a citizen."[5]

Americans obtained their information about politics from the daily and weekly newspapers that covered the partisan debates with an intensity that resembles modern attention to professional sports. Each party had its own newspapers to advance the cause, and no pretense of objectivity stood in the way of reporting the news. A Democratic paper might describe a party convention as enthusiastic and optimistic. The Republican counterpart in the same town would call the gathering underattended and demoralized. Newspapers did carry the full text of speeches, reported on local and state conventions in copious detail, and dissected political machinations of the other party in their editorials at length. The debates in Congress and the progress of bills were followed in rich detail, often with elaborate discussion of what one faction or the other was doing. The political universe of the Gilded Age pervaded American life.

REPUBLICANS IN THE GILDED AGE

> The Republican party does things, the Democratic party
> criticizes; the Republican party achieves, the Democratic
> party finds fault.
>
> —Thomas B. Reed[6]

Despite their apparent dominance of American politics since
1860, the Republicans' hold on power was precarious. They still
faced a daunting electoral arithmetic when their candidates
sought the presidency. Because their unbreakable grip on the
South was assured, the Democrats could always count on about
135 electoral votes from Dixie and the border states no matter
who their presidential candidate might be. If the Democrats
could then add New York and Indiana to their total, they would
be very near the 185–190 electoral votes needed to win. The
Democratic doctrines of limited government and states' rights
gave them a powerful national base in a country where suspicion
of the federal government and its power still prevailed.

The position of the Republicans was much less secure. The
party's strength was rooted in the Northeast and Middle West,
but only in the states of upper New England such as Maine, Vermont, and New Hampshire was victory assured in presidential
contests. There the Democratic Party was weak, and Republican loyalties, formed during the 1850s and confirmed during
the Civil War, remained strong. Middle western states such as
Indiana, Ohio, and Illinois were disputed battlegrounds where
Democrats were a significant presence. The Middle Atlantic
states, New York, New Jersey, and Pennsylvania, also were hotly
contested because of their diverse populations. The Republicans
had to win almost every one of these key states to have any
chance at the presidency. For them, unlike the Democrats, there
was no margin for error in a race for the White House.

The Republicans confronted difficult choices during the late
1870s and into the 1880s. Reconstruction seemed to have failed,
and the fate of African Americans, while useful as a campaign
rallying cry, did not sway voters who were not already fierce par-

tisans. Republicans complained with much justification that African Americans ought to have the right to vote in the South and were blocked from doing so by the extralegal tactics and outright violence of white Democrats. But what was to be done? Military government could not be restored, and expensive government programs to help the former slaves ran up against a national feeling that a large federal government was dangerous. Whenever the Republicans took even small steps in this direction, Democrats denounced them in racist terms for their friendship with black Americans.

Cultural issues did as much to divide the party. Republicans with strong Protestant leanings wanted local, state, and national governments to promote a more godly society by prohibiting the sale of alcohol, requiring a strict observance of the Sabbath, and mandating that public schools teach their courses in English rather than the language of the immigrants. These ethnocultural arguments galvanized Republicans in the Middle West, but they also aroused strong feelings among immigrant groups who saw these policies as discriminatory against Catholicism and restrictive toward personal liberties. Party leaders asked if the pursuit of these ideals lost as many votes as they gained for Republican candidates.

The legacy of corruption from the 1860s and early 1870s continued to be a problem for the party. Since Republicans believed that they were morally superior to the Democrats, the scandals of the Grant years had been embarrassing. The Whiskey Ring, the Salary Grab, the Crédit Mobilier—all these and other examples of wrongdoing compromised the portrait of the Republicans as the party of virtue and honesty. As a former Radical Republican from Indiana said in 1877, the party "lies wallowing in the mire of its apostasy, the helpless victim of its leaders and the spectacle of the nation."[7]

On an ideological level, the Republicans also had a tough sell for prospective voters. Many Americans in the late nineteenth century looked with suspicion on a government that taxed imported goods, used grants and subsidies to stimulate corporate expansion, and poked into local affairs on behalf of African

Americans or militant Protestantism. While Americans applauded the benefits that came from the Republican policies, including railroads, military bases, and land distribution, average citizens retained a fondness for the Democratic argument that emphasized "the master wisdom of governing little and leaving as much as possible to localities and individuals." These considerations led one reporter to warn President Rutherford B. Hayes in 1877 that the Republicans, as they existed in the 1870s, had to change. The party "must have a broadened base and reinforcements, or it is gone and the Democratic party will come into power for a generation."[8]

Predictions of an imminent Republican demise would appear at other times in the party's history. Then, as in the 1870s, they would be overstated. Because of the Civil War, the Republicans were associated with preserving the Union and ensuring the survival of the American experiment in self-government. That patriotic link remained strong across the North in such powerful pressure groups as the Grand Army of the Republic, an alliance of Union veterans. As the wife of an Ohio senator wrote many years later in describing Gilded Age attitudes, "The Republican party had saved the Union. It was the Union." Men who had fought in the conflict forged an emotional attachment to Republicanism that endured for decades and was passed on to their children. Growing up in Ohio in this period, the novelist and diplomat Brand Whitlock recalled the Republican Party as "a synonym for patriotism, another name for the nation." To Whitlock's family and friends, "it was inconceivable that any self-respecting person could be a Democrat."[9]

The belief that the Democrats were proponents of disloyalty and disunion still permeated the Grand Old Party. Republicans rejected the Democrats' argument that the United States was a collection of individual states with a weak federal government. "The United States is a nation and not a mere confederation of states," said one Republican state party platform during the 1870s. New York Republicans in March 1876 avowed that the Democratic Party was "the same in character and spirit as when it sympathized with treason."[10]

Contempt and derision toward the Democrats were staples of Republican thinking during the late nineteenth century and went beyond merely the usual ribbing of politicians. Jokes abounded about Democratic ineptitude. It was said that the Democratic Party was like alcohol: it killed everything that was alive and preserved everything that was dead. *The New York Tribune,* in those days a leading Republican newspaper, editorialized in July 1882 that "to join the Democratic party is to go down among the dead men at once, and to chain one's self to the dead past forever."[11]

The disdain of Republicans for their political rivals went beyond bemusement at the follies of their opposition. The Democrats were simply unworthy to govern and incapable of doing so effectively. Senator George Frisbie Hoar of Massachusetts articulated the feelings of many in his party in 1889:[12]

The men who do the work of piety and charity in our churches; the men who administer our school systems; the men who own and till their own farms; the men who perform skilled labor in the shops; the soldiers, the men who went to war and stayed all through; the men who paid the debt and kept the currency sound, and saved the nation's honor; the men who saved the country in war, and have made it worth living in peace, commonly, and as a rule, by the natural law of their being, find their place in the Republican party; while the old slave-owner and slave-driver, the saloon-keeper, the ballot-box-stuffer, the Kuklux, the criminal class of the great cities, the men who cannot read and write, commonly, and as a rule, by the natural law of their being, find their congenial place in the Democratic party.

The Republicans during the Gilded Age did possess a higher degree of internal unity than the Democrats. Despite the intraparty feuds that often marked campaigns and conventions, the Republicans displayed a cohesion and common purpose that more often eluded the Democrats. The reigning belief in the

Grand Old Party was that no single party member was more important than the fate of the Republicans as a whole. In Congress during the 1870s, one reporter characterized the Democrats as a "headless undisciplined force." The Republicans, on the other hand, were "an organized well-disciplined army." Nowhere was that unity more evident than in the Republican conviction that the protective tariff ought to be the driving force in national economic policy.[13]

REPUBLICANS AND THE TARIFF

Under the Protective system, agriculture, manufactures and commerce have flourished in equal degree.

—James G. Blaine[14]

One issue on which most Republicans agreed during the Gilded Age was the protective tariff. The doctrine stood at the heart of Republican thinking about the economy. From the vantage point of the start of the twenty-first century when the Republican Party, according to President George W. Bush, embraces the concept of free trade on economic and moral grounds, it is hard to envision an era when the core belief of the Republicans was protectionism. In that period the tariff was "the sacred temple of the Republican party." For several generations a test of a Republican's fidelity was a devotion to tariffs and the ideology of nationalistic government that it represented.[15]

In the years before the income tax was adopted in 1913, the federal government raised its revenues from two main sources. Taxes were imposed on the sale of alcohol and other luxuries on the domestic side, while the remainder of the government's funds each year derived from taxes imposed on imported goods. In 1881, for example, customs revenues brought in $198,160,000 while internal revenues accounted for $135,264,000. From 1866 to 1893 the government ran budget surpluses as tariff revenues from the growing international trade with the United States swelled the nation's coffers.

While Democrats believed that tariffs should be set low and the amount of revenue available to the government kept small, Republicans argued that a tariff policy that raised rates on foreign imports brought a number of positive results. First and foremost, it provided security for American manufacturing firms as they struggled to meet competition from overseas. Tariff rates, said GOP members, should be "so levied as to give full and adequate protection to the laborer, the producer, and the industries of the United States." A related pro-tariff argument contended that such an approach also safeguarded the jobs of American workers who bore the brunt of job losses when cheap, imported goods flooded the domestic market. Although Democrats said that protection served only the interests of employers and industrialists, the doctrine appealed to skilled workers who connected retention of their jobs to the higher tariffs in what protectionists called "the home market."[16]

Protection was more than just an economic policy. In the hands of the Republicans, it also sounded themes of nationalism and patriotic pride. James G. Blaine and later William McKinley were Republican leaders who were particularly adept at making this link. "Vote the Republican ticket," said McKinley in 1886, "stand by the protective policy, stand by American industry, stand by that policy which believes in American work for American workmen, that believes in American wages for American laborers, that believes in American homes for American citizens." Since the major free trade nation of the world was Great Britain, which imposed no protective tariffs on goods that it imported, tariff protection tapped into anti-British feelings in a manner that solidified the Republican appeal to ethnic groups, such as the Irish, who were otherwise loyal to the Democrats.[17]

Drawing on ideas that had their origins in the Whig Party, Republicans contended that American society was a network of interdependent producers. As a result, the tariff did not favor a single class but spread its benefits across all levels of society by ensuring markets and jobs for all Americans. Since there was a natural harmony of interests across the nation, it was wrong to claim that the tariff favored the wealthy or privileged few, as the Democrats often did. To use such rhetoric in campaigns, said Republicans, pitted one class against another in conflicts that were more characteristic of European socialism than the United States.

Objective circumstances made the tariff an urgent matter to Americans in the Gilded Age. Foreign competition reached across many areas of the economy. Farmers and ranchers who raised beef and produced cattle hides faced rivals in Argentina. American lumber and coal vied with the products of Canadian forests and mines. Cheaper British, German, and French goods brought clothes, eyeglasses, agricultural machinery, and jewelry into the country to challenge the dominance of American manufacturers.

While the tariff had mainly succeeded for the Republicans as a political creed, there were negatives as well. Higher customs duties raised prices for consumers of protected goods, a point that the Democrats stressed when they accused their rivals of championing high taxation on the American people. The financial and ideological links between the Republicans and large segments of the business community made the party susceptible to charges that the protective tariff was simply a payback for the support of industrialists and corporations. There was a community of interest between the Republicans and the groups their policies favored, but the advocates of the tariff believed in their doctrine as firmly and with as much conviction as their modern Republican counterparts believe in free trade.

As the size of business grew in the 1880s, many Americans worried about the emergence of the "trust" as a form of corporate organization. The many state laws that barred a corporation in one state from doing business in another led lawyers to devise the "trust" concept. Shareholders in oil companies in several states turned their shares over to trustees of the Standard Oil Trust and received trust certificates in return. The trustees then used their control of the various companies to establish a national strategy for dominating the oil business. The Democrats charged that the protective tariff, by encouraging the rise of big business, also spurred the establishment of these trusts—or, as they put it, the tariff was "the mother of all trusts." Moreover, said Democrats, the economic size of the trusts made them a threat to small business everywhere. Republicans countered these arguments by claiming that the tariff fostered prosperity while the low-tariff or "free trade" policy of the Democrats led to hard times. During the 1880s, the issue became a significant dividing line between the two parties.[18]

James G. Blaine: The Man from Maine

> To his extraordinary power of attracting friends, Blaine added an inexhaustible capacity for making enemies.
>
> —John J. Ingalls[19]

When Republicans and their historians look back on the late nineteenth century, what is most significant about Rutherford B. Hayes, James A. Garfield, Chester Alan Arthur, and Benjamin Harrison is that these presidents have fallen into an obscurity that makes them almost indistinguishable to modern readers. The classic expression of this view was well rendered by the novelist Thomas Wolfe when he wrote some years later of these presidents as "The Four Lost Men":[20]

> For who was Garfield, martyred man, and who had seen him in the streets of life? Who could believe his footfalls ever sounded on a lonely pavement? Who had heard the casual and familiar tones of Chester Arthur? And where was Harrison? Where was Hayes? Which had the whiskers, which the burnsides; which was which?
>
> And were they not lost?

If the Republican presidents of the Gilded Age have slipped into historical limbo, they at least are counted among the list of American chief executives. The most exciting, controversial, and interesting Republican of the period, James G. Blaine, has disappeared from the roster of important members of the Grand

Old Party, except among a few specialists in the historical study of the period. However, Blaine, more than any other Republican of his time, shaped the destiny of the party for two decades while making the tariff the centerpiece of Republican thinking. Born in 1830, he grew up in Pennsylvania, taught school in Kentucky and in his home state, and then moved to Maine in the mid-1850s as a journalist. Soon his oratorical talents, encyclopedic memory, and personal magnetism led him into politics. After service in the Maine legislature, he was elected to the United States House of Representatives in 1863 and became Speaker in 1869. In his prime, Blaine sported a full beard and had his hair combed over the right side of his head. And from the beginning of his political life, Blaine inspired strong feelings. The saying in Washington was that he caused men to go crazy over him in pairs, one for and one against. The most dedicated of his followers called themselves "Blainiacs."[21]

Blaine was one of those politicians, like Franklin D. Roosevelt, John F. Kennedy, Richard Nixon, and Bill Clinton, whose mastery of American politics extended to the smallest detail. Ask Blaine about an obscure county in the Middle West, and he could discuss its politics and election returns accurately. He never forgot a face and could instantly recall a conversation with someone he had met years before. No politician of the Gilded Age was better at articulating Republican doctrine and making its appeal clear to the voters.

The tariff was an issue he grasped fully, and he regarded it as a topic that could move the party into the next phase of its history. He believed in the effective use of national power to promote industrial growth and diffuse economic benefits. The war had persuaded him that "every thing which may be done by either Nation or State may be better and more securely done by the Nation."[22] For Blaine this philosophy involved sharing government revenues with states to assist their educational programs, and in foreign affairs, a system of reciprocal trade treaties to open up foreign markets to American goods.

For all his political talents and wide support within the Republican Party, Blaine had problems with personal corruption

that made him controversial and in some sense a political liability. While he was Speaker of the House, he pushed through legislation helpful to the owners of a railroad in Arkansas in 1869
and wrote some indiscreet letters in the process. When the
episode came to light in 1876, he explained away how he had
later sold stock for the railroad, but this rationale did not satisfy
his critics. Blaine was one of the earliest examples of the truism
that the cover-up may be worse than the crime itself.

To prove his case he recovered from a clerk named Mulligan
some of the damaging letters he had written, and he read portions of these missives on the House floor. His performance stilled
doubts for a few days. Then when his critics read the full text of
the letters in the newspapers, they claimed that Blaine had lied to
protect himself. Since he had written at the bottom of one of the
letters, "Burn this letter when you have read it," he had provided
damning evidence for his enemies to use against him.[23]

Blaine gave his political opponents plenty of ammunition in
other respects. He and his family lived well, and he refused to
discuss the source of his income. There was always a sense that
Blaine lived on the ethical edge. The Gilded Age did not have
conflict-of-interest laws, and political morality was not as well
defined as it would be a century later. Blaine was probably no
better and no worse than most of his contemporaries, Republican and Democratic, in his financial transactions. But because he
was so charismatic a figure, he simply attracted more press attention and newspaper coverage. In significant ways he anticipated the celebrity political culture of the century to come.

Half Breeds and Stalwarts

> We are in a period when old questions are settled, and
> the new ones are not yet brought forward.
>
> —Rutherford B. Hayes[24]

Blaine's spectacular political feud with Roscoe Conkling, which
culminated in the "turkey gobbler strut" encounter during the
1880s, helped define Republican politics in the 1880s. Distinct

factions emerged around the two men. The "Stalwarts," led by
Conkling and his New York machine, clung to the issues of Reconstruction and believed that the sectional appeals, such as the
"bloody shirt" that had worked in the 1860s and the first half of
the 1870s, were still viable. Blaine and the men who followed his
lead were known as "Half Breeds" because of their willingness to
depart from Stalwart orthodoxy. They shared the disappointment that the Republicans had been shut out of southern politics, but they also were convinced that the Republican Party
could grow only if it addressed some of the issues that industrialism demanded. That did not mean government regulation of
business. Half Breeds endorsed instead a protective tariff, revenue sharing with the states, and federal assistance for educat-
ing both blacks and whites in the South.

These contrasting positions embodied the Republican struggle during the late 1870s and into the 1880s. During the one-
term administration of Rutherford B. Hayes, the Stalwarts
fought the president's efforts to assert executive authority over
the system of patronage and appointments that dominated national politics. Hayes favored the growing cause of civil service
reform, the idea that nominees for federal positions should be
qualified for selection by more than just their political connections. He believed that selecting officials because of their partisan loyalty led to the graft and scandals that embarrassed the
party. Hayes hoped to find Republicans who would administer
federal offices honestly.

That led the president into conflict with Roscoe Conkling,
who wanted to control the federal offices in New York. The key
post was the customs house in New York City, through which
flowed much of the nation's trade. The Collector of Customs received a percentage of the customs duties, and the position was
thus one of the favored patronage positions in the federal system. Hayes nominated two men to fill vacancies, but Conkling
persuaded his fellow senators to defeat them for confirmation. A
year later Hayes ousted Conkling's friends and won Senate confirmation of his own choices. The episode received national cov-

erage and was interpreted as a victory for presidential power and a defeat for senators who opposed civil service procedures.

These frequent disputes between president and influential senators explain why the issue of civil service reform became so central to Gilded Age politics. As it showed, powerful lawmakers who controlled the government offices in their states or localities limited the power of the president to improve the quality of government employees. Professionalizing the government service appealed to those who wanted trained experts to replace political amateurs. It also curbed the power of a state party leader relative to the national government. Some advocates also saw it as a means of limiting the power of the average citizen to play a role in politics since expertise, rather than just political loyalty, would be needed. In any case, the question of limiting the part that patronage played in late-nineteenth-century politics made the civil service question a constant source of contention within the Republican Party.

REPUBLICANS IN POWER, 1877–1885

> Madam, I may be President of the United States, but my private life is nobody's damned business.
>
> —Chester Alan Arthur[25]

In the eight years after the disputed election of 1876, three Republican presidents—Hayes, Garfield, and Arthur—held office. Each in his way sought to increase presidential power and authority, but circumstances made their efforts less than successful. Rutherford B. Hayes performed creditably in his single term, Garfield's bright promise fell victim to an assassin's bullet, and Arthur turned out to be a decent caretaker of his political inheritance. None of them was able to move the Republicans toward the status of a majority party that so many party members coveted.

In his four years, Hayes sought to conciliate the South as he had promised during the disputed election, but the Democrats in Dixie turned a deaf ear to his blandishments. Building a viable Republican Party around African Americans and whites attracted to the Grand Old Party's economic views proved untenable as the race issue predominated and the Democrats surged back into clear dominance of southern politics between 1877 and 1881. The Republicans experienced much internal discontent during the process, but there was little support for a return to Reconstruction. Short of that, the reduction in Republican influence below the Mason-Dixon line became inevitable.

In other areas, Hayes, sensitive to the situation of workers and farmers, saw his party become more intertwined with the interests of the industrial sector and the business community. The nationwide railroad strike of 1877, sparked by pay cuts to rail workers during the persistent depression, brought walkouts and the threat of violence. Governors called out their state militias, but some units declined to fire on strikers whom they knew from their own communities. As the crisis worsened, Hayes dispatched army units to keep the peace. Middle-class Americans applauded the president's actions. Unhappy workers blamed the Republicans for the defeat of the strike.

With hard times still lingering from the Panic of 1873, Democrats and some western Republicans wanted to move away from the policy that every dollar in circulation was backed by an equal amount of gold in the government's vaults. Using silver, which was more plentiful than gold, would lead to some inflation and a rise in prices for farmers. In 1878, the Bland-Allison Act was passed over the veto of President Hayes, who deemed the measure inflationary. It provided for the government to buy a fixed amount of silver each month, which did little to inflate the currency. Hayes's action pleased business interests, who favored a stable currency, but unhappy farmers would raise the issue of lifting crop prices again in the decade ahead.

Hayes had promised to serve only one term, and so in 1880, the Republicans looked again for a winning candidate. Conkling and the Stalwarts pushed for a third term for Ulysses S. Grant, who, after eight years in office and four touring the world, was now deemed ready to be president. Blaine was the Half Breed hopeful, but his ethical lapses remained. In the end, the party turned to James A. Garfield, an Ohio congressman with the requisite Civil War record who had Blaine's appeal without his liabilities. To run with Garfield, the national convention selected Chester Alan Arthur, a New Yorker and friend of Conkling, to balance the ticket as the vice presidential candidate.

The Republicans emphasized the tariff issue in 1880, and Garfield eked out a narrow victory over the Democratic nominee, Winfield Scott Hancock. Garfield's majority was a scant 9,000 votes in the popular vote over his rival, but he had a 214–155 lead in the electoral tally. In his brief presidency, Garfield faced down Roscoe Conkling over appointments in New York State and seemed to have established the authority of the president over that of powerful senators. With Blaine as his Secretary of State, Garfield looked forward to expanding the nation's economic presence in Latin America and uniting the Republicans behind a program of tariff protection and economic nationalism. On July 2, 1881, while waiting at the Washington train station to leave on a vacation from the stifling heat of the capital, Garfield was assassinated by Charles J. Guiteau, an insane man who believed that he was entitled to a federal job. Guiteau shouted, "I am a Stalwart and Arthur is President," as police took him away.[26] Garfield died of his wounds in mid-September, and Chester Alan Arthur became president. Guiteau was tried and executed for his crime.

Although he had been a Conkling ally, Arthur proved to be his own man as president. Blaine was dropped as Secretary of State, and the president took charge of his own administration. Congress enacted the Pendleton Civil Service Law to end some of the abuses of the patronage system and to construct a better workforce for the government. The lawmakers also passed a Chinese Exclusion Law to limit the number of immigrants from that Asian country. Finally, the passage of a tariff law in 1883 did not satisfy either side in the debate over protection, and the measure was such an awkward compromise that it became known as the Mongrel Tariff.

BLAINE VERSUS CLEVELAND

> Campaign eloquence burdens the air, the public be crammed.
>
> —*St. Paul Dispatch*[27]

Arthur wanted the Republican nomination in 1884, but he was in poor health and, in addition, as an interim president, did not have much real support within the party. Everyone agreed that Blaine's turn at the nomination had come. His liabilities remained a major problem. So many questions had been raised about his finances that some Republicans in the Northeast threatened to bolt the party if he was selected. These vocal proponents of civil service, political ethics, and smaller government had become known as "Mugwumps" (an Indian word meaning big chief). They made up in noise what they lacked in numbers, and they hated Blaine. Carl Schurz, the former Liberal Republican and a leading Mugwump, proclaimed that Blaine had "wallowed in the spoils like a rhinoceros in an African pool."[28]

The Republican National Convention nominated Blaine and his running mate, John "Black Jack" Logan of Illinois, and the Mugwumps dutifully bolted to the Democrats. Two young Republicans, Theodore Roosevelt and Henry Cabot Lodge, stayed with the party, thereby preserving their political futures. Blaine wanted to run on the tariff issue, and he went out on a speaking tour to arouse Republican enthusiasm. The candidate knew it would be a tough year for the party since the Republican vote had been in a slight decline nationally. Moreover, the Democrats were united behind their standard-bearer, the governor of New York, Grover Cleveland.

The 1884 campaign soon degenerated into one of the noisiest and dirtiest races in American history. Rumors of scandals in Cleveland's past had circulated for some time, and they broke open when he admitted that he had been sexually involved with a woman named Maria Halpin. Cleveland did not know for certain that he was the father of Halpin's child, but he accepted responsibility and paid for the young boy's education. Republicans jumped on these revelations to embarrass their rivals. The Democrats countered with charges that Blaine and his wife had been married only three months when their first child was born. Blaine responded that the couple had married in secret two years earlier. Charges and countercharges about these indiscretions filled the air. American cities and towns echoed with the slogans of the rival candidates as military-style campaigners marched in huge rallies.

The most sensational event of the campaign occurred shortly before the election itself. On October 29, Blaine attended a reception for predominantly Protestant clergymen in New York City. Presiding over the gathering was Reverend Samuel D. Burchard of a Methodist church in the Murray Hill section of the city. Addressing Blaine, he said, "We are Republicans and don't propose to leave our party and identify ourselves with a party whose antecedents have been rum, Romanism, and rebellion." Blaine did not rebut the anti-Catholic slur, and within a few days a storm of controversy arose over the episode. Since New York State went narrowly for Cleveland and cost Blaine the election, the Burchard remark has often been labeled as a slip that denied the Republican candidate the White House, and so it has passed into the folklore of American politics.[29]

The night of Burchard's remark, Blaine addressed a fundraising dinner with an audience of business leaders and corporate executives at Delmonico's restaurant. The Democrats called it "Belshazzar Blaine and the Money Kings" in their cartoons (after the biblical king who saw his doom in the handwriting on the wall). The contrast between the opulence of the dinner and the plight of the working poor in the United States was underlined in the campaign literature of the Cleveland forces during the waning days of the race. The dinner only underscored the emerging links between the Republican Party and the business community.

When the votes were tallied, Cleveland had won New York

State by just over 1,000 votes, but that was enough to give him the state and the election. The Democrat won 219 electoral votes to 182 for Blaine, and the twenty-four-year Republican lock on the White House had been broken. In retrospect, neither the Burchard episode nor the Delmonico's feast could be blamed for the loss. Blaine had run better than any other candidate could have done for the Grand Old Party. The Republican share of the national vote fell from 48.3 percent in 1880 to 48.2 percent four years later, while the Democratic share rose 2 percent over what they had achieved in 1880. The election of 1884 was one of those close Gilded Age contests where the result could have gone either way based on a host of causes in specific states. Blaine had rallied the Republican base and enabled the party to stay cohesive for another winning race four years later.

The Cleveland Years

> The Democrat represented the faith in the responsibility of the individual; each individual being like a "little dynamo working automatically for the good of the community." The Republican, on the other hand, represented a faith in centralized power, in the capacity of the few who are in authority at the centre of the state or the municipality to regulate the many and manage the affairs.
>
> —Beatrice Webb[30]

If the Republicans had hoped Grover Cleveland would be a political failure in the White House, they were disappointed. While the Democratic president did not inspire enthusiasm within his own party, where his patronage policies irritated the faithful, he was a competent executive who performed his duties honestly and efficiently. The Republicans achieved some gains in the congressional elections of 1886, and everyone expected another close and hotly contested election two years later.

During Cleveland's presidency, currents of social change accelerated in both the industrial and rural regions of the nation in ways that challenged both parties. In May 1886, for example, working people in Chicago staged a rally to protest the role of police in a strike against the McCormick company, a manufacturer of harvesting machines. When the police tried to break up the gathering, a bomb exploded, killing one police officer. His comrades fired into the crowd, and a riot ensued. Eight alleged participants in a bombing conspiracy were tried and convicted, and four were executed. The Haymarket incident seemed to signal to the middle and upper classes that social violence was a real possibility.

The growing presence of immigrants from southern and eastern Europe created additional unrest. The American Protective Association, an anti-Catholic organization with ties to Republicans in some middle western communities, sought to limit the role of immigrants in national politics with restrictive legislation. Local politics in the major cities saw urban machines arise. These institutions, run by a city boss and based on a network of operatives in each ward of such places as New York, Chicago, and Philadelphia, were predominantly Democratic in character. Relying as they did on the votes of immigrants and ethnic minorities, they pitted genteel, "respectable" Republicans, usually from the middle and upper classes, against the power of the bosses who ran the organizations.

At the same time, conditions in rural America worsened. The expansion of agriculture brought bumper crops of wheat and cotton during the 1880s, and farm prices sagged. On the Plains and in the South, unhappy agrarians joined the Farmers Alliance, seeking ways to raise prices and to reduce the burden of debt that plagued farmers. Many settlers had bought lands at high interest rates earlier in the decade. In the South, the Alliance spelled trouble for the Democrats. In Kansas, Nebraska, Minnesota, and the soon-to-be states of North Dakota and South Dakota, the Republicans felt the sting of farm protest. Among the ideas being promulgated was to increase the supply of available currency by abandoning the gold standard and coining silver, which was in ample supply. With an increase in the amount of money in circulation, debts would be easier to pay and the prices for commodities would rise. Republicans in the Northeast scorned such schemes, fearing that inflation would erode the value of the dollar and promote economic instability.

During the 1880s, the trust problem moved to the center of political debate. Both parties soon felt the wave of public unease about what corporate bigness might do to smaller entrepreneurs, but the issue cut more deeply for Republicans with their strong base in the business community. The anger against railroad abuses had resulted in the enactment of the Interstate Commerce Act in 1887 and the creation of the Interstate Commerce Commission through bipartisan legislation. Now Democrats charged that big business and its impact was robbing "the body of our citizens by depriving them of the benefits of natural competition," and they blamed the Republicans for the threat that trusts posed to traditional values of small business, individual enterprise, and economic freedom.[31]

The 1888 presidential election was another opportunity for the two parties to present their competing visions of what constituted a good society. In December 1887, President Cleveland decided to devote his entire annual message to Congress to a single subject: the need for reform in the tariff system. Republicans leaped to the challenge with evident eagerness. They believed that a presidential race focused on the protective tariff issue would enable them to maximize their strength at the polls. The day after Cleveland's written message was delivered to Congress, James G. Blaine, on vacation in Paris, shared his reaction with a reporter for the *New York Tribune*. Blaine maintained that a low tariff policy would produce instability for American business, drop wages for workers, and force companies to confront devastating competition from Great Britain and other European countries. In short, said Blaine, "the Democratic Party in power is a standing menace to the prosperity of the country."[32]

The Republicans could have nominated Blaine to make the case for tariff protection, but the party realized that his candidacy would only dredge up the issues of 1884. Benjamin Harrison of Indiana had been a Civil War general, a one-term senator, and a successful attorney. Small in stature, "Little Ben" was effective on the campaign trail. His logical, well-delivered speeches appealed to large audiences. His personal integrity seemed impeccable. (Only after his presidency and the death of his first wife did a few insiders learn of his long-running affair with his wife's niece.) In 1888, Harrison could make the tariff case, carry Indiana, and give the Republicans a chance to win.[33]

The resulting election proved to be significant on several fronts. The success of the Republican campaign for the protective tariff confirmed the perception that the party's interests were those of business. While the tariff also appealed to labor, the link with business stuck in the public mind, and business responded accordingly. To help finance the Republican campaign, businessman John Wanamaker embarked on a systematic effort to raise money from big corporations through a businessmen's committee. Other Republicans with ties to the business community did likewise. This technique became known as "frying the fat" out of corporations. The money paid for the torrent of pro-tariff literature that the party poured out. Meanwhile, Harrison stayed home and spoke to the delegations that came to visit him. He made eighty speeches to more than 300,000 guests, articulating the Republican message in a crisp manner.

The election ended in a Harrison victory, the Republican candidate winning 233 electoral votes to 168 for Cleveland. In the popular vote, Cleveland had a 89,000-vote majority largely based on the Democratic vote in the South where black Americans were more and more excluded from politics. The Republicans had control of the House of Representatives by a margin of 166 to 159, and they held a 2-vote majority in the Senate. In surveying the results, the consensus was that the protective tariff had played a major part and the Republicans had outworked and outfought their Democratic rivals. Now they had control of the legislative and executive branches of government. It remained to be seen what they would do with their narrow but important victory.

THE BILLION DOLLAR CONGRESS

> The danger in a free country is not that power will be exercised too freely, but that it will be exercised too sparingly.
>
> —Thomas Brackett Reed[34]

Despite their narrow seven-vote margin in the House of Representatives, the Republicans hoped to enact an ambitious agenda in the Fifty-first Congress that convened a year after the presidential election in December 1889. President Harrison wanted action to raise tariff rates and legislation to safeguard the voting rights of black Americans in the South. Democratic efforts to strip the franchise from African Americans had made the Republican presence in the South more fragile as the years passed. Mindful of the 1890 elections, some Republican lawmakers wanted to address the trust issue with laws to curb the expansion of monopolies. Responding to growing discontent in the farm belt, Republicans from that area hoped to enact measures to inflate the currency through coining more silver.

Democratic obstructionism in the House of Representatives proved an immediate obstacle. For years efforts to enact legislation had run up against what was known as "the disappearing quorum." Democratic lawmakers sat silent when the clerk called their names for the purpose of establishing a quorum (the minimum number of members who had to be present for the House to take any legislative action). A determined minority could thus thwart the progress of any bill. Eager to defeat Republican initiatives, the minority party found this delaying tactic quite to their liking.

In December 1889, the Republican majority selected Thomas B. Reed of Maine as the new Speaker of the House. A giant of a man at three hundred pounds, Reed had a sarcastic wit that served him well in debate. In one famous response to a Democrat who boasted, echoing Henry Clay, that he would rather be right than president, Reed responded, "The gentleman need not be disturbed, he will never be either." Once he spoke to an audience that included many Democrats and claimed that a photograph taken of their party would reveal they were doing some "mean, low-lived and contemptible thing." The crowd jeered and howled. Reed smiled and said, "There, I told you so."[35]

Beyond his sardonic demeanor, Reed believed that the Republican majority ought to be able to pass bills. In late January 1890, Reed ruled that members who were present but refusing to vote could be counted toward a quorum. The Democrats complained and sought to block any further business through obstructive tactics. Reed also contended that the majority had the power to disallow motions that were designed simply to prevent legislation from going forward. In the end, the Democrats gave in and the House was able to move forward with the Republican program. The result attested to the Republican determination to impose their activist program and their commitment to making government work.

The Congress that followed during the remainder of 1890 provided important and constructive laws for the nation. Key measures included the McKinley Tariff (named after the chair of the House Ways and Means Committee, William McKinley of Ohio), which raised rates on industrial products and initiated a system of reciprocal trade treaties with Latin American nations. The Republicans also enacted the Sherman Antitrust Act that declared monopolies and combinations "in restraint of trade" illegal. The language was clearly directed against monopolies, but the definition remained vague, as generations of antitrust lawyers could attest. The measure was not enforced much during its first decade, but it became the basis for subsequent antitrust prosecutions under Theodore Roosevelt after 1901.

Meanwhile, the surge in protest from the farm sector that had begun during the late 1880s persuaded Republicans that they needed to make at least a symbolic gesture to placate agrarian sentiment. While they drew back from coining silver into money without limits, they did try to assist the expansion of the currency by having the government buy a fixed amount of the white metal each month. The government could then coin it into money or not as it saw fit. Called the Sherman Silver Purchase Act, named after Senator John Sherman of Ohio, it was a mild compromise, but in the minds of some eastern Republicans and their Democratic counterparts, it was a long step toward the abandonment of the gold standard.

The major Republican disappointment occurred on the issue of voting rights for blacks. Representative Henry Cabot Lodge of Massachusetts introduced an elections bill that would have given the federal courts the right to name bipartisan panels to regulate voter registration and administer elections. The judges could also name investigators to examine complaints of voting discrimination. The South erupted in protest at what was soon dubbed "the Force Bill" because it would compel Dixie to allow black Americans to vote. Grover Cleveland called it "a dark blow at the freedom of the ballot," and an Alabama newspaper said it would "deluge the South in blood." The bill passed the House on a party-line vote of 155 to 149 and then went on to the Senate. There it lingered until after the election of 1890 when the Democrats and some western Republicans killed it. These Republican dissenters were more interested in inflationary solutions such as free silver than in the rights of African Americans. With the bill's defeat went the last meaningful civil rights legislation for almost three-quarters of a century. As had happened so often in the past, mild Republican steps in the direction of political equality ran into unyielding Democratic opposition.[36]

As 1890 proceeded, Republicans sensed that their activism and agenda were meeting with voter resistance. Confident of the rightness of their cause, they pressed ahead. On the local level in the Middle West, other Republicans sought to implement their own programs in ways that compounded the party's problems with the voters. Convinced that they could use the law to produce a more godly and pious society, party activists in states such as Wisconsin, Illinois, and Iowa pushed for laws to close sporting events and taverns on Sunday, to mandate that public schools receiving state support teach their classes in

English (usually instead of German or Polish), and to obtain stronger controls on alcohol. These measures alienated Irish Catholic and German Lutheran voters who made up important swing blocs in key states. To many it seemed as if the Republicans wanted bigger and more intrusive governments at all levels. The Democrats saw their opportunity.

The election of 1890 ended in serious reverses for the Grand Old Party. The Democrats went on the offensive and attacked all aspects of the majority's program. To make the case that the tariff raised prices, the Democrats sent out peddlers to visit homes and tell residents that their goods now cost more because of the tariff. One Democratic speaker told a crowd in Detroit: "The McKinley bill is with us always, at the table, at the bedside, in the kitchen, in the barn, in the churches and to the cemetery." The Democratic contention that the Republicans were the party of higher taxes and excessive government spending caught on with voters. After all, the Fifty-first Congress had been the first to appropriate 1 billion dollars. That made for a terrific negative slogan for the Democrats—the Billion Dollar Congress. Tom Reed countered that the United States was a "billion dollar country," but few voters bought that argument.[37]

Adding to the Republican problems in 1890 was the arrival on the political scene of the farm discontent that had been mounting since the mid-1880s. With farm prices falling, usually reliable Republican supporters in the Middle West listened as the new Farmers Alliance and their People's Party (or Populists) declared that the old ways of political life no longer suited the needs of the depressed farm sector. It was time for a party that would inflate the currency, raise prices, and make debts easier to pay. In Kansas and Nebraska, orators such as Mary Elizabeth Lease, the "Kansas Pythoness," urged farmers to leave their Republican roots, join the Populists, and "raise less corn and more hell." Republicans reported that the Farmers Alliance "wants to cut a day in two, and the free coinage men are ripe for revolt." An agrarian revolution seemed to be sweeping the South and West.[38]

The election of 1890 proved a disaster for the Republicans,

one of the worst defeats in their history. The party dropped 78 seats in the House, and the next Congress would have 235 Democrats to only 88 Republicans in that body. The Republicans who went under in the Democratic tide represented both the party's past and future. Joseph G. Cannon, a future Speaker, Robert M. La Follette of Wisconsin, and William McKinley all saw their seats turned over to the Democrats. Surveying their defeat, McKinley told his friend Joe Cannon that perhaps the setback was all for the best. There would be time for a well-earned rest and the chance to make some money with the law business in Canton, Ohio. Cannon was more realistic. "That's what I tell all the boys, but, Mack, don't let's lie to one another."[39]

In Republican strongholds such as Massachusetts, Illinois, Iowa, and Ohio, Republican House seats had become Democratic. Meanwhile, the Populists made striking gains and elected nearly forty House members who were outright Farmers Alliance men or sympathetic to the agrarian cause. The next two years would determine whether a farm-based party might actually supplant the Republicans in the American political system. Tom Reed caught the spirit of the GOP after their reverses: "Every woman who went to a store [and found the higher prices that the Democrats had imposed for the election] and tried to buy went home to complain, and a wild unrest filled the public mind. The wonder is that we got any votes at all."[40]

Gilded Age Republicans felt the pain of the 1890 defeat. They believed that they had offered the voters a moderate, reasonable program of economic and political growth. But the public had not liked the higher tariffs, the federal elections bill, and increased spending that went along with Republican initiatives. With no apparent need for bigger government, the Republicans had been rebuked for their presumption. The defeat of the federal elections bill represented a particularly painful setback since it reflected a partial attempt to make southern politics more equitable. As Henry Cabot Lodge noted in his diary, "The sting of the present defeat lies in the fact that the Republican party never since the war deserved so well." That was scant consolation for a party that had been repudiated so strongly by the voters.[41]

The run of bad luck for the Republicans continued during the two years that followed. The defeat in 1890 signaled that President Harrison would have a difficult time winning another term two years later, but there were equal dangers in rejecting an incumbent president. Harrison had named Blaine as his Secretary of State, and the two men worked together reasonably well during the initial stages of Harrison's presidency. By 1891, tension between the two men had increased, and some Republicans looked to the possibility of a Blaine candidacy to bail the party out of trouble. Blaine was only sixty-one, but he was already an old man, with chronic illnesses and a sense of melancholy caused by deaths in his family. Still, leaders who did not like the cold and aloof Harrison warmed to the thought of a Blaine candidacy and the chance to recapture the excitement the Plumed Knight had once evoked.

By the late spring of 1892, Blaine had left the Harrison administration and launched a last-minute bid for the Republican nomination. At the national convention in Minneapolis, the party decided not to ditch Harrison, and Blaine's last foray in Republican politics went down to defeat. Harrison's chances of winning in the fall against Grover Cleveland, nominated a third time by the Democrats, were not much better. Disenchanted with Harrison's leadership, the Republicans prepared themselves for a likely defeat and looked ahead to 1896. Matthew S. Quay of Pennsylvania told the press as he watched Minneapolis shimmer in the summer heat: "It looks as though it might snow."[42]

The 1892 election foreshadowed future events and the social turmoil that was to mark the rest of the 1890s. In June 1892, the Carnegie Steel Company lowered wage rates at its Homestead Steel Plant outside of Pittsburgh. A strike followed with violence in its wake as union members battled with strike breakers and Pinkerton detectives in bloody encounters. Since Andrew Carnegie and his associate Henry Clay Frick were notable Republican business leaders, the Democrats made much of what the tariff and big business had meant to the average worker in 1892. Other strikes dotted the United States. Labor militance that aroused antipathy against big business and the Grand Old Party helped the Democrats as the election neared.

The nature of elections themselves were changing. The days of marching men and spectacular rallies were yielding to what were now called "campaigns of education." Parties reached voters by pamphlets, newspaper advertising, and magazine articles. The glory days of the eloquent stump speakers were sliding into the past. This new approach was costly, and the parties turned to corporations for the funds necessary to pay for documents and ads. The Democrats adjusted to this kind of politics in 1892 better than did their rivals, and Cleveland had a well-funded campaign while Harrison, whose defeat seemed all but certain, did not.

The presidential election of 1892 was a three-cornered race. The People's Party put a national ticket in the field with James B. Weaver as its candidate. The Democrats and the Populists were energetic and enthusiastic. The Republicans largely went through the motions of a campaign. The result was a clear triumph for Cleveland, a rejection of Harrison, and a mixed result for the Populists. Cleveland carved out a popular vote margin of almost 400,000 ballots, the most decisive result since Ulysses S. Grant defeated Horace Greeley in 1872. The Democrat won 277 electoral votes to 145 for Harrison and 22 for Weaver, who carried four western states. The Democrats also controlled both houses of Congress. A Republican senator from Connecticut, Orville H. Platt, summed up the situation: "The Republican party has been defeated in this election because the Democrats have induced all the people in the country who think that they want something which they have not got, to vote the Democratic ticket in the expectation that that party in power will give them what they want."[43]

In the aftermath of the election, the Republicans seemed adrift and at a loss about their future. Both Rutherford B. Hayes and James G. Blaine died in January 1893, and their passing appeared to mark the end of an era in which Republicans had sought to become the nation's majority party. A young college professor named Woodrow Wilson said in a magazine article that "the Republican party is going, or at any rate may presently go, to pieces."[44] Few Republicans anticipated that a looming economic crisis would divide the Democrats, restore the Republicans to national power, and begin a long period in which the Grand Old Party would shape the political destiny of the United States.

Chapter 4

McKINLEY TO ROOSEVELT,
1893–1904

DURING THE SUMMER and fall of 1896, people came to Canton, Ohio, from all over the North and the Middle West. In addition to their regular service, railroads scheduled special trains to convey Republicans of every stripe to William McKinley's hometown. The McKinley Escort Troop of forty-six men brought the delegations to McKinley's house on North Market Street, where he and his wife, Ida, had lived when they were first married a quarter of a century earlier. After noon each day the delegations assembled, McKinley mounted a chair, a box, and eventually a special stand, and then the Republican presidential candidate addressed them. Some 750,000 Americans, voters and nonvoters, journeyed to Canton during the campaign of 1896 for what became the height of the "front-porch campaign" style of electioneering.

The people gathered at Canton were looking for relief from the hard times of the Cleveland administration. The economy had been depressed since 1893, and the angry electorate had defeated congressional Democrats in great numbers in the 1894 elections. McKinley was running against William Jennings Bryan and those Democrats who favored inflation of the currency as a way of promoting a return to prosperity. In contrast, McKinley stressed the need to maintain the dollar at its current value relative to gold bullion and to return to the policy of tariff protection. The crowds cheered his remarks, and the bands played such election anthems as "The Honest Little Dollar's Come to Stay." There was a feeling that it was a Republican year, and the people in Canton sensed that McKinley would soon be president. The political winds that had brought the Democrats into office four years earlier now blew in the direction of the Grand Old Party. The change signaled a transformation in American politics; it was the beginning of an era of Republican dominance.[1]

The Democrats Collapse

> Business is at a standstill and the people are becoming thoroughly aroused. Their feeling is finding expression about as it did during the War of the Rebellion.
>
> —James J. Hill[2]

For years the Republicans had warned the American public that Democratic low-tariff policies would put an end to economic prosperity and plunge the nation into prolonged hard times. In the spring of 1893 these predictions began to come true. Another panic erupted in April 1893 as hundreds of railroads, banking houses, and industrial enterprises failed. As the economy collapsed into a prolonged downturn, unemployment rose, despair spread, and confidence in the future disappeared. The crisis was not the fault of President Grover Cleveland and his new administration, but his record in office would be judged by how well he met the economic challenge.

Cleveland chose to blame the entire economic problem on the Sherman Silver Purchase Act of 1890 that had the government purchase a fixed amount of silver each month. Believing that the law hurt business confidence and undermined the gold standard, he summoned Congress into special session in August

1893 to repeal the offending law. The Democrats were divided. Their eastern, urban, commercial wing supported gold and sound money. Western and southern Democrats, predominantly rural, wanted inflation and an easing of their debts. Faced with Cleveland's support of gold, the Democrats broke into competing factions. In the 1892 election, Cleveland and his party had promised reform of the tariff. But that would have to wait until the Sherman Act was repealed.[3]

Using the protective tariff as their major program, Republicans built their own campaign themes in the 1893 state elections around the failures of their opposition. "On every hand can be seen evidences of Democratic times," said the party in Pennsylvania, "the deserted farm, the silent factory and workshop, and in the large cities soup societies (the only industry created by the Democratic party) abound." The conclusion was obvious. "Theories of tariff reform will not answer the demand of the people for bread." The tariff question would receive even more emphasis in the congressional elections of 1894.[4]

THE REALIGNING ELECTION OF 1894

> We were told in the old times that the rich were getting richer and the poor poorer; and to cure that imaginary ill, our political opponents have brought on a time when everybody is getting poorer.
>
> —Benjamin Harrison[5]

While the economy foundered, the political situation for the Republicans brightened during the rest of 1893. Most of their members of Congress stood behind Cleveland in the fight to repeal the Sherman Act, though silver sentiment ran high among Republicans from the Plains and mountain states. But whatever tensions might exist within the GOP over silver were dwarfed by the party consensus about the wisdom of increasing the tariff to fight the depression. For many Republicans, using the power of the national government to relieve the suffering of the unemployed made sense. As Benjamin Harrison put it, "The Republican theory has been all along that it was right to so legislate as to provide work, employment, comfort to the American workingman. We believe that the National Government has a duty in this respect, as well as the city council and the board of county commissioners." This position stood in marked contrast to the unwillingness of the Cleveland administration to take any direct steps to ease the effects of the depression, to put people back to work, or even to understand the plight of those unemployed. Democratic orthodoxy, as Cleveland understood it, meant that "while the people should patriotically and cheerfully support their government, its functions do not include support of the people."[6]

Throughout 1893 and into 1894 the political situation of the Democrats deteriorated as the Cleveland administration blundered its way through the enactment of a tariff measure intended to produce the reform promised in the presidential campaign. Because their control of the Senate was narrow, the Democrats had to write a revenue bill that conciliated various interests within their party. As a result, what came out of the House as a measure to lower the tariff turned into much more of a protectionist hodgepodge in the Senate. There, the Democratic leader, Arthur Pue Gorman of Maryland, tried to assemble a coalition that could pass some sort of tariff.[7]

The Republicans on Capitol Hill looked on with barely disguised glee as their adversaries wandered deeper into political trouble. In the Senate, the Republicans, said Henry Cabot Lodge of Massachusetts, were "not disposed to enter upon any extreme filibustering; they are determined that the bill shall be thoroughly and fairly discussed in all its items and that its inconsistencies and injustices shall be thoroughly shown up." The resulting Wilson-Gorman Tariff, passed in August 1894, raised rates on some industrial products but represented a travesty of the promised tariff reform. President Cleveland let the bill become law without his signature. "The distrust caused by the Democratic threats of a tariff revolution has produced its bitter fruits," said Republican congressman Nelson Dingley of Maine, "and the end is not yet."[8]

The popular discontent that the depression produced only made things worse for the Democrats. The army of the unemployed, led by Jacob S. Coxey, had come to Washington in the spring of 1894 and were turned away before their petitions could be heard. Later that summer, a strike begun in Chicago against the Pullman Palace Car Company mushroomed into a national railroad walkout led by Eugene V. Debs and the American Railway Union. Meanwhile, the president seemed insensitive to the plight of the average American when he was reluctant to use government power to aid those out of work.[9]

The protest vote was up for grabs between the Populists, with their commitment to inflation in the form of free silver, and the Republicans, who were emphasizing the tariff. While an expanded currency appealed to debt-ridden farmers in the South and West, it had less relevance for industrial workers on a fixed income. The Populists sought to transcend their sectional appeal in 1894, but they were not able to outdo the Republicans in the crucial states of the Middle West and the Northeast.[10]

The 1894 campaign saw a united Republican Party making its case for a national majority against divided and dispirited Democrats. "The drift is all our way!" exclaimed Theodore Roosevelt in September 1894. To ensure Republican success, such popular leaders as Tom Reed and the governor of Ohio, William McKinley, took to the campaign trail and pounded the Democrats for their errors in policy. "Prosperity does not perch upon uncertainty," said Reed. "It can never ripen fruit as long as these noisy boys are shaking and clubbing the tree." McKinley gave 371 speeches in sixteen states during the canvass, and he came out of the election as one of the most likely possibilities for the party's nomination in 1896.[11]

Before the votes were cast in 1894, Reed predicted that "the Democratic mortality will be so great next Fall that their dead will be buried in trenches and marked 'unknown.' " If anything, Reed was too cautious. Even the most optimistic Republican professionals were surprised by the magnitude of the party's victory. On the eve of the election, the Republicans held 127 seats in Congress. After the results came in, they had 244 seats. The Democratic loss of 113 seats marked the greatest transfer of strength from one party to another in the nation's history. Though they gained 5 seats in the Senate, the Republicans did not quite achieve control there, but the future trend was clear.[12]

The outcome in 1894 had an even larger significance for Republicans. It represented what political scientists call a "realigning" election in which the electoral landscape of the nation was transformed. The stalemated politics of the Gilded Age had ended, and an era of Republican dominance of Congress had begun. The GOP would not relinquish control of the House for sixteen years, until the Taft-Roosevelt split of 1910. After the Wilson era from 1912 to 1918, the Republicans would control the House again from 1918 to 1930. This congressional election was one of the most important in the nation's history because it laid the basis for a long period of Republican legislative dominance.[13]

The Republicans had benefited from the disarray of the Democrats, to be sure. The timing of the Panic of 1893 and the inept performance of Cleveland had provided the Republicans with a chance to establish their ascendancy. But with the Populists in the field it was by no means certain that angry voters would necessarily choose the GOP. For the middle-class electorate of the Northeast and Middle West the Republican program of tariff protection, promotion of enterprise, and assertion of national authority seemed a wise answer to the depression. Industrial workers agreed that the tariff and a sound currency were more attuned to their specific needs than the inflationary policies of the People's Party.

THE ADVANCE AGENT OF PROSPERITY

McKinley is in it with the masses in nearly every state in the Union, from New Hampshire to Wyoming, and from

Minnesota to the Gulf. The politicians are making a hard fight against him, but if the masses could speak, McKinley is the choice of at least seventy-five percent of the entire Republican voters in the Union.

—Senator Francis E. Warren (R–Wyoming)[14]

Even a decisive victory in the off-year elections does not always presage success in the presidential contest. Much depended on the candidate that the Republicans selected in 1896. As the party prepared to look at presidential hopefuls in 1895, a number of credible aspirants hoped to gain the prize and capitalize on the Republican triumph in the election that seemed so certain. Tom Reed was the candidate of the forces within the party, largely in the Northeast, who wanted to make an unequivocal commitment to the gold standard and against inflation. Unfortunately for Reed, his sarcasm had made him as many enemies as friends. From the Middle West, Senator William Boyd Allison of Iowa hoped to be a compromise choice if the convention deadlocked. Yet the cautious Allison seemed an unlikely prospect. More and more, as 1895 progressed, it seemed apparent that the front-runner for the nomination was the former congressman and governor of Ohio William McKinley.[15]

In the history of the Republican Party, William McKinley occupies an important place, but one that has become increasingly obscure as his presidency recedes in history. He had the bad fortune to serve before Theodore Roosevelt, and McKinley's reputation has never escaped from the shadow of Roosevelt's tumultuous years in the White House. Another drawback for McKinley's historical standing was his involvement in the Spanish-American War and the Philippine insurrection. Now regarded as misguided imperialist ventures, these conflicts have diminished McKinley's historical stature. When his contributions as a president and a Republican are put in proper context, however, his central place in the history of the GOP in the 1890s is clear.

William McKinley was fifty-three years old in 1896. After a

Civil War career in which he rose to the rank of major (and was known by that title to his friends thereafter), McKinley practiced law in Canton, Ohio, before his election to Congress in 1876. He served there for the next fourteen years. From the outset of his legislative service he steeped himself in the complexities of the protective tariff and became the embodiment of its appeal to the Republican rank and file. In 1890, he helped shape the McKinley Tariff as chairman of the House Ways and Means Committee.[16]

Defeated for reelection in the Democratic sweep in 1890, he won election as governor of Ohio in 1891 and was reelected in 1893. His ability to carry that key midwestern state, along with his popularity as an orator, made him a likely front-runner for the nomination in 1896. His labors for the party in 1894 along with his many friendships across the country created a groundswell of support for him that none of his rivals could match.[17]

McKinley was a short man at five feet six, and he dressed to make himself seem taller than he was. A British reporter who visited him in 1896 described the candidate's "strong, clean-shaven face" that had "clear eyes, wide nose, full lips—all his features suggest dominant will and energy rather than subtlety of mind or emotion." McKinley smoked cigars constantly, but was careful not to be photographed with one. Later, when he was president, a French journalist who came to interview him was told by a diplomat: "You are going to see the Emperor in a dress suit." "His face is as serious and distant as that of a Roman Emperor," decided the reporter. Because he listened more than he talked and displayed few emotions, McKinley was a hard man to know and an easy person to underestimate.[18]

One reason that McKinley has been a mystery for historians to decipher was his reluctance to commit his private thoughts to paper. On the surface, McKinley's letters are terse and unrevealing. His invalid wife and his own discretion closed off his family affairs from public scrutiny. Few men, even those closest to him, really understood McKinley, and his skill and determination as a politician have not been recognized. Underneath his genial exterior was a cold, resourceful mind. An associate, Senator Charles Dick, put it well in 1906: "I don't think that McKinley ever let anything stand in the way of his own advancement. McKinley was not altogether to blame for this trait in his character. He had been petted and flattered until he felt that all the fruit on the tree was his."[19]

McKinley also had the unstinting aid of a prominent Ohio industrialist, Marcus A. "Mark" Hanna. Their friendship has often been caricatured and usually misunderstood. McKinley, not Hanna, was the dominant figure in the relationship between the two men. Hanna supplied access to the business community and money for the McKinley campaign, but he neither made the key decisions nor set the overall strategy. As a Chicago publisher observed, Hanna's approach to McKinley was "always that of a big, bashful boy toward the girl he loves."[20]

Nonetheless, Hanna became one of the important figures in the history of the Republicans because of his friendship with McKinley. The Ohio business executive proved to be a favorite target for cartoonists, who depicted him as the stereotypical example of the excesses of big business. The notion that Hanna directed McKinley's fortunes translated into the perception that big business gave the orders and Republicans jumped to obey. The reality was more complex than that, but the image endured.

Hanna did assist McKinley financially at one key moment. During the Panic of 1893, a friend for whom McKinley had cosigned some debts went bankrupt. As a result, McKinley faced financial ruin. Hanna led the effort to raise funds for his friend to pay off his debts. However, the money-raising, even though it was done in public view, did not hurt McKinley with the voters. It made him seem more human during economic hard times.

The key to McKinley's appeal in 1896 was his identification with the tariff and his wide popularity within the Republican Party. To demonstrate his strength he campaigned as "the Advance Agent of Prosperity" and styled his canvass as "the People Against the Bosses." Republican leaders in the East tried to block

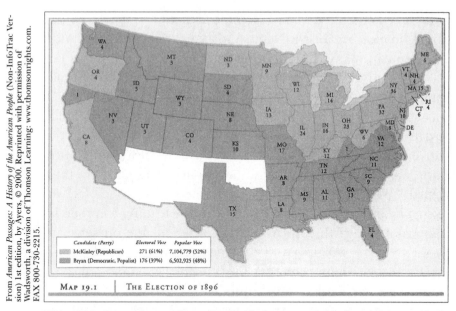

Candidate (Party)	Electoral Vote	Popular Vote
McKinley (Republican)	271 (61%)	7,104,779 (52%)
Bryan (Democratic, Populist)	176 (39%)	6,502,925 (48%)

MAP 19.1 | THE ELECTION OF 1896

This 1896 electoral map shows the divide between the industrial East and the agrarian South and West when McKinley won the White House.

his nomination by supporting Tom Reed or a group of favorite sons in hopes that a compromise candidate might surface. Instead, McKinley went to the Republican National Convention in St. Louis with a first-ballot victory in sight.

GOLD VERSUS SILVER IN 1896

> *The mills are a-stoppin', an' the markets are a-droppin'*
>   *An' we want yer, McKinley, yes, we do;*
> *The last four years of Grover, thank the Lord, are almost over*
>   *An' our hearts are a-turnin', Mack, to you*
> *We've been thinkin', till we're sad, of the good old times we had*
>   *Up to eighteen ninety-two*
> *An' you see we do not care if t'was called a "robber tariff,"*
>   *We want yer, McKinley, yes, we do.*
>
>   —McKinley campaign song, 1896[21]

The most contentious issue of the convention was that of national finance. Against a Democratic Party for which inflation was popular, many Republicans, especially from the industrial East, wanted to make an unequivocal endorsement of the gold standard. Western Republicans, from states where free silver was strong, hoped for more conciliatory language. McKinley and Hanna, who was managing his candidate's fortunes at the convention, agreed with the platform's declaration that the party was "unreservedly" for sound money. The platform then added: "We are therefore opposed to the free coinage of silver, except by international agreement with the leading commercial nations of the earth, which agreement we pledge ourselves to promote." The wording was designed to indicate to the westerners that McKinley, while backing the gold standard, left some room for compromise. But a number of western Republicans bolted the party, despite the "international agreement" phrasing. The upshot of the convention was the fixed impression that the Republican Party had become the unwavering champion of the gold standard.[22]

As anticipated, McKinley achieved his first-ballot victory, and the party selected Garret A. Hobart of New Jersey to balance its midwestern presidential candidate with an eastern vice president. The Republicans expected to carry the Northeast easily, and the battleground of the election became the large states of the Midwest. If the Democrats picked anyone identified with the Cleveland administration and its problems, a landslide Republican victory seemed possible.[23]

The Democrats then did the unexpected. They chose William Jennings Bryan as their nominee. Bryan was a two-term congressman from Nebraska who had established himself as the champion of free silver and rural values. His famous "Cross of Gold" speech at the Democratic convention in Chicago had electrified the nation with the line "You shall not crucify mankind upon a cross of gold." The People's Party also nominated Bryan. He could count on the Solid South and much of the far West. During the summer, the youthful, dynamic Bryan (he was only thirty-six) seemed the popular favorite to win the election, unless the Republicans could counter his charismatic style. Bryan soon was out on the stump attracting large audiences and building his momentum.[24]

The Republicans responded with what became known as a "campaign of education." First, the GOP raised impressive amounts of money, probably between $3.5 and $4 million from eastern Republicans and corporate leaders fearful of a Bryan victory. In history, this large amount of cash has often been described as a slush fund used to buy voters and to coerce industrial workers. The reality was more prosaic. The money went for advertising and pamphlets.[25]

McKinley struck the keynote: "This is a year for press and pen." The Republicans used their money to pay for some 200 million pamphlets and a torrent of newspaper advertising. Special inserts appeared each week in small-town papers about McKinley, his wife, and his family. In many languages, the stories described the virtues both of the candidate and a sound dollar. McKinley allowed himself to be filmed, and the party employed the crude movie in the campaign. Hanna watched over all these tactics with his shrewd organization sense. Theodore Roosevelt said that Hanna had advertised McKinley like a patent medicine.[26]

The candidate himself carried the brunt of the actual campaigning from his front porch in Canton, where he gave more than three hundred speeches to three-quarters of a million listeners. The candidate coordinated his speeches in advance with visiting delegations to avoid any unscripted mistakes. Each day McKinley reiterated the keynotes of his campaign, and each day the nation's newspapers reported on what he said. The Republican candidate seemed calmer and more statesmanlike in this domestic setting. Thus, McKinley controlled the agenda of the campaign and blended an allegiance to sound money with a reiteration of the virtues of tariff protection.[27]

Bryan's initial surge faltered as the autumn of 1896 approached. His party was split, with a Gold Democrat ticket in the field. The public's initial fascination with free silver ebbed away, and the one-dimensional aspect of Bryan's campaign became evident. As Hanna put it, the Democratic candidate was "talking silver all the time and that's where we've got him." Bryan called the East "the enemy's country," and his monetary doctrines did not appeal to workingmen and small-business owners in the Middle West.[28]

As the election neared, the Republicans cast their campaign as a patriotic appeal, and American flags became a feature of their rallies. The identification of their party with the nation and the suggestion that the Democrats were less committed to the cause of the country and its honor were too tempting for Republicans to ignore. In the East, attacks on Bryan and his supporters as anarchists and revolutionaries reached levels of near hysteria. Theodore Roosevelt reflected this spirit when he told an English friend in October, "All the men who pray for anarchy, or who believe in socialism, and all the much larger number who have not formulated their thoughts sufficiently to believe in either, but who want to strike down the well-to-do, and who have been inflamed against the rich until they feel that they are willing to sacrifice their own welfare, if only they can make others less happy, are banded against us."[29]

To counter this Republican groundswell, the Democrats pounded away at McKinley's alleged subservience to Mark Hanna. Cartoons depicted "Dollar Mark" with a little McKinley strapped to his waist. Democrats alleged that major corporations and businesses coerced their workers to make them vote for McKinley. No doubt some of McKinley's more impassioned supporters in the business community did try to strong-arm their employees, but laboring men on fixed incomes also had good reason to dislike inflation and the economic uncertainty that would have accompanied a Bryan election.[30]

The outcome of the election of 1896 was a thorough Republican triumph. McKinley won 271 electoral votes to Bryan's 176, and received 7,035,638 popular votes to 6,467,945 for the Democratic ticket. The Republicans held on to the control of the

House with a large majority. Their grasp of the Senate was more tenuous.

The election galvanized public interest. In the North, more than seventy-eight percent of the eligible voters went to the polls. These totals would not be repeated during the entire twentieth century. McKinley's victory brought together an enduring coalition of voters—urban dwellers in the North, prosperous farmers, and large elements of industrial workers. The Republican appeal reached into most ethnic groups with the exception of the Irish. The election of 1896 solidified the result in 1894 and meant that the Republicans were now the majority party of the nation everywhere but in the Solid South.

THE WAR WITH SPAIN AND ITS CONSEQUENCES

> Territory sometimes comes to us when we go to war in a holy cause, and whenever it does the banner of liberty will float over it and bring, I trust, blessings and benefits to all the people.
>
> —William McKinley[31]

While McKinley's election was fought out on domestic issues, the keynote of his administration became overseas expansion. The Cuban revolt against the rule of Spain, which had begun in 1895, emerged two years later as the leading foreign policy question, and a significant sentiment in both parties sought American intervention to stop the conflict that was devastating the nearby island. Because this action culminated in the Spanish-American War and led to American intervention in the Philippines, McKinley's leadership in 1898 and beyond has been one of the most criticized aspects of his presidential tenure.

In his first year in office, McKinley began the revival of the presidency, following the low point it had reached during the Cleveland years. He cultivated good relations with the press and brought the newsmen into the White House by setting up tables of their own on the second floor. The new president traveled and used these junkets to push his programs with the electorate. Relations with Congress also improved as McKinley listened to what lawmakers of both parties had to say about the nation's policies and future course.[32]

On the domestic side, the new administration saw a protective tariff law through Congress. The Dingley Tariff (named after Nelson Dingley, then chair of the Ways and Means Committee) raised rates on industrial goods. The law also contained language allowing the president to negotiate reciprocal trade treaties with other countries, a program that McKinley pushed hard during his tenure as chief executive. To promote a wider use of silver, McKinley named a commission to talk with the French and the British, but that endeavor failed when Great Britain refused to endorse an effort to open the mints of India to the white metal. With prosperity returning because of gold discoveries in the Yukon and South Africa, pressure for silver eased. The administration endorsed the Gold Standard Act of 1900 that put the nation behind a single standard of value for its currency.[33]

But the Cuban uprising against the Spanish in Cuba dominated the first year of McKinley's presidency. Unlike Grover Cleveland, who had sympathized with Spain and let them try to subdue the revolt, McKinley made it clear that his administration disapproved of continued turmoil and wanted the rebels and the Spanish to talk about a settlement. He insisted that any agreement be acceptable to the Cubans, which meant the ouster of Spain and independence for the revolutionaries. During 1897 and into 1898, McKinley struggled to find a peaceful solution on the basis of these principles. Since Spain believed that Cuba was part of their nation and would not surrender it peacefully, a solution was difficult to reach.[34]

The Republican Party generally favored intervention to end the fighting in Cuba, as did the Democrats during this period. By early 1898, a crisis with Spain loomed. The administration had sent the battleship U.S.S. *Maine* to Havana harbor as a goodwill gesture in January. When the ship exploded in February, Americans believed that Spain was responsible. Diplomatic relations with Madrid worsened, and Congress pressed for war. Despite these moves, the president, who hoped to achieve Cuba's independence from Spain without violence, delayed as long as he could to find a way out of the crisis. In the end, since neither Spain nor the United States would give way, war came in late April. Contrary to the historical canards about his performance, McKinley had worked hard for peace until war became inevitable. Once the fighting broke out, he used his power as president to bring the war to a speedy and victorious resolution.[35]

The rapid series of American victories on land and sea in the summer of 1898 enhanced McKinley's prestige and identified the Republicans with another military triumph. The president pursued the war in a nonpartisan manner, allocating commissions to Republicans and Democrats in equal measure. When the fighting ended in August and it came time to send commissioners to Paris to negotiate a peace treaty, he dispatched a panel that contained members of both parties, several of them senators who would vote on any pact that resulted from the talks.[36]

While most Americans applauded the eviction of Spain from Cuba, there was less consensus on the fate of the Philippine Islands. The United States sent a fleet to that Asian possession of Spain as part of a war plan to pressure Madrid to seek peace terms. The victory of Commodore George Dewey at Manila Bay on May 1, 1898, had given the United States a strong claim on the archipelago, and as the summer progressed, the McKinley administration became more identified with an imperialistic policy that sought to establish an American presence in Asia. Democrats largely dissented from these developments, and an anti-imperialist wing of the opposition emerged during the last months of 1898.

The Republicans faced the congressional elections in 1898 as the party associated with the victory over Spain, but they still anticipated the losses that the incumbent party usually suffered two years after a successful presidential election. President McKinley capitalized on the opportunity that celebrations of the American triumph provided to make a speaking tour of the Middle West in October 1898. No chief executive had gone on

such a journey during an off-year election since Andrew Johnson's disastrous "Swing Around the Circle" in 1866.[37]

While McKinley did not ask the voters to elect Republicans,
he sounded the notes of expansionism and made the case for retaining the Philippines. He also asserted that prosperity was returning. "Business looks hopeful and assuring everywhere, and
our credit balances show the progress which the country is making." What the president said, and the crowds he attracted,
helped to hold down Republican losses in the House of Representatives. The GOP lost nineteen seats, while the Democrats
gained fifty seats, many of those from the Populists. The Republicans added six seats in the Senate, and thus the party now controlled both houses.[38]

These majorities would not take office until December 1899
under the system of congressional sessions that operated in the
late nineteenth century. The Treaty of Paris now became the
focus of partisan conflict. Signed in December 1898 between
the United States and Spain, it removed the Philippine Islands
from Spanish control and awarded possession to the United
States. That treaty would be debated in the lame-duck session of
the Senate that ran from December 1898 to March 1899. The
Democrats in the Senate saw an opportunity to embarrass the
administration by defeating the pact.

McKinley displayed solid presidential leadership in getting
the treaty ratified in the months that followed. He spoke in the
South on behalf of sectional harmony and thus subtly pressured
southern Democratic senators. The administration used patronage, backroom deals, and the leadership of Senate Republicans
on behalf of the document. William Jennings Bryan also helped
when he advocated ratifying the treaty and fighting the issue in
the 1900 elections. The Senate ultimately approved the Treaty
of Paris on February 6, 1899, by one vote more than the two-
thirds necessary for ratification.[39]

But the administration had a difficult year ahead because of
the insurrection in the Philippines that broke out against American rule in February. There was the task of governing Cuba and

Puerto Rico as well. The president successfully handled these crises by using his power as commander in chief to create military governments without congressional oversight. McKinley's speaking tours in 1899 stilled popular doubts over possible imperialism among the public. Meanwhile, the Republicans proclaimed that prosperity had returned. When the GOP achieved success in the 1899 state elections, a Republican told McKinley that the campaign "has settled the issues and the candidates for the presidential election in 1900."[40]

There were two issues, however, that promised future trouble for the Republicans. The late 1890s saw an upsurge of racial violence as southerners imposed segregation firmly on the African-American population there. A riot in Wilmington, North Carolina, left eleven blacks dead. McKinley said little about such events, and his policies looked more toward reconciliation with the white South. Black leaders fumed about the president's position. He was, said T. Thomas Fortune, "a man of jelly, who would turn us loose to the mob and not say a word."[41]

McKinley's record was better than that, but only just. Like many white Americans, he and his party had concluded that efforts to pursue policies of racial justice in the South were doomed to failure. The most that black Republicans could hope for was patronage positions and a role of furnishing delegates from Dixie at the national conventions. Compared to the Democrats, that was enough to retain the loyalties of those few African Americans who could still vote in the South. Nonetheless, the party had sacrificed a portion of its original purpose that proved hard to recapture.[42]

More pressing was the Republican attitude toward the burgeoning number of large businesses popularly known as "trusts." In the wake of prosperity, corporations had absorbed competitors at a dizzying pace. During 1899, some twelve hundred companies were bought out or taken over. Newspapers were filled with stories about the wave of corporate mergers. Just what the Republicans planned to do about these developments was not clear. "Jamming a stick into the machinery will only throw us back," said one Republican. Many party members shared the view of Senator Mark Hanna (he had been appointed to the upper house in 1897 and elected in 1898) that "a man had a right to do what he pleased with his own."[43]

The McKinley administration responded to these concerns with speeches that laid the groundwork for federal action in the second term. McKinley, however, did not authorize use of the Sherman Antitrust Act against the large corporations, though he recognized that "there must be a remedy for the evils involved in such organizations." McKinley knew that the protective tariff was a particular point of vulnerability for the GOP since the Democrats were arguing that high tariffs promoted the growth of trusts. The president pushed for reciprocal trade treaties as a way of defusing the tariff issue without destroying the protective system. Many within his own party disagreed, and reciprocity seemed likely to be a contentious Republican issue in a second term.[44]

The impression that the Republicans were the party of big business was solidifying. Their senators were identified with corporate affairs, and the party's early emphasis on the unity of capital and labor was giving way to a sympathy with business at the expense of other segments of society. As Americans thought of themselves more and more as consumers, Democratic charges that big business meant higher prices eroded support for Republicans among middle-class voters. As a journalist noted in 1900, "The Republican party may suffer innocently from a bad name, but I do not believe that one voter in ten in the United States honestly thinks that, if continued in power, it will wage successful war upon the trusts."[45]

THE ROOSEVELT CANDIDACY

Senator, I am not a candidate for Vice President, and I don't want the nomination. What I want is to be Governor of New York.

—Theodore Roosevelt, June 1900[46]

As the election of 1900 neared, the most pressing business for the party was the choice of a new running mate for President McKinley. Vice President Hobart had succumbed to heart disease in November 1899, and the national convention would pick his successor. Talk swirled around the new governor of New York, Theodore Roosevelt, but neither McKinley nor Senator Hanna liked that option. The administration wanted a more reliable, predictable vice presidential choice.

Keeping Theodore Roosevelt out of the limelight was no easy task. He was forty-one in 1899 and had been a celebrity since his first days in politics in the New York Assembly in the early 1880s. Following the death of his first wife in 1884, Roosevelt raised cattle in the West, where his reputation as a two-fisted hero spread. After six years on the Civil Service Commission, from 1889 to 1895, he served on the board of police commissioners in New York City, was Assistant Secretary of the Navy under McKinley, and left for the war with Spain as an officer in a volunteer regiment in April 1898. The unit became known as "Roosevelt's Rough Riders," and its spectacular charge up Kettle Hill on July 1, 1898, made Roosevelt a national hero. Winning a tough race for governor of the Empire State in the fall of 1898 precipitated talk about his aspirations for higher office. Hobart's death turned the possibility into a reality.[47]

While Roosevelt enjoyed immense popularity, he made old-line Republicans uneasy. A century later, when Roosevelt has become a revered American icon, it is difficult to explain why he triggered such qualms among his fellow Republicans. Part of it was his hesitancy in embracing the protective tariff. He had flirted with free trade in his youth, and many proponents of protection correctly sensed that Roosevelt had little familiarity with the subject. His aristocratic disdain for business enterprise was another element in the equation. Finally, the young Roosevelt seemed impetuous and erratic. As McKinley put it, "Roosevelt is always in such a state of mind."[48]

On the other hand, he was very popular, especially among younger party members in the West. Although he hated the name and no one who knew him well ever called him "Teddy," the nation styled him "Teddy" Roosevelt and followed his large family, his public exploits, and his vivid personality. As a result, he would bring excitement and energy to the ticket and would campaign with his accustomed intensity. The sticking point for those promoting Roosevelt was the candidate's own hesitance in early 1900. Seeing 1904 as his best chance to run for the Republican nomination, he knew that if he ran for another two-year term as governor, he would be out of office in 1903 without a secure political base. Roosevelt thought that a Cabinet post or a stint as governor-general of the Philippines might round out his credentials as a presidential hopeful, but none of these options appealed to the White House. Within New York, the boss of the party's organization, Senator Thomas Collier Platt, wanted Roosevelt out of the state. The governor had been too eager to take steps to publicize corporate abuses, and his activism ill-suited the Republican hierarchy. So Platt encouraged Roosevelt's vice presidential hopes.[49]

In the end, the administration could not find a credible alternative to Roosevelt. The Republican convention met in Philadelphia, where Roosevelt showed up on the floor wearing the Rough Rider headgear that had become his trademark. "That's an acceptance hat," noted one observer, and so it proved. McKinley gave way to the inevitable. Senator Hanna fumed: "Don't you know there's only one life between that madman and the Presidency?" But the tide was too strong, and Roosevelt was swept onto the ticket. The GOP went into the campaign brimming with confidence. A magazine editor named Albert Shaw, himself a Republican, caught a cautionary note amid the self-congratulation. "The Republican party was never outwardly so harmonious as it is now since it was organized half a century ago, and, apparently, it was never as strong as it is now. But it is a little too fat and sleek and prosperous and its moral tone is not quite what it ought to be. It looks back with pride, rather than forward with aspiration."[50]

McKinley observed the custom among incumbent presidents of not campaigning for reelection, so the bulk of the work fell to Roosevelt and Republican surrogates. The Democrats nominated Bryan for a second time. At first the Democrat tried to make imperialism the key issue of the campaign, but McKinley defused the matter in his speech and letter of acceptance. Colonial government in the Philippines, the president argued, was preferable to Bryan's proposal for independence and a trusteeship status for the islands. Bryan then switched his emphasis to the trust question and then back to free silver. The Democrats never found a consistent theme for their campaign nor offered the voters a reason to turn McKinley out of office.

The result was a decisive McKinley victory in the second race with Bryan. The president won 292 electoral votes to 155 for his rival. The Republican ticket garnered 51.7 percent of the vote to Bryan's 45.5 percent. McKinley increased his popular-vote majority over Bryan by 200,000 votes. The Republicans also enjoyed a forty-six-seat majority in the House and had a twenty-four-seat edge in the Senate. McKinley told friends that "I am now President of the whole people."[51]

Tragedy at Buffalo

> My wife, be careful, Cortelyou, how you tell her—oh, be careful.
>
> —William McKinley[52]

During the first half of 1901, McKinley made it clear that he intended to push for revision of the tariff through ratification of reciprocity treaties with Argentina and France. In June, he stated that he would not be a candidate for a third term in 1904. Noting the continued growth of trusts, the president discussed with aides what might be done in the way of revitalizing the Sherman Antitrust Act. In September 1901, McKinley fulfilled a commitment to visit the Pan-American Exposition in Buffalo, New York. In a speech on September 5, he told the crowd: "The period of exclusiveness is past. The expansion of our trade and

commerce is the pressing problem. Commercial wars are unprofitable. A policy of goodwill and friendly trade relations will
prevent reprisals. Reciprocity treaties are in harmony with the
spirit of the times; measures of retaliation are not."[53]

McKinley understood that the tariff issue, long a source of
strength for the GOP, was becoming a political liability. As prosperity returned, prices rose, and industrial consolidation
spread, discontent with protection appeared in key states such
as Iowa where farmers resented the cost of agricultural imple-
ments and other supplies for their business. The "Iowa Idea,"
that tariffs should be lowered on trust-made products, gained
attention during the spring and summer of 1901. McKinley saw
his treaties as a way of modifying the protective system in a gradual and controlled manner without abandoning the tariff altogether. Many Republicans were suspicious of what the president
proposed, but his credentials as the "Napoleon of Protection"
were so good that he could not be criticized personally for his
apparent heresy.

How the history of the Republican Party might have differed
had McKinley lived to serve his full second term is conjecture.
Much of what happened under Theodore Roosevelt—lawsuits
against the trusts, the canal across Central America, and settlement of the boundary dispute with Canada over Alaska—all
these would likely have occurred in a second McKinley term. Although the Senate would not have accepted quietly the reciprocity treaties, in the end the lawmakers would likely have
acquiesced. Progressive reform would have begun in a more se-
date and measured way. Would the GOP have escaped division
and discord in 1912? No one can say.

On September 6, 1901, while McKinley was standing in a
receiving line at the Temple of Music at the Pan-American Exposition, an assassin shot him. The president died eight days
later, whispering the words of "Nearer My God to Thee." His
heartbroken Secretary of State, John Hay, said that McKinley
"showed in his life how a citizen should live, and in his last hour
taught us how a gentleman could die." McKinley had been a

major architect of Republican success in the 1890s and a forceful innovator of presidential power. Now the nation turned to
see how his youthful successor would perform in the White
House.[54]

THE UNITED STATES AND A NEW CENTURY

> Circumstances—education, the claims upon vitality, the
> natural pride of a self-governing people—have raised
> the standard of American life to a height hitherto unre-
> alized in civilized society."
>
> —Archibald R. Colquhoun[55]

When Theodore Roosevelt came to the presidency, the United
States had left behind the hard times of the 1890s and now enjoyed the fruits of prosperity that had come during the waning
years of the nineteenth century. According to the census, there
were almost 76 million Americans, most of them white, with
more than 9 million blacks and 238,000 Native Americans. Most
people lived in the Northeast and north central areas, some 56
million in all. More citizens lived in rural than in urban areas,
but the trend toward city life was accelerating. In the first full
year of Roosevelt's administration, almost 649,000 newcomers
entered the United States from abroad. The tide of immigration
swelled throughout Roosevelt's presidency. Some welcomed the
new diversity; others among the older American stock tried to
restrict immigration. These cross-currents shaped politics in the
decades ahead.

In economic terms, the country was well off. The gross national product had reached almost $20 billion by 1901, and per
capita income had reached $569 by Roosevelt's first term. The
money that Americans earned faced no income tax on either the
state or national level, and other levies were low, except on luxuries and imports. Yet for all the collective wealth that Americans enjoyed at the beginning of the twentieth century, the
nation confronted serious social inequities.

Victims of work-related injuries, which included some twenty thousand deaths a year and another half-million maimed or hurt, had little insurance or medical assistance. Skilled workers received some protection through craft unions such as the American Federation of Labor, but unskilled laborers were at the mercy of the marketplace. There were few old-age pensions and no federal unemployment insurance. The welfare state as the twentieth century would know it did not yet exist.

Power in society rested with corporations and banks, which dominated the economy. The antitrust law had been rendered largely impotent, and there was real doubt about the power of the federal government to supervise business. Theodore Roosevelt believed that it was necessary to alter that balance. "The absolutely vital question was whether the government had power to control them at all. This question had not yet been decided in favor of the United States Government."[56] For the majority of Republicans in 1901, the dominance of business presented no philosophical problems. For Roosevelt and dissident Republicans in the Middle West who were starting to call themselves progressives, the party needed to engage the issue of bringing corporations to heel.

Two changes in American attitudes would shape the future of the Republicans during the decade that followed. Increasingly, citizens called for the government to do more to regulate an industrial society at the state and national levels. That pressure challenged the Republicans who believed in a strong government to promote economic growth but not in interfering with business itself. The other new force was a developing suspicion of the value of political parties. After more than a generation in which parties were regarded as necessary to the working of democracy, more and more people began to ask whether parties contributed to the problems of society and needed to be limited in their influence and power. Because they were the majority party, the Republicans became the focus of measures limiting the power of partisan politics to shape national policy.

THE YOUNGEST PRESIDENT

> You will have hard work to keep the pace with Roosevelt
> and sometimes I fancy you must be frightened at the
> spirit you have helped to unchain.
>
> —Eugene Hale[57]

Theodore Roosevelt was forty-two years old when he became
the twenty-sixth president of the United States. He had been a
Republican since his boyhood, but his allegiance to the Grand
Old Party was not that of a regular partisan. He had little interest in the protective tariff and was not a fan of businessmen or
the process by which they made their money. Instead, as a member of the New York aristocracy, he saw his duty as representing
the American people in their adjustment to the promises and
perils of industrial growth.

For Roosevelt the Republicans were the party of constructive
nationalism, and the new president believed that government
power could be employed to enable all citizens to share in the
bounty of an expanding economy. In time he would come to believe that some government regulation of the economy was also
necessary. Democrats were the party of ineptitude and states'
rights who could be counted on to thwart the constructive work
of Roosevelt and his party. While Roosevelt was adroit at the political maneuvering that allowed him to win the Republican
nomination in 1904, over the long haul he was not skilled at persuading his fellow party members to follow his policies.

Where Roosevelt excelled was in the public conduct of his office. He governed with energy and excitement. For the first time
the president became a celebrity in his own right, and the newspapers avidly followed the president's frenetic schedule, the an-
tics of his brood of young children, and the social life of his
daughter from his first marriage, Alice Roosevelt. When a friend
told him that his daughter's lifestyle, which included a pet
snake, fast cars, and many parties, needed restraint, Roosevelt
replied, "I can be President of the United States, or I can control

Alice. I can't possibly do both."[58] Roosevelt was the first president to use his family in a conscious way to enhance his own appeal.

Roosevelt was also the first president to make the most of the celebrity potential of the office. Newspapers covered him as though he were a modern film star. "When Roosevelt was in the neighborhood," wrote a journalist who did not like the president much, the public could "no more look the other way than the small boy can turn his head away from a circus parade followed by a steam calliope." Roosevelt conducted public quarrels with a number of Americans, which only added to the fun of his years in the White House. Leaving the White House, Roosevelt attributed part of his success to the publicity value that the presidency had given him. "I have got such a bully pulpit," he told a reporter in February 1909.[59]

In the initial months of his administration, Roosevelt pledged to carry on McKinley's policies, and in substance that is what he did. He soon demonstrated that he had a flair for the dramatic and the timely that his predecessor had not displayed. To build up support among southern Republicans, Roosevelt entertained the African-American leader Booker T. Washington at the White House in October 1901. The South reacted with outrage when the news leaked out that a black had dined with the president and his family. The episode illustrated the continuing power of racism in early-twentieth-century America. It did not stop Roosevelt from pursuing Republican delegates for 1904 among the shrinking number of GOP members in Dixie.

In one key respect, however, Roosevelt did abandon a McKinley initiative, and the consequences of that decision proved difficult for the Republicans. The reciprocity treaties that McKinley had championed were still pending before the Senate, and it would take a fight to gain approval for them. For Roosevelt, who found the tariff boring, the prospect of such a struggle was dismaying. As a result, he deferred to the Senate leadership, including Nelson Aldrich of Rhode Island, and gave the pacts only a tepid endorsement. The Senate did not act on them, and they lapsed.

What that meant was that no meaningful action on the tariff could take place in Roosevelt's first term. When he again postponed the issue in his second term, the task of dealing with protection fell to his successor. Meanwhile, the tensions between advocates of tariff revision in the Middle West and defenders of protectionism in the Northeast and Mid-Atlantic states intensified. Democratic assaults on the tariff as a cause of higher prices and industrial bigness added to Republican vulnerability on the issue. The return of inflation and rising consumer prices during the first decade of the century gave Democratic arguments more bite with middle-class consumers. But Roosevelt left the issue alone to fester and divide Republicans.

THE SQUARE DEAL

> The great corporations which we have grown to speak of rather loosely as trusts are the creatures of the State, and the State not only has the right to control them, but it is in duty bound to control them whenever the need of such control is shown.
>
> —Theodore Roosevelt[60]

The new president elected to emphasize control of big business as one of his salient priorities. In February 1902, the Justice Department filed an antitrust suit against the Northern Securities Company, a holding company for railroads in the Northwest. Unpopular in the region that these lines crossed, the company had been under legal attack by the governors of the states affected. Roosevelt was determined to demonstrate that the power of the federal government was more potent than any combination of private capital. Once that supremacy was established, Roosevelt believed that the government could then encourage socially useful enterprises ("good trusts") and discourage ones that misbehaved ("bad trusts") through an ongoing regulatory process.

Roosevelt's assault on Northern Securities prompted the financier J. P. Morgan to hurry down to Washington to express his personal concern about the treatment of a firm he had helped put together. In a celebrated White House meeting on February 22, 1902, the investment banker told Roosevelt, "If we have done anything wrong, send your man to my man and they can fix it up." Roosevelt and his attorney general, Philander C. Knox, informed Morgan that "we don't want to fix it up, we want to stop it." Roosevelt assured Morgan that his other interests would not be attacked "unless we find out that in any case they have done something we regard as wrong." Once Morgan had left, Roosevelt told his attorney general, "That is a most illuminating illustration of the Wall Street point of view. Mr. Morgan could not help regarding me as a big rival operator who either intended to ruin his interests or else could be induced to come to an agreement to ruin none."[61]

The episode and Roosevelt's comments expressed one part of his attitude toward big business. By taking Northern Securities to court and obtaining a favorable ruling from the Supreme Court, as he did in 1904, he demonstrated that the government was more powerful than any single corporation. Once he had done so, however, he followed a policy that worked along the lines Morgan had suggested. The White House distinguished between socially useful corporations, such as United States Steel, and the ones that operated in a more predatory fashion, such as Standard Oil or the so-called Beef Trust of meat packers. The "good trusts" received government support for their economic programs; the "bad trusts" risked antitrust prosecution.[62]

Roosevelt's case against Northern Securities enhanced his popularity in 1902. He added to his standing with the voters when he intervened in the Anthracite Coal Strike in the fall, thereby averting an economic crisis in those areas of the country that depended on coal for their winter heat. Summoning the mine owners and the union leaders to the White House, Roosevelt's intervention led to a settlement that ended the threat of a walkout. The most important aspect of the episode was the implicit recognition that the president gave to labor. It represented a philosophy that Roosevelt called "the Square Deal," one that refuted the popular idea that "the Republican party always legislates to aid the rich and oppress the poor."[63]

The settlement of the strike helped the Republicans in the 1902 congressional elections. The census of 1900 served to increase the size of the House of Representatives, and so each party gained seats. The Democrats added twenty-seven seats; the Republicans gained eleven. The GOP still held a majority of thirty in the lower house. Roosevelt was "well contented with the elections."[64]

Although there were no public opinion polls at the beginning of the twentieth century, Republicans recognized that Roosevelt had captured the nation's attention and regard by early 1903. Within the party he had already obtained more than half of the nearly five hundred delegates needed to assure his nomination in 1904. Some of these successes had occurred in the South, where the incumbent president usually controlled the predominantly black delegations. But the enthusiasm for Roosevelt extended across the entire rank and file of the GOP.

Nominated in His Own Right

> I think I can truthfully say that I now have to my credit a sum of substantial achievement and the rest must take care of itself.
>
> —Theodore Roosevelt[65]

One important segment of the Republicans remained cool to the new president. Businessmen feared that he might go further in the direction of government regulation than he had already. In the year before an election, though, these qualms were muted and not widely discussed. Some leaders hoped, however, that an alternative to Roosevelt might emerge. They looked to Senator Mark Hanna to supply them with that option.

By 1903, Mark Hanna had achieved a legendary reputation in American politics as both the architect of McKinley's success in 1896 and his political confidant during the ensuing presidency. Opponents of the Ohio senator had characterized him as "Dollar Mark," who fostered trusts and oppressed the working-man. In fact, Hanna envisioned a society where business and labor cooperated for common ends, and he looked with scorn on those employers who refused, as he put it, to meet their men halfway. He was far from the reactionary force that the Democrats assailed.

But Hanna's reputation outran his real power in the Republican Party. Much of his influence had rested on his presumed closeness to McKinley. When the president died in September 1901, much of Hanna's clout died with him. The senator was not in good health, either. Most of all, he knew that a presidential nomination obtained after the defeat of a popular incumbent would be worth very little. The Republicans were hardly likely to select the politician who symbolized corporate power after rejecting a trustbuster. There was a degree of improbability in Hanna's candidacy from the outset.[66]

Nonetheless, the Ohio senator wanted to be consulted about the nomination and said in August 1902 that it was "out of place to permit so much discussion about the future selection of the candidate for the Republican party." He wanted to see how well Roosevelt did and keep his options open to support another candidate in 1904. But that was not what Roosevelt wanted to hear. Passionately concerned with being elected in his own right, Roosevelt saw conspiracies against him everywhere. He expected unwavering support for his nomination from Republicans, and he had little patience with Hanna's equivocation.[67]

A political enemy of Hanna's in Ohio, Senator Joseph B. Foraker, saw a chance during the spring of 1903 to embarrass his colleague and help Roosevelt's candidacy. Hanna's allies in Ohio said that the Republican state convention, meeting in May, would not endorse Roosevelt's candidacy so far ahead of the national convention. Foraker immediately announced that because Roosevelt was "the best known and most popular man in the United States," the convention should express its support for his candidacy in 1904.[68]

THE VALUE OF THE BINDER IN HARVEST-TIME

(Apropos of the pledging or "binding" of various State delegations to support Mr. Roosevelt in the

inating convention.)

Theodore Roosevelt locked up the Republican nomination well before the party's convention in 1904. Here the cartoonist for the *Brooklyn Eagle* shows the president gathering up delegates with his "practical politics" binder.

Hanna wired Roosevelt to ask that he not support Foraker and force the issue of an endorsement. Roosevelt wired back that "those who favor my administration and nomination" would favor a resolution of endorsement and "those who do not will oppose them." When confronted with the issue on those terms, Hanna had little choice but to accept a convention endorsement of the president in what one senator called a "back-action-double-spring feat." The episode settled the issue of the 1904 nomination for all practical purposes.[69]

Nonetheless, Roosevelt still wanted to obtain a formal statement of support from Hanna. That did not occur before Hanna's death in February 1904, much to the unhappiness of the White House. Roosevelt believed that he faced a conspiracy among the anti-Roosevelt, pro-business side of the Republican Party. Though there was uneasiness about his policies from that quarter, much of the problem was a function of Roosevelt's obsession with being nominated on his own. With Hanna gone from the scene, that concern faded away, and the months before the national convention became a kind of triumphal procession for the president.

THE REPUBLICAN APPEAL

If Republican policies are approved at the ballot box at the coming election, commerce will not need to furl her sails and industry will not need to prepare to meet surprises which change of administration sometimes brings.

—Charles Warren Fairbanks[70]

Roosevelt's reelection seemed a sure thing during the spring of 1904. In the domestic arena, he had the Northern Securities case (which the Supreme Court decided in the government's favor); the coal Strike, the start to conserve natural resources; and a general level of prosperity. As a world leader he had resolved a boundary dispute with Canada about Alaska and, more important, had secured a zone in Panama through which an isthmian canal could be built. The Democrats had tried to make an issue of Roosevelt's methods in Panama, but most Americans thought his strong position toward Colombia, which had opposed a treaty to obtain the zone, was justified. They endorsed Roosevelt's succinct summation of his approach to foreign policy: "There is a homely old adage which runs 'Speak softly and carry a big stick; you will go far.' " Few presidents have had more going for them as they approached an election than Theodore Roosevelt in 1904.[71]

The Republican National Convention was not an exciting affair. Everyone among the nearly one thousand delegates knew that Roosevelt would be nominated unanimously. As his running mate, the party selected the cautious and careful senator from Indiana Charles Warren Fairbanks. The only exciting moment came when a State Department telegram was read aloud. A man named Ion Perdicaris had been seized in Morocco by a bandit known as the Raisuli. In the diplomatic negotiations, the United States wired Morocco: "We want either Perdicaris alive or Raisuli dead." The disclosure of the telegram did not affect the ultimate decision to release Perdicaris, but it made for great political theater and reinforced Roosevelt's image as a man of action.[72]

The Democrats recognized their weakness and sought to make it a positive asset. Instead of opposing Roosevelt as someone who had not done enough to curb corporations, they elected instead to run to the right of the president. Thinking that Roosevelt's forceful presidency had alienated conservative Americans, the Democrats nominated a candidate whose life had been spent in the quiet of the judicial chamber. Alton B. Parker was a New York state judge who had won a sweeping victory in his race for office in 1897. To the Democrats that meant he could carry New York against Roosevelt. Added to the electoral votes of the Solid South, a win in New York for Parker would put the Democrats very close to victory. So the Democrats turned away from their commitment to William Jennings Bryan and the South and West. They saw Parker as the safe and sane alternative to Roosevelt's flamboyant conduct in office.

"Cortelyou and Corruption"

> He got down on his knees to us. We bought the son of a
> bitch and then he did not stay bought.
>
> —Henry Clay Frick[73]

Parker proved to be a dud candidate who inspired no one. His
speech of acceptance "fell upon his party like a wet blanket." He
conducted a front-porch campaign from his home in Esopus,
New York, a remote spot that attracted few visitors. Moreover,
the public liked Roosevelt's energy and fun. They applauded his
policies and endorsed the Square Deal. It soon became apparent
that Parker was what one midwestern Republican called "a
blank cartridge." With memories of Grover Cleveland still fresh,
the electorate outside the South was not about to opt for another
New York Democrat.[74]

Even though it was clear that Roosevelt was heading for a
landslide victory in 1904, the president took an intense interest
in the campaign and his fortunes. He grudgingly observed the
custom by which incumbent presidents did not campaign for
their own reelection. The most that he could contribute personally was a speech when he accepted the nomination and the letter of acceptance that became a main campaign document.
Roosevelt chafed at the enforced inactivity. "I wish I were where
I could fight more offensively," he told his old friend Henry
Cabot Lodge in July 1904. "I always like to do my fighting in the
adversary's corner."[75]

Roosevelt had to let surrogates do the campaigning for him,
and the Republicans rallied behind a winning effort. The campaign manager, former presidential secretary and head of the
Department of Commerce and Labor, George B. Cortelyou,
managed an efficient canvass. Republicans reached out to a wide
array of ethnic groups and religious voters. African-American
voters were told to recall "the silent legions which sleep to-night
in Northern churchyards and the forgotten buried trenches on
the Southern battlefield." Roosevelt had conciliated the Catholic

hierarchy during his first term by protecting the Church's interest in the Philippines and also making presidential appointments on a nonsectarian basis. These steps led an editor of a newspaper to say that the president was "a man without prejudice, sectarian bias or intolerance." Meanwhile, party orators proclaimed that Republicans rode "in the chariot of American glory; the Democratic party in the hearse of dead and discredited theories."[76]

Most of the 1904 election was quiet. The military-style campaigning during the Gilded Age had largely vanished in favor of pamphlets, newspaper appeals, and advertising. Voters displayed less interest in the issues, and observers noted that enthusiasm was wanting. "This is the most apathetic campaign ever heard of since James Monroe's second election," wrote Albert Shaw of the *American Review of Reviews.* Instead of charismatic speakers, the nation now responded to "a half dozen bulging browed youths, a set of encyclopedias and a report of the Bureau of Statistics."[77]

With the Democrats headed for a resounding defeat, Parker decided to take up a new issue as the election neared. The Democratic candidate charged that the Republicans were receiving campaign donations from large corporations in return for protection from government regulation. A Democratic newspaper called the issue "Cortelyou and Corruption." As Secretary of Commerce and Labor, Cortelyou had access to corporate records and, so the Democrats charged, knew where to tap business for funds. Parker also received information from Democratic businessmen who had attended a meeting where Roosevelt asked for campaign contributions. The event occasioned the later accusation that Roosevelt had been bought but then refused to comply with his implied agreement with corporate leaders.[78]

Fearful of his victory despite all the favorable signs, Roosevelt had been meeting with corporate leaders such as railroad magnate E. H. Harriman. Whether Roosevelt actually asked him for money became a source of controversy later. Cortelyou and other Republican campaign officials were getting donations from Standard Oil and other firms. Roosevelt did not know what was going on, but neither did he ask too many questions about where the money originated.

Parker's charges outraged the president. He insisted that the money from Standard Oil be returned, and he flooded Cortelyou with letters refuting the Democratic charges. When Parker stepped up his attacks on November 3 with an assault on Cortelyou's "organized importunity," Roosevelt could not keep silent. He released a statement on November 5 stating that Parker's charges were "unqualifiedly and atrociously false." Now the burden fell on Parker to prove his claims. Without access to Republican campaign records and with his informants confidential, Parker could not connect the dots to show that Roosevelt and the Republicans had accepted corporate funds in exchange for promises of special treatment. Parker's lame response convinced few people as the election neared.[79]

While the episode was not significant in terms of the election, it did indicate a mounting popular interest in the influence of business in politics. The question of corporate power and its impact on the Republican Party would become more acute within the next two years. Some reformers even discussed placing legal limits on the amounts of money that corporations could contribute to a candidate or a party. The roots of campaign-reform legislation extend back to the early years of the twentieth century.

When the voters went to the polls on November 8, 1904, they recorded a landslide victory for Theodore Roosevelt and the Republicans. As the votes came in, Roosevelt met with reporters in his private office in the Executive Office Building. Roosevelt dictated a statement to the press. He thanked the American people for their verdict and then took himself out of any race for another term in 1908. The time he had already spent in the White House "constitutes my first term. The wise custom which limits the President to two terms regards the substance and not the form, and under no circumstances will I be a candidate for or accept another nomination."[80]

Roosevelt's statement was no spur-of-the-moment decision, as is often claimed. He had discussed the move with Senator Winthrop Murray Crane of Massachusetts and probably with his wife, as well as several other people. Though it turned out to be a political mistake, the declaration made sense at the time. Roosevelt remembered how the press had reacted favorably to McKinley's renunciation of a third term in 1901. More important, the statement would counter Democratic charges that he had ambitions to be president for life. He could pursue his agenda in his second term without being accused of personal gain or partisan motivation.

Even if all that was true, Roosevelt had still erred. To the extent that politicians believed it, and Roosevelt reaffirmed it over the next several years, the choice confirmed his status as a lame duck. Congress knew that Roosevelt would be gone on March 4, 1909, and behaved accordingly. At the same time, friends and enemies of Roosevelt parsed his statements to see if there might be a chance he would change his mind. In the end, Roosevelt had managed to box himself into a corner as far as his future ambitions were concerned, as he would learn to his cost in 1912.

The election of 1904 represented a decisive success for the president and the Republican Party. Roosevelt won 56.4 percent of the vote to 37.6 percent for Alton B. Parker; the president garnered 7,628,875 votes to 5,084,442 for his Democratic opponent. The Socialist candidate, Eugene V. Debs, and the Prohibitionist Party candidate trailed the two-party nominees. Roosevelt had 336 votes in the electoral college to 140 for Parker, and that represented the most electoral votes any candidate had received up to that time. By carrying the border state of Missouri, the president made a small dent in the Solid South.

The Republican ticket had assembled staggering majorities in such party strongholds as Ohio and Pennsylvania, but Roosevelt had also carried New York, Connecticut, and New Jersey by large margins. The argument against Roosevelt as a potential dictator had fallen flat. Instead, the president ran well among most ethnocultural groups.

Two important sub-themes affected the election. Turnout fell from 1900, with about 400,000 fewer ballots cast than four years before. The estimated turnout in the northern states, which had stood at nearly seventy-two percent in 1900, was just under sixty-five percent in 1904. Democratic ballots went down dramatically, with 1,300,000 fewer votes cast for Parker than for William Jennings Bryan in 1900.

Yet the Democrats also elected five governors in states that Roosevelt won, most notably Massachusetts, Missouri, and Minnesota. The ties of party loyalty were beginning to fray compared with the late nineteenth century. Split tickets indicated that Republicans dominated in the presidential balloting in the first ten years of the twentieth century, while Democrats retained residual strength in the states. Beneath the surface of an overwhelming Republican triumph, voter trends suggested that the majority coalition of the 1890s was under some pressure.

The election of 1904 was the culmination of the political changes that had begun during the depression of the 1890s. Republicans had come to power behind a program that embraced the protective tariff, a foreign policy of overseas expansion, ethnic inclusiveness, and the return of prosperity. A charismatic and appealing president had brought all these currents together through his vivid personality. But there were signs that a nationalism that promoted economic growth would not be enough to keep the Republicans in power indefinitely. Americans discussed whether government should do more to regulate the economy. That issue was much on Theodore Roosevelt's mind in late 1904. He dreaded a nation in which the political landscape was "divided into two parties, one containing the bulk of the property owners and conservative people, the other the bulk of the wage workers and less prosperous people generally."[81] To avoid such a situation, Roosevelt believed, the government must do something to curb corporate power and clean up politics. Whether the majority of Republicans agreed with such a shift in priorities would be an issue that determined the fate of Roosevelt and his party in the eight years that followed.

Chapter 5

THE TAFT-ROOSEVELT SPLIT, 1905–1912

NO ONE WHO attended the Republican National Convention in Chicago in June 1912 easily forgot the experience. In a week of tumultuous proceedings, the Grand Old Party broke into competing factions for Theodore Roosevelt and William Howard Taft. The delegates hurled insults at each other, accused their opponents of theft and worse, and vowed revenge for every slight. William Allen White sat in the reporters' gallery, where he looked "down into the human cauldron that was boiling all around me." A Democratic visitor to the proceedings remembered "a flat, flat lake, sizzling asphalt pavements, bands circling and zigzagging along Michigan Avenue, tooting and booming, 'Everybody's saying it, Roosevelt, Roosevelt.' " For Roosevelt, as he left the party of his birth after pulling out of the convention, the choice was starkly simple: "We stand at Armageddon, and we battle for the Lord."[1]

How had this epochal Republican rupture happened? Taft and Roosevelt had been close friends in Washington. They often told associates how their personal ideas meshed in running the government. Together they represented the reforming energies of the Republicans during the period of change that historians have dubbed the Progressive Era. It seemed unthinkable that the party they led could somehow fall from the electoral heights it had scaled in 1900 and 1904. Yet, because of Roosevelt's efforts, the party had been forced to reckon with an issue that was a source of increasing contention. To what extent should the national government regulate the increasingly complex industrial society that the United States had become? Coming up with a response to that central question tested the resilience and cohesion of the Republican Party as it had not been tried since the days of its birth in the 1850s. In the end, the GOP decided that it would not embrace government regulation of business; it would seek to limit and control such a policy.

Republicans in Control

It was a good thing to have the people decide for the candidate and the party representing the positive side—the side of achievement in many directions—instead of for the colorless candidate and the party whose position had become one of negation, criticism and obstruction merely.

—Theodore Roosevelt[2]

In November 1904, the Republican Party stood at the pinnacle of American politics. Theodore Roosevelt's defeat of Alton B. Parker was the first true landslide victory in the modern sense of the term. The Republican presidential candidate had swamped his rival in both the popular and electoral votes, something that had not happened in more than thirty years. The GOP also held secure majorities in both the House and the Senate. Happy party members asked each other, "What are we going to do with our victory?"[3]

In light of their apparent cohesion and unity, the last thing that would have seemed possible was a crippling party split into a progressive and a conservative faction within eight years. Yet following the second term of Theodore Roosevelt, an increasingly divided party emerged under Roosevelt's designated successor, William Howard Taft. The friendship between Taft and Roosevelt dissolved, and the two men became bitter rivals for the presidential nomination in 1912. By that fateful summer the Republicans had degenerated into a quarreling family that was easy prey for the Democrats and Woodrow Wilson.

One reason for this unexpected turn of events was the nation's change in priorities by the time Roosevelt was inaugurated in his own right on March 4, 1905. The United States was moving away from the agricultural society of the nineteenth century and toward an industrialized, urbanized social order. While the country had not yet fully completed this process, the dominance of big business, the swelling tide of immigration, and the shift from country to city seemed unstoppable in the decades ahead. New demands would confront Republicans and Democrats alike, and older philosophies of government would be tested in ways that shifted the ruling assumptions of both major parties.

There were almost 84 million Americans in 1905, augmented by a constant flow of immigration. One million immigrants entered the country that year, and similar numbers followed during the next two years. More than three-quarters of the new residents had come from central, eastern, and southern Europe. They provided labor for a robust and growing economy that had left the depression of the 1890s far behind. How these newcomers would sort out in political terms remained to be determined. Some Republicans of old-stock American backgrounds regarded immigrants with dismay and suspicion. Others, including Theodore Roosevelt, wanted to bring them into the party's governing coalition.

Prosperity dominated the economic scene in 1905. The gross national product stood at $24 billion, compared with $13 billion just a decade earlier. Yet the new riches of society rested on a foundation of hard work by millions of laborers who did not share in the growing abundance. American workers toiled almost sixty hours a week on average for about twenty-four cents an hour. The annual income of the average worker was less than $600 per year. The rising rate of inflation cut into the purchasing power of many families. There was no federal income tax, but there were also few pension plans, little in the way of unemployment insurance, and no medical coverage beyond what an individual family could afford to pay. If a breadwinner lost a job, the family made do or slipped into poverty.

Republican orators hailed the good times achieved since the start of the McKinley administration eight years earlier. The Dingley Tariff, in their view, had restored business confidence and protected capital and labor from the damaging effects of foreign competition. It was, said one Republican senator in November 1904, "largely to be credited with our wonderful prosperity and present impregnable business position." The best policy was to "let well enough alone" or, as Senator Mark Hanna had said, using the old poker phrase, to "stand pat." Defenders of that position were soon called "standpatters" within the party.[4]

In Congress, the Republicans of the "stand pat" persuasion held the levers of power in the Republican Party as Roosevelt's second term commenced. The Republican leader in the Senate was Nelson Wilmarth Aldrich of Rhode Island. Aldrich, along with Orville H. Platt of Connecticut, John Coit Spooner of Wisconsin, and William Boyd Allison of Iowa, constituted "the Four" who directed the policies of the upper house. Conservative in their views, and defenders of the business community and the protective tariff, they and the Republicans they led had little sympathy with the idea of regulating the economy. Still, they could read the changing popular sentiment. Roosevelt would get some of what he proposed during his second term, but he would have to fight to do so. The scope of Aldrich's influence embodied the dominance of the Senate by wealthy Republicans from safe seats who stood against the rising tide of reform.[5]

Across the capital, the leader of the House was Joseph G. Cannon of Illinois. First elected to Congress in 1872 at the age of thirty-six, the bearded, cigar-smoking Cannon, sporting a smashed felt hat that he wore everywhere, was fondly called

"Uncle Joe" by his friends. His enemies who chafed under his firm control of House procedure and substance labeled him "Czar Cannon." He had been elected Speaker in 1903 and soon gained fame for his blunt, often profane language. He was so conservative that it was said if he had been present when the universe was created, he would have voted for chaos. Or, as Cannon himself remarked, "I am god-damned tired of listening to all this babble for reform."[6]

An Agenda for Reform

The Republican party must be dominated by the spirit of progress. While not yielding to the demands of insane radicalism, it must not be terrorized into inaction by the threats of those who have all they want, and more than they deserve.

—Albert Baird Cummins[7]

Despite Republican reluctance to heed them, there were signs in 1905 that middle-class Americans were worried about their own place in society and the country's well-being. That large corporations controlled the productive means of the nation and greatly influenced politics seemed more and more disturbing to average citizens fearful of losing economic opportunity. Daily newspapers reported on corrupt campaign contributions that were revealed during an investigation of the insurance industry in New York. Across the nation, other disclosures about officials with illicit ties to business and favored treatment from corporate allies became commonplace. Investigative journalists uncovered municipal scandals and revealed shoddy practices in the patent medicine and meatpacking industries.[8]

More and more Americans wondered why the government could not do something on the state and federal level to root out these evils. "Corporations have, and ought to have, many privileges," said Governor Albert B. Cummins of Iowa, "but among them is not the privilege to sit in political conventions or occupy seats in legislative chambers." The answer, said such "progressive" Republicans, was an expanded role for the government. As Theodore Roosevelt put it in January 1905: "Neither this people nor any free people will permanently tolerate the use of vast power conferred by vast wealth, and especially by wealth in its corporate form, without lodging somewhere in the government the still higher power of seeing that this power, in addition to being used in the interests of the individual or individuals possessing it, is also used for and not against the interests of the people as a whole."[9]

Roosevelt was not talking about the modern welfare state but, rather, about using government to preserve a balance among competing economic interests, as he had envisioned in the Square Deal of his first term. The president's first priority in that regard was the railroad industry, which had become the target of complaints from shippers and consumers about high rates for rail services. At the turn of the twentieth century, railroads were the main mode of transportation, occupying a place in the popular mind roughly akin to the oil industry a century later. In his annual message of December 1904, Roosevelt asked whether the regulatory powers of the Interstate Commerce Commission (ICC) should be increased to deal with high railroad rates and illegal practices by the major lines. Fundamentally, he was asking whether the traditional Republican doctrine of promoting economic growth through government action now had to give way to increased regulation from the executive branch.[10]

During the eighteen months that followed, Roosevelt used his presidential powers of persuasion to achieve passage of the Hepburn Act of 1906, which did enhance the authority of the ICC. His repertoire included a series of public speeches, leaks to friendly journalists, the threat of legal actions against major rail lines, and pressure on lawmakers to support his program. Conservatives in the Senate, led by Aldrich, tried to block Roosevelt by giving the federal courts the broad power to oversee ICC decrees. There was a protracted legislative struggle that began when Congress assembled six months later, in December 1905.

As a result, Roosevelt did not obtain everything he wanted in what became the Hepburn Act. He did get substantially increased powers for the ICC to oversee the rail companies. Nonetheless, the president believed the final form of the law was "a fine piece of constructive legislation, and all that has been done tends toward carrying out the principles I have been preaching." Many conservative Republicans wondered if Roosevelt's regulatory sermons did not include a healthy dose of heresy from party doctrine.[11]

By 1906, Roosevelt's reform principles included other measures to expand the power of the national government. For several years journalists had been revealing fraud and deadly products that plagued the patent medicine industry as well as the dangers within the nation's food supply from unsafe meatpacking. Legislation to ensure pure food and drugs languished in Congress where the Republican leadership, protecting the interests of the patent medicine and packaged-food trade, had kept it buried in committee. But when the unhealthy practices in the Chicago stockyards were revealed in sickening detail in Upton Sinclair's novel, *The Jungle,* the disgusted public clamored for governmental remedies in 1905–1906.[12]

Roosevelt responded first to the meatpacking controversy. The White House supported an amendment to the agricultural appropriation law providing for stricter meat-inspection rules. The resultant publicity intensified demands to pass the pure food and drug law. With Roosevelt now solidly behind a law that the public wanted, the legislation won passage in late June 1906. Roosevelt had succeeded in moving the Republicans toward greater regulation, calling the three regulatory measures "a noteworthy advance in the policy of securing Federal supervision and control over corporations." That same spring, Roosevelt came out for a federal inheritance tax, "a tax so framed as to put it out of the power of the owner of one of these enormous fortunes to hand on more than a certain amount to any one individual; the tax, of course, to be imposed by the National and not the State Government." In that way, the president believed, extremes of wealth and poverty in the United States could be reduced.[13]

The rationale behind Roosevelt's commitment to greater regulation was simple. If the federal government did not address the major social inequities in American society, then agitation for more drastic reforms would gain converts. After all, Eugene V. Debs and the Socialists had won more than 400,000 votes in 1904, and there was evidence of growing support for Socialist candidates in states such as Massachusetts and Wisconsin. As Roosevelt himself wrote in 1908, "We seek to control law-defying wealth in the first place to prevent its doing dire evil to the Republic, and in the next place to avoid the vindictive and dreadful radicalism which, if left uncontrolled, it is certain in the end to arouse."[14]

The Republican Progressives

> Reform was in the air. In forging new weapons of democracy in the state legislatures and in the Congress, the people were setting out on a crusade.
>
> —William Allen White[15]

The midwestern Republicans who regarded themselves as the progressive wing of the party applauded Roosevelt's actions, even if they sometimes wished to go even further than the president. Among those identified with reform were Governor Cummins of Iowa and Senator Robert M. La Follette of Wisconsin. A mixture of motives underlay their desire for a stronger federal presence. Railroads were a particular grievance, as were the high tariff rates that drove up prices on goods their agrarian constituents purchased. These Republicans also disliked the existing party structure that often shut them out of office and power. Insurgents in California, Kansas, Iowa, Minnesota, Wisconsin, and New Hampshire, for example, endorsed direct primaries to choose candidates and reform of campaign funding and practices. These changes would lessen the clout of these older, entrenched Republican leaders who had relied on party caucuses, rigged conventions, and backroom deals to stay in power. Now Republican voters could select primary candidates.

The progressive creed that Republican reformers espoused did not attack capitalism as the mainstay of the American economy. Instead, they wanted their party to do more to challenge the power of corporations. That would make tariff rates less onerous for consumers and reduce railroad rates. Once the proper balance had been restored, then the role of government could be pared back.

Robert La Follette became the national embodiment of this spirit among Republicans. "Battle Bob," as he was known, was a short, feisty man with a pompadour and a strident speaking style. As a two-term governor of Wisconsin, he had defied the Republican organization in his state by setting up a direct primary, pursuing railroad regulation, and imposing higher taxes on corporations. He also used the academic resources of the faculty of the University of Wisconsin to shape his reform program in what became known as "the Wisconsin Idea." Elected to the Senate in 1905, he came to Washington a year later with his eye on the White House. He had to defer to Roosevelt, but a mutual suspicion soon grew between the two men. Roosevelt regarded the Wisconsin lawmaker as an impractical visionary. La Follette saw the president as too willing to compromise with corporate interests.[16]

The progressive Republicans were vocal and articulate; they attracted a good deal of press attention. Yet outside of their regional base, they remained a minority among Republicans. While the party rank and file admired Roosevelt's vote-getting appeal and tolerated the progressive ideas he championed, there was a growing unease among the conservatives, strong in the Northeast and in the older states of the Middle West such as Ohio and Indiana, about the direction of the party. What were the implications of increasing the power of the government and limiting the economic freedom of corporations, asked such standpatters as Joseph G. Cannon, Nelson Aldrich, and Joseph B.

Foraker. The emergence of regulation as a critical issue forced Republicans to reappraise their party's priorities. Perhaps Democrats should not be the only champions of states' rights and local power.[17]

Some of these crosscurrents were evident in the 1906 congressional elections. The Democrats joined with the American Federation of Labor (AFL) to mount a determined challenge to the Republican majority in the House of Representatives and the rule of Speaker Cannon, who had become the symbol of Republican conservatism. By 1906 some Republican progressives in the House saw the Speaker as the major obstacle to the enactment of reform legislation.

A sore point for many Republicans by 1906 was the protective tariff, the centerpiece of the party's economic doctrine. Prosperity had brought about inflation after 1900, and rising consumer prices gave Democrats a tempting target. The high tariff rates of the Dingley Law, they charged, hiked prices for what the average American purchased every day. Middle western Republicans, for whom the issue cut deeply, contended that a downward adjustment of rates was needed. The president and the Congress should pursue "a rational revision of the tariff along protection lines." But Speaker Cannon disagreed. He believed that the Dingley Tariff was, "all things considered, the most perfect and just customs law ever enacted." As a result, the Republicans sent out contradictory messages on their main issue in 1906.[18]

Roosevelt threw himself into the fight to save the House for the Republicans. He dispatched Cabinet officers to the stump, wrote public letters, and tried to stoke enthusiasm among the party's candidates. His efforts, combined with Democratic miscues, held down Republican losses in the House to twenty-eight seats. The Republicans retained control of the lower house and picked up strength in the Senate. While the party had escaped disaster, the internal tensions splitting the Republicans over the tariff and the question of government regulation did not augur well. With Roosevelt out of the 1908 race, a bitter battle for the nomination loomed.[19]

Though Roosevelt several times reaffirmed his 1904 declaration that he would not be a candidate again, the president did
not intend to leave the choice of his successor to the party faithful and the nominating process. He knew that such an approach
would result in a candidate who did not share his progressive
views, so he made it clear that he would not accept a nominee
who failed to "carry out the governmental principles in which I
believe with all my heart and soul." With that posture, Roosevelt
virtually guaranteed the selection of the candidate he wanted,
given his enduring popularity with the voters.[20]

By 1907–1908, a substantial element among the Republicans
had decided that Roosevelt was too much of a reformer for their
tastes. His regulatory policies, his advocacy of resource conservation in the West, and his endorsement of an inheritance tax drove
conservatives to paroxysms of rage. A reporter told a prominent
senator in mid-1907 that Republicans disliked "the present fire
works administration because it squints too much in the direction
of Socialism, that is paternalism from which may easily follow various encroachments on property rights and the rights of individual states." These feelings intensified when a severe financial
panic occurred in late 1907. For conservatives the business slump
and resulting bank failures were the direct result of Roosevelt's
"ill-considered recommendations and hasty policies."[21]

So both progressives and conservatives in the GOP looked to
1908 as their chance to shape the party's future direction. The
Republicans were in the midst of a succession crisis that would
affect the next twelve years. With Roosevelt out of the running,
a number of conservatives hoped to emerge from a crowded
field in 1907–1908. There were other progressive aspirants for
the prize as well, but none of these potential nominees had any
chance of receiving President Roosevelt's endorsement.

Among the conservatives with an eye on the White House
were Charles W. Fairbanks of Indiana, Speaker Cannon, and
Joseph B. Foraker. Fairbanks was a colorless soul who had once
been described as too scared to say boo to a goose. "Uncle Joe"
Cannon had developed into a political symbol of a reactionary
Congress, and he had little support outside of his home state.[22]

Senator Foraker presented a different problem for the White House. Although the Ohio senator had once been friendly with the president, the two men had split over the Hepburn Act; the Ohio senator was one of the few lawmakers to oppose on the final vote. Then a more bitter rupture happened. In August 1906, a shooting incident took place in Brownsville, Texas, where white residents charged that African-American soldiers stationed in the town had been responsible for the violence. The soldiers, to a man, denied any involvement, and the historical evidence supports their case. The army and eventually Theodore Roosevelt concluded that some of the troops were responsible and that every member of their unit knew who the culprits were. Therefore, he dismissed all three companies from the service in November 1906, a few days after the congressional elections.[23]

Foraker sprang to the defense of the soldiers and accused Roosevelt of unfairness. The senator saw political advantage in appealing to black Republican voters in the North, but he also believed that a miscarriage of justice had occurred. The president and the senator had a nasty public quarrel at the annual dinner of the Gridiron Club of journalists in late January 1907. Theodore Roosevelt did not forgive and forget. Thwarting Foraker's presidential bid would enable Roosevelt to defeat a conservative and also punish a Republican who had impugned his integrity as a chief executive.[24]

The problem of designating an acceptable successor remained. If the choice was made purely on a personal basis, the president would probably have picked his Secretary of State, Elihu Root. But Root had several political disabilities. At the age of sixty-three, he was perceived as too old, and his background as a corporation lawyer also worked against him. On the more progressive side of the party, Roosevelt might have designated the newly elected governor of New York, Charles Evans Hughes, who had won in 1906 after revealing scandals in the insurance industry. But Hughes was too independent for Roosevelt's taste. The other possibility, Robert La Follette, was seen as too radical, and, moreover, he and Roosevelt were not friendly.[25]

Roosevelt and Taft

> To none will I show preference
> To me it makes no difference,
> The party may choose any man
> Who is a good Republican
>   Just so it's Taft
>
> —*Kansas City Times*[26]

Looking around his Cabinet, Roosevelt's eye fell on his Secretary of War, William Howard Taft, and Roosevelt soon decided that he had found the man he needed to carry on what Roosevelt termed "my policies." This decision grew out of a blend of personal interaction and political calculation that often animated Roosevelt's judgment, but it proved to be a fateful one for the Grand Old Party.

In many respects, Taft was a sensible selection. He had a strong record as governor-general of the Philippines from 1900 to 1904 and had been a valuable subordinate as Secretary of War. As the two men worked together, they formed what appeared to be a strong friendship. Roosevelt believed in 1906 that Taft "would be an ideal President" and "the best man to receive it." The links between president and secretary were genuine but were based to some extent on a misunderstanding of where each of them stood politically within the Republican ranks.[27]

As an attorney, Taft believed in orderly procedures and the rule of law. His fondest ambition was to be the chief justice of the United States and he had declined two offers from Roosevelt to go on the Court as an associate justice because of his desire for the highest judicial place. Within the administration, Taft felt that Roosevelt's willingness to stretch presidential power to accomplish his regulatory goals sometimes went too far. He also thought that Roosevelt went behind the backs of his Cabinet too often and dealt directly with their subordinates. Pulled along by the force of Roosevelt's personality, Taft became identified with the progressive thrust of the administration even though he had reservations about how far such policies should be pushed. He remained a loyal lieutenant to Roosevelt, and the two friends never really examined their potential differences over issues such as conservation, the tariff, and the trusts.

By mid-1906, Taft seemed the logical choice from Roosevelt's perspective. He could be counted on to implement regulation, and he was not identified with the conservatives. Roosevelt's enthusiasm for Taft shot up dramatically after the Brownsville controversy erupted in the fall. Since Taft was from Ohio, his candidacy would have the added benefit of frustrating Foraker's hopes. By early 1907, the president had made it clear to everyone in Republican politics that Taft had his full backing.

One key person in the Taft camp resented the time it had taken Roosevelt to come around for the Secretary of War. Helen Herron Taft wanted to see her husband become president. In fact, she had been a major force in persuading him not to accept a Supreme Court nomination. Mrs. Taft believed that Roosevelt had been too slow to endorse the Secretary of War, and her distrust of Roosevelt grew from that point onward. Another person wary of the president was newspaper publisher Charles P. Taft, the candidate's half-brother and the financial mainstay of his campaign. While Taft remained loyal to the president, the same could not be said for his family and friends.[28]

Throughout 1907 the Taft campaign gained momentum as Roosevelt emphasized who his first choice was. Meanwhile, the ideological split in the party deepened. Roosevelt became more emphatic in his denunciation of business after the panic of 1907. A message to Congress in late January 1908 renewed Roosevelt's earlier call for inheritance taxes and stronger legislation to curb corporations. Conservative Republicans reacted with outrage at this presidential endorsement of greater regulation.

Relations between Roosevelt and the Republican Congress only worsened during the spring of 1908 as the president pushed for antitrust legislation that Speaker Cannon and his allies then rejected. The progressives urged the party in Congress to do more on social justice, downward revision of the protective tariff, and reform of the banking system in the wake of the 1907 panic. But the conservatives balked, and the session proved less than productive. Roosevelt complained that "the ruling clique in the Senate, the House and the National Committee seem to regard every concession to decency as merely a matter of bargain and sale with *me*, which *I* must pay for in some way or fashion."[29]

The Taft campaign, meanwhile, rolled ahead toward a first-ballot victory for the Secretary of War. As the national convention approached, the conservatives (or the "Allies," as they were known) tried to make a stand on the legitimacy of some of the Taft delegates from the South. By this time the Republican Party in Dixie had become largely a shadow organization that existed solely for the purpose of providing delegates. Patronage favors and even outright bribery often explained which national candidate secured the votes of southern delegates. The Taft-Roosevelt forces in 1907–1908 had proven superior in providing inducements to support the Secretary of War. With the president and his supporters securely in control of the convention machinery and the Republican National Committee, these challenges from the Allies were repulsed and the Taft delegates seated.

Once the procedural roadblocks had been removed, Taft achieved a decisive first-ballot victory at the convention in Chicago. But the real story of the gathering was that Taft and Roosevelt were forced to accept a more conservative platform than they had hoped for. The most noteworthy language in the document pledged to revise the tariff, but the document did not specify in what direction the rates should be changed. The new presidential candidate had to take a conservative congressman, James "Sunny Jim" Sherman of New York, as his running mate. Coming out of the convention, the Republicans anticipated a tough contest with the resurgent Democrats, particularly since Theodore Roosevelt would not be on the ballot. Running William Jennings Bryan for a third time, the Democratic Party looked to success since they did not have to face a Republican incumbent. "This election is not going to be an open-and-shut affair," wrote a Republican reporter.[30]

Behind the scenes, the friendship between Roosevelt and

From Albert Shaw, A Cartoon History of Roosevelt's Career

LOADING THE BAND WAGON

Despite the efforts of other candidates, William Howard Taft, with Roosevelt's assistance, moved toward a first-ballot victory in 1908. Charles Evans Hughes, Philander C. Knox, Charles W. Fairbanks, and Joseph G. Cannon watch their states responding to Roosevelt's siren song for Taft in this cartoon from a Spokane, Washington, newspaper.

Taft suffered the first misunderstandings that would only grow as the months passed. Upon receiving the news that he was the Republican candidate, Taft casually remarked to Roosevelt that he wanted the members of the president's Cabinet "to stay just as they are." Whether Taft meant that all these men would be retained in office if he became president is not clear. With his usual ebullience, Roosevelt conveyed to all the Cabinet that Taft was planning to keep them on after the election.[31]

Meanwhile, the nominee was confronting the festering quarrels within his divided party. Conservatives wanted Taft to keep the progressives on the sidelines and be sure that men like La Follette did not become prominent. To send La Follette out to speak, said a conservative Montana senator, "seems to be like going on a hunt with a kicking gun." The progressives, for their part, believed that the congressional leaders, most notably the unpopular Speaker Cannon, should be kept under wraps. "Our party has got to keep abreast of the times—to consider the interests of the country and free itself from the domination of the Aldrich and Cannon regime," concluded Senator Joseph L. Bristow of Kansas.[32]

Taft proved to be an effective candidate on the stump. Despite warnings from the campaign managers to avoid speaking tours where he might make a verbal slip, Taft went to the Middle West, parts of the South, and through the critical state of New York. In all these places, he attracted sizable and enthusiastic audiences. He endorsed the role of labor unions, pledged downward revision of the tariff, and promised to implement the regulatory legislation on the trusts that Roosevelt had obtained from Congress. Taft's goal, said one commentator, was "to strengthen the impression that the Republican Party is a more trustworthy instrument of government than the Democratic."[33]

But a restless Roosevelt could not sit idly in the White House. While he could not by custom go out and tour for Taft, he could infuse "a little vim into the campaign by making a publication of my own." The public letters that Roosevelt issued made the president the unofficial campaign manager and cheerleader of Taft's race for the White House. By overshadowing the party's candidate, however, Roosevelt added to the popular sense that he and not Taft was the party's leader. This development did not sit well with Mrs. Taft and others close to the presidential candidate.[34]

Meanwhile, the Democrats and Bryan did not find a winning theme against Taft. The opposition tried to capitalize on the tariff, popular concerns about corporate contributions to the Republicans, and calls for the direct election of senators by the people rather than state legislatures. "Shall the people rule?" asked William Jennings Bryan, and the answer was not what the Democrats expected.

Taft won a substantial victory on November 3, 1908. He received 321 electoral votes to 162 for Bryan; the winner gained 7,675,000 popular votes to 6,412,000 for the loser. The turnout was about sixty-five percent of the eligible electorate, as participation continued to recede from the high levels of the late nineteenth century. Taft polled almost 50,000 more votes than Roosevelt in 1904, in an even more significant indicator of potential change, but Bryan gained nearly 1,400,000 more ballots than Alton B. Parker.

So within the victory were some ominous signs for the Republicans. In five states that Taft carried, Democrats elected governors. Ticket-splitting showed that the intense partisanship of the previous generation was breaking down, a trend that worked to the disadvantage of the Republicans. Appeals to party unity counted for less as independent voters increased. As Elihu Root put it, "Discontent hurts only the party in power." The factionalism among the Republicans meant that both progressives and conservatives looked to the president-elect to resolve their growing differences. As one newspaperman wrote to Theodore Roosevelt, "Are we to hope that Taft will be a bigger man than the party?—and that is the hope in which most progressive men are supporting him." The expectations of both wings that he would be their champion proved to be one of Taft's greatest burdens once he was in the White House.[35]

A PERILOUS TRANSITION

> I have done my work; I am perfectly content; I have
> nothing to ask; and I am very grateful to the American
> people for what they have done for me.
>
> —Theodore Roosevelt[36]

A key to party unity was the maintenance of the friendship between Taft and Roosevelt, but that concord began to fall apart within days of the election results. On November 7, 1908, the president-elect sent Roosevelt a thank-you letter, telling the president that "you and my brother Charlie made that possible which in all probability would not have occurred otherwise." Though he said nothing at the time, Roosevelt resented being bracketed with Taft's wealthy half-brother. He later remarked that it was as if someone said "Abraham Lincoln and the bond seller Jay Cooke saved the Union." Roosevelt would have more to fret about during the weeks leading up to the inauguration on March 4, 1909.[37]

The Cabinet selections produced the first tangible rift. Having forgotten his comments in June 1908 or not regarding them as a binding pledge, Taft proceeded to make appointments that did not include some of the key members of Roosevelt's official family. The Secretary of the Interior, James R. Garfield, and the Secretary of Commerce, Oscar S. Straus, were informed that they would not be retained. Straus said to Roosevelt that "through influence or surroundings Taft did not wish to take those who distinguished themselves under" the outgoing president. As Roosevelt later put it to another Cabinet officer who was not to be reappointed, "Unfortunately you have been too close to me, I fear."[38]

Tension between the Roosevelt and Taft families also contributed to the emerging split. Helen Herron Taft pressed for the right as the incoming first lady, even before the inauguration, to make changes among the White House ushers and doormen, a move that Edith Roosevelt resented. The Tafts told the

president-elect "to be his own king" and resist close identification with Roosevelt. When the outgoing president and Congress
feuded in the waning days of his term over controversial issues
such as Roosevelt's use of the Secret Service to investigate
wrongdoing by lawmakers, Taft kept silent. An uneasy state
of affairs persisted through the inauguration. The Roosevelts
had the Tafts stay over at the White House on March 3, but the
evening went awkwardly. Taft once described the occasion as
"that funeral."[39]

The next day a severe snowstorm pelted Washington. Roo-
sevelt said, "I knew there would be a blizzard when I went out."
The inauguration had to be held in the Senate chamber, where
Taft read his speech. Roosevelt and Taft then shook hands, and
the former president departed for his home in Oyster Bay, New
York. President and Mrs. Taft then rode together to the White
House, the first presidential couple to do so.[40]

Because his single term fell between the dramatic presidencies of Theodore Roosevelt and Woodrow Wilson, William
Howard Taft's status has been relegated to mediocrity in the
pantheon of chief executives. His embrace of Republican conservatism also hurt his historical reputation. To some extent,
Taft was defined as much by his weight (he tipped the scales at
nearly three hundred pounds at times during his presidency)
and perceived indolence as his actual record in office. A quip
from Senator Jonathan P. Dolliver, an Iowa progressive, seemed
to sum up all one needed to know about the Taft presidency.
Taft, he said, was "an amiable island; entirely surrounded by
men who know exactly what they want."[41]

TAFT AND THE REPUBLICANS

> I am not so constituted that I can run with the hare and
> hunt with the hounds.
>
> —William Howard Taft[42]

In real life, Taft was a more interesting person as president and
politician than his critics at the time realized. He brought a phi-

losophy to the presidency that grew out of his training as a lawyer. Where Roosevelt believed that the president could do anything that the Constitution did not prohibit, Taft looked for a clear basis for presidential policy in the Constitution and existing law. He was convinced that Roosevelt often had stretched the law unduly in support of what he deemed worthy causes. When Roosevelt and his aides ascribed "an undefined residuum of power to the President," they were advancing, according to Taft, "an unsafe doctrine" that "might lead under emergencies to results of an arbitrary character doing irremediable injustice to private right." Taft saw his role as carrying out Roosevelt's policy goals in what he felt was a more legal and constitutional manner.[43]

Taft's background was in administration, and his sense of how Washington should work in his presidency grew out of that experience. He was fifty-three years old in 1908, a native of Cincinnati, Ohio, and a graduate of Yale. He had little experience with elective politics before he ran for president. What Taft did have was a perceptive mind and the capacity to work hard when his interest was engaged. He lacked Roosevelt's brilliance but made up for it with common sense. On an issue such as antitrust, he was more of a dedicated believer in breaking up big corporations than Roosevelt was. To that extent, Taft had more in common with middle western progressives than Roosevelt did.

Where Taft came up particularly short, though, was in the public relations that the presidency demanded. His relations with the press had been good when he was the Secretary of War, but he shut out journalists when he moved to the White House. More damaging, Taft paid little attention to his public image. He loved to play golf as a form of exercise for his weight problem. As a result, he frequented country clubs with rich friends at a time when golf was seen as an elitist diversion. The president liked to travel around the country, but the purpose of these speaking junkets did not come through to the public. As a decision-maker, it took him time to make up his mind, and yet he could be swayed toward another course of action at the last minute. When he was angry, Taft displayed a mean and petty streak, which led Roosevelt to conclude that he "was one of the best haters he had ever known." One journalist summed up Taft's abilities as a leader well. The president's "bump of politics" was "a deep hole."[44]

Taft had also inherited an abundance of problems from Roosevelt. The first and most divisive was the tariff since the new president intended to carry out the pledge in the 1908 platform to revise customs duties. Since the Republicans had not specified the direction that revision would take, Washington braced for a prolonged tariff battle. That prospect set out a flurry of lobbying from all affected interest groups. And to get any tariff bill through Congress required the support of Speaker Cannon, who by early 1909 had become more unpopular in the country than ever. Yet a majority of conservative Republicans in the House stood strongly behind the Speaker. With Roosevelt's endorsement, Taft declined to help Republican progressives in the House who were challenging Cannon's leadership in March 1909. Standing with the House Republican leadership made good sense for Taft, but it stirred suspicions about the incoming president within the reform wing of his party.

During the weeks that followed the inauguration, Roosevelt departed for Africa and a long-planned hunting safari that would take him out of the country for a year. In his absence, Taft would be out from under the ex-president's shadow. (The joke in Washington was that on Wall Street everyone hoped that a lion would do its duty.) While he was away, Roosevelt did not correspond with Taft, as both men waited for the other to make the first move. In that vacuum, hard feelings and suspicions grew between the two leading Republicans.

Meanwhile, Taft engaged the vexing tariff question. He summoned Congress into special session on March 15, 1909. The House approved a measure in early April that lowered rates on such key items as iron (important for construction), sugar (a key to consumer products), and lumber (for home building), and also put coal and hides of cattle on the free list. Named after the chair of the House Ways and Means Committee, Sereno E. Payne of New York, the bill went to the Senate where it faced an uncertain future.

In the upper house, the Republicans had a secure majority of sixty-one to thirty-one. According to the press, the GOP leader, Nelson Aldrich, was supposed to be the virtual dictator of that body. Like so many other assumptions about the history of the Republicans, this picture was misleading. By 1909, between seven and ten Republicans from the Middle West, such as Robert La Follette, Jonathan P. Dolliver, and Albert J. Beveridge of Indiana, were prepared to oppose Aldrich on the tariff. That put Aldrich's real majority down to around ten votes. Both eastern and western Republicans, eager to protect products of their states, pushed Aldrich for concessions that favored the economic interests of their states in the final law. The bill that came out of the Senate Finance Committee had eight hundred amendments, many of which raised rates upward. The progressives howled and attributed the result to Aldrich's disdain for popular opinion. Their protests eroded Republican unity, but Aldrich had kept his fragile coalition together. His version of the bill passed on July 8, 1909, by forty-five to thirty-four, with ten Republicans voting no.[45]

Taft was in a bind. The progressives sought his support, but the president did not want to abandon Aldrich. Taft believed in lower rates, but he did not want to accept an amendment in the bill that would have added an income tax. In Taft's mind, only a constitutional amendment could authorize such a levy. In the end, Taft negotiated a tax on corporations and language endorsing an income tax amendment. In the conference committee to reconcile the Payne and Aldrich bills, Taft secured enough concessions, particularly on free cattle hides, to persuade him to sign what was now known as the Payne-Aldrich Tariff. He rebuffed calls from the progressive Republicans that he should veto the bill. To maintain as much party unity as possible, Taft believed that he had to accept the new law.

The congressional debate over the Payne-Aldrich Tariff

marked another turning point for the Republican Party. While there would be other protective measures passed under Republican congresses in 1922 and 1930, the Payne-Aldrich measure represented the last time that the tariff issue would be at the heart of party doctrine. When the Democrats enacted an income tax in 1913, they permanently changed how government revenues were collected. Customs duties became less important, a diminishing percentage of the funds for government operation. Republican attitudes toward taxation, spending, and trade policy would commence a long and slow evolution away from the tariff and toward the commitment to free trade that would characterize the party by the end of the twentieth century. Such a prospect would have seemed rank political heresy to Nelson Aldrich and the defenders of protectionism in 1909.[46]

Taft's approval of the Payne-Aldrich law in August 1909 evoked little anger from a public that could not follow the intricate details of tariff-making. To further promote party unity, Taft decided to praise the law and all who voted for it. But by extension he was also condemning those who had opposed Aldrich and the Senate bill. In Winona, Minnesota, on a speaking tour in September 1909, Taft called the Payne-Aldrich measure "the best tariff bill that the Republican party has ever passed." The regulars were delighted. The progressives seethed and could only conclude that Taft had cast his lot with Aldrich, Cannon, and the party conservatives.[47]

The political picture became more complex for the Republicans during the rest of 1909. Consumers were angered at the rising cost of living that continued into 1910. In the regular session of Congress that opened in December 1909, a dispute between Secretary of the Interior Richard A. Ballinger and Chief Forester Gifford Pinchot, a close ally of Roosevelt, further tarred the Taft White House as antagonistic to Roosevelt's legacy. Speaker Cannon, too, became ever more of a liability, and House Republicans accepted restrictions on his power in March 1910. Absorbing the impact of these setbacks, Taft and congressional Republicans then worked together to pass the Mann-Elkins Act, which increased the regulatory power of the Interstate Commerce Commission. Other pieces of progressive legislation were also enacted. By the time Congress left town, the president concluded, "I think things are coming our way a little more than heretofore."[48]

This proved to be misplaced optimism. The Democrats sensed that they had an excellent chance to retake the House for the first time since 1894, and they were able to put aside their differences in the interest of unity. They indicted the Republican tariff policy as a major cause of inflation. With strong candidates such as Woodrow Wilson in New Jersey seeking gubernatorial seats, the Democrats were, as one of them put it, "a courageous, vigilant, hopeful, militant band, not only ready but eager for the fray."[49]

Some Republicans hoped that Theodore Roosevelt would return from Africa and use his popularity to salvage the situation in the fall. It was not to be. While Roosevelt had been on safari, the bonds of friendship with Taft had frayed. The major irritant had been Taft's dismissal of Pinchot. Roosevelt regarded conservation as his wisest policy gift to the nation. Taft believed that Roosevelt had been careless in some of his decisions about natural resources. He and Secretary Ballinger tried to rein in the chief forester, who had enjoyed autonomy under Roosevelt. Through allies in the press, Pinchot charged that Ballinger was corrupt, citing his decisions about Alaska coal lands. This public attack led Taft to fire Pinchot for his insubordination toward a fellow government official. A congressional probe revealed no wrongdoing on Ballinger's part, but the controversy damaged both the secretary and the White House.

The real political consequence of the Ballinger case was contained in Roosevelt's reaction to the dismissal of his close friend and confidant. During the autumn of 1909, the former president's associates had sent him letter after letter with negative news about Taft's performance. When he heard the news of Pinchot's ouster, he said, "It seems to me absolutely impossible that there can be any truth in this statement." But when the report was confirmed as Roosevelt made his way home, his disillusionment about his successor and the administration's policies was plain. Roosevelt was forced "to admit" that Taft "had gone wrong on certain points; and then I also had to admit to myself that deep down underneath I had known all along he was wrong on points as to which I had tried to deceive myself, by loudly proclaiming to myself, that he was right."[50]

By this time many of Roosevelt's progressive friends wanted him to run in 1912. They formed "Back from Elba" clubs to spur him on. Still a Republican, he downplayed such overtures but did not repudiate them with a definite statement in support of Taft. The president wanted such an endorsement, but Roosevelt was unwilling to do so. The former president was genuinely torn about his next move. He had loved being president, and private life was boring after the excitement of the White House.

For Roosevelt to maintain his standing with progressives and remain in the public eye, he had to keep open the chance that he would run in 1912. The longer that option was on the table, the more likely it became that Roosevelt would exercise it. Meanwhile, he convinced himself that he would be the agent through which party unity would be restored. In that sense, Roosevelt was casting himself as the real leader of the party and relegating Taft to a subordinate role. Since Taft was the president, what Roosevelt was envisioning was impossible to sustain.

Toward the New Nationalism

> Our position is that we don't know what Oyster Bay is going to do and we don't give a damn.
>
> —Charles D. Norton[51]

Roosevelt returned from Africa to wide popular acclaim based more on his celebrity status than the idea that he should be president once again. Republican progressives wanted him to take a clear stand against Taft's administration. At first Roosevelt said he was out of politics, but pressure from his friends soon had him back in the fray in New York State where the Republicans were in trouble. Taft still wanted Roosevelt's endorsement for reelection in 1912, but the former president hedged on the issue, and suspicion mounted between the two camps. Taft said, "I do not see how I am going to get out of having a fight with President Roosevelt."[52]

The animosity between Taft and Roosevelt only intensified during the summer of 1910. By September, the resulting tension permeated Republican ranks. The deeper significance for the party lay in the policy ideas that Roosevelt advanced during a three-week speaking tour of the West that he launched in late August. His goal, he said, was "to announce myself on the vital questions of the day, to set the standard so that it can be seen, and take a position that cannot be misunderstood."[53]

In Denver on August 29, Roosevelt criticized the courts' tendency to nullify legislative enactments that promoted reform. His key statement came two days later at Osawatomie, Kansas, in what became known as the "New Nationalism" speech. Roosevelt defined his brand of Republicanism as it had developed during his second term and in the year since he left office. He called for a "New Nationalism" that would have the federal government be more than the neutral umpire he had advocated during the Square Deal. Roosevelt wanted the government to intervene to achieve a higher degree of social justice. "When I say that I am for the square deal, I mean not merely that I stand for fair play under the present rules of the game. But I stand for having those rules changed so as to work for a more substantial equality of opportunity and of reward for equally good service."[54]

In practical terms, Roosevelt advocated policies that very much looked forward to the modern welfare state. He endorsed such progressive reforms as limits on corporate power in politics, greater regulation of big business through government agencies, and laws to curb child labor, provide minimum wages, and workers' unemployment compensation. "A graduated inheritance tax on big fortunes" and income taxes "on big fortunes" were large elements of his agenda. "The really big fortune, the swollen fortune, by the mere fact of its size acquires qualities which differentiate it in kind as well as in degree from what is possessed by men of relatively small means," he argued.[55]

This was Republicanism that went further in the direction of governmental activism than many in the party were willing to accept. Roosevelt was fusing the nationalism that had always been a hallmark of the party with a faith in regulatory power that conflicted with the business orientation of the Grand Old Party. Roosevelt's ideas, said a New York conservative, "had startled all thoughtful men and impressed them with the frightful danger which lies in his political ascendancy." Roosevelt muted his position in response to criticism from conservatives, but there was no doubt that he proposed to take the party in a dramatic new direction.[56]

Roosevelt's efforts to achieve party unity behind his philosophy backfired, and the Republicans went into the 1910 contests more divided than ever. The voters watched the spectacle of Republicans feuding and heeded the Democratic calls for electoral change. With his customary wisdom, Elihu Root captured the spirit of the impending defeat. The country was like "a man in bed. He wants to roll over. He doesn't know why he wants to roll over, but he just does; and he'll do it."[57]

The voters rolled over the Republicans on November 8, 1910, as the party lost control of the House. The GOP dropped fifty-eight seats to the Democrats and saw another ten United States senators defeated. Woodrow Wilson won the governorship of New Jersey for the Democrats and was immediately mentioned as a likely nominee in 1912. Progressive Republicans claimed that they had done better at the polls than their conservative counterparts. That was true because the Democrats were weak in the states where Republican reformers were strong. Where the two parties were competitive, the conservative Republicans incurred large losses. Roosevelt was the big loser in the election. The Democrats carried New York, where the former president's hand-picked gubernatorial candidate lost.

Taft made the quickest adjustment to the new political realities, and during the first half of 1911, he moved well ahead in the race for his party's nomination a year later. He selected a new personal secretary, Charles D. Hilles, who got the president's campaign for renomination under way during the summer of 1911. Meanwhile, Taft launched a series of initiatives, including freer trade with Canada and arbitration treaties to resolve international disputes, which conveyed an impression of strong executive leadership. By the fall of 1911, Hilles estimated that Taft was closing in on a majority of Republican convention delegates.

The progressives had trouble pulling together behind a single challenger to the president. Senator La Follette wanted to make the race, and he spent a good deal of time organizing a campaign. But there was little support outside Wisconsin for someone whose radical opinions and French name (evoking echoes of the revolution in that country) stamped him as an extremist. A reporter said that the senator could not count on "one delegate from East of Ohio."[58]

The wild card in Republican calculations was Theodore Roosevelt, who had suffered through the first half of 1911 after his humiliation following the outcome in 1910. While the former president appeared to be in eclipse, his relations with Taft had warmed somewhat. Roosevelt admitted to worried Republican friends that "as things are now it would be a serious mistake from a public standpoint, and a cruel wrong to me, to nominate me." Roosevelt did not take the irrevocable step of endorsing Taft or rejecting any chance of accepting the Republican nomination. The possibility that he might change his mind kept Republicans on edge as 1912 neared.[59]

THE FINAL BREAK

My hat is in the ring, the fight is on and I am stripped to the buff.

—Theodore Roosevelt[60]

Then a series of incidents during the summer of 1911 revived Roosevelt's doubts about Taft. As La Follette's campaign also stalled, he in turn became suspicious of Roosevelt's intentions. The political situation among Republicans of all stripes had reached a very volatile stage by the end of October. Then the news broke that the Department of Justice had filed an antitrust lawsuit against the United States Steel Company. The wording of the indictment helped trigger the final, decisive break between Roosevelt and Taft.

In the charges, the Taft administration alleged that Roosevelt had been deceived by the steel company during the Panic of 1907. At the height of the financial crisis in that year, Roosevelt had let the steel giant acquire a competing firm, Tennessee Coal and Iron, without fear of an antitrust prosecution. Roosevelt had maintained in public and private that he had done so to protect the economy and had not been duped by the management of U.S. Steel. The Justice Department was now stating in public that the former president had been fooled. For Roosevelt, it was bad enough when Democrats had made the charge in the summer of 1911, but to have a Republican administration say so was to play "small, mean and foolish politics in this matter."[61]

The crucial element about the U.S. Steel indictment was its effect on Roosevelt's thinking about the 1912 Republican nomination. Up to that point he had turned aside overtures from progressive Republicans that he declare his candidacy. But when he attacked the administration's trust policy in public after the lawsuit and made clear his doubts about Taft, the clamor for him to run intensified. His 1904 pledge not to seek another nomination posed an immediate problem, but Roosevelt said that the statement did not rule out a former president "who is out of office." He avowed that he should not be a candidate unless "the bulk of the people wanted a given job done, and for their own sakes, and not mine, wanted me to do that job." Such language gave his supporters a green light to demonstrate to Roosevelt their fervent enthusiasm for him as a candidate. Soon letters poured in to Roosevelt at Oyster Bay urging him to challenge Taft.[62]

Confronted with the evidence of the popular will, Roosevelt moved toward a willingness to accept the nomination after all. The question was how to announce his candidacy in a way that made it appear he was responding to the urgings of reform Republicans and not just his own ego. It was decided that a group of progressive governors would send him a letter asking him to become a candidate for the party's nomination, and he would respond with a letter agreeing to do so.

As this scenario developed, the lingering problem of Senator La Follette and his claims to be a progressive eased in a dramatic fashion. At a banquet on February 2 before an audience of newspaper publishers in Philadelphia, the senator gave a disastrous speech. He was dead tired, distracted by illness in his family, and aware of Roosevelt's impending candidacy. He spoke too long, indulged in vitriolic attacks on the press, and generally made a public spectacle of himself. Those progressives such as Gifford Pinchot and James R. Garfield, who had nominally been with La Follette, jumped ship and went over to Roosevelt. It looked for a few days as if La Follette might get out of the race altogether. That did not happen, but Roosevelt's allies capitalized on the moment to put Roosevelt into the race.

Events proceeded as the Roosevelt camp had planned. The letter from the seven governors was received, Roosevelt issued his reply, and on February 21, 1912, the candidate said to the press corps that he would be in the race for the Republican nomination at the national convention. Indeed, said Roosevelt, he felt like a bull moose. The cartoonists lost no time in depicting a political moose disrupting Republican politics.

Roosevelt's decision to run was a crucial moment in the history of his party. Personality and policy were almost indistinguishable in his thinking. He differed with Taft over antitrust and other issues, and he did hope to implement the New Nationalism. He also believed that Taft would take the Republicans down to defeat against the resurgent Democrats. But Roosevelt's reasons had a personal dimension. As a political celebrity, he craved the attention that a presidential race would bring him.

He had felt most alive when he was in the White House, and nothing else quite rivaled it in terms of excitement and interest.

But Roosevelt had not really thought through his situation. If he won the nomination, what would that prize be worth after a debilitating fight with Taft? Assuming that he lost, it was improbable that he would endorse Taft. The chances were that Roosevelt would then bolt the party and run on his own. Roosevelt could make a good case that the Republican Party had not treated him fairly or given his ideas much respect, but at the same time the former president seemed to think that he had become bigger than the party in which he had spent his entire career.

Taft and his supporters responded by putting party success at a lower premium than their personal feelings. It was likely that, in the face of a united Democratic Party, only Roosevelt had a good chance of keeping the White House in Republican hands in 1912. But to conservative Republicans that meant accepting all or part of the New Nationalism and its expansion of governmental power. In 1912, they were unwilling to do so, and the defeat of Roosevelt transcended any temporary success of the party as their ultimate goal.

Roosevelt's campaign got off to a rocky start. He made his initial speech to the Ohio Constitutional Convention, calling for the recall (or review) of state judicial decisions through popular elections. That meant that rulings of the courts would be subject to the will of the people as expressed at the ballot box. In the early twentieth century, the conservative wing of the Republican Party held the state and federal courts in high esteem as bulwarks against the forces of popular reform and radicalism. To suggest that what judges decided could be overturned in an election was heresy. Many moderate to conservative Republicans shrank from endorsing Roosevelt on those grounds alone.

With time slipping by and much organizational work to be done, the Roosevelt forces had to devise a way to offset the impression, fostered by Charles Hilles and the Taft headquarters, that the president was gaining delegates every day and moving toward a first-ballot nomination. The Roosevelt campaign decided to challenge the delegates chosen from southern states where Taft was amassing a big lead. Although the Roosevelt men knew that the president would likely end up with most of these delegates, putting them under challenge disguised the former president's predicament. In the newspapers, where running counts of delegates appeared daily, readers saw Roosevelt and Taft with roughly the same number of delegates and a larger number in the disputed category. The national convention would have to decide the contests.

THE RACE FOR THE NOMINATION

> We believe that this country will not be a permanently good place for any of us to live in unless we make it a reasonably good place for all of us to live in.
>
> —Theodore Roosevelt[63]

To demonstrate how popular he was with rank-and-file Republicans, Roosevelt called for presidential preference primaries to determine what the party members thought about the nomination contest. These elections allowed Republican voters to allocate the delegates for their states directly, rather than going through a system of party conventions. Six states decided to have primaries, and these encounters, to be held in April and May, were Roosevelt's main hope. Meanwhile, the president continued to accumulate delegates.

With the nomination slipping away unless he stopped Taft's momentum, Roosevelt went out on the campaign trail at the end of March. He won the primary in Illinois and picked up fifty-nine delegates. He added another sixty-seven in Pennsylvania and won victories in Maine, Nebraska, and Oregon in state conventions. Suddenly, Roosevelt had the advantage. As the campaign heated up, all vestiges of Roosevelt and Taft's onetime friendship disappeared. Roosevelt charged that Taft had no real support beyond what he could acquire through patronage. Otherwise, as he said in Omaha, Nebraska, on April 17, "Mr. Taft's strength would be trivial and indeed negligible in the present

contest." He charged that Taft followed a "policy of flabby indecision and helpless acquiescence in the wrongdoing of the
crooked boss and the crooked financier."[64]

Taft responded angrily to these attacks on his character.
Roosevelt had failed to give him a "square deal." In Lowell,
Massachusetts, he announced, "I was a man of straw but I have
been a man of straw long enough; every man who has blood in
his body and who has been misrepresented as I have is forced to
fight." Or as Taft said on another occasion about himself, "Even
a rat in a corner will fight." Taft warned that once the two-term
tradition was breached, Roosevelt would want to serve "as many
terms as his natural life would permit."[65]

Beyond the two main combatants, Republicans debated the
future direction of their party. Nicholas Murray Butler, the president of Columbia University, told the delegates to the New York
Republican State Convention that "this contest within the party,
and this presidential election, may decide whether our government is to be Republican or Cossack." Republican progressives
saw the contest as the last chance to make the party more responsive to the needs of modern society. For Taft supporters the
issue was equally stark. As one of them said, "Roosevelt's doctrines, and still more himself, spell out the complete overturn of
our institutions, revolution and the establishment of a one-man
autocracy for life."[66]

After the primary battles, Roosevelt had 278 delegates and
had received 1,157,397 votes from Republicans. Taft had polled
761,716 votes and had secured 78 delegates. La Follette trailed
with 351,013 votes and 36 delegates. Other delegates were selected in state conventions and party caucuses. On the eve of the
convention, Roosevelt had 411 committed votes, Taft had 201,
and La Follette had 36. Of the remaining delegates, there were
166 counted as "uninstructed" (meaning they were not pledged
openly to any particular candidate and could vote as they
pleased). Another 254 were contested. Actually, Taft could count
on most of the "uninstructed" votes, including the large delegation from New York State because party leaders there, while
pro-Taft, wanted to preserve their bargaining power. How the

contests were decided would determine which candidate had the 540 delegates that were needed for the nomination.

The Republican National Committee met in Chicago during the early days of June to resolve the contests. The panel was controlled by Taft supporters, who allocated 235 delegates to the president and gave Roosevelt 19. On the merits, Taft was entitled to at least 200 of these southern delegates that the Roosevelt forces had challenged in early 1912. The president's supporters in the South had followed the party rules and simply outworked the Roosevelt supporters in Dixie. For Roosevelt's part, he deserved about 30 more delegates than he received. Had he won those seats, Roosevelt might have impaired Taft's control of the convention, but he would not have had a majority of the convention behind him. In deciding the contests, the Taft operatives on the national committee voted for the president as the basis of their decisions. Of course, had the Roosevelt men held the upper hand, they would have done the same thing. Resolving delegate contests was not an episode where anyone was seeking true justice.

Roosevelt believed that he had won a majority of the delegates fairly and squarely. He either did not remember or conveniently forgot that the contests in the South had been largely a pro forma exercise, and he did not think back to the 1908 GOP convention when the national committee, with his endorsement, had acted in much the same way to secure Taft's first nomination. As the national committee in 1912 seated Taft delegates from the key states of Arizona, California, Texas, and Washington, states where Roosevelt had a strong case, the former president concluded that Taft was stealing the nomination that was rightfully his.

CONFRONTATION AT CHICAGO

I'll name the compromise candidate. He'll be me. I'll name the compromise platform. It will be our platform.

—Theodore Roosevelt[67]

Faced with what he deemed to be outright theft, Roosevelt decided to go to Chicago and the GOP convention in person, in defiance of political convention. By now he was also making plans for a third-party race if that became necessary. "I have absolutely no affiliation with any party," he wrote the week before the convention started. Roosevelt's loyalty to the Republicans had now frayed to such an extent that only a nomination to lead the party could keep him in the fold.[68]

The national convention in 1912 was thus a seminal event in the history of the Republicans. The political humorist Finley Peter Dunne depicted his main character, Mr. Dooley, predicting in Irish dialect what would happen when the Republicans assembled. It would be "a combynation iv th' Chicago fire, Saint Bartholomew's massacree, the battle iv th' Boyne, th' life iv Jesse James, an' th' night iv th' big wind." The conclave exceeded such predictions. Roosevelt delegates shouted "Steam roller!" and "Liar! Liar!" at the Taft forces. One Taft supporter recalled that "a tension pervaded the Coliseum breathing the general feeling that a parting of the ways was imminent."[69]

Roosevelt appeared on June 15, the night before the Republicans kicked off the proceedings, and told supporters in the Chicago auditorium that "a great moral issue" faced the party. He was entitled to sixty or eighty more delegates than he had received, and the nomination was being stolen from his grasp. To prevent fraud, only the delegates whose seats were not in question should be allowed to vote. That would give the former president a majority of the delegates and control of the convention. Assailing Taft bitterly, he then told his audience that "fearless of the future, unheeding of our individual fates; with unflinching hearts and undimmed eyes; we stand at Armageddon, and we battle for the Lord."[70]

It made for wonderful political theater, but it did not change the hard reality that the Taft men had control of the machinery of the convention. Charles D. Hilles told his daughter that "Mr. Roosevelt's movement is the most horrible attack on Constitutional Government with which we have yet been confronted." As a result, the president's forces were determined to deny all efforts to block his nomination. The Roosevelt forces first sought to elect a friendly politician, the governor of Wisconsin, as temporary chairman of the convention. Instead, Elihu Root was named to the post by a vote of 558 to 501. The votes of Senator La Follette and his delegates helped block Roosevelt and gain the victory for Root.[71]

Next came the attempt by the Roosevelt men to have seventy-two of their delegates seated in place of those pledged to Taft from the disputed states. That initiative went down by 567 to 507. There was still a possibility that Roosevelt could win the nomination. Taft's position was not secure, and had Roosevelt been able to unite with the La Follette forces and other potential defectors, he might still have prevailed. In any case, there was always a chance for a compromise candidate such as Governor Herbert S. Hadley of Missouri. But Roosevelt made it clear that he was not going to back down and allow someone else to be selected.

Instead, Roosevelt had decided to bolt the party. He and his supporters began discussing how to organize a third party and to raise enough money to make it work. In the meantime, he issued a statement to the convention that accused it of seating "fraudulent delegates" and said it was "in no proper sense any longer a Republican convention." Thus, he instructed his delegates to sit mute and let the proceedings go forward. That made things easy for Taft, who was nominated on the first ballot with 561 votes to 107 for Roosevelt and another 41 votes for La Follette. The party platform said that the Republicans were "a party of advanced and constructive statesmanship." The document promised social justice and praised courts as the guardians of the rights of the people. The party had been "genuinely and always a party of progress; it has never been either stationary or reactionary."[72]

While Roosevelt went off to organize a third party, the Republicans were left to contemplate their situation. Unless the Democrats slipped badly, chances for a Republican victory in the fall seemed slim. But for the Republicans who opposed Roosevelt, his departure from the party was what mattered. Taft's vice president, Jim Sherman, was convinced that "it was essential for the life of our party and the continuance of our Government" that Roosevelt be "side-tracked." The important question was who retained control of the party, and on that point the regulars (as the Taft men styled themselves) felt secure that they had prevailed.[73]

There was enough blame to go around for everyone involved in the 1912 debacle. Senator La Follette had allowed his personal ambition to stymie progressive hopes to nominate the only candidate with a realistic chance to win. President Taft, although likely to lose in the fall, pursued his candidacy against all odds, and he, too, prevented any kind of compromise candidate from emerging. Taft was an honest man, but in the heat of the nomination campaign, he made deals with some of the shadiest individuals among the party's conservatives to ensure his own success. The Republican notion that no one was bigger than the party was nowhere to be found in 1912.

Most of the onus for the disaster belonged to Theodore Roosevelt. He began the race for the Republican nomination with the unspoken assumption that he would follow the rules of the party if he won, and reserve the right to bolt if he lost. At no time did Roosevelt think through what he would do in the unlikely (to him) event that he lost. In the most basic sense, Roosevelt never had a majority of the delegate votes at the Republican convention, so the nomination was never his to lose. What Roosevelt could not admit to himself was that Taft had proven the better politician in the nomination contest.

While Roosevelt had initially acted from bitterness and principle, and his ambition in seeking the nomination, his loss still dealt a blow to the Republicans that went beyond 1912. His belief in social progress, his willingness to accept social change, and his eagerness to engage national problems gave an energy and commitment that the Republicans needed. His absence made the GOP less receptive to the issues that came with regulating an industrial nation. Although the party talked of its devotion to progress, its emphasis was more focused on party unity, political caution, and conservative ideas. A certain degree of stagnation and rigidity had crept into Republican thought and governed how the party dealt with national issues for the three decades that followed.

In the months after their convention, Republicans watched as Theodore Roosevelt formed the Progressive Party in August and began a wide-ranging campaign on behalf of the New Nationalism and against the candidate of the Democrats, Woodrow Wilson of New Jersey, and his philosophy of the New Freedom. The Republicans were relegated to the periphery of this exciting debate. President Taft, observing the tradition that an incumbent president did not campaign, stayed in the White House. Vice President Sherman was ill with heart disease and died during the campaign. Hilles took over the Republican campaign as chair of the national committee, but he faced insurmountable obstacles as far as fund-raising was concerned. With inevitable defeat in the offing, party contributors closed their wallets. The general sentiment among the party faithful was: "We can't elect Taft and we must do anything to elect Wilson so as to defeat Roosevelt."[74]

A difficult and painful year for the Republican Party finally came to an end on November 5, 1912, when the voters elected Woodrow Wilson in a Democratic sweep. The winner received 435 electoral votes from forty states, Roosevelt garnered 88 electoral votes from six states, and Taft trailed with the 8 electoral votes of Vermont and Utah. The Democrats won control of both houses of Congress.

Yet amid the wreckage, there was Republican hope. Wilson was a minority president with only 41.9 percent of the popular vote. Roosevelt and Taft had 27.4 percent and 23.2 percent, respectively, and the Socialist, Eugene V. Debs, got almost 3 percent. If they remained united, the Republicans were still the majority party. However, in a two-man race against either Roosevelt or Taft, Wilson would likely have been the favorite because of his party's increased strength after 1904 and the Republican division. But in the long run, the Republicans were likely to win back some of the progressives who had left with Roosevelt and regain their position as the leading challenger to the Democrats. In the meantime, the conclusion of most of the party was, as one of them wrote, "If the Republican party is to have a future, it must be on conservative lines; it must be the great conservative party of the nation." The eight years of Woodrow Wilson's presidency would test the validity of that judgment.[75]

Chapter 6

REPUBLICANS DURING THE WILSON YEARS, 1913–1921

BY CHRISTMAS 1918, age had even caught up with the prodigious energy of Theodore Roosevelt. In and out of hospitals during the year for a variety of ailments, he had worsened since his youngest son, Quentin, a pilot with the American Expeditionary Force, had been shot down and killed in France the previous July. The emotional shock of this personal loss had been devastating for both Roosevelt and his wife, Edith. Amid his family tragedy, Roosevelt continued to criticize the policies of President Woodrow Wilson toward the defeated Germans and the plans for a League of Nations to preserve the peace. Wilson, the former president said, "is a conscienceless rhetorician and he will always get the well-meaning foolish creatures who are misled by names."[1]

To thwart Wilson, Roosevelt placed renewed emphasis on the role of the Republican Party he had forsaken six years earlier. Returning to the GOP in 1916 in hopes he could block Wilson's reelection, he had become more partisan during the last years of his life. But his renewed allegiance to the party had not changed his conviction that the Republicans should champion social justice measures such as those he had advocated in 1912, including old-age pensions and a program of medical insurance. His goal remained "to make the Republican Party the Party of sane, constructive radicalism, just as it was under Lincoln."[2]

Roosevelt's reinvigorated partisanship and strong distaste for Wilson made him the logical choice to seek the presidency again in 1920. Republicans assumed that he would be the nominee, especially after the party regained control of Congress in the 1918 elections. But it was not to be. Although he was only sixty in October 1918, Roosevelt's years of exertion and the effects of rheumatism, heart trouble, malaria, and other ailments put him back in the hospital in November. He was released in late December and returned to his home in Oyster Bay, New York. On January 5, 1919, he wrote a brief memorandum to himself. It spoke of Will Hays, chairman of the Republican National Committee, and party unity:

> Hays see him; he must go to Washington for 10 days; see Senate & House; prevent split on domestic policies.[3]

With this last concern for the Grand Old Party on his mind, Roosevelt died in his sleep early on the morning of January 6, 1919. His passing posed one of the great what-if's of Republican history. Had Roosevelt been nominated and elected in 1920, would the Republicans have embraced his domestic program? No one can say. But certainly Roosevelt's agenda would not have squared with that of Warren G. Harding, who became president when the Republicans swept back into power over the discredited policies of Woodrow Wilson. By the early 1920s, Theodore Roosevelt and the reforms he championed seemed a fading episode in Republican history as the party moved further to the right in both the domestic and foreign arenas.

THE AFTERMATH OF 1912

> It was party methods and not party principles that caused estrangements between parts of the party last summer.
>
> —Herbert S. Hadley[4]

In 1912, the Republican Party nominated William Howard Taft for a second term. After his defeat, Taft went on to become the chief justice of the United States. Four years later, the party selected Charles Evans Hughes to run against Woodrow Wilson. After his loss, Hughes became Secretary of State and then the chief justice of the United States. In 1920, the Republicans nominated Senator Warren G. Harding of Ohio, who won a landslide victory in the fall contest. In his brief administration, Harding would go on to be rated one of the worst presidents in the history of the United States.

How did the Republican Party that had selected two such distinguished candidates as Hughes and Taft decide to nominate a genial second-rater such as Warren G. Harding? After all, as Alice Roosevelt Longworth put it, Harding was "not a bad man. He was just a slob." The political logic of Harding's selection in 1920 revealed much about the Republicans' transformation during the presidential terms of their hated rival, Woodrow Wilson. In these eight years, the Republicans turned away from the moderate progressive reform impulses of Theodore Roosevelt and emerged as the conservative party it would remain for the rest of the twentieth century.[5]

Their 1912 defeat left the Republicans in a temporary state of confusion and disarray. After sixteen years of national power, they had lost control of the presidency and the Congress at the same time, and they faced the bitter legacy of the divisive rupture between Roosevelt and Taft. While they might have some confidence that the Progressive Party would soon collapse, no one could be certain that Roosevelt and his allies would fail in their attempt to supplant the Grand Old Party. Republicans could only hope that Woodrow Wilson would repeat the mistakes of Grover Cleveland and that Democratic failure would provide a Republican opening. Meanwhile, as Joe Cannon wrote, in his state and elsewhere "the party landed in Purgatory, from which place according to orthodox teaching there is an escape. We have to be thankful we didn't land in that other place from which it is said there is no escape."[6]

The general Republican attitude toward the new president

was one of suspicion and more than a little contempt. Wilson's shift from a Democratic conservative to a more progressive stance between 1908 and 1910 struck many Republicans as evidence of inconsistency and expediency. The president's condescension toward those with whom he disagreed also grated on Republican sensibilities. His status as a minority president led some Republicans to question his position. But GOP members quickly learned that Wilson was a skillful politician with a good sense of the public mood. In addition, he seemed to be a politician on whom Lady Luck smiled, at least during the first six years of his presidency. A Washington wag in 1916 observed that if Wilson "was to fall out of a sixteen-story building . . . he would hit on a feather bed."[7]

Some committed progressives wanted to rewrite party rules to institute presidential preference primaries and reduce the influence of the southern delegates. These initiatives attracted much newspaper attention in the early months of 1913 but did not lead to important results. Most party members preferred to leave things as they were and wait for Wilson to slip up.

The new Democratic president did not oblige his opposition. In rapid succession during his first year in office, he and the Democratic Congress passed the Underwood Tariff that reduced rates on imports and put an income tax in place, established the Federal Reserve system, and dealt with the trust issue in what became the Clayton Antitrust Act. The president had promised to implement his New Freedom program during the 1912 campaign, and now he had done so. After the Underwood Tariff had passed, a magazine editor said that the Democrats had "done much to remove the grounds for the criticism which has been consistently and justly leveled against their party in the past, that it is incapable of positive action."[8]

The enactment of the income tax did not diminish the importance of the tariff for the Republicans in the years before World War I. In their 1916 platform, they pledged that the party stood "now, as always, in the fullest sense for the policy of tariff protection to American industries and American labor."

While the party's commitment to protectionism would endure for another fifty years, the greater reliance on the income tax as a funding source for government shifted the debate about federal revenues away from customs duties. The changes in world trade in the years up to and after World War II also discredited protection as an economic doctrine. What had been the main tenet of Republican ideology began a gradual shift away from the center of political debate.[9]

The Republicans were thrown off stride by the spectacle of an effective progressive Democrat in the White House, but Wilson's skill did not mean that Republican opposition vanished. His status as a minority president meant that some Republicans regarded him as a transitory, even illegitimate, phenomenon whom they could challenge with their traditional arguments. From the outset of the new administration, Republicans predicted that lowering the tariff and regulating big business would hurt the economy. During the second half of 1913, they took some modest steps to reduce the disproportionate effects of southern delegates at the national convention, but they stopped short of calling a special meeting of the party or national committee to ratify such changes. Off-year elections brought gains for the party and signs of waning support for the Progressives and Roosevelt. As 1914 began, political observers detected omens of a Republican electoral revival in the making.[10]

During the first seven months of the year, the trend seemed to be running toward the Republicans. A downturn in the economy, reflecting worldwide economic problems, revived memories of the 1890s on which the GOP leaders capitalized. The party attacked Wilson for not doing more to stop unrest and violence against Americans in revolutionary Mexico, criticized him for being heavy-handed in his patronage practices, and accused him of antibusiness attitudes. Of the administration's antitrust legislation in 1914, the Republican leader in the House, James R. Mann of Illinois, said, "There is nothing in any of the Democratic anti-trust bills that will build a fire that is now out, start a factory, or in any way encourage business."[11]

During the early years of the Wilson administration, it was by no means certain which of the two parties would embrace Roosevelt's legacy of progressive reform. Along with Wilson's activism coexisted a strong and long-held strain of suspicion among Democrats about governmental power. Southern Democrats, once again "in the saddle," supported segregation in government departments in Washington, D.C., where blacks had gained some jobs under Republican presidents. These lawmakers also wanted to repeal the Fourteenth and Fifteenth Amendments and were suspicious of such reforms as woman suffrage. While the GOP had moved in a conservative direction after 1912, there remained vestiges of the spirit that Roosevelt had imparted to the party in such areas as conservation. The political situation was fluid and uncertain as the summer of 1914 commenced.[12]

But if anything, the portents favored the Republicans. "Reports reaching the national capital daily are far from encouraging from a Democratic point of view," said a Republican newsman in late July 1914. There was also talk that Theodore Roosevelt might be considering a return to his old party. The former president could see that progressives were drifting back toward their Republican moorings. Many reformers disliked and distrusted Wilson, who was "a sheep in wolf's clothing." Wilson was too much the Democrat for these progressives who favored government programs to address child labor and other social issues. The conclusion that grew out of these developments was that "the administration is losing support at an astonishing rate."[13]

THE WORLD WAR AND AMERICAN POLITICS

Folks are just hamstrung with the fear of war and huddled together in their parties without much sense. I do not think in all Kansas there is a Republican, whose name would reach beyond his county line, who would announce for Wilson today. And I do not think there is

a Democrat of any importance who would not be for
Wilson.

—William Allen White[14]

Throughout the first fourteen years of the twentieth century,
foreign policy issues played a secondary role in American politics. The Republicans had been the exponents of empire in the
late 1890s under William McKinley, and under both Roosevelt
and Taft they favored a greater degree of overseas involvement.
The Democrats opposed international adventures, sought independence for the Philippines, and advocated a smaller Army
and Navy. Although the United States had become a world
power, isolationist sentiment had a strong base in both parties.
Americans believed that European quarrels were far away and
best avoided.

The sudden outbreak of World War I in late July and into
August 1914 changed all this. A century of American separation
from European conflicts ended abruptly. Both sides in the war
sought to placate the United States but found that their causes
often demanded a confrontation with the American government. The outbreak of war added a new dimension to the history of both parties, and the Republicans first felt the effects in
the 1914 congressional elections. The Democrats capitalized on
the popular desire to remain aloof from the conflagration then
engulfing Europe. The president said that he would not campaign for Democratic candidates because of the crisis and confined himself to public statements that labeled the Republican
Party "utterly unserviceable as an instrument of reform." Democratic managers, meanwhile, proclaimed, "War in the East!
Peace in the West! Thank God for Wilson!" The nation was expected to rally around the president, and if the Republicans did
not do so, they risked being depicted as unpatriotic. That was a
new position for GOP members, and one they resented, especially coming from Wilson and the Democrats they had so often
criticized.[15]

The outcome of the voting still favored the Republicans in

November 1914. They gained sixty-six seats in the House, where they reduced the Democratic margin to forty seats. In the Senate, where popular elections occurred for the first time, the Democrats gained five seats. The Progressives lost ten of their eighteen members in the House and did not do well nationally. Roosevelt's third party was collapsing. Republicans believed that these results portended a victory in 1916.

Most of the Republicans who won in 1914, such as Boies Penrose in a Pennsylvania Senate race, were on the conservative side of the party, and the future indicated that a progressive-conservative split would dominate partisan conflict between Republicans and Democrats. Republicans were convinced that they would have recaptured the House but for the outbreak of war. Once again, the wily Wilson had escaped their grasp. Yet, with the likely return to the fold of progressive Republicans who disliked Wilson, the chances of the Grand Old Party winning in 1916 still seemed promising. The GOP did not take into account how the president would use the war and a timely shift toward progressive programs to gain another four-year lease on the White House.

The war put unexpected strains on the Republican electoral coalition. President Wilson asked Americans to be neutral between the Allies (Great Britain, France, Russia, and later Italy) and the Central Powers (Germany, Austria-Hungary, and later Turkey). Eastern Republicans, meanwhile, identified with the British cause, and some leaders, such as Roosevelt and Elihu Root, even thought that the United States should intervene to ensure an Allied victory. German Americans, strong in the Middle West, supported their fatherland and wanted true neutrality or even an anti-British stance. They regarded Wilson as anti-German and looked to the Republicans to sustain their cause. Most Americans, whatever their point of view, believed that the country should not enter the war. Republicans of a progressive bent felt strongly that only big business and Wall Street would gain from such hostilities.[16]

As Theodore Roosevelt moved away from the Progressive

Party in 1915, he did so in large part because of his unhappiness with Wilson's foreign policies and his hatred for the president. In Roosevelt's mind, these considerations outweighed any effort Wilson might be making to enact elements of the progressive agenda. Wilson was practicing a cowardly diplomacy, Roosevelt believed, that placed him in a class with other inept Democrats such as James Buchanan and Thomas Jefferson. When a German submarine sank the British liner *Lusitania* on May 7, 1915, Roosevelt asserted that the United States should have declared war on the Germans for an act of piracy. He ridiculed Wilson's statement that a nation could be "too proud to fight" in such a crisis. Throughout the months that followed, Roosevelt kept up his private and public attacks on the president. His ideas won the backing of Republicans sympathetic to the Allied cause. Much of the country worried, however, that Roosevelt would take the United States into the European war should he become president once again.[17]

During the first half of 1916, President Wilson moved the Democrats leftward in order to nail down the votes of former members of the Progressive Party. His efforts included the nomination of Louis D. Brandeis for the Supreme Court, support for a bill regulating child labor, and endorsement of federal loans for farmers. Wilson had also come out for limited woman suffrage. The Democrats were thus expanding the role of government and identifying themselves with social reform. Wilson's Secretary of the Interior, Franklin K. Lane, exulted at the change: "The Republican party was for half a century a constructive party and the Democratic party was the party of negation and complaint. We have taken the play from them. The Democratic party has become the party of construction." Republicans would have disagreed with this assessment, but Wilson's platform of peace, progressivism, and wartime prosperity would prove to have a powerful appeal at the polls.[18]

In 1916, the Republicans needed to select a presidential candidate who could satisfy both the Roosevelt and Taft partisans, the advocates of neutrality and the proponents of the Allies, and the progressives as well as the conservatives. None of the declared candidates in 1915–16 displayed much real strength along all these lines. Albert B. Cummins, once a progressive, low-tariff governor and now a senator from Iowa, as well as Robert M. La Follette had little appeal outside of their home states. Elihu Root could do well with eastern Republicans but was poison in the Middle West as a corporation lawyer and pro-Allied figure.

Roosevelt wanted the nomination desperately in order to defeat the hated Wilson. The president, Roosevelt wrote in February 1916, "is a very adroit and able (but not forceful) hypocrite." But Roosevelt recognized in March 1916 that he would win the nod from the Republicans only if "the country has in its mood something of the heroic." Roosevelt criticized German Americans for disloyalty, and he repeated his belief in the need for American intervention in speech after speech. He hoped to leverage what remained of the Progressive Party either to secure his own nomination by the Republicans or, at worst, to have a strong anti-Wilson candidate jointly named by the Republicans and his third party. The more Roosevelt spoke out, however, the more apparent became the limits of his support and influence with Republican voters outside of the East.[19]

The obvious answer for the Republicans and their electoral dilemma was Supreme Court justice Charles Evans Hughes. Hughes's candidacy had many attractive attributes for a beleaguered party. He had been a progressive governor of New York who got to Albany after he exposed wrongdoing among insurance companies. In 1906, he had defeated the notorious publisher William Randolph Hearst to win the governorship, and in 1908, he had made a speech attacking William Jennings Bryan's presidential candidacy that politicians remembered as a devastating performance. Taft had named him to the high court in 1910, and his judicial duties kept him out of the fray in 1912 when he turned down overtures to be a compromise candidate.

The wife of a Democratic congressman remarked in June 1916, "Who knows what opinions lurk beneath Hughes's primly parted hair." The last presidential candidate of a major party to wear a beard, Hughes appeared to be a moderate reformer who had no allegiances to political bosses, an ideal combination for the Republicans. Once he won the nomination, however, he would have to take on questions, especially those relating to neutrality and the war, where the party was divided. Like the Democrats' nomination in 1904 of Alton B. Parker, a jurist detached from the fray struck many Republicans as the best answer to the political challenge that Woodrow Wilson posed.[20]

The Republicans and the Progressives met in Chicago in early June in separate conventions, though they kept in constant touch about their activities. Hughes was nominated on the third ballot, and Charles W. Fairbanks of Indiana, Roosevelt's vice president in the second term, once again served as a running mate. Any attempt to select Roosevelt was rejected, and the dejected former president told his sister, "We are passing through a thick streak of yellow in our national life." He promised to support Hughes if the candidate agreed with Roosevelt's attitude toward foreign policy. Roosevelt's new loyalty to the GOP was carefully measured and conditional.[21]

The Republican platform tried to attract progressive voters while also reflecting the conservative temper of the delegates and the party. It reaffirmed the party's commitment to the protective tariff, declaring that "the Underwood tariff act is a complete failure in every respect." The Republicans came out for woman suffrage and a child labor law, but they also asserted that, while the party favored "rigid supervision and strict regulation" of railroads and "great corporations," Republicans believed "in encouraging American business as it believes in and will seek to advance all American interests." On foreign affairs and the war, it endorsed a "firm, consistent and courageous foreign policy" as well as "a strict and honest neutrality," without specifying how those contradictory goals were to be realized.[22]

Roosevelt maintained control of the Progressive convention until Hughes was selected. He then turned down the nomination of the party he had created four years earlier. In so doing,

Roosevelt made sure that his former colleagues did not select a candidate who might cripple Hughes, and the Progressive Party expired when Roosevelt told them on June 22 that they should endorse the Republican ticket. Men who had supported Roosevelt in good faith went away bitter and disillusioned. Roosevelt claimed that Wilson had "raised indecision, hesitancy and vacillation into a settled governmental policy" while Hughes would ensure that "the government will once more work with vigor and force." Many Progressives accepted Roosevelt's argument; others did not and gravitated toward Wilson. The effect on the Republican ticket remained to be seen.[23]

"He Kept Us Out of War": Republicans and the 1916 Campaign

> We believe that peace and neutrality, as well as the dignity and influence of the United States, cannot be preserved by shifty expedients, by phrase-making, by performances in language, or by attitudes ever changing in an effort to secure votes or voters.
>
> —Republican platform, 1916[24]

With Hughes as their candidate, the Republicans again sought to be as progressive as they could to suit voter attitudes in 1916 while not giving up their conservative posture on domestic issues. For Hughes that choice meant that he would have to move rightward to please the party's base or move left by accepting reform ideas while criticizing Wilson's methods. But foreign policy posed even more delicate issues for the Republican nominee. Hughes could not support Roosevelt's aggressive program toward aiding the Allies without alienating German Americans and letting Democrats take over the peace issue. But if he appealed to the German Americans and other Americans distrustful of the Allies, then the Democrats would assail his patriotism and imply that he was not truly being neutral.

Wilson and his party made the problem more acute for

Hughes when they adopted the slogan "He Kept Us Out of War" and stressed peace, prosperity, and reform as the major issues at their national convention. Under Wilson's leadership in 1915–16, the Democrats had moved leftward to embrace an activist national government on such issues as child labor and farm credits (but not race relations). The president had dropped much of his earlier suspicion of government as a means of pursuing social justice and openly identified himself with progressive goals.

These legislative accomplishments impressed those former members of the Progressive Party who advocated similar measures. The Democrats were making an explicit appeal on class-conscious issues in a manner that anticipated the similar posture of the party during the New Deal. Their literature declared that "for the first time in history the financial needs of the American Farmers have been recognized as of equal importance with the insatiable demands of Wall Street and the Big Interests." In 1916, the Republicans did not answer these charges as effectively as they could have.[25]

As the Republicans struggled with a changing opposition, they were forced into the unpleasant realization that Hughes was not the exciting candidate they had hoped he would be. His acceptance speech did not awaken voters, and he did not do much better in a campaign tour across the country in August. Hughes focused his attacks on Wilson's sometimes mediocre appointments to office and the president's mixed record on the civil service, but these did not come across as riveting topics. When the Republican candidate touched on the tariff, he pleased party regulars but said little to win over progressives. Democrats charged that "Mr. Hughes apparently is touring the country telling the people small, petty things which amount to nothing." Meanwhile, the Democrats emphasized the prosperity that had come with orders for war materials from the Allies, thus defusing the traditional Republican association of the Democrats with hard times.[26]

The Republican campaign organization, usually a positive element in the party's winning races, proved weak and ineffective in 1916. William Willcox, the man Hughes chose as national chairman, was a dud, and the headquarters made poor use of the ample funds it received. A British journalist told his superiors in London that "no American campaign that I have seen has been worse managed than the Republican one," and this occurred even though "the Republicans have lots of cash; the Democrats not much."[27]

Every move that the Hughes managers made seemed to backfire. When they organized a campaign train tour of women who supported Hughes because of his endorsement of woman suffrage, the wealth of these surrogate speakers became a liability. Since some of the participants were socialites, the Democrats dubbed it "The Billionaires Special." Hughes himself slipped up in California where he appeared to snub Hiram Johnson, a Senate candidate and popular governor. As one reporter argued, "Hughes is dropping icicles from his beard all over the west and will return to New York clean shaven."[28]

How to distinguish himself from Wilson on the war issue bedeviled Hughes through the fall campaign. The German Americans, who disliked Wilson intensely, seemed a likely source of Republican votes. To gain their allegiance without providing opportunities to the Democrats was a challenge Hughes could not master. The candidate met with German-American leaders, and his speeches emphasized the need for American neutrality. But neither Wilson nor Theodore Roosevelt would let the Republican candidate off the hook on the issue.

Roosevelt took to the stump himself to attack Wilson's foreign policy and Germany. His language was harsh and his desire for war with Germany evident. In one speech, Roosevelt alluded to Wilson's summer residence at Shadow Lawn, New Jersey. "There should be shadows enough at Shadow Lawn; the shadows of men, women and children who have risen from the ooze of the ocean bottom and from graves in foreign lands" where Wilson's policies had put them. When Hughes did not criticize Roosevelt's rhetoric, defections occurred among German-American voters in the Middle West.[29]

Wilson and the Democrats exploited Hughes's vulnerability on the loyalty issue with skill in the fall of 1916. When an Irish-American leader attacked the president as pro-British, Wilson rebuked him with a stinging telegram. At the same time, the Democratic candidate suggested "that the certain prospect of the success of the Republican party is that we shall be drawn, in one form or another, into the embroilments of the European war." The implication that the Republicans were both bellicose and somehow unpatriotic rankled leaders such as Henry Cabot Lodge and Theodore Roosevelt. However, Hughes never found a way to counter the impression that Theodore Roosevelt would influence him to take the United States into the conflict.[30]

While foreign policy occupied attention throughout the 1916 campaign, the Republicans and their opponents were also further split on domestic issues and the role of the federal government. In September, Wilson pushed the Adamson Act through Congress to avert a national railroad strike. The measure gave the railroad workers the eight-hour day they had long sought instead of the ten- to twelve-hour workday common in the industry. Tilting toward the labor unions struck Republicans as outrageous. Hughes and the party attacked the president for pandering to a special interest group. The Republican candidate said he "would not submit to dictation from any power in the country, no matter what the consequences."[31]

Beneath the surface of political debate, the campaign became bitter and ugly. Republicans charged that Wilson was pro-southern, and the party's orators brought out the bloody shirt among midwestern voters. Gossip circulated regarding Wilson's second marriage in 1915 to Edith Bolling Galt and the president's earlier relationship with a woman named Mary Hulbert Peck. When these stories got back to the White House, Wilson became even less inclined to cooperate with the Republicans. Since he would have to work with the opposition during World War I, this reluctance proved politically damaging.[32]

By the time the election neared, the odds seemed to favor Wilson's reelection, although everyone sensed that the contest would be close. So inept had been the Hughes campaign that a decisive Democratic win seemed likely. Roosevelt wished that Hughes had made "a straight-from-the-shoulder fighting campaign," but he still hoped for a Republican victory. On election night, the initial returns from the Northeast and Middle West disclosed a Republican trend. Hughes carried New York, Pennsylvania, New Jersey, and the rest of the Northeast, with the exception of a narrow loss (fifty-six votes) in New Hampshire. Michigan, Indiana, and Illinois also fell into the Hughes column. Only Ohio in the Middle West stayed with Wilson. It seemed as if Hughes would win. But then the tallies from the West indicated gains for Wilson in usually Republican states such as Kansas and Nebraska. In an age of paper ballots and slower communication, several days went by with the result in doubt. When California's late returns went for Wilson three days after the polling, it was clear that Hughes had been defeated.[33]

The final results attested to how evenly divided the country was in this contest. Wilson had amassed 9,100,000 votes and carried thirty states with 277 electoral votes to 8,500,000 popular votes for Hughes that gave the Republican eighteen states with 254 electoral votes. Almost sixty percent of eligible voters in the North went to the voting booth, though this was another presidential election in which participation was below the late-nineteenth-century levels. The Republicans did not recapture the Senate, but only the votes of independents and socialists kept the Republicans from retaking control of the House.

Although Wilson and the Democrats had won two consecutive terms, making him the only Democrat since Andrew Jackson to do so, the Republican electoral dominance established in the 1890s would soon resurface. The president had brought together themes of prosperity, progressivism, and peace in just the right mix to stave off the Grand Old Party and Hughes. If any one of these disparate elements turned in favor of the Republicans, they would likely regain the White House in 1920. With Roosevelt as their anticipated leader and the strife of 1912 in the past, the Republicans could look forward with optimism. As it happened, Wilson's political skills and the run of good luck he had enjoyed up to 1916 deserted him soon after the election. Within a few months the fragile Democratic electoral coalition started to collapse.

The campaign left abundant hard feelings between the two major parties. Wilson believed that the Republicans had smeared him with attacks on his private life. Republican leaders trusted the president even less than they had before the campaign began. Henry Cabot Lodge contended that Wilson had made "a sordid and base appeal" to defecting Republicans who were swayed by the peace issue. The president and the senator had gone through a bitter exchange of charges in the waning days of the campaign that left both men convinced of the other's dishonesty. Edith Roosevelt complained "that another four years must pass with this vile and hypocritical charlatan at the head of the nation." The sense among Republicans that Wilson was president only because of a dishonest campaign and demagogic issues shaped their strategy during the nasty and partisan warfare in which both parties engaged over the ensuing four years.[34]

POLITICS IS NOT ADJOURNED

> Unless a Republican Congress comes into control the present tendency toward indiscriminate and wholesale socialization of industries and utilities will not be wisely checked.
>
> —Richard Barry[35]

Within a few months after the 1916 election, the United States was drawn into the world war as the Germans launched unrestricted submarine warfare at the end of January 1917. President Wilson had tried to mediate an end to the conflict in December, but his efforts had failed, and by April the administration had decided to seek a declaration of war against the Germans. Republicans supported this step in public, but in private they were scathing about Wilson. Lodge said that the president "lowered the American spirit and confused the popular mind" by coming out for war after he had earlier sought "peace without victory" as the only sensible solution to the conflict. Theodore Roosevelt was more blunt: "Wilson and his crowd should be in the Boche trenches."[36]

Wilson indicated that as far as Republicans were concerned, entering into the war would be largely a Democratic affair. Wilson thought he was being bipartisan in his approach to the conduct of his office. After all, he gave Elihu Root a diplomatic assignment to aid the democratic Russian government during the summer of 1917, and he named William Howard Taft to the War Labor Board. In fact, Republicans did not regard these subsidiary assignments as credible examples of taking their party into the counsels of government in a serious way. It was not clear just what Wilson was supposed to do to satisfy the opposition, but he clearly fell short, in the minds of the GOP hierarchy, of an even-handed policy.

For many Republicans a decisive example of Wilson's aloof attitude was his reaction to Theodore Roosevelt's efforts in the spring of 1917 to raise a volunteer division for service in France as he had done with his Rough Riders during the war with Spain. On military grounds the aging Roosevelt, already blind in one eye, was a dubious warrior. The former president saw his major role as a booster of Allied morale. He told friends, including Elihu Root, that if he went to France, he did not expect to return alive. Root pointed out that if Roosevelt could give Wilson that assurance, the president would probably let him go! The administration turned down the offer, and Wilson had the better of the case on the merits since Roosevelt would have likely been a difficult subordinate sooner or later. The exclusion of Roosevelt from the war and the failure to find an overseas command for General Leonard Wood, a Republican general, enhanced the impression within the Grand Old Party that the president had no real use for Republican help.[37]

Amid the mobilization for fighting, social issues also called for resolution. By 1917, momentum on behalf of woman suffrage had intensified as its proponents contended that democracy should include all of the white population without regard to gender. The Democrats were divided on the issue since many southerners were opposed to an expansion of the franchise that might eventually include African Americans. The Republicans provided more substantial support for suffrage in Congress. The Grand Old Party also moved more quickly during this period toward giving female members of the party a greater role in its affairs. Women such as Ruth Hanna McCormick, daughter of Mark Hanna, and Mary Garrett Hay of New York contended for a more powerful voice in party deliberations with what proved to be largely nominal success.[38]

During 1917, the Republicans gained ground as problems engulfed Wilson and his party on the home front. The Democratic coalition frayed, and the Republicans reaped the political rewards. Congress passed the Lever Act that contained language allowing the president to fix prices on certain farm products. The goal was to encourage production and stem inflation. In the normally Republican grain states of the Middle West, some of which had gone for Wilson the previous year, farmers looked to receive higher returns on their crops and chafed at the possibility of price controls. Southern Democrats, in their turn, using their control of congressional committees, made sure that no regulations limited the rise of cotton prices. When Wilson fixed the price of wheat at $2.20 a bushel in the summer of 1917, farmers grumbled that they were being denied profits while cotton growers went unregulated. "The Iowa farmer," said a newspaper in that state, "would be satisfied with the present price of wheat if he did not know that the Georgia cotton farmer is allowed to sell his product on an unregulated market. He thinks there is politics in that situation, and he is right."[39]

Republicans also criticized the tax policies of the Democratic Congress. Its leaders believed that Americans in the cities with high incomes should bear the burden of the war while their rural constituents should be less penalized. This sectional disparity did not escape Republican notice. The party complained that Wilson and the Democrats were targeting the prosperous Northeast, an argument that appealed to voters there in 1918. Additionally, the repressive policies of the Wilson administration toward those who opposed the war rebounded against the White House. While Republicans applauded the hard line toward peace advocates and socialists, they resented it when the government criticized Roosevelt and others who wanted more vigorous prosecution of the war.[40]

Although the tide of events ran toward the Grand Old Party in 1918, the Republican organization still reflected the tensions of 1912 and 1916. In February 1918, the Republican National Committee convened to select a new chairman who would replace the holdover from the Hughes campaign. The front-runner appeared to be John T. Adams of Iowa, but he had the liability of pro-German statements he had made during the period of American neutrality. After a close vote of twenty-four to twenty-one, the party turned to Will H. Hays of Indiana. Not yet forty, the slight Hays styled himself as a "100 percent American." After graduation from Wabash College, he had risen through the ranks of the Hoosier Republican Party until he chaired the state's delegation to the 1916 national convention. His efforts enabled Hughes to carry the state, and he had endorsed the return of Theodore Roosevelt and the Progressives to the party fold. His selection, wrote Harold Ickes, a former Progressive, "has paved the way for a reconstructed party organization that can win and hold the confidence of all members of the party."[41]

Hays proved to be just what the Republicans needed in a national chairman. His aggressive tactics restored party morale as the November 1918 contests neared. Hays emphasized Republican unity in all his pronouncements. "Our party has no yesterdays," he wrote. "We do not care how a man voted in 1912, 1914 or 1916; nor his reasons for so doing." He contended instead that the Republicans were doing more to support the Wilson administration in fighting the war than many of the congressional Democrats. As the campaign got under way, Hays proclaimed, "Every Republican vote cast is another nail in the Kaiser's coffin, every Republican Congressman elected is another stone piled on his tomb."[42]

The Republicans especially bridled when President Wilson sought to identify the administration and the Democrats with the war and national patriotism. During a special election for the Senate in Wisconsin in April 1918, Wilson attacked the Republican candidate, Irvine Lenroot, for his "questionable support of the dignity and rights of the country on test occasions." Vice President Thomas Riley Marshall claimed that the Lenroot campaign relied on the "sewage" vote of German sympathizers in the state. This episode drove Republicans together, and Lenroot won the race. In another sign of growing Republican cohesion, Taft and Roosevelt staged a well-publicized, if somewhat bogus, reconciliation in late May 1918.[43]

From the spring of 1918 onward, the Republicans were on the offensive. Wilson took the lofty position that "politics is adjourned," but both parties continued their partisan warfare with abandon. Theodore Roosevelt attacked Wilson for "inefficiency, incompetence, hesitation, and delay," while Chairman Hays denounced "the socialistic tendencies of the present government." The administration's tax policies, reliance on bureaucracies for managing the food supply and overseeing American industry, and its apparent closeness to organized labor all proved tempting areas for Republican criticism. They alleged that Wilson's policies favored unions and penalized business. A British journalist said that the Republicans "are trying to create a party of what I suppose they would call stalwart nationalism."[44]

As the election neared, Allied fortunes on the battlefield improved, and the Germans asked for peace terms. The Republicans dropped their criticism of Wilson's war tactics and now demanded a harsh peace settlement for the beaten foe. "We stand not for a Democratic peace but an American peace," Roosevelt said in October 1918. With the Republicans arguing that only they could keep Wilson and the Democrats in check with control of Congress, the president concluded that he should make a personal appeal to Americans to cast their votes for Democratic candidates. It proved to be a fateful political gesture.[45]

On October 25, 1918, Wilson's statement went out to the nation. Republicans had "unquestionably been pro-war, but they have been anti-administration." To elect Republicans, Wilson said, would be seen "on the other side of the war as a repudiation of my leadership." The statement, with its implication that the GOP had been less than helpful in the war effort, evoked Republican outrage. "The President makes the demand of unconditional surrender upon the Republican voters of the United States. We asked for meat and he gives us a stone," wrote Charles D. Hilles. Across the country, "the Republicans of California can view the President's appeal as hardly less than an insult."[46]

When Republicans attacked Wilson and his party, they did so as part of what they conceived to be their patriotic duty in a nation at war because they disagreed with the way the president was conducting the war. But for the Democratic president to defend his party and seek its electoral success while the fighting took place seemed to many Republicans an assault on their patriotism. One aspect of Wilson that irritated his Republican foes was his adoption of the issue of allegiance to the nation that for so long had appeared to be a Republican monopoly. Wilson's strategy for the congressional election backfired, but had he kept silent, Republicans would have chastised him for abandoning his party. By November 1918, partisan feelings had reached such an intensity that any sort of accommodation across party lines was an impossibility.

The Republicans emerged victorious on November 5, 1918, in one of the most important congressional elections of the first half of the twentieth century. The Democrats suffered the losses to be expected in the sixth year of a two-term presidency, and the delicate majority they had assembled since 1910 disappeared. After the votes were counted, the Republicans had 240 seats in the House to 190 for their rivals. Republicans picked up 6 seats in the Senate to gain a 49 to 47 majority. Most of the hotly contested Senate races broke for the Republicans in the last weeks of the campaign. The issue of sectionalism and wheat prices cost the Democrats 21 House seats in the farm states. The Wilson coalition collapsed into internal bickering, and the Republican majority of the 1890s reappeared. For the moment, the voters had had enough of higher taxes, government regulation, labor unrest, and progressive reform.

The 1918 elections were more than just a sweeping Republican victory. For the party they represented the triumph of the conservatives after the turmoil that began at the end of Theodore Roosevelt's presidency. The decision that William Howard Taft and his allies made in 1912 to retain control of the machinery of the party had long-term consequences. The conservatives were in a position to enforce their agenda as progressive Republicanism faded away in the face of Wilson's activist programs. When the Democrats moved left under Wilson, the Republicans took up a conservative posture on regulation of business, the role of taxation, and the size of the government that remained in place for the rest of the twentieth century. The Democrats had not yet firmly decided to become the party of liberal reform and government regulation; that would not occur until the ascension of Franklin Delano Roosevelt in the early 1930s. But the position of the Republicans on the right side of the political spectrum was now one of the foundation points of American partisan life.

THE FIGHT OVER THE LEAGUE

> My first duty is to keep the Republican party in the Senate together.
>
> —Henry Cabot Lodge[47]

The armistice brought World War I to an end six days after the 1918 election, and the nation turned its attention to the problem of moving from war to peace amid concern over the way in which President Wilson would negotiate a treaty to provide for a lasting settlement. While the 1918 election had been bitter and hard fought, it proved only a prelude to a more impassioned struggle over the League of Nations that defined the foreign policy positions of both parties for decades to come.

One major figure in the history of the Republican Party did not live to see the outcome of the battle between Woodrow Wilson and the Republican Senate over the nascent League of Nations. On January 6, 1919, Theodore Roosevelt died in his sleep at his home in Oyster Bay, New York. In his last days, he was thinking of the unity of his party and its duty to provide a progressive, responsible brand of political conservatism. Roosevelt was a controversial part of Republican history, and his legacy is still debated within the Grand Old Party today. For all of his vigorous nationalism and defense of American interests overseas, Roosevelt also believed that the Republicans needed to address the nation's domestic problems at home. Had he lived, Roosevelt would have had to come to terms with the conservative tone of the party after 1918. Perhaps his anti-Wilson sentiments would have been enough to keep him loyal as he had not been in 1912. In any case, the Republicans had to look for another presidential candidate in 1920.

The Republicans emerged victorious in both the struggle with Woodrow Wilson over foreign policy and in the electoral battle with the Democrats in 1920. In the case of the League of Nations and in the election of Warren G. Harding in 1920, the short-term result advanced Republican fortunes. But both episodes were historical setbacks for the Grand Old Party, since the defeat of the League and the elevation of Harding came to be seen as evidence of the party's narrow view of the world and its tolerance of mediocrity in its presidential candidates.

The Republicans found the political environment even more favorable to their cause in the eighteen months that followed the 1918 balloting. Control of Congress enabled them to expose the weaknesses and failings of the Democratic administration. Meanwhile, Wilson himself pursued policies that angered the Grand Old Party and undercut his own coalition. Each month seemed to augment the bitterness that suffused American politics during the first months of the postwar era.

President Wilson sought to realize his dream of a League of Nations in 1919, but he did so in a high-handed manner that intensified Republican hard feelings. When he traveled to Paris to negotiate the peace treaty for World War I, he refused to take any prominent Republicans in his delegation. Had he decided to include any senators in his diplomatic party, as William McKinley had done with his negotiators in 1898, he would have been compelled to ask Senator Henry Cabot Lodge, the new chair of the Foreign Relations Committee, to go with him. Since Lodge and the president hated each other with a passion that was rare at any time in American politics, inviting Lodge was not an option. Lodge told a friend, "With the exception of Roosevelt there is no one the President dislikes more than he dislikes me." As he had done during the war, Wilson decided not to add other prominent Republicans such as Taft or Elihu Root to his team. The president regarded both men as hopeless partisans and his intellectual inferiors. The man he did invite to join his negotiating delegation, Henry White, was a veteran Republican diplomat but not a partisan identified with GOP fortunes.[48]

While Wilson was in Europe for six months, the Republicans delayed action on key bills in a lame-duck Congress from December 1918 through March 4, 1919. Since the new Congress was not scheduled to meet again until December 1919, that meant the president would have to summon a special session where Republicans would be in control. Under the leadership of Lodge, Republican senators also circulated a "round-robin" document that insisted on changes in the proposed League of Nations before they would accept any treaty. Enough senators added their names to deny a two-thirds majority for approval of a pact. An irritated Wilson had to renegotiate some key provisions in Paris to appease his domestic critics.[49]

Wilson returned to the United States in July 1919 with the

Treaty of Versailles, the central provision of which was the League of Nations. Article Ten of the treaty bound member nations to come to the assistance of any state in the organization that was the victim of aggression as the League defined it. That meant a diminished role for Congress in deciding whether the nation went to war overseas. Lodge and other Republicans called this clause an infringement of American sovereignty since it would compel possible military action without the consent of lawmakers. Lodge told his colleagues, "We would not have our country's vigor exhausted, or her moral force abated, by everlasting meddling and muddling in every quarrel, great and small, which affects the world." Most Senate Republicans shared Lodge's view to some degree. Those known as "Irreconcilables" wanted no treaty at all. Others labeled "Mild Reservationists" would accept a pact with amendments in the less binding form of reservations.[50]

Whether the Treaty of Versailles succeeded or failed depended on the competition between Lodge and Wilson for the wavering Republicans in the middle. The president tried to appeal over the heads of the senators and made a speaking tour to rouse public opinion in September 1919. But by the end of the month, as he spoke out for the treaty in the West, Wilson's health collapsed. He returned to Washington where he suffered a disabling stroke on October 2. When the nation realized the severity of Wilson's condition, the sentiment against the Democrats mounted. Beyond the League issue, rising prices, repeated strikes, race riots, and an anti-Communist Red Scare convinced voters that the nation was in a crisis of significant dimensions. There seemed for a time to be no effective government in Washington. Rumors circulated that Wilson had gone mad and his wife was in charge. A change in political leadership seemed inevitable.

While Wilson recuperated, the League of Nations came up for a vote in the Senate. The president insisted that his treaty be approved without change. On November 19, both the treaty without amendments and the version with Lodge's reservations were defeated. The Senate made another try in March 1920 in a vote on the treaty, this time with Lodge's language. Wilson told the Democrats to oppose the deal. With the Democrats doing the president's bidding and the Irreconcilables voting no, the treaty came up seven votes short of approval. The United States stood aloof from the League and continued to ignore its deliberations throughout the 1920s.[51]

This did not mean that the Republicans opposed American involvement in the world during the 1920s. Lodge, Root, and Charles Evans Hughes believed that the United States had to exert its power on the international stage. As Secretary of State for Warren G. Harding, Hughes played a constructive and creative part in dealing with issues of European war debts, the Far East, and disarmament. A tradition of strong international power that reached back to William McKinley and Theodore Roosevelt maintained a place in the hearts and minds of eastern Republicans.

But in defeating Wilson, Lodge had also accommodated senators from the Middle West and the West who were suspicious of world power. The arrangement that Lodge had achieved also meant the emergence of a more isolationist foreign policy position among Republicans that was suspicious of military power, imperialism, European diplomacy, and overseas commitments. The sense that the United States could and should play a limited role in the world established itself as political dogma in many areas of the nation's heartland where the Republicans were strong after 1920. The increasing influence of this faction in the party would have serious consequences during the rise of the dictators in the 1930s. For now, the United States and many Republicans could think of themselves as safe behind the comforting barrier of two oceans.[52]

"Mr. Harding, You're the Man for Us"

[Harding] is a regular Republican, believing in the necessity and efficacy of solid party action as the only effec-

tive means of interpreting the will of the people into constructive progress.

                                    —William Howard Taft[53]

After their success in the League of Nations battle, the Republicans could taste victory in the fall of 1920 as they prepared to select their presidential nominee. The process by which Senator
Warren G. Harding of Ohio prevailed as the GOP candidate
soon became the stuff of American political legend. His selection, so the story went, occurred on June 11, 1920, when a cabal
of conservative senatorial king-makers gathered in a smoke-
filled room and anointed the flawed Harding as the Republican
choice. There was such a room, and there was a meeting with
the candidate, but after that the legend yields to a more complex
reality.

For the first time since 1888, the Republicans had no clear
front-runner or incumbent president to place on their ticket.
There were a number of hopefuls. General Leonard Wood campaigned as the heir of Theodore Roosevelt but lacked his idol's
interest in social justice. He recommended that the nation follow
the advice of a clergyman who proposed that suspected Bolshe-
viks be sent away "in ships of stone with sails of lead, with the
wrath of God for a breeze and with hell for their first port."
Frank O. Lowden was the governor of Illinois, an important
state, and had ample campaign funds from his wife's links to the
Pullman railroad car millions. Neither man did well in the primary season leading up to the convention. Whatever remained
of Republican progressivism resided with Senator Hiram Johnson of California. With only one hundred delegates, he had an
outside chance at best.[54]

The fourth major candidate in the race was Warren G.
Harding. A newspaper publisher in Marion, Ohio, who was finishing his first senatorial term, Harding would be fifty-five by
Election Day. Rank-and-file Republicans warmed to the affable
politician. William Allen White recalled him in his youth as "a
handsome young dog, a little better than six feet tall, straight,
with well-carved, mobile features, a good shock of black hair,

dark olive skin, fine, even teeth, and an actor's mouth." No one thought of Harding as a brilliant intellect, but the party had seen enough of intelligent candidates in Roosevelt, Taft, and Hughes. As the governor of Kansas put it, "I have a feeling that we have had all the superman business the party is likely to want and what the period really needs in my judgment is the man who is a product of our institutions and not the product of a peculiar period." Handsome and a pleasing orator, Harding reassured voters that he would not press for reform in office. In his most famous statement of his placid philosophy, he avowed: "America's present need is not heroics, but healing; not nostrums, but normalcy; not revolution, but restoration; not agitation, but adjustment; not surgery, but serenity; not the dramatic, but the dispassionate; not experiment, but equipoise; not submergence in internationality, but sustainment in triumphant nationality."[55]

Known only to a few intimates and his neighbors in Marion were Harding's personal failings. Although his alleged illicit romance with Nan Britton seems to have been only a product of her fertile imagination, the senator had pursued an extramarital affair with Carrie Phillips, the wife of a friend in Marion. The romance became "a primrose detour from Main Street which Florence Kling [Harding], the Duchess, had chosen to ignore." In his ardor, Harding had written Carrie letters that could have occasioned blackmail or embarrassment had they become public. Harding's managers, led by Harry M. Daugherty, made sure that word about these indiscretions did not reach the press and public. Harding did not do well in the Republican primaries, but his backers saw him as a logical compromise choice after the initial balloting of the convention concluded. Daugherty touted Harding as the second-choice candidate who could unite the party in victory.[56]

The Republicans met in Chicago and made a bow toward the memories of progressivism with their promise in the platform of "an enlightened measure of social and industrial justice." What that entailed was not defined. For the most part, however, conservative themes dominated the document. The Wilson administration was guilty of "complete unpreparedness for war and complete unpreparedness for peace." The platform writers attacked high taxes, promised "honest money and sound finance," and pledged that they would "free business from arbitrary and unnecessary control." As for the League of Nations, the delegates endorsed "an international association" as long as it was "based upon international justice." Above all, the Republicans vowed "to end executive autocracy and to restore to the people their constitutional government."[57]

The national convention unfolded according to the script of the Harding strategists. Lowden and Wood stalled in the early ballots with about three hundred delegates each. Harding trailed with only sixty delegates. By the time the convention adjourned for the night late on June 11, 1920, the stalemate was evident. Rumors flew that Harding was the choice of influential senators. The candidate had been summoned to a room at the Blackstone Hotel where he was asked if he knew of any reason why he should not be president. Aware of bogus rumors in Ohio that he had African-American ancestors, his dalliance with Carrie Phillips, and his weak heart condition, Harding nevertheless responded that he saw no reason why he could not be selected.[58]

These events did not produce a seal of approval for Harding, however, or make his nomination inevitable. For the next three ballots on June 12, the front-runners remained deadlocked. Harding, meanwhile, crept up to 133½ votes by the eighth ballot. After a three-hour recess, the ninth ballot saw Harding surge into the lead with 374½ votes. On the next tally, he became the nominee. Harding himself said it best: "We drew to a pair of deuces and filled." In the context of 1920, Harding made sense as a compromise candidate. He could carry Ohio, he had no serious enemies within the party, and he made a winning figure on the stump. Ohio had produced another Republican who looked like a president.[59]

Party leaders wanted to balance the selection of Harding with Senator Irvine Lenroot of Wisconsin, but the weary delegates preferred a more popular choice, one not tainted with any links to the reform ideas of Robert M. La Follette. During a police strike in Boston the previous year, Governor Calvin Coolidge had proclaimed, "There is no right to strike against the public safety by anybody, anywhere, anytime." Although Coolidge had not been instrumental in resolving the labor dispute, his ghost-written words caught the nation's conservative trend in 1919–20. In a wave of enthusiasm, his name was placed in nomination, and he easily swamped Lenroot.[60]

The Harding-Coolidge ticket faced a demoralized Democratic Party. President Wilson had some late delusional thoughts of a third nomination, but his friends advised him that the convention delegates would reject him. Democrats opted for another Ohioan, former governor James M. Cox, to lead the ticket. Franklin Delano Roosevelt, the Assistant Secretary of the Navy and a distant cousin of Theodore, became the running mate. The Democrats never had a chance of victory in light of Wilson's pervasive unpopularity. The only real question would be the size of Harding's triumph.

The Republican campaign in 1920 reflected the organizational skills of Will H. Hays and the advertising techniques of Albert Lasker, who brought his talents in public relations to Harding's cause. Lasker's advertisements featured Harding's picture in every possible place where it could be displayed. He brought in actors from New York, including Mae Marsh, Pearl White, and Al Jolson, to endorse the Republican candidate in his hometown. Jolson contributed his own melodic tribute to Harding under the title "Mr. Harding, You're the Man for Us":

> *We need a man to guide us*
> *Who'll always stand beside us*
> *One who is a fighter through and through*
> *A man who'll make the White House*
> *Shine out just like a lighthouse*
> *And Mister Harding, we've selected you.*
> *Harding, lead the G.O.P.*
> *Harding, on to Victory!*
> *We're here to make a fuss!*
> *Mr. Harding, you're the man for us!*[61]

Rather than make an overtly ideological appeal to the voters, the Grand Old Party sought to capitalize on the pervasive voter discontent with Wilson and the Democrats. The Harding managers wanted to assemble as many votes as possible without alienating any large interest group in society. Antilabor elements in the party found their message muted so that Harding could reach out to workingmen. Even former Progressives were given a reason to support the Republican ticket.

In 1920, women voted for the first time in a national election. The suffrage amendment had been adopted in 1919 and then ratified in the late summer of 1920. Republicans had a better claim to the credit for the adoption of the reform since many southern Democrats had opposed the expansion of government power inherent in extending the vote to females. The Republicans, however, had not moved as quickly as their Democratic counterparts to integrate women into their party structure. At the Republican convention, twenty-seven women were duly elected delegates; another 277 women served as alternates. Women were on committees and made half a dozen seconding speeches for presidential candidates. The party welcomed women into its ranks, and the platform contained language endorsing a number of issues important to female voters. Yet equality for women in the political operations of the Republican organization was still decades in the future.[62]

In the 1920 campaign, Republicans saw a chance to attract black votes in the North from African Americans whom the segregationist policies of the Wilson administration had alienated. Harding met with black leaders and promised a sympathetic hearing for their grievances. The initiative soon encountered problems that would bedevil Republican efforts in this area for the next eighty years. Migration of blacks to the North during the preceding decade had begun to create large blocs of potential Republican supporters in major cities. At the same time, the movement of whites from the North to warmer southern states meant that Republican chances of cracking the Solid South looked more promising than they had been since Reconstruction. The dilemma was that the policies that spoke to one group alienated the other. If Republicans such as Harding promised to support measures in Congress to stamp out lynching, they risked the wrath of southern whites who would flow back toward their Democratic home. Yet if they advanced policies that pleased the South, such as "lily-white" Republican parties from which African Americans were excluded, they would encounter the displeasure of northern black voters.[63]

So the Republicans tried to have the best of both worlds. Harding met with groups of black leaders during the campaign and listened to their complaints about the Wilson administration. He advocated in July that "the Federal government should stamp out lynching and remove that stain from the fair name of America." The Republicans also made a strong effort to rally black voters in Tennessee, one southern state that they thought might go for their ticket. At the same time, when Harding appeared in a border state such as Oklahoma, on October 9, a local newspaper carried Harding's answers to questions about segregation and black voting. The presidential candidate wavered: "You can't give one right to a white man and deny it to a black man. But I want you to know that I do not mean that white people and black people should be forced to associate together in accepting their equal rights at the hands of the nation."[64]

The race issue surfaced toward the end of the campaign when the charge that Harding had black ancestors appeared in several places. This rumor had been circulating in Ohio politics for years, and the Republicans responded with a listing of Harding's family roots that said he came from "a blue-eyed stock from New England." Afraid of a popular backlash, Democrats refused to touch the rumor in the press, and the episode did no damage to the Republican candidate's chances of election.[65]

Harding's overall campaign began as a replay of William McKinley's front-porch style in 1896, and large crowds came to Marion to view the candidate. As the election neared, demands for Harding to be seen led to tours of the Middle West and the East. The candidate equivocated at first on the League of Nations and then settled on a stance of strong opposition. None of these issues really did anything to disturb the Republican march to victory because the public was ready for a change. "The election of Harding will end Wilson and his works, and the sentiment seems to be growing very strong against Wilson and the administration," predicted one Republican.[66]

The election, said Woodrow Wilson's secretary, Joseph Tumulty, "wasn't a landslide. It was an earthquake." In one of the most sweeping Republican victories in the party's history, Harding amassed over 16 million popular votes to over 9 million for Cox. In the electoral tally, Harding gained 404 to 127 for Cox, who carried only the still solidly Democratic South. The Republicans won thirty-seven states and had achieved big majorities in the House and Senate. Women voters cast their first-time ballots for Harding. So did many other normally Democratic ethnic groups such as Irish Americans and Italian Americans. Bitterness over the territorial settlements of the League of Nations accounted for some of these ethnic defections. The Democrats slipped back into minority status as the Republicans reestablished themselves as the nation's majority party.[67]

Two turbulent decades had elapsed since William McKinley stood in the receiving line at Buffalo and shook the murderous hand of Leon Czolgosz. Theodore Roosevelt's two terms brought an acceptance of some government regulation as part of an enlightened conservatism for an industrial society and its problems. The exercise of national power to regulate business could be justified, as Roosevelt tried to do, as a way of staving off more radical changes. But for a majority of Republicans after 1910, the more preferable course was to limit the role of government and oppose regulation. Some restraints on business could be tolerated, but not many. A place for organized labor existed in American society, but its power should be constrained. As the two parties struggled with the question of how to manage an urbanized, industrial polity, the Democrats edged leftward (except on race) while the Republicans increasingly occupied the right side of the spectrum in opposition to more government power and more regulation. The pattern of political discourse created in the age of progressivism proved to be enduring on domestic issues for the eight decades that followed.

The task that lay ahead for Warren G. Harding and the Republicans was an imposing one. The Wilson years had left a legacy of social unrest, government debt, and popular suspicion of the political system. High taxes and an intrusive government seemed to be the legacy of a generation of progressive reforms. The dominant sentiment in 1920 endorsed what Harding had promised in his campaign: a nation "where childhood had a right to happiness, motherhood to health, everyone to education, and all Americans the right to our equal opportunity." But it was not the job of the president to supply these wants or to regulate the behavior of the American people in furtherance of social justice. As the 1920s began, Republicans looked once again to the energies of business enterprise and the individual initiative of the American people to provide what government could not.[68]

Chapter 7

THE AGE OF REPUBLICAN DOMINANCE,
1921–1933

THE PRESIDENT DIED suddenly and unexpectedly in the midst of his first term in August 1923, and the nation mourned. The funeral train that took his body across the United States encountered the grief-stricken all along the way. When the procession reached the Middle West, great crowds lined the route and continued through Chicago. In Pittsburgh, industrial workers stood crying as the train passed by. An outpouring of sorrow marked the entire country as people wept for their fallen leader. Yet within a decade the memory of Warren Gamaliel Harding would become a kind of national joke, his presidency shrouded in scandal and ineptitude.[1]

Few periods in the history of the Republican Party have received more scorn and criticism than the brief presidential tenure of Warren G. Harding. One of the most famous scandals in American history, Teapot Dome, symbolized the sordid record of a man whose performance fell well short of the high standards of his office. By the time he died of a heart attack in August 1923, Harding knew that he would face the embarrassment of seeing some of his close associates under investigation for official misdeeds. While these transgressions did not touch Harding personally, they reflected his inadequacy as president. How did Harding, now generally depicted as one of the worst chief executives in the nation's history, evoke such reverence when he was alive and reap such devastating criticism after his death?

A point about Harding often forgotten is the lowly reputation of Woodrow Wilson when he left office in March 1921. Even some liberal voices welcomed the change from the repudiated Democratic president. Harding did not have an inaugural ball, and the promised simplicity in office elicited wide praise. The new first lady, Florence Kling Harding, opened up the White House after the seclusion of the world war and the president's illness, and made it more accessible to visitors. This shift back toward a president who was only "the First Citizen" provided Harding a surge of popularity during his early days in office.[2]

Harding was a kindly man. Eugene V. Debs, the Socialist leader, had been imprisoned during the Wilson years for antiwar sentiments, and the Democratic president had vowed that he would remain there until the end of his term. After some initial hesitation, Harding pardoned Debs in December 1921, and other radical prisoners were released during the remainder of Harding's tenure. On racial issues Harding made some mild gestures toward African Americans and attacked lynching in a message to Congress in April 1921, but the administration did not follow up on this initiative with support for an antilynching bill then in Congress. Nor did Harding attack the Ku Klux Klan, which was growing in power, or encourage his Department of Justice to investigate the hooded order's violent policies. But Harding did not endorse the repressive racial policies of the Wilson years.[3]

AMERICA IN THE HARDING ERA

Our eyes never will be blind to a developing menace, our ears never deaf to the call of civilization. We recognize the new order in the world, with the closer contacts which progress has wrought. We sense the call of the human heart for fellowship, fraternity, and cooperation. We crave friendship and harbor no hate. But America, our America, the America builded on the foundation laid by the inspired fathers, can be a party to no military alliance. It can enter into no political commitments, nor assume any economic obligations which will subject our decisions to any other than our own authority.

—Warren G. Harding[4]

The United States over which Harding now presided was one transformed from the nation that Theodore Roosevelt governed in September 1901. A generation earlier, agriculture and rural life had shaped the values and experience of a majority of citizens. Now the 1920 census revealed that a majority of Americans lived in cities and towns of 2,500 or more inhabitants, rendering those who resided in the countryside a minority. Throughout the next decade Americans left the country for the city in growing numbers. They brought with them attitudes and mores bred on the farm, but they embraced the bustle of Chicago, the excitement of New York, the glamour of Los Angeles as their future. The rural-urban split that ensued hurt the Democrats most in the 1920s, but the Republicans did not escape its effects, either.[5]

After a slow start in the first two years of Harding's presidency, the economy boomed, up through 1927. The gross national product rose forty percent from 1922 to 1927, and in the latter year unemployment stood at only four percent. Republican dominance of American politics rested on the surge of prosperity and economic change. A new consumer culture brought cars, appliances, and the mass media to millions of homes. Movies and radio shaped the common experience of the average citizen. Labor unions lost power and influence as business installed the nonunion "open shop" (in contrast to the all-union "closed shop") and offered more benefits through what was called welfare capitalism. The social conflict of the Progressive Era, while it had not disappeared from national life, seemed to have receded from the minds of most political leaders and the public. Magazines asked what had happened to the prewar reformers.[6]

One sector of the economy, however, did not share in the rising economic tide. In the nation's agricultural belt, overproduction of crops marked the decade as wheat and cotton prices slumped from their wartime levels. Farm incomes remained well below what city dwellers were earning. A "farm bloc" of Republican senators pushed for government help for their constituents throughout the 1920s, a drive that both the Harding and Coolidge administrations resisted. The result was often Republican discord in Congress as these senators also opposed greater American involvement overseas and business-oriented trade policies.[7]

For organized labor the 1920s were a time of retreat and confusion. The antiunion sentiment that followed the world war discredited the American Federation of Labor (AFL) and its leader, Samuel Gompers. Composed of craft unions and skilled workers, the AFL did not reach out to organize the unskilled, lower-paid workers who faced the most economic hazards. Court decisions limited the power of unions to strike effectively, and the White House under Harding and Coolidge was unsympathetic to organized labor's agenda. Opposing Coolidge in the 1924 presidential election did not improve the standing of the unions with Republican leaders.[8]

A central element of public policy during the 1920s was the effort to shut down the flow of immigration into the United States following World War I. In 1921, 805,000 people entered the country, a number that aroused the fears of immigration restrictionists in and out of Congress. Lawmakers responded with an emergency bill to limit immigration from Europe to 600,000 per year. Three years later, Congress approved the National Origins Quota Act that restricted annual immigration from Europe to 150,000 people, with preference given to those who came from northern Europe. Congressman Albert Johnson, a Washington Republican and chair of the House Committee on Immigration, observed in 1927, "The day of unalloyed welcome to all peoples, the day of indiscriminate acceptance of all races, has definitely ended."[9]

The 1920s have become almost a historical cliché, and one of the most hidebound notions of the era has to do with the controversial social reform of Prohibition. A program that grew out of the tensions between city and country and a desire to purify politics from the corrupt influence of brewers and liquor dealers, alcohol control came in with the passage of the Eighteenth Amendment in 1917 and its ratification two years later. The Volstead Act of 1920 implemented the specifics of Prohibition. Far from being as ineffectual as its critics have contended, Prohibition brought down drinking during the early 1920s and then waned in effectiveness as the decade went on. Republican prohibitionists (drys) tended to come from the rural Middle West and New England. Those opposed to the policy (wets) were stronger in urban areas. Neither national party said anything about Prohibition in its 1920 platform. The burden of national enforcement fell on the Harding and Coolidge administrations. While it never divided the Republicans as it fractured the Democrats, Prohibition did become a source of factional discord within the party in some key states.[10]

The rise of the Klan reflected the social tensions of the early 1920s. Going beyond its antiblack heritage from Reconstruction, the Klan assailed Jews, Catholics, and immigrants. In some states of the Southwest, Middle West, and West, Klansmen became politically powerful and pursued its nativist policies on the state level. Democrats felt the problem of the Klan in their rural base in the South and West.[11]

HARDING IN THE WHITE HOUSE

I never find myself done. I never find myself with my work completed. I don't believe there is a human being who can do all the work there is to be done in the President's office. It seems as though I have been President for twenty years.

—Warren G. Harding[12]

Though Warren G. Harding was far from a great president, his brief administration could claim some tangible accomplishments. Aware of his own limits, the new president sought to enlist "the best minds" in the key Cabinet posts. He selected Charles Evans Hughes as his Secretary of State and named Herbert Hoover as Secretary of Commerce. Hoover proved to be an energetic and determined Cabinet officer who respected few boundaries among the other departments and whose reach extended into much of the government. Another key Harding selection was Andrew Mellon, the Secretary of the Treasury, whose connections to his family's banking interests in Pittsburgh reassured the financial community of the president's conservatism and fiscal soundness.[13]

The rest of Harding's Cabinet was undistinguished. The president selected Albert B. Fall, an old friend from the Senate, to head the Department of the Interior. From that post Fall would set in motion the events that led to the Teapot Dome scandal. Harding's attorney general was his campaign manager and political associate from Ohio, Harry Daugherty, who proceeded to compromise the ethical standards at the Justice Department. Under his lax rule, the criminality of the "Ohio Gang" flourished as favors and pardons were bought and sold through some of Daugherty's cronies. Harding knew little of these developments, but he allowed them to happen.[14]

Yet the administration achieved some creditable results. The Republican Congress passed the Budget Act of 1921, setting up the Bureau of the Budget to give the government a means of managing its annual expenditures. In the first two years of the presidency, ambitious plans for government reorganization went forward but had not yet reached fruition when Harding died. The president named conservatives to fill the regulatory agencies that the progressives had created, demonstrating that political reform could have unexpected consequences.

In foreign affairs, while not recognizing the League of Nations, the administration did summon the Washington Conference on Naval Disarmament in 1922, and Secretary of State Hughes secured important reductions in the naval strength of

Britain, Japan, and the United States. That same year Congress
enacted the Fordney-McCumber Tariff that undid some of the
provisions of the Underwood Tariff of 1913 as far as rates were
concerned, and restored much of the protective structure that
had existed under the Payne-Aldrich Tariff of 1909. Protectionism was still alive and well within the core beliefs of the GOP.[15]

Ultimately, the first two years of the Harding presidency did
not satisfy the voters, and the Republicans suffered serious reverses in the 1922 congressional elections. The postwar slump
continued, and unemployment hovered at around eleven percent. Meanwhile, the antilabor sentiment that the war had also
fostered had weakened the unions. As hard times intensified,
strikes became more common and more violent. Republicans
sensed that voter unhappiness would be intense, but little prepared them for the depth of resentment that the Congress and
the presidency encountered. The departure of Will H. Hays
from the chairmanship of the Republican National Committee
for a profitable job in the movie industry added to the party's
disarray as the election approached. In the balloting, Republicans lost nearly eighty seats in the House and eight in the Senate. The GOP retained control of both houses, but by very
reduced margins. Conservative Republicans were particularly
vulnerable, and their loss moved the party in Congress more toward the center. If Harding expected to win reelection in 1923,
he would have to improve Republican chances with the American people during the next two years.[16]

Warren G. Harding worked hard at being president, but
after two years in office he regarded the position as a burden
and a punishment more than a place to improve the lot of Americans. The duties of the nation's chief executive had increased
dramatically as the position became more bureaucratic after
World War I and with the increasing focus on the presidency itself. Harding struggled to deal with the flood of letters the president received. No longer able to control his own schedule as he
had in the Senate, he complained to one Republican: "I am not
fit for this office and should never have been here." While most

presidents gripe at some point about the rigors of the job, Harding felt the disconnect between his ambitions and his abilities with more acuteness as his presidency developed.[17]

In early 1923, Harding's friends sought to quell doubts about his intention to run again in 1924. Harry Daugherty told reporters in March that "President Harding will be a candidate for renomination." The president thought the declaration a little premature since he intended to make a speaking tour of the Pacific Northwest, not as an announced candidate but as the president, during the summer of 1923. Meanwhile, his health was deteriorating. A bout with the flu in January 1923 intensified his existing heart problems, and his blood pressure rose above 175 in the spring. Despite these warning signs, Harding remained a heavy smoker and did not obey his doctor's orders to slow down. Overweight and experiencing chest pains, Harding was a classic candidate for a heart attack.[18]

By this time scandals had begun to dog the White House. The president's appointee to the Veterans Bureau, Charles Forbes, had been forced to resign in February 1923 after disclosures of kickbacks and secret deals in contracts for his agency. At the Justice Department, Daugherty had let a crook named Jess Smith gain special access from which pardons, appointments, and contracts were sold. Smith and his cronies traded on their alleged closeness to Harding. Harding confronted Smith about his conduct in late May, and the day after their meeting, Smith blew his brains out in a Washington apartment. Harding did not know about the looming Teapot Dome scandal in any detail, but by the time he left for the West, he sensed that his administration was under a cloud. According to William Allen White, the president told him, "My God, this is a hell of a job! I have no trouble with my enemies. I can take care of my enemies all right. But my damn friends, my God-damn friends, White, they're the ones that keep me walking the floor nights!"[19]

Harding and his party left for the West on June 20, 1923. His speeches seemed to go well, and the president told the press that the American people were "hopeful and confident of the future and manifestly glad to live in this wonderful republic of ours." Harding then left for Alaska, where his speeches pleased his audiences, but his health suffered further reverses. After retreating to the care of his doctors in late July, he succumbed to a fatal heart attack on August 2, 1923. The nation went into mourning.[20]

In the years after Harding's death, macabre stories circulated about the circumstances under which he died, suggesting murder by his wife or presidential intimates. Sensation seekers and confidence men provided lurid accounts of how the conspiracy had supposedly been carried out. Since there was no autopsy of the president, theories about his death stemmed from this grain of fact and became ever more elaborate. The simple reality was that Warren G. Harding was a middle-aged man with a bad heart who indulged in all the wrong habits for a person in his condition. That he suffered a fatal heart attack was hardly a surprise.[21]

But the most sensational scandal associated with Harding's presidency did not become public knowledge until after his death, and it did not involve the president himself. Teapot Dome was a rock formation in Wyoming that when viewed from the proper angle vaguely resembled a teapot. Underneath the surface were reserves of oil that had been administered by the Navy for use in the event of war. In 1922, Secretary of the Interior Albert B. Fall convinced Harding to transfer control of this reserve and another in California to the Interior Department. The oil reserves were subsequently leased to oilmen Harry F. Sinclair and Edward L. Doheny. Subsequent probes revealed that Fall had received more than $400,000 in loans and government bonds from the two oil executives. Congressional inquiries in late 1923 and into 1924 spread the story on the nation's front pages, posing a problem for Harding's successor, Calvin Coolidge. At no time were there credible suggestions that Harding was aware of, approved of, or profited from Fall's transactions.[22]

The revelations of corruption in his administration sent Harding's reputation into a downward slide from which it has never recovered. Historical efforts to rehabilitate his record have demonstrated that Harding worked hard at his job, was personally honest, and sought to implement the conservative policies that his party favored and that the American people wanted after a generation of reform. By no means an above-average president, Harding reflected a return to a kind of pleasing mediocrity in the White House that accorded with the temper of his times.

KEEPING COOL WITH COOLIDGE

> I am going to try to do what seems best for the country, and get what satisfaction I can out of that. Most everything else will take care of itself.
>
> —Calvin Coolidge[23]

Calvin Coolidge received the news of Harding's death while he was working on his farm in Plymouth Notch, Vermont. By candlelight his father administered the oath of office to the new president. Coolidge later told a friend that the presidency held few terrors for him. "I thought I could swing it," he said.

Calvin Coolidge has enjoyed something of a resurgence of popularity in recent years, especially among Republican conservatives, as a kind of tax-cutting precursor of Ronald Reagan and supply-side economics during the 1980s. His belief in limited government and economic self-reliance has added to his reputation in those quarters. In fact, Ronald Reagan replaced Harry S. Truman's portrait in the Cabinet room of the White House with one of Coolidge when he became president in 1981.[24]

Leaving contemporary parallels aside, Coolidge was an interesting figure for the 1920s. He avoided the scandals of his predecessor and was shrewd enough to retire from office before the emergence of the economic problems that would engulf Herbert Hoover. In his handling of the office of the presidency, moreover, Coolidge was more of an innovative executive than historians have realized. He employed image-making techniques effectively before Franklin D. Roosevelt did. He was adept on the radio, relied on his wife's glamour as first lady to increase popular support for his administration, and mastered the political environment of his party. Even in his frequent press conferences, Coolidge belied his reputation as a man of few words. He could be quite voluble with reporters without saying much of substance. He was also adroit at deflecting blame onto other officials for the problems of his administration. In many respects, Coolidge merits a careful reevaluation.[25]

Calvin Coolidge celebrated his fifty-first birthday on July 4, 1923, a month before he became president. Born in Vermont, he was educated at Amherst College and then read for the law in Northampton. Soon he was active in Republican politics, and in 1905 he married Grace Goodhue, a teacher at a local school for the deaf. A friend said of her romance with the taciturn Coolidge that "having taught the deaf to hear, Miss Goodhue might perhaps cause the mute to speak." Coolidge served in a variety of local posts in Northampton and spent two one-year terms in the Massachusetts House of Representatives. By 1911 he was in the state senate, moved on to lieutenant governor in 1915, and three years later was governor of the state. The Boston police strike in 1919 made Coolidge a national figure and put him on track to reach the White House in 1923.[26]

There was always a sense about Coolidge that his achievements had more to do with luck than his own abilities. When he was selected to be Harding's vice president, a Boston newspaperman at the convention offered to "bet all comers that Harding, if elected, would be assassinated before he had served half his term." Warned by his colleagues that "any talk of assassination was unwise and might be misunderstood, for the Armistice was less than two years old and the Mitchell Palmer Red hunt was still in full blast," the reporter refused to stop talking. "I am simply telling you what I know. I know Cal Coolidge inside and out. He is the luckiest ——— in the whole world!"[27]

Coolidge was not an activist president in the mold of Theodore Roosevelt and Woodrow Wilson. He believed in his party's conservatism with more conviction than Harding had displayed, and he resisted efforts to expand the role of the government. "I favor the American system of individual enterprise, and am opposed to any general extension of government ownership and control," he said in accepting the Republican presidential nomination in 1924. He also believed that the high taxes inherited from World War I were a drag on business enterprise, and with the support of Secretary of the Treasury Mellon, he sought to have them lowered or repealed.[28]

Before he could implement any specific programs, however, Coolidge had to ensure his own nomination for president in 1924. Given his relative obscurity within the Republican Party and the prospect of more scandals, his chances did not seem promising during the summer of 1923, but he quickly demonstrated an ability to relegate possible rivals to the sidelines. Coolidge named C. Bascom Slemp, a West Virginia Republican, as his secretary. Slemp knew the southern Republican Party from the inside, and he was indispensable in rounding up delegates for Coolidge. As a result, potential candidates such as Governor Gifford Pinchot of Pennsylvania, Henry Ford of Michigan, and William E. Borah of Idaho found that Coolidge had outmaneuvered them, rendering remote their chances of beating him at the national convention.[29]

The Teapot Dome scandal broke in the months shortly after Coolidge became president, but the apparent opportunity for the Democrats to wound the new administration did not come to pass. While the probes on Capitol Hill revealed Fall's involvement with oilmen Sinclair and Doheny, there was no smoking gun linking Harding to what had happened. Moreover, in his testimony before Congress, Doheny revealed that a number of leading Democrats had accepted payments from him for legal work and other services. The most notable example of these relationships was that of former Secretary of the Treasury and Wilson son-in-law William G. McAdoo. McAdoo was a leading candidate for the Democratic presidential nomination in 1924, but Doheny's revelations left him as damaged political goods.

The public soon tired of the hearings on the scandal, and the case did not prove to be the political bonanza that the Democrats had anticipated.[30]

Meanwhile, the new president eased out of office those Harding holdovers who might be an embarrassment in 1924. It took some delicate maneuvering to convince Attorney General Daugherty to depart, but Coolidge secured his resignation in late March. In his place, Coolidge selected Harlan Fiske Stone, a distinguished lawyer who went on to become chief justice of the United States. Wrongdoing in the Federal Bureau of Investigation, also tainted under Harding, was cleaned up as the new director, J. Edgar Hoover, installed more honest agents and more modern investigative procedures.

By the spring of 1924, Coolidge had outdistanced all of his possible rivals, and the only issue was his running mate. The president hoped to persuade the maverick Republican from Idaho, William E. Borah, to run with him. The story goes that Coolidge said he wanted Borah on the ticket, to which Borah is said to have replied, "Which place, Mr. President?" But Borah would have presented some problems since he was involved in a torrid affair with Alice Roosevelt Longworth, wife of Nicholas Longworth, the House Republican leader. Washington wags joked about "Aurora Borah Alice."[31]

With Borah eliminated, Coolidge decided to pick Charles G. Dawes, an old McKinley associate, a former director of the Bureau of the Budget, and a banker in Chicago. The Republican National Convention was broadcast on the radio, a sign of the increasing role of the mass media in national politics. Once nominated, Coolidge faced two rivals in the presidential campaign. After a protracted and bitter convention in New York City that took 104 ballots to decide, the Democrats named John W. Davis, a corporate lawyer, to head their ticket. Senator Robert M. La Follette ran as the candidate of the Progressive Party, an alliance of reformers and organized labor. From the outset it was clear that Coolidge was in the lead. The Republicans painted La Follette as a dangerous radical, portraying the choice for the voters as either "Coolidge or Chaos." Meanwhile, Davis and the Democrats were obscured, "concealed in the crowd like a bootlegger at a wedding," wrote H. L. Mencken, the acerbic columnist.[32]

The sudden, tragic death of the president's son, Calvin Coolidge, Jr., during the summer spared the incumbent the need to campaign in person. As Coolidge told reporters, "I don't recall any candidate for President that ever injured himself very much by not talking." He did make some effective radio addresses as Election Day neared, but none of this really mattered in the long run. The Republicans had an ample war chest and an abundance of surrogate speakers for Coolidge, and the return of prosperity after 1922 lifted the campaign. The protest vote that La Follette expected did not materialize, and Davis proved to be a boring speaker on the stump. The Republican campaign again used Hollywood stars to its advantage. A delegation came to the White House to pose with the president and first lady. Grace Coolidge led the cinematic assemblage in the campaign theme song: "Keep Cool with Coolidge."[33]

In 1924 the voters decided that retaining the president in office made sense, and he won a landslide victory over Davis and La Follette. The president had 15,700,000 popular votes to almost 8,400,000 for Davis and another 4,800,000 for La Follette. The president won fifty-four percent of the vote and amassed 382 electoral votes. Voter turnout, which had been declining since 1900, rose slightly in 1924 to just over fifty-one percent of the eligible voters casting ballots. The Republicans gained a strong majority in the Senate and had a solid margin in the House as well. With the Democratic Party in disarray and the Republicans united behind the president, there seemed little likelihood of a return to power for the opposition party. That the Democratic share of the vote in northern cities grew during the decade was not yet seen as a real threat to the continuation of Republican rule.[34]

The most famous words that Calvin Coolidge uttered as president came in the waning days of his first term when he was

With Calvin Coolidge directing its movement, the Republican elephant stamps out the snake of radicalism in this Grant Hamilton cartoon from 1924.

speaking to the American Society of Newspaper Editors, on January 17, 1925. He said that "a press which maintains an intimate touch with the business currents of the nation is likely to be more reliable than it would be if it were a stranger to these influences. After all, the chief business of the American people is business." Taken out of context, Coolidge's words have been seen as a justification for whatever business did during the 1920s. While he was no enemy of business, to be sure, Coolidge thought that material success was only justified as a means to a better society.[35]

One key to that endeavor was, in the president's mind, lowering tax rates and government expenditures as well as paying the national debt. (In that sense, Coolidge's tax reduction program was not a 1920s version of the supply-side doctrines of the 1980s under Ronald Reagan.) Accordingly, in 1926 the president proposed to Congress that tax rates be lowered. The resulting legislation reduced the surtax on individuals who made more than $100,000 each year, lowered the tax on estates to twenty percent, and ended the gift tax. The exemption for married couples was set at $3,500, a figure that few Americans earned. Only about 4 million Americans submitted tax returns annually during the 1920s. The measure did raise the corporate tax rate, however. As a sign of the growing importance of the income tax, the rate of federal income taxes averaged more than three percent of the Gross National Product, up from the rate of one percent before World War I.[36]

The continued problems of American agriculture during the 1920s challenged financial policy in another way. Faced with huge surpluses that they could not sell, farmers found themselves confronted with falling prices for their crops. They looked to Washington for assistance on behalf of what was known as the McNary-Haugen plan, named after its Republican sponsors, Charles L. McNary of Oregon and Gilbert N. Haugen of Wisconsin. McNary-Haugen proposed to solve the farm problem through government purchase of the farm surpluses at the market price, after which it would dump the goods on the world market. The resulting monetary loss would be covered by an "equalization fee," or processing fee, that would be charged to the farmers whose crops benefited from the government program. The major criticism of the plan was that it forced the government into the process of fixing prices for an agricultural commodity. Increasing prices would also increase production, of course, and thus only exacerbate the overproduction problem that caused the farm crisis in the first place. The powerful farm bloc passed the McNary-Haugen measure twice, and Coolidge vetoed it twice, in February 1927 and again in May 1928. In his first veto the president called the proposal both unconstitutional and, in its support for a particular economic interest group, against "the spirit of our institutions." The farm problem would not go away and remained a source of vexation for Coolidge's Republican successor, Herbert Hoover, and Franklin D. Roosevelt's New Deal.[37]

The 1920s are often portrayed as a decade of American isolationism as the United States stood aloof from the problems that would culminate in the rise of the dictators and the onset of the Great Depression. But while neither Harding nor Coolidge reversed the Senate's decision to stay out of the League of Nations, neither did they turn their backs on all world issues. Under Harding the Washington Naval Conference pursued disarmament in the Pacific. Coolidge pushed for the nation to join the League of Nation's Permanent Court of International Justice (known as the World Court), but the Senate insisted on so many limiting amendments for United States entry that the campaign for membership collapsed in 1925 and 1926. The Republican administrations sought to expand American business across the globe, relying on business executives to fill ambassadorial positions in key countries. The United States also remained much involved in the turbulent affairs of Mexico, where American oil interests were threatened with expropriation, and in Nicaragua, where civil war flared periodically.[38]

The United States became involved in the intricate structure of international debts and reparations payments that followed the end of World War I. In the Treaty of Versailles, Germany was forced to pay reparations for its role in the war. During the Coolidge years, the administration pushed for a series of agreements to reduce the amount of debt that Germany had to pay the Allies. It has often been written that President Coolidge was reluctant to reduce the debts that Great Britain and France owed the United States from the war. The phrase he was said to have used was "They hired the money, didn't they?" While it was something Coolidge might well have said, the evidence suggests that it was one of those presidential tales that gathered around

Coolidge. The structure of international loans and debts that the Coolidge administration put in place in the 1920s proved to be impossible to sustain when the Great Depression hit, but it represented what was possible and feasible at the time.[39]

In the 1926 congressional elections, six years after the election of Warren G. Harding, the Republicans suffered the losses usually expected following an extended hold on national power. The GOP lost ten seats in the House of Representatives and dropped another seven in the Senate where their control now rested on a shaky three-seat margin over the Democrats. The president had supported a Republican Senate candidate in his home state who was defeated despite the party's argument that "the issue in Massachusetts this year is Calvin Coolidge." The outcome of the congressional contests foreshadowed more legislative trouble for the White House, but no one thought that Coolidge was in any political trouble should he decide to run again in 1928.[40]

After four years in office, Coolidge could likely have had the Republican nomination in 1928 simply by indicating that he wanted it. The country was prosperous and at peace, the Democrats were still divided between their urban and rural wings, and the Republicans had united behind the president. In Coolidge's mind, however, the situation had a different look. The death of his son in 1924 had cast a permanent pall over his presidency. Moreover, his health and the health of the first lady were more fragile than the public realized. Coolidge had chronic, severe allergies, and his heart was also weak. Whether Coolidge sensed the economic storm over the horizon is impossible to tell, although Mrs. Coolidge told a friend, "Poppa says there's a depression coming." The president was convinced that another term would mean spending ten years in Washington, and that seemed to him too long. As he wrote in his autobiography, "An examination of the records of those Presidents who have served eight years will disclose that in almost every instance the latter parts of their term have shown very little in the way of constructive accomplishments. They

have often been clouded with grave disappointments." Sometime in the spring and summer of 1927, Coolidge made his decision not to seek another term.[41]

With typical Coolidge understatement, he picked the fourth
anniversary of his accession to the presidency, August 2, 1927, to
drop his political bombshell—while the Coolidges were vaca-
tioning in the Black Hills of South Dakota. That day there was a
press conference scheduled at a local high school. As the reporters filed in, Coolidge handed them a small piece of paper on
which appeared the sentence, "I do not choose to run for President in nineteen twenty-eight." The decision was Coolidge's
alone. He had not even mentioned it to his wife before he distributed the announcement.[42]

The statement set off a flood of speculation about whether
Coolidge was orchestrating a draft to be nominated or whether
he sincerely meant to leave politics. In the end, that did not matter much. Once Coolidge stepped aside, the competition for the
Republican nomination in 1928 began in earnest. The best evidence suggests that leaving politics was Coolidge's intention all
along: He made no further efforts to have his name pushed forward as a Republican candidate, nor did he align himself with
any of the leading hopefuls for the party's nomination. With his
usual political sagacity, Coolidge had decided to leave while he
was still admired and wanted, and he let his successor grapple
with national issues.

As president, Coolidge embodied competence rather than
distinction. He deserves credit for the prosperity that Americans
enjoyed during the 1920s, but he did little toward the end of his
term to dampen the speculative fever that preceded the Stock
Market Crash of 1929. He left the government's finances in
good shape, the national debt lowered, and the budget in balance. Politically, he mastered the Republican Party as it was but
did little to expand its base among urban ethnics or to reaffirm
the historical allegiance of African Americans to the Grand Old
Party. Neither the boob that later Democrats portrayed him as
nor the precursor of supply-side economics as depicted by some

Republicans in the 1980s, Coolidge carried out his duties proficiently but without distinction.

THE NEW DAY OF HERBERT HOOVER

> I cannot think off-hand of any big-league politicians who were unqualifiedly for Hoover, who really wanted him. Most of them were openly or covertly against him.
>
> —Alice Roosevelt Longworth[43]

The front-runner for the nomination soon became the Secretary of Commerce, Herbert Hoover. Because of the repudiation he suffered four years later during the depths of the Great Depression at the hands of Franklin D. Roosevelt, Hoover's political abilities have often been underestimated. In 1928, however, he was a strong candidate for a Republican Party still riding the crest of national prosperity. The Democrats had not yet overcome their cultural divisions, and when they nominated Governor Alfred E. Smith of New York, a Roman Catholic, they ensured that the 1928 election would bring to light the prejudices and social divisions that animated American politics in that decade. Historians have raised the question of whether any Democrat could have beaten Hoover in 1928, and the consensus is that in a Republican year he was the strongest nominee the party could have chosen.[44]

In 1928, at the age of fifty-four, Herbert Hoover seemed to be one of the dazzling success stories of American politics. Orphaned at a young age and raised by relatives in Iowa and Oregon, he had attended Stanford University, studied geology, and then pursued a career as a mining engineer. For a decade and a half he amassed a personal fortune before retiring to pursue more fulfilling interests. He and his wife, Lou Henry Hoover, had raised two children and in their spare time translated and edited a Latin treatise on mining. After the outbreak of World War I, he helped provide food to millions left destitute by the fighting, first in Belgium and later in Russia. When the United

States entered the conflict in 1917, Hoover came home to direct
the Food Administration for Woodrow Wilson. His efficiency in
providing the resources that the Allied cause needed made him
a world figure. In 1920 he made a brief run at the Republican
presidential nomination and then accepted the post of Secretary
of Commerce in Harding's Cabinet.[45]

Hoover proved to be the most dynamic member of the new
Republican administration. He expanded the role of Commerce
and involved himself in the business of other departments as
well. Through an efficient public relations staff who talked up his
accomplishments, Hoover became the best-known official in the
government below the president. Fighting floods, making policy
on the radio industry, and promoting the interests of corporate
America, Hoover was everywhere in the 1920s. This blend of the
efficiency of an engineer and the humanitarianism of a progressive appealed to Americans as a method of achieving social justice in a less costly manner. Hoover became known as "the
busiest man in Washington," and reporters gushed over his abilities and the potential of a Hoover presidency if Coolidge should
not run in 1928. President Harding had called Hoover "the
smartest 'gink' I know," and most political observers seemed to
agree with that verdict.[46]

When the president stepped aside in August 1927, Hoover
emerged as the front-runner for the Republican nomination almost at once. President Coolidge was not thrilled with this result
because Hoover had so often upstaged him, but he could not do
much to stop his Cabinet officer. The president said to a friend
about Hoover, "That man has offered me unsolicited advice for
six years, all of it bad!" But even without Coolidge's enthusiastic
support, Hoover quickly surged to the front of the Republican
pack. By the time he announced officially in February 1928,
Hoover was well ahead of any challengers and, according to one
reporter, "widening the gap every day and every hour." Hoover
swept most of the primaries and soon had a total of 400 delegates of the 545 needed for the nomination. In May, Hoover
told Coolidge that he would be glad to release his delegates to
the president if he changed his mind about running. Coolidge

answered dryly, "If you have four hundred delegates, you better keep them."[47]

The Republican National Convention in Kansas City selected Hoover on the first ballot and named Senator Charles Curtis of Kansas as the running mate. The platform proclaimed that under Coolidge "the country has been lifted from the depths of a great depression to a level of prosperity." The delegates praised the tax reduction policies of the Coolidge years, reaffirmed their belief "in the protective tariff as a fundamental and essential principle of the economic life of this nation," and indicted any Democratic effort to increase the role of the federal government, which "weakens the sense of initiative and creates a feeling of dependence which is unhealthy and unfortunate for the whole body politic." The Republicans also sought a larger role for women in politics and renewed their call for a federal act to eradicate lynching.[48]

Accepting the Republican nomination on August 11, 1928, at Stanford, California, Hoover spoke the words that four years later would come back to haunt him: "We in America today are nearer to the final triumph over poverty than ever before in the history of any land. The poorhouse is vanishing from among us. We have not yet reached the goal, but given a chance to go forward with the policies of the last eight years, we shall soon with the help of God be in sight of the day when poverty will be banished from this nation." In the heady days of prosperity in 1928, such a lofty goal seemed plausible. The Gross National Product in 1928 stood at $98 billion, with only 4.4 percent of the workforce unemployed, up slightly from the preceding year but far below the levels of the Depression decade to follow. In his campaign speeches, Hoover emphasized the spread of automobiles to American families, the labor-saving benefits of electric power, and the bigger homes in which Americans lived. As he later remarked in New York City during the campaign, "Every man and woman knows that their comfort, their hopes and their confidence for the future are higher this day than they were seven and one-half years ago."[49]

Because his likely opponent in the presidential election

would be Governor Alfred E. Smith of New York, a well-known opponent of Prohibition, Hoover also spoke out on that controversial reform. In his acceptance address he came out against repeal of the Eighteenth Amendment because the nation had "deliberately undertaken a great social and economic experiment, noble in motive, and far-reaching in purpose." In later years the phrases would be compressed, and he would be erroneously credited with calling Prohibition a "noble experiment." For now, his identification with the dry cause sharpened the cultural divisions that separated the two candidates in 1928.[50]

Two weeks after the Republican convention, the Democrats met in Houston to nominate Al Smith. Because Smith was the first Roman Catholic to receive the nomination of a major political party, the 1928 election became a contest where religious feelings ran high. Protestant fears about a Catholic president fueled bigotry directed against Smith that dominated political discourse throughout the fall of 1928. Historians have devoted much attention to the "Brown Derby campaign" (the governor wore a derby hat), both for what it reveals about the emergence of the Democratic electoral coalition of the 1930s and as a precursor to John F. Kennedy's successful run for the White House in 1960.[51]

While Al Smith was a very attractive personality in 1928, he had political liabilities as well that the Republicans intended to exploit. Within the spectrum of the Democrats, Smith, for all the social reform that he endorsed in New York State, was a conservative candidate who proclaimed that "government should interfere as little as possible with business." Rather than focus on issues such as public ownership of electric power companies and Republican tax policy, Smith came across as someone who was very close to Hoover on most issues other than Prohibition. On that divisive issue the Democratic candidate made clear his commitment to changing the alcohol laws. As a result, Smith did little to ease the feelings of Americans outside the Northeast about whether he understood their lifestyle.[52]

More important, Smith's religion aroused suspicions in large parts of the West and South. The Republicans faced a possible backlash if they made Smith's Catholicism an issue themselves, but they did not have to do so publicly in 1928. The press and the Protestant churches did that for them in what became a vituperative attack on the Democratic nominee. The contrast between the eastern cultural provincialism of Smith, who was very much the New Yorker, and the rural cultural provincialism of many Hoover supporters worked to the advantage of the Republican candidate.

Throughout the Republican campaign, Hoover's public stance indicated that he was above the battle and the specifics of attracting votes. He did not make many speaking tours and confined himself to seven public speeches at regular intervals. Hoover did not much like the process of campaigning, so the radio's ability to reach large audiences suited his shyness and dislike of personal contact. In 1928 it did not matter that his delivery was flat and uninspired. Against Smith, it was enough that he sounded like a competent engineer who would manage the country's affairs with efficiency and honesty.[53]

The Republicans exploited radio effectively with surrogates for Hoover, known as the "Hoover minute men," a variation of the "Four Minute Men" of the World War I era who made speeches on behalf of war bonds. A radio division of the campaign supervised the activities of the men and women who spoke out for Hoover. The Republicans used some theatrical celebrities such as Walter Huston in their appeal. Most of the Republican effort was directed at the smaller rural communities of the nation where the Grand Old Party was strong.[54]

As the campaign deteriorated into religious name-calling against Smith, the Hoover headquarters maintained an air of detachment from the controversy. Behind the scenes, however, Hoover quietly encouraged attacks on Smith and the skillful exploitation of anti-Catholic sentiments. One of the main Republican assailants against the Democratic nominee was Mabel Walker Willebrandt, an assistant attorney general in the Department of Justice. Famous for her efforts against Prohibition, she

gained more notoriety when she became the first female to chair
a committee at the 1928 Republican National Convention. During the campaign she went after Smith's record on Prohibition
in a highly publicized tour. Her denunciations of Smith aroused
a storm of protest, such that the Republican campaign sought
to distance itself from her efforts. In her correspondence with
campaign officials, she protested that "I have not made a
single speech that has not been arranged through your office."
In these and other ways the Republicans gave anti-Smith propaganda a discreet push from the sidelines without leaving any
traces. State and local Republican campaigns distributed anti-
Catholic leaflets and literature against Smith.[55]

Both sides in the 1928 campaign sought to exploit the race
issue in the South. Hoover launched a variant of what would be
known in the 1960s as a "southern strategy" when he appealed
to whites in Dixie by eliminating language from the platform fa-
voring enforcement of the Fourteenth and Fifteenth Amendments. The pledge against lynching was widely regarded in the
black community as empty language, and southern whites did
not take it seriously. Republicans also alleged that Smith had
encouraged racial intermarriage in New York City, and they circulated photographs showing mixed couples and literature discussing Smith's racial tolerance. The Democrats charged that
Hoover had abolished segregation in the Department of Commerce, an allegation that the Republican candidate's camp vigorously denied. "I can state to you positively that there has been
no change whatever in the Department of Commerce since the
Wilson administration regarding the treatment of colored people," said Hoover's secretary in late October 1928. While most
black voters stayed with the Republican ticket in the Hoover-
Smith race, the African-American leadership, alienated by the
Republican courtship of southern whites, began to drift toward
the Democrats in a process that accelerated in 1932.[56]

After all the sound and fury of the 1928 election, the voters
finally decided the issue on November 6. Hoover and the Republicans achieved a decisive victory over Smith and his party.

Hoover amassed 21,400,000 popular votes to 15,000,000 for Smith. In the electoral total, Hoover won 444 votes to 87 for Smith. The Democratic candidate carried only Massachusetts and Rhode Island in the North as well as six states in the South. Hoover broke the Democratic hold on Dixie with victories in Texas, Florida, Tennessee, North Carolina, and Virginia. The Republicans piled up big majorities in both houses of Congress. Hoover told the press that "there has been a vindication of great issues and a determination of the true road of progress. The Republican Party has again been assessed with a great responsibility."[57]

Since the Republican triumph proved short-lived and the New Deal coalition emerged within a few years, much attention has been given to the ways, if any, in which Al Smith's showing in 1928 anticipated the success of Franklin D. Roosevelt four years later. In that sense, Hoover's 1928 victory was soon eclipsed and forgotten. But Hoover also anticipated what would happen to the Republicans after the trauma of the Great Depression. In the 1950s, as the Democrats became more identified with the cause of civil rights and the votes of African Americans, the strategy that Hoover had applied to the South would be reborn under Dwight D. Eisenhower and Richard Nixon. The coalition that Hoover built turned out to be fragile in the short run and a portent of the future in the longer term.

Herbert Hoover's presidency ended in such disaster for the Republican Party that it is hard to imagine the contented mood of the country during much of the first year of his administration. With prosperity still secure during 1929, Hoover focused his activism on the nation's problems. He summoned Congress into special session to address the farm problem, looked into reform of the federal prison system, and launched initiatives for international disarmament in foreign policy. One newspaper review of his early performance concluded that "Washington is a center of news these days, not because a corps of hard-working newspaper correspondents is doing its best to pick up tidbits out of a great laissez-faire but because a quick-witted and aggressive

Executive is plainly on the job." *The Literary Digest,* in its issue of September 21, 1929, summarized the overall praise of the press for "six months of Hoover's presidential engineering."[58]

HOOVER AND THE DEPRESSION

> Shall we establish a dole from the Federal Treasury? Shall we undertake Federal ownership and operation of public utilities instead of the rigorous regulation of them to prevent imposition? Shall we regiment our people by an extension of the arm of bureaucracy into a multitude of affairs?
>
> —Herbert Hoover[59]

By the time that issue of *Literary Digest* was published, the first signs of trouble in the New York Stock Exchange had appeared. Stocks had peaked on September 3 and then prices decreased throughout September and into October. Still, brokers and their customers remained optimistic. *The New York Times* index of industrial securities had been at 245 in 1927. In 1928 it had risen to 331. The increase continued until the index stood at 452 in September 1929. A Yale economist, Irving Fisher, played down warnings that the market might be overvalued. Stocks had "reached what looks like a permanently high plateau," he said.[60]

But on October 24, 1929, traders discovered that there were no buyers for the stocks that they wished to sell. Prices sagged as 13 million shares were traded, then a record day. Bankers under the leadership of J. P. Morgan and Company stepped in to settle the market and succeeded in doing so for several days. The panic resumed on October 29 when more than 16,400,000 shares were traded. The *Times* index dropped 43 points on what became known as Black Tuesday. The entertainment newspaper *Variety* ran a famous headline: "Wall Street Lays an Egg."[61]

The stock market crash was a calamitous event, but it did not lead inexorably to the Great Depression of the 1930s. Economists and historians still debate what destroyed the prosperity of the 1920s and brought about a downturn that would not disappear until the United States geared up to fight World War II. Various causes have been singled out. The Federal Reserve, the Smoot-Hawley Tariff of 1930, the intricate relationship between war debts and loans following World War I, the Democratic Congress of 1931–32, and the speculative fevers of the 1920s have all been blamed at one time or another. In terms of the history of the Republican Party, however, the causes of the Depression are less important than the way President Hoover responded to the economic crisis.

Hoover's performance following the crash has also been the subject of much controversy. On one level he did much more to fight the Depression than any previous president had done when faced with a similar economic downturn. Hoover rejected the view of some in his party and his government that the collapse of the economy was a natural event that simply had to be endured before a return to national well-being could take place. The president knew that such a policy, following the precedent of Grover Cleveland during the 1890s, would be political suicide. Naturally an activist himself, Hoover believed that the president could encourage his fellow citizens to work together to lift the country out of the doldrums. His policies sought to instill renewed confidence in the country that the Depression would soon come to an end—but without expanding the role of government to fight the economic crisis more than was necessary.[62]

In the process, Hoover broadened government's ability to help the unemployed through a variety of voluntary programs in which the government sponsored and coordinated what private groups did. As time passed and the limits of voluntary programs became evident, Hoover endorsed such programs as the Reconstruction Finance Corporation (RFC) that Congress created in 1932 to lend money to banks, railroads, and insurance companies in danger of collapse. The RFC showed that the government had to take action during a depression, and it represented a turning away from private answers and inaction from Washington during a downturn.[63]

After the stock market crash, the Depression took a while to hit with full force. The market recovered somewhat during 1930, and it seemed as if the economy might straighten itself out. The president struck an encouraging note in late 1929, saying, "The fundamental business of the country, that is production and distribution, is on a sound and prosperous basis." In 1930, Congress passed the Smoot-Hawley Tariff, thus returning the Republicans to their protectionist roots. Republicans contended that the answer to the business problems of the nation was tariff protection for industry and farmers, and Hoover signed the measure despite some reservations. When they became a free-trade party during the 1980s, Republicans often blamed the Smoot-Hawley Tariff for the Depression rather than Hoover's policies. The adverse effects of the bill have probably been exaggerated in comparison with other causes of the Depression, but this last gasp of Republican orthodoxy on the tariff certainly did not help promote world trade and revive American business.[64]

By mid-1930 the effects of the Depression became more evident. Bank failures grew and corporate profits declined. Unemployment moved upward until by October 1930 nearly nine percent of the labor force was looking for work, a problem that worsened during the year that followed. Unemployment stood at sixteen percent by 1931. Farm prices fell as production of crops continued to increase. The homeless and unemployed took to the railroads and the highways seeking work anywhere they could find it. Gradually, the animus against Hoover rose. The shanty towns outside of the big cities became known as "Hoovervilles," and an empty pocket turned outward as a sign of poverty was dubbed "a Hoover flag." Jokes about the president proliferated. It was said that if you put a rose in his hand, it would wilt. Another described Hoover as asking the Secretary of the Treasury for a nickel so he could call a friend. "Here's a dime," said Mellon. "Call all your friends."[65]

Although he had been a master of public relations during the 1920s when times were good and his reputation was riding high,

Hoover proved to be inept at inspiring national confidence during the Depression. At first, White House reporters anticipated an open administration as they remembered how accessible Hoover had been as Secretary of Commerce. In the presidency, however, Hoover became more terse and dismissive, and the press corps soured on the administration. To stimulate confidence, Hoover called business leaders to the White House, and they duly issued positive statements about the future of the economy. When the Depression did not improve, these occasions had less effect and even undermined what the president sought to do.

The Hoover administration displayed difficulty in understanding what Americans were going through in the hard times. After a drought hit the Middle West in 1930 and 1931, Congress allocated $60 million to help those in need acquire food and fuel. Hoover agreed that farm animals could be fed, but he disapproved of the idea of spending money on farmers and their families. An Arkansas Democrat alleged that the administration believed in feeding "jackasses but . . . not starving babies." Hoover's administration was more sensitive to the crisis, but the president's dogmatic belief in maintaining the limited role of the federal government proved politically disastrous for himself and his party.[66]

The 1930 congressional elections occurred before the full effects of the Depression were felt. Nonetheless, the Republicans suffered a fifty-one-seat loss in the House, retained only a one-seat margin, and gave that up by the time Congress convened in December 1931. The GOP also kept control of the Senate by a single vote. The Democrats did not make the Depression itself a major issue, but they were able to tap into resentments over the Smoot-Hawley Tariff, the problems of agriculture, and Republican factionalism. In Nebraska the Republican National Committee endeavored to oust Senator George W. Norris, an insurgent party member, through sleazy tactics that backfired when they were revealed after the election. The president failed to distance himself from what had been done to Norris, who was returned by the voters.[67]

The Democratic National Committee and its publicity director, Charles Michelson, also mounted a very effective, unrelenting assault on the administration that the administration often let go unanswered. Meanwhile, the governor of New York, Franklin D. Roosevelt, won a landslide reelection victory by 750,000 votes and was immediately discussed as a strong Democratic challenger to Hoover in 1932.[68]

By 1931 the Depression hit the nation with full force, and the president's political situation rapidly deteriorated as a result. When the lame-duck Congress met in December 1930, the calls for more presidential action to provide relief for distressed farmers and the unemployed rose dramatically. Hoover resisted these efforts on the grounds that direct assistance would sap the self-reliance and healthy spirit of the population. In a speech in mid-June 1931, he asked his audience, "Shall we abandon the philosophy and creed of our people for 150 years by turning to a creed foreign to our people? Shall we establish a dole from the Federal Treasury?" For the moment, Hoover's commitment to a less active government than many Democrats and insurgent Republicans desired continued to hold sway, but the tide was turning against the president as the unemployment figures worsened throughout 1931. Other indices told the same story, as the Gross National Product had fallen some thirty percent since 1929.[69]

When the Democrats took control of the House of Representatives in December 1931, the Hoover administration in response proposed the creation of the Reconstruction Finance Corporation (RFC). Later in the session, Hoover approved the Emergency Relief and Construction Act, albeit with severe limitations, to provide some relief funds for states to start projects to put people to work. Further than that the president would not go.[70]

As the government's finances worsened, Hoover believed that balancing the federal budget was imperative. The Democratic Party leadership in Congress concurred, despite the opposition of some Democrats and progressive Republicans who sought more spending on public works. The end result was a tax law that raised rates on income and lifted taxation on luxuries and gifts. Maintaining the confidence of the banking industry and the business community was the rationale for this step. At a time when the balanced budget still represented economic orthodoxy, the idea that the government should deliberately spend money to stimulate economic growth was anathema to conservatives in both parties. The economic effect, of course, was to worsen the impact of the Depression by taking money out of the economy at a time when it was most needed.[71]

As the 1932 election loomed, with the potential for a disastrous Republican defeat, party members looked around for a possible alternative to Hoover, but none had much credibility. With the memories of 1912 still fresh, the idea of a protest candidacy against the president that might split the party seemed unlikely. Few alternatives to Hoover presented themselves anyway. Former president Coolidge, already ailing with the heart condition that would kill him in early 1933, had no interest in taking on Hoover. Charles G. Dawes was an improbable choice, and a boomlet for Pennsylvania governor Gifford Pinchot encountered a frosty response. While most Republicans expected Hoover to lose, they stuck with his candidacy.[72]

Hoover and his vice president, Charles Curtis, were chosen to run again at the Republican convention in June. The platform praised Hoover as a "wise, courageous, patient, understanding, resourceful" leader who had acted to meet the economic distress of the nation. The party pledged to maintain a balanced budget, to keep the currency sound, and to eliminate waste. Meanwhile, the gathering attacked Democrats in Congress for offering "proof of the existing incapacity of that party for leadership in a national crisis."[73]

Another sensational incident tested Hoover's leadership in the weeks after the Republican convention. After World War I, Congress had authorized the payment of a bonus to members of the American Expeditionary Force (the World War I Army in Europe) to be made in 1945. Veterans of the war asked in the Depression why the bonus could not be paid to them when they needed it so badly. Congress was reluctant to appropriate money for the bonus, and legislation failed to pass. To put pressure on lawmakers the veterans marched to Washington where they encamped on Anacostia Flats while Congress deliberated. The presence of the Bonus Marchers in the nation's capital stirred fears of social unrest and perhaps a violent revolution. After Congress adjourned in mid-July, pressure mounted on the District of Columbia police force to disperse the marchers from their encampment.

Late in the month the police were ordered to remove the marchers from government buildings they had occupied. In a melee that ensued, two Bonus Marchers died. Hoover ordered in federal troops commanded by General Douglas MacArthur to restore order. The resulting panic when the Army attacked was recorded on newsreels. The Hoover administration labeled the marchers as Communists, and many newspapers applauded the president's action. But the incident did not assist Hoover's flagging popularity, and for those opposed to him it seemed further confirmation of his insensitivity to the plight of struggling citizens caught in the Depression.[74]

Within another month the campaign for the presidency had begun. As the Democratic candidate, Franklin D. Roosevelt exuded optimism and a sense of confidence about the future. Roosevelt was a distant relation to Theodore, and his wife, Eleanor, was the former president's niece. The New York governor had followed the Democratic tradition of his father and had gained an appreciation for an active federal government during his eight years as Assistant Secretary of the Navy under Wilson. The Republican descendants of Theodore Roosevelt, whose family residence was in Oyster Bay, New York, did not like or trust their Democratic relative who lived in Hyde Park, New York. The tension between the two Roosevelt branches endured for generations.

Franklin D. Roosevelt's specific plans for fighting the Depression were vague, and he criticized Hoover as a big spender and for doing too little to address the economic crisis. This inconsistency irritated Republicans in 1932, and they regarded Roosevelt as an opportunist. For his part, the president made more formal speeches than he had delivered in 1928, most of them written in longhand and spoken in a dry, impassive manner. Some of his campaign stops attracted only apathetic or hostile crowds. Elsewhere the audiences were enthusiastic. But all the informed Republicans expected Hoover to lose. He was glum; Roosevelt was confident. Hoover was still in favor of Prohibition; Roosevelt offered the prospect of repeal. Few listened when Hoover said that the Democrats were out "to change our form of government and our social and our economic system." For Hoover in 1932, the large differences between his views and Roosevelt's on how to fight the Depression and the future direction of the nation proved to be irrelevant.[75]

The election results bore out the gloomy predictions that Republicans had been making throughout 1932. Roosevelt swamped Hoover by more than 7 million votes and rolled up 472 electoral votes to 59 for the president. Hoover carried Pennsylvania, Delaware, Connecticut, Rhode Island, New Hampshire, Vermont, and Maine. Roosevelt won everything else. In Congress the Democrats gained big majorities in both houses. The Republican coalition that had dominated American politics during the 1920s collapsed along with the economy.

Protest against the Depression was the major element in the Republican debacle in 1932, but other reliable sources of GOP support faltered in the Hoover-Roosevelt race. For the campaign, Republican fund-raising, impacted by the economy, was down dramatically from 1928, and only $2.54 million came in compared with nearly $7 million four years earlier. Prominent businessmen split their donations between the two parties instead of tilting Republican. In the western states, Republican factionalism between progressives and conservatives gave the Democrats an edge in a region that had usually been solid for the Republicans. While black voters remained loyal to the Republicans by and large, there were signs in such cities as New York that unhappiness with the party was mounting among

African Americans. The early years of the New Deal would ac-
celerate that trend.

Amid the ruins of the Hoover campaign and the Republicans' stinging defeat in 1932, they could find little consolation.
They had been blamed for the Depression and all of its atten-
dant ills. The Democratic campaign had capitalized on popular
unhappiness and Roosevelt's skills as a candidate to crystallize
the mood of protest. In all probability, given the severity of the
Depression, Hoover never had a chance to gain reelection, and
the Republicans were bound to suffer for his political sins.

Despite all of these obstacles, the Republican Party retained
the allegiance of more than 15 million American voters who represented forty percent of the electorate in 1932. If a candidate
with such grave liabilities as Hoover could rely on a base of support, then a more effective challenger to a Democrat might revive the party's fortunes four years later. For all the loose talk
about the decline in Republican effectiveness, the party was still
a potential force on the national political scene. Much would de-
pend on how Franklin D. Roosevelt implemented his promise of
a "New Deal" for the American people.

In American political history, the election of 1932 would become a major turning point between the welfare state that
emerged from the New Deal era and the business-dominated
politics that had preceded it. For twenty-four out of the first
thirty-two years of the century, the Republicans had controlled
the nation's political destiny. In that time they had accomplished
some notable legislative and policy achievements. These included the Hepburn Act and the Pure Food and Drugs Act
under Theodore Roosevelt, the Budget Act under Harding, and
tax reduction under Coolidge.

But by 1932 the United States was also a nation that did not
provide old-age pensions for its retired workers, did not fully
recognize organized labor, did not regulate its banking and securities systems in a meaningful way, did not limit the impact of
child labor on its youngest citizens, and did not have the national means of lessening the effects of mass unemployment.

There were ideological and political reasons that the Republican Party had not moved to enact any of these measures during its years of power; each reform would have threatened a major constituency of the Republican coalition.

Yet these conditions meant that the United States confronted the worst economic depression in its history with an unmet agenda of pressing social reforms to make the society more equitable and just for all its citizens. The Republican Party had possessed the capacity to address these problems during its long tenure of power but had chosen not to do so. In the 1930s it felt the effects of its historic failure at the ballot box.

Chapter 8

THE REPUBLICANS IN THE AGE
OF THE NEW DEAL, 1933–1945

IT WAS HOT in Philadelphia in June 1940. Delegates to the Republican National Convention crowded into Convention Hall, a structure built with just such gatherings in mind. The seating capacity was fifteen thousand people. Everyone who was there remembered the galleries packed with supporters of Wendell Willkie, chanting "We want Willkie." The Republicans were on the verge of nominating a convert from the Democratic Party to run against Franklin D. Roosevelt. Representative Charles S. Halleck, a Willkie supporter from his home state of Indiana, asked the crowd as he placed his man's name in nomination: "Is the Republican party a closed corporation? Do you have to be born in it?" The galleries rocked with the response: "No, no."[1]

Some Republicans were less thrilled with Willkie. When he told former Senator James E. Watson of Indiana that he had once been a Democrat, Watson replied, "Well, Wendell, you know that back home in Indiana it's all right if the town whore joins the church, but they don't let her lead the choir the first night." But the specter of World War II hung over the nation. Democracy seemed to be under assault, and Republicans concerned about the place of the United States in the world wanted a candidate who would defend the country against the danger of Nazi Germany and Imperial Japan. They also looked for someone who could beat Franklin D. Roosevelt. If a former Democrat could do that, these Republicans were prepared to nominate him. The shouts from the gallery rocked on: "We want Willkie!" After six tumultuous ballots, the Willkie supporters got their wish. Their new candidate told them he would wage "an aggressive, fighting campaign." As he left the podium, the organist played "God Bless America," and the delegates sang in unison as the convention ended. It was a moving moment in an era of defeat and discord for the Republicans as they watched Franklin D. Roosevelt dominate American politics during the New Deal.[2]

The nomination of Willkie began a twenty-year struggle between the eastern wing of the party, more conservative than the Democrats but willing to accept some aspects of the New Deal, and the Republicans of the nation's heartland, who believed the party must oppose Roosevelt and all his programs. The battle was always between differing visions of a conservative ideology, but the Republicans who wanted to endorse the more popular aspects of the New Deal and expand the nation's world role became known as "liberals" within the party. While their strength in Congress was always marginal, their ability to install their candidates as the GOP's presidential nominees between 1940 and 1960 produced continuing irritation from their more conservative brethren. In the end, however, the conservative version of Republicanism prevailed.

THE REPUBLICANS FACE THE NEW DEAL

> There are as yet no signs that the Republican party has found an issue on which it can unite. In fact there are many signs which indicate that the schism which rent it in 1912, was healed in 1920, and broke out again in 1932, is deeper than ever.
>
> —Walter Lippmann[3]

> DONT LET IT GET YOUR GOAT!

By early 1934, as the New Deal took hold, Republican progressives flirted with Roosevelt and the Democrats. In this Clifford K. Berryman cartoon, the shade of Abraham Lincoln urges his party to recapture the straying GOP members from the West.

The 1932 presidential election represented a massive political repudiation for the Republican Party. Things then got even worse. Herbert Hoover and Franklin D. Roosevelt wrangled during the four-month transition over what, if anything, could be done for an economy with failing banks and mounting unemployment. Hoover's efforts to tie his successor to his own policy answers collapsed by March 4, 1933. A friend of Hoover's said that it would be "hard on H. to go out of office to the sound of crashing banks." By the time Roosevelt was inaugurated, the banking system stood on the edge of disaster.[4]

In his inaugural address and decisive actions during the Hundred Days that followed, Roosevelt administered a dose of political energy to the government that represented a striking contrast to Hoover's dour approach to his job in 1931–32. The New Deal, as Roosevelt called his program, began with a flourish of activity that galvanized Congress and the American people. So responsive was Capitol Hill to what Roosevelt requested that some of the early New Deal measures were enacted unanimously.

The New Deal has taxed the ability of historians to explain its impact because it did so much in so many areas. For Republicans the key points of disagreement were Roosevelt's willingness to use the power of government to establish permanent programs such as Social Security, his sympathy for organized labor, and his reliance (albeit reluctantly in some cases) on deficit spending to pay for his initiatives. New groups—blacks, union members, ethnics—flocked to the Democratic banner, and the Republican dominance of the voters faded away. Roosevelt and his party seemed to be everywhere. There were projects to put people to work, to encourage theater and the arts, to develop the resources of the Tennessee Valley. A man of wealth, Franklin D. Roosevelt was betraying his own background, igniting class warfare, and making the Republicans swallow everything. Opposition turned to bitterness and in some instances even hatred for "that man in the White House."

As many historians have noted, much of what Roosevelt did worked at cross purposes to the goal of economic recovery. His initial measures to cut government spending, to restore the banks, and to legalize 3.2 beer did not embody long-term solutions to the crisis of an economy working at less than full capacity. But even these limited steps were more than the Republicans offered during the spring of 1933 and in the months that followed.[5]

While the small cadre of Republicans in Congress could do little to counter the wishes of the Democratic majority in 1933–34, some opposition members managed to influence aspects of key legislation. Senator Arthur Vandenberg of Michigan pushed for federal insurance of bank deposits as a means of shoring up banks that were not part of large urban banking companies. Vandenberg's campaign led to the incorporation of the idea in the Glass-Stegall Act of 1933, and the provision became one of the most important results of the early New Deal because it introduced stability into the financial system.[6]

Throughout Roosevelt's first two years in office the Republicans groped for a way to deal with the popular Democratic president. Heavily in debt after the 1932 campaign, the Republican National Committee unproductively assailed Roosevelt's policies at a time when the man in the White House was riding high. As a result, moderate Republicans sought ways to couch their appeal in more attractive terms by creating new committees among House and Senate Republicans to help candidates in the 1934 congressional elections. These panels would try to adopt a more constructive tone than the national committee followed.[7]

The Republicans now faced a dilemma that dominated their internal debates for the next dozen years and beyond. Conservatives argued that the best and most intellectually honest course was to oppose the New Deal and all its works from the start. As an Ohio senator told Herbert Hoover, "I would rather be defeated in antagonizing this program of economic absurdities than to have been elected either by advocating them or sneaking in as noncommital." On the other hand, Republicans in the Northeast, where Roosevelt's policies had much resonance with the voters, contended that simply naysaying would be political suicide. A New Yorker observed, "It is no longer good political strategy to abuse and denounce everyone and everything without regard to the facts or the temper of the times."[8]

SETBACK IN 1934

The measures undertaken by the Democratic Administration are alarming. Whatever may be said for them as emergency measures, their permanent incorporation into our system would practically abandon the whole theory of American government, and inaugurate what is in fact socialism.

—Robert A. Taft[9]

In 1934 neither ideological purity nor political expedience did much to help Republican congressional candidates before the New Deal tide. The usual pattern of the opposition party gaining seats two years after a presidential election did not hold up. Going into the voting, the Grand Old Party held 117 seats in the House. They saw their numbers drop by 13 in that chamber. Another 10 senators went down to defeat as well, leaving the party with only 25 senators to oppose Roosevelt. The bulk of the losses Republicans suffered were in the Northeast and Middle Atlantic states. In the Middle West, more moderate Republicans were defeated so that the conservative bloc of Republicans in the House was actually strengthened in terms of its influence within the party. Disgruntled conservatives blamed their losses on timely relief payments that the Roosevelt administration had made in key states. Moderates in the party contended that the results showed the party had to move to the center. Exultant Democrats shared the sentiment of their national chairman, James A. Farley: "Famous Republican figures have been toppled into oblivion. In fact we must wonder who they have left that the country ever heard of."[10]

Following the 1934 elections, the New Deal moved further leftward during the spring of 1935 as Congress passed Social Security, the Wagner Act to provide bargaining rights for organized labor, the Public Utility Holding Companies Act, the Banking Act of 1935, and some $4.8 billion for relief. The Roosevelt administration also introduced major legislation to raise income tax rates on the wealthiest Americans. These measures intensified the existing Republican opposition to Roosevelt and his programs. The business community, some of whose members had been sympathetic to early New Deal measures such as the National Recovery Act in 1933, moved back toward the GOP and lent their financial support to the beleaguered Republican treasury.[11]

In Congress, Republican lawmakers fought a rearguard action against what historians have called "the Second Hundred Days" during the spring and summer of 1935. Their dissents anticipated the critiques that the party would make of Roosevelt and the New Deal for several decades. On Social Security, Republicans saw "no compelling reason" for dealing with this reform prior to recovery. Taking money out of the economy to pay for old-age pensions was not a step that would put people back to work. The White House claimed, on the other hand, that some kind of provision for people's welfare in their old age was necessary. Republicans disagreed profoundly with this movement away from individual self-reliance. Congressman James Wadsworth of New York contended that "once we pay pensions and supervise annuities, we cannot withdraw from the undertaking no matter how demoralizing and subversive it may become." Charles Eaton of New Jersey charged that "the ultimate aim of the New Deal is to place all American industry, business, and individual liberties under the control of Government here in Washington." After failing in an effort to have Social Security sent back to committee, most Republicans then went on record as endorsing the popular bill on final passage.[12]

As for the Wagner Act, Republicans stood against the "closed shop" that mandated union membership when organized labor won an election in a factory or business. They also condemned Roosevelt's 1935 tax measure that increased levies on inheritance, gifts, and high individual incomes. Senator Vandenberg called it "a tin foil measure which snipes inconclusively at wealth, but will neither produce revenue commensurate with our spending nor achieve any useful social purpose." The Republican reaction to the Second Hundred Days was not monolithic. Western Republican progressives, such as George W. Norris of Nebraska, gave a greater degree of support to the Democratic administration than did their eastern conservative counterparts. Yet, overall, congressional Republicans were becoming more conservative and more cohesive as the New Deal progressed.[13]

By 1935, discontent with Roosevelt among some conservative Democrats sparked the emergence of the American Liberty League, designed to counteract Roosevelt's dominance within his own party. Such dissent from the president's policies encouraged Republicans to believe that the political tide might be turning. One newspaperman on the right observed in August 1934 "that the chance of a Republican comeback has been strengthened." A year later, after the Second Hundred Days, increased contributions from business helped the Republican Party pay off its debt from 1932. The Republicans devoted themselves to restoring party unity and, more important, finding a presidential candidate who could win in 1936. If the conservative elements in both parties worked together, defeat of Roosevelt and the Democrats actually seemed possible.[14]

The key to success against Roosevelt, so Republican strategists believed, was to bring the normally Republican states of the Northeast and Middle Atlantic regions back into harmony with the Plains and middle western states. In short, the Republicans needed to re-create the coalitions that had elected William McKinley, Theodore Roosevelt, and Warren G. Harding. In light of that theory, it made sense to look for a presidential candidate from west of the Mississippi River who could appeal to both sections. But after the 1934 disaster, there were not many attractive candidates who fit that set of requirements.

As Maine Goes . . .

> I still believe in fairies, and I still hope that the Republican party will have enough sense to know that it can't go back to McKinley. If it tries to go back to McKinley, it will keep on going past Lincoln and Fremont to Franklin Pierce to the end.
>
> —William Allen White[15]

Only one incumbent Republican governor had been reelected in 1934, Alfred M. Landon of Kansas. The other GOP presidential possibilities did not arouse much enthusiasm. Herbert Hoover hoped for another nomination even though most realistic Republicans knew his selection would spell disaster. Under pressure from party regulars, he withdrew from contention in

September 1935. Senator William E. Borah of Idaho, a progressive on domestic issues and an isolationist in foreign policy, was seventy years old and had little strength outside the Rocky Mountain region. Other contenders such as Frank Knox of Illinois and Arthur Vandenberg were not credible alternatives.

Landon seemed in 1935 to have real potential as a rival to Roosevelt. He had supported Theodore Roosevelt in 1912, but since then had backed Republican candidates. Some styled Landon a "Kansas Coolidge." His ally, William Allen White, called him "a bigger man than Coolidge was the day he went to the White House" and a candidate who "outsizes most of the Republican aspirants." Landon was forty-nine in 1936, a successful oil operator in Oklahoma, and a liberal on social matters. But otherwise his economic opinions tracked Republican orthodoxy. He supported a balanced budget, opposed attempts to inflate the currency, and believed Roosevelt and the New Deal had shifted too much power from the states to Washington.[16]

In the absence of a serious challenge, Landon glided toward the Republican nomination during the first five months of 1936. He united his western support with the big states of the East and locked up the nomination on the first ballot. At first the convention leaders wanted to name Senator Styles Bridges of New Hampshire as the running mate until someone pointed out the dangers of "Landon Bridges falling down." Frank Knox became the vice presidential nominee. In the platform the party charged "America is in peril" from a New Deal that had "dishonored American traditions and flagrantly betrayed the pledges upon which the Democratic Party sought and received public support."[17]

The platform then endorsed in principle a number of New Deal programs, including Social Security, the right of labor to organize, and the desirability of regulating business. The delegates promised to balance the budget by cutting expenditures rather than raising taxes. In foreign affairs they pledged not to join the League of Nations or the World Court and to seek resolutions of disputes among nations through international arbitration. The foreign policy section was very brief for the last time in the twentieth century. The Democrats were not overtly criticized, though the Republicans balanced uneasily between their conservative impulses and the need to craft language that supported popular New Deal programs in principle.[18]

The course of the Landon campaign refuted all the optimistic forecasts of his electoral appeal and the possibility of real voter discontent with Roosevelt's leadership. Landon proved to be a lackluster candidate who was no match for Roosevelt at the peak of his reform and popularity. As his chances receded, Landon attacked Roosevelt more and more from the right, and thus ceded to the president the middle ground, which is where the voters were in 1936. The Republicans made the sunflower their symbol and "Oh Susanna" their campaign song. Nostalgia did not work in 1936, nor did predictions of imminent national doom from the right. The *Chicago Tribune,* under the leadership of Colonel Robert R. McCormick, had its switchboard operators tell callers as the election neared the number of days that remained for the Republic to be saved from Roosevelt and tyranny.[19]

The Republicans did carry Maine, which in those days voted in September. If the familiar slogan "As Maine Goes, So Goes the Nation" were true, then Roosevelt might have been in trouble. The *Literary Digest* magazine offered polls that showed Landon competing well with the president. Unfortunately, the *Digest* surveyed only those voters with telephones, missing the massive surge for Roosevelt among those who were less well off. When Landon carried only Maine and Vermont in November, the chairman of the Democratic National Committee retorted, "As Maine goes, so goes Vermont."[20]

The Landon-Roosevelt race furthered a sharp ideological division between the two parties. Landon said that only his election would preserve "the Constitution and the American form of government." The New Deal, he charged, believed "in an all-powerful chief executive" as well as "the destruction of states' rights and home rule." In short, the Roosevelt administration had "betrayed" American principles. Roosevelt reciprocated with tough rhetoric of his own. In his final speech at Madison Square Garden in late October, he linked the Republicans with "organized money," which was "unanimous in their hatred for me— and I welcome their hatred." He promised that in his second term "the forces of selfishness and lust for power" would meet "their master." This strident language intensified the already powerful Republican dislike for the president.[21]

The 1936 campaign also saw the business community rally behind the Republican ticket and supply the bulk of the party's funds for the national campaign. Some segments of corporate America, such as the du Ponts, who had large chemical holdings, had contributed to the Democrats in 1932, and they moved back into the ranks of the GOP. Most major business leaders, however, had endorsed Hoover with their checks in 1932 and did the same for Landon four years later. The Republicans spent $14 million in 1936; the Democrats and their allied groups expended more than $9 million, though the Republicans charged that the president and his supporters used ample government funds, especially relief payments, to bolster the incumbent's chances for victory. In the end, the defeat of Landon left the Republicans with a $900,000 deficit.[22]

Roosevelt did achieve a landslide of seismic proportions in the 1936 race. He won nearly 28 million popular votes to almost 17 million votes for Landon. The Republican candidate actually increased the party's total over Hoover in 1932, but Roosevelt gained almost 5 million votes over his previous showing as well. The electoral vote tally was 523 for Roosevelt with only 8 for Landon. The Democrats controlled the Senate eighty to sixteen. There were only eighty-nine Republicans left in the House of Representatives. The Republicans seemed to have reached such a low ebb that there was talk of their imminent demise as a party.

President Roosevelt soon took care of reviving Republican fortunes, but on the national level he had assembled an electoral coalition that would win five of the next seven presidential elections. The New Deal coalition became a dominant fact of American political life for a generation, and its ultimate breakdown in the 1960s was what enabled the Republicans to dominate during the last third of the twentieth century. The component parts of Roosevelt's electoral team comprised contradictory and unstable elements, but when they worked together effectively, as they did in 1936, the Republicans were at a disadvantage.

The oldest building block was the still solidly Democratic white South. The Depression restored Dixie to its traditional Democratic allegiance as New Deal programs poured in money and jobs to the region. The newest component was the vote of African Americans in the North; they had moved there during the "Great Migration" of blacks from the South during and after World War I. Beginning slowly in 1932 and with increasing speed in the four years that followed, blacks had left the Grand Old Party and identified themselves as Roosevelt Democrats. The Roosevelt administration was cautious in assisting African Americans because of the power of southern Democrats in Congress, but even the modest steps that the White House took to distribute relief payments and provide government jobs for blacks brought its reward at the polls. Eleanor Roosevelt's evident sympathy for the aspirations of African Americans helped as well.

Urban voters formed another key part of the New Deal alliance, and organized labor provided a final key component. The various measures that assisted the American Federation of Labor and the Congress of Industrial Organizations moved union members into the Democratic alliance. As Alf Landon put it, "The labor leaders are all tied up with this administration." As long as these disparate forces remained in the Democratic column, the Republicans faced an uphill battle in a presidential contest.[23]

In light of the endurance of the New Deal coalition, conservatives have described the period from 1933 to 1968 as one of liberal ascendancy. Whether it was "twenty years of socialism" from 1932 to 1952 or "the old liberal order" that began under Roosevelt and lasted until Lyndon Johnson, the consensus on the right was that liberal Democrats controlled the levers of power and policy at this time. In fact, the actual story was more complicated and the political control of the Democrats more tenuous than many Republicans realized then or later. The "dominance" of liberalism in American politics for the two decades after 1932 is largely a myth.[24]

After all, the Roosevelt landslide in 1936 demonstrated that even with a very weak candidate and facing a popular president, some forty percent of the voters remained loyal to the Republicans. Once the natural balance of American politics reasserted itself and the economic crisis ebbed, the Republicans would move back to a competitive status with their rivals. That historical trend was confirmed during the two years that followed the 1936 result. Because of fissures within the Republican Party and the skill of Roosevelt as a president and campaigner, the return of the Republicans to power on the presidential level took longer.

The other significant aspect of the 1936 presidential contest was the way it underscored the lineup of ideologies in the process of development since the 1916 Wilson-Hughes campaign. Following the era of Theodore Roosevelt, a progressive, reformist group resided within the Republican Party, albeit with diminishing influence during the 1920s. By the mid-1930s, conservatism prevailed as the dominant policy position of the party on domestic issues. "Liberal" Republicans were willing to accept some aspects of the New Deal for electoral reasons. Moderates were less enthusiastic about this strategy but would go along when a winning campaign seemed a likely prospect. Conservatives who made up the majority of the party believed that the New Deal represented a revolutionary shift in American values that should be rolled back when the party regained political power. The faith in national power that had been at the heart of Republican thinking during the mid–nineteenth century was now replaced by an increasing commitment to states' rights, smaller government, and a limited executive, all of which became hallmarks of twentieth-century Republicanism.

THE REPUBLICANS REBOUND

> If we extend Federal power indefinitely, if we concen-
> trate power over the courts and congress in the execu-
> tive, it will not be long before we have an American
> fascism.
>
> —Robert A. Taft[25]

From the heights of his electoral triumph in 1936, Franklin D. Roosevelt committed a monumental blunder that enabled the Republicans to move out of the political wilderness for the first time in the 1930s. In February 1937, Roosevelt launched his plan to transform the Supreme Court by adding new justices, up to as many as six, to the existing nine members. The "court packing plan," designed to make the high court more liberal and responsive to popular opinion, backfired. Even some liberals who disliked the Court's anti–New Deal decisions did not approve of Roosevelt's initiative. At a time when the Court was still held in awe, Roosevelt created a controversy that united some liberal and many conservative Democrats in opposition to the scheme. A firestorm of protest erupted.

The small minority of Republicans in Congress naturally opposed what Roosevelt wanted to do, but they recognized that their public displeasure might drive Democrats back into Roosevelt's camp. With Democrats in the Senate attacking the Court plan, the Republicans kept relatively silent and let the Democrats fight among themselves. The result was a stinging defeat for Roosevelt: He achieved from Congress only a much watered-down version of his original proposal that left the Supreme Court intact. This controversy prompted conservative Democrats in Congress to explore ways in which they might cooperate with their Republican colleagues to stymie additional New Deal measures.[26]

Other forces aided the revival of Republican fortunes in 1937–38. Labor militance, expressed in sit-down strikes in the automobile and steel industries, brought outbreaks of violence

that frightened middle-class citizens who were otherwise sympathetic to the administration. The Congress of Industrial Organizations (CIO), which tried to organize unskilled industrial
workers into unions, became the symbol of labor's new aggressive posture. An advertisement in a Boston newspaper sought to
capitalize on the apprehensions that the sit-down strikes evoked:
"Come on down to Cape Cod for a real vacation where the CIO
is unknown and over 90 percent are Republicans who respect
the Supreme Court."[27]

The final lift for the Republicans in 1938 came from the
deep recession that started in the spring of 1937 and belied the
promises of the president that the Depression was on the run.
Industrial production sagged some thirty percent during the
sixteen months after April 1937. Unemployment surged from
about 5 million in August 1937 to 9.6 million the following
spring. Roosevelt's efforts to balance the budget, the reduced
purchasing power brought on by Social Security taxes, and the
loss of business confidence all contributed to the abrupt downturn. Blame fell on the president and his policies. Republicans
talked of the "Roosevelt recession," even the "Roosevelt Depression."[28]

The Republicans saw their fortunes revive even further during 1937 when Thomas E. Dewey won election as district attorney
in New York City and sometime Republican Fiorello La Guardia
also gained reelection as mayor. As 1938 opened, polls showed
Republican gains in the Middle West. Meanwhile, the Democrats
divided into warring factions when the president sought to
"purge" conservatives within his own party. After six years Roosevelt's popularity sagged at what everyone assumed would be
the end of his presidency.

For the first time in a decade the Republicans were on the offensive, and their newspapers proclaimed "American Voters Return to Sanity." When the results of the 1938 elections were
tabulated, the GOP had reestablished itself as a real alternative
to the Democrats. The party picked up seven senators, elected
twelve governors, and added seventy-five seats in the House.

Some new Republican faces emerged on the national scene. Robert A. Taft, son of the former president, won a Senate seat in Ohio. Harold Stassen was elected governor of Minnesota, and even Thomas E. Dewey's close but losing race for governor of New York made him an up-and-coming figure in the party.[29]

The surge of Republican strength in Congress, combined with southern Democratic unhappiness with Roosevelt over both his economic policies and the race issue, facilitated the rise of the conservative coalition that dominated the legislative stage for the next twenty-five years. As a result, the New Deal had to face lawmakers in 1939–40 who were intent on cutting back social programs such as the Federal Theater Project. An ambitious White House effort to reorganize the executive branch had produced a bitter struggle on Capitol Hill during 1938, and the president had to compromise to get some of what he sought in 1939.[30]

The political events of 1938 took place while the international scene darkened for both the European democracies and the United States. The Munich Conference dismembered Czechoslovakia at the behest of Adolf Hitler while the tide of anti-Semitism rose in Germany. Japan seemed an aggressive challenger to the American position in the Pacific, and tensions between the two nations mounted. Foreign policy surged to the forefront of the national debate, revealing the serious internal divisions over foreign affairs that plagued the Republicans.

In the nation's heartland, far from Europe and its troubles, sentiment to stay out of the quarrels of the Old World commanded wide support among Republicans. Disillusion with the outcome of World War I, antipathy toward Great Britain, some degree of anti-Semitism, and sympathy for Germany moved together in various degrees to feed the argument on behalf of continued isolation. Senators such as William E. Borah of Idaho and Gerald P. Nye of North Dakota led the bloc of Republicans in the upper house who wanted to stay out of European disputes. The *Chicago Tribune* under Colonel Robert McCormick provided a powerful editorial voice for this brand of Republican thought.

The American hero, Charles A. Lindbergh, contended that Germany "alone can either dam the Asiatic hordes or form the spearhead of their penetration into Europe."[31]

In the East, other Republicans looked with apprehension at the string of German triumphs in 1938 and worried about the foreign policy dangers to the country if Hitler prevailed. These interventionists wanted the United States to aid Great Britain and France after World War II began with the German invasion of Poland on September 1, 1939. Such newspapers as the *New York Herald Tribune* carried the cause in their editorials. Less conservative on domestic issues than their middle western counterparts, these Republicans believed in a strong national defense and aggressive opposition to German designs. With money from the business and banking communities and good connections to the mass media through such magazines as Henry Luce's *Time,* the interventionist side had greater capacity to influence Republican conventions on behalf of the candidate they favored.[32]

"WE WANT WILLKIE"

> Every time Mr. Roosevelt damns Hitler and says we ought to help the democracies in every way we can short of war, we ought to say: "Mr. Roosevelt, we double-damn Hitler and we are all for helping the Allies, but what about the $60 billion you've spent and the 10 million persons that are still unemployed?"
>
> —Wendell Willkie[33]

As 1940 loomed, the choice of the Republican presidential candidate was not at all clear. The party's victory in 1938 had made the Republican nomination worth having, especially if Roosevelt decided to step down at the end of his second term. None of the Democrats mentioned as the president's possible successor seemed of heavyweight caliber. In that setting the Republican nomination seemed a very attractive prize, and a number of hopefuls entered the race.

Senator Robert A. Taft had already followed the course that would earn him the title "Mr. Republican." Party conservatives admired Taft's intellectual rigor and commitment to pre-1932 party doctrine of small government that favored business enterprise. Later, Taft would endorse a government intervention in the form of public housing that would raise eyebrows on the right, but before the war he was a staunch exponent of anti–New Deal thinking and strong isolationist sentiments. But he was also dull. Alice Roosevelt Longworth said that having Taft follow Roosevelt "would be like drinking a glass of milk after taking a slug of benzedrine." From the beginning of the race, Taft's appeal to the voters was hampered by his cold and stern personality. Balding, with steel-rimmed glasses and a dry speaking style, Taft was austere and aloof. The best one of his advocates could do to humanize him was to tell the 1940 convention that Taft was "as common as an old shoe."[34]

The ostensible front-runner in early 1940 was Thomas E. Dewey, the district attorney of New York City. Just thirty-seven years old in 1939, the diminutive, mustachioed Dewey had built a reputation as a racket-busting prosecutor who had taken out "Murder Incorporated," as the New York tabloids dubbed organized crime. He had lost the governor's race to Herbert H. Lehman in 1938 but had come so close to the popular incumbent that it was in essence a moral triumph. Dewey had a very pleasant speaking voice on the radio, and he told his audiences, "There is no limit to America. There is a force in America that has been held in check which, once released, can give us the employment we need." For all Dewey's charm in general, he impressed some who met him in person as cold and arrogant. An aide later called him "cold—cold as a February icicle." The Democrats mocked his youth. Secretary of the Interior Harold Ickes quipped that when Dewey announced for president, he threw his diaper into the ring. Despite these difficulties, Dewey forged a lead over Taft and Senator Arthur Vandenberg when he won primaries in Wisconsin and Nebraska in April and May.[35]

Then the international scene further deteriorated. On May 10, 1940, the Germans invaded Holland and Belgium, and soon

were deep into France with their Panzer divisions. As the cause
of democracy in Europe wavered and Germany seemed ascen-
dant, previous calculations of Republican politicians went out
the window. Neither Dewey nor Taft seemed up to the job of
managing the country's defense in a time of crisis. Talk began in
Democratic circles that the president might seek an unprecedented third term in the White House. As the Republicans assembled for their national convention in steamy Philadelphia in
June 1940, they faced a situation as confused and uncertain as
any in the party's history. Many Republicans argued that the
best course was the selection of a man who only a few short years
earlier had been a utility company executive and a Democrat,
Wendell Willkie of Indiana.[36]

Few events in the history of the Republican Party were more
improbable than Wendell Willkie's capture of the presidential
nomination in 1940. In May 1940, Willkie was the choice of only
three percent of Americans in a presidential poll, but that result
was hardly surprising. The forty-eight-year-old Willkie was not
known to most Americans that troubled spring. He grew up in
Elwood, Indiana, graduated from Indiana University with a law
degree, and went to work for the Commonwealth and Southern
Corporation, a public utility. In 1935 he became the company's
president. From that position he came into conflict with the
Roosevelt administration over its Tennessee Valley Authority
project to provide inexpensive electric power to that region.
Willkie was an effective and articulate defender of the interests
of private power companies, and his views soon attracted the attention of other corporate executives and opinion makers in the
East. As a conservative Democrat, Willkie had few realistic options other than to move toward the Grand Old Party.[37]

The burly Willkie was only an average orator with a prepared text, but when he spoke ad lib he had the ability to excite
a crowd. He was especially appealing to women, who found that
he had "the well-organized bulkiness of a healthy bear, and sin-
gularly brilliant eyes." His marriage was long since over in fact,
but his wife kept up the pretense that they were a happy couple.

To the public, Willkie seemed a breath of political fresh air: a critic of the New Deal and its excesses who also maintained some balance about what was valuable within the Roosevelt record. As war engulfed Europe, Willkie's belief in aiding the Allies struck internationalist Republicans as what the leaders of their party should be saying. To the conservatives of an isolationist bent, the candidacy of this lapsed Democrat was dismaying and dangerous.[38]

Willkie registered as a Republican before local elections in New York in November 1939. Then in the April 1940 issue of *Fortune* magazine, Willkie proclaimed, "It makes a great deal of difference to us—politically, economically and emotionally— what kind of world exists beyond our shores." With words like that, Willkie set himself apart from the isolationist attitudes of Taft and Vandenberg as well as the equivocations that Dewey had expressed in the many speeches he made that same spring.[39]

While the Republican National Convention was in progress, President Roosevelt surprised the delegates and the nation by naming two prominent Republicans to his Cabinet. He selected Henry L. Stimson as his Secretary of War and Frank Knox as Secretary of the Navy. Stimson had served as William Howard Taft's Secretary of War a generation earlier and had then been Hoover's Secretary of State. Knox had run with Landon four years earlier. Angry Republican leaders said that the two men were no longer party members in good standing, but the episode illustrated Roosevelt's skill in co-opting his political enemies and defusing the appeal of the opposition.[40]

In 1940 it was still possible for a candidate such as Willkie to come from nowhere and seize the Republican nomination. Although primaries were held, they did not lock up the nomination in advance for any single candidate, and the party structure was fluid enough to enable an insurgent to outwit the established Republican leadership. Many elements contributed to Willkie's striking victory. The course of the war in Europe made all the other candidates seem wrong for the presidency. With no clear front-runner to beat, Willkie divided and conquered. He had intense popular enthusiasm on his side. Younger Republicans, led by an attorney named Oren Root, Jr., created Draft Willkie for President clubs that sprang up across the nation among young professionals who identified with the moderate wing of the party. The candidate also had the support of such publishing giants as Henry Luce, the Cowles family of *Look* magazine, and other print moguls. Advertising men also lent their expertise to what one of them later characterized as "one of the best engineered jobs in history."[41]

So it may have been, but the rumpled, heavyset, plainspoken Willkie caught the imagination of Republicans in the summer of 1940 who did not want their party to stand aside from the dangers of impending war. The leaders of the Willkie bandwagon provided the fuel for the vehicle, but popular enthusiasm and the sense that Willkie could beat Roosevelt propelled the Hoosier newcomer toward the nomination. The packed gallery, the chanting crowd, the telegrams that deluged the delegates, all attested to the charisma of this new Republican hero. Willkie still might have been stopped had the Taft and Dewey delegates combined, but that alliance did not occur because neither candidate would defer to the other. Once Willkie had won, the convention chose Senator Charles L. McNary of Oregon as his running mate.[42]

The platform that the convention delegates adopted in Philadelphia reflected the crosscurrents among Republicans as World War II intensified. "The Republican Party is firmly opposed to involving this Nation in foreign war" was the first line in the plank on national defense. Elsewhere in the platform was a promise to "revise the tax system and remove those practices which impede recovery" in favor of policies "which stimulate enterprise." The delegates urged Congress to submit the Equal Rights Amendment to the states. They also condemned "the New Deal encouragement of various groups that seek to change the American government by means outside the Constitution" and pledged "the Republican Party to get rid of such borers from within." The GOP platform writers did not specify whether such threats came from Nazis or Communists in 1940, but the underlying suspicion of the patriotism of the Democrats lingered on.[43]

Had Willkie gone on to capture the presidency in 1940, his nomination would not have had the traumatic effect on the party that it did. But since he lost to Franklin D. Roosevelt in November, the choice of Willkie came to be seen as the first of several cases in which eastern Republicans thrust a supposedly electable liberal nominee on the middle western and western conservatives, only to go down to defeat anyway. The argument that more conservative choices would have done even worse against Roosevelt in 1940 and 1944 and Harry Truman in 1948 was plausible but impossible to prove. The right wing of the party believed it had been betrayed for expediency's sake and had nothing tangible to show for the degrading experience.

Willkie's candidacy peaked the day he was nominated. In his acceptance speech he referred to "you Republicans." From the outset of his race against Roosevelt he demonstrated an insensitivity to party regulars by installing a new Republican National Committee chair after promising to retain the incumbent. The Republican nominee was not well organized, nor did he have a consistent strategy to beat President Roosevelt. So chaotic did the Willkie campaign train become that one of the speechwriters said, "This place is like a whorehouse on a Saturday night when the madam is out and all the girls are running around dropping nickels in juke boxes."[44]

Willkie started out by looking for the middle ground. He agreed not to attack Roosevelt's pro-Allied deal with the British that exchanged obsolete American destroyers for British bases in North America. The deal strengthened American defenses against Nazi submarines. However, Willkie moved rightward as the campaign progressed. By October, when polls showed him trailing Roosevelt, Willkie played the isolationist card with increasing vehemence. "We can have peace but we must know how to preserve it," he told the nation over the radio. "To begin with, we shall not undertake to fight anybody else's war. Our boys shall stay out of Europe." Still, Willkie's energy and the appeal of his dynamic personality helped the challenger close the gap as the election neared a climax.[45]

The 1940 election was hard-fought and bitter, and its residual impact on the Republicans was profound. The issue of Roosevelt's unprecedented third term received much attention. GOP buttons proclaimed, "Two times is enough for any man." Others said, "We don't want Eleanor either," a reference to Mrs. Roosevelt's growing status as a controversial advocate of African-American rights. Democrats countered with a button that said, "Better a third-termer than a third-rater." Secretary of the Interior Harold Ickes called Willkie "a simple, barefoot Wall Street lawyer." The campaign strengthened Republican resolve that no president in the future should be allowed to duplicate Roosevelt's three-term tenure.[46]

Behind the scenes, Republicans gained access to letters that the Democratic vice presidential candidate, Henry Wallace, had written to a personal adviser who happened to be an Eastern mystic. The missives painted Wallace in a naive and foolish light. Roosevelt was determined to play hardball, too. A White House conversation was taped on a crude device in the president's office that Roosevelt had installed. In the recording, Roosevelt planned to counter any anti-Wallace effort with a whispering campaign against Willkie. It would reveal the Republican candidate's long-standing extramarital relationship with Irita Van Doren of the *New York Herald Tribune*. In the end neither side used its damaging personal material.[47]

As the presidential race tightened, Roosevelt went out on the stump. In two statements FDR seized the initiative from his rival. During a speech at Boston Garden on October 30, 1940, Roosevelt promised: "I have said this before but I shall say it again and again and again. Your boys are not going to be sent into any foreign war." The speech outraged Willkie when he heard it on the radio. "That hypocritical son of a bitch! This is going to beat me." In a final speech at Madison Square Garden in New York City, Roosevelt assailed three isolationist Republicans in the House by name: Joseph W. Martin of Massachusetts, and New Yorkers Bruce Barton and Hamilton Fish. He gained roars from the crowd when he denounced "Martin, Barton, and Fish." As the president pressed the crowd to identify Republican culprits on issues of defense and preparedness, the throng shouted back "Martin, Barton, and Fish." The isolationist wing of the Republicans proved Willkie's heaviest burden in 1940.[48]

Willkie made the election close, but he fell short of victory. The Republican candidate came within 5 million votes of the president but lost decisively in the electoral result by 449 to 82. The Republican ticket did well in the Middle West and made gains among Irish Americans who resented the emerging alliance with Great Britain, and Italian Americans who bridled at the president's criticism of Benito Mussolini. Roosevelt ran strongest in the cities and piled up large margins in precincts where lower-income Americans lived. Dominance in that area as well as the impact of the war offset Willkie's robust showing in the suburbs, the Great Plains, and the Pacific Coast. The continuing Democratic stranglehold on the South gave Roosevelt a strong base that Willkie's impassioned race could not overcome.[49]

The 1940 election result produced a permanent sense of grievance within the conservative base of the Republicans. Reliance on the moderate Willkie and the eastern Republicans who supported him had not brought victory and the ouster of Roosevelt. Instead, in their view, the party had compromised its core principles without winning national power. Some Republicans believed that Willkie's nomination had been engineered by eastern media interests for the express purpose of denying the nation an honest choice between Roosevelt's pro-war policy and genuine isolationism. Had Willkie taken a clear position against war and Roosevelt's pro-Ally stance, this argument ran, the Republican candidate would have made a better showing in the Middle West. The sense that the Republicans needed to be true to their fundamental beliefs would animate conservatives for the next four decades.

The Loyal Opposition in World War II

> There is only one party when it comes to the integrity
> and honor of the country.
>
>   —Representative Joseph W. Martin[50]

In the aftermath of the 1940 election, however, Republicans remained at odds with one another. Roosevelt's initiative to help
Great Britain through the Lend-Lease program, announced in
early 1941, sharpened the animosity between Republicans such
as Willkie, who saw the United States as tied to the fortunes of
the Allies in the global conflict, and party members such as Senator Taft, who believed that the country must not be drawn into
Europe's battles. The idea of making war matériel available to
Britain during the fighting and receiving payment only after the
war was won seemed fiscally unsound and, worse yet, a blatant
betrayal of neutrality. As Senator Taft told a friend in January
1941, "I feel very strongly that Hitler's defeat is not vital to us,
and that even the collapse of England is to be preferred to participation for the rest of our lives in European wars."[51]

The political battle that ensued over Lend-Lease in 1941 led
some Republicans to support the Roosevelt administration's
stance on national defense, aid to Great Britain, and, after June
1941 and Hitler's invasion of Russia, assistance to the Soviet
Union. William Allen White, the Kansas editor, for example,
formed the pro-interventionist Committee to Defend America
by Aiding the Allies. Willkie testified on behalf of Lend-Lease. In
the midst of his appearance, Senator Gerald P. Nye of North
Dakota asked him if he still believed, as he said during the presidential race, that Roosevelt would have the nation in the war by
April 1941. Willkie responded that what he had said "was a bit
of campaign oratory." The candid remark outraged Republican
conservatives who believed that it revealed Willkie's true colors
on foreign policy. Their 1940 candidate had never truly been
committed to the Republican cause, or so they thought.[52]

These conservative Republicans comprised the other side of

the foreign policy divide in their opposition to Roosevelt, the British, and American involvement in the war. The America First Committee movement attracted their support, especially in the Middle West. Organized in September 1940, the committee achieved its greatest prominence during the Lend-Lease debate. Republicans used the committee and other such foreign policy interest groups to make their case against the president and his proposal. Among them were Alice Roosevelt Longworth, Herbert Hoover, and Arthur Vandenberg. The Michigan senator noted in his diary when Lend-Lease passed the Senate that he "was witnessing the suicide of the Republic." Led by Senator Taft, seventeen Republicans voted against Lend-Lease on final passage. Ten GOP senators voted with the administration.[53]

Republican isolationists in 1941 proved in the end to have chosen the wrong side of the historical issue. They voted overwhelmingly against the extension of the selective service law as a means of drafting young Americans into the armed forces when it came up for a vote in the House in August. Their strong opposition accounted for the tough fight that Speaker Sam Rayburn and the House leadership faced in passing the measure by a single vote. In the months that followed, Republicans in the Senate also opposed more money for Lend-Lease and the arming of merchant ships.

Later revelations about the Holocaust and the enormity of Adolf Hitler's and the Nazis' crimes have complicated the debate about the prewar period. Why the United States did not do more sooner to defeat Germany and Japan has seemed a salient historical issue. While the position of the isolationists was misguided, it was honestly held and reflected deep currents of American thinking about the world. That Franklin D. Roosevelt was not always candid in his diplomatic and military efforts to aid the British and their allies in 1940–41 is also clear, and some of the tactical criticism that he incurred about his undeclared naval war with Germany in late 1941 had validity. Republican warnings about the dangers of unchecked presidential power would also seem prescient a generation later in the Vietnam

War. Nonetheless, the way in which war came to the United States and the consequences that followed undermined the doctrine of Republican isolationism within the Grand Old Party of the 1940s. Still, the impulses that isolationism reflected did not easily die away.

The Japanese attack on Pearl Harbor on December 7, 1941, ended the debate over the United States' active participation in World War II. Republicans rallied behind the administration in the immediate aftermath of the assault. Willkie's running mate in 1940, Senator McNary, said that "our first duty now is to knock down the ears of those little yellow rats of the Orient." Senator Taft told the press, "Undivided and unlimited prosecution of that war must show the world that no one can safely attack the American people."[54]

But the attack on Pearl Harbor represented a major intelligence failure for the military that became, for his Republican opponents, even more sinister evidence of Franklin D. Roosevelt's duplicity. During and after World War II, the perception grew within the GOP that Roosevelt had been deliberately criminal in his manipulation of secret intelligence about Japanese intentions before December 7, 1941. He had, as Clare Boothe Luce put it, lied the nation into war when he could not lead it. The issue has not faded away. A journalist friendly to Republicans stated in May 2002: "FDR had ordered the fleet to put in at Pearl to make it easier for the Japs to destroy it and suck America into the war." That these conspiracy theories have been discredited for years among diplomatic historians has not made any difference as far as Roosevelt's Republican critics are concerned. That Roosevelt was culpable in endangering the lives of American sailors for personal or political advantage seemed perfectly plausible to many in the GOP.[55]

While pledging their endorsement of the war in principle, Republicans did not believe that there was any reason to abate their political criticism of the Roosevelt administration. As Taft put it: "I believe there can be no doubt that criticism in time of war is essential to the maintenance of any kind of democratic government." The Republicans in Congress argued that war was no time to continue costly New Deal programs, especially since the return of prosperity had ended any need for them in the first place. Republicans insisted that such initiatives as the National Youth Administration, the Civilian Conservation Corps, and the Works Progress Administration be stopped within six months in the interest of the war effort. Faced with a Congress where conservatives dominated, the Roosevelt administration reluctantly acquiesced in terminating the New Deal.[56]

Nor did the war end the Republicans' internal debate over foreign policy and the nation's future role in the world. To some degree the aftermath of Pearl Harbor intensified the disagreement between isolationists and interventionists. Both the Democrats and the Republicans remembered World War I and the experience of Woodrow Wilson with the League of Nations. Roosevelt looked for ways to avoid the mistakes of his Democratic predecessor while the Republicans sought to prevent a commitment to a modern variant of the League. The result was a contentious foreign policy dialogue that continued throughout the war and beyond it.

While the war evoked a surge of patriotic fervor in early 1942, the Democrats did not gain a political advantage from the fighting. For most of the year the war news was bad. The Japanese advanced in the Pacific with stunning speed, taking the Philippines. The enemy's naval power in the Pacific was checked at the Battle of Midway in June, but the turn of the tide on the ground did not come until the struggle for Guadalcanal ended in early 1943. In Europe the Germans once again seemed on the march in Russia until the battle of Stalingrad took shape late in the year. American forces did not go on the attack until the invasion of North Africa five days after the congressional elections in November 1942.

World War II produced new political circumstances to which both parties had to adapt. Government spending on the conflict fueled the economic boom that ended the Depression once and for all. It has become an article of Republican faith that New

Deal spending failed to relieve the hard times until the war lifted the economy. Of course, the war instigated government spending at a rate that would have been unthinkable a few years earlier.

While World War II would become enshrined in the 1990s as the heyday of "the Greatest Generation," the home front endured its share of social turmoil and wrenching change. The Japanese relocation program, race riots in major cities, wartime profiteering, and the ever-present casualty lists were also part of the American experience between 1942 and 1945. The nation was more prosperous than ever before, even if citizens had little on which to spend their increased paychecks. As war workers moved to follow the relocation of many industries to the Sunbelt and other Americans began the trek to the suburbs, a shift toward conservatism and traditional social values vied with the painful memories of the Great Depression in shaping political attitudes toward the Republicans and their presidential candidates.

The war and its aftermath was the probable cause of the Grand Old Party's inability to regain national power for two additional presidential contests, in 1944 and 1948. The Republicans did enjoy greater success at the congressional level in the 1940s, yet their internal differences over foreign policy limited their effectiveness in shaping alternatives to the overseas initiatives of the Democrats.

In 1942 the Republicans gained another victory in the congressional races. The slow pace of the war along with recurrent Allied defeats stirred unhappiness with the Roosevelt administration. Isolationist views were still strong in the farm states of the Middle West where voters also disliked the price controls that had been imposed on food crops to stem inflation. Turnout in the elections was very low, especially among the low-income groups that formed the Democratic base. With soldiers away, only 26 million voters went to the polls, a sharp drop from the 1940 performance.[57]

The Republicans added 44 seats in the House to raise their

total to 208. They were now within sight of a majority for the first time in twelve years. The GOP added 9 Senate seats, which increased their delegation to 37. The working arrangement with southern Democrats that had started in the late 1930s meant that the Senate was not a reliable asset for the Roosevelt administration. "The vote seems to me," wrote Senator Taft, "a protest against unnecessary and inefficient regulation, particularly as it affects the war effort."[58]

The big winner in the 1942 election was Thomas E. Dewey. He achieved a decisive victory over divided Democrats in New York State in his bid to become governor. Dewey bested his lackluster opponent James Mead by more than 647,000 votes. Elsewhere, Earl Warren became governor of California, Harold Stassen won the Minnesota statehouse, and John W. Bricker, a Taft conservative, triumphed in Ohio in his bid for a third term. Bricker's victory made him a potential presidential contender, too, as a leader of the conservatives and isolationists. In 1943 both Taft and Vandenberg took themselves out of the 1944 contest, and the battle for the prize shaped up as a contest among Willkie, Dewey, and Bricker.

Despite his continuing national popularity, Willkie saw his standing among Republicans erode in 1942 and 1943. His defense of the Roosevelt administration on foreign policy did not help him, nor did his decision to make a round-the-world tour rather than campaign for GOP candidates in 1942. Above all, Willkie's internationalist views made him anathema to the party's rank and file. Neither Taft nor Dewey liked or trusted Willkie, whom Dewey derisively called "my fat friend" in private. As Willkie became yet more internationalist and more critical of his party leaders, his Republican base shrank. "Willkie is undoubtedly out to make as much trouble as possible for the Republican party," wrote Taft in July 1943.[59]

Dewey saw his fortunes improve at Willkie's expense. As governor of New York he did well on issues such as housing, agriculture, and taxes. He also staked out a moderate position on foreign policy between Taft and Willkie. A private poll of the

1940 convention delegates showed Dewey ahead of Bricker thirty-six percent to twenty-one percent. Willkie trailed badly, as did General Douglas MacArthur. When prominent Republicans assembled at Mackinac Island in Michigan in 1943 to discuss postwar foreign policy, Dewey grabbed the headlines when he proposed an alliance between the United States and Great Britain after the fighting ended. The move irritated isolationists. The *Chicago Tribune*, ever ready to rebuke signs of internationalism, responded with a banner headline: "Tom Dewey Goes Anti-American." The episode made Dewey seem a moderate within his party.[60]

The Mackinac Conference, designed to smooth over Republican tensions, generally achieved its desired result by scripting language on foreign policy that all factions of the party could endorse. The resulting document spoke of "responsible participation by the United States in postwar cooperative organization among sovereign nations to prevent military aggression and to attain permanent peace with organized justice in a free world." That inclusive rhetoric enabled Republicans, whether isolationists or internationalists, to coexist without fratricidal debates over foreign affairs as they headed into the 1944 presidential race.[61]

During the first half of 1944, Willkie's star dimmed among Republicans. When Dewey trounced him in the Wisconsin primary in April, Willkie withdrew from the presidential race. By the fall of 1944 he was dead of pneumonia and a heart attack. His role in Republican politics in the 1940s receded from memory quickly as the party moved further to the right during the rest of the decade. Yet Willkie had been an important Republican during his all-too-brief season in the party's leadership. He provided a voice for the internationalist wing and the more moderate policies associated with eastern Republicans. Had the GOP sought to rely on only its isolationist base during the 1940 and 1944 presidential contests, Roosevelt would likely have won more decisive victories. By keeping the Republicans closer to the middle in both domestic and foreign affairs, Willkie maintained their competitive posture. In that sense, Willkie was an important transitional figure for the presidency of Dwight D. Eisenhower.

After Dewey ousted Willkie, the 1944 nomination was his to win. The determined New Yorker believed that he could beat President Roosevelt on themes of economic conservatism and moderate social policies, a combination that had worked for him as governor. As he told newspaper publishers in late April, he rejected the view espoused by the New Deal that the economy "can continue to function only by constantly taking ever more expensive patent medicine." Instead, Dewey affirmed that "America is still young, still vigorous, still capable of growth." Privately, he vowed that if the electorate "can give their full attention to domestic problems, they will vote Roosevelt out unanimously."[62]

PRESIDENTIAL POLITICS IN WARTIME: 1944

> It is time to elect a President who will clear everything, not with Sidney, but with Congress and the American people.
>
> —John W. Bricker[63]

As Dewey neared victory for the nomination, latent conservative restiveness about the candidate and his political style simmered. Someone, perhaps Ethel Barrymore but not Alice Roosevelt Longworth, had said that the dimunitive New Yorker looked like "the little man on the wedding cake." Imperious and disinclined to suffer fools, Dewey did not ingratiate himself with his GOP colleagues. But with the New Yorker well ahead in the delegate race and with John Bricker fading as the conservative alternative, the right wing of the party saw Dewey as their only hope to unseat Roosevelt.[64]

The convention met in Chicago summer heat that hovered around 100 degrees, and the proceedings went forward in a kind of stupor. Dewey wanted Earl Warren to be his running mate, but the Californian declined. That left Bricker, whom

Alice Roosevelt Longworth had dubbed "an honest Harding." A man noted for his dynamic oratory but not for his brains or political flexibility, Bricker was the darling of the right. As a newspaper columnist noted after Bricker went on the ticket: "Mr. Average Delegate's mind and judgment is all for Dewey, but his heart belongs to Bricker."[65]

The platform at Chicago was largely the work of Senator Taft. It incorporated the language of the Mackinac Conference directly into the platform plank on "the War and Peace." On other subjects, the convention again endorsed the Equal Rights Amendment, favored a two-term limit on the presidency, and attacked lynching and the poll tax. The platform also charged that "four more years of New Deal policy would centralize all power in the President, and would daily subject every act of every citizen to regulation by his henchmen; the country would remain a Republic only in name."[66]

Yet after twelve years of the New Deal, the Republicans also endorsed many Democratic programs, albeit with a greater emphasis on the role of the states. They favored the extension of Social Security "to all employees not already covered." Calling their party "the historical champion of free labor," the delegates accepted "the purposes of the Wagner Act, Social Security, and the Wage and Hour Act" as well as other "Federal statutes designed to promote and protect the welfare of American working men and women." They did "reject the theory of restoring prosperity through government spending and deficit financing." Nonetheless, the rhetoric of the GOP's official statement of party policy went further in the direction of the welfare state than would have seemed possible a few years earlier.[67]

The 1944 presidential campaign proceeded in the context of war news that was increasingly bright for the Allies and their cause. Nazi Germany was clearly on the defensive as Allied armies surrounded it from east and west. The Americans were driving the Japanese back across the Pacific and invaded the Philippines in the autumn. The Roosevelt administration received credit for the good war performance, though the White

House knew that hard fighting still remained. By 1944, people close to Roosevelt recognized that his health was failing and he was unlikely to serve another four-year term. The Democrats selected Senator Harry S. Truman to be the president's running mate, and many people expected him soon to occupy the Oval Office if Roosevelt was reelected. Yet the Republicans faced risks if they invoked the issue of the president's health. They had to rely on public perceptions about Roosevelt's physical condition, and there Roosevelt proved adept at defusing the problem.[68]

Dewey and Bricker raised a number of domestic issues in their effort to throw the president off-stride. One topic that received much press attention turned on the role of the Congress of Industrial Organizations (CIO) and its Political Action Committee (PAC), headed by labor leader Sidney Hillman, which raised money for Democratic candidates. Hillman became notorious when the president issued instructions during the Democratic National Convention, that aides should "clear" the vice presidential choice with Hillman. The tag "Clear it with Sidney" quickly passed into political folklore as evidence of the power of left-wing labor leaders in the Democratic Party. The Hearst newspapers ran a "Sidney Limerick Contest" where readers were invited to turn their poetic talents to mocking that Roosevelt deference to labor.[69]

The turning point in the campaign came in late September. A Republican congressman named Harold Knutson charged that Roosevelt had wasted taxpayer money on his pet Scottish terrier, Fala. During a trip to the Aleutians, Fala had supposedly been left behind, and allegedly a destroyer had been dispatched to retrieve the presidential pet. Roosevelt pounced. During a speech to the Teamsters on September 25, he ridiculed the charge as an example of chronic Republican exaggeration of his failings. As for Fala: "When he learned that the Republican fiction writers had concocted a story that I had left him behind on the Aleutian Island and had sent a destroyer back to find him—at a cost to the taxpayer of two or three or twenty million dollars—his Scotch soul was furious. He has not been the same dog since." The sarcastic attack on the Republicans energized the Democrats while enraging Dewey and his aides.[70]

During the later stages of the campaign, Dewey and his running mate turned to an issue that would loom larger for Republicans in the years that followed. Addressing alleged ties between the Roosevelt administration and the American Communist Party, especially its leader, Earl Browder, Republican campaign literature asserted that Dewey and Bricker owed their political standing "to no pressure group, to no Communists and pinks who would discredit the American system." Bricker made the link explicit. In a speech to a Texas audience he said that "to all intents and purposes the great Democratic party has become the Hillman-Browder communist party with Franklin Roosevelt as its front." With the Russians fighting the Germans and driving toward the enemy's homeland, the invocation of domestic Communism as an issue did not yet have the resonance it would gain just a few years later. But since Republicans believed that the New Deal was inherently anti-American in its general thrust, a linkage with subversive elements was a natural connection to make.[71]

Another incident in the campaign illustrated the mutual suspicion and rancor that marked the Dewey-Roosevelt interaction. Many Republicans believed that the president had been criminally negligent, if not duplicitous, in the case of the Japanese surprise attack on Pearl Harbor. Rumors that the government had broken the Japanese diplomatic code before December 7, 1941, circulated freely in Washington during 1944. Republicans concluded from these leaks that Roosevelt had been aware of the impending Japanese strike. While the diplomatic code-breaking gave clues to Tokyo's intentions in 1941, it did not supply the time or place of the attack. That information was contained in the naval codes that were not being read in late 1941 in sufficient amounts to provide clues to what the Japanese Navy planned.

More important, the United States was still reading the Japanese cable traffic between Tokyo's ambassador in Berlin and his superiors, and the decoding was a source of valuable intelligence. If Dewey made an issue of the matter and the code-breaking success was revealed to the Japanese, this window into Nazi strategy would be closed. General George C. Marshall, acting on his own, prevailed on the Republican candidate to keep the matter out of politics. Dewey did so, and the secret was preserved. However, the belief that Roosevelt had been at fault remained an article of Republican faith.[72]

The last month of the 1944 race became quite bitter as Dewey pressed the attack while Roosevelt campaigned in person to still rumors about his health. His eight-hour ride in pouring rain through New York City did much to rebut the whispering about his probable demise. But the two candidates felt an abiding dislike for each other. Roosevelt said of Dewey on election night, "I still think he is a son of a bitch."[73]

In a heavy turnout of 48 million voters, Roosevelt beat Dewey and won his fourth consecutive presidential election with fifty-three percent of the vote and a 432-to-99 result in the electoral race. The margin of the popular vote was about 3.5 million ballots. Dewey carried nine states, including Bricker's Ohio, but not his own state of New York. Meanwhile, Senator Taft won re-election and emerged as a presidential candidate in 1948. The Republicans expected that with the war at an end before 1948 and Roosevelt not a candidate, they would have a better than even chance four years later. The defeat in 1944, said Taft, "was attributable primarily to a strong feeling of a small percentage of the people that we had better not take out a winning pitcher in the eighth inning."[74]

In January 1945, an ailing Roosevelt left for a final wartime conference with Joseph Stalin and Winston Churchill at Yalta in the Crimea. The resulting deliberations produced one of the long-running political controversies of the Cold War era. The Allies agreed to divide Germany into occupied zones, designating four-power status on Berlin among Russia, the United States, Great Britain, and France. The best Roosevelt could get out of Stalin was a pledge to have free elections in Poland at some time in the future. Roosevelt's bargaining space was limited since Russian armies occupied Poland and other Eastern European countries. But when the details of the agreements reached at Yalta became known, Republicans believed that the president had made concessions to the Soviets that put Eastern Europe in Communist hands. As the 1952 platform put it, Yalta had aided "Communist enslavement." And, Republicans wondered, were there secret agreements of an even more dastardly nature? The idea that Roosevelt had been swayed by Communists inside the government was introduced. The Democrats were not just inept and deceitful; as far as many on the right of the Republican Party were concerned, they had flirted with treason.[75]

On April 12, 1945, Franklin D. Roosevelt died in Warm Springs, Georgia, and Harry S. Truman succeeded to the presidency. After twelve years of the New Deal, its Democratic architect was no more. In his diary Senator Vandenberg wrote that day that "a truly great and gallant spirit, despite all his flaws, was gathered to his fathers." Senator Taft told reporters that Roosevelt was "the greatest figure of our time." Behind these private and public expressions, Republicans knew that the political ground had shifted. Truman was an unknown quantity, and their adversary in four losing presidential elections had passed from the scene.[76]

During his years in office, Roosevelt had reshaped American politics by creating the welfare state and broadening the nation's role in the world. The Republican Party had been divided about both achievements, and that fracture persisted after Roosevelt was gone. On the right of the GOP, sentiment was strong to repeal as much of the New Deal as the voters would allow. More moderate elements among the Republicans, while equally critical of the premises of Democratic programs, wished to retain the popular and workable results of the Roosevelt era while trimming away excessive bureaucracy and holding down spending. On questions of foreign policy, Republicans diverged about whether the United States should revert to an isolationist past or continue its participation on the international stage. During the early months of the Truman administration, as the war in Europe ended and then the Japanese surrendered, Republicans watched the new president and looked ahead to the 1946 congressional elections. Those contests loomed as their first opportunity to return to national power. But the onset of peace also brought disturbing signs that victory over Germany and Japan had not ended the challenges facing the nation. Tensions with the Soviet Union mounted as 1945 unfolded. The era of Roosevelt was over. The Cold War was beginning.

Chapter 9

FROM "HAD ENOUGH?"
TO MODERN REPUBLICANISM, 1945–1961

THE REPUBLICANS WERE once again meeting in Chicago in
July 1952 amid intense passions as Robert A. Taft and Dwight D.
Eisenhower struggled for the nomination. After twenty years
out of power, victory against the Democrats in the fall now
seemed probable. But first the party had to decide between "Mr.
Republican" and the American military hero of World War II.
The contest was close, hinging on a cluster of disputed delegates
from the South. The Eisenhower forces charged that Taft's men
were trying to steal delegates, and they sought "fair play." The
Taft camp believed that their man was being cheated out of a
nomination that was rightfully his. Once again, eastern Republicans were thwarting the will of the party's middle western base.
A decade and a half of strife between the factions boiled to a climax.

The symbol of frustration for the Taft forces was New York
governor Thomas E. Dewey, the losing presidential candidate in
1944 and 1948. Now Dewey was the brains behind the effort to
put Eisenhower in the White House and the spirit behind the
claim that Taft "can't win." At a key moment in the struggle over
the delegates, the Taft leaders decided to make Dewey the issue.

They selected Senator Everett M. Dirksen of Illinois to speak on Taft's behalf during the debate over the issue of contested delegates. The senator's real task was to take on Dewey and his controversial role in the party. With his wavy hair and stentorian voice, the grandiloquent Dirksen assailed the New Yorker. Spotting Dewey in the audience, he said, "We followed you before and you took us down the path to defeat."[1]

Dirksen's words set off a tumultuous, spontaneous outpouring of Dewey denunciation. Boos rang through the hall, some of them for Dirksen, but most directed at Dewey. From the galleries, jeers rained down on the imperturbable New Yorker. A national television audience (or as national as it was in those days) watched as the pent-up animosities of two decades of the New Deal and the Fair Deal coursed through the convention. The next day the Taft leaders styled Dewey "the greatest menace that the Republican party has."[2]

In the end, Dewey's cause triumphed and Eisenhower was nominated, but the long-term victory would rest with the conservatism that Taft and Dirksen represented. During the 1940s and 1950s, the Republicans sought and then won national power. Nonetheless, their own sense of themselves as a party remained in flux during the years between the end of World War II and the presidential candidacy of Richard Nixon in 1960.

POLITICS IN THE TELEVISION ERA

> Political leaders in all sections of the country agreed that no individual running for office could afford to ignore television's influence, but there was substantial division of opinion on whether this influence always would be socially desirable.
>
> —Jack Gould[3]

That television viewers saw for themselves Dirksen's convention attack on Dewey was one major indicator of how American politics had changed for both parties after the end of World War II.

Following the Republican takeover of Congress after the 1946 elections, some predicted internal feuding. This Clifford K. Berryman cartoon from January 16, 1947, shows Senators Wallace White, Robert Taft, and Eugene Millikin working in harmony.

Cartoonist Reg Manning depicts President Eisenhower handing the presidential baton to himself as he starts his second term. Not all Republicans were pleased with Eisenhower's performance after 1957.

In 1948, fewer than one percent of American homes had a television set. By 1952 the number had risen to more than thirty-four percent. Televised hearings of Senator Estes Kefauver's investigation of organized crime attracted big audiences in 1951. A new age of American politics was dawning as the old alignments that had dominated public life since the turn of the century gave way to a new political culture of celebrity and mass media that tested the resilience of both major parties.

Although many Americans feared that the depression of the 1930s might return once the fighting stopped, the exact opposite occurred. The nation had become so prosperous during wartime that consumers built up large amounts in their savings as their weekly wages rose by almost one hundred percent. Government spending on veterans also increased in the late 1940s. With money at their disposal and marriage rates soaring, couples poured savings into suburban homes for the baby boom offspring that arrived in staggering numbers by the end of the decade. Mothers stayed home to raise their families while they also acquired cars, appliances, and all the trappings of the good life. With prosperity came a move to warmer climates as veterans who had been stationed in the Sunbelt returned there to make a new start. Fresh from the Navy and then Yale, George Herbert Walker Bush ventured into the oil business in west Texas, and soon his growing family found other Republican-minded friends in Midland and later in Houston. Barry M. Goldwater welcomed newcomers to Phoenix after the war, and though still a liberal Democrat, Ronald Reagan witnessed Los Angeles explode in size with new arrivals after 1945. Richard Nixon accepted the invitation of local Republicans to seek the congressional nomination in his southern California district that same year.

Many Roosevelt Democrats found their allegiance to that party eroding as they acquired a home and achieved prosperity in their businesses. The militance of labor unions now seemed a threat to social stability, and attacks on management now had less resonance. Other forces also undermined the New Deal

coalition. As Communism loomed, Democrats of Eastern European extraction saw their party as less concerned about the
Russian threat and the plight of the satellite nations. A gradual
drift to the Republicans began. The influx of blacks into the
North strengthened the Democrats, but the resulting racial tensions also strained white ties to the party of Roosevelt and Truman. These pressures emerged slowly but by the 1950s were
tilting voters toward the Republicans.

In the South, Democrats chafed at the evident sympathy of
their northern colleagues for the aspirations of African Americans following World War II. They began to think of either a
third party to express southern interests or the even more profound heresy of making common cause with the Republicans.
But white migrants to Atlanta, Houston, Birmingham, and other
southern cities found only a shell of a Republican Party in most
instances. For decades the Grand Old Party had existed only to
distribute patronage when Republicans held the White House
or to furnish delegates at the party's national conventions. These
entrenched leaders did not seek out new converts during the
late 1940s even as the size of their electorate expanded for the
first time since after the Civil War. New Republicans would make
a powerful statement when Dwight D. Eisenhower ran for president.[4]

The style of national politics also shifted during the postwar
era. Radio in the 1920s and 1930s had provided an aural window
into a culture that had not changed much since the late nineteenth century. Newspapers reported conventions and rallies in
some detail, and the full text of key speeches often appeared in
major urban dailies. The media only covered what politicians did
and had little effect on how politicians conducted themselves.
Television proved a devastating solvent to "business as usual" for
politicians. Lengthy speeches were boring when cameras looked
on. Contested conventions proved embarrassing to winner and
loser alike when the proceedings ran into the night and dis-
rupted video schedules. Photogenic qualities trumped sober substance.

Television also produced new ways for parties to market their ideology through commercials. With access to a mass audience came the costs associated with a national medium. Soon the expenses of campaigns escalated in an inflationary cycle that made fund-raising a key part of a politician's skill. Dependence on large donors, whether personal or corporate, became a renewed fact of American political life. Republicans in the 1950s and 1960s combined cultivation of small givers among their rank and file with the largesse of corporate America.

The century-long trend of declining interest in politics accelerated. Despite periodic surges in voter interest, such as the 1952 and 1960 elections, the voters took a smaller role in partisan affairs during the second half of the twentieth century. Other diversions—ample leisure time, television, professional sports—wooed people away from politics year after year. The number of self-styled independents rose to one-third of the eligible voters. Parties became the arena where activists dominated, and as a result, ideological differences between Republicans and Democrats became more intense.

THE COMMUNIST ISSUE

The Russians undoubtedly gained 3 to 5 years in producing the atomic bomb because our government from the White House down has been sympathetic toward the views of Communists and fellow travelers, with the result that it has been infiltrated by a network of spies.

—Harold Velde[5]

The issue of Communism and internal subversion was perhaps the most striking element in the postwar political equation. The emergence of the Cold War and the rivalry with the Soviet Union and later Communist China had turned victory in World War II into a dangerous worldwide struggle with a totalitarian ideology. That the USSR took advantage of its military triumph over Germany to dominate Eastern Europe was not sufficient

explanation in the eyes of Republicans. Nor did the ability of the
Chinese Communists to capitalize on the weakness and corruption of their Nationalist rivals appear to explain the "fall" of
China. Franklin D. Roosevelt and his administration must have
been sympathetic to Communism or been taken in by Soviet
agents working in the government. Since some Republicans believed that the New Deal was an alien creed on its own terms, a
connection between Roosevelt and the Communist threat was
easily made.[6]

Subsequent revelations taken from Soviet archives and American code-breaking have disclosed the presence of an active Soviet
espionage network in the United States. Its membership and impact is still a matter of intense dispute. To assert today, for example, that Alger Hiss was a spy is to ignite a clamorous controversy.
While the weight of the evidence does indicate that Hiss was indeed a Soviet agent, the work of Hiss, Harry Dexter White, and
others did not fundamentally change the direction of American
foreign policy between 1941 and 1947. Cooperation with the Soviets during World War II made sense since the Red Army was
the main force confronting the Wehrmacht until 1943 or 1944.
Historians on the left now believe, moreover, that Harry Truman
was too much the belligerent anti-Communist in 1946–47 rather
than the dupe of left-wing advisers.[7]

But Republican attacks on Democrats for their alleged softness on Communism offered tempting rewards beyond asserting
a position that many in the GOP accepted as an article of faith. It
provided the prospect of recapturing the allegiance of voters of
Eastern European ancestry who disliked the Soviets. Roman
Catholic voters also found the Republicans more acceptable because of their stance against the Soviets. Anti-Communism put
the Democrats on the defensive on the issue of patriotism, while
it served to emphasize the differences within the majority party
about how to handle the Soviets. There seemed to be no political
risks in the campaign since being too patriotic against Communism could never be perceived as a liability among Republicans.

The practical effect was another matter, however. Rooting

out the real Soviet spies was a laborious process for law enforcement and not something done well in the glow of publicity. Labeling as security risks all those in government who had once sympathized with Communism disregarded the changes that had occurred in people's thinking during the 1940s after such events as the Nazi-Soviet Pact of 1939. Moreover, the effort to instill conformity on anti-Communism wasted much valuable energy without producing real results in the struggle with the Soviets themselves. But for more than a decade allegations of disloyalty became a staple part of Republican attacks on the Democrats.

"HAD ENOUGH?" THE ELECTIONS OF 1946

> Today's major issue is between radicalism, regimentation, all-powerful bureaucracy, class exploitation, deficit spending, and machine politics, as against our belief in American freedom of the individuals under just laws fairly administered for all, preservation of home rule, efficiency and pay-as-you-go economy in government, and protection of the American way of life against either fascist or Communist trends.
>
> —Republican National Committee[8]

Though Harry S. Truman is now generally regarded as a great president, his administration got off to a clumsy start in 1945–46. The dropping of the atomic bombs in August 1945 ended the war with Japan, and the economy lurched into peacetime in the months that followed. Organized labor sought to realize wage gains that had been deferred during the fighting, and strikes became a chronic part of American life. Price controls added to the further dislocations that consumers experienced. Truman stumbled from one crisis to another without the united support of his own party. Liberal and conservative Democrats battled for influence within the new administration over civil rights, foreign policy, and the economy. Martha Taft quipped "To err is Truman," and much of the American middle class took up the refrain. As the Republicans put it to the voters: "Had Enough?"[9]

The Republicans also fielded new faces among their candidates. In California a young Navy veteran named Richard Nixon ran against the liberal congressman Jerry Voorhis with an indictment of the incumbent's record "as more Socialistic and Communistic than Democratic." Joseph R. McCarthy in Wisconsin portrayed himself as "Tail-Gunner Joe" (an exaggerated statement of his military record with the Marines in the South Pacific) in his race against Senator Robert M. La Follette, Jr., in the state's Republican primary. John Bricker of Ohio ran for the Senate and won, as did John Sherman Cooper in Kentucky, while Henry Cabot Lodge won reelection in Massachusetts.[10]

The issue of Communism loomed large in the Republican surge. The chairman of the Republican National Committee, B. Carroll Reece, told voters that "the choice which confronts America this year is between Communism and Republicanism." Senator Taft was at the forefront of this effort. He argued that the Democrats were "so divided between Communism and Americanism" that the party's "foreign policy can only be futile and contradictory and make the United States the laughing stock of the world." A single phrase summed up this aspect of the Republican campaign. The Democrats were guilty of the "Three C's," which were "Confusion, Corruption, and Communism."[11]

In fact, the election results produced a Republican sweep. The party gained 13 seats in the Senate to establish control with 51 senators to 45 for the Democrats. In the House their net gain was 55, and they had a strong working majority with 245 members. The Republicans also elected twenty-five governors in what the *Chicago Tribune* called "the greatest victory for the Republic since Appomattox." For the first time since 1930 the GOP had control of Congress, and prospects for 1948 now seemed bright.[12]

Congressional Republicans, flushed with success, thought they knew what the election meant. As Taft put it, the party should "restore those principles of freedom which had been the foundation stone of America's historical development." Most of the new members agreed that they had a popular mandate to repeal as much of the Roosevelt program as President Truman would accept. This post-election enthusiasm was misguided. The Republicans had not campaigned on the issue of overturning the New Deal and repudiating the policies of the past fourteen years. The party had won because of discontent with the excesses of organized labor and the early ineptitude of the Truman administration. By going too far in their zeal to reject the New Deal, the Republicans in Congress played into Harry Truman's hands in 1948.[13]

THE EIGHTIETH CONGRESS: REPUBLICANS IN POWER

> A vast amount of New Deal rubbish will have to be removed before even the outline of our free institutions will become visible.
>
> —Daniel Reed[14]

In the Eightieth Congress that began in January 1947, Robert Taft was the major Republican leader. He did not take the post of majority leader, but he dominated the upper house on domestic issues. "Congress now consists of the House, the Senate, and Bob Taft," said the *New Republic*. Although conservative on most subjects, he advocated government support of housing and federal aid to education. In a few instances Taft even voted with such New Deal stalwarts as Claude Pepper of Florida. These departures from Republican orthodoxy aroused suspicion among some of his more militant colleagues. His conservative counterpart from Nebraska, Kenneth Wherry, observed of his leader: "I like him, goddamit, even if we have had a hell of a time to keep him from climbing up in Claude Pepper's lap. . . . He doesn't want to make half the fight of it I do."[15]

The main Republican voice on foreign policy was Arthur Vandenberg, who had renounced his earlier isolationism in favor of the internationalism of Roosevelt and Truman. He and Taft coexisted uneasily because the Ohioan was suspicious of the administration's attempts to involve the United States overseas. As a result, the Republicans rarely spoke with a coherent voice as the White House evolved the containment policy against the Soviet Union in 1946–47.

The House, under the leadership of Joseph W. Martin of Massachusetts, was more determined than the Senate to roll back the New Deal. Legislation came out of the lower chamber that often put the Republican senators in the awkward posture of disagreeing with their Republican House colleagues or accepting legislation that would hurt the party's chances in 1948. The reluctance of the House to compromise provided the president with ample evidence to use against the Republicans when 1948 rolled around.

Divisions among the Republicans frustrated the hopes of Robert A. Taft and his colleagues to build a platform on which the party could run. In foreign affairs, the Grand Old Party fell in behind the administration on the main components of containment. As for domestic issues, Congress did pass the Taft-Hartley law aimed at organized labor in 1947 over Truman's veto. Despite charges that it was unfair to unions, even a "slave labor" measure, the Taft-Hartley Act became an enduring part of American labor law. Labor most resented the measure's abolition of the closed, all-union shop where every worker had to be a union member. In the short run, therefore, organized labor's unhappiness with Taft-Hartley helped Truman's reelection chances.[16]

On the issue of Communism, Truman took much of the sting out of the Republican attacks. Aid to Greece and Turkey in 1947, along with the Marshall Plan to rebuild the war-torn economies of Western Europe, showed that the White House was as anti-Communist as the GOP. Truman also launched a large-scale government program to root out alleged subversives, a tactic that preempted that issue. As left-wing elements in the Democratic Party moved away from Truman and toward the potential presidential candidacy of Henry Wallace, Truman came to be even more of a battler against Communist influence in the United States.[17]

Meanwhile, the congressional Republicans made substantial cuts in farm programs, declined to increase the minimum wage, and rejected housing legislation that Senator Taft had introduced and supported. The assumption that the American people wanted to have the New Deal overturned proved to be out of step with the popular mood in 1947–48. Yet the congressional Republicans declined to modify their conservative positions even when it came to helping their party's chances in the 1948 presidential race.

THE VICTORY THAT NEVER WAS: DEWEY VERSUS TRUMAN

> Mr. Dewey asserts without equivocation or reservation that he is for unity, peace and prosperity. Although he did not specifically commit himself on this point, one may confidently assert that he is also against sin.
>
> —Gerald W. Johnson[18]

That contest proved to be the last of the New Deal confrontations between Republicans and Democrats. When the year began, the fundamentals appeared to be on the side of Truman. The nation was prosperous and once again at peace within the context of the Cold War. But in political terms, dark clouds threatened the incumbent's chances. On the left, the candidacy of Henry Wallace attracted many Democrats who were not convinced that a hard-line policy toward the Soviet Union was needed. In the South, resistance to Truman's ambitious civil rights program stirred talk of a revolt among Dixie Democrats (Dixiecrats) against party loyalty because of the race question. The Democratic coalition, so long an amalgam of contradictory elements, seemed to be coming apart.[19]

The Republicans appeared to have a good chance of winning against Truman, whose popularity remained vulnerable to political downdrafts. But their available candidates as 1947 began had weaknesses that made the possibility of an outside candidate more attractive. So in late 1947, much talk went around within both parties about the potential of Dwight D. Eisenhower as a presidential candidate. The general had not yet revealed his strong Republican leanings. His Republican supporters entered him in the New Hampshire primary, and Eisenhower, now president of Columbia University, was forced to respond. Not wishing to enter politics at that time, he wrote a public letter to the publisher of the *Manchester Union-Leader* that conveyed his decision "to remove myself completely from the political scene."[20]

That left the Republicans with their main hopefuls, Thomas E. Dewey of New York, Robert A. Taft of Ohio, and Harold Stassen of Minnesota. Though he would later turn into a political joke, Stassen had real appeal in 1948 as a young (he was forty), dynamic, and self-professedly liberal Republican. Behind the attractive facade was an empty suit, but that was not so clear then as it would later become. Stassen won a number of primaries in the spring but stumbled when he debated Dewey during the Oregon primary. The Minnesotan advocated outlawing the Communist Party, Dewey demolished his argument, and Stassen faded as a candidate.

Senator Taft still had to overcome the tag that he could not win because of his dour personality. A public relations campaign to humanize the Ohio senator only ended up emphasizing his sterner qualities. Taft may have been "Mr. Republican," but there persisted in the ranks of the faithful the nagging sense that he would be a poor choice in a presidential contest against Truman. Neither he nor his supporters really liked Dewey and his icy efficiency, but Taft's lack of charisma was his main stumbling block in 1948.

Despite his loss in 1944, Thomas E. Dewey appeared to be the strongest Republican choice. The defeat by Roosevelt was blamed on wartime conditions, and in an election against the less commanding Truman, Dewey's victory was probable. He could carry his home state against the president and would do well on the eastern seaboard. With Republican strength in the farm belt and the West, a winning electoral coalition seemed to be within reach. Dewey had been a popular governor in New York, where he blended fiscal conservatism with moderation on social issues. During the primary season, Dewey put special emphasis on the struggle with Communism and urged the American people to "insist that our government stop listening to the left-wingers, the communist propaganda and its own fears and doubts and start believing whole-heartedly in our system and telling all the world about it."[21]

While Dewey stood in the mainstream of Republican thought, he did not believe his party could win simply by denouncing the New Deal and all its works. Yet by offering more conservative policy alternatives that still sympathized with the goals of the Democrats, he came across to many of his fellow Republicans as a "me-too" candidate. As a result, conservatives thought, Dewey did not attack the opposition with sufficient vigor and passion. A street fighter by instinct, as he had proved in his war with organized crime in New York City in the 1930s, Dewey concluded that his slashing attacks on Roosevelt in 1944 had not worked, and he resolved to take a higher road against Truman toward what seemed an inevitable victory.

Dewey was also plagued by what many felt was an unattractive personality. The wife of a Republican leader in New York once said, "You have to know Mr. Dewey very well in order to dislike him." The working press regarded him as secretive and arrogant. Dewey's mustache put voters off, but his wife liked it and he refused to change his appearance. With a poll-driven organization that pretested his views on disputed issues, Dewey often came across as soulless and calculating. As long as he seemed like a winner, the GOP would tolerate him, but he never won the party's heart in his two presidential campaigns.[22]

With Truman beset on all sides during the first half of 1948, Dewey disposed of Harold Stassen in the primaries and won the nomination on the third ballot over Taft and the other candidates at the Philadelphia convention. Both parties met in the same city that year because network television coverage through the coaxial cable enabled them to reach the small number of set owners in the Northeast. For his running mate, Dewey selected Earl Warren, the popular governor of California. But the two men did not get along, and Dewey criticized Warren's intelligence in private.

In his acceptance speech on June 24, 1948, Dewey sought to rise above the partisan fray and strike a note of unity and national resolve. "Our people are turning away from the meaner things that divide us," he told the delegates. The Republicans "must be the instrument of that inspiration." In its lofty tone it read and sounded more like an inaugural address than a call to arms. From the outset of the campaign, the Republican assumption that victory was theirs informed the strategy that Dewey followed. Their platform was moderate in its tone and centrist in its substance. It called for the Equal Rights Amendment, stood for broader civil rights including abolition of the poll tax, and proposed a "reduction in the enormous burden of taxation." While there was a pledge "to expose the treasonable activities of Communists," the language did not link the Democrats with subversion. There was a plank supporting the United Nations and the concept of "collective security."[23]

The Republicans left Philadelphia confident of their success in November. The post-convention polls gave Dewey a "bounce," and he was reported to be eight to ten points ahead of Truman, whose troubles persisted. Southern Democrats, angry about the administration's civil rights program, split off to form the States' Rights Party, with Strom Thurmond of South Carolina as its presidential nominee. The Progressive Party behind Henry Wallace was certain to draw off voters from Truman's left. How then could the Democrats ever expect to win? As Dewey's campaign manager, Herbert Brownell, later wrote, "Our optimism for a Republican victory in November was based in large part on Truman's political woes."[24]

Republican confidence in victory bred a sense of impending

entitlement within the party that had large consequences for the future. With polls showing Dewey well ahead, Republicans made plans for a move to Washington in January 1949. Partisans readied their resumes and thought about how new policies would be developed. All that remained was the formality of the election itself before the Republicans would retake control of the government and resume their natural role as the majority party.

Nothing went as the Republicans had planned. Truman made a hard-hitting acceptance speech at the Democratic convention that assailed the Eightieth Congress as the worst in American history. He promised to summon the lawmakers back into a special session in late July (on "Turnip Day," as the president put it) to address the nation's unmet needs on housing, education, civil rights, and economic issues such as rising prices. The strategy was risky since the Republicans could easily enact some substantial laws and leave Truman looking foolish.[25]

The Republicans chose principle over tactics during the special session. The lawmakers deadlocked on most issues, even proving unsympathetic to Dewey's needs. The candidate wanted modifications in the restrictive law governing the admission of refugees from Europe that had alienated urban Catholic and Jewish voters. The Republicans on Capitol Hill took no action on the measure. The episode and other roadblocks solidified the stereotype about a "Do-Nothing" Congress that Truman was now using as a whipping boy in his reinvigorated campaign.[26]

Both Dewey and Truman campaigned in the fall in the last of the railroad-oriented presidential contests. The Republican and his team rode the "Victory Special," with polls showing him some thirteen points ahead in mid-September. Dewey let Taft, Stassen, and other Republican leaders do the heavy lifting in attacking Truman and his policies. Dewey himself stumped like an incumbent facing a beaten opponent. His propensity for sonorous banalities soon became a trademark. In Arizona on September 23, he told his audience, "You know that your future is still ahead of you." The next day at the Hollywood Bowl he proclaimed, "We will go forward to develop our resources." Several weeks later in

Kansas City, Dewey intoned that "as never before we need a rudder to our ship of state and a firm hand on the tiller."[27]

Dewey's speeches did have substance, but they often resembled dry position papers more than exhortations to the faithful to turn out and vote. But Truman and the Democrats were rarely mentioned, and the record of the Republican Congress received little attention. Like a team with a secure lead in the fourth quarter, the Dewey camp planned to run out the clock. The problem was that President Truman did not plan to perform the political equivalent of "taking a knee." As Dewey's momentum slowed, the president kept hammering away at his "Give 'Em Hell" campaign to large and enthusiastic crowds. In his battle, Truman sometimes touched his remarks with demagoguery; in late October he likened Dewey to a "front man" for fascism on the model of Hitler's Germany and Mussolini's Italy. Dewey wanted to strike back hard but backed off on the advice of his strategists. He chided Truman for a "new low in mudslinging" but went no further.[28]

These events would become part of Republican lore. Dewey's defeat convinced many conservatives that only an all-out attack on the Democrats would work in the future. If Truman could raise the specter of fascism, then Republicans could invoke the more damaging image of Communism at home and abroad. In the mutual exchanges of invective that mark American politics, both parties enjoyed playing hardball when they were pitching. The Dewey-Truman campaign inflicted lasting scars on the GOP, and they would not soon again be outdone in vitriol on the trail.

A key element in Dewey's defeat had little to do with ideology but emerged from a sector of the economy where the GOP had done well in the past. A revolt in the farm community, unanticipated by Republicans, cost Dewey crucial electoral votes and the presidency. With crop surpluses at high levels, farmers needed storage capacity for their products, or they would have to sell their goods for whatever the market would bear. The Eightieth Congress had not funded the expansion of such facilities when it reauthorized the Commodity Credit Corporation.

So when farm prices fell in the fall of 1948, middle western farmers blamed the Republicans for their plight. As a gentleman farmer from New York, Dewey seemed less interested in the problem than did Truman who had been a Missouri farmer himself. The issue collapsed Dewey's support in key farm states as the election neared.[29]

On Election Day, November 2, 1948, everyone expected a Dewey victory. Small boys in the suburban Republican precincts of Stamford, Connecticut, were told that Dewey was a sure thing before they went to bed that night. Some pollsters had even stopped taking surveys in late September because Dewey was perceived as so far ahead. The conventional wisdom was that voters made up their minds by Labor Day and rarely changed after that date. In fact, Dewey lost supporters and Truman picked up votes as the campaign concluded. Still, as the returns started to come in and Truman moved into the lead, commentators expected Dewey to bounce back and pull the contest out based on the rural vote in the West.

It never happened. Truman won more than 24 million votes; Dewey received just under 22 million. The president garnered 303 electoral votes to 189 for Dewey, while the States' Rights Party carried four southern states with 39 electoral votes. Henry Wallace and the Progressive Party came in a badly beaten fourth. The Democrats also regained control of the House and Senate. Truman carried much of the old Democratic South and border states, did well in the Middle West, and scored solidly west of the Rockies. Dewey ran strongly in the East, picked up Michigan and Indiana, but carried only four states west of the Mississippi. Despite the excitement of the election, fewer voters went to the polls than expected. Republican turnout was not robust, probably because Dewey's success seemed so certain. The campaign that had begun with so much confidence for the Republicans ended in one of the great electoral surprises in the nation's history.[30]

The Republicans spent the post-election season dining on political crow. The *Chicago Tribune,* convinced that the Republicans had won on election night despite all the negative indicators, came out with its banner headline the next morning: "Dewey Defeats Truman." Alice Roosevelt Longworth quipped as the returns came in: "You can't make a soufflé rise twice." The defeated candidate well summed up Republican feelings in private: "What do you know? The son of a bitch won."[31]

The outcome of the 1948 contest hinged on Dewey's lapses as a candidate. Had he campaigned with half of Truman's vigor and invective, he would have spurred Republicans who stayed home in their confidence of success. Had Dewey been more approachable and trusting of the voters, he could have blended his skill as an administrator with just a touch of humanity. As it was, the American people sensed that Dewey was not really one of them.

The results of the 1948 election produced important long-term results for both parties. The Democrats were a tired organization by 1948 after sixteen years in power. While Truman was an effective foreign policy president and a pioneer in civil rights, his administration lacked the energy and talent of the New Deal. It was probably time for a change. Had Dewey triumphed, the Korean War would have been fought under Republican auspices and the issue of domestic Communism might not have taken the virulent form that it did. The country was not as liberal as Truman's victory made it appear, and Dewey's administration would probably have reflected the country's real mood.

As it was, the Republicans were convinced that the combination of Truman's demagogic campaigning and Dewey's ineptitude had cost them an election that was rightfully theirs. If Truman could toss charges of fascism against them, then why shouldn't the GOP hurl charges of Communist subversion against their political rivals? After all, most Republicans believed in their hearts that these allegations were true. As Senator Ralph Flanders of Vermont put it, "Our late, departed saint, Franklin Delano Roosevelt, was soft as taffy on the subject of Communism." Similar opinions circulated about Truman. If exploring the Communist issue attracted new voters to the Republicans, that was a pleasant dividend from their honest patriotism. Soon the issue would find a spokesman who would shape the nature of the debate about subversion for almost five years.[32]

After Dewey's loss, the conservative and moderate wings of the party argued about the cause of the 1948 debacle in a debate that raged for another decade. One influential conservative, Clarence Budington Kelland, complained in February 1949 that the party had "appeased groups and blocs. We have fished for racial voters or sectional votes with evasions. We have not realized our duty to our party, to our country and to posterity." Faced with a tide of Democratic efforts to take away freedoms in the name of liberalism, Kelland continued, the Republican Party, "if it deserves to survive, must erect itself as a restraining dam to contain and hurl back this flood."[33]

Dewey himself contended in a speech that same month that the Republicans could not win national elections if they joined those "who honestly oppose farm price supports, unemployment insurance, old age benefits, slum clearance, and other social programs." Should the Republicans come out against these measures, "you can bury the Republican party as the deadest pigeon in the country." The Republicans allied with Dewey's point of view made speeches while the conservatives and their supporters worked at the grass roots to reaffirm their dominance within the party. Liberal Republicanism in its twentieth-century form always had an air of electoral expediency rather than real conviction about it. As a result, that faction's hold on the GOP was more tenuous than it seemed.[34]

The Democratic victory in 1948 soon turned sour as the Republicans reasserted themselves in and out of Congress. The coalition of Republicans and southern Democrats on Capitol Hill stalled most of the initiatives, including a civil rights program that Truman proposed in 1949. At the same time, a series of foreign policy shocks raised questions about the Truman administration's competence and revived the controversy about Communism in government. In the first half of 1949, the position of the Nationalist Chinese deteriorated, paving the way for a Communist takeover in December. The trial of Alger Hiss on charges that he had lied under oath about spying for the Soviets was in the headlines. Most ominous was the news in September 1949 that the Russians had exploded an atomic bomb. The American nuclear monopoly no longer existed.

Joseph R. McCarthy and the Republicans

> One of the most serious problems we inherited from Truman was Joe McCarthy. As a Democratic friend put it to me, "Joe has been a snake in the grass for us. If you're not careful he'll become a viper in your bosom."
>
> —Richard M. Nixon[35]

Republican criticism of the Truman administration's performance intensified throughout the year. Bipartisan foreign policy continued since Republican votes helped pass the pact creating the North Atlantic Treaty Organization in the spring. On other issues, however, Republican ire mounted, particularly against Secretary of State Dean Acheson, who seemed to embody the administration's perceived failure to take a harder line toward the Soviets. Haughty and aristocratic, Acheson drove his political enemies to distraction, especially when he did not rush to condemn the accused spy Alger Hiss. With the administration under siege, the Republicans looked to win back some of the ground they had lost in the House and Senate in 1948.

Though few recognized it at the time, the political landscape in the United States shifted in February 1950. In a speech to the Ohio County Women's Republican Club in Wheeling, West Virginia, Joseph R. McCarthy, an otherwise obscure Republican senator from Wisconsin, told his audience that "I have in my hand fifty-seven cases of individuals who would appear to be either card-carrying members or certainly loyal to the Communist party" in the State Department. McCarthy went on to say that "the reason why we find ourselves in a position of impotency is not because the enemy has sent men to invade our shores, but rather because of the traitorous actions of those . . . who have had all the benefits that the wealthiest nation on earth has had to offer—the finest homes, the finest college educations, and the finest jobs in Government we can give."[36]

From this speech followed McCarthy's rise to national influence as the embodiment of the anti-Communist spirit that dominated the early 1950s. "McCarthyism" soon became a label. More than half a century since, McCarthy's place in the history of the Republican Party still stirs acrimony and debate. The man himself was forty-one on February 9, 1950, when he spoke in Wheeling. He had been elected as a circuit judge in 1939 at the age of twenty-nine and then served with the Marines as an intelligence officer in the Pacific. While his actual war record was perfectly creditable, McCarthy inflated his performance to include dangerous missions and phony war wounds. In 1946, he defeated the Republican incumbent in the primary and then went on to win a Senate seat during the Republican sweep in November.

Once McCarthy gained national fame, legends about the impetus behind the speech proliferated. Facing a difficult reelection campaign in 1952, he needed a winning theme, but he had not yet fixed on subversion in government when he appeared in Wheeling. The intense public response to his remarks made McCarthy realize what a rich vein he had tapped, and his campaign took shape from there. As numerous students of McCarthy have noted, he proved to be a master of publicity who used the press on behalf of the sensational charges he could never sustain in fact. But for Republicans in 1950, McCarthy was a political asset, and the party establishment in the Senate approved his efforts. "If one case doesn't work, bring up another," Taft told McCarthy. From the outset of McCarthy's rise, there were Republicans such as Margaret Chase Smith of Maine who disapproved of his methods and questioned his effectiveness. For the most part, however, Republicans fell in line behind McCarthy through the 1952 election.[37]

The Wisconsin senator's profile increased as the troubles of the Truman administration multiplied during the second half of 1950. The outbreak of the Korean War in late June 1950 produced a brief moment of bipartisan support behind the president, but soon Republicans resumed their criticism of the administration. Taft remarked on June 28 that "this entirely unfortunate crisis has been produced, first, by the outrageous, aggressive attitude of Soviet Russia, and second, by the bungling and inconsistent foreign policy of the administration."[38]

Republicans were on the offensive in 1950 as the congressional elections approached. Popular unhappiness with the war in Korea, where Truman had introduced American troops to stop the North Korean advance into the South, helped the GOP. Republicans argued that a lack of readiness and a soft policy toward Communism accounted for the initial military setbacks that the country experienced in Korea. As Harold Stassen said on the eve of the voting, the administration had practiced "five years of coddling Chinese Communists, five years of undermining General MacArthur, five years of snubbing friendly, freedom-loving Asiatics, and five years of appeasing the arch-Communist, Mao Tse-tung."[39]

The elections produced Republican gains but fell well short of a landslide on the scale of 1946. In the Senate, the GOP picked up five seats. In California, Richard Nixon defeated Helen Gahagan Douglas in a bitter campaign dominated by the issue of Communism. Nixon and the Republicans believed that he had made a hard-hitting race against a Democratic liberal. The Democrats asserted that Nixon had smeared Douglas as "the pink lady." Everett M. Dirksen easily beat the Democratic majority leader in the Senate, Scott Lucas, in Illinois. Taft won a smashing reelection victory in Ohio, despite the stiff opposition of organized labor, and conservative Eugene Millikin prevailed in Colorado. The Democrats kept control of both houses of Congress, but the Truman administration was now on the defensive with no political mandate.

Joseph McCarthy was the big winner in 1950. He spoke widely around the country as the best drawing card for the GOP.

His efforts were credited with bringing down Democrat Millard Tydings in Delaware and in assisting Republican candidates in general. The accepted judgment in Washington was that defying McCarthy over Communism was political suicide. For the next two years, fears of his wrath shaped the nation's discourse about Communism.

When the president relieved General Douglas MacArthur of his command in April 1951, Republican outrage at Truman boiled over. Tension between the general and the president had been building for months, and the Republicans took MacArthur's side in the dispute over military strategy in Korea. MacArthur believed that with the Communist Chinese now deeply involved in combat in Korea, the war should be extended into Communist China and total victory pursued even at the risk of using nuclear weapons. The administration countered that such moves would risk an even wider war with the Chinese and the Soviet Union with no guarantee of victory in the end.

The general's ouster occurred after MacArthur praised a speech by Republican House leader Joseph W. Martin that proposed using the forces of Nationalist China from the island of Taiwan to open a second front against Communist China. In the letter that he wrote to Martin after he read the speech, MacArthur renewed his own call for triumph in Korea by attacks on the Communist Chinese inside their nation. "As you pointed out, we must win," MacArthur said. "There is no substitute for victory." Truman had decided to fire MacArthur before his letter to Martin became public, but the general's response encapsulated what MacArthur was proposing to Republicans and to the nation.[40]

MacArthur returned home later in April 1951, addressed Congress in a sensational speech, and was met with a wave of popular adulation. Republicans sang his praises and decried Truman, Secretary of State Dean Acheson, and the British government for his dismissal. The GOP in Congress called for hearings on the war and its aims which the Democrats had no choice but to hold. Yet the discussion of foreign policy did not produce the political bonanza that the Republicans expected. As the Joint

Chiefs of Staff rebutted MacArthur's arguments for a wider war in Korea and China, some of the steam went out of the general's presidential bid when the public realized the dangerous implications of his aggressive approach. However, the Republicans did maintain that a negotiated settlement of the war that left Korea divided between North and South was unacceptable. As Senator Taft put it in July 1951, "There is no satisfactory protection against socialism at home and against war and ignominy abroad except an overwhelming Republican victory in 1952."[41]

"THOU SHALT NOT STEAL": EISENHOWER VERSUS TAFT

> Eisenhower has the support of the crowd who, three times before, have been back of a "me-too" campaign.
>
> —Congressman John Taber[42]

The urgent question among Republicans in 1952 was the identity of their presidential candidate. With no major moderate-conservative hopeful left on the scene after the defeat of Dewey, it looked at long last to be Senator Taft's turn. On October 16, 1951, he summoned reporters to a news conference where he said that he would make the race for the GOP nomination. In the weeks that followed, Taft forged ahead among the Republican regulars, and by the end of the year he estimated that he had as many as six hundred delegates who were "clearly favorable" to him. That total would put him within a few votes of a convention victory. By the start of 1952, Taft was the front-runner by all conventional measures of Republican sentiment.[43]

Behind Taft's apparent strength lay two nagging issues that would cause some Republicans to look for an alternative. The first was the well-known fear that the Ohioan could not be elected. Beyond his lackluster personality on the campaign trail, Taft's record of opposition to so many of the domestic programs of the Democrats led even those favorably disposed to him to wonder "whether he can revise his thinking and be positively for something." More damaging was the perception that Taft was a dedicated isolationist who would pull the nation back from its recent commitments to the defense of Europe. Eisenhower later revealed that he had offered to stay out of the 1952 race if Taft would agree to a larger role for the United States abroad, but Taft refused. As Herbert Brownell, later a manager for Eisenhower, put it, "Taft's candidacy threatened to set the party and the country, if he were to win the presidency, on a foreign-policy course I thought dangerous."[44]

The logical choice for internationalist-minded Republicans was the military hero of World War II, General Dwight D. Eisenhower. Ever since his withdrawal from elective politics in 1948, Eisenhower had been courted by Republicans of all stripes to run in 1952. These party members were convinced that only someone of his popular stature could ensure a GOP victory and the White House. In addition, Eisenhower would see to it that internationalist ideas prevailed in the party, which added to the general's appeal among eastern Republicans. On domestic issues, Eisenhower's thinking was as conservative as Taft's, perhaps even a little more to the right than the senator on a question such as government support for housing, but Eisenhower came across as a moderate, balanced politician who would not approach public issues in a radical way.

Underrated as a politician while he was alive and downgraded by historians during the 1960s and into the 1970s, Eisenhower is now recognized as a forceful chief executive and a very canny politician. In fact, the extent to which he dominated the national scene in the 1950s is still being revealed as research into his life and administration continues. Yet his place in the history of his party is more difficult to assess. Deeply suspicious of many aspects of the New Deal, he recognized the wide public support for measures such as Social Security and believed that attacking such programs was suicidal. For many Republicans on the right, that made Eisenhower an apologist for what Franklin D. Roosevelt had done. Accordingly, the eventual triumph of conservatism among Republicans after 1964 somewhat diminished Eisenhower's standing as a party leader. His policies became the target of Barry Goldwater and his followers in the late 1950s, and he looms smaller in historical perspective for Republicans than either Richard Nixon or Ronald Reagan.[45]

Eisenhower was no liberal, and he became more conservative as his presidency advanced. Unlike many of his contemporaries, however, he believed that the changes the New Deal had produced could not be overturned without lasting damage to the Republican cause. He had little regard for Democrats and liberals, but he was equally scathing about the right wing of his own party which he believed was impractical and often reckless. His disdain was reciprocated. While Eisenhower believed in a strong national defense, he thought that the Pentagon often asked for more than it needed, and he was convinced that a balanced budget and fiscal prudence were as important an index of the nation's health as another weapons system. His emphasis on arms control also put him at odds with members of his party, particularly conservative Republicans who believed that the president was closer to the New Deal than he really was.

Eisenhower's first task in 1952 was to win the Republican nomination. And although Taft was far ahead in the delegate race, Eisenhower had an asset in his broad popularity with the American people that his rival could not match. It became clear as Eisenhower got into the race in the spring of 1952 that his allure as a military hero above political strife crossed partisan barriers. He had some learning to do about campaigning and national politics, but he proved to be a very quick study. With the support of Dewey and his organization, several prominent eastern media outlets, including *Time* and the *New York Herald Tribune,* and rank-and-file Republicans across the country, Eisenhower had drawn nearly even with Taft in delegate strength by the time the national convention arrived in Chicago in June 1952.

The Eisenhower forces were close to nabbing the nomination, but Taft likely would still prevail unless some of his pledged delegates could be jostled loose. Eisenhower's candidacy had prompted a surge of enthusiasm in the South where conservative white Democrats in states such as Texas had flooded into Republican caucuses. Old-line Republicans who had dominated the party's deliberations for years fought with these newcomers (in some cases fisticuffs occurred) and then used their control of the party machinery to send pro-Taft delegations to Chicago. The Eisenhower Republicans, in turn, contested these results and dispatched competing slates on the grounds that the Taft leaders had acted outside the rules. As had happened in the race between Taft's father and Theodore Roosevelt in 1912, the issue of honesty arose, and the Eisenhower leaders maintained that "the Taft forces are now convinced he cannot win the nomination fair and square, so they are out to steal it."[46]

The Eisenhower camp knew that if Taft had his disputed delegates from Texas, Georgia, and Louisiana seated at the convention, then the general's candidacy was doomed. Their strategy became to adopt a "fair play" amendment to the convention rules that would preclude the Taft delegations from these states from voting on their own right to be seated (as had been done in past conventions). Equally important was the need to cast this battle as a struggle between virtue (Eisenhower) and old-style machinations (Taft). When the credentials committee tried to meet in secret, the Eisenhower managers clamored for television coverage of the committee's proceedings. The Taft men had to give in on that point, and the televised deliberations of the committee built support for Eisenhower outside the convention hall. As a result, the convention adopted the fair play amendment, which meant that Taft's total vote was reduced. Then debate began on the issue of seating the Georgia, Louisiana, and Texas slates.[47]

Senator Dirksen then launched his attack on Thomas E. Dewey and illustrated the fissures that remained in the party from the defeats of Willkie and Dewey in the preceding three elections. The spectacle again worked in Eisenhower's favor since the Taft delegates seemed to be the embodiment of an older political tradition of backroom deals. Eisenhower succeeded on all the key votes about seating contested delegates, and the number of votes committed to him rose. Clearly, Taft could not win the nomination. While Eisenhower did not yet control a clear majority, he had the best chance of gaining the delegates pledged to favorite-son presidential candidates such as Earl Warren of California and Harold Stassen of Minnesota. These two hopefuls looked to a deadlocked convention and the chance to be a compromise selection.

On the first ballot, Eisenhower was within nine votes of success. When Stassen threw the Minnesota delegation to Eisenhower, the nomination was his. Taft was gracious in defeat, and despite the strains of the bitter contest, Republicans hoped that Eisenhower could bring them victory. For the fourth time in succession, the Republicans had turned to the candidate with the best perceived chance of victory in the autumn instead of the politician who reflected the real philosophy of the party. Future Republican conservatives would be less willing to accept such compromises. In subsequent elections, the party would find ways to align its true feelings with its electoral goals for the White House.

The convention's final task was the selection of Eisenhower's running mate. The choice of Senator Richard M. Nixon of California was a decisive step for the party's future, and much writing has been devoted to how Nixon won the prize. Well before Eisenhower even got into the race, shrewd political insiders had seen the young California senator as a logical choice. Eisenhower was sixty-two and needed youth to balance the ticket. California's electoral votes might be crucial in a close election, and Nixon had proved he could carry the state with his decisive defeat of Helen Gahagan Douglas two years earlier. Nixon's reputation as a foe of Communism, established during the House hearings against Alger Hiss, made him an ideal foil for Eisenhower's foreign policy skills. In all respects, Nixon complemented Eisenhower as no other potential Republican vice president did. Taft did not want to leave the Senate, Earl Warren was too liberal for the regulars, Stassen was a lightweight, and Nixon's senatorial colleague, William Knowland, was too far to the right.

Because of the subsequent events in Nixon's career that culminated in the Watergate scandal of the 1970s, his biographers have devoted many pages to his clandestine efforts to obtain the vice presidential nomination in 1952. He did undercut Earl Warren's presidential chances within the California delegation and maintained ties with the Eisenhower camp to keep himself available as a potential running mate. Nixon's machinations revealed him to be a shrewd politician who maximized his opportunity to achieve high national office at a young age. The scars that he left among the California Republicans loyal to Warren would soon lead to the major crisis of the 1952 Republican presidential race.[48]

Following his nomination, Eisenhower prepared to face the Democratic nominee, Governor Adlai E. Stevenson of Illinois, in the fall. Although he was eligible to serve another term, President Truman had recognized the decline in his fortunes and had withdrawn from the race in March 1952. The Democrats chose the witty and articulate Stevenson because he seemed to have the best chance to rally a divided party against Eisenhower. While a gifted speaker at his best, Stevenson proved to be only a competent candidate who was no match for the popular Eisenhower.

The bitter Republican convention left some hard feelings, and so Eisenhower met with Taft in New York City on September 12. The candidate was already under attack for the lack of energy in the Republican campaign. The influential Scripps-Howard newspapers, which spoke for the Republican middle, said that Eisenhower was "running like a dry creek." The two men got together on Morningside Heights, and Taft received most of what he wanted from Eisenhower. Since the nominee shared Taft's views on most domestic issues, the concessions were not hard for Eisenhower to accept. He agreed to keep the national budget at $60 billion, to reduce tax revenues, and to retain the essence of the Taft-Hartley law. Critics called it "the surrender of Morningside Heights," but the episode actually underscored the unified Republican commitment to oust the Democrats in November 1952.[49]

Once the Republican campaign got on track, the GOP had ample ammunition to hurl at their opponents. The political formula K1 C2 seemed to embody the main points: Korea, Communism, and Corruption. Eisenhower would deal with the Korean issue and end the unpopular war. Meanwhile, campaign surrogates such as Nixon and McCarthy would pound the Democrats on the subversion issue. Stevenson, said Nixon, had received "a Ph.D. from Dean Acheson's cowardly college of Communist containment." In a television broadcast, McCarthy referred to "Alger—I mean Adlai." Democratic attempts to answer these allegations with attacks on Eisenhower's performance as president of Columbia University fell flat.[50]

The Republicans capitalized on the ethical problems of the Truman White House. Aides of the president had been involved in episodes of influence peddling (including the receipt of freezers and mink coats) that cast a cloud over Truman's presidency. When he failed to act vigorously to clean house, Republican critics had more political fodder. Eisenhower had called his campaign a "crusade," and for Republicans the twenty years of Democratic rule had descended into a mass of sleaze.[51]

In this setting, the news that Richard Nixon was the beneficiary of a secret fund of $18,000, collected from his supporters in California, that paid his office expenses disrupted the Republican cause. Disgruntled Republicans in California, angry over how Nixon had treated Earl Warren during the convention, leaked news of the fund to the national press, and the story gradually came out. To some extent Nixon was the victim of a bum rap. He did not spend the money for personal needs but only for his political actions and projects. However, there was evidence of tangible benefits for some donors. The seeming contradiction between Eisenhower's ethical standards and Nixon's apparent transgression precipitated a wave of criticism. Calls arose for Nixon's removal from the ticket. Thomas E. Dewey urged the vice presidential candidate to give a full accounting on national television. The episode became legendary in American politics because of Nixon's refusal during his half-hour address to return one gift, a cocker spaniel named Checkers that his daughters had received. The public responded enthusiastically to Nixon's earnest, open demeanor. Nixon suggested shrewdly that telegrams be directed to the Republican National Committee (not the Eisenhower campaign), and Nixon's place on the ticket was assured.[52]

The controversy, however, introduced a note of political reserve into Eisenhower's relations with his vice president. Nixon did not appreciate being told that he must be "as clean as a hound's tooth." Eisenhower's initial indecision sparked anger from his running mate: "There comes a time on matters like these when you've got to shit or get off the pot." Eventually, when Nixon had clearly gained popular acclaim, Eisenhower told him, "You're my boy."[53]

With the Nixon campaign fund fracas behind him, Eisenhower put the election away when he announced late in the campaign that he would go to Korea as president-elect to inspect the military situation. Since the general would not make the trip to intensify the war, the implications of the pledge were clear. Stevenson and the Democrats were clearly outmatched as the voters clamored for a change in political leadership in 1952. The result was a landslide for Eisenhower. The Republican ticket received 442 electoral votes to 89 for Stevenson. In the popular vote, Eisenhower led by 6,600,000 ballots. The Republicans gained control of both houses of Congress. Eisenhower won four states in the South, including Texas, and initiated the long-term buildup of Republican strength in that region. After two decades, Democratic dominance of American politics had ended. In Boston a happy Republican displayed a banner that read: "Thank God."[54]

THE HIDDEN-HAND PRESIDENT

Beneath his captivating personal appearance was a lot of finely tempered hard steel.

—Richard Nixon[55]

In historical perspective, the presidency of Dwight D. Eisenhower would come to seem a period of peace and prosperity before the tumult of the 1960s. Eisenhower's standing among historians has risen accordingly, and he is now one of the twentieth century's most effective chief executives. For Republicans, however, Eisenhower's legacy was more contentious. By the end of the 1950s, his policies were under assault from the right for not being conservative enough. Meanwhile, Eisenhower's campaign to make his party more attractive to a majority of the electorate, what he called "Modern Republicanism," largely failed to make any impression on the GOP.

Eisenhower was a strong conservative, becoming more so as his presidency progressed. But he was not an intense partisan in his Republicanism, and he regarded many on the right as impractical and often obstructionist of his administration. Of Senate Majority Leader William F. Knowland, he once remarked to his diary: "In his case, there seems to be no final answer to the question, 'How stupid can you get?' " In terms of foreign policy, for example, he did not believe in military power as an end in itself and was convinced that simply accumulating nuclear weapons did not enhance the nation's security. He was thus willing to negotiate with the Soviet Union over arms control in ways that dismayed the Republican right. Given Eisenhower's military credentials, it was almost impossible to make a credible case that he was too soft on the Soviets even though many Republicans chafed at the president's efforts at arms control. Eisenhower resisted GOP attempts to limit presidential power in foreign affairs. The Bricker Amendment to curb the impact of treaties on the Constitution, which Senate Republicans endorsed, was defeated largely because of Eisenhower's unrelenting opposition.[56]

In their 1952 platform, the Republicans had spoken of the need to reject the doctrine of containment that the Truman administration followed toward the Soviet Union from 1947 onward. That policy, which aimed at blocking Soviet expansion until that nation collapsed from its own inefficiencies, was "neg-

This photograph of Abraham Lincoln by Mathew Brady was taken in February 1860 as he was coming to prominence as a potential Republican candidate for president.

In some respects, Andrew Johnson does not qualify as a Republican president, but this photograph conveys the stubbornness and sense of his own rightness that so often put him at odds with Republicans in Congress.

Ulysses S. Grant was a better president than he is given credit for, but his eight years in office were marred by scandals and the end of Reconstruction.

Rutherford B. Hayes, the victor in the disputed election of 1876, restored a sense of honesty to the White House despite the circumstances that brought him to the presidency.

The Republican National Convention, 1880: A photographer in the Gilded Age captured the crowded hall as the party met to nominate James A. Garfield for the presidency.

James A. Garfield represented one of the great might-have-beens of Republican history. His promising presidency was cut short by an assassin's bullet in 1881.

Chester Alan Arthur did better as president than even his friends expected, but illness and the lack of a political base limited him to finishing out Garfield's term.

The most popular Republican politician of the late nineteenth century, James G. Blaine lost a close presidential race to Grover Cleveland in 1884 but helped shape GOP policy toward the protective tariff.

"Little Ben," as President Benjamin Harrison was known, brought efficiency and a sense of purpose to the Republicans, but his one term was beset with problems. He is shown here in a campaign poster from 1888 at the upper left with his running mate, Levi Parsons Morton of New York.

Marcus A. Hanna, an Ohio industrialist, helped put William McKinley in the White House in 1896 and came to symbolize the party's ties to the new industrial order.

Republican presidential candidate William McKinley poses with women of the party during "Ladies' Day" in Canton, Ohio, in 1896; Ida McKinley sits to her husband's left.

Theodore Roosevelt provided youthful energy and vigor to the White House, but his regulatory policies strained Republican unity.

The portly and conservative William Howard Taft found it difficult to follow Roosevelt, and his one term was troubled and contentious.

The last bearded presidential candidate, Charles Evans Hughes proved to be a disappointment against Woodrow Wilson in 1916 and lost in a close race to the incumbent. This photograph was taken in 1906.

The Republican National Convention in 1920 was a heated affair. Multiple ballots were required to nominate Warren G. Harding for the presidency.

Warren G. Harding loved to play golf during his presidency. This photograph shows him out on the links.

Calvin Coolidge was famous as a man of few words, even on the telephone, but he kept the Republicans in power after the impact of Harding's scandals.

The Great Depression burdened the presidency of Herbert Hoover. Here he receives a ticket from the actress Mary Pickford for a benefit staged by Hollywood stars for the relief of the unemployed.

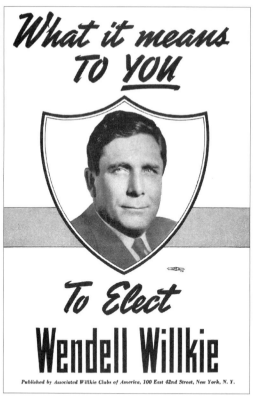

Wendell Willkie stormed to the Republican presidential nomination with the help of the Willkie clubs, which put out hundreds of documents such as this one.

President Dwight D. Eisenhower, having survived a heart attack in 1955, sits in the Oval Office in early 1956 as he contemplates a second run for the White House as the Republican candidate.

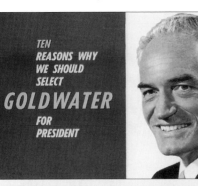

TEN
REASONS WHY
WE SHOULD
SELECT
GOLDWATER
FOR
PRESIDENT

WHY WE NEED SEN. BARRY GOLDWATER

1. Barry Goldwater is the unifying force for the GOP—the single most popular man in all sections of the country, north, south, east and west.
2. Barry Goldwater is an experienced lawmaker with 11 years service in the United States Senate, our Nation's most important legislative body.
3. Barry Goldwater has traveled widely and is a widely acclaimed expert in foreign affairs who will lead the Free World to greater unity and resolution in the Cold War.
4. Barry Goldwater is a fiscal conservative who believes in a balanced budget and a tax structure which will promote economic growth and individual initiative.
5. Barry Goldwater is a staunch defender of personal freedom and the rights of every American, regardless of race, creed or color.

6. Barry Goldwater is a practical businessman who successfully managed a business and met a payroll, even during the Depression.
7. Barry Goldwater is a World War II veteran and jet pilot—presently a major general in the U. S. Air Reserve—who knows we must remain militarily strong.
8. Barry Goldwater is a man devoted to his family, with a lovely wife and four children.
9. Barry Goldwater is an extraordinary all-American man — author, explorer, linguist, historian, pilot, photographer, "ham" radio operator, and athlete.
10. Barry Goldwater is a dedicated Party man who will actively support every Republican running for office at the local, state and Federal levels.

BARRY GOLDWATER IS THE REPUBLICAN OPPORTUNITY TO WIN IN 1964!

Barry Goldwater's nomination for the presidency in 1964 came about because of the grassroots efforts of the GOP's rank and file. Advertisements such as this one spread the conservative message about the Arizona senator.

In 1964, Senator Margaret Chase Smith was the first woman to make a serious attempt to gain the Republican presidential nomination. She is shown here arriving at the GOP convention in San Francisco.

Richard Nixon restored the Republicans to national power in the campaign of 1968. Here he and his wife, Pat, enjoy the cheers of an enthusiastic crowd.

Gerald Ford faced unique challenges as an unelected president after the Watergate scandal. His dignity and honesty in office won him popularity but could not provide him with a presidency in his own right in 1976.

Ronald Reagan was an ingratiating salesman for Republican ideas, and he charmed a hostile Washington press corps when they came to his office.

George Herbert Walker Bush is shown with his 1988 running mate, Dan Quayle, shortly after the announcement at the national convention in New Orleans that they would be the Republican ticket.

General Colin Powell was the most prominent African-American Republican in the party's history. Often spoken of as a potential vice presidential choice, he became the secretary of state in the administration of George W. Bush.

George W. Bush won the presidency after the disputed election in 2000 and took the party into the twenty-first century.

ative, futile and immoral" and with regard to Eastern Europe, the United States, "as one of its peaceful purposes, looks happily forward to the genuine independence of those captive peoples." The idea of "rolling back" Communism and freeing the Soviet satellites seemed much more appealing than merely containing the Soviets. Republicans also expected that once in office and in control of documents, they would find government records to confirm Roosevelt's alleged secret agreements at Yalta, finally revealing Democratic softness toward Communism during World War II.[57]

Yet once the Eisenhower administration was in power, it found that the containment policy was easier to denounce than to abandon. The archives contained no stunning secrets about Yalta. The concept of liberating the captive nations faded away in the face of the reality of Soviet power in that region. On defense policy, even though it was called the "New Look," the Eisenhower White House relied on nuclear weapons to deter the Soviets, much as Truman had done. Promising "massive retaliation" in the event of Soviet aggression did not answer the question of when such action was justified. Eisenhower did negotiate a truce in Korea based on the current military balance and an acceptance of a divided peninsula between North and South Korea. He also resisted efforts by the French to involve the United States in a direct military intervention in Vietnam in 1954 to avert a defeat at the fortress of Dien Bien Phu. When the Hungarians revolted against their Soviet masters in 1956, the United States accepted the presence of Russian tanks to crush the uprising. Republican critics of Eisenhower noted with dismay the continuity with the Truman years and expressed their disappointment that the government had not been more willing to have a showdown with Moscow.[58]

While Eisenhower worked hard to hold down government spending and achieve a balanced budget, he did not share the suspicion of Social Security that some conservative Republicans felt. As he told his brother Edgar, "Should any political party attempt to abolish social security and eliminate labor laws and farm programs, you would not hear of that party again in our political history." He was convinced that Social Security and unemployment insurance helped maintain national stability and economic health. For conservative Republicans who wanted to overturn the New Deal, Eisenhower seemed to offer a council of expediency rather than principle.[59]

Eisenhower had never liked the methods of Senator Joseph McCarthy but had tolerated them in 1952 in the interests of party harmony and his own election. When the Wisconsin senator continued his course of exposing alleged Communists after January 1953, Eisenhower bristled at tactics that embarrassed a Republican administration. Unwilling to get into a public confrontation or, as he put it, "to get into a pissing contest with that skunk," Eisenhower allowed the senator to hang himself. McCarthy did so by 1954 in the celebrated Army-McCarthy hearings over alleged subversion in the military. Viewers who saw McCarthy's badgering of witnesses and arguing with fellow senators found the senator a less attractive figure. When McCarthy attacked fellow Republicans, he went too far. The Senate rebuked McCarthy and ended his political influence. A broken, alcoholic McCarthy died three years later. The episode left scars on the right among those Republicans who believed that McCarthy had not gone far enough in rooting out subversives. Some even suggested that Eisenhower had served the Communist cause.[60]

Had Eisenhower's approach to the Republicans proved successful at the polls for candidates other than himself, he might have persuaded his Republican critics of the merits of his view of the electorate. Unfortunately for the president, the GOP suffered losses in the three congressional elections that followed Eisenhower's elevation to the presidency. In 1954, the Republicans lost eighteen seats in the House and one in the Senate as the Democrats reestablished control of Congress. Two years later, even though Eisenhower was reelected, the Republicans dropped another House seat and one in the Senate. The big loss for the GOP came in 1958 when their party suffered a fifty-eight-seat loss in the House and saw twelve Senate seats go into the opposition column. The Republicans would not regain majority status in the Senate for more than two decades and in the House for thirty-six years.

The first half of the 1950s reshaped American politics for the rest of the century. In foreign policy, the 1954 defeat of the French in Indochina and the division of that country into North and South Vietnam left the United States the main financial and military supporter of the anti-Communist regime in Saigon. Propping up that new government in South Vietnam increased American economic and diplomatic involvement in Southeast Asia, creating a new and more dangerous commitment in that region. During that same year, the Supreme Court ruled in the case of *Brown v. Board of Education* that racial segregation in public schools was unconstitutional. Soon the civil rights revolution introduced new opportunities and problems for the Republicans as white and black Americans responded to shifting racial attitudes.

The decade was prosperous as the baby boom and consumer spending lifted the economy. The spread of television transformed the nature of politics, placing greater emphasis on the personal appeal of the individual candidates and leaders. The role of the parties themselves lessened as independents became as common as Republicans and Democrats. By the end of the 1950s, the fears of internal Communism faded even as a resurgent Soviet Union posed greater global challenges. An era of apparent conformity, characterized by an apathetic younger generation, had taken root in the United States. Some social critics forecast an end to ideology and an era of political calm.

On the issue of civil rights, the Republicans received some credit from blacks for the *Brown* decision, but Eisenhower, who shared the southern view on race, did little to push integration during his first term. The Democrats retained their dominance in congressional races in the South even though Eisenhower did well personally in that region in 1956. Throughout the 1950s, the Republicans were still a sectional party, though the increasing Democratic identification with civil rights was opening the door for Republican gains a decade later.

To capitalize on Eisenhower's strength with southern white voters, the Republican National Committee created a southern arm of its organization and launched "Operation Dixie" in 1957 to expand the GOP base below the Mason-Dixon line. The initiative appealed to the expanding postwar white electorate of former Democrats defecting in the wake of their party's rising identification with black aspirations. The enhanced GOP presence in the South helped conservatives such as Barry Goldwater find an audience and future supporters. In the early 1960s, Operation Dixie provided the foundation for the emergence of the southern Republican Party during the presidency of John F. Kennedy.

REELECTING IKE: THE 1956 ELECTION

> Not since the Democratic convention of 1936 has a president dominated a political rally the way the president is dominating this one.
>
> —James Reston[61]

Any Republican ideological restiveness about Eisenhower as a party leader was well submerged in the 1956 presidential election. Eisenhower had suffered a heart attack in September 1955, but his recovery and his party's need for a strong candidate justified his decision to seek a second term in early 1956. The president toyed with the idea of replacing Richard Nixon on the ticket until it became clear that there was no acceptable alternative. Coolness between Nixon and Eisenhower lingered.[62]

At the national convention, the platform sang Eisenhower's praises while reflecting some elements of his desire to move the GOP away from its staunchly conservative posture. The delegates promised "to seek extension and perfection of a sound social security system" as well as a balanced budget and a "gradual reduction of the national debt." As they had done since 1940, the Republicans endorsed "the submission of a constitutional amendment providing equal rights for men and women." On the time-honored issue of the tariff, the party now said that "barriers which impede international trade and the flow of capital should be reduced on a gradual, selective and reciprocal basis, with full recognition of the necessity to safeguard domestic enterprises, agriculture, and labor against unfair import competition." Protectionism was slowly yielding to the new world of free trade. The delegates praised Eisenhower's record in the world that allowed "our people to enjoy the blessings of liberty and peace."[63]

The 1956 presidential race was never a real contest. Adlai Stevenson was again the Democratic nominee, but his campaign lacked focus and energy. When the Democratic candidate called for a ban on nuclear testing, Nixon and others denounced Stevenson's idea as impractical. Republicans said the proposal demonstrated that Eisenhower was a trusted world leader and Stevenson was not. Outside events, including the Hungarian Revolution and the Suez Canal crisis, convinced most voters that Eisenhower should remain at his job. The reluctance of the United States to get involved on the side of the rebellious Hungarians demonstrated, however, that "rolling back" Communism had been largely a rhetorical device. The result of the Eisenhower-Stevenson contest was a landslide victory that saw Eisenhower roll up 457 electoral votes and compile a margin of 9.5 million popular votes over Stevenson. More disappointing was the GOP's failure to regain control of Congress as the Democrats, benefiting from ticket-splitting for their candidates, made small gains in the House and Senate. Eisenhower proclaimed: "Modern Republicanism has now proved itself. And America has approved Modern Republicanism."[64]

After World War II, the Republicans had fought hard to win approval of the Twenty-second Amendment that limited all presidents to two elected terms. But in their zeal to prevent another Franklin D. Roosevelt, the GOP had also circumscribed itself. With no chance to run again, Eisenhower's political clout diminished when his lame-duck status became apparent. Although Eisenhower grew more conservative on budgetary issues during his second term, his efforts to reshape the Republicans proved more and more futile. Richard Nixon would inherit Eisenhower's mantle in 1960, but the party itself was beginning a move to the right that would repudiate Eisenhower's legacy during the 1960s.

Throughout the 1930s and 1940s, conservatism had not rested on a sustained philosophical basis. With the rise of the New Deal and the expansion of the federal government, Democrats in and out of politics contended that the programs and goals of the Roosevelt era were now a permanent part of American life. Liberalism, broadly defined, seemed to be the dominant ideological force driving American history. Liberals themselves might not have seen the situation in such positive terms given the reluctance of Congress to expand the New Deal. Nonetheless, the Democratic version of the political struggles of the first half of the twentieth century seemed firmly established as an integral part of American thought. Some historians contended that the actual differences between the two parties were small and trivial compared to the many issues on which a fundamental consensus existed.[65]

Conservatives dissented from this posture during the 1940s and 1950s. They regarded the New Deal as a sharp, revolutionary break with American traditions. Its programs, they maintained, had been destructive of the national character by fostering a dependence on money from Washington. As the United States confronted the threat of Communism after World War II, liberalism was attacked as a precursor of a Soviet takeover that softened up citizens for the collectivism to come. Conservatism came in many shapes and sizes in the postwar era. Some of its adherents attacked the income tax as the basis of national decline; others in the South regarded racial integration as evidence of the malign intentions of big government. Antiunion sentiment played a large role in business support for conservative periodicals. Conservatism also looked to the long-held suspicion of a powerful national government that went back to the days of Andrew Jackson and Thomas Jefferson.[66]

Whatever the motives, conservatism stirred and then gained momentum in the 1950s. William F. Buckley's *National Review,* founded in 1955, provided the nascent movement with a national voice through which contrasting views could be heard. On college campuses, recruiting for the Young Republicans proved fruitful. Further to the right, the John Birch Society, founded by Robert Welch in 1958, attracted followers for its militant anti-Communism and conspiratorial view of the world.[67]

Because of their rules that allowed representation at all levels of the party's conduct, a determined Republican faction could gain control of the grassroots machinery. The impact of these new conservative forces therefore began to be felt as the 1950s came to an end. Their presence did not yet threaten Richard Nixon's control of the 1960 presidential nomination, but the tension between Eisenhower's brand of conservatism and the more ideological brand on the right foreshadowed the party's struggles in the 1960s.

During his second term Eisenhower sought to move the GOP toward a greater acceptance of a strong presidency, more involvement overseas through foreign aid, and an enhanced willingness to have programs such as Social Security while still constraining their growth. At the same time, Eisenhower wanted this "Modern Republicanism" to remain true to the long-standing commitments for a balanced budget and a smaller federal government. As a military expert the president believed that defense spending could be held down through a close scrutiny of weapons systems and a reasonable appraisal of the Soviet threat. Republicans saw social spending as a better target for cuts. Eisenhower could not share information about the relative weakness of the Soviet Union that intelligence had amassed without disclosing his sources. As a result, he and his defense policy became vulnerable to attacks from both left and right as the 1950s wound down.[68]

The president's 1957 budget proposed $71.8 billion in spending, up some $2.8 billion over the previous year. Secretary of the Treasury George M. Humphrey urged Congress to make substantial cuts in the budget that Eisenhower had submitted. If expenditures were not pared back for years to come, he told reporters, "I predict you will have a depression that will curl your hair." The administration soon faced a Republican revolt, with leading senators denouncing the spending plans in the budget.[69]

The new champion of the resurgent right of the GOP was a first-term Arizona senator named Barry M. Goldwater. Elected in 1952, Goldwater was handsome, photogenic, and a compelling speaker before a friendly audience. Whether portrayed flying a jet or striding through the halls of Congress, Goldwater at age forty-eight imparted an energy and vigor to his cause. After he looked over Eisenhower's budget, he denounced the excessive spending that only confirmed how Eisenhower had been beguiled by "the siren song of socialism." Goldwater also rejected the support of New Deal programs that Eisenhower was advancing. More money was needed for national defense, he said, but funds for what he termed "squanderbust government" were out. The result was some congressional trimming of what Eisenhower had proposed before the budget passed.[70]

The ambiguities of Republican policy became evident in the early months of Eisenhower's second term. The civil rights law enacted that year, though a mild nod toward increased voting rights for African Americans, was a forward step for which the Republicans could claim some credit. The crisis over integration in Little Rock, Arkansas, later that year, however, set back Republican hopes in the South when Eisenhower used National Guard troops to enforce court decisions that allowed black students to attend Little Rock High School. The Soviet launch of the Sputnik satellite in the fall allowed Democrats to raise more questions about the state of the nation's defenses. Again, Eisenhower knew but could not say for security reasons that the United States was well ahead of the USSR in retaliatory power.

The bête noire of the right in the GOP in 1957–58 was organized labor and its political clout, most notably expressed through Walter Reuther and the United Auto Workers. In the

1958 elections, the Republicans advanced an antilabor theme across the country through an emphasis on "right-to-work" laws that prevented closed, union shops. The tactic backfired by galvanizing labor in key states. Adding to the Republican problems were the allegations of corruption against White House chief of staff Sherman Adams who had accepted gifts from a favor-seeking friend. The embattled aide stepped down a month before voters went to the polls.[71]

When the effects of a sharp recession were added to the political mix, Republican defeats in the sixth year of a two-term presidency were to be expected. Their scope, however, staggered the party. The loss of such conservative stalwarts as William F. Knowland and John W. Bricker underlined the sweeping nature of the setback. Goldwater won reelection to a second term, confirming his status as the darling of the conservatives. On the other side of the country, Nelson Rockefeller secured the governorship of New York and was recognized as a contender for 1960. Yet the likely nominee remained Richard Nixon who had piled up political credits while campaigning for party candidates during 1958.[72]

Nelson Rockefeller soon emerged as a wild card in the Republican contest, but in the process he alienated himself from the mainstream of the party. The distaste for the New York governor was not so much about his views, which tended to be conservative except on civil rights. The problem was that Rockefeller seemed to think that his money and celebrity appeal entitled him to leadership, and he made little secret of his disdain for the opinions of rank-and-file Republicans. Dominant in New York where his money and a divided Democratic Party helped him, Rockefeller was not a very good national politician. Along with indecision went a tin ear for Republican attitudes, and his casual approach to his marriage vows compounded his problems. But through an array of publicists and sympathetic journalists, he could make noise about Republican issues whenever he chose.[73]

After testing the waters and finding that Nixon had a lock on the nomination, Rockefeller announced in late December 1959 that he would not be seeking the Republican nomination in 1960. Rockefeller had no way of knowing that his best chance for getting the party's nod had now passed. His withdrawal cleared the way for Nixon, or so it seemed. But the first half of 1960 produced a series of crises that seemed to threaten the standing of the United States in the world. The shooting down of the U-2 spy plane, the failure of Eisenhower's summit with the Soviets, and Democratic complaints that the country was falling behind in defense because of a "missile gap" with the USSR put the Republicans on the defensive in an area that was usually their own. The Democratic front-runner, John Kennedy, was already sounding the theme of getting the nation "moving again."[74]

Into this volatile mix stepped Rockefeller in early June with the announcement that he was back in the race for the GOP nomination. He urged the party "to save the nation by saving itself." Selecting him, so the argument went, would put in the White House someone committed to rebuilding national defense and pushing civil rights. Rockefeller's strategy was Willkie-like. By making an issue of the convention's platform on foreign policy, he hoped to unsettle the race and sway the delegates to his cause. The approach made little sense. In the unlikely event that Nixon was to be stopped, the delegates would be much more inclined to switch to Goldwater who already had a good deal of latent support as a vice presidential candidate. So there was an air of unreality about Rockefeller's campaign.[75]

Faced with a Rockefeller insurgency whose power he overestimated, Nixon decided to make concessions to his putative rival. The two men met at Rockefeller's lavish apartment in New York City on July 22, 1960, and produced a joint declaration that became known as the "Compact of Fifth Avenue." In it, Nixon came out for an increase in defense spending to meet the Soviet challenge, implicitly accepting the criticisms of Eisenhower's stewardship in foreign affairs. Nixon backed other social causes, including a plan seeking vigorous support for civil rights and black protesters who had begun "sit-ins" at lunch counters across the South.[76]

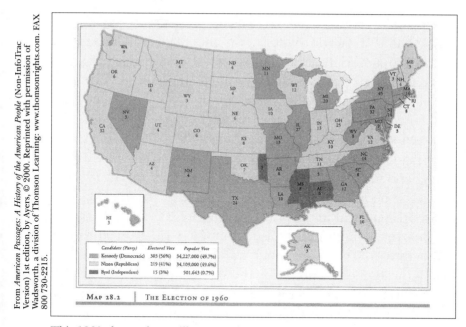

Candidate (Party)	Electoral Vote	Popular Vote
Kennedy (Democratic)	303 (56%)	34,227,000 (49.7%)
Nixon (Republican)	219 (41%)	34,109,000 (49.6%)
Byrd (Independent)	15 (3%)	501,643 (0.7%)

Map 28.2 | The Election of 1960

This 1960 electoral map illustrates the closeness of the Nixon-Kennedy race.

The outreach to Rockefeller backfired. It irritated Eisenhower, who did not appreciate having his defense policy repudiated. More important, it infuriated Barry Goldwater and his conservative base. Goldwater declared that what Rockefeller and Nixon had agreed to, if it became part of the platform, "will live in history as the Munich of the Republican party." A rebellion brewed among southern delegates over civil rights. Nixon decided that retaining Eisenhower's support was more important than southern electoral votes. The nominee dropped the criticism of Eisenhower and agreed to make the civil rights plank more assertive.[77]

GOLDWATER, NIXON, AND THE 1960 ELECTION

This great Republican party is our historic house. This is our home.

—Barry Goldwater[78]

A compromise was worked out that allowed everyone involved to rally behind a facade of unity on the platform. Rockefeller dropped out officially, Nixon received the nomination, and a divisive floor fight was avoided. A united Republican Party presented a positive face to the voters. But there was one unscripted, spontaneous moment that cast a spotlight on the Republican future. On Wednesday night of the convention, when nominations were made, Barry Goldwater's name was placed before the delegates. The Arizona senator then rose to make a speech of withdrawal; it became the first move in the 1964 presidential race and a pivotal event in the history of the GOP.

Before a tumultuous crowd, Goldwater proclaimed that as conservatives "This great Republican party is our historic house. This is our home." Denouncing the Democrats as a "party which has lost its belief in the dignity of man," he urged that Nixon be elected. In his closing, Goldwater told the throng: "Let's grow up, conservatives. If we want to take this Party back, and I think we can someday, let's get to work." Goldwater did not say from whom the Republican Party should be reclaimed, but he meant Rockefeller and by extension Richard Nixon. For Goldwater the task was to make a conservative political party even more conservative.[79]

The presidential election of 1960 was the most exciting and closely contested race for the popular vote of the second half of the twentieth century. Nixon's narrow defeat at the hands of Jack Kennedy has produced a number of plausible explanations for the Republican setback. Had Nixon pulled out a victory, the course of American history could have been very different, but a train of circumstances frustrated the Republican nominee in his first race for the White House.

Eisenhower delivered the opening rebuff to Nixon in August. Asked at a press conference several times how Nixon had contributed to the decisions of the administration, the president deflected his questioners. Finally, a reporter at the end of the session sought "an example of a major idea of his that you had adopted." Eisenhower replied, "If you give me a week, I might think of one. I don't remember." The comment, which may have reflected some of Eisenhower's private doubts about his vice president, dogged Nixon throughout the campaign.[80]

Nixon also faced problems of his own doing. Overconfident about his debating abilities, he agreed to four televised encounters with his Democratic opponent. The first debate, in which Nixon was both recovering from the effects of illness and poorly prepared in terms of makeup and overall readiness, elevated Kennedy to an equal status with his Republican rival. The two men did equally well in the remaining debates, but the political damage to Nixon had been done.

Promising to campaign in all fifty states, Nixon spread his energies too thin and never developed a clear electoral strategy for winning. The choice of Henry Cabot Lodge as his running mate also was whimsical. Lodge was not going to help Nixon in Massachusetts, which Kennedy was sure to carry, and Lodge's patrician style of campaigning was lazy and self-indulgent.

Still, despite all the advantages that Kennedy had, including more favorable press coverage, Nixon very nearly won. Last-minute campaigning from Eisenhower, a strong late campaign by the candidate himself, and doubts about Kennedy's youth and Catholicism tightened the race at the end. Nixon came within one percentage point and 118,000 popular votes of beating Kennedy. The Democrat captured 303 electoral votes to 219 for Nixon. In his memoirs a generation later, Nixon blamed the press, especially television, for his unfavorable coverage. The Kennedys themselves also stirred his wrath. The Republicans were "faced by an organization that had equal dedication and unlimited money, that was led by the most ruthless group of political operators ever mobilized for a presidential campaign." He resented the way that, in his mind, the Democrats had capitalized on the issue of Kennedy's religion. Any criticism of Kennedy's relationship to the Catholic Church was denounced as bigotry, but the Democratic candidate also stressed his faith in appealing to his coreligionists.[81]

These elements entered into the equation, but they did not

account for Nixon's failure to focus his campaign on a winning strategy, make the case for the need to extend the Eisenhower record, and present his message in a clear and forceful manner. Conservative Republicans also thought that Nixon had not given the party's base a reason to turn out and vote for him. Oddly enough, these same Republicans believed that Nixon should have used Eisenhower more as a campaigner, especially on foreign policy, when it was the president's record on which Nixon was campaigning and that the conservatives disdained.

Years later, during the aftermath of the disputed 2000 election, Nixon gained plaudits as a statesman for not encouraging Republican efforts in November and December 1960 to challenge Kennedy's victory. The reality was less simple. Nixon did not concede defeat until three days after the election, and Republicans pressed inquiries into the Illinois and Texas votes. The Republican probe came up short in Illinois, which made any further inquiry into the Texas result moot. Nixon needed to change the result in both states to shift the outcome.[82]

The defeat in 1960, while frustrating to the Republicans, did not represent a decisive setback. So anemic had been Kennedy's coattails that the Democrats lost a few seats in the House and Senate. Thus, the new president came to Washington without a mandate for his ambitious agenda of domestic change and foreign policy activism. Nixon's loss and the eclipse of Rockefeller left a vacuum in the party that the conservative troops enamored of Barry Goldwater intended to fill in 1964. The process of taking back the Republican Party for conservatism was under way days after Nixon's concession. A new and tumultuous era in the history of the GOP had opened.

Chapter 10

FROM GOLDWATER TO WATERGATE, 1961–1974

MANY IN SAN Francisco's Cow Palace on that July evening in 1964 had been waiting for this moment for four years and more. Through precinct conventions and county caucuses, they had pledged themselves to the cause of conservatism and its Republican champion, Senator Barry Goldwater of Arizona. The eastern press had called them extremists, and Governor Nelson Rockefeller of New York had denounced them just a few days earlier. But they knew that their cause was right and that Barry would carry them to victory in November against the socialistic policies of the hated Lyndon Johnson and the Democrats. The delegates on the floor and the passionate throng in the galleries had seen Goldwater nominated. Now it was time for the acceptance speech that would be a prelude to the White House.

In other years at other Republican conventions, unity had been the theme after the nominee was chosen. Conservatives had been made to swallow Wendell Willkie, Thomas E. Dewey twice, Dwight D. Eisenhower twice, and then Richard Nixon. Even when Eisenhower had led them to victory, winning seemed to come at the price of principle. Eisenhower had promised a crusade to take back America for conservative ideals and instead delivered the "modern Republicanism" that Goldwater and his followers detested. Richard Nixon had rebuffed Goldwater and then lost to John F. Kennedy in another "me-too" campaign that failed to be conservative enough. But those days were over, and conservatives believed their time had come at last.

The business of the final night of the convention was done quickly. Goldwater's personal pick for vice president, Congressman William E. Miller of New York, was nominated almost unanimously. Richard Nixon then introduced Goldwater, and the Republican nominee strode to the podium. Handsome, spectacled, and determined, Goldwater had not come to conciliate his party's defeated moderates or to reach out to undecided voters across the country in the biggest audience he would ever command. He had stepped forward to issue a call to arms to the conservative faithful in the hall and the armies of like-minded Republicans across the country.

And so he did. Like an Old Testament prophet, Goldwater urged the nation to return to the tried-and-true America that he believed had disappeared since the New Deal. The United States must not "stagnate in the swampland of collectivism" or "cringe before the bully of Communism." Democrats had let the nation's defenses weaken and allowed a billion people to be "cast into Communist captivity." The key element in Goldwater's address came near the end in two sentences that summed up his appeal and foreshadowed his electoral fate several months later. "I would remind you that extremism in the defense of liberty is no vice," he said as the applause responded. Then, after a pause, he added, "And let me remind you that moderation in the pursuit of justice is no virtue."[1]

The crowd cheered lustily as Goldwater began his campaign to oust Lyndon Johnson from the presidency. Though the Republican went down to defeat in November 1964, the Republican Party of the second half of the twentieth century had been born. The course of its development would not be smooth nor its progress without setbacks. Nonetheless, the Goldwater speech marked a pivotal juncture after which the Republican

"I HAVE *NEVER* SEEN HIM SO HAPPY."

Animosity toward the press and the television networks was an important aspect of the Barry Goldwater campaign. This John Fischetti cartoon from 1964 emphasizes the feelings of the Goldwater supporters about their journalistic enemies.

Party moved ever rightward. As one commentator said after Goldwater had lost, "The GOP will either go forward as the conservative party or it will disappear, and conservatism will be forced to create another vehicle."[2] The move to the right begun in 1912 and accelerated thereafter had not dispensed with all the moderate or even liberal elements from the party. After 1964, however, the ideological center of gravity of the party moved ever rightward as Republicans explored the legacy of Barry Goldwater and his loyal legions.

THE CHANGING POLITICAL LANDSCAPE OF THE 1960S

The center that had more or less held in the late 1950s cracked in the 1960s, exposing a glaring, often unapologetic polarization that seemed astonishing to contemporaries.

—James T. Patterson[3]

At the beginning of the 1960s, the United States was prosperous, powerful, and troubled. After a decade and a half of the Cold War, the balance of nuclear terror between the United States and the Soviet Union had preserved the peace, but the nation was uncertain about the future of its relations with the Soviet Union. Across the world it appeared as though Communist countries were aggressively challenging American security. Cuba had become a Communist-bloc bastion under Fidel Castro during the late 1950s. South Vietnam grappled with a Communist insurgency sponsored by North Vietnam, and other Southeast Asian nations, such as Laos and Cambodia, faced similar threats. A new president, John F. Kennedy, who took office in January 1961, warned that the United States faced "the hour of maximum danger" and a "long twilight struggle with Communism."[4]

At home the civil rights revolution gained momentum as sit-ins and "freedom rides" attested to the growing discontent of African Americans. The rising tide of black aspirations stirred resentment and fears among whites who saw their way of life and hard-won economic gains imperiled. In colleges and universities, students on the left and right chafed against authority, sought personal fulfillment through political action, and prepared to march. Conservatives formed the Young Americans for Freedom in 1960–61; Students for a Democratic Society followed in 1962 with the Port Huron Statement that expressed their alienation from the emptiness of American affluence. But by and large the status quo prevailed. For most college students in the early 1960s, draft calls for the men were low, marriage and family were the prescribed routes for the women, and life in suburbia seemed the eventual destiny.[5]

While social upheaval dominated in the South because of civil rights, the early 1960s were not characterized by the great tumult that would mark the rest of the decade. The fad for rock and roll seemed to have passed, and folk music shaped the rhythms of summers. That the nation might soon be torn apart politically and culturally would have appeared improbable in the months before John F. Kennedy's assassination. The 1950s consensus about politics lived on as Republicans and Democrats remained evenly balanced in their electoral alignments. Social thinkers debated whether ideology had ended as a force in American politics.

THE REPUBLICANS DURING THE NEW FRONTIER

The aggressive post-war club of conservative young Republicans from the small states of the West and South are seizing power, displacing the Eastern party chiefs who have dictated Republican policy and candidates for a generation.

—Rowland Evans and Robert Novak[6]

The Republican Party looked the same outwardly in the aftermath of Nixon's defeat in 1960, but beneath the surface the nature of the GOP was shifting. The party's establishment, rooted mainly in the East, saw its power and influence ebb as the Republican center of gravity moved to the South and West. To some extent the core of the rightward trend lay in the Sunbelt states. Whites who had migrated to California, Arizona, and the old Confederacy after World War II hated Communism, distrusted the federal government, wanted to protect their stake in society, and feared for the moral future of the nation. A desire to counter the civil rights struggles of Latinos and African Americans underlay a sizable proportion of the conservative endorsement of states' rights and limited government as well. Belief in the values of Christianity and a virtuous lifestyle also impelled the new adherents of conservatism in the early 1960s.[7]

Barry Goldwater's ghostwritten book, *The Conscience of a Conservative* (1961), embodied conservative Republicanism in the early 1960s. It sold millions of copies and inspired a generation of young people to adopt the causes that the senator espoused. Before the demands of the campaign trail in 1963–64 tempered his rhetoric, Goldwater offered a heady appeal of

drastic change. "I have little interest in streamlining government or making it more efficient for I mean to reduce its size. I
do not undertake to promote welfare for I propose to extend
freedom. My aim is not to pass laws but to repeal them." The
Arizona senator called federal matching funds for the states the
equivalent of bribery, asked that farm subsidies be ended, and
sought the dismantling of the income tax and annual reductions
of ten percent in the federal budget. Social Security was also a
questionable idea that at best should be voluntary.[8]

Goldwater declared that the Communists were winning because timid liberals were fearful of standing up to the USSR. As
a result, the Soviet Union was on the march as liberals made concession after concession. Goldwater was skeptical of the United
Nations, arms control, and the idea that nuclear weapons had established a balance of terror in the world. Winning a war, even
one with nuclear arms, was the main point for the United States,
and the American people should be willing to take risks for
peace. In the end, the Soviets would back down before the threat
of a resolute United States.[9]

A central element of Goldwater's creed was his stance on civil
rights. Since he had quietly supported the rights of African
Americans in his native Arizona, including contributions to the
National Association for the Advancement of Colored People, he
was confident that he was not guilty of racism—a conviction
he shared with many whites in the 1960s. If the senator endorsed, as he did, states' rights and the power of the people of
the South and Southwest to make segregation the law in their
states, then Goldwater believed that the freedom to do so was a
higher value than black equality. That stance had a powerful
pull for white voters in the South who identified the national
Democratic Party more and more with the interests of African
Americans. Goldwater had once said that in seeking votes the
Republicans should go hunting "where the ducks are," and
southern whites, particularly males, would prove to be a key element in the new Republican electoral coalition.[10]

In the first three years of the 1960s, Goldwater had become

the charismatic figure of the Republican right that they had long sought. But Goldwater's firm beliefs precluded the possibility of compromise, and Goldwater himself rarely examined the premises of his own convictions. Political campaigns in Arizona in 1952 and 1958 had not tested his skills on the stump, and friendly newspaper reporters had never pressed him to define his policy positions. As a result, Goldwater was a novice as a national candidate when he began his race for the White House. While he could dish out the hot rhetoric that pleased his audiences, it was not clear how he would do when the Democrats attacked him.

Pushing Goldwater in the early 1960s was a broad alliance of conservative activists that ranged from William F. Buckley through the young party members on college campuses to fringe groups such as the John Birch Society. The society was named after a Baptist missionary in China and sometime American agent whose death at the hands of Communists in 1945 was, to founder Robert Welch, at least, proof of the extent of the State Department's culpability in the ultimate loss of China to the Reds. Welch's organization was very popular among rank-and-file conservatives, but his views troubled conventional members of the right. When Welch charged that Eisenhower was not just a dupe of the Communists but an active Soviet agent, he alienated the *National Review* and other usually sympathetic allies. Yet the Republicans could not disavow the Birchers completely without losing supporters and contributors. The charge of extremism that clung to Welch and his society would prove to be a significant weakness for conservatives in the political battles of the early 1960s.[11]

While historians of John F. Kennedy's presidency have stressed his caution on domestic issues, his mixed record with Congress, and the limited nature of his program, the Republicans, particularly conservatives, depicted the New Frontier as a continuation of the Democratic charge into collectivism. In foreign policy they criticized Kennedy's failure at the Bay of Pigs to provide sustained air cover for the anti-Castro Cubans in April

1961. Goldwater and other Republicans contended that the 1,500-man invasion would have defeated the 240,000 Cuban defenders if sufficient American airpower had been employed. A year and a half later, during the Cuban Missile Crisis, Republicans pressed for more aggressive action against the Soviet forces on Castro's island and felt that Kennedy's agreement to the dismantling of Soviet missiles in Cuba fell short of a firm solution to the nuclear crisis. American involvement in Vietnam and the ostensible failure to pursue victory there was another target for Republican criticism.[12]

The first chance for the GOP to test the popularity of the Kennedy administration came in the 1962 congressional elections. The party was not in robust shape from an organizational standpoint. The debt from Nixon's 1960 campaign persisted, and the party's leadership in Congress, Senator Everett Dirksen of Illinois and Congressman Charles Halleck of Indiana, were not effective in their televised "Ev and Charlie Show" before the cameras. Richard Nixon, the titular party leader, was making an unsuccessful race for governor of California. The former vice president, assuming that Kennedy would win in 1964, looked upon the California statehouse as a base for a possible try at the White House in 1968. Still, the party anticipated gains in the off-year contests until the Cuban Missile Crisis revived the Democrats. The results were disappointing on the national level for the GOP since the Democrats held down their losses in the House to two seats and gained four seats in the Senate.[13]

Conservative Republicans took heart from the results in key individual contests. Nixon's loss in California removed him from the 1964 nomination derby. In New York, Nelson Rockefeller won reelection, but his margin was reduced by the presence on the ballot of a Conservative Party candidate who took votes away from the incumbent. Meanwhile, in the South where Operation Dixie was still functioning, Republicans gained five House seats, came close to winning a Senate seat in Alabama, and did well in the losing battle for governor of Texas. With anger mounting among white voters at Kennedy's civil rights policies, the prospects for the Republicans in 1964 seemed limitless, especially if Senator Goldwater faced off against Kennedy.[14]

While Goldwater gained strength, Nelson Rockefeller fatally wounded his own candidacy. In the spring of 1963, he divorced his wife of more than three decades and a month later wed Margaretta "Happy" Murphy, herself a recent divorcee with four young children. For mainline Republicans mindful of what a later generation would call family values, Rockefeller's actions exemplified eastern liberalism at its worst. Although with typical obtuseness he stayed in the race for the nomination, his chances were extinguished. Other potential moderate candidates, such as Governors George Romney of Michigan and William Scranton of Pennsylvania, were much talked about in the press but lagged well behind Goldwater at the party's base.[15]

Goldwater was the beneficiary of one of the most efficient and well-organized grassroots efforts in modern American politics. The campaign to gather delegates was orchestrated by a New Yorker named F. Clifton White who operated out of Suite 3505 in a Washington office building. Short of cash but not of dedication, the Draft Goldwater Committee set up enthusiastic rallies and courted potential delegates. When Goldwater, doubtful about his chances, hesitated to become a presidential candidate in January 1963, one supporter told the core group around White: "There's only one thing we *can* do. Let's draft the son of a bitch."[16]

The Republican Party in 1963–64 was readily responsive to the draft-Goldwater effort. The Republican National Committee was now chaired by Congressman William E. Miller of upstate New York, who supported Goldwater's cause. Throughout the rest of the party, from the Young Republicans to the National Federation of Republican Women, conservative activists had come to the meetings, elected their members of key committees, and drafted pro-Goldwater resolutions. Moderate Republicanism, which looked so imposing both in terms of governors in the East and Middle West and in opinion polls, was actually a hollowed-out shell. The days when money men from New York and the dictates of eastern newspapers would prevail in choosing Republican candidates were about to end.

So confident were the Goldwater leaders and followers that they boasted that President Kennedy could be defeated in 1964 if their champion won the Republican nomination. Had Kennedy lived, a race with Goldwater would have been much closer than the Lyndon Johnson–Goldwater match-up. Goldwater would have run stronger in the South and would probably have carried Texas, for example. Yet his problems as a national campaigner would still have made him vulnerable to Kennedy's superior skills as a candidate.

In any case, Kennedy's murder on November 22, 1963, changed the political equation for the Republicans and impaired Goldwater's chances for victory. In the long run, Lyndon Johnson would prove to be an inept leader of his party, but from late 1963 through November 1964, sympathy arising from Kennedy's death, his mastery of Congress, and his command of the foreign policy apparatus appeared to make Johnson the proponent of prosperity at home, the heir of Roosevelt, Truman, and Kennedy, and the preserver of peace abroad.

After some initial hesitation about whether he still wanted to run in 1964, Goldwater made his formal declaration from his home in Phoenix on January 3, 1964. He promised "a choice, not an echo" against Lyndon Johnson and Democratic liberalism. The American people should not become "just cogs in a vast government machine." Upon his announcement, Goldwater trailed Johnson badly in the major public opinion polls. The president had already put the GOP on the defensive with his legislative activism and ambitious program for a civil rights bill, a tax cut, and soon a war on poverty. Goldwater, however, regarded Johnson as an unworthy opponent and a politician "who never cleaned the crap off his boots."[17]

The opening months of the 1964 campaign produced mixed results for Goldwater's candidacy. In the contest for convention delegates, his bandwagon rolled on, picking up votes in the South, Middle West, and West with striking efficiency. As he went out to meet the voters in person and came under intense press scrutiny for the first time, his defects as a candidate emerged. While Goldwater could work hard when he wished, he lacked the discipline to stay on message in this early phase. These inconsistencies tended to confirm the senator's self-evaluation to a newsman in August 1963: "You know, I haven't got a really first-class brain." He could have avoided the New Hampshire primary, but he decided to make a test of his strength there. The Arizonan campaigned hard but produced some damaging gaffes that haunted him for the rest of the year.[18]

Goldwater liked to speak off the cuff and answer questions informally. That had worked for him in Arizona where the obliging press had tidied up his awkward prose and smoothed out his mistakes. Now the reporters began to print most of what he said. In answer to a question in New Hampshire, he said that Social Security ought to become a voluntary program. "If a person can provide better for himself, let him do it. But if he prefers the government to do it, let him." Conservatives at the time and since have contended that it was mistaken to assume, as opposing newspapers immediately did, that Goldwater wanted to end Social Security. Leaving aside Goldwater's imprecise language, there remained the point that if Social Security was made voluntary, its character as a system of old-age insurance would be fundamentally altered. To offer that idea as a casual response to an inquiry illustrated Goldwater's amateurish approach to a presidential campaign in early 1964.[19]

A similar slip occurred over the candidate's stand on nuclear weapons. While Goldwater's ideas about the North Atlantic Treaty Organization commanders having the authority to use nuclear weapons in the case of a Soviet attack reflected government policy, the senator discussed the issue in a way that suggested a rather cavalier attitude toward the matter. By raising the question in the context that he did, Goldwater enabled first Rockefeller and later Lyndon Johnson to depict him as unreliable and intemperate on the topic of nuclear weapons. The later complaints by Goldwater defenders that these charges were unfair obscure the harder political truth that allowing opponents to define a candidacy is no way to win an election.[20]

Goldwater lost the New Hampshire primary to Henry Cabot Lodge, the American ambassador to South Vietnam, who gained from a deft write-in campaign organized by two young supporters. That slip in Goldwater's fortunes did not interrupt the senator's progress toward the nomination. The climactic encounter with the flagging campaign of Nelson Rockefeller came in early June in the California primary. Rockefeller had won the Oregon contest in which Goldwater did not participate. If the New York governor could defeat his conservative rival in that large state, he might disrupt Goldwater's momentum enough to deadlock the convention. Given the passion with which the delegates favored Goldwater, if his candidacy had been stopped, the convention would never have endorsed Rockefeller. The New Yorker had become little more than a potential spoiler.

In a hard-fought primary, Rockefeller's money met Goldwater's volunteers in an ugly contest. Both sides hurled charges at the other. Rockefeller had a slight edge in the polls as the voting neared, but then the picture changed during the days just before the election. His new wife gave birth to their first child, recalling the Rockefeller divorce, especially when the New Yorker left the state to be with Happy and the new baby. Goldwater partisans asked, "Do You Want a Leader or a Lover in the White House?" Goldwater's victory was narrow, with only 68,000 votes separating the two men. Nonetheless, he had beaten Rockefeller and was now on a clear path to the nomination at the national convention.[21]

Faced with the prospects of Goldwater's nomination, moderate Republicans had no credible alternative to challenge him. Professionals regarded the candidacy of Senator Margaret Chase Smith of Maine, the first woman to seek the GOP nomination, as only an amusing sideshow. But the men running to stop Goldwater were hardly more believable contenders. Between the California primary and the national convention in mid-

July, abortive stop-Goldwater efforts from Pennsylvania governor William Scranton proved futile. The Goldwater delegates were not to be shaken loose from their man, especially not at the eleventh hour by an eastern moderate. Despite qualms about Goldwater's chances in the fall, the effective opposition to him dwindled as the convention in San Francisco's Cow Palace neared.[22]

GOLDWATER AND CIVIL RIGHTS

The structure of the federal system, with its fifty separate state units, has long permitted this nation to nourish local differences, even local cultures.

—Barry Goldwater[23]

While Goldwater was locking up the nomination, events in Congress posed a test for his leadership and for his party in response to the rising tide of the civil rights movement. The Kennedy administration had proposed a bill in the summer of 1963 that provided access to public accommodations for all Americans regardless of race. After Kennedy's death, Lyndon Johnson made civil rights a keystone of his legislative program. Passage in the House came with the crucial support of 138 Republicans. Then Johnson insisted that the Senate act on the measure in 1964. The White House pushed hard to break the filibuster of southern senators against the measure. Everett Dirksen assembled a majority of Republican senators whose votes were indispensable to ultimate passage. By the summer of 1964 it was evident that the bill was going to become law.[24]

Goldwater had supported the civil rights laws of 1957 and 1960, but he stopped short on the 1964 proposal. The Arizonan believed, based on the opinions of legal advisers such as William Rehnquist and Yale professor Robert Bork, that the measure was unconstitutional. As a result, Goldwater decided that he would vote against the law on final passage in the Senate. "The problems of discrimination cannot be cured by laws alone," he told his colleagues. States' rights prevented the government from interfering with local issues such as race relations, Goldwater maintained.[25]

Goldwater's position mixed conviction and expediency. His hopes of winning the presidency hinged on a strong showing in the South where he hoped to get the largest share of votes needed to prevail in the electoral college. This judgment represented an important shift in the party's strategy for presidential contests and would anticipate subsequent Republican campaigns. A vote for the civil rights law would doom his chances and leave the South in Johnson's hands. With Governor George C. Wallace of Alabama, an avowed segregationist, embarrassing the Democrats with his presidential campaign in their primaries, talk of a "white backlash" against civil rights suggested that opposition to civil rights might not be bad politics in the North, either. Moreover, a dislike of an intrusive federal government brought conservative Republicans into an alliance with defecting southern Democrats and restive ethnic Democrats in the North, fearful of desegregation in their all-white neighborhoods, that offered rich prospects for the GOP.[26]

Citing Goldwater's financial support for the National Association for the Advancement of Colored People in Phoenix and his role in desegregating the Air National Guard in that state, as well as the senator's declared lack of racial prejudice, Goldwater's biographers attribute his opposition to the 1964 law to constitutional principle, not race. Fear of an oppressive federal government telling the states what to do in private matters was Goldwater's worry. In time the South would see the error of segregation. Until then, patience and noninterference were the proper approaches.

Black Americans and Democratic critics found Goldwater's logic flawed since he clearly placed greater emphasis on the rights and opinions of white southerners than the fair treatment of African Americans in public places and employment. Goldwater and his allies had made an electoral calculus. There were more white votes to be gained by opposing the civil rights law than black votes to be lost. As Lyndon Johnson told Bill Moyers after the law was enacted, "I think we just delivered the South to the Republican party for a long time to come." The balance did not go the Republicans' way in 1964, but in the years that followed, the GOP gathered in a rich harvest of ballots in the South and elsewhere from white Americans who prized social order. Like the Democrats in the nineteenth century, the Republicans found that states' rights, calls for limited government, and lower taxes had an enduring appeal. To what extent that also meant making the GOP the party of white Americans remained to be seen in the years that followed. The percentage of black Americans who identified themselves as Republicans skidded from twenty-three percent four years earlier to twelve percent on Election Day 1964.[27]

The Republican National Convention proved two points beyond question. Goldwater and his conservative supporters had gained control of the Republican Party. More important, they intended to win or lose the presidency on their own terms. The convention was well controlled by the Goldwater managers through an elaborate system of telephones and walkie-talkies. Despite this conservative discipline, the delegates and galleries let a national television audience know about their passion for their cause. They cheered when Dwight D. Eisenhower attacked the news media in passing, and they booed Nelson Rockefeller when he spoke on behalf of a platform plank denouncing extremism. The plank was defeated, but the way Rockefeller was treated backfired against the Goldwaterites.[28]

The Republican platform, as adopted by the delegates, backed away from the 1960 document on civil rights by promising on the one hand "full implementation and faithful execution" of the new civil rights law while at the same time asserting that the elimination "of any such discrimination is a matter of heart, conscience, and education, as well as of equal rights under law." The delegates supported an amendment to allow prayer in public places, endorsed Social Security "with improved benefits to our people," and sought a reduction of at least $5 billion in government spending. In foreign policy the GOP opposed the admission of Communist China to the United Nations, promised victory in South Vietnam, and pledged to "never unilaterally disarm America." While couched in conservative language, the Goldwater platform was less confrontational than some of the delegates might have wished in that it did not seek abolition of Social Security, denunciation of civil rights, and repudiation of other New Deal measures.[29]

Conciliation or even electoral success was not Goldwater's priority, as evidenced by his choice of a running mate and his acceptance speech. The selection of Congressman William E. Miller, the chair of the Republican National Committee, was made primarily on the grounds that his slashing political oratory would, in Goldwater's phrase, drive Lyndon Johnson "nuts." Miller added little to the ticket, despite his Catholicism. Goldwater had no hope of carrying New York, Miller's home state, and the congressman proved an indifferent campaigner. The nominee would have been better advised to have selected a figure from a border state or the Middle West, but Goldwater made his choice without consulting any major party leaders.[30]

The acceptance speech provided Goldwater with a last chance to woo Republican moderates back to his camp and to convince independent voters that he was not the demon that had appeared in the media since January. Goldwater was understandably angry about the treatment he had received from the press and other Republicans. Some commentators had questioned his mental balance, and others had attacked his intelligence. As a result, Goldwater saw the speech not as a time to heal wounds but as a moment to chart "a new course in GOP national politics." So the rhetoric of the speech was intensified. Unlike the inclusive Ronald Reagan sixteen years later, Goldwater's approach did not increase the chances of winning the White House. He and his speechwriters, particularly Professor Harry Jaffa of Claremont McKenna College, wanted to send a message to the American political world. Thus, the famous statement about "extremism in the pursuit of liberty" became the way Goldwater's acceptance speech will always be remembered.[31]

Seasoned politicians such as Richard Nixon understood that the Republican nominee, often unfairly attacked about his alleged ties to the John Birch Society, had handed his enemies a rhetorical gift. Not only did Goldwater fail to close the rifts in the party and heal its wounds, Nixon recalled, "he opened new wounds and then rubbed salt in them." The Goldwater campaign deflated as soon as the words were delivered. One reporter in the crowd said, "My God, he's going to run as Barry Goldwater." Patrick Buchanan, the father of Nixon's speechwriter, was more terse: "He's finished." The Republican candidate had provided the opposition with evidence to support their charges that Goldwater himself harbored extreme views. That the Democrats and moderate Republicans used Goldwater's words against him was hardly surprising.[32]

While some Republicans loyally stayed with the national ticket, others made clear that they were either not voting for Goldwater or providing only token support for his candidacy. The Johnson administration found it easy to recruit Republicans for financial support and as members of Republicans for Johnson organizations. While the moderates defected, Goldwater moved his friends into key positions within the GOP and the Republican National Committee. Arizonans whom the presidential candidate had known for years ran the campaign and excluded outsiders. Even among conservatives the Goldwater forces proved less inclusive than was prudent. Goldwater was never comfortable with those outside of his inner circle. The resulting campaign was very insular and ineffective.[33]

GOLDWATER VERSUS JOHNSON

You know in your hearts that something is wrong in our land. . . .

—Barry Goldwater[34]

As a contest the 1964 race for the presidency was one-sided in its results and ugly in its tone. Little in the campaign itself affected the final outcome. Lyndon Johnson enjoyed a big lead in the polls over Goldwater in August 1964, and that advantage expanded into a landslide Johnson victory in November. Everything seemed to go Johnson's way. The Tonkin Gulf episode in August, when confusing naval encounters between North Vietnamese and American ships occurred in the waters off North Vietnam, enabled the incumbent to appear both strong in defending American interests and moderate in his response to what was portrayed as Communist action to challenge the United States. For a public that did not want war in Southeast Asia but sought a defense of American rights, Johnson's actions appeared to be appropriate. The arrest of a key White House aide, Walter Jenkins, on a morals charge in October did not give the Republicans any leverage in claiming that Johnson headed a corrupt administration.[35]

The importance of the contest lay in its enduring effects on American politics for the next three decades. The defection of moderate Republicans from the Goldwater-Miller ticket assured continuing conservative dominance of the party once the election results were counted. Whatever moderate Republicanism was, that faction of the party had both shrunk and shifted rightward at the same time to remain within the party. Although Goldwater lost in a national rout, he established a more permanent base for the GOP in the South. The Republican candidate carried Alabama, Georgia, Louisiana, Mississippi, and South Carolina, and ran well in Florida and the rest of the Deep South even in states that he lost. In South Carolina, Senator Strom Thurmond made a public conversion to the GOP that proved significant for the party in the future. The process by which the South became a GOP bastion took time to unfold, but Lyndon Johnson correctly anticipated the impact of the Democratic adherence to civil rights and the Goldwater candidacy on the political allegiance of the states of the old Confederacy.

The Goldwater-Johnson contest featured a degree of negative campaigning, especially on television, that anticipated the techniques common by the end of the twentieth century. The Republicans believed that the Johnson White House had gone well beyond the boundaries of political fair play in its advertising against Goldwater and the GOP. The major exhibit in this argument was the so-called Daisy Field commercial that showed a little girl with daisy petals that dissolved into a nuclear explosion. Johnson's voice intoned under these images: "These are the stakes—to make a world in which all of God's children can live, or go into the dark." Aired only once but repeated often on news broadcasts, the "daisy" became a symbol to the Republicans of the willingness of Johnson and his aides such as Bill Moyers to stop at nothing to defeat Goldwater. Moreover, those close to Goldwater were sure that the president used the Federal Bureau of Investigation to tap phones and place listening devices on Goldwater's campaign plane.[36]

The 1964 campaign was not virtue against vice in the campaign tactics of the two parties, however. Goldwater's campaign gained from widely circulated anti-Johnson literature such as J. Evetts Haley's *A Texan Looks at Lyndon* and Phyllis Schlafly's *A Choice, Not an Echo*. The GOP prepared a tough film about Johnson and the Democrats, but withdrew it at Goldwater's orders. Spots that were aired emphasized crime in the streets and Johnson's shady past. Since they were always on the defensive, the Republicans were not able to "go negative" on Johnson as effectively as they would with other Democrats in the future. Nonetheless, the 1964 race would linger as a touchstone for Republicans that the Democrats were the first to use attack ads on national television.

From a historical perspective, the most significant moment of the Goldwater campaign did not involve the presidential candidate himself. A former Democrat turned Republican, Ronald Reagan delivered a nationally televised speech on October 27, 1964, called "A Time for Choosing." In it, Reagan invoked many of the policy themes and much of the appealing rhetoric that would mark his political career. "We'll preserve for our children this, the last best hope of man on earth, or we'll sentence them to take the last step into a thousand years of darkness." The speech, delivered with Reagan's oratorical skill, sparked a flood of contributions, made Reagan a national political personality, and encouraged talk of a race for governor in 1966. Though Barry Goldwater did not yet realize it, his moment as a leader of conservatism within the Republican Party ended even before his presidential campaign did.[37]

When the votes came in on election night in 1964, Goldwater's candidacy went down to a crushing defeat. The Republican candidate carried six states, five in the South and Arizona. He trailed Johnson in the popular vote total by more than 16 million ballots, and his 27 million popular votes were nearly 7 million fewer than Nixon received four years earlier. The Goldwater-Johnson race brought a smaller percentage of Americans to the polls than the exciting Kennedy-Nixon encounter.

The Democrats controlled both houses of Congress by wide margins, and the president had the legislative muscle he needed to enact his Great Society program that embraced a war on poverty, medical care for the elderly, and sweeping environmental legislation, among other initiatives. The pundits likened the contest to a rerun of the 1936 debacle for the GOP. Some analysts were even quick to prepare a Republican obituary. Goldwater, wrote James Reston in *The New York Times*, "has wrecked his party for a long time to come and is not even likely to control the wreckage."[38]

These forecasts of the demise of the GOP would once again prove premature. Within two years the Republicans bounced back, and four years later Richard Nixon was in the White House. Lyndon Johnson's impressive victory proved transient as the combination of racial tensions, domestic unrest, and the costs of the Vietnam War unhinged the Democratic presidency. Barry Goldwater brought conservatives to dominance within the Republican Party, but other men such as Richard Nixon and Ronald Reagan inherited his mantle and returned the GOP to national competitiveness in the mid-1960s.

In fact, the aftermath of the 1964 presidential election demonstrated that Democratic grip on American politics was not permanent. Although he had assured voters that he sought no wider war in Vietnam, Johnson escalated the conflict in 1965 with bombing of North Vietnam and the introduction of American ground troops in the summer. Republicans endorsed these moves, eager to stop Communism in Southeast Asia. Richard Nixon said in September that Johnson "has got to make it clear to the world and to the people of South Vietnam that our objective is a free and independent South Vietnam with no reward and no appeasement of aggressors." Other Republicans criticized Johnson for not using enough military force, for his willingness to negotiate with North Vietnam, and for his reluctance to pursue total victory. The nature of this total victory was not usually defined with any precision, but the idea that some other course, whether more intense escalation or the threat of nuclear weapons, might have brought an end to the conflict became embedded in conservative thinking.[39]

Like many young people during that troubled time, future Republican leaders responded differently to the demands and trials of the conflict. Some men who would be prominent in the GOP three decades later fought for their country, often in heroic circumstances. These individuals included John McCain, Oliver North, Chuck Hagel, Jeremiah Denton, and James Webb. Others who were advocates of military action in future conflicts and critical of Bill Clinton's failure to serve in Vietnam had themselves not entered the military because of physical and student deferments. Among the most prominent of these Republicans were Newt Gingrich, Phil Gramm, Dick Cheney, Rush Limbaugh, and David Stockman. Cheney spoke for many of these men when he said he had "other priorities" during the 1960s. Dan Quayle and George W. Bush gained enlistment in their state's National Guard units during a time when waiting lists for such places were long and the chances of combat service almost nonexistent. By the first decade of the twenty-first century, Republicans who had not served in the military during the Vietnam era but were advocates of war in the Persian Gulf and elsewhere were derisively labeled "chicken hawks." The legacy of Vietnam for the Republicans proved as long as it did for the Democrats.[40]

In their divergent responses to Vietnam, young Republican

men of the 1960s reflected the ambivalence of the nation about the Asian war. But once the war was lost in the mid-1970s, an idea gained currency within the GOP that the Democrats under Johnson a decade earlier had not pushed the war to victory. The answer the next time was to amass overwhelming force and allow the military, and not civilian politicians, to make the key strategic decisions. In that way, the Democratic errors of slow escalation and an unwillingness to use the full weight of military power that had doomed the American cause in Vietnam would not be repeated. The rise on the left of Democratic protest against the war provided abundant evidence to the Republicans about a lack of true patriotism among their political rivals. Erasing the "Vietnam syndrome" that wars could not be won became a goal of GOP foreign policy in the 1980s and beyond.[41]

While the Vietnam War stirred political controversy, the conflict in Southeast Asia had general popular support in 1965–66. What eroded backing for the Great Society was the surfacing of the issue submerged in the Johnson-Goldwater contest—race. During the summer of 1965, the Democratic Congress, with the crucial support of twenty-three of thirty-two Republicans in the Senate, passed the Voting Rights Act of 1965. Though it was not apparent at the time, the civil rights movement had reached its high tide, as had Republican support for the goals of African Americans.[42]

Within a week the Watts riots in Los Angeles erupted and continued for five days. The National Guard had to restore order after thirty-four people died and much property was destroyed. In the three years that followed, "long hot summers" brought racial uprisings in major cities. Advocates of "black power" represented the more militant opinions of African Americans. Democratic liberalism became identified with the resentments and demands of the black underclass. Whites who had supported the party since Franklin D. Roosevelt began to defect. Two British politicians who toured the country after the elections of 1966 "found an undercurrent of resentment concerning civil order and gains made by the Negro population."[43]

The Republicans Bounce Back

The 1966 campaign was one I thoroughly enjoyed.

—Richard Nixon[44]

The Republicans came into the 1966 elections well positioned to capitalize on the sudden Democratic disarray. On the organizational side, a new chairman of the Republican National Committee, Ray Bliss of Ohio, brought efficient fund-raising and ideological tolerance to his duties. While Bliss emphasized the problem of inflation as a gut issue in the fall elections, the question of race was barely beneath the surface. A poll taken in September 1966 found that fifty-two percent of Americans believed that the Johnson administration was moving too fast on the civil rights issue.[45]

A particular target for Republican complaints was the Supreme Court under Chief Justice Earl Warren. The decision in *Miranda v. Arizona* that affirmed the right of criminal suspects to remain silent during police questioning was denounced as pro-criminal and antipolice. Richard Nixon would promise in 1968 to appoint judges who would favor law and order. The nation needed men in law enforcement, said Nixon, "with an awareness of the severity of the crime crisis, men with a new attitude toward crime and criminals." The Republican themes resonated with an electorate worried about social stability and the prospect of becoming a victim of crime.[46]

Republican criticism of Democrats as soft on law and order issues, ranging from racial unrest to antiwar demonstrations on college campuses, resonated with voters in 1966. Vice President Hubert Humphrey said at the convention of the National Association for the Advancement of Colored People that if he lived in a ghetto, he would "lead a mighty good revolt." Republicans responded that "high officials of this Administration had condoned and encouraged disrespect for law and order." The Johnson administration found itself on the defense and never located a persuasive theme to offset the GOP attacks.[47]

The election results revived Republican spirits after the 1964 debacle. The GOP gained forty-seven seats in the House, elected three new senators, and won eight gubernatorial races. The party suddenly had fresh faces to present to the American people. Spiro T. Agnew won the Maryland statehouse. Across the country, Ronald Reagan defeated the incumbent governor, Edmund G. "Pat" Brown, and Charles Percy won a Senate seat in Illinois by ousting longtime liberal Paul Douglas. In Massachusetts, Edward Brooke gained a Senate seat and became the first African American to sit in that body since Reconstruction. "We've beaten the hell out of them," said Richard Nixon, "and we're going to kill them in '68." The natural balances of American politics were reasserting themselves after the one-sided 1964 race.[48]

In the long-range perspective, the most significant result in 1966 was Ronald Reagan's victory in California. Building on his television appearance for Goldwater in 1964, the personable, attractive Reagan won the GOP nomination and easily defeated the overconfident Brown. While his views were as hard-edged as Goldwater's, Reagan presented them with charm, plausibility, and a winning smile. Not for the last time did the Democrats underestimate Reagan's skill as a campaigner and communicator of conservatism. His opposition to the Civil Rights Act of 1964 no longer seemed unreasonable in the wake of Watts. The student upheavals at the University of California at Berkeley gave Reagan even more appeal to middle-class voters who wanted calm as well as patriotism on their nightly news programs. The so-called hippies who personified the drug culture of the 1960s were an inviting target for Reagan's devastating barbs. They "act like Tarzan, look like Jane and smell like Cheetah."[49]

Some of Reagan's supporters began thinking of a presidential race in 1968 as the dimensions of his landslide over Brown emerged. The big winner in 1966, however, was Richard Nixon, who now saw his path to the nomination in 1968 open up. Widely written off as a political has-been after his loss to Pat Brown in 1962, Nixon had supported Goldwater two years later when so many other Republicans stayed home or supported

Lyndon Johnson. When the Democrats ran into trouble, he went out on the campaign trail on behalf of Republican candidates in 1966. The political credits he gained would turn into delegate votes two years later.

President Johnson gave Nixon a lift as the congressional elections neared. After the Republican assailed the president's policy on Vietnam, Johnson fired back that Nixon was "a chronic campaigner." Nixon responded that the remark represented "one of the most savage personal assaults ever leveled by the President of the United States against one of his political opponents." Johnson had treated him as a major Republican leader, and this allowed Nixon to depict GOP gains as a triumph for himself personally.[50]

Nixon's fortunes prospered during the rest of 1967. He built a well-financed campaign organization and went on a series of foreign tours that provided even more visibility to his candidacy. The key for Nixon was to erase the "loser" image that he had acquired in 1960 and 1962. As the Vietnam War stalemated and urban rioting plagued the domestic scene, Nixon seemed like a moderate, credible alternative to Johnson's failing policies.

The main Republican rival of Nixon in 1967 was Governor George Romney of Michigan. Handsome and impressive-looking before television cameras, Romney had served three terms and blended public service with executive experience in the automobile industry. But the governor was not a gifted speaker or a fast thinker, and his campaign was always vulnerable to a verbal slip. After a trip to Vietnam, a reporter asked him why his position on the war had changed to one of opposition to American involvement. Romney responded that "when I came back from Vietnam, I just had the greatest brainwashing that anybody can get when you go over to Vietnam, not only by the generals but also by the diplomatic corps over there." Ignoring the substance of Romney's comments, the press treated the brainwashing remark as evidence that Romney lacked the smarts to be president. Private polls soon showed him well behind Nixon. As a result, the Michigan governor took himself out of the race in late February 1968.[51]

The other potential challengers for Nixon were Nelson

Rockefeller and Ronald Reagan. Rockefeller was never a serious threat because of the hatred he aroused among conservatives. Reagan, however, was already beginning to create the buzz among Republicans that he would continue to generate for the next quarter of a century. He represented a real threat to Nixon's quest for the GOP nomination if he could dispel the impression that the former vice president had a lock on the prize. A quiet struggle between Reagan and Nixon for supremacy among Republicans ensued during the first half of 1968.

Nixon's the One in 1968

> I am not going to campaign for the black vote at the risk of alienating the suburban vote.
>
> —Richard Nixon[52]

The nation experienced a chaotic first three months of 1968. The Democratic Party shook itself to pieces as first Senator Eugene McCarthy of Minnesota and then Senator Robert F. Kennedy of New York sought the nomination against Lyndon Johnson. The Tet offensive of North Vietnam undermined popular confidence in the outcome of the war. Then Johnson's surprise withdrawal from the race on March 31, 1968, as his political base collapsed, further scrambled the political scene. All these events worked in favor of Nixon and the Republicans. In the New Hampshire primary, Nixon trounced Rockefeller, who was not a formal candidate, by an eight-to-one margin. Only the potential threat of a Reagan candidacy stood in Nixon's way.

In later years, the allegation that Nixon had claimed to have "a secret plan" during the campaign to end the Vietnam War produced much debate. Publicly, he proclaimed his intention to provide "new leadership" that would "end the war and win the peace in the Pacific." That goal would be achieved "if we mobilize our economic and political and diplomatic leadership." Though he did not say so, Nixon intended to play the Soviet Union and China against each other to pressure North Vietnam into a negotiated settlement of the conflict. At the same time, American troops would be pulled out and the war put in the hands of South Vietnam. Nixon said that he could not reveal specific details of his approach lest he interfere with Johnson's leadership or commit himself on his own presidential agenda. So ambiguous was Nixon's stance that opponents of the war and those who wanted a victory could both take comfort in Nixon's words.[53]

The Nixon campaign's priority at this point was to change the way the press viewed the candidate himself. Though he disliked and distrusted journalists after his 1960 campaign, Nixon knew that careful management of the media was essential to a successful run. The candidate gave few press conferences and emphasized events, such as scripted meetings with voters, that were staged for television. Nixon and his campaign portrayed him as a "new Nixon," a man of more mature judgment and a less volatile temper than earlier in the decade. One of his aides put it well: "It's not the man we have to change, but rather the *received impression.*"[54]

Johnson's departure from the race further aided Nixon's candidacy. Reporters had been clamoring for the details of Nixon's Vietnam ideas, but the surprise announcement of Johnson's withdrawal allowed the Republican front-runner to remain silent while the president opened the negotiations with North Vietnam that Johnson had coupled with his departure from politics. Meanwhile, Nelson Rockefeller had concluded by the end of the month that Nixon could not be beaten. He declared on March 21 that he would not run. The statement outraged and embarrassed Spiro Agnew who had started a Draft Rockefeller Committee. Nixon and Agnew began quiet conversations about the future.

Then a month later, urged by President Johnson (who at that time feared the race might be between Nixon and Senator Robert F. Kennedy on the Democratic side) and others, Nelson Rockefeller reappeared as a candidate. The strategy of the New Yorker was bizarre. He argued that he was electable and Nixon was not, based on public opinion polls. The polls he commissioned did not show the support the New Yorker anticipated. Rank-and-file Republicans, most of whom hated Rockefeller, were not buying. Should Nixon falter, they would turn to Ronald Reagan, but the front-runner did not collapse under the Rockefeller barrage. By the early part of June 1968, the inept Rockefeller campaign was moribund.

The spring of 1968 brought traumatic events for an already crippled nation. Martin Luther King, Jr., was murdered in early April, and the assassination of Senator Robert F. Kennedy occurred after he won the Democratic primary in California. While the Democrats descended into bitter infighting, Nixon campaigned on themes that would resonate with voters for decades to come. The Republican candidate stressed the needs of "the silent center, the millions of people in the middle of the political spectrum who do not demonstrate, who do not picket or protest loudly." Moreover, there was, he said, "a rebellion against taxes, and against the ever-higher piling of Federal tax on state tax on local tax."[55]

Nixon's election chances seemed promising as the summer of 1968 unfolded. On the Vietnam issue, Nixon worked to be as close to Johnson's negotiating stance as he could. He feared that the president might announce something approaching peace before the election, boost the Democrats, and undercut Republican hopes. Vice President Hubert Humphrey, the likely Democratic nominee after Robert Kennedy's death, was trying and failing to escape from the embrace of Johnson's Vietnam policy that was so unpopular with members of Humphrey's party. Nixon was moving closer to the White House. "The GOP may be of more help to us than the Democrats in the next few months," Johnson observed. This meant that, hedging his bets, Nixon was opening up back channels to the South Vietnam government that could be used to send private messages to the politicians in Saigon in the event Johnson started a peace offensive that could hurt the chances of the GOP in the election.[56]

As the Republican convention neared in early August,

Nixon's victory seemed assured, barring the emergence of a Rockefeller-Reagan coalition to block the front-runner on the first ballot. The former vice president's camp had long feared the charismatic appeal of the California governor to Republican conservatives. Although his administration in Sacramento got off to a shaky start, Reagan displayed an ability to rouse the party faithful to even greater heights of enthusiasm than Goldwater had achieved. Inevitably, the Californian's campaign had to be something of a stealth enterprise. He dared not oppose Nixon openly, but he could watch for a chance should Nixon falter. With his usual political wariness, Nixon recognized the threat that Reagan posed. According to Nixon's memoirs, Reagan appealed to southern Republicans because he "spoke their conservative language articulately and with great passion, and there was always a possibility that Southern delegates could be lured at the last minute by his ideological siren song."[57]

Reagan entered the race just before the GOP convention started. A media event with the California delegation provided the platform and hinted at the "Great Communicator" to come. The Reagan slate adopted a resolution requesting that Reagan be "a leading and bona fide candidate for President." The governor then strode into the room and told the group, "Gosh, I was surprised. It all came out of a clear blue sky." If Reagan was to win, he would have to dislodge Nixon's grip on Republicans from below the Mason-Dixon line. Should Nixon waver on the race issue or, worse yet, choose a northern, liberal Republican as his running mate, then a break for Reagan might take place.[58]

Nixon moved to forestall Reagan on two fronts. He and his surrogates assured southerners that, while he believed in desegregation of schools, he was opposed to busing children outside their home neighborhoods in pursuit of racial balance. Moreover, he thought that the South should be allowed to comply voluntarily with judicial decrees before being compelled to do so. Second, in these private sessions with Dixie delegates, Nixon made clear his opposition to federal judges who interfered with local schools. "I think it is the job of the courts to interpret the

law and not make the law," Nixon commented. The assistance of
Strom Thurmond of South Carolina was crucial in attesting to
Nixon's devotion to the South. Nixon subdued any potential
Reagan rebellion among southerners and held on to the crucial
delegate votes there. The actual voting for the nominee went as
the Nixon camp had anticipated. Nixon went over the top on
the first ballot with twenty-five more votes than he needed.
Although Reagan, Rockefeller, and several minor candidates
trailed badly, their combined total revealed how narrow Nixon's
victory had been. Now it was up to the candidate to choose his
running mate. Above all, Nixon sought to avoid a repetition of
the mistake he had made in 1960 with the lackluster and lazy
Henry Cabot Lodge.[59]

Weeks earlier, Nixon had concluded that Spiro Agnew was
the best choice. On the surface, the Maryland governor had
much to recommend him in terms of Nixon's emerging strategy
toward the South. In 1966, Agnew had defeated a racist Democrat to claim the Maryland statehouse. After the embarrassment
of supporting Rockefeller before his withdrawal, Agnew moved
toward Nixon, especially in his own view of civil rights. He also
reacted to the rioting that followed the murder of Martin Luther
King, Jr., with stern denunciations of black leaders and attacks
on urban unrest. Here was the man Nixon required to help him
win the South and border states by appealing to white voters.
With Governor George C. Wallace running as a third-party candidate, Agnew seemed an ideal choice to defuse Wallace's allure
without getting into the racial gutter with the Alabama leader.

One thing Nixon had not done was launch an investigation
into Agnew's background and financial affairs. Nor had Nixon
or his men questioned Agnew about potential problems that
might affect his fitness to serve as vice president. Nixon had
made a mistake. Agnew was involved in several conspiracies in
Maryland that included bribery, tax fraud, and extortion. He
had been taking payments and kickbacks from state contractors.
These arrangements continued once he became vice president,
and so Nixon had chosen an active participant in criminal enterprises as his choice for the nation's second highest office.[60]

At the convention, Nixon made symbolic offers of the vice presidency to two other Republicans, both of whom declined. Nixon then chose Agnew and made the announcement to a surprised press corps. It became apparent that Agnew was not a strong choice, but he suited Nixon's purposes in August 1968. The criticisms of the media were only nagging distractions for Nixon as he prepared for his moment of vindication and triumph.

In his acceptance address, Nixon made himself the champion of "the great majority of Americans, the forgotten Americans, the non-shouters, the nondemonstrators." He contended that "America is in trouble today not because her people have failed but because her leaders have failed." The problems of Vietnam, racial unrest, and crime were compelling reasons that "it's time for new leadership for the United States of America."[61]

Nixon began the campaign with obvious advantages over his main opponent, Vice President Humphrey, and George C. Wallace. He was well ahead in the public opinion polls with a 45-to-29 spread over Humphrey, and Wallace trailing with 18 percent. The electoral map also looked promising for the GOP. There were many states in which Nixon was certain of victory. Humphrey had no such cushion. The Republicans had built up a big lead in campaign funding and had more than $30 million in the Nixon war chest. For all of his assets, however, Nixon's candidacy relied on voter discontent with the Democrats, not on any ideological appeal. Unlike Goldwater four years earlier, the Nixon effort was empty of programmatic content. If the Democrats reunited and Humphrey closed the gap, then Nixon and the GOP might be in difficulty. As a Nixon aide, William Safire, later wrote, "Nixon was playing not to lose."[62]

At first it seemed that Nixon had very little to fear in his cautious approach to the campaign. The turbulent Democratic National Convention, blighted by riots and the heavy-handed tactics of the Chicago police, pushed Humphrey even further behind. With his lead, Nixon could devote his resources to those states where his candidacy seemed strong. Had Wallace not been in the race, a Republican landslide would likely have occurred since the majority of voters for the Alabama governor would have gone Republican. By the end of September, the prospect of a decisive Nixon triumph seemed possible, especially because the underfunded Humphrey campaign was doing so badly.

Yet problems lingered. Nixon seemed stuck at around forty to forty-five percent of the vote; as one GOP strategist observed, "This race is by no means in the bag for Nixon." Wallace faltered as October began, in part because organized labor attacked him strongly in the North. Like many third-party candidates, Wallace lost ground when voters realized he could not be elected. Meanwhile, Nixon ran to protect his lead rather than seeking to expand it. Nor did he run in a way that energized the campaigns of other Republican candidates for the Senate and the House. Safely tucked behind his campaign apparatus, which was out of sight of the media, Nixon sought to run out the clock as the election neared.[63]

Humphrey revived his candidacy by breaking away from Johnson on the Vietnam issue in late September. A few weeks later, prospects for negotiations with North Vietnam improved and peace hopes rose. By October 24, Humphrey was eight points down in the polls and closing the gap as traditional Democrats returned to their party. In the last two weeks of the election, the margin between Nixon and Humphrey tightened almost daily.

The final days of the 1968 contest saw an intricate interplay between President Johnson and Nixon over a bombing halt in Vietnam. Both sides played hardball. Nixon used his back channel to Saigon to prevent South Vietnam from backing Johnson's initiative. The president brought in the FBI and used wiretaps to keep track of what the Nixon camp was doing. In the end, the bombing halt did not lead to peace talks because of Saigon's reluctance to sit down with the North. Although the public knew little of these events, the process had large consequences. Having endured political surveillance from a Democratic president, Nixon and his men came to believe that they could take similar actions when they were in power.[64]

Despite the last-minute Democratic surge, Nixon and the Republicans held on to win in 1968. The victor secured 31,770,237 popular votes to 31,270,533 for Humphrey. Wallace trailed with 9,906,141. Nixon garnered 43.4 percent of the vote to 42.7 for Humphrey and 13.5 percent for Wallace. In the electoral college, Nixon had the votes of thirty-two states for 301 electoral votes to Humphrey's thirteen states and the District of Columbia with 191 electoral votes. Wallace captured five states and 46 electoral votes.

While the election represented a massive repudiation of the Democrats, it was not a major endorsement of the GOP. In four years the Democrats had lost 12 million votes from Johnson's 1964 total, and Nixon had run 4 million votes better than had Barry Goldwater. The big element in the shift was race. The Republicans benefited from the movement of white voters away from the Democrats. The Republicans now had the prospect of majority status if the party could solidify the gains that the 1968 presidential contest had produced.

The GOP came out of 1968 with several enduring advantages over their opponents. The Republicans had learned how to frame issues so that key elements of the Democratic coalition defected from that party. Nixon drove a wedge into the South with his "southern strategy," and Republicans duplicated that feat in subsequent presidential contests. Indeed, in the 1970s, the South moved toward its ultimate role as Republican bastion, despite the temporary victory of Jimmy Carter in 1976.

The success of Nixon's fund-raising also proved to be a lasting GOP strength. While Nixon had not helped Republican congressional and senatorial candidates much, the base of small and large donors meant that the party could always be competitive nationally. Finally, the organization that Nixon put together in 1968 helped created a cadre of seasoned political operatives in the Republican presidential races that followed. Whoever the Republican candidate was after 1968, he could count on practiced GOP strategists and advocates to sign on for another national campaign. From 1968 onward, at the purely nuts-and-bolts level of politics, the Democrats were outmatched.

NIXON, THE PRESIDENCY, AND WATERGATE

> What history says about this administration will depend
> upon who writes history.
>
> —Richard Nixon[65]

For all these positive strides, the Nixon presidency and the Watergate scandal that ensued proved a dramatic setback to Republican hopes of building a national majority for the party. Even though Nixon won a huge reelection victory in 1972, the Democrats retained control of both houses of Congress throughout his presidency. Nixon's resignation in 1974 and the brief presidency of Gerald R. Ford laid the basis for the election victory of Jimmy Carter in 1976.

Widely perceived as a Republican partisan for most of his pre-presidential career, the fifty-six-year-old Nixon had worked hard for GOP candidates nationally in many of the congressional races from 1954 to 1966. In those days, such a course established political friendships that helped Nixon both times when he ran for president in 1960 and 1968. Once in the White House, however, Nixon proved less interested in the success of his party than in his own reelection. The president was not willing to risk much of his own political capital to help other Republicans prevail in down-ballot races.

Of all the Republican presidents in the twentieth century, Richard Nixon is the most complex and controversial. He had great ability as a practitioner of foreign policy, and his administration was innovative in many areas of domestic concerns. So activist was his presidency on environmental matters, welfare reform, and Native American issues of tribal rights that Nixon has been called, with a touch of irony, the last liberal president. In many respects, Nixon was a Republican moderate, to the left of his mentor Dwight D. Eisenhower on a number of social and economic questions. In his rhetorical animus against the size of government and his dislike of bureaucracy, of course, Nixon articulated more conventional Republican thinking.[66]

For all of Nixon's abilities as a politician and diplomat, he had comparable flaws that led him into disaster by 1974. The new president trusted almost no one, and he viewed the world with deep suspicion. Convinced that he had been cheated out of the presidency by the press, liberal Democrats, and the Kennedys in 1960, he regarded himself as surrounded by enemies while he sat in the White House. So he sought to use the power of the presidency to strike back in an often bitter, ruthless fashion. As he told his aide H. R. Haldeman in September 1971, "Bob, *please* get me the names of the Jews, you know, the big Jewish contributors of the Democrats. . . . All right. Could we please investigate some of the cocksuckers? That's all." Out of this sense of persecution and potential betrayal came a need to control all aspects of the political environment, even by illegal means if necessary. Politics for Richard Nixon was not like war, it was war.[67]

This deep-rooted conviction led Nixon to view the apparatus of the Republican Party as inept and insufficiently ruthless for his needs. He wanted to advance the interests of his party but was not willing to make the GOP organization the means of doing so. To a greater degree, the Republican National Committee became a figurehead with no real power or authority. Nixon and his aides ran the 1972 presidential election as a separate operation apart from the Republican parties in the states. The chairman of the RNC in 1972, Senator Robert Dole of Kansas, put it with his usual brand of sarcastic realism: "The Republican party was not only not involved in Watergate, but it wasn't involved in the nomination, the convention, the campaign, the election or the inauguration."[68]

Despite his reputation as a fierce Republican partisan, Nixon often was not in step with his fellow GOP members. He once remarked to John Connally that, compared with the Democrats, "the Republicans are more inhibited, more restrained, more proper. The Democrats let it all out and love to shout and laugh and have fun. The Republicans have fun but they don't want people to see it. The Democrats, even when they are not having fun, like to appear to be having fun." Nixon even contemplated, before and after the 1972 election, creating a new party to replace the GOP. The new organization would be the right side of the spectrum but would be moderate on social policy and conservative in foreign affairs and the economy. In that sense, Nixon shared sentiments that Dwight Eisenhower had expressed a decade or so earlier.[69]

For their part, conservative Republicans eyed Nixon with suspicion as well. They had to tolerate a president who sponsored such initiatives as a guaranteed annual income, the Environmental Protection Agency, greater spending on social programs at a rate higher than under Lyndon Johnson, and affirmative action on racial policies. In foreign policy, while Nixon sought to achieve "peace with honor" in Vietnam, he also pursued détente with the Soviet Union and opened up relations with the Communist leaders of China. Even before all these Nixonian policies were in place, Patrick Buchanan, a speechwriter for the White House, observed in a January 1971 memorandum: "The President is no longer a credible custodian of the conservative political tradition of the GOP."[70]

Nixon wanted the Republicans, as he conceived them, to become the majority party during his presidency. He dreamed of redefining American politics as Franklin D. Roosevelt had done during the 1930s. To reach that goal, Nixon exploited the changes in political demography that the 1960s had produced. As Nixon began his presidency, talk of a new Republican majority was all the rage. Kevin Phillips published *The Emerging Republican Majority* (1969) which explored the future of the GOP in the South and West where explosive population growth and conservative values offered ripe pickings for the Republicans. Other commentators made a similar case that Republicans, with a conservative agenda that appealed to Middle Americans, could outgain the Democrats with key voting groups. These Americans became known in the Nixon White House as the Silent Majority.

The Nixon administration moved with skill and determination to attract these voters. Division and discord among the Democrats after 1968 made these White House initiatives successful among many Americans. Outside the South, Nixon targeted blue-collar Democrats in the Middle West, especially those who belonged to the unions of the AFL-CIO and members of Jimmy Hoffa's Teamsters. A timely commutation of Hoffa's prison sentence in December 1971 helped win Teamster support for Nixon in the 1972 presidential race. The White House also reached out to Catholics with public statements of his opposition to abortion and his belief that the federal government should assist parochial schools.

A key component of Nixon's political equation was the South, but the president had to tread carefully because of the sensitivity of the civil rights issue. The Republican administration was generally popular with southerners because of Nixon's opposition to busing and his efforts to appoint a southerner to the Supreme Court. At the same time, the Nixon administration brought public school segregation in the South to an end and advanced affirmative action programs in the North. Although these activities produced grumbling from the unions and scattered unhappiness in parts of the South, Nixon and the Republicans did not suffer at the polls. The blame for civil rights advances always fell on the Democrats. The Republicans were recognized in the North and South as the party of states' rights and for their willingness to restrain the aspirations of black Americans.[71]

The congressional elections of 1970 offered the first test of the success of Nixon's political approach. He had begun to withdraw American troops from South Vietnam and to pursue "Vietnamization," which gave Saigon more responsibility for their own defense. The president had thus defused some of the antiwar sentiment. It flared again in the spring of 1970 with the invasion of Cambodia, the death of students at Kent State University in Ohio and Jackson State University in Mississippi, and a resulting wave of student protest. With the economy lagging, the best tactic for the White House and the GOP in the fall seemed to be a concentration on law and order issues. As Nixon said, "Emphasize-anti-Crime-anti-Demonstrations, anti-Drug, anti-Obscenity."[72]

The campaign itself did not go as the White House had hoped. The Democrats co-opted many of the social issues and thus offset the GOP offensive. Vice President Agnew was supposed to be the point man for the Republicans, but he proved ineffective. To save the situation, Nixon campaigned himself during the last two weeks. In San Jose, California, an angry crowd taunted the president who stood on the hood of his car and waved the "V" sign at the protesters. The White House released a film of another Nixon campaign address on election eve that backfired because of the poor quality of the images themselves and the president's frenetic appearance. A response by Democratic Senator Edmund Muskie countered Nixon with a calm, well-produced statement of the issues.[73]

The results of the 1970 elections left Nixon and the GOP deeply disappointed. The Republicans gained two Senate seats—in New York, where conservative James Buckley was elected, and in Tennessee, where Bill Brock defeated Albert Gore, Sr. In another key Senate race, Lloyd M. Bentsen, Jr., defeated George H. W. Bush in Texas, in what was a particularly bitter loss for the White House. The Democrats added nine House seats and added eleven governorships. Nixon declared the results a success because the Republicans had not suffered greater defeats two years after their presidential victory. Yet the prospects for Nixon's reelection two years later now seemed more problematic.

The Democratic victory, which turned mostly on a weaker economy and Republican miscues, was illusory. When it came to nominating a candidate to run against Nixon, the fault lines in the opposition, which were first opened up in 1968, were still evident and raw. The Democratic Party's new rules for electing delegates, which made their process more open to determined minorities, created problems for a moderate centrist seeking support from activist liberals. In short, Nixon and the GOP faced a wounded, demoralized Democratic Party in the runup to

1972. Senator Edward M. Kennedy had been compromised by the 1969 drowning of a woman who was a passenger in his car late at night on Martha's Vineyard. The apparent Democratic front-runner, Edmund Muskie, was untested in national politics beyond his 1968 vice presidential run, and he came from a small state. His likely challengers, George S. McGovern of South Dakota and Hubert Humphrey, also had serious flaws as potential candidates.

The conclusion that Nixon and his aides drew from the 1970 outcome, however, was that the president's reelection effort had to be directed from the White House. Although he spoke to the men around him about "introducing dynamic campaign management into the Republican National Committee," the president wanted little to do with the Republican professionals at the committee or in the various states. The obvious choice in Nixon's mind was to have at hand "the formidable political muscle that goes with being the party in the White House." Democrats had done it since Franklin D. Roosevelt, Nixon wrote later, and "I planned to take no less advantage of it myself."[74]

Convinced from the outset of his presidency that he faced a coordinated and ruthless opposition from Democrats and a liberal media, Nixon had already taken steps to employ "formidable political muscle" in clandestine ways. Wiretaps of White House aides and reporters, done on Nixon's orders, had begun as early as 1969. The Internal Revenue Service, building on what Kennedy and Johnson had done in probing right-wing enemies, had audited the tax returns and launched investigations of radical groups, journalists, and Democratic critics of the president. In 1971, after Daniel Ellsberg leaked the Pentagon Papers to *The New York Times* and *The Washington Post,* the administration created "The Plumbers," a secret group of illicit operatives, to forestall further leaks by illegal means. Other White House insiders coordinated efforts to disrupt Democratic political campaigns. Meanwhile, in 1971, the White House installed an audio taping system that was recording Nixon's conversations in the Oval Office. All the elements for a major scandal were in place, but few Republicans outside of Nixon's immediate circle had any hint of what was happening.[75]

For conservative GOP members who remained loyal to Nixon in public, the president's policies in 1971 were troubling. Nixon's endorsement of Keynesian economics as well as his commitment to wage and price controls hardly represented right-wing orthodoxy. More problematic still was the dramatic opening to China, which outraged many conservative journalists, including William F. Buckley and his colleagues at the *National Review*. The resulting hard feelings led Congressman John Ashbrook of Ohio to mount an ineffective challenge to Nixon's renomination that drew only minimal support in the two primaries that the maverick lawmaker entered. On the left, Congressman Pete McCloskey of California mounted an antiwar insurgency against Nixon that drew few Republican voters. Discontent with Nixon faded as the 1972 campaign loomed and the traditional unity among Republicans reasserted itself.[76]

The 1972 presidential race was no contest. The Democrats selected their most vulnerable candidate, Senator George S. McGovern, whose liberal campaign encountered endless troubles, produced Democratic defections to Nixon among key voting groups, and never found a winning theme on major issues. The Republicans depicted McGovern as out of touch with mainstream opinion because he favored a negotiated settlement in Vietnam. The Democrats were painted as advocates of drug use and abortion. As a result, the president hardly needed to campaign as McGovern's candidacy collapsed. The Nixon camp did not intend, however, to rely on the mistakes of their opponents. "We have to develop a sense of mission," Nixon said to Haldeman, "and not back into victory by default."[77]

Nixon and Spiro Agnew achieved the landslide that they sought. Nixon won every state but Massachusetts and the District of Columbia, received more than an 18-million-vote margin over his rival, and gained 60.7 percent of the vote. He made inroads into such former bastions of Democratic strength as union members and Roman Catholics. Only African Americans and traditional Democrats stayed with their party. On a personal level, Nixon had built the New Majority he had been proclaiming during his first term.

It was not yet a new Republican majority. Down the ballot, the Democrats held their own. The Republicans picked up a dozen seats in the House, not enough to threaten Democratic control. The GOP dropped one Senate seat. In Maine the lone woman in the Senate, Margaret Chase Smith, was defeated after four terms in Washington. A sometime thorn in Nixon's side, Smith had not seen the president campaign for her. During the 1972 campaign, Nixon again did not risk his own political capital to advance the hopes of the GOP on Capitol Hill.

In the aftermath of the 1972 election triumph, Nixon intended to move back toward conservatism by restructuring the federal government to make it smaller and less intrusive. The president believed that only stern measures "can get the government under control before it gets so big that it submerges the individual completely and destroys the dynamism which makes our American system what it is." To that end he sought the resignations of most senior officials in the White House and the government within days of his reelection, a move that badly shook morale within the administration. It also reflected Nixon's lust for personal power. Having achieved an end to United States involvement in Vietnam by early 1973, Nixon now saw domestic change as his main agenda. Like Eisenhower before him, he intended to "revitalize the Republican Party along New Majority lines." Having allowed the government to get larger as he pursued reelection, Nixon now proposed to do in his second term what he had not had the will to do in his first administration.[78]

Of course, Nixon's mandate of 1972, such as it was, never went into operation in the ambitious form that the president envisaged. By early 1973 the Watergate scandal was already operating like a corrosive acid on the administration and to a significant extent on the Republican Party as well. The break-in at the Democratic Party headquarters in the Watergate complex in

June 1972 had been part of the effort of the Nixon White House to manage what the president and his men regarded as a hostile political environment. Along the same lines, Nixon had authorized criminal acts against Democrats, dissenters, and journalists. By late 1972 a variety of "White House horrors," in the words of Attorney General John Mitchell, were being covered up lest the public, Democrats, and law enforcement learn about them. The reporting of *The Washington Post* by Bob Woodward and Carl Bernstein was laying out much of the scandal, but their revelations were not widely believed during the second half of 1972.[79]

The Watergate scandal began to unravel early in 1973 and continued to come apart until Nixon's resignation in early August 1974. For Republicans the disintegration of Nixon's administration was protracted and painful. Although many prominent leaders within the party had long harbored private doubts about Nixon's character, Democratic attacks on the White House in 1973 elicited staunch defenses of the president from GOP members on Capitol Hill. Barry Goldwater had once labeled Nixon "a two-fisted, four-square liar," but he stood behind the president until the spring of 1973 when he likened Watergate to the Teapot Dome scandal of Warren G. Harding a half century earlier. "I mean, there's a smell to it. Let's get rid of the smell."[80]

Other Republicans had different reactions. George H. W. Bush, the new chairman of the Republican National Committee after the 1972 election, commented that Nixon "has said repeatedly he wasn't involved in the sordid Watergate affairs. I believe him." Ronald Reagan defended Nixon against the attacks of what the California governor privately called "a lynch mob" until just a few days before the president's resignation.[81]

As the evidence of Nixon's wrongdoing accumulated, Republicans were important participants in revealing the extent of the scandals in the White House. Senator Howard Baker of Tennessee became a key figure on the Senate committee to probe the scandal during the spring of 1973. Baker's famous question, "What did the President know and when did he know it?" zeroed in on the main issue of the Watergate affair. A year later, Republican senator James Buckley of New York called for Nixon's resignation because he had lost "credibility and moral authority." When Nixon made a damaging partial release of White House tape recordings, Republicans such as Hugh Scott of Pennsylvania called the disclosures, which contained Nixon's coarse language and machinations, "shabby, disgusting, and immoral." On the House Judiciary Committee, four GOP members provided key votes against Nixon and joined with conservative Democrats in a coalition that sealed the president's fate when impeachment votes were taken.[82]

As the Watergate scandal ran its course, the leadership of the GOP changed in ways that scrambled the party's future. Vice President Spiro Agnew proved to be a criminal who had continued to take bribes as vice president. His resignation in a plea bargain with federal prosecutors removed a potential conservative rival to Ronald Reagan in 1976. Agnew's departure posed a more immediate challenge for the embattled Nixon who had to select a successor that Congress would confirm as vice president.

Nixon had long been infatuated with John Connally of Texas as a potential president, but the former Treasury Secretary and defector from the Democrats faced a bruising fight for confirmation because of his questionable financial past. There was talk of George H. W. Bush, also of Texas, but doubts about his capacity to be president ruled him out. The Republican leader in the House, Gerald R. Ford of Michigan, seemed a popular choice who would face no difficulty in winning the approval of his fellow lawmakers. Ford also offered Nixon insurance against impeachment because legislators, so the president believed, would not want to replace the incumbent with such an untrained man. In fact, as Watergate pressed on in 1974, Ford's personal honesty appeared a refreshing contrast with Nixon's criminality.

The Watergate mess hit the Republican Party at the ballot box in 1974. The Republicans lost several special elections in the spring, caused by the death or resignation of incumbents, including Gerald Ford's own seat in Michigan. An electoral disaster loomed in the November contests as the GOP faced the voters in the sixth year of a two-term president. With a presidential impeachment becoming likely, the Republicans had little joy in the summer of 1974.

By that time, however, Nixon's political position was collapsing. The Republicans in Congress contended that Nixon must be proved guilty of an illegal act for impeachment to occur. When a tape of a Nixon conversation of June 23, 1972, was released in July 1974, it showed the president involved in the cover-up of the Watergate break-in. This "smoking gun" made Nixon's departure from the presidency inescapable. Congressional Republicans informed the president that he had only a few remaining supporters on Capitol Hill. On August 8, 1974, Nixon resigned, and Gerald Ford became president. In his first address to the nation, Ford proclaimed that "our long national nightmare is over."[83]

Richard Nixon's public relationship with the Republican Party, which stretched over nearly three decades, from 1946 to 1974, has yet to be understood in all of its complexity. Because of his participation in Watergate, he remains an embattled figure and a reminder to Republicans of one of their shabbier hours. As historians and political scientists have chronicled the increased government spending and expanded social programs that marked Nixon's tenure, conservatives have discovered even less to admire. The foreign policy accomplishments—détente with the Soviet Union, the opening of China, and the end of the Vietnam War—are regarded by many on the right as negative features of Nixon's record. Whether he was the last liberal president or not, he was not a conservative true believer in the mold of Ronald Reagan.

Yet Nixon left important legacies to the GOP in both substantive and tactical ways. His conviction that he faced ruthless enemies bent on his destruction harmonized with the sentiment among conservatives that liberals and Democrats were not just political adversaries but active opponents of American values.

Unrelenting efforts to achieve complete electoral dominance were thus more than justified since Democratic victories lacked basic legitimacy. The training that Republican politicians received in Nixon's hard school carried into campaigns during the rest of the twentieth century.

While Congress under the Democrats sought to reform fund-raising practices in 1974, the ties that Nixon had established with the business community in 1968 and 1972 translated into a continuing access to big money for the GOP. As electioneering became a year-round endeavor, the Republicans outstripped their opponents in both resources and expertise without serious challenge until the arrival of Bill Clinton on the national scene in the early 1990s.

Although he lived until the mid-1990s, Richard Nixon seems like a throwback to an earlier era—the age of anti-Communism, a divisive war, and a protracted political scandal. The ousted president spent the rest of his life trying to rebuild his reputation and had largely succeeded at the time of his death. Yet it seems unlikely that Nixon will ever enter into the pantheon of GOP heroes. As happened with the presidencies of Ulysses S. Grant and Warren G. Harding, a stain of scandal and disgrace will always color Nixon's career, unlike the esteem that Republicans feel for Lincoln, Theodore Roosevelt, and Ronald Reagan, whose moment in the sun dawned with Nixon's ruin.

Chapter 11

REPUBLICANS IN THE REAGAN ERA,
1974–1988

THE 1980 PRESIDENTIAL election was still close as the Democratic president, Jimmy Carter, and his Republican challenger, Ronald Reagan, prepared for their only debate in late October. The two candidates had been jockeying for position on the debate issue since the campaign began. While the Carter campaign had originally thought Reagan would be a pushover for the president, they had come to have respect for the Republican candidate's skills in public settings. The Reagan camp, on the other hand, needed to have their candidate on the same stage with Carter to reassure Americans that, contrary to the claims of some Democrats, the Republican standard-bearer was not a menacing figure who was likely to imperil the nation. After much deliberation, the aides to the two presidential hopefuls agreed to hold a single debate late in the campaign, on October 28, 1980.

Two moments defined the encounter. The first came as Carter was discussing the issue of arms control and nuclear weapons. Perhaps to underline his empathy with the younger generation, perhaps to show his sensitivity on the matter generally, the president said, "I had a discussion with my daughter, Amy, the other day, before I came here, to ask her what the most important issue was. She said she thought nuclear weaponry and the control of nuclear arms." Carter's invocation of his daughter as an element in his thinking fell flat.[1]

The more crucial moment came when Carter went after Reagan for his opposition to Social Security and Medicare in the 1960s when he was a conservative spokesman and later a candidate for governor of California. The president's hard-edged criticism gave Reagan his chance to display his skill as a platform debater. When Carter contended that Reagan had begun "his career campaigning around the nation against Medicare," Reagan looked at his adversary and simply said, "There you go again." In a phrase the Republican summed up how many Americans felt about the president's preachy tone and his strident attacks on his presidential rival. Reagan had crystallized the doubts about Carter's personality and political leadership. At that moment the tide that had been running in Reagan's favor turned into a torrent, and a landslide victory ensued when the voters went to the polls a week later.[2]

THE REPUBLICAN PARTY IN 1974

Has the Republican vessel been so severely damaged in the Watergate battering that it is no longer seaworthy?

—Patrick Buchanan[3]

The Watergate scandal and the political fate of President Richard M. Nixon defined the Republican Party in the early 1970s. While their national leader was resigning in temporary disgrace in August 1974, within the Grand Old Party itself new issues and new forces were arising that would shift its direction during the remainder of the decade. Conservatism was becoming more ideological and confrontational, underscoring the existing Republican opposition to Democratic liberalism on economic matters. Even the Republican stance on the economy would soon grow more fervently attached to the idea of lower taxes under almost all circumstances.

In retrospect, the second half of the 1970s came to be identified with Ronald Reagan's emergence as the party's national
leader on the way to the presidency in 1981. Yet Reagan's rise to
power derived from a fresh generation of activist Republicans
who transformed the energy of Barry Goldwater and his supporters in the 1960s into a new brand of social conservatism that
spoke to the fears and hopes of middle- and lower-class Americans during a disturbing period for the nation.

Neither of the two major parties had been especially hos-
pitable to women before the 1970s, but the Republicans were
marginally more inclusive than the Democrats. The GOP had
specified in the party's national convention rules in 1940 that
women should have equal representation on committees of the
Republican National Committee and mandated a similar status
on the platform committee of the national convention four years
later. From 1940 through 1960 the Republican platform had
endorsed the Equal Rights Amendment (ERA). By 1964 the
statement was gone when the Goldwater delegates wrote the
document. It reappeared in 1968 with Nixon. Four years later,
when Richard Nixon was renominated, the convention delegates in the platform "continued our support of the Equal
Rights Amendment to the Constitution" and promised to work
toward its ratification.[4]

But the mood within the party was changing. Phyllis
Schlafly, who had written a best-selling book, *A Choice, Not an
Echo,* in support of Barry Goldwater in 1964, came to the forefront among opponents of the Equal Rights Amendment after
Congress sent it to the states for ratification in March 1972. Although thirty states had endorsed the amendment within a
year, Schlafly rallied opponents of the ERA to block the ratification process. She charged that it would infringe on the rights
of mothers and housewives while at the same time promoting
homosexual rights, unisex toilets, and taxpayer-funded abortions. Whatever the merits of the arguments against the ERA,
Schlafly's STOP E.R.A. campaign drew conservative women
into Republican politics at all levels. The ERA was not ratified,

and the Republicans moved into opposition of much of the feminist agenda in the 1970s. In the process, the Republicans enjoyed the allegiance of conservative women in the South and West who found what feminists were calling for to be anathema.[5]

The United States Supreme Court decision in the case of *Roe v. Wade* in 1973 further persuaded social conservatives to move toward the Republicans. The high court's ruling made abortion legal in the United States, thereby triggering protests from opponents of abortion who presented themselves as defenders of the unborn. Roman Catholics were at the forefront of what became known as the pro-life movement, with evangelical Protestants going in the same direction during the mid-1970s. The goal of these groups was to amend the Constitution to outlaw abortions. Their power at the ballot box, along with the similar convictions of many Republican lawmakers, impelled GOP leaders to identify the party as antiabortion.

Similar to what had happened a century earlier when Republicans in the 1880s pushed for temperance laws and Sunday closing measures, pietistic Protestants found the GOP a ready vehicle for implementing their religious values. At this time, however, Catholics made common cause with their onetime religious rivals in the interest of blocking abortions. The inroads that Republicans made among previously Democratic Catholic voters, especially men, provided a crucial difference for the GOP in the elections of the late 1970s and early 1980s.[6]

The Republican Party during this period was also strengthened by the appearance of "neoconservatives" within the party's ranks. Drawn from former Democrats put off by their party's liberal views on domestic and especially foreign policy issues, these intellectuals and polemicists found the Republicans more congenial as the 1970s wound down. As one of their leaders, Irving Kristol, later wrote in the wake of George McGovern's nomination in 1972, "Though none of us was a Republican, and few of us even knew any Republicans, our political landscape was in the process of being transformed."[7]

These individuals included Jeane Kirkpatrick, Ben Wattenberg, and Michael Novak, and they moved into well-funded conservative think tanks in Washington, most notably the American Enterprise Institute. There they preached their doctrines of a strong national defense, militant anti-Communism, and economic policies of deregulation and a smaller national government. The neoconservative movement proved to be a bridge for many of these writers and their children, in the case of Irving Kristol's son, Bill Kristol, to move into Republican politics.[8]

Neoconservatives applauded the desire of Republican conservatives to present the arguments for their doctrines in a more positive and upbeat light during the mid-1970s. The traditional GOP dislike of unbalanced budgets and deficit spending meant that the party often seemed willing only to retrench and pare back government programs, which came to be known on the right as "root canal" economics.

By the mid-1970s, however, a more appealing presentation of Republican orthodoxy evolved. Opponents of federal and state taxation contended that substantial tax cuts would in time generate so much economic growth that government revenues would increase, not go down. This approach became known as "supply-side economics," and it soon captured the allegiance of many Republicans. Ronald Reagan, who had paid high taxes as a movie star, embraced the idea eagerly. Congressman Jack Kemp of New York and Senator William Roth of Delaware advocated trimming income tax rates by thirty percent. Other Republicans argued that the capital gains tax rate should be reduced.

The tax reduction ethos had long been part of Republican thinking, but now it could be presented as a fresh and innovative way to overcome the economic stagnation that plagued the United States during the mid-1970s. Conservatives no longer had to stand in the way of liberalism by saying no to social change. They could be the proponents of progress while they painted Democrats and especially liberals as reactionary defenders of big-government policies that no longer served the needs of the American people. In the process, Republicans denounced unpopular manifestations of big government such as welfare and finessed discussion of the popular programs such as Social Security and Medicare that would also have to be cut back if the size of government was to be reduced.[9]

New political fund-raising rules favored the GOP in the mid-1970s. In the wake of the excesses of the Watergate scandal, Congress had updated the laws on raising money for political candidates. A key provision of the measure, passed in 1974, limited individual contributions to $1,000, and $5,000 for political action committees (PACs). With their superior base of small contributors and their ties to corporations that sponsored PACs, the Republicans soon outpaced the Democrats in the money available for campaigns in presidential and congressional elections.

In 1976, the Federal Elections Commission decided, and Congress wrote the ruling into law in 1979, that parties could raise unlimited amounts of money for general activities of a party-building nature, yard signs, leaflets, and voter registration. These functions were not regulated, and the funds that sustained them came to be known as "soft money," as opposed to supervised "hard money" that went directly to a candidate. While soft money did not explode into American politics until the late 1980s, the concept would serve the interests of Republicans because of their greater access to corporate resources.[10]

Republicans also benefited from the rise of direct-mail political fund-raising developed by Richard Viguerie and other conservative activists in the 1970s. Using mailing lists of contributors from the campaigns of Barry Goldwater and Alabama governor George Wallace, Viguerie framed messages of stark simplicity that spoke of imminent disaster if liberal initiatives were not fought with a timely donation. The response was usually gratifying, and the power of such groups as the National Conservative Political Action Committee (NCPAC) grew as they mobilized conservative Protestant evangelical voters for Republican causes. These voters would find their champion in Ronald Reagan in 1980.[11]

The Politics of Limits in the 1970s

> We are in a recession. Production is declining and un-
> employment, unfortunately, is rising. We are also faced
> with continued high rates of inflation greater than can be
> tolerated over an extended period of time.
>
> —President Gerald R. Ford
> December 1974[12]

The Republican assault on liberals in the mid-1970s coincided
with a serious recession following the boom years of the 1960s. A
number of worrying developments came together in the last
years of the Nixon presidency to shake confidence in the future.
After years of postwar prosperity, the prospects for the nation
seemed less bright and promising. American workers were no
longer as productive as they had been a decade earlier. The
goods they made, especially automobiles, did not compete well
in world markets. The manufacturing sector was falling behind
the rest of the world. In the early 1970s, inflation and unemployment rose at the same time in what was called "stagflation."
By 1974 the jobless rate stood at 7.2 percent, the highest in almost a decade and a half.[13]

A major shock to the economy was the Arab oil embargo of
late 1973. A brief war between Israel and the Arabs in October,
"the Yom Kippur War," raised international tensions and caused
the Middle Eastern oil producers to withhold oil shipments for
several months. The cartel that controlled world oil supplies, the
Organization of Petroleum Exporting Countries (OPEC), raised
oil prices shortly thereafter. The resulting dislocation in the
United States produced temporary oil shortages, long lines at
gas stations, and chronic inflation. The United States no longer
seemed to be in control of its own economic destiny. A long debate ensued about whether the nation should try to produce
more oil, whatever the cost to the environment, or rely on conservation and accept a permanent set of limits on prosperity for
the future. From the outset, the Republicans endorsed a policy

of opening public land to oil exploration and placing less weight on energy conservation as a solution to the problem.[14]

The economic shocks of the mid-1970s came at a time when the cultural wars of the 1960s were still playing themselves out in the public arena. The women's movement, beyond the Equal Rights Amendment and the abortion issue, pressed forward to achieve greater economic and social equity. The protests of gay Americans, which began in the late 1960s, challenged traditional values as well. On the left, sympathy with gay rights grew in this period when the American Psychiatric Association decided in 1973 that being homosexual was not a psychiatric disorder. Conservatives saw permissiveness and lower moral standards encroaching on the established order in disturbing ways. The Republican Party seemed the best political option for countering these unwelcome trends.[15]

Overseas, the dominance that the United States had enjoyed since World War II now seemed in doubt. The Nixon administration had terminated American involvement in Vietnam in 1973, but the collapse of South Vietnam two years later ended the longest war and the most painful military defeat in the nation's history. Meanwhile, the Soviet Union appeared disinclined to follow the policy of détente on which Nixon and Secretary of State Henry Kissinger had based much of their international diplomacy. Moscow had helped Egypt against Israel in 1973, the Soviets were abusing human rights and jailing dissidents, and worst of all, they were building missiles in what many conservatives argued was a clear effort to gain nuclear superiority over the West. The future of the country looked to be at greater risk despite all the sacrifices and social turmoil Americans had endured since John Kennedy's death.[16]

A FORD, NOT A LINCOLN

Can you imagine Jerry Ford sitting in this chair?

—Richard Nixon[17]

The weight of these problems fell first on Nixon's successor, Gerald R. Ford, whose brief presidency began abruptly on August 8, 1974. A longtime congressman from Grand Rapids, Michigan, Ford had risen to lead the Republican minority in the House in the mid-1960s. He was a decent man whose conservatism lacked a hard exterior; his many friends on both sides of the aisle applauded his elevation to the vice presidency after Spiro Agnew's departure in October 1973. Ford was not a glib man, and in a Washington where being able to speak quickly was taken for a bright mind, he gained a reputation as someone whose brain was average at best. Lyndon Johnson summed up the Washington consensus in a cruel quip about Ford: "He can't fart and chew gum at the same time."[18]

These judgments were unfair. While Gerald Ford was no intellectual, his record at Yale Law School demonstrated his aptitude. He was not an inspiring speaker, but his character and sincerity shone through in his public appearances. Ford was not a good administrator, and it took him some time to pull together a functioning team in the White House. His reliance on Henry Kissinger in foreign policy evoked qualms among many on the right who regarded the Secretary of State as too willing to negotiate with Moscow. Nonetheless, Ford proved to be more than a competent president.

Ford enjoyed a brief honeymoon with the press and the nation. After the tensions of the Nixon years, the Ford family seemed refreshing and open. Betty Ford's problems with drugs and alcohol were not yet fully known even to her own family. Pictures of the new president making breakfast, his attractive children gathered around, added to Ford's favorable image.

The euphoria lasted one month. On Sunday morning, September 8, 1974, Ford told a national television audience that he had pardoned Richard Nixon for any and all crimes connected with Watergate. A storm of protest followed. Ford's press secretary quit in disgust. The new chief executive came across as no more than another Washington insider ready to cut a deal with one of his cronies. His standing in the polls sagged from seventy-one percent to fifty percent in the week following his announcement. Ford's presidency and the chances of the Republicans in the 1974 and 1976 elections never really recovered from the episode.[19]

By and large, pardoning Richard Nixon was a defensible step. A prolonged trial for the former president would have been a major political distraction for the White House. Even if convicted, Nixon would not have received jail time, so the whole exercise would have been largely symbolic. Where Ford and his men failed in the first month of his presidency was in making the case that a pardon was necessary. Instead, the action came out of the blue and left the impression of another insider deal that the voters so disliked about Washington in the mid-1970s. There was no bargain between Ford and Nixon, but the look of the arrangement aroused suspicions that the president then had to spend time putting to rest.

With only two months to go before the congressional elections, the Republicans faced dire prospects in the wake of Watergate and Nixon's departure from the White House. The poor economy worked against GOP candidates who were already demoralized by the scandal. Adding to Republican woes was Ford's nomination of Nelson Rockefeller as vice president to fill that vacancy. Seeing their old adversary elevated to the second highest office outraged the right wing. Ford did his best to campaign for Republican candidates, but nothing worked to help the beleaguered GOP. The Republican National Committee ran advertisements asking: "When has it been easy to be a Republican?"[20]

When the votes came in, the GOP dropped forty-three seats in the House and another four seats in the Senate. Ford now faced a Democratic majority in the House that could override his vetoes and a Democratic Senate where Republican filibusters were less of a threat with only thirty GOP members. The new Congress was more liberal and more reformist. As a result, legislative confrontations with Ford loomed while the 1976 presidential election approached.

Ford Versus Reagan

> How can you challenge an incumbent president of your own party and *not* be divisive?
>
> —Gerald R. Ford[21]

The president's major political problem among Republicans was the impending challenge from Ronald Reagan. The California governor came to the end of his second term in Sacramento in the autumn of 1974. Already sixty-three, Reagan had to make decisions about his future quickly, or the window of opportunity to seek the White House might be closed to him. If Ford won the presidency in 1976, he could run again in 1980. That would leave Reagan well past the age of seventy and too old to seek the White House. Reagan had no interest in a United States Senate race. For him, 1976 was an up or out year as far as politics was concerned. In addition, Reagan had little respect for Ford, a sentiment that the president reciprocated. "Ford thought Reagan was a phony, and Reagan thought Ford was a lightweight, and neither one felt the other was fit to be President," said a Ford aide, Robert Hartmann, in his memoirs.[22]

But going up against an incumbent Republican was a problematic course in a party that placed such a premium on unity, continuity, and loyalty. Reagan himself had often invoked what he called the Eleventh Commandment: "Thou shalt not speak ill of another Republican." But the imperative of winning the White House and implementing his program persuaded Reagan that this self-created limitation could be breached. As Ronald Reagan was to demonstrate over the next decade and a half, he was a Republican to whom the customary rules of the party did not apply, both in his appeal to the broad spectrum of the GOP and his mastery of the arts of national politics.

Bringing Ronald Wilson Reagan into clear focus is not a simple proposition. Republican devotion to his legacy has become so pronounced that Reagan has evolved into a totemic, almost deified figure. In the minds of his admirers, there should be a

Reagan memorial in every state, a fifth face on Mount Rushmore, and his image on the dime like (or instead of) Franklin D. Roosevelt. As Abraham Lincoln has faded from Republican sainthood, in part because of his staunch nationalism, Reagan has stepped forward as the embodiment of all the modern GOP virtues. For one historian, Steven F. Hayward, even the president's frequent exaggerations and tall tales can be excused because they were "always about the deeper meaning of America, both what was right with America and what was wrong with America." But as Reagan continues to rise within the political pantheon, appraisals of his impact on the Republican Party slip away from reality.[23]

Reagan was sixty-five years old when he began his race against Gerald Ford in 1976. He had been a Republican officially for fourteen years, switching his registration from an independent in 1962. But for much of his life Reagan had been a Democrat with an admiration for Franklin D. Roosevelt. Though he campaigned for Hubert Humphrey and other liberals in the late 1940s, Reagan's political views in the 1970s recalled an older style of Democratic conservatism that was much akin to the new Republican thinking. He was, for example, a committed proponent of free trade but was not comfortable with the protectionism that had been so much a part of the Republican past.[24]

Even more powerful was Reagan's belief in the idea of states' rights and local government. He had opposed the Civil Rights Act of 1964 and the Voting Rights Act of 1965 as unconstitutional because of their enhancement of national power. In his inaugural address on January 20, 1981, Reagan asserted that the states existed before the creation of the federal government, a concept with which Abraham Lincoln and several generations of Gilded Age Republicans would have disagreed. But as a means of limiting federal power over natural resources in the West, the ability to regulate business activities, or in the area of civil rights, states' rights became an essential part of Reagan's conservatism.[25]

Reagan was a "conviction politician" who brought a well-developed set of ideas to national affairs. The federal government was too big, too costly, and too ready to tax the American people. Reining Washington in on the domestic side was both crucial and in the end, Reagan believed, not too difficult. What was required was a leader with the will to cut spending and abolish unnecessary programs. Since the federal government was, in Reagan's opinion, rife with fraud and abuse, reducing expenditures was simply a matter of determination and persistence. "There isn't any problem we can't solve," Reagan observed, "if government will give us the facts."[26]

In foreign policy, Reagan saw the United States as engaged in a death struggle with the Soviet Union that by the mid-1970s his nation was losing. "The evidence mounts that we are Number Two in a world where it's dangerous, if not fatal, to be second best," he said in 1976. As a result, an immediate buildup of American strength was imperative. More important yet was to follow a diplomatic course that identified the Soviets as the major source of evil in the world who threatened "the last island of freedom" with oblivion. Reagan rejected détente as the Nixon and Ford administrations practiced it. The Republican candidate did not like the idea of containment in principle and saw the eventual end of the USSR as a key goal for the United States.[27]

Other Republicans, most notably Barry Goldwater, had offered variants of Reagan's views, but accompanied by a biting anger and tough demeanor. Goldwater in 1964 had seemed perpetually angry at America's plight. Reagan shared Goldwater's dismay, but his sunnier disposition, affirming optimism, and nonthreatening manner conveyed his ideas to the nation in a much more positive way. Not since Theodore Roosevelt had the Republicans found a politician who so skillfully combined ideology and celebrity. Dwight D. Eisenhower had rarely used his popularity in the cause of party doctrine even when he advanced "Modern Republicanism" in the 1950s.

Reagan came to politics from Hollywood and show business where he had been a successful film star and a highly competent actor. To say that Reagan was not a performer of the top rank in Hollywood is true but misses the point. If a group of excellent screen actors surpassed Reagan, he still stood near the top of his profession. That made him so much better a speaker and advocate of political ideas than his contemporaries, Republicans and Democrats alike, that he had no equals in the period from 1970 to 1990. Reagan had spent a lifetime mastering the camera and the TelePrompTer. He held his body in just the right position and recounted anecdotes with genial charm. Thus, he easily conveyed sincerity and conviction on the campaign trail. So effortless did his carefully calculated performances appear that the Ford White House in 1976 and later the Democrats underestimated how profoundly Reagan connected with the American people.

Engaging the substance of public policy was not one of Reagan's strengths. A complex issue made it more difficult to explain in compelling phrases. But Reagan wasn't interested in the nuances of policy. He knew what he knew about the major questions in which he was interested, and he only refilled his store of anecdotes on occasion without probing his own assumptions. Reagan's power as a communicator lay in his simplicity of expression. For him the truth of an episode or illustration mattered less than its capacity to sway an audience. Much as a screenwriter "adapted" a nonfiction story to be more compelling on screen, Reagan used tales about welfare queens or racial integration in place of policy analysis. While critics might point out a resulting inaccuracy, an untouched Reagan had moved on to another speech and another story.

Reagan entered the race on November 19, 1975, with an attack on a national government that "has become more intrusive, more coercive, more meddlesome and less effective." He went after Ford over his foreign policy and pledged to transform Washington to make the nation more secure. Few Washington insiders seemed to think that Reagan had a chance to win the contest against Ford.[28]

The Ford campaign was already making plans to squash the Reagan candidacy. Richard Nixon reassured one Ford operative that "Ronald Reagan is a lightweight and not someone to be considered seriously or feared in terms of a challenge for the nomination." Perhaps Nixon simply forgot the problems that a less well known Reagan had posed for his own candidacy in 1968. In any case, the Ford campaign was searching for Reagan's vulnerabilities, and they thought they had found one based on a speech Reagan had delivered in September 1975. In the address in Washington, he had contended that transferring federal government programs to the states "would reduce the outlay of the federal government by more than $90 billion." With that one stroke, balancing the federal budget would become a realistic possibility, Reagan asserted.[29]

The statement at first received little press coverage because of the troubles that the Ford White House itself was experiencing during the autumn of 1975. As Reagan's candidacy loomed, the presence of Nelson Rockefeller as a potential running mate in 1976 continued to irritate the right wing of the party. Ford asked Rockefeller not to be a candidate for vice president in 1976 because staying on "would hurt him in getting the nomination." Rockefeller obliged with a public statement on November 3, 1975. A day earlier, Ford had sought the resignations of Secretary of Defense James Schlesinger and Director of Central Intelligence William Colby as the president shook up his foreign policy team. The resulting impression of disarray caused Ford to slump in the polls. By the time Reagan announced, Ford trailed him by twelve points.[30]

The President Ford Campaign was nominally in charge of the effort to reelect the incumbent, but the main direction for the president came from Richard B. Cheney, the White House chief of staff, along with Stuart Spencer, a former adviser to Reagan in the 1960s. Their team decided to emphasize Ford as an effective president while going after Reagan for his $90 billion in spending reductions. Their strategy hinged on the New Hampshire primary when they charged that Reagan's proposed cuts in federal taxes would necessitate corresponding increases on the state level, not an appealing position for Reagan to defend in a state with no income or sales tax. Although Reagan had a big lead over Ford initially and campaigned well in the state, Ford's effort closed the gap. The president eked out a close victory on February 24, 1976, by a little more than 1,300 ballots out of a vote of 109,000. Since Ford had exceeded expectations and Reagan had fallen short of these same standards, the win revived the president's chances for the nomination. Two weeks later, Ford won the Florida primary, a race that turned when Reagan came under fire among senior citizens for saying that the government should invest Social Security funds in the stock market.[31]

With Reagan's campaign apparently on the ropes, the challenger assailed the administration's foreign policy, especially the volatile question of the fate of the Panama Canal. The government had been attempting to negotiate a resolution to Panamanian grievances over the Hay-Bunau-Varilla Treaty of 1903 that had given the United States perpetual control of the ten-mile-wide Panama Canal Zone as if the United States were the sovereign. Diplomatic talks had stalled; on the right, deep suspicions existed over the Panamanian ruler General Omar Torrijos, a friend of Cuban dictator Fidel Castro. Reagan asserted that the Canal Zone and the canal itself were part of the United States and should not be ceded to Panama. As he put it to cheering audiences, "When it comes to the canal, we built it, we paid for it, it's ours, and we should tell Torrijos and company that we are going to keep it." The Ford administration reacted too slowly to this offensive from Reagan because of the assumption that his campaign was failing.[32]

Reagan's turnaround happened on March 23 in the North Carolina primary. Helped by the efficient organization of Senator Jesse Helms, Reagan beat Ford with fifty-two percent of the vote. Suddenly it was the president who seemed to be in trouble. Reagan swept Texas on May 1 with its big bloc of delegates, and won three other states in the week that followed. Reagan was ahead in pledged delegates and appeared to have momentum. Ford's advantage was in the states that chose delegates at state conventions rather than primaries. Exploiting all the benefits of incumbency, Ford wooed the uncommitted delegates. As the convention in Kansas City neared, both Ford and Reagan were close to victory, but neither candidate had yet achieved a majority.

Then the Reagan campaign gambled. To shake up the race and win voters for his candidate in the East, John Sears, Reagan's campaign manager, proposed that the vice presidential nomination be offered to Senator Richard Schweiker of Pennsylvania, the most liberal Republican in the Senate. When Reagan did so, conservatives erupted in anger, and the challenger to Ford actually lost delegates. Moreover, Schweiker did not deliver any votes from Pennsylvania, and the tactic made Reagan appear to be a reckless opportunist. Ford now had a tenuous hold on the nomination as the convention began.

The Kansas City convention in 1976 never became a repeat of earlier nomination battles such as the Taft-Roosevelt showdown in 1912 or even the bitter Taft-Eisenhower confrontation of 1952. To avoid any bruising floor fights that might sway delegates to Reagan, the Ford forces compromised on major platform issues such as foreign policy. Secretary of State Kissinger was kept out of sight until the final night lest he stir the juices of the right. The platform reflected Reagan's thinking about Eastern Europe and relations with the Soviet Union. On abortion, the convention supported "the efforts of those who seek enactment of a constitutional amendment to restore protection of the right to life for unborn children." In a bow toward Betty Ford, who championed the Equal Rights Amendment, the platform endorsed the "swift ratification" of the ERA. The delegates also supported lower taxes if spending cuts were made, but then added "without such spending restraint, we cannot responsibly cut back taxes."[33]

Ford won the nomination by a vote of 1,187 to 1,070. For his running mate, Ford selected Senator Robert Dole of Kansas, largely at the behest of Reagan who did not want the second spot on the ticket himself. Dole added little to the Republican chances since Kansas was safely in the GOP column, and the senator's abrasive campaigning style later proved a drawback. Ford gave as good an acceptance speech as he was capable of delivering, but the most dramatic moment of the convention came when the nominee, in a gesture of harmony, invited Reagan to join him on the podium and "say a few words at this time."[34]

Reagan endorsed the platform and the party but never mentioned Ford's name. Instead, he spoke of the future and whether Americans a hundred years from 1976 would enjoy the same freedoms and live in a world that had avoided the threat of nuclear weapons. It was vintage Reagan—broad, thematic, uplifting, and evocative of Republican themes. It if did not do much to help Gerald Ford, it signaled that if the president failed to win in the fall, the hearts of most Republicans were already pledged to Reagan and his vision of the future.[35]

Of course, Gerald Ford did not beat Jimmy Carter in November 1976. The Democratic nominee started the campaign with a big lead over the president, based on Carter's appeal as a fresh face who was not a Washington insider. A very effective Republican advertising campaign, coupled with Carter's mistakes as a novice in national politics, soon brought the Democratic candidate down in the polls. The Republican ticket did not do well in the vice presidential and presidential debates. In his encounter with the Democratic vice presidential nominee, Walter Mondale, Senator Dole said that "if we added up the killed and wounded in Democrat wars in this century, it would be about 1.6 million Americans, enough to fill the city of Detroit." The implied attack on the foreign policy record of the opposition in the twentieth century did not enhance Dole's reputation.[36]

Ford and Carter debated three times. In the second, Ford, responding to a question about American attitudes toward the Soviet Union and Eastern Europe, misstated a line from his predebate briefing book. "There is no Soviet domination of Eastern Europe, and there never will be under a Ford administration." When the reporter who posed the question gave Ford a chance to clarify his answer, the president stepped into trouble again: "I don't believe that the Poles consider themselves dominated by the Soviet Union," he said, and added that "the United States does not concede that these countries are under the domination of the Soviet Union." The episode renewed doubts about Ford's grasp of the issues, and he slipped in the polls. Ford did not repudiate his comments for a week, and the Republican campaign never quite overcame the Democratic advantage that Carter had taken into the election.[37]

The result was still very close. Carter won 297 electoral votes with 49.9 percent of the vote to 241 electoral votes and 47.9 percent for Ford. The congressional results were a standoff. In the House, the Republicans dropped one seat and the Senate alignment remained the same, with the Democrats in strong control. On the surface, the Democrats held the major components of national power. Yet the Democratic success was illusory. Carter had run well in the South among whites because of his religious appeal as a Baptist and "born-again" Christian. Combined with the reliable African-American vote, the return of some conservative Democrats to the party meant that Carter had a strong electoral base in Dixie. The long-term success of the GOP in the South stalled for a moment. But the Democrats would now have to run the government, an assignment that would prove to be their undoing. Democratic mistakes would bring converts to the GOP during the Carter years.

THE CARTER PRESIDENCY: REPUBLICAN OPPORTUNITY

> There is something seriously wrong with the White House leadership today. They have no faith in the people of this great country.
>
> —Gerald R. Ford[38]

Most crucial of the drawbacks of the Carter administration was the poor economy. In 1976, the Democrats had made much of the "misery index" that the country endured under Ford, a combination of the inflation rate of six percent and an unemployment rate of eight percent. Under Carter, however, while unemployment went down to six percent in his first two years, inflation mounted. In 1978, inflation stood at ten percent annually, and the "misery index" of the Democrats rose to sixteen and then kept climbing.[39]

The administration proposed and Congress passed energy legislation that Republicans attacked for its emphasis on conservation and government regulation. In foreign policy, Carter negotiated a Panama Canal Treaty that relinquished control of the waterway to Panama by the end of the century. Although the Senate approved the pact, with the support of key Republican senators such as Howard Baker of Tennessee, the issue proved a popular theme for Ronald Reagan in his stump speeches in 1978–79. Panama also galvanized the base of the GOP by eliciting a flood of contributions for the National Committee and political action committees.

Taxes became the major focus of the 1978 congressional elections, especially when California voters approved a major tax-cutting proposal in the state, Proposition 13. Other states followed suit. The debate over the proper level of taxation developed as the potential key to Republican economic policy and victory in the impending congressional races. One of the effects of rising inflation in the 1970s had been to push more taxpayers with lower and middle incomes into higher tax brackets. What had once been a progressive federal income tax that affected the upper end of the income scale now hit the middle class with effective tax rates above twenty percent. Combined with rising state and local sales and property taxes, the impact of federal income taxes aroused additional popular unhappiness and greater receptivity to Republican calls for reductions in tax rates and curbs on government spending.[40]

The Republicans took advantage of this political windfall to develop the tax-cutting policy that has been the hallmark of the party's domestic ideology ever since. Their strategy, famously identified with the term "supply-side economics," has become one of the most controversial courses of action in GOP history and within the historical legacy of Ronald Reagan. Conservatives and liberals still debate the economic effects of the policy and whether the way the party implemented tax rate cuts in the

1980s helped or hurt the nation's economy in the short and long run.

The proposals for cuts in income tax rates bubbled up from a number of Republican sources in the mid- to late 1970s. Economist Arthur Laffer advanced the argument that rate cuts would stimulate economic activity, as did Congressman Jack Kemp, a former pro football quarterback and Republican from upstate New York. The supporters of these cuts in income tax rates did not say that the improvement in the economy that resulted would restore all the lost government revenue, but they did assert that some compensating gains in revenues would occur. To throw the Democrats off stride, the supply-siders identified themselves with John F. Kennedy's tax cuts of the early 1960s (which some congressional Republicans had then opposed). That move allowed them to depict the GOP as the party of change and energy. The Democrats thus became the defenders of the status quo and the repository of tired, big-government ideas.[41]

The prospect of tax rate cutting caught on in American politics in 1978 but did not appear quite soon enough to translate into large Republican gains in the congressional elections of that year. The GOP added twelve seats in the House and another three in the Senate. Democratic control of Congress persisted. Yet the evolving trends favored the Republicans.

Among the new faces that voters sent to Congress were Newton "Newt" Gingrich from Georgia and Richard B. "Dick" Cheney from Wyoming. Gingrich, in particular, soon laid ambitious plans to recapture the House for the GOP. In the South, the Republicans scored a notable victory when William L. Clements won the governorship of Texas, the first GOP member to do so since Reconstruction. The support for President Carter was waning in his home region as he moved too far leftward for the taste of southern conservatives. The elections also produced the ouster of several liberal senators by Republican challengers.

On Election Day, the government of the Shah of Iran collapsed, and an anti-American regime of Muslim fundamentalists took power. The foreign policy position of the United States in the Middle East seemed to be under siege. Meanwhile, the Soviet Union appeared to be gaining power at American expense. Soon the Carter administration was under attack from both the Democratic left and the resurgent Republicans who saw a return to power in 1980 as a tantalizing prospect. The seizure of American embassy personnel by Iranian militants in November 1979 underscored the persistent problems that the Carter White House faced as the presidential election approached.

The larger national mood was becoming more Republican as the Carter presidency faltered. One of the keys to the president's victory in 1976 had been the support of evangelical Christians in the South who had been attracted by the president's public piety. Disillusioned with Carter's performance, they found more to admire in a new organization headed by Jerry Falwell of Lynchburg, Virginia. The Moral Majority, which Falwell created in 1979, used modern fund-raising techniques, including direct mailings, and proved an effective means for evangelicals to identify with the Republican Party and its issues.

By 1978 the amount of funds that Republicans raised far exceeded what their rivals collected. In 1980, for example, the Republican National Committee brought in $77 million, compared to $16 million brought in by the Democratic National Committee. The base of small donors that grew out of the Goldwater Campaign in the 1960s and the efforts of Republican National Committee chair Ray Bliss in that decade continued to pay dividends for the GOP. In addition, the Republican organization built the party at the state and local levels with far more success than the Democrats achieved, devoting their resources to finding Republican voters and getting them to the polls. While the Democratic organization withered under Lyndon Johnson and Jimmy Carter, the GOP was constructing a modern system that gave it a decided edge in the two-party competition throughout the 1980s.

"Are You Better Off?" The 1980 Election

> A recession is when your neighbor loses his job. A depression is when you lose *your* job. And recovery will be when Jimmy Carter loses *his*.
>
> —Ronald Reagan[42]

With the Republican presidential nomination in 1980 a likely stepping-stone to the White House, a number of hopefuls put their names forward. Senator Howard Baker of Tennessee, John Connally of Texas (a convert to the party), Congressman Philip Crane and Congressman John Anderson of Illinois, Senator Robert Dole, and George H. W. Bush all sought to position themselves as the alternative to Ronald Reagan. Each one thought there was either enough potential opposition to Reagan or that the front-runner might stumble and give them a legitimate chance at the nomination. As events were to prove, these optimistic scenarios bore little relation to the reality of Reagan's overwhelming popularity within the party. George Bush scared the Reagan campaign with a victory in the Iowa caucuses, but Reagan rebounded to win the New Hampshire primary and then move toward a first-ballot nomination.[43]

At the 1980 convention, Reagan briefly explored the idea of putting Gerald Ford on the ticket, but the two men and their aides could not work out an acceptable division of presidential responsibility. Reagan then turned to George H. W. Bush for the second spot. There were reservations about Bush in the Reagan camp because he had been critical of the tax cut proposals that the front-runner had advanced. At one point Bush had called the idea "voodoo economics." Bush was also widely believed to favor some abortion rights. His advocacy of population control while in Congress during the 1960s had earned Bush the nickname "Rubbers." Reagan insisted that Bush "support me on the issue of abortion," and the Texan agreed. The new vice presidential candidate dropped his earlier backing of the Equal Rights Amendment as well.[44]

The Republican platform in 1980 reflected Reagan's beliefs and the thinking of GOP conservatives who were able at last to tailor the document to their liking. On economic policy the delegates called for lower tax rates and a balanced budget. In a decisive move away from the party's past, they contended that "protectionist tariffs and quotas are detrimental to our economic well-being." The platform called for a constitutional amendment "to restore protection of the right to life for unborn children." On the Equal Rights Amendment both sides of the argument were recognized as engaged in "legitimate efforts." As for civil rights and African Americans, "Republicans will not make idle promises to black Americans and other minorities. We are beyond the day when any American can live off rhetoric or political platitudes."[45]

Jimmy Carter's foreign policy received a tongue-lashing from the Republican platform. "For three and one-half years the Carter administration has given us a foreign policy not of constancy and credibility, but of chaos, confusion, and failure." Not since 1941 on the eve of Pearl Harbor had the nation faced such peril, argued the platform writers. Accordingly, they would "build toward a sustained defense expenditure sufficient to close the gap with the Soviets and ultimately reach the position of military superiority that the American people demand." The various proposals included rebuilding nuclear forces and defense systems against a Soviet surprise attack.[46]

Given the disarray of the Carter presidency, Reagan had a clear advantage going into the 1980 election. The American hostages were still being held in Iran, the Soviet Union had invaded Afghanistan, and the United States seemed powerless. The White House had failed in a military mission to free the hostages in the spring, and in the ensuing months negotiations to free the captives had produced no results. At home the weak economy dragged down Democratic hopes. In the summer of 1979, Carter had shaken up his administration after a nationally televised address that warned the American people of a crisis of confidence in their country. Though Carter never used the word "malaise" in his speech, the term became associated with the president's troubles, and the Republicans made much of the issue. Carter had to stave off a challenge to his nomination from Senator Edward M. Kennedy of Massachusetts, a battle that left scars on the Democrats. To further bedevil Carter's chances, the candidacy of an independent, John Anderson, a former Republican, gave anti-Carter voters who did not like Reagan a place to go. Carter's only remaining hope was that Reagan would make a fatal slip either on the stump or in a debate.

Reagan did show a propensity for verbal gaffes in the early phase of the campaign, but he hit his stride as the election neared. Carter sought to paint the Republican candidate as an extremist in harsh terms, but this tactic backfired when the president came across as strident and Reagan as optimistic and confident. The polls indicated that the election was still close, with the voters undecided about the merits of the two major rivals for the presidency.

The election finally turned on October 28, 1980, when Reagan used his "there you go again" line with such effectiveness. Moreover, he posed to voters the devastating question: "Are you better off than you were four years ago? Is it easier for you to go and buy things in the stores than it was four years ago?" When the issues were framed in that way, the undecideds broke for Reagan in the waning days of the campaign, and an electoral landslide resulted. Reagan piled up fifty-one percent of the vote to Carter's forty-one percent and achieved an even more decisive sweep in the electoral college. Reagan won forty-four states with 489 electoral votes to Carter's five states with 49 electoral votes. The independent candidacy of John Anderson won 7 million popular votes.[47]

The triumph for the Republicans in 1980 swept across the board. The GOP turned twelve Democratic senators out of office and regained control of the upper house for the first time since 1955. Republican candidates also picked up thirty-two seats in the House. While the Democrats retained control under Speaker Thomas P. "Tip" O'Neill, the Republicans had a good chance of forging a working majority with the assistance of conservative southern Democrats fearful of defeat in 1982 if they did not cooperate with a popular incumbent president. The prospect of a realignment of American politics in a rightward direction, and the establishment of an enduring Republican majority, was much discussed in the wake of Reagan's triumph.

The 1980 presidential election illustrated how much the Republican Party had changed since the 1950s. One new area of electoral strength was the South where Reagan was held in high esteem by white voters. In Mississippi, for example, Reagan carried sixty-two percent of the white vote, and he recorded similar margins across the region. The nature of Reagan's appeal, and indeed that of the Republicans in the South generally, is very controversial because of the race question. To what extent had the GOP replaced the Democrats as the party of white Americans in the South by the 1980s, and to what degree did these new Republican loyalties rely on the longtime racial animosities of white southerners toward their black neighbors?

Ronald Reagan opened his national campaign after the Republican convention at the Neshoba County Fair in Philadelphia, Mississippi. Sixteen years earlier, four civil rights workers had been murdered in that county in one of the most notorious examples of white violence against those seeking to integrate the South. Reagan's speech defended states' rights and private property before a friendly, almost all-white audience of ten thousand listeners. "I believe in people doing as much as they can at the private level," Reagan maintained. With memories of his opposition to the Civil Rights Act of 1964 and the Voting Rights Act of 1965 still fresh, Reagan couched his conservative message in language that pleased white voters in the South. Like Richard Nixon's southern strategy, Reagan's speech could be defended as racially neutral but which a southerner unhappy with black progress could also interpret as an affirmation of his opinions. Black southerners in the 1980s disliked Reagan, but his popularity among whites more than neutralized the impact of African-American animosity. During the decade that followed, former white Democrats moved in huge numbers over to the Republicans to make the southern GOP the bastion of the white racial attitudes that had for so long been the property of Democrats in the region.[48]

Appealing to the white vote paid large electoral dividends for the Republicans and Ronald Reagan during the 1980s. Southern white voters, especially males, comprised a key element in the party's winning coalitions. With the South, Plains states, and Rocky Mountain region securely in the GOP column in most presidential elections, the party had what one commentator called "a lock" on the presidency in the electoral college. But with the immediate advantages came long-term problems as well. As southerners moved into positions of power and influence within the GOP, their racial views, cultural conservatism, and religious moralism sometimes grated on other sections of the nation. Like the Democrats before them, the Republicans would find that having a "Solid South" was a mixed advantage.

Another characteristic of the changed Republican party was the new president's attraction among religious conservatives. Despite his own lack of churchgoing and strong public piety, Reagan knew what the religious right wanted to hear. He stood against abortion, supported voluntary prayer in the public schools, and questioned whether evolution was a valid scientific theory. Careful not to push the agenda of the Moral Majority into substantive legislation, Reagan gave these groups and their leaders enough rhetorical endorsement to keep them reasonably contented throughout his administration.[49]

REAGAN IN THE WHITE HOUSE

America is back and standing tall.

—Ronald Reagan[50]

As president, Reagan continued to identify the federal government as the major source of the nation's woes. "In the present crisis, government is not the solution to our problems; government is the problem," he said in his inaugural address. The new president intended to reduce taxes, balance the budget by 1984, and restore national defenses to offset the threat from the Soviet Union. The extent to which Reagan and the Republicans succeeded in these goals during the 1980s has persisted as a source of bitter controversy between the two parties since Reagan left office in January 1989. Reagan's partisans contend that he revolutionized American politics, restored the authority of the presidency, and laid the basis for victory in the Cold War. On the other hand, critics point to the substantial budget deficits he left behind, the social costs of his economic policies, and the mistakes of his second term, such as the savings and loan scandal and the Iran-Contra affair.[51]

In his first four years in office, Reagan put in place the economic and defense policies he had promised in his race for the White House. Congress enacted an even more generous version of his tax proposals during the summer of 1981. Meanwhile, lawmakers approved the sizable buildup of the nation's defenses that the new president proposed. The failed assassination attempt on Reagan on March 31, 1981, and his bravery during the aftermath raised the president's popularity. So, too, his firm stance against striking air traffic controllers a few months later confirmed his strength as a chief executive. By the end of 1981, despite worsening economic conditions, Reagan dominated the political scene.[52]

The Republican Party did not benefit immediately from Reagan's stature. Turning the economy around took longer than the White House had anticipated, and the nation experienced a sharp recession in 1981–82. Democrats complained about the impact of "Reaganomics," which included some 9 to 11 million people out of work and a substantial number of business failures. Reagan's personal approval rating dropped to forty-one percent by the end of 1982. The prospect of achieving a balanced budget by 1984, as Reagan had promised during the campaign, faded away.

The Democrats were the short-term beneficiaries of these developments. In the 1982 elections, the opposition added twenty-six seats in the House while the Republicans retained control of the Senate. Reagan urged his fellow Republicans to "stay the course" and predicted that his economic policies would produce a turnaround before the 1984 presidential race. Reagan's forecast proved correct, but not for the reasons he offered. The administration backed away from its tax-cutting policy with a law, passed in August 1982, that lifted taxes to close the budget deficit. In addition, the Federal Reserve loosened up on the money supply. The stock market rose in August, and the economy itself began a sustained expansion in late 1982 that continued during the rest of Reagan's presidency.

As the economy improved and memories of the 1970s faded, Reagan and the GOP received credit for the nation's good health. The president seemed impervious to adverse criticism, and critics said "Teflon" caused negative comments to bounce off the affable Reagan. The president was a likable, engaging leader whose image was carefully cultivated to present his policies in their most appealing form. The Reagan White House staged his daily activities with an eye to the impact on nightly television news. The upshot was that Reagan remained popular even when his policies were less so.[53]

In foreign policy, Reagan's staunch defense of traditional values and stringent criticism of the Soviet Union also resonated with the voters. The comment in March 1983 that the Soviet Union was an "evil empire" resounded with Americans. Two weeks later the president advanced the Strategic Defense Initiative (SDI) to protect the United States against a Soviet missile launch. The attack on Grenada in October 1983 to oust a left-wing government also contributed to an impressive upturn in Reagan's standing as the 1984 election approached.

THE REPUBLICAN APPEAL

> We are Republicans, and we believe in government that
> is our servant and not our master.
>
> —Pat Robertson[54]

Under Ronald Reagan's leadership, the ideas of the Republicans set the agenda for American politics in the 1980s. The dominant themes of the GOP were the dangers of big government and the failures of liberalism since the New Deal. At the 1984 national convention, George H. W. Bush declared that "for over half a century the Liberal Democrats have pursued the philosophy of tax and spend, tax and spend" while the Republicans were saying to "the tax raisers, the free spenders, the excess regulators, the government-knows-best hand wringers, those who would promise every special group everything" that "your time has passed, your time has passed." The answer to America's economic problems, Bush said, was "a dynamic private sector that provides jobs, jobs with dignity. The answer lies in limited government and unlimited confidence in the American people."[55]

Restricting government above all meant a reduction in the size of the federal establishment and a lowering of the tax burden. "We in the Republican party," said Congressman Phil Gramm of Texas in 1984, "understand that when somebody gets something for nothing from the Federal Government, that some poor taxpayer is getting nothing for something." Ronald Reagan believed that in fighting poverty and relieving national ills, "it was time we ended this reliance on the government process and renewed our faith in the human process." Accordingly, Reagan added, "it was time for tax increases to be an act of last resort, not first resort."[56]

A suspicion of the efficiency and value of the national government as a proper force in regulating the economy underlay much of the GOP's ideology. The market was a much better way of dealing with inequities and dislocations. "In many fields," said the Republican platform in 1984, "government regulation either did not achieve its goals or made limited improvements at exorbitant costs." One of the administration's proudest accomplishments, achieved in conjunction with Democrats and Republicans in Congress, was the deregulation of the savings and loan industry in the early 1980s. Reagan and other Republicans believed that government should promote economic growth

through favorable tax policies, enterprise zones for economically disadvantaged areas, and subsidies for research and development. On the other hand, programs to supply welfare to the
poor must reduce the federal role in that area because "Federal
administration of welfare is the worst possible, detached from
community needs and careless with the people's money."[57]

The Reagan years also demonstrated Republican suspicion
about governmental action on behalf of the environment.
Though the Environmental Protection Agency (EPA) had been
created during the Nixon years, GOP leaders saw it as a leading example of overregulation. The 1980 platform argued that
"environmental protection must not become a cover for a 'no-
growth' policy and a shrinking economy." The Reagan administration reflected the influence of westerners, embodied in the
"Sagebrush Rebellion" against government interference, who
wanted pro-development policies in the West. Secretary of the
Interior James Watt led this effort until he was forced out of office in 1983 after a series of indiscreet public comments. Meanwhile, the EPA and Interior were now run by individuals with
close ties to the business interests they were to oversee.[58]

In the suburbs of the Northeast and Middle West, Republican voters did not share the zeal for unchecked growth that
animated their western counterparts. The GOP advocates of
moderate environmental regulation reminded their legislators
of their opposition to dirty streams, a lack of open spaces, and
urban sprawl. As a result, a minority of Republican members of
Congress combined with the Democrats to act as a restraining
force against development. The fault line in the party in this
area would become more significant during the 1990s.

For all the distrust of government in the economic sphere,
Republicans in the Reagan era saw areas in which an expanded
federal presence was necessary and desirable. "We are waging
all-out war against narcotics in our schools, in our neighborhoods, and across the land," said George H. W. Bush at the 1984
convention. The "War on Drugs," begun under Nixon, expanded during the Reagan presidency, especially because of

Nancy Reagan's "Just Say No" program to change teenage behavior. The GOP platform also pledged to "vigorously enforce constitutional laws to control obscene materials which degrade everyone, particularly women, and depict the exploitation of children." On the controversial topic of abortion, the party believed that "the unborn child has a fundamental individual right to life which cannot be infringed." This principle entailed government intervention on a variety of levels to implement opposition to abortion.[59]

Republicans grappled as well with the role of government toward civil rights. Efforts to increase the party's share of African-American voters did not bear much fruit. Rhetorical deference to the Civil Rights Act of 1964 was compromised by an opposition to efforts to implement affirmative action programs. "Just as we must guarantee opportunity, we oppose attempts to dictate results," said the 1984 platform. "Quotas" in hiring "are the most insidious form of discrimination: reverse discrimination against the innocent."[60]

The need to attract black and Hispanic votes often ran up against the party's growing reliance on white support, especially in the South and West. The president proclaimed his lack of personal bigotry even as his Justice Department sought to grant tax-exempt status to Bob Jones University, which maintained exclusionary racial policies toward minorities. The White House also opposed the extension of the Voting Rights Act of 1965 and only accepted a national holiday for Dr. Martin Luther King, Jr., in 1983 when it was clear that congressional passage was inevitable. As President Reagan argued, "If you happen to belong to an ethnic group not recognized by the federal government as entitled to special treatment, you are the victim of reverse discrimination."[61]

While defining themselves by what they were for, the Republicans in the 1980s also stressed how different they were from the existing Democratic Party which was depicted as soft on the issue on Communism and the continuing Soviet threat, permissive on cultural issues, and prone to "class warfare" in economic matters.

Making such a case involved finding virtues in past Democratic presidents that few Republicans had avowed when these men were in office. Ronald Reagan began this process in his 1980 acceptance speech. He quoted Franklin D. Roosevelt's speeches from 1932 on balanced budgets to show how far the Democrats had strayed from their onetime principles. By the 1984 Republican convention, party orators were praising Harry Truman, John F. Kennedy, and Hubert Humphrey as "mainstream" Democrats in contrast to the leaders of the party in the 1980s. As Senator Paul Laxalt of Nevada put it, "The once-great Democratic party is now the home of the special interests, the social welfare complex, the anti-defense lobby, and the glitter set, lighter-than-air liberals, and it's getting worse every year."[62]

The GOP by the 1980s had detached itself from most of its own history. There were occasional references at party gatherings to Abraham Lincoln, a quotation or two from Dwight D. Eisenhower, and respectful comments about Gerald Ford. Theodore Roosevelt had essentially vanished from the Republican record, as had the Gilded Age chief executives, the presidents of the 1920s, and Richard M. Nixon. The ideological turmoil that had marked the 1940s with Wendell Willkie and Thomas E. Dewey had not deposited even faint traces. Moderate or liberal Republicans, not to mention Modern Republicanism, had vanished as if they had never been a force in party affairs. For the moment, conservatism among Republicans carried all before it. It was as if the Republican Party had sprung from the forehead of Ronald Reagan without a past to burden its affairs.

Morning in America: The 1984 Campaign

> Let us ask for their help again to renew the mandate of 1980, to move us further forward on the road we presently travel, the road of common sense, of people in control of their own destiny, the road leading to prosperity and economic expansion in a world at peace.
>
> —Ronald Reagan[63]

The 1984 campaign for the presidency was a cakewalk for the Republicans, but an important missed opportunity as well. There was never any real doubt that Ronald Reagan and George Bush would be reelected. The Democratic ticket of Walter Mondale and Geraldine Ferraro brought together a colorless presidential candidate and an obscure New York congresswoman whose presence as a vice presidential hopeful owed most to her gender. Mondale's statement at the Democratic National Convention that he would raise taxes if elected gave Republicans all the ammunition they needed. Mondale enjoyed one bright spot when Reagan faltered in the first of their two debates, but even that temporary triumph really never altered the political balance. As a campaign official said to Lesley Stahl of CBS News, "We have built an electoral fortress in the South and West. We can withstand anything in this campaign—any mistake, anything at all, and still win."[64]

The 1984 election was thus made to order for the creation of a sustained GOP majority united behind a set of ideological goals. But there were two problems with such an approach. Reagan himself was more popular than his domestic policies. Pushing the envelope by coming out for private control of Social Security, more stringent controls on abortion, and abolishing the Energy and Education Departments, for example, might disrupt the voters and alienate potential support. These limits raised the question of whether a conservative transformation of American society was a feasible goal. The Reagan Revolution was a timid affair once taxes had been cut and defense spending increased. If a president with the political capital of Ronald Reagan in the summer of 1984 could not advance the harder edge of the Republican agenda, it was difficult to see when such an array of initiatives could be launched.

The second problem arose from the need for the president to explain and rationalize these controversial items if they were made part of his campaign. While opinions differ on how much Reagan had aged by 1984, when he was seventy-three, there was a strong sense within the Reagan political operation that the burdens of the campaign should not rest on his shoulders. While Reagan had his good days, he had uncertain ones, too, and a slip in a public appearance, while not likely to impair his reelection, could arouse doubts about his ability to govern. Thus, the decision was reached to run an issueless campaign that affirmed the faith most Americans had in Reagan but tried to do little else. Skillfully produced commercials proclaimed that it was "Morning in America" to make voters feel good about the choice of their president. It was a campaign, recalled Richard Darman, "that managed to bypass conventional substance altogether." The GOP used the national pride generated by the Los Angeles Olympic Games to reinforce their upbeat message.[65]

Unlike other previous incumbents such as Lyndon Johnson and Richard Nixon who had not debated their challengers as they rode to landslide victories, Reagan agreed to confront his challenger twice, while Geraldine Ferraro and George H. W. Bush squared off once. After his debate with his Democratic counterpart, Bush announced that "we tried to kick a little ass last night." Bush's eager participation as the attack man for the Reagan campaign attested to his concentration on the Republican nomination in 1988.[66]

As for Reagan, his first appearance with Mondale went badly. The president was listless, appeared confused at times, and rambled in answer to some questions. So poor was Reagan's showing that the age issue, which had not bothered the president up to that time, became the center of concern. The Republicans attributed Reagan's indifferent showing to overpreparation and promised a better result two weeks later. In fact, Reagan improved only marginally over the first debate, but he did deliver a devastating one-liner that made the difference. Faced with a question about his age, Reagan said, "I will not make age an issue in this campaign. I am not going to exploit, for political purposes, my opponent's youth and inexperience." For a nation that wanted Reagan to prevail over the fifty-six-year-old Mondale, that statement was comforting assurance enough.[67]

On Election Day, Reagan achieved a personal landslide. He carried forty-nine states and 525 electoral votes. Mondale won his home state of Minnesota and the District of Columbia for 13 electoral votes. With fifty-nine percent of the popular vote, Reagan confirmed his status as a champion vote-getter among all the men who had ever run for president as a Republican. Yet the president proved to have short coattails. The GOP lost two seats in the Senate and gained a handful of House seats. With Reagan's political future settled, political speculation within the party turned to the succession issue in 1988 and the hopes of Vice President Bush.

The second Reagan term brought about more problems than political revolutions for the Republicans. The president saw his White House team that worked well during the first term split up. Tired by the exertions of the first term, the successful managers of Reagan's presidency wanted new challenges. White House Chief of Staff James A. Baker moved over to the Treasury Department. In turn, Secretary of the Treasury Donald Regan took over the White House post. The change, which was developed by the two men and then presented to Reagan, was not an improvement. Regan proved to be heavy-handed and devoid of political skill. The White House lost much of its mastery in showcasing the president.

The events of the latter half of the 1980s tested Reagan's ability to lead. Mounting budget deficits impelled Congress to devise a method of keeping federal spending under control. Republican senators Phil Gramm of Texas and Warren Rudman of New Hampshire, along with Democrat Ernest F. Hollings of South Carolina, confronted Congress with mandated spending cuts or the prospect of across-the-board reductions in key programs. Their initiative on the spending cuts pleased most lawmakers and the White House even though it put off most of the hard choices until after the 1986 elections.

The major legislative achievement for the Republicans in Reagan's second term was sweeping tax reform in 1986. Although the White House pushed for the concept in general, the significant credit for enactment of the measure belonged to Senator Robert Packwood. The Oregon Republican, chair of the Senate Finance Committee, took up the bill following House passage in late 1985. By April 1986, the prospects for tax reform seemed dim since most senators were bent on loading up the bill with special deals. Packwood drafted a new bill that provided much lower rates and ended a host of long-standing deductions. The bill went through the legislative process, and Reagan signed it into law in September 1986. The new tax act simplified and reduced taxes in a way that helped the economy.

During Reagan's second term, the economic boom continued and the nation experienced a wave of money-making and mergers. Wall Street operators such as Ivan Boesky and Michael Milken sponsored large corporate acquisitions through the issuance of "junk bonds." The salaries of top executives shot upward. In the midst of the "merger mania," attention focused on such controversial figures as real estate operator Donald Trump in New York City who developed opulent casinos in Atlantic City, New Jersey.

The culture soon learned about young, urban professionals, labeled "yuppies" by an adoring press. These affluent individuals gathered in the areas of the East and West Coasts where computers were transforming expectations of how the economy would function in the future. For Republicans, all these developments provided evidence that the policies of the Reagan years were achieving sustained growth as the GOP had always promised. "Contrary to all the doomsayers," said Jack Kemp, "we have witnessed an entrepreneurial renaissance. It's electrified the world. It's raised our standard of living."[68]

Unfortunately for the Republicans in the 1986 elections, the prosperity of the decade did not produce a continuation of their political success. In the sixth year of a two-term presidency, when losses usually take place for the party in power, the GOP dropped six Senate seats. The Reagan tide in 1980 had swept in some marginal figures to the upper house, and these weaker candidates, without Reagan on the ballot, succumbed to Democratic challengers when the opposition regained control of the Senate. With the 1988 presidential election over the horizon and Reagan's presidency winding down, the Democrats thought that recapturing the presidency was more possible than anyone could have believed after the Reagan triumph of 1984.

On Election Day in 1986, the Iran-Contra scandal broke in what became the most serious crisis of Reagan's presidency. The revelation of the arms-for-hostages deal with Iran and the diversion of funds to the Nicaraguan Contras staggered the administration. Disclosures that White House staff members, including Colonel Oliver North of the National Security Council, had negotiated with the Iranians and sent money to Nicaragua suggested that a separate foreign policy apparatus had been established outside the possible restraints of Congress. Republican officials had regarded the Constitution not as a check on their power in conducting foreign policy but rather as a troubling obstacle to be circumvented by any means necessary to achieve their ends. In that sense, Reagan's conservative administration displayed quite radical tendencies toward the traditional procedures of the United States government.

The episode took some of the luster off Reagan's relations with the American people in 1987–88, but he rebounded with the foreign policy successes he forged in negotiations with the Soviet Union in the same period. Contrary to what the Democrats believed when the news of the scandal broke, the political fallout did not hurt the GOP. The Iran-Contra episode figured as an issue of much less importance in the 1988 elections than seemed probable when the news came out in late 1986.

From a long-range perspective, the most significant episode at the end of Reagan's presidency was Robert Bork's nomination to the United States Supreme Court. President Reagan had already made history when he selected Sandra Day O'Connor as the first woman nominated for the high court in 1981. Five years later Reagan elevated Justice William H. Rehnquist to the position of chief justice of the Supreme Court after Warren Burger stepped down. To fill Rehnquist's place, the president named

Antonin Scalia, a brilliant legal conservative and appeals court judge. The conservative cause did not yet have a secure majority on the Court. When Justice Lewis Powell resigned on June 26, 1987, Reagan turned to Bork, a judge on the U.S. Court of Appeals for the District of Columbia. A political firestorm then erupted.[69]

A prolific legal writer and professor at the Yale Law School, the scraggly-bearded Bork specialized in antitrust law but had provocative views on a number of hot-button issues. He had opposed the 1964 Civil Rights Act for intruding on the rights of citizens. Bork disagreed with the Court's ruling on privacy in such matters as birth control and was widely believed to harbor doubts about abortion rights and the decision in *Roe v. Wade*. As a member of the Justice Department, Bork had fired Special Prosecutor Archibald Cox during the "Saturday Night Massacre" of the Watergate period. There were no personal or financial skeletons in Bork's past. His opponents found his views distasteful and disliked him on ideological grounds.[70]

Liberal groups and Democratic senators went after Bork's opinions in the manner of a political campaign with hard-edged advertising and strong rhetoric. Senator Edward M. Kennedy of Massachusetts said, in remarks that especially angered Republicans, that "Robert Bork's America is a land in which women would be forced into back-alley abortions, blacks would sit at segregated lunch counters, [and] rogue police could break down citizens' doors in midnight raids" among other transgressions. The use of movie star Gregory Peck in anti-Bork ads, before celebrity political ads had become common, also seemed out of bounds to Republican supporters of the nominee.[71]

Republicans charged at the time and later that this kind of examination of Bork's opinions represented an intrusion of politics and ideology into a Supreme Court appointment. While scrutiny of a Supreme Court nominee's views had not generally occurred, there had been exceptions. In 1916, Republicans had opposed Woodrow Wilson's selection of Louis D. Brandeis because he was a liberal and a Jew. Fourteen years later, labor and civil rights groups had defeated the nomination of John J. Parker under Herbert Hoover. In 1968, Republicans such as Strom Thurmond had opposed Abe Fortas for chief justice based on the Court's decisions about crime and pornography as well as Fortas's finances.

In 1987, the White House was unprepared to make the case for Bork and let the initiative slide to his well-organized opponents. Bork himself was not an effective witness on his own behalf when he testified before the Senate Judiciary Committee. In the end, the nomination went down fifty-eight to forty-two, with a few Republicans deserting Bork on the final vote. After another slip-up in the nomination of Douglas Ginsburg, who had used marijuana while a Harvard Law School professor, the White House turned to Anthony Kennedy, an appeals court judge, and he was unanimously confirmed in early 1988.

The real consequence of the Bork episode was a persisting sense of Republican grievance. A qualified nominee had been "Borked" because he was a smart conservative, and the Democrats would pay for their "gutter" tactics in the future. American politicians like to play "hardball" best when they are throwing rather than being the target. In the Bork case, Republicans found themselves in an unfamiliar position for the 1980s: under Democratic assault. Whatever the circumstances, the episode would continue to resonate with conservatives in the GOP. A decade and a half after Bork's nomination failed, his rejection still came up when Republicans were criticized for their tactics against Democratic officeholders or judicial appointees. For Republicans, the Bork nomination was the moment when the Democrats had made judicial nominations all-out war. By the 1990s, the methods that had characterized the Bork case had moved down to appeals court nominees from both parties. A series of "mini-Borks" raged on into the early years of the twenty-first century.

The reasons for the ideological bitterness that marked American politics during the late twentieth century have been often discussed but rarely analyzed. The members of the two parties in Congress, more isolated in their own caucuses, did not socialize as they had in the past, and the partisan divide widened in the absence of nonpolitical contacts. The increased emphasis on social and cultural issues such as abortion, religion, and values put a premium on consistency and loyalty to the point that adversaries became enemies in a kind of warlike setting. Demonizing an opponent produced more campaign contributions from supporters, and so the process fed on itself. Both parties routinely deplored what was happening, but like the Cold War image of two scorpions in a bottle, neither the GOP nor the Democrats wanted to take the risk of a first move away from intense partisan strife.

By the time the aftershocks of the Bork case had eased in early 1988, the Republicans were well on their way to selecting their nominee to succeed Ronald Reagan as the party's leader. Already efforts to measure the impact of Reagan's presidency had begun, and they have continued ever since. In some respects, it is still too early to offer even a preliminary estimate of how history will measure this important Republican president. The record of his presidency is gradually being opened at the Reagan Library in California. That pace has not served Reagan well since it has retarded inquiries into his performance that would be more balanced than partisan evaluations from either the left or right. In addition, the selection of Edmund Morris as his designated biographer produced the semifictional *Dutch* in 1999, a book that obscured as much as it revealed. Some analytic studies of Reagan have now begun to come out, and the coming decades should see many more.

In the history of the Republican Party, Reagan is now seen as its greatest president and most important single leader. Abraham Lincoln has receded because of his nationalism and racial views, while Theodore Roosevelt's concern for social justice and expanded government power makes him a difficult choice for contemporary conservatives. Dwight D. Eisenhower's "Modern Republicanism" disqualifies him, and Richard Nixon is flawed because of Watergate. So Reagan stands supreme as the embodiment of GOP virtues and conservative ideals.

Reagan transformed the Republican Party into a conservative unit with a diminishing band of moderates on its fringes. His advocacy of smaller government, deregulation, and private enterprise commanded general assent while he was in office. In foreign affairs, the debate over whether he helped the nation win the Cold War as president attests to the power of his ideas and personality in the international arena. As a media communicator and presence on the campaign trail, only Franklin D. Roosevelt plausibly exceeded Reagan in those roles.

Reagan thus serves as a talisman of what it means to be a Republican. Although his anti-Communism was made superfluous by his own success in opposing the Soviet Union, his belief in tax cuts and increased defense spending are pillars of Republican orthodoxy. Given a world threatened by terrorism, a strong defense has now become a bipartisan truism. Tax cuts as a perennial policy present a different issue. Within a short time as American politics goes, the baby boom generation will claim its Social Security and Medicare benefits. To avoid a budgetary collapse, the government will in all likelihood have to reduce benefits or raise taxes to meet these obligations. If a Republican president is in office or if the GOP controls Congress, then Ronald Reagan's legacy will meet its most exacting test. As Reagan's immediate successor, George H. W. Bush, learned to his cost in 1990–92, raising taxes as a Republican was tantamount to political suicide.

Chapter 12

BUSH TO GINGRICH TO BUSH,
1988–2000

IT WAS A clear, crisp day in Washington as three hundred Republican members of the House of Representatives and GOP
congressional candidates assembled on the steps of the Capitol
on September 27, 1994. Behind them was a large blue sign that
read "Contract With America." In front of the Republican crowd
an array of television cameras and microphones was ready to
relay the party's message to the American people. The architect
of the event, Newt Gingrich of Georgia, the minority whip and
the presumed next Speaker of the House, came forward to present the message that he had been perfecting for fifteen years.

Ever since he came to Congress in 1979, Gingrich had
worked and thought about a Republican majority. He was convinced that the Democrats had become a corrupt, power-
hungry organization, committed to a vision of America that no
longer worked. He sought "to smash 'tax-and-spend liberalism'
which has dominated our domestic politics for sixty years," said
a Gingrich friend. The whole concept of an activist federal government, so beloved by the Democrats, was misguided, Gingrich
believed. Accordingly, the Democrats represented a set of ideas
that were historically obsolete.[1]

In the fall of 1994, with Republican fortunes on the rise,

Gingrich and like-minded Republicans had the wind at their backs. Demoralized Democrats tried to distance themselves from the unpopular administration of President Bill Clinton, while resurgent Republicans, energized by conservative radio-talk-show hosts, longed for Election Day to make their anger known. Suddenly what had once seemed impossible, a Republican takeover of the House of Representatives after forty years of Democratic rule, now appeared to have a chance of coming true. And once in power, Gingrich and his allies had an even larger vision. With the Contract With America enacted, they would move forward to recapture the presidency, implement the Conservative Opportunity Society of Gingrich's dreams, and make the nation Republican for a generation or more. But as countless Republicans in the party's past could have attested, it was much easier to want to change American public life than to accomplish that goal. Gingrich got what he sought—victory in the election and the speakership of the House—only to find that history had other plans for his vision and his party.

WIMP OR WARRIOR?:
THE CANDIDACY OF GEORGE H. W. BUSH

> We don't need radical new directions—we need strong, steady, experienced leadership.
>
> —George H. W. Bush[2]

The relentless rhythms of American politics meant Republicans were already looking to the future of their party in 1988 even as they paid tribute to the legacy of Ronald Reagan. At the end of Reagan's eight years there was a moment when the party's future was more open and less settled. Whoever emerged as the party's nominee, if he then won the White House, would determine the direction of the GOP well into the future.

On the other hand, the Republican Party tended to have a clear line of succession already established even in moments of flux. Reagan had made it clear that he believed his vice president, George H. W. Bush, should be the next nominee. That fact, as well as Bush's loyalty to the administration and the GOP over the years, gave him a presumptive claim on the nomination. Of course, Bush might falter in the run-up to the primaries, but the money, organization, and traditions of the party all favored Bush's chances in 1988.

Still, a crowded field of candidates vied for position as the process of choosing a candidate began in 1987. By this time the rituals of narrowing the candidates down embraced a series of straw votes, public debates, and party caucuses around the country. These "cattle shows" allowed Republican activists a chance to see their prospective leaders perform under pressure and measure their conservative credentials. Changes in state elections laws during the 1980s had grouped major state primaries on a single date, especially in the South. There, a number of elections would occur on the same day, Super Tuesday, in March 1988. The candidate who won those contests would likely be the nominee.

The Republican aspirants in 1988 divided into two groups: those looking for political lightning to strike a long-shot candidacy and the serious contenders for the prize. In the first group were former Secretary of State Alexander Haig, Congressman Jack Kemp, Governor Pierre S. "Pete" du Pont of Delaware, and Pat Robertson, a television evangelist. The two serious rivals were Senator Robert Dole of Kansas and Vice President Bush.

Dole had become the GOP leader in the Senate after Howard Baker left politics in 1985. An effective lawmaker best known for his tart tongue and refreshing candor, Dole had flopped as Gerald Ford's running mate in 1976, but he saw his chance twelve years later. A decorated veteran who had been gravely wounded in World War II, Dole knew that Bush would be his most dangerous foe. The Kansan hoped to beat Bush in the Iowa caucuses and the New Hampshire primary, thus winning the nomination quickly. If the race went on too long, Dole lacked the organization and the money to fight the vice president in the southern primaries on Super Tuesday.[3]

Bush, on the other hand, had surface weaknesses and residual strength. Born in 1924 and, like Dole, a World War II veteran, Bush had graduated from Yale after the conflict and made a success of the oil business in west Texas. He had then moved to Houston and entered Republican politics. He first ran for the Senate in 1964 and lost in the Democratic tide of that year. Bush spent two terms in the House of Representatives, from 1967 to 1971, and voted for the 1968 Civil Rights Act. In 1970, Bush made another Senate race but again lost, this time to Lloyd M. Bentsen, Jr.[4]

For the next decade Bush held appointive positions in the Nixon and Ford presidencies: chairman of the Republican National Committee, ambassador to the United Nations, United States representative to China, and director of Central Intelligence. These posts added to Bush's exposure and reputation as a Republican team player. Nevertheless, doubts about his abilities and commitment to conservatism persisted in GOP circles. When his name came up as a possible running mate for Ronald Reagan in 1980, the presidential candidate said of the potential choice, "I have strong reservations about George Bush. I'm concerned about turning the country over to him."[5]

Reagan had come to like and respect Bush as his vice president, but within the GOP at large there was still less regard for Bush as a man and a candidate. The conservative columnist George Will wrote in 1986 of the vice president as a potential successor to Reagan: "The unpleasant sound Bush is emitting as he traipses from one conservative gathering to another is a thin, tinny 'arf'—the sound of a lapdog. He is panting along Mondale's path to the presidency." Will was unkind, but his opinion resonated on the right of the party.[6]

A serious problem for Bush was the degree of his knowledge and involvement in the Iran-Contra scandal that broke in 1986. Bush asserted that he had not been "in the loop" of decision-making about the arms-for-hostages deal with Iran. Yet there was always the chance that evidence would surface to show he had greater knowledge than he had disclosed. For the most part, the vice president succeeded in keeping the issue at a distance during the early phase of the 1988 campaign.[7]

As events were to prove, it was easy to underestimate George

H. W. Bush as a candidate in 1988. Behind his Ivy League demeanor and patrician habits was a man who wanted the presidency and was ready to do whatever he deemed necessary to achieve it. First, he had to secure the Republican nomination, and his campaign encountered problems during the early stages.

Since Bush had won the Iowa caucuses over Ronald Reagan in 1980, it was assumed that he would have the advantage eight years later. But with Reagan's farm policies unpopular in a state that went Democratic later that year in the general election, Bush's campaign was in trouble in January 1988. The vice president's immediate problem was his role in the Iran-Contra scandal. To defuse the issue and demonstrate Bush's toughness, his campaign turned to the mass media. He had a live interview scheduled with Dan Rather of *CBS News* on January 25. Widely regarded in the GOP as the embodiment of the "liberal media," Rather was an excellent target for Bush's wrath. The vice president stood up well to Rather's aggressive questioning and gave as good as he got. The encounter helped Bush with the still-suspicious conservative base. "It was stronger than grits in the South," said campaign aide Lee Atwater. "Rather is a guy people love to hate down there." The staged confrontation eased the perception that Bush lacked courage or was a political "wimp."[8]

The Rather interview did not turn the tide for Bush in the Iowa caucuses, however. The vice president came in third behind the winner, Dole, and the well-organized effort to rouse evangelicals by Pat Robertson. Suddenly, Bush's campaign was in trouble again, and some of the press even pronounced his political obituary. That judgment was premature. Bush was the only Republican with true national support and a viable organization. His status as the designated heir of Ronald Reagan meant that the conservative base of the party was his if he could beat Dole in the New Hampshire primary.

Bush went into that contest behind Dole in the polls by a narrow margin but with all the advantages of money and organization rolling his way. Dole was not a good administrator, and his campaign lacked a defining theme beyond his Senate record. Bush had the backing of Governor John Sununu and a hard-hitting advertising strategy that attacked Dole's votes for tax increases in the Senate. Bush forsook his preppy ways and campaigned as a regular fellow in the retail politics of New Hampshire. As a result, Dole was simply overwhelmed as Bush achieved a nine-point win over his main challenger. The campaign then turned south with Bush securely in the lead.[9]

The importance of Super Tuesday in the Republican nominating process underscored how central the South was becoming in GOP affairs by the 1980s. Originally designed to give Dixie extra clout in the Democratic nomination race, the cluster of presidential contests now had a similar impact for the Republicans. If a candidate scored big in the South, an insurmountable lead in delegates could be established. That was what the Bush forces sought in March 1988.

Though he was far from the only southern Republican involved in the Bush campaign, Lee Atwater of South Carolina emerged as the defining presence in Bush's 1988 race both in the primaries and the general election. Atwater, who had had his thirty-seventh birthday in March 1988, had come up through the rough school of his state's politics as a protégé of Senator Strom Thurmond and a contemporary of Governor Carroll Campbell. Steeped in the blues culture of African Americans, a devotee of the guitar, and a confirmed ladies man, Atwater played politics with verve and an instinct for the throat. Atwater managed a GOP congressional candidate's race against a Democrat who revealed that he had received electric shock treatments for depression. When the Democrat accused Atwater of dirty tricks, his dismissive answer was "I'm not going to respond to that guy. What do you expect from someone who was hooked up to jumper cables?"[10]

Atwater understood how important southern Republicans were to Bush's chances for the nomination in 1988. The blend of cultural and economic conservatism that played well in the region tapped into feelings about race and religion that had once been the hallmark of Democrats. Now white voters in the South found in the GOP those same qualities. On Super Tuesday, Bush recorded victories in all the southern states and put Dole's candidacy on the ropes. Further successes in the spring left the vice president the likely Republican nominee.

How much that prize would be worth was still in question during the spring of 1988. The Democrats were on the verge of selecting Governor Michael Dukakis of Massachusetts as their candidate, and public opinion polls gave him a lead of as much as sixteen points over Bush. A moderate, centrist Democrat, Dukakis seemed a fresh face who might be able to tap into a public desire for gradual change after eight years of Ronald Reagan and the Republicans. Accordingly, Bush and his campaign team explored ways to turn the temporary assets of Dukakis into permanent weaknesses.

An additional task for Bush was the selection of a running mate to be unveiled at the Republican National Convention in New Orleans in mid-August. By the time the Republican delegates assembled, Bush had already cut into the poll lead that Dukakis had once held. The Democratic candidate had started to show the vulnerabilities on issues that plagued him during the fall campaign. So Bush knew that if present trends continued, he was likely to win. What could his running mate contribute to what now seemed inside the vice president's campaign to be a likely presidency?

The field of possible choices was large but not promising. Senator Dole had run second in the primaries, but he had already been a vice presidential candidate once in 1976 and had not done well. More important, he and Bush disliked each other, with Dole complaining after the New Hampshire primary that Bush had lied about his record. Once Dole was eliminated, sentiment appeared for Congressman Jack Kemp of New York. An enthusiastic and articulate tax cutter, Kemp was also perceived as a loose cannon who could not be relied on to stick to campaign themes without adding comments of his own.

Bush then became intrigued by a young second-term senator from Indiana, J. Danforth "Dan" Quayle. Much of the appeal of Quayle, a staunch conservative, was cosmetic since Bush was certain to carry Indiana anyway. A Bush aide wrote that Quayle looked "like Robert Redford, only he is better looking. He symbolized youth for the future of the Republican party." Bush had trouble connecting with women voters. The gag was that he reminded every woman of her first husband. The handsome, energetic Quayle seemed a solid contrast. The problem was that in the haste of the preconvention countdown, a thorough vetting of Quayle's strengths and drawbacks did not occur.[11]

When the choice was announced, Quayle made a lackluster impression. He gushed with enthusiasm to Bush in their joint appearance on camera but could not handle press questions about his enlistment in the Indiana National Guard in the late 1960s. Since Guard units were unlikely to be called to active duty during the Vietnam War, they had become a favorite option for fortunate young men who wanted to serve but not to fight. Quayle came across as not fast on his feet mentally, and his repeated verbal gaffes did little to refute that impression. One Republican later called the selection "a perfect example of computer dating gone wrong." Bush had erred, as he noted in his private diary, but there was no choice but to press forward with Quayle once he had made his selection.[12]

The high point of the convention came with Bush's acceptance speech to the delegates. He had been the subject of ridicule from the Democrats at their convention. Ann Richards had stung with a line about Bush being born "with a silver foot in his mouth." With the polls showing him pulling ahead of Dukakis, a strong speech would give Bush momentum going into the general election. Republican speechwriters, most notably Peggy Noonan of the Reagan White House, crafted an oration with key applause lines. One of these remarks would propel Bush to victory in 1988 but also foreshadowed the ultimate problems of his presidency.

Before a cheering crowd, Bush assailed Dukakis's record on cultural issues. As governor of Massachusetts the Democrat had vetoed a bill requiring schoolchildren to recite the Pledge of Allegiance. Bush attacked his rival for failing to get right on this matter. He ended his speech by leading the delegates in the Pledge himself. The other phrase that resonated was Noonan's description of America's private charities as "a brilliant diversity spread like stars, like a thousand points of light in a broad and peaceful sky."[13]

What made Bush's oration so memorable, however, was his statement about taxes. He contrasted his unwillingness to raise income taxes and other levies with Dukakis's reluctance to "rule out raising taxes." The Republican nominee predicted that "Congress will push me to raise taxes, and I'll say 'no,' and they'll push, and I'll say 'no'; and they'll push again, and I'll say to them, 'Read my lips. No new taxes.'" The last line, borrowed from Hollywood star Clint Eastwood's films, produced exuberant applause from the delegates and defined Bush's revamped persona. Gone was the "wimp" image. The short-term political gain was large, but Bush had also made himself hostage to unexpected events when he became president.[14]

The 1988 campaign shifted toward the Republicans after the national convention. Dukakis did not respond in a timely manner to the attacks on his character and record, and he performed poorly in the debates with Bush. The GOP pounded away on the issue of the Pledge of Allegiance and Dukakis's "liberalism" to create the perception that the Democratic candidate lacked the stature to be president. When Dukakis rode in a tank with a helmet on, he looked like a parody of a military leader, a point the Republicans emphasized with relish. In all of this jockeying, however, Bush was never really compelled to put forward his own vision of where the nation should be going. From an ideological point of view, it was another empty campaign for the GOP.[15]

One aspect of the canvass was fixed indelibly in the public memory. As part of their effort to indict the Dukakis record, Republicans criticized one of the policy decisions of the Massachusetts governor: the granting of furloughs to convicted felons in the state's prisons. The furlough program began during the term of the Republican predecessor to Dukakis, but it was continued by Dukakis. Under the policy, an African-American convict named William J. Horton, Jr., who was serving a life sentence for murder, was released on a weekend furlough. Horton fled to Maryland where he assaulted a couple, raping the woman. A Massachusetts newspaper brought the case to light. One of Dukakis's Democratic rivals, Senator Albert Gore, Jr., attacked the furlough policy (but did not mention Horton) in a Democratic debate in December 1987.[16]

Looking for issues with which to dent Dukakis's poll numbers, Republicans found the furlough issue an inviting target. The Horton case had been well aired in Massachusetts and had become the subject of a widely circulated *Reader's Digest* article. What made the issue explosive was the transformation of William Horton into "Willie Horton" and the creation of commercials featuring his mug shot, made by pro-Bush groups not directly affiliated with the vice president's campaign. While the Bush organization distanced itself from the Horton ads, they also did not mind that the case received abundant media coverage. "The great thing about the issue was that any way you spin it, Dukakis loses," said one campaign aide. After black leader Jesse Jackson visited Dukakis at his home, Lee Atwater told the press in his sarcastic public manner that the Democratic nominee might "put this Willie Horton on the ticket after all is said and done."[17]

The Republicans had a legitimate issue in the furlough policy. They rarely mentioned that Ronald Reagan had pursued a similar arrangement as governor of California. While denying racial motivation in the Horton controversy, the GOP strategists in the Bush campaign made only pro forma gestures to still the furor over the advertisement and its implications. The episode attested to the extent that racial attitudes more common to the South had permeated the ethos of the party.[18]

The most memorable and difficult moment for Dan Quayle in the campaign came when he debated the Democratic vice presidential candidate, Senator Lloyd M. Bentsen, Jr., of Texas.

Seeking to rebut charges that he was young and inexperienced, Quayle compared his legislative record and accomplishments to those of John F. Kennedy before he became president. Bentsen had prepared in his predebate trials for such a comment and responded, "Senator, I served with Jack Kennedy, I knew Jack Kennedy. Jack Kennedy was a friend of mine. Senator, you are no Jack Kennedy." Quayle's popular standing slipped further.[19]

Bush prevailed in the debates over Dukakis since the Democrat came across as emotionless and cold, especially in response to a question about whether he would endorse the death penalty for a man who raped and murdered his wife. When the votes were counted, Bush recorded a seven percentage point win over his rival, fifty-three percent to forty-six percent. The result in the electoral race was 426 to 112. The Republicans still had their "lock" on presidential contests, but there were small signs of erosion. The Democrats carried ten states and came close to winning several others. Dukakis did well among skilled workers, a growing segment of the electorate. A more effective Democratic campaigner could build on the centrist argument that Dukakis made to give Bush and the Republicans a real challenger four years later. However, such a scenario seemed unlikely in 1988 with four more years of a Republican administration coming to power.[20]

The presidency of George H. W. Bush boasted many historically significant events in its four years in power: the end of the Cold War, the collapse of the Soviet Union, and victory in the Gulf War. More specifically for the Republicans, however, the crucial moment came in 1990 when President Bush abandoned his "no new taxes" pledge and started the GOP on its way to an unexpected and stunning defeat in the 1992 election.

THE GEORGE H. W. BUSH PRESIDENCY

> The problem with my old man is that he thinks you can solve problems one at a time with good character, good judgment, a good team, and all that stuff.
>
> —George W. Bush[21]

During his first two years, George H. W. Bush seemed an activist and a very effective chief executive. More involved in governance than Ronald Reagan had been, he promised "a kinder, gentler nation." Like the shift from Theodore Roosevelt to William Howard Taft in 1908–09, the transition from Reagan to Bush was more like a transfer of power to the opposition than a baton pass from one Republican president to another. On the surface, everything was amicable between Reagan and Bush. Behind that facade, Reagan loyalists believed that their presence was not wanted in the new White House team. A close friend of Reagan's later griped that there had been "a very systematic purge" that included "anyone with any association with the Reagan-Nixon-Goldwater wing of the party."[22]

The new administration was, by most standards of American politics, very conservative. Bush named his old friend and campaign manager James Baker as Secretary of State. After a misstep with the selection of former senator John Tower as Secretary of Defense, who was rejected by the Senate, Bush named Richard Cheney to the post. The rest of the Cabinet, which combined conservatives and moderates, was well within the GOP mainstream. To run the White House, Bush picked the former governor of New Hampshire, John Sununu, the man whose help had been so critical in the New Hampshire primary against Bob Dole.

Bush distinguished between politics, which he disliked, and governing, which engaged his hyperactive energies. His record in the White House proved creditable. In foreign policy, he and his team managed the fallout from the Soviet Union's collapse with skill. He sent troops into Panama to capture strongman and drug dealer Manuel Noriega. The Bush White House had its greatest triumph with the Gulf War and the expulsion of Saddam Hussein from Kuwait. On the domestic side, the Americans with Disabilities Act and the resolution of the savings and loan scandal inherited from Ronald Reagan were both to Bush's credit.

By 1990, however, the political quandary that Bush confronted was the issue of taxes. The pledge that he had uttered at the 1988 convention was one that he meant at the time and intended to keep as long as he could as president. But if flexibility was required, Bush had the example of Reagan before him. Dedicated tax cutter that he was, Reagan had still agreed to a number of what were in fact tax hikes during the 1980s. What Bush and his advisers such as Richard Darman did not grasp was that Republican conservatives allowed Reagan these temporary heresies because of their confidence that in his heart he favored lower tax rates. With Bush there was no such faith in his motives. After all, Bush had once been for birth control and had criticized Reagan's supply-side policies in the 1980 campaign. To staunch conservatives, Bush always had the feel of someone with well-concealed moderate leanings. Many in the GOP feared that Bush, like Robert Dole, did not mind big government in some areas and the taxes that funded it. As the party moved to a stance that regarded all tax increases for whatever reasons as a betrayal of the core values of the Republican Party, any wavering at all on Bush's part was bound to spark intense criticism within the GOP.[23]

In the 1990s, when Bill Clinton and the Democrats claimed that their tax increases in 1993 had led to the economic boom of that decade, some Republicans countered that George H. W. Bush's acceptance of a tax rise in 1990 had jump-started the process of recovery by restoring fiscal stability. There was an element of truth in that judgment, but any credit Bush received for his change of mind occurred only after the Republicans had lost the White House in 1992. At the time, the move outraged Republicans, who saw the essence of their party under assault.

The Bush shift took place in two stages during the spring and early summer of 1990. On May 8, 1990, the White House announced that in dealing with congressional Democrats over the budget, there would be "no preconditions for negotiation," which in itself implied that revenues might rise. The Republican base was angered. A month and a half later the president issued a statement in which he said that dealing with the deficit might require "tax revenue increases." The 1988 pledge had been breached.[24]

Republicans in and out of Congress were infuriated. The chair of the Republican Congressional Campaign Committee, Ed Rollins, warned that the broken pledge might cost the party as many as ten seats in the House races in the fall. Newt Gingrich of Georgia, a rising star in the GOP and minority whip in the House, made clear to allies that he would oppose whatever came out of the budget negotiations with the Democrats if it included increased taxes. "An angry Newt Gingrich decides to go his own way," wrote one columnist.[25]

The Bush negotiators, John Sununu and Budget Director Richard Darman, did produce a deal with the Democrats in October 1990. The deficit reduction package proposed to raise the highest marginal tax rate, but it would be offset with cuts in proposed increases in the gasoline tax. Because of Democratic support, the measure passed, even though almost three-quarters of the Republicans in the House and Senate voted against the administration. Gingrich's position, not that of President Bush, represented the true attitude of the GOP. The belief that tax cuts were good in every circumstance and under all conditions was now, more than ever before, a fundamental principle of the party. Conversely, tax increases were to be resisted with the most intense fervor possible.[26]

At first it did not seem that Bush would suffer any lasting consequences from his political apostasy over taxes. The Iraqi invasion of Kuwait in the summer of 1990 and the events that led to the Gulf War in February 1991 lifted President Bush's popularity to record heights, making the furor among Republicans over the budget deal seem secondary. The congressional elections cost the GOP eight seats in the House and one in the Senate, but with Bush and his party riding high after the Gulf triumph a reelection in November 1992 seemed a predictable conclusion. Leading Democrats decided to duck the opportunity to face the incumbent. And Bush's own burgeoning popularity gave him little incentive to take steps toward building up his Republican base. In the president's mind, when 1992 came around there would be ample time for the Republican partisanship that the president now regarded as a necessary evil.

Partisanship flared when Supreme Court Justice Thurgood Marshall retired in 1991 and the White House selected Clarence Thomas, an African-American appeals court justice, to succeed him. When Thomas was accused of sexual harassment by a black law professor named Anita Hill, a controversial Senate hearing ensued. Republicans on the Judiciary Committee defended Thomas and attacked Hill's credibility. Republicans believed that a talented, qualified nominee had been the victim of a smear campaign, much like the one Robert Bork had faced five years earlier. Thomas was confirmed by a narrow vote, but the passions his case aroused spilled over into the political arena in 1992 and beyond.[27]

THE 1992 ELECTION

> This was the most poorly planned and executed incumbent presidential campaign in this century.
>
> —Dan Quayle[28]

Although on the surface President Bush's reelection in 1992 still seemed likely in the second half of 1991, the ground was shifting under the feet of the Republicans. A brief, sharp recession, the first in eight years, aroused fears about the future among voters. Many large businesses embarked on a process called "downsizing." The payrolls of important companies shrank. The millions of jobs that were to be created in the Bush administration materialized primarily in low-paying service posts. Resentments rose against both multinational corporations and new immigrants who secured jobs once held by longtime residents.[29]

With deficits weighing on the government, Americans asked whether the benefits of Social Security and Medicare would be available for them when they reached retirement age. Citizens told pollsters that the nation was on the wrong track and that national leaders were out of touch with ordinary people. Congress suffered its own internal scandals about its bank and overdrafts that members had written. The Democratic Speaker, Jim Wright, was forced out of office over his ethical lapses in 1989. Other disturbing revelations about congressional misbehavior marked these years.

An antipolitical mood, fed by the economic troubles and the sense that national leaders had failed to deal with serious problems, coursed through the electorate as party loyalties weakened. Both parties seemed detached from pressing concerns, and the possibilities for a third party or a popular insurgency brightened. As a Republican operative told President Bush in November 1990, "There is a sense of government apathy, unawareness, or insensitivity to the growing problems." The success of the Gulf War had masked these concerns during the first half of 1991, but they continued to eat away at backing for Bush and, by extension, for the party he led.[30]

The high levels of poll ratings that Bush had achieved after the Gulf victory slipped away in 1991 as the White House seemed to become immobilized by the economy. Yet through these months the president appeared oblivious to what was happening to his reelection hopes. An old friend, not otherwise identified, pressed Bush in August 1991 about planning for the campaign by asking, "Are you about ready to give us some work to do?" The answer was "Sooner or later. I don't see any reason to do anything now. Do you?" Even a skid in his job approval rating of almost twenty points in the early fall of 1991 did not seem to jolt Bush out of his self-imposed lethargy.[31]

Meanwhile, the political scene worsened for the GOP. In a special election to fill a vacant Senate seat in Pennsylvania, Richard Thornburgh, a onetime governor of the state and attorney general in the Bush cabinet, lost to Harris Wofford, a Democrat named to hold the place until the voters could speak. Wofford used the failure of the Bush administration to address the issue of expanded health care for the elderly and Thornburgh's connections to Washington to pull off a big upset. In

Louisiana the Republican gubernatorial candidate was David Duke, a former leader of the Ku Klux Klan. The national Republican Party repudiated Duke and he lost, but the GOP had been embarrassed.

Meanwhile, the perception that Bush was out of touch with the concerns of Americans hurting in the hard economic times continued to spread. The president was aware of what citizens were going through in an abstract way, but he was unable to connect with the public at large. The sense that he did not understand the problems that Americans faced came through when a Democratic pollster asked focus groups in mid-1991 whether the president evoked memories of characters in children's stories. Answers such as Rip Van Winkle and Little Boy Blue led the list.[32]

By December 1991, Bush had jettisoned the unpopular and maladroit White House chief of staff John Sununu, whose nastiness had become legendary in Washington. But no one of stature came in to manage the Bush reelection effort, and the leaders of the president's campaign never found a theme or a purpose to persuade voters that Bush should receive another four years in the Oval Office. Bush particularly missed the advice of Lee Atwater. Previously head of the Republican National Committee, Atwater had died of a brain tumor in 1991. Bush himself could not articulate his own message, as one of his friends admitted: "If you asked him why he wanted to be reelected, he'd have to look at his note cards. That's the fundamental problem at the core."[33]

While Bush was looking for the proper moment to revive his faltering candidacy, he faced a challenge to his own renomination. Former Nixon and Reagan aide Patrick "Pat" Buchanan left his cable television political show to run against Bush in a symbolic protest of the president's "moderate" policies. The challenger advocated "a new patriotism where Americans begin to put the needs of Americans first." After a rocky start, Buchanan found his argument in New Hampshire against "King George," aided by the wounded state of the economy in New England.[34]

In the New Hampshire Republican primary in February 1992, Bush easily defeated Buchanan by fifty-three to thirty-seven percent, but the showing of the insurgent embarrassed the president. Although Bush then locked up the nomination in the southern primaries, Buchanan had become enough of a nuisance that he would require delicate handling at the national convention in August. The need to repel Buchanan at the polls showed that Bush had alienated about a quarter of the GOP electorate. The upshot was that the president had to move rightward, which was not something that helped his chances in the general election.[35]

By the spring of 1992, Arkansas governor William Jefferson "Bill" Clinton had become the Democratic front-runner. But because Clinton was compromised by personal problems, including marital infidelity, the Bush camp did not see him as a major threat in the fall campaign. Like Dukakis four years earlier, Clinton would wilt under the negative campaigning of the GOP. A Bush campaign aide wrote the president in late April: "The swing voters have dismissed Bill Clinton as a serious alternative to President Bush."[36]

In the same memo, the Bush operative noted a new force on the political scene during the volatile year that was 1992. "The swing voters are very intrigued with Ross Perot." A Texas billionaire who had made his name in the computer service industry, Perot was a feisty, hard-talking individual who had long disliked Bush and his family. During the winter, Perot announced his candidacy for president on Larry King's call-in show. A wave of enthusiasm engulfed the Perot effort, and soon he had shot ahead of both Bush and Clinton in the polls.[37]

The troubles of the Bush campaign plagued the Republicans. In late April, rioting broke out in Los Angeles when four white police officers were acquitted by a white jury in the beating of an African-American motorist. Bush responded slowly to the domestic unrest, and press critics unfavorably compared his passive civil rights stance to the activism that Lyndon Johnson had displayed a generation earlier.

As the summer began, the political climate further deteriorated for Bush and the GOP. Media probing into Ross Perot's background revealed his personal quirks and brought his poll numbers down, thus leaving Clinton the major alternative to another Bush term. On the eve of the Democratic National Convention, Perot dropped out of the race. Meanwhile, the Democrats nominated Clinton, who chose Senator Albert Gore, Jr., of Tennessee as his running mate. The impression of energy and dynamism that the Democratic ticket provided lifted that party in the polls. Clinton had opened up a substantial lead in the polls over Bush as the Republican National Convention drew near.[38]

The GOP conclave renominated Bush and Quayle, despite some misgivings among the president's aides about the electoral value of the vice president. On the whole, the convention proved to be a public relations disaster for Bush and his party. To appease Buchanan, he was allowed to speak on the first night, and he made the most of his chance in the spotlight. "There is a religious war going on in this country. It is a cultural war as critical to the kind of nation we shall be as the Cold War itself." He denounced the wife of the Democratic candidate, Hillary Rodham Clinton, and the liberal forces that supported her, and he spoke with particular asperity toward homosexuals. The Bush leaders recognized that Buchanan struck a discordant note, but he had tapped a vein in Republican thinking. Since the Civil War, Republicans had seen Democrats not just as political opponents but as a threat to the nation's existence. As a Bush aide put it, "We are America. Those other people are not America." The trouble with Buchanan was not that he rejected core Republican values but that he articulated them with damaging clarity.[39]

Bush regained some lost ground with his acceptance speech, and he got a small bounce in the public opinion polls. But on a basic level the Republicans entered the fall campaign with a dispirited candidate and an inept organization. Bush's reelection effort was one of the worst-run in the history of the party. Although James A. Baker left the State Department to manage the Bush campaign, even he could not save the president's collapsing candidacy. Angry at the way the press had treated his withdrawal, Perot reentered the race in October, which hurt Bush's chances still more. The president also did not perform well in several three-cornered debates with his two rivals.

As the election approached, some Republicans saw the popular vote polls narrowing and Bush closing the gap with Clinton. Then five days before the voting, Lawrence Walsh, the independent counsel investigating the Iran-Contra affair, indicted Reagan's Secretary of Defense, Caspar Weinberger, for his role in the affair. The court documents filed with the charges indicated that Bush as vice president had known of the effort to exchange arms for hostages, an allegation that Bush had long denied. Some Republicans became convinced that had the Walsh indictment not come down, Bush could have prevailed. Though that was not a likely scenario, the belief informed GOP opinion toward Bill Clinton and his right to hold office when he became president in January 1993.[40]

The outcome of the 1992 election was a devastating personal defeat for Bush. He garnered only a little more than thirty-seven percent of the popular vote to forty-three percent for Clinton and nearly nineteen percent for Ross Perot. Clinton won 370 electoral votes to 168 for Bush. Perot was shut out in that category. The GOP picked up one Senate seat and ten House seats, but still did not have control of either branch of Congress.

The major cause of Bush's defeat was the economy, which had begun to turn around in the waning months of the year but did not arrive in time to push the Republican president into another term. A second administration for George H. W. Bush would have been bereft of ideas in any case. The campaign against Clinton had been negative and had not offered a vision of where Bush proposed to take the nation. After a dozen years in office, the momentum of the Republican surge that began in the late 1970s seemed to have ebbed. The nation had not voted for conservatism or liberalism. It had voted for a change.

The Republican Party Out of Power

> Clinton's empathy—the "I feel your pain" emotion—is as
> powerful a public relations tool as Reagan's "Morning in
> America" vision.
>
> —Frank Luntz[41]

When the Clinton presidency got under way, the Republican
Party regrouped to examine its political future. As before in its
long history, the GOP consisted of disparate groups with differing visions of what the party should be and where it ought to go.
The presence of a Democratic president in the White House allowed the Republicans to concentrate on what they were against
during the 1990s without having to set out exactly what they
stood for, beyond their dislike of income taxes. That problem of
ideological focus would linger beyond the Clinton era.

By 1992 the Republicans in electoral terms were solidly in
control of two main geographical areas of the nation. In the
heartland of the Middle West and Rocky Mountain states, the
Democrats rarely posed a significant challenge in presidential
contests. A newer area of dominance was the South where
George H. W. Bush still carried seven states in his national loss
to Clinton. In the South, white voters went in large numbers for
Bush while blacks gave the Democratic candidate almost ninety
percent of their support. However, the party was becoming less
securely based in the Northeast and along the Pacific Coast,
where the Democrats were establishing an ascendancy.

In economic terms, Republican policies won their greatest
endorsement from the business community, particularly small
and middle-sized firms. Corporations provided a dependable
source of campaign contributions that gave the GOP a wide
edge over the Democrats. Most Republican lawmakers believed
in the pro-business, antigovernment agenda that attracted such
financial support. They asserted that their independence had
not been impaired because of their monetary links to lobbyists.
In fact, when they took control of Congress in 1995, Republican

leaders punished firms that had donated money to Democratic candidates in the past or dared to do so in the future.[42]

The increasingly close relationship between the party and the lobbyists often influenced policy on such issues as gun control, the environment, and health care issues. The National Rifle Association (NRA) found in the GOP an ardent backer of its efforts to prevent gun control legislation. The party's constituency among white males in the 1990s made a link with the NRA a natural connection. Similarly, the Republican suspicion of regulation often guaranteed GOP support of industry groups' attempts to retard environmental legislation and block government efforts to implement such laws. The insurance industry found the GOP a congenial ally against national health insurance and campaigns to put insurance for mental health problems on the same plane as other diseases. Within the party's ideological core, there were those who wanted to overturn the major programs of the New Deal and the Great Society: Social Security and Medicare. Others dreamed of abolishing the income tax in favor of a national sales tax or other consumption-based levies.[43]

While economics secured many votes and led interest groups into the GOP coalition, the party's stance on social issues attracted countless others. Antiabortion forces saw the Republicans endorse their goals in the 1980s and 1990s to the extent that supporters of abortion were an endangered minority within the party. Other goals that Christian voters sought from the Republicans included an amendment on prayer in the public schools and restrictions on the rights of homosexuals. The gay members of the GOP, organized in a group such as the Log Cabin Society, found its economic thought appealing but often were at odds with the leadership about the antihomosexual tenor of the religious right. For the Christian conservatives, any economic goals proved secondary to the use of government power to achieve social change. Such a posture did not sit well with Republicans of a more libertarian bent.[44]

Republicans were not of one mind on foreign policy, either.

A strain of isolationism and unilateralism persuaded a number of GOP members to oppose international organizations such as the United Nations, the World Trade Organization, and the International Court of Justice. Involvement of American military forces overseas on behalf of "nation-building" was another strategy that large numbers of Republicans disliked.[45]

Yet the GOP also attacked the Democrats for an unwillingness to project national power around the world to safeguard American interests against terrorists and "rogue nations." For the GOP, one attractive feature of the strategic defense initiative, to protect the United States from a surprise attack, was that it maximized military power. At the same time it relied primarily on American technology and ingenuity, rather than foreign commitments or unreliable allies. Within the party the tension between isolationist sentiments and internationalist responsibility persisted.[46]

A similar fault line existed on the issue of immigration. Some in the party, such as Patrick Buchanan, wanted to cut off the flow of legal and illegal newcomers into the country. In California, Proposition 187, which passed as a ballot initiative, prevented illegal immigrants from receiving state education and health benefits. The Republican governor of the state, Pete Wilson, was at the forefront of advocates of the proposition's passage, which came in November 1994. Other Republicans, mindful of the burgeoning Hispanic population in the country, wanted the party to be more inclusive and tolerant. Asian immigrants also seemed a logical target of GOP recruiting campaigns because of their economic and cultural conservatism. The party's ability to resolve these tensions would determine its future in an increasingly pluralistic society.[47]

The 1990s also produced an upsurge of political ideas that diverged from the intellectual origins of the Republicans a century and a half earlier. Senator Trent Lott, the party's leader in the upper house after 1996, and Senator John Ashcroft of Missouri, for example, praised neo-Confederate groups and at least suggested that the Civil War had been wrongly decided. Lott on several occasions indicated that the nation would have been better off if the segregationist policies advocated by Strom Thurmond in 1948 had been pursued instead of the civil rights revolution. Gale Norton, Secretary of the Interior under George W. Bush, indicated that the Union victory in 1865 and the subsequent adoption of the Fourteenth Amendment had pushed the nation too far toward centralization.[48] The United States Supreme Court, under the leadership of William Rehnquist and Antonin Scalia, wrote decisions that shifted power back to the states in an apparent effort to redress imbalances that in their minds the Civil War and its aftermath had created. The Court even advanced the view—one that Abraham Lincoln never shared—that the states had been sovereign before the Union was formed.[49]

The federal courts themselves became a battleground for the Republicans with their Democratic adversaries. Mindful of the cases of Robert Bork and Clarence Thomas, Republican senators used their power to slow down the scrutiny of Bill Clinton's judicial nominees to lower court vacancies and in some instances to block their confirmation. Democrats protested these tactics but emulated them when they had control of the Senate, and a kind of partisan tit-for-tat ensued into the early years of the next century.

REPUBLICANS AND THE CLINTONS

> Mr. President, you should realize there are people in my party who just hate you.
>
> —Peter King[50]

A major element in Republican cohesion during the 1990s was the shared distaste, sometimes verging on hatred, for President Bill Clinton and his wife, Hillary Rodham Clinton. Since the 1992 presidential election had been, in the minds of Republican leaders, a shocking deviation from the natural order of American politics, it followed that Clinton's victory was not an authentic expression of the will of the American people. As a result, Clinton was president in fact but not in legitimacy. Robert Dole said after the election that the GOP in the Senate would represent the fifty-seven percent of Americans who had not voted for Clinton while Representative Richard "Dick" Armey of Texas told House Democrats that the incumbent was "your president." A modern variant of the Civil War–era Republican suspicion of the Democrats as not true Americans had again appeared.[51]

Since Clinton had run and won as a centrist Democrat, the extent of Republican animosity toward him went beyond ideology. The first baby-boomer president represented all the elements of the 1960s that Republicans disliked: self-involvement, cultural looseness, and sexual infidelity. Moreover, Clinton was a strong partisan infighter, something Republicans had not seen in a Democratic president since Harry S. Truman. Hillary Clinton's apostasy from being a Goldwater Girl in 1964, with a stop to work on the Nixon impeachment effort in the House in 1974, to a Democratic champion of health care in 1993 made her another GOP target.

The animosity against Clinton moved beyond intense political opposition into loathing that sometimes unhinged Republican judgments. Many on the far right of the party depicted the president as a drug addict, cocaine dealer, murderer, and potential dictator with covert plans to perpetuate himself in office and to end democracy in the United States. In the eyes of Republicans, Clinton was alternately a ruthless immoral man and an ineffectual bumbler. The American people had been deluded when they elected and reelected the man. The GOP need only put the facts about Clinton before the public, and the American people would come to their senses. Republicans seemed to forget how the Democrats had said the same things about the voters and Ronald Reagan.[52]

Clinton gave the Republicans ample cause to put their teeth on edge. Self-indulgent and reckless, he behaved like a modern John Kennedy in his sexual adventuring. He brushed the limits of legality and arguably crossed the line of criminality in his fund-raising practices. His word was good for that day and time only, and he showed an uncanny capacity to talk his way out of tight spots. Republicans always had him in their sights but found him an elusive prey.

THE GINGRICH REVOLUTION

> This is not about a bigger welfare state or a cheaper welfare state. This is about replacing a system that is killing our children.
>
> —Newt Gingrich[53]

The first two years of the Clinton presidency unfolded as if the Republicans had written the script. Clinton's administration stumbled out of the gate with flaps over Cabinet selections and the president's endorsement of gays in the military. The Branch Davidian episode at Waco, Texas, with its fiery climax, in April 1993 convinced far-right critics of Clinton and Attorney General Janet Reno that the White House intended to disarm law-abiding citizens, end religious freedom, and impose tyranny on conservatives.

It was the tax-increase measure, however, which the Democrats pushed through Congress in the summer of 1993, that united the Republicans. Not a single member of the GOP voted for the law, which narrowly passed the House and then squeaked through the Senate with Albert Gore's tie-breaking vote. Designed to reduce the burgeoning deficit and to assure the financial markets of the nation's fiscal integrity, the bill used tax hikes on upper-income taxpayers and spending reductions to trim the deficit for 1993 to $255 billion and for 1994 to $203 billion.

The Republicans in Congress pounced. The law, they said, was the largest tax increase in the history of the world (Reagan's 1982 tax bill was actually larger in constant dollars). Moreover, none of the supposed benefits to the country that Clinton had promised would come true. Instead, Republican speakers predicted, economic ruin impended. "It is a recipe for disaster," observed Dick Armey. "Taxes will go up. The economy will sputter along. Dreams will be put off, and all this for the hollow promise of deficit reduction and magical theories of lower interest rates." Newt Gingrich forecast "a job-killing recession" if the bill was enacted. In the Senate, Phil Gramm of Texas said that "hundreds of thousands of Americans will lose their jobs because of this bill."[54]

The tax fight energized the Republicans nationally but did little to arouse Democrat support behind the disorganized Clinton White House. In the fall of 1993, the Republicans made gains in state races. The most notable was New Jersey, where the GOP candidate, Christine Todd Whitman, running on an anti-tax program, came from far behind in the polls to oust a Democratic incumbent who had raised taxes. Suddenly, the tide of events was with the Republicans as 1994 loomed.

A key component of the Republican surge was the growing phenomenon of talk radio, exemplified in its most famous practitioner, Rush Limbaugh. A former sportscaster turned conservative advocate, Limbaugh spoke to millions of listeners daily over his "Excellence in Broadcasting Network" where he taught "Advanced Conservative Studies" with "talent on loan from God." So enraptured were his fans and so effusive was their on-air praise of Limbaugh that to save time callers were asked simply to say "ditto" when echoing earlier encomiums. Listeners or "dittoheads" relished Limbaugh's denunciations of feminists as "feminazis" and his decrying of "environmentalist wackos." As for Clinton, his presidency had resulted in "America held hostage." Among those who listened to talk radio more than ten hours a week, a striking majority of the audience were Republicans. Limbaugh's hard-edged anti-Democratic rhetoric, like that of other conservatives on the air such as G. Gordon Liddy (a former participant in Watergate), appealed particularly to white males in the South who were unhappy with Clinton, gun control, and higher taxes. Democrats never found a compelling alternative to Limbaugh and the talk radio craze.[55]

As Republican prospects brightened, Newt Gingrich of Georgia saw a chance to achieve what had previously seemed politically unthinkable: winning a GOP majority in the House of Representatives and making himself the new Speaker. Fifty-one years old in 1994, the burly, rumpled Gingrich, who dressed in the same casual manner as Wendell Willkie in 1940, had been in Congress since 1979. From the outset he had wanted to be Speaker. Taking advantage of the newly televised proceedings of the House on C-SPAN to build an audience in nightly special-order speeches, he and his like-minded colleagues harassed the Democratic leadership. Gingrich's intention was to transform the House into a Republican stronghold. Passing legislation by cooperating with the Democrats was not one of his priorities. His biggest coup had been ousting Speaker Jim Wright of Texas in 1989 over ethics charges. Now Gingrich reached for power of his own.[56]

A former college history professor who thought in large terms about national and world trends, Gingrich employed military metaphors (he had been an Army brat) and the language of the new technology. Eager to dish out insults, he did less well on the receiving end of political barbs. In Gingrich's mind the Democrats in the House had been corrupted by being in power since 1955. The majority party was identified with the over-centralization of the Great Society and was moving away from true American values. When a mother drowned her children in South Carolina, Gingrich saw her act as an example of Democratic permissiveness. Left unsaid amid all the moralistic language was anything about Gingrich's own personal lifestyle, which included an abrupt divorce from his first (and older) wife while she suffered from cancer and his clandestine affair with the congressional aide who ultimately became his third wife.[57]

As a political strategist, Gingrich had a talent for organization and a good sense of the weaknesses of his opponents. In addition to his innovative use of television, he had taken over a political action committee, GOPAC, in 1987 to channel money to Republican House candidates. Gingrich used the group to train Republicans to become more effective politicians, and thus he built up a network of supporters in the House as his efforts brought more GOP members to the body. By late 1993, Gingrich sensed that his historical moment had arrived. The incumbent Republican leader in the House, Bob Michel of Illinois, announced that he would not run for reelection in 1994. Gingrich was the putative Republican leader and informed a journalist: "We're going to be a modern revolutionary party that really wants to replace the welfare state and get back to common sense so everything I am going to be near is going to move that way."[58]

Gingrich had extensive polling done with focus groups to determine which issues resonated with these panels of voters. The data obtained were then combined in "A Contract With America" that pledged to take action on a balanced budget amendment, term limits for members of Congress, and laws to make Congress conform to the rules that they imposed on the rest of society. All these ideas would be addressed within the first one hundred days of the next Congress. If the public got the notion that they would be passed during that period, so much the better. Republican poll numbers were rising, and the Democrats saw the prospects for extending their control of the House eroding from week to week.[59]

The crux of the GOP strategy was to nationalize the election and make it a referendum on the Clinton presidency. Talk radio, effective advertising to rally the GOP base, and Democratic mistakes all worked to Gingrich's advantage. By this time conservative animus against the administration had intensified. A complex and costly health care program, endorsed by Hillary Rodham Clinton, had become an albatross for the Democrats. They could not pass it, but neither would it go away because insurance companies ran effective ads against it. A crime bill that included a ban on assault weapons activated the National Rifle Association and stoked the anger of conservative white males. Campaign contributions poured in from groups and individuals who applauded Gingrich's agenda. A cohesive Republican Party stood poised to capitalize on the anti-Clinton, anti-Democratic tide of the moment. As Gingrich told audience after audience, "It is impossible to maintain civilization with twelve-year-olds having babies, fifteen-year-olds killing each other, seventeen-year-olds dying of AIDS, and eighteen-year-olds receiving diplomas they cannot read."[60]

The climax of the Republican campaign came on September 27 when Gingrich and the three hundred Republican representatives and congressional candidates made their appearance on the Capitol steps for their photo opportunity. At the time, the Democratic response to these initiatives seemed to be always a step behind the political sentiment of the country. The elections saw the Republicans gain fifty-two seats in the House of Representatives and regain control for the first time in forty years. The GOP also won back the Senate, which they now controlled fifty-three to forty-seven. Republicans also won key governors' races, in New York with George Pataki and in Texas with George W. Bush, the oldest son of the former president, ousting Ann Richards. Gingrich became the Speaker of the House, and Robert Dole, an all-but-announced presidential candidate for 1996, was named Senate majority leader.[61]

At the specific moment it happened, the return of the Republicans to majority status in the House appeared to be a shift of historic proportions. The immediate result reversed a political condition that had existed in the mature lifetimes of most House members. Yet the longer term impact suggested that the 1994 elections lacked the staying power of the realignment that took place after the 1894 elections a century earlier. Instead of creating a new Republican majority, the election opened a period of political deadlock between the White House and Congress. Unlike the depression of the 1890s, the 1990s were a time of prosperity that helped sustain the popularity of Bill Clinton even in the face of Republican attacks. And for Newt Gingrich, his moment of triumph proved to be bittersweet and short-lived.

The House Republicans under Newt Gingrich set about implementing the Contract With America with great energy in the winter of 1995. The shift away from Democratic power intro-

duced new GOP congressional leaders to the nation, some of
whom became objects of controversy. The majority leader, Dick
Armey, asserted that "the market is rational and the government
is dumb." The new majority whip, Tom DeLay, also of Texas,
believed that the Environmental Protection Agency was "the
Gestapo of government pure and simple." To offset the effects of
liberal interest groups on Capitol Hill, Armey and DeLay pressured lobbyists not to contribute to Democratic candidates and
brought in business executives to help draft environmental legislation. While they denounced big government, the Republican
congressional leadership began directing federal appropriations
away from Democratic districts and toward the districts composed of the more affluent supporters of the GOP. Dick Armey
would later remind critics of the Democratic aphorism from the
Jacksonian era: "To the victor belong the spoils." But the Republican commentator William Kristol observed that if the
congressional party worked only "for special interests, it's going to be hard to show the Republican party has fundamentally
changed the way business is done in Washington."[62]

The Republicans set a busy pace through the spring of 1995
with the proposals that were part of the Contract With America.
The balanced budget amendment that Gingrich's friends in the
House proposed failed by a single vote in the Senate. The law
preventing Congress from imposing its mandates on the states
without sufficient funding was adopted. A constitutional amendment to impose term limits on members of Congress also failed.
By April, Gingrich and his allies proclaimed that they had either
enacted or brought for a vote most of the Contract and had thus
fulfilled their one-hundred-day pledge.

The horrific terrorist bombing of the federal building in
Oklahoma City on April 19, 1995, that killed more than 160 people changed the political landscape. Dismissed as irrelevant just a
few days before this sad event, President Clinton regained his
standing with the nation when he spoke eloquently at a memorial service for the victims. The bombing shifted the political momentum in favor of the president.

Meanwhile, the Republicans in Congress assailed environmental legislation and sought to remove restraints on business. The White House counterattacked, and Clinton used his veto against the GOP measures. However, Republican efforts to turn personal scandals in Arkansas against the president yielded few results.

One central battle with the Democrats in the budget fight was over the issue of Medicare. In their effort to secure a tax cut and to restrain the growth of federal spending, Republicans provided that the money allocated per patient would rise from $4,800 per year to $6,700 per year over the succeeding seven years. They bristled when Democrats described this process as "cutting" Medicare, and they said their goal was to "preserve, protect and strengthen" the Medicare program. Democrats countered that the government would have to spend $8,000 per year to maintain services at the 1995 level. The episode indicated the continuing GOP vulnerability on Medicare issues.[63]

Looking ahead to 1996, Republicans thought about General Colin Powell and hoped he might join the party. For most of the year Powell remained silent about his intentions. That left Senator Dole as the likely front-runner, with Phil Gramm of Texas and Lamar Alexander of Tennessee as the alternatives. Dole was seventy-two, had a long-standing reputation for a tart tongue, and looked to be an underdog to Clinton.

By the end of the year, the Republican Congress was itching for a showdown with the president. With no budget agreement in prospect, militant GOP members in the House thought that shutting down the government would pressure the president to agree to their terms. They could then have the satisfaction of humiliating their hated rival. It was not to be. Two government closures in November and December resulted in the Republicans getting the blame for the stalemate. As that perception sank in, the GOP leadership in Congress agreed to reopen the government on January 6, 1996. The first round in the 1996 presidential contest had gone to the Democratic incumbent.[64]

'WELL, WE'VE TAKEN OUR BALL AND GONE HOME... NOW WHAT DO WE DO?'

Newt Gingrich and the Republican elephant ponder their options after the effort to shut down the federal government in 1995–1996 has ended in political defeat.

THE 1996 ELECTION

> Don't you think it's time to elect a President who will keep Bill Clinton's promises? And that man is Bob Dole.
>
> —Kay Bailey Hutchison[65]

Clinton still seemed vulnerable as talk of financial scandals swirled around him and his wife. The Republicans were not able to connect the dots to make a compelling case against the president and first lady. The Democrats had raised ample sums of money, some of it from foreign corporations, and had begun a saturation advertising campaign to improve the president's poll ratings and drive down the numbers for his Republican rivals.

The Republican field was crowded, with Senator Dole the clear front-runner after Powell announced that he would not run. Dole lost an early race in New Hampshire to Pat Buchanan and faced the ample war chest of millionaire publisher Steve Forbes. Despite these obstacles, Dole did well in the southern primaries and was in sight of the nomination. He was also out of money and unable to fend off Clinton's advertising. With his candidacy in the doldrums, Dole resigned his Senate seat in June 1996 and ran as a man without an office or power in Washington. The poll numbers did not move.

With the election looming and control of the Republican House at stake, the GOP leadership in Congress decided to cooperate with Clinton in the adoption of welfare reform. Such legislation would bolster Clinton's credentials as an effective president and a "New Democrat" not tied to the failures of liberalism. By the end of July a compromise measure had cleared Capitol Hill. It ended the Aid for Dependent Children program and replaced it with block grants for the states. The federal responsibility of dealing with impoverished Americans, set up during the New Deal, was over. The law also cut back on benefits for illegal aliens during their first five years in the United States. During the remainder of the Congress, the minimum wage was increased, over Republican objections. The GOP sought wording in appropriations bills that would deny public education to the children of illegal immigrants but lost that fight.[66]

At the GOP national convention, Senator Dole sprang two surprises. He promised a fifteen percent cut in tax rates over a three-year period that would produce "a fairer, flatter tax." Many among the Republicans disliked the progressive income tax and had been advocating that the existing tax structure be replaced with a single, low tax rate on income for all Americans. Since there would be a loss of federal revenues at the start of Dole's plan, Democrats claimed that what Dole proposed would "blow a hole in the deficit," but the Republican candidate promised to find spending reductions that would offset the revenue losses.[67]

The second bold move was his selection of former congressman Jack Kemp of New York as his running mate. A champion of tax cuts, Kemp was supposed to be popular with African Americans, and he had the glamour of having once been a quarterback in the National Football League. However, he brought little electoral appeal to the ticket since Dole had no chance of carrying New York State against Clinton. Kemp also turned out to be a mediocre campaigner. Dole got a modest bounce out of the Republican convention, but Clinton's lead soon widened again.

In the campaign, Ross Perot once again launched a third-party effort, but without the enthusiasm or success of 1992. Dole and Clinton debated twice, with the Texan not present. In neither encounter did Dole inflict any serious damage. By mid-October, Clinton seemed far ahead, and the Democrats saw a chance to recapture the House and Senate. Then news reports surfaced about campaign contributions to the president from the Far East, with the possible involvement of Communist Chinese and Indonesian business interests. The revelations ate at the Democratic lead, and the race tightened somewhat. Dole conducted a last-minute whirlwind tour of the country to show that his age was no obstacle to being president. Yet when his blitz was over, the result of the election still seemed predictable.[68]

Clinton secured a second term with 379 electoral votes and forty-nine percent of the vote to forty-one percent for Dole and eight percent for Perot. Dole won 159 electoral votes from reliable GOP states; for the second presidential election, the Republican popular vote percentage had been under forty-one percent. The Republicans also lost some seats in the House of Representatives but held on to a ten-seat majority. In the Senate, the Republicans gained two seats but with fifty-five votes were still short of the sixty votes needed to halt a Democratic filibuster. Divided government remained in place.[69]

CLINTON IMPEACHED

So what you're saying is we have to impeach the bastard.

—Robert Livingston[70]

The two parties worked together in 1997 to achieve a budget agreement to balance the government's books for the first time in decades. With a booming economy and a soaring stock market pouring in tax receipts, the trend pointed to the end of the budget deficit. Clinton claimed that his policies, beginning with the 1993 tax bill, had produced that positive result. Republicans answered that their control of Congress had led to fiscal discipline and the brightening budget situation. Either way, by 1998 the nation could look forward to an unheard of change: an actual budget surplus.

In the House, unhappiness with Speaker Gingrich culminated in an effort by rebellious Republicans to oust him in the summer. Their perception was that Gingrich had failed too often to defeat Clinton on budget issues and other confrontations. An attempted coup against the Speaker collapsed in mid-July 1997 when the plotters could not agree on his successor. The episode left the House GOP in some disarray, but Gingrich had survived. Among his more fervent supporters there was even talk of a possible presidential candidacy in 2000 despite his weakened position in the House. Other hopefuls included Senator John McCain of Arizona and, assuming he was reelected in 1998, Governor George W. Bush of Texas. For the moment, with prosperity at a high level and Clinton's presidency enjoying popularity, the 2000 election seemed to favor the Democratic candidate.[71]

Then a dramatic development scrambled American politics and renewed Republican optimism about 2000: the revelation of President Clinton's affair with White House intern Monica Lewinsky and the possibility of his impeachment for perjury and other crimes in connection with this sordid episode. While Republicans had no doubts about Clinton's guilt, the situation presented delicate alternatives for the opposition. As the year unfolded and it became clear that the public did not want the president removed, the GOP was forced to reconcile its distaste for Clinton with political reality. In the end, the party decided to press forward with the impeachment out of a sincere belief in the president's complicity in perjury and obstruction of justice.[72]

Having made that decision, however, Gingrich and his congressional allies then failed to develop a strategy that could achieve Clinton's conviction and removal from office. The legislative arithmetic was simple. A majority in the House could pass articles of impeachment. Since Republicans assumed that the 1998 election would increase their majority in the House, their capacity to place Clinton on trial was assured. The Senate was another matter. Sixty-seven votes were needed there for conviction. Assuming that all fifty-five GOP senators voted to convict Clinton, the Republicans still needed to win over twelve Democrats to achieve the president's removal. Thus, the success of impeachment hinged on bipartisanship and conciliation of the Democrats in both houses. The Republicans adopted a confrontational approach, however, and risked alienating the Democrats rather than seeking their support.

Gingrich and the House Republican leadership saw the autumn of 1998 as the chance to increase their slim majority since the voters would punish the Democrats for their loyalty to Clinton. They expected that the president's speech on August 17 admitting some "inappropriate" conduct would lay the basis for a GOP rout. Accordingly, they disseminated the report of the independent counsel, Kenneth Starr, which made the case for impeachment even though the document contained lurid, graphic details of Clinton's sexual behavior. These tactics backfired. The partisanship of the Republicans galvanized the Democrats, and the results of the voting produced a stunning shift. The Democrats gained five seats in the House and cut the Republican majority to 221–211. Reporters had to look back to the early nineteenth century to find an instance when the party holding the White House added seats in the sixth year of a two-term president. The Senate alignment remained unchanged.[73]

The unexpected outcome of the election sealed the fate of Newt Gingrich. Restive Republicans now saw his leadership as a liability. With his support for reelection to the speakership in doubt, he decided to step down. His successor was supposed to be Robert Livingston of Louisiana. Revelations about his extramarital affairs doomed his candidacy at a time when personal rectitude was deemed a necessity. The battered Republicans chose Dennis Hastert of Illinois to be Speaker. Gingrich then resigned his House seat, ending one of the most fascinating legislative careers of the twentieth century. The Georgian had transformed the House of Representatives in ways that would have seemed impossible when he first arrived in Washington, but his weaknesses of temperament, rhetorical overkill, and personal morality made him a casualty of the hypercharged political atmosphere he had created.[74]

Notwithstanding the election result, the Republicans pressed ahead with the impeachment of Clinton in December 1998. Efforts to frame a solution short of impeachment had found little GOP support. The writing of four articles of impeachment and the eventual adoption of two of them were all done in a partisan atmosphere with only a handful of Democratic votes. By the time the trial opened in the Senate in January 1999, any chance of obtaining the dozen Democratic votes needed for conviction had long since disappeared. Republicans complained that Democrats had not displayed bipartisan statesmanship such as the GOP had shown during the Watergate controversy. Yet the Republicans in 1998 had forgotten to seek the votes of the Democrats if they really meant to oust Clinton. The Senate proceedings were anticlimactic, and Clinton was acquitted on both counts. The Senate Republicans did not achieve a majority of senators voting for conviction on either count.[75]

Anger at Clinton and perhaps an unwillingness to make Vice President Albert Gore an incumbent president clouded Republican judgments about the impeachment process. The GOP was serious enough about removing Clinton to initiate the process, but in the end it did not have sufficient determination to put aside partisanship and reach out to Democrats. That strategy might not have worked, but at least it offered some reasonable chance of success. As a result, Republicans had trivialized impeachment as a meaningful constitutional weapon.

THE 2000 ELECTION

> We are a new Republican Party. A compassionate, con-
> servative party, one that concedes no issue, one that re-
> gards every voter as an opportunity.
>
> —Tom Ridge[76]

By mid-1999, Republican thoughts turned to 2000 when Clinton would not be on the ballot. The field was once again a
crowded one for the GOP, but there were only two credible aspirants for the nomination. In 1998, George W. Bush had won a
landslide victory over weak Democratic opposition in his race
for a second term as governor of Texas. His triumph included
strong Hispanic support, an evident plus for a party that was
having difficulty attracting minority voters nationally. Under the
leadership of his skilled campaign manager, Karl Rove, Bush
promised to pursue "compassionate conservatism" in social policy. That meant an emphasis on education, long a Democratic
issue, and a large cut in income taxes. Rove told reporters that
Bush had the potential to do for the Republicans in 2000 what
William McKinley had accomplished for the GOP in 1896: build
a majority coalition that endured for decades.[77]

Bush soon established himself as the leader in the GOP race.
His fund-raising was so successful that he did not accept federal
matching funds. His war chest for the primaries soon exceeded
$100 million. With his record as governor to run on, Bush
promised "to change the tone" in Washington and restore bipartisan harmony that had been missing under Clinton. He
called himself "a uniter, not a divider," and his reassuring message played well with Republican audiences.

Bush also had vulnerabilities. Sober since the mid-1980s, he
had been dogged by rumors of alcohol abuse and even some
drug use as a young man. He brushed aside questions about
these matters as only of historical interest. His military record in
the National Guard in the early 1970s had unexplained gaps in
his service. Although he was intelligent, he had not shown at

Yale, Harvard Business School, or in private business an ability to frame an argument about public policy in an unscripted setting. His record in the oil business and professional baseball also suggested that he had not been an entrepreneur so much as a beneficiary of the largesse of Republican businessmen who were impressed by his name. The governorship of Texas, a constitutionally weak office, had not tested his leadership skills. The press, which had probed every aspect of the lives of the Clintons, largely accepted George W. Bush at his own evaluation of himself and made only sporadic inquiries into his background and character.

The main challenge to Bush came from Senator John McCain of Arizona who brought to the race a heroic war record, a reputation for plain speaking, and personal charisma. A conservative on most issues, McCain was susceptible to maverick moments when he actually worked with Democrats. The most notable such apostasy was his alliance with Senator Russell Feingold, a Wisconsin Democrat, on behalf of campaign finance reform. Outraged by the corrupting flow of money into American politics, McCain attacked the links among cash, access, and votes. The perception was, he told the Senate in 1998, "the more you give, the more effectively you can petition your government."[78]

For the GOP campaign, finance reform was unpalatable, especially if it only curbed corporations and did not address the role of labor unions in bankrolling the Democrats. The amount of money given to the Republicans by corporations and their political action committees far outweighed the contributions of organized labor, but GOP lawmakers equated the funds that came from these two sectors.

McCain was an attractive candidate whose appeal to the press did not derive only from the media's desire to see a fight for the GOP prize, but he had drawbacks of his own. Many of his fellow Republicans believed he was a loose cannon who was prone to excitable outbursts. In his personal life there were incidents of financial improprieties and romantic lapses that could hurt him in a general election. His brand of reformist Republicanism, which some of his admirers linked to Theodore Roosevelt, worried the GOP when its leaders contemplated a McCain presidency.

McCain upset Bush in the initial primary test with a decisive victory in the New Hampshire primary. The Arizona senator did well in primaries where independents could vote. When the candidates headed south to territory where Democrats and independents had a smaller role, however, Bush's strong campaign organization, his financial deep pockets, and a hard-hitting, even vicious series of attacks on McCain from the right reestablished Bush as the front-runner. In South Carolina, for example, Bush allies used McCain's adoption of a young Asian girl to tap into racial prejudices in that state. Though McCain won some other primaries, Bush had the nomination locked up by the spring of 2000.

Vice President Gore had secured the Democratic nomination. With the prosperity of the Clinton years not yet faded, Gore seemed to have the advantage over Bush. Yet the vice president was not an appealing campaigner, and the legacy of the Clinton scandals dogged him. So, too, did the national press corps whose members spoke openly of their dislike of Gore and their desire to see him lose. The Bush campaign found reporters to be eager consumers of the anti-Gore materials that the GOP generated with its customary skill. The "liberal media," always something of an imaginary Republican construct, was an ally of Bush throughout most of the general election season.

At the Republican convention in Philadelphia, Bush was nominated in a well-produced spectacle that emphasized his appealing qualities. His vice presidential choice was Richard B. "Dick" Cheney of Wyoming. The Republican candidate made his proposal for a $1.6 trillion tax cut, to take effect over a ten-year period, the centerpiece of his campaign. Directed primarily at upper-income taxpayers, the tax reductions would distribute money to the people that, in Bush's view, properly belonged to them and not the government. In foreign affairs, Bush said, "we have seen a steady erosion of American power, and an unsteady exercise of American influence." As for Bill Clinton and Al Gore, "The administration had its moment. They've had their chance. They have not led. We will." The new Republican ticket got a good bounce from the convention, and Bush's lead over Gore was in double digits as the Democratic convention opened.[79]

Gore, too, did well in his convention, and after the delegates dispersed, the Democrat again led in the polls in September. The election seemed likely to turn on the three televised debates where the conventional wisdom gave Gore, perceived as a seasoned debater, the edge over Bush. In the actual confrontation, both candidates were at best mediocre. The press had set expectations of Bush so low, however, that he came out the apparent winner.

In addition to his tax cut ideas, Bush also raised the volatile issue of Social Security, usually a risky course for any GOP member. Bush proposed to allow workers to invest a portion of their Social Security payroll contributions in private accounts that could take advantage of any future gains in the stock market. He promised that benefits would not be cut for those "nearing" retirement. The result, the Bush campaign contended, would be protection of the fiscal integrity of the system and greater wealth for Social Security recipients. With doubts about the fiscal soundness of the system growing, Bush's idea seemed to its proponents to provide a simple answer at a very low cost. Two years later, after Bush was in office, the electorate learned that the president's real goal was to make Social Security a voluntary system.

Advocates of the Bush changes during the 2000 campaign called the idea "privatization" of Social Security. Amid the positive rhetoric, problems were minimized. No clear definition emerged of what "nearing" retirement meant, and it was not apparent whether the presidential candidate was specifying a person in his or her early sixties or mid-fifties. The press, which praised Bush for political courage, showed little interest in how the plan would work. That some recipients would face benefit cuts and that the financial transition to the new system would be in the hundreds of billions of dollars seemed evident. For the moment, the Republicans had co-opted a Democratic issue.

In foreign policy, Bush and the Republicans attacked the involvement of the Clinton administration in overseas commitments of American troops. Bush told a Tennessee audience just before the election that "I'm worried about an opponent who uses nation building and the military in the same sentence. See, our view of the military is for our military to be properly prepared to fight and win a war and, therefore, prevent war from happening in the first place." Bush opposed a supervisory foreign policy for the United States over other countries. In a debate with his Democratic opponent, he argued that "I'm not so sure the role of the United States is to go around the world and say, 'This is the way it's got to be.' " In these comments, the Republican presidential candidate was articulating his party's suspicion of Democratic military commitments in the Balkans, Haiti, and elsewhere in the world.[80]

The race tightened as Election Day neared. Revelations about his drunk-driving conviction twenty-five years earlier slowed Bush's momentum in the run-up to the voting. Still, the Bush team thought, and so assured the press, that the Republican candidate would likely have a clear, even decisive lead in the popular vote but that the race for the electoral vote would be close.

The opposite occurred. Gore on election night held a lead in the popular vote that eventually proved to be a 540,000-vote plurality. In the electoral vote, however, the result was very close. Gore had won or was leading in states with 266 electoral votes. Bush had 246 electoral votes in his column. Florida, with the decisive 25 electoral votes, was first placed in Gore's column by the television networks and then called for Bush, and finally deemed too close to call. The Republicans, however, interpreted the network decision for Bush as one that established the legitimacy of his victory in the presidential race. Gore's forces, meanwhile, charged that ballot irregularities and errors in the Florida count had deprived him of the votes that would put him over the top.[81]

From the moment the controversy began, Republicans insisted that Bush had won Florida. The cohesion of the GOP and their refusal to lose gave them the upper hand over the Democrats, who never settled on a definitive strategy in the dispute. When vote-counting in a Florida county seemed, in the minds of Republicans, slanted against their party, a vocal demonstration of angry GOP operatives shut down the process. Much as in 1876, the ingrained Republican sense of entitlement as the natural governing party proved useful, while the Democrats were depicted in the press as obstructionists, deceitful, and unpatriotic.[82]

The nation watched as lawsuits and court proceedings, along with recounts in various Florida counties, dominated television coverage through November and into December 2000. The dispute reached the United States Supreme Court in December, and the justices ruled 5–4 in *Bush v. Gore* that the Florida vote as recorded by state officials appointed by Jeb Bush, brother of the Republican candidate, should be final. The recount in Florida ended. Gore accepted the decision, and George W. Bush was the president-elect. He was inaugurated as the forty-third president on January 20, 2001, and became the eighteenth Republican chief executive since the party's founding in 1854.[83]

The Republicans kept control of the House, again by a narrow margin, and the Senate split into a fifty-fifty tie. For the third consecutive presidential race, the Republicans had not secured a plurality of the popular vote. While the party's base in the South and West was secure, the results indicated that the West Coast and the Northeast were becoming more Democratic when the White House was at stake. The Bush campaign in 2000 had achieved a victory by combining fragile elements that would require and receive constant attention from the GOP and the White House in the years ahead. The tight result of the election allowed Republican analysts to predict the makings of a GOP majority coalition in the future, while Democratic observers

Election 2000
States Won, Percent of Votes Won, Electoral Votes Gained, and Voter Turnout Per State

This 2000 electoral map shows the tightness of the Bush-Gore contest.

were equally convinced that long-term trends favored their party.[84]

THE REPUBLICANS AT THE MILLENNIUM

> Republican policies are comprehensive and national, yet always conservative and safe, and never lacking in creative energy and constructive power.
>
> —James S. Clarkson[85]

The Republican Party that won the White House in 2000 reflected the dramatic changes that the twentieth century had produced in the party's electoral base and ideology. Comparing the Bush-Gore outcome with the race between William McKinley and William Jennings Bryan in 1900, for example, yielded intriguing results. Republican McKinley and Democrat Gore carried sixteen states in common, and their respective strengths were each concentrated on the West Coast, in the Middle West, and the Northeast. Bush and Bryan, on the other hand, dominated the South, with Bush running more strongly in the Plains and Rocky Mountain regions than Bryan did. Nonetheless, the regional shift in the political balance of the two parties, the realignment of their bases of support over the course of the century, was striking.

One hundred years earlier, the Democrats had been the party of states' rights, limited government, free trade, anti-imperialism, and white supremacy in the South. A leavening of anticorporate sentiment also animated the Democrats. The Republicans had been the party of business within the context of tariff protection, economic nationalism, overseas expansion, and an activist federal government. By 2000 the GOP was still pro-business, but otherwise it had taken over key aspects of the Democratic creed of the Bryan era: states' rights, small government, free trade, and limits to overseas involvement. On race, the Republicans had not adopted the creed of white supremacy, but they did represent the view that too much had been done for African Americans and other minorities during Democratic administrations. In the South, however, many leading Republicans saw the party as a means of maintaining the ascendancy of whites in the region.

The Republican endorsement of states' rights and restricted federal government arose from the GOP dislike of government regulation of business, a foundation of the party's ideology after 1912. Opposition to the income tax began in 1913 and intensified as the levy became part of funding the New Deal and the Great Society. The social welfare programs of the New Deal, most notably Social Security, also seemed to Republicans ill-conceived in theory and destructive of individual initiative in practice. The Republican shift on race stemmed from the defection of black voters to the Democrats after 1932 and then the allure of southern white ballots in the 1960s and beyond. As free trade replaced the protectionist international economy of the nineteenth century, the GOP moved toward a view of world commerce that maximized the market and afforded a smaller role to the government.

Despite its transformation into an updated version of many

features of the older Democratic Party, important aspects of an earlier Republican commitment to activism persisted. The party that had emphasized a more moral nation through prohibition laws and Sunday closing measures in the second half of the nineteenth century saw no contradiction a century later in encouraging the national government to outlaw abortions, mandate prayer in schools, and enforce traditional values such as heterosexual marriage only, antipornography laws, and a war on drugs. Deference to the religious right had become a central tenet of Republicanism since the 1960s, and with it came a reliance on governmental power that would have been anathema if applied to economic activities.

Where will the Republican Party go in the twenty-first century? The answer to that question lies beyond the vision of a historian. More than a century ago the British writer James Lord Bryce laid out in *The American Commonwealth* an intriguing prescription for Republican survival:

> In a country so full of change and movement as America new questions are always coming up and must be answered. New troubles surround a government, and a way must be found to escape from them; new diseases attack the nation, and have to be cured. The duty of a great party is to face these, to find answers and remedies, applying to the facts of the hour the doctrines it has lived by, so far as they are still applicable, and when they have ceased to be applicable, thinking out new doctrines conformable to the main principles and tendencies which it represents.

To the degree that Republicans can follow Bryce's recommendations, so, too, will the party remain as integral a part of democracy in the United States. Such it has been since delegates first gathered in Michigan in the summer of 1854 to create a party that would be, as William McKinley proclaimed in 1891, "a mighty force in the future, as it has been a mighty force in the past."[86]

CONCLUSION

THE HISTORICAL LEGACY OF
THE REPUBLICAN PARTY

> I became the first Republican I ever saw because a great
> teacher explained to me that people who were determined to
> make it on their own belonged in the Republican party while
> those who needed help were Democrats.
>
> —*Randy Ridgel*[1]

IN 2004, THE Republican Party will observe its 150th birthday
as a political organization in the United States. During that span,
the Grand Old Party won twenty-two presidential elections to
fifteen for the Democrats, saw eighteen members of its party occupy the presidency, and for a majority of the time controlled
the agenda of American politics.

Belonging to the Republican Party was one of the great com-
munal experiences for millions of Americans over that 150
years. Some, such as Christine Todd Whitman of New Jersey,
went through "growing up Republican," as she discussed in the
biography of that title. Others started out in life as Democrats,
like Ed Rollins who entered politics as a supporter of John and
Robert Kennedy and became an aide to Ronald Reagan. Then
there were the unheralded loyal Republicans who did the work
of the party at the local level, persons such as Sheldon Buck, a
crude-oil producer in West Branch, Michigan, who served in the
1950s, 1960s, and 1970s on the Ogemaw County Republican
Committee. Each of these countless individuals, famous and not
so famous, in his or her own way created the fabric of Republican history.[2]

What has the Republican Party meant to the United States?

After its inception as a radical, reformist political movement, it has become the conservative party of the nation, offering resistance to the activist programs of Democrats to its left. Begun as a party of nationalism and positive government, the Republicans have evolved into the champions of states' rights and limited federal power. The historical foe of slavery, Republicans find that their policies now attract almost no electoral support from blacks. Once the party of the protective tariff, it is now the most reliable ideological proponent of free trade. Imperialistic at the start of the twentieth century, the GOP has since been by turns isolationist, anti-Communist, and to some degree unilateralist in foreign policy. Across the sweep of American history, as issues changed, the Republicans have moved in directions that would have seemed improbable to its members only decades earlier. Of course, the same can be said for the Democrats, whose ideological journey has been at least as convoluted.

Leaving aside thematic consistency as a political impossibility, a balanced assessment of Republicans from an historical standpoint yields mixed results. The party's founding principle—the need to restrict the expansion of human slavery—was unquestionably sound. Even if, as modern critics of the Republicans have contended, racism flawed the Republican position in the 1850s, their belief that slavery had to be placed, in Lincoln's words, "in the course of ultimate extinction" identified them with the highest aspirations of the Declaration of Independence.[3]

The crisis over slavery and the Civil War, with its huge cost in lives and blood, is still a point of contention. That this titanic conflict was necessary to save the nation and end slavery is an issue that historians still debate and on which some modern Republicans, attuned to the seductive music of states' rights, have wavered. If one believes that the United States played a constructive role in the twentieth century in world affairs in World War I, World War II, and the Cold War, then it is hard to argue that a dismembered nation, part of it practicing slavery, would have had a comparable impact. Lincoln expressed that thought well when he called the nation "the last, best hope of earth."[4]

Once the Civil War was over, the Republicans faced the monumental task of Reconstruction in the South. For decades the main criticism of the radical Republicans was that they had done too much for the freed slaves, that their vindictiveness toward the South had produced an unwise experiment in racial justice. Since the mid-twentieth century, the charge has been that the Republicans, unable to rise above the nation's pervasive racism, have not done enough to change the South and the nation as a whole. In recent years, other Republicans have even identified the Fourteenth Amendment as too centralizing and have attacked their political ancestors as unwitting proponents of big government in the 1860s and 1870s.

That Reconstruction failed cannot be denied. But if it did so, it happened not because the Republicans offered too conservative a program but because the Democrats, north and south, resisted even the moderate changes that the northern Republicans proposed in the political rights of black Americans. Out of this turmoil came three enduring results: the Thirteenth, Fourteenth, and Fifteenth Amendments to the Constitution. While the retreat from Reconstruction abandoned African Americans to segregation and second-class citizenship once again, these amendments prevented a reemergence of slavery and offered the possibility of eventual equality. It was far from enough for the black Americans who suffered under segregation for so many years, but without these amendments the nation would have been set back even further.

So in the Civil War era, the Republican Party saved the Union, abolished slavery, and laid a foundation for political equality that could occur whenever the nation was ready to cast off old ideas about human potential. It was an impressive set of accomplishments of which any political party could be proud. That Republicans in the present time seem uncomfortable about their Civil War legacy attests to how much the party has changed in the decades since Reconstruction ended.

Two decades after it was founded, the Republican Party turned to a new set of issues, those concerning how the nation would pursue its economic development in the new world of industrial growth. The Republicans coalesced around the doctrine of the protective tariff as the best means of using the government to stimulate the growth of the economy. Drawing on its Whiggish past, the Grand Old Party contended that the interests of business and labor would harmonize behind the banner of protection. During the 1880s and 1890s, with the help of Democratic ineptitude amid the Panic of 1893 and afterward, the protectionist, nationalizing Republicans emerged as the majority party. The elections of 1894 and 1896 completed this process. William McKinley proved to be the architect of this enduring electoral coalition.

As industry matured and the rise of big business went forward, new inequities in society emerged. Voices from both political parties argued that the government must do more to regulate the injustices that industrialism produced. Reliance on the free market was not enough. For the first dozen years of the twentieth century, a new domestic challenge pressed for resolution. Under the leadership of Theodore Roosevelt from 1901 to 1909, the Republicans took up the question of how closely states and the national government should regulate the economy in order to mitigate the injustices of the now dominant industrial order.

With Roosevelt goading them, the Republicans adopted such regulatory measures as the Hepburn Act (1906) to oversee the railroads and the rates they charged, and the Pure Food and Drugs Act (1906). In the presidency of William Howard Taft that followed, GOP lawmakers went further to strengthen government oversight of the railroads and create other supervisory mechanisms. Opinion within the party remained divided on these issues, and the battle between Roosevelt and Taft in 1912 saw the conservatives emerge victorious with control of the GOP machinery. As Woodrow Wilson and the Democrats pushed for greater regulatory controls and legislation for labor unions, social justice for women and children, and increased appropriations for the South in the New Freedom years, the Republicans adopted a posture of skepticism concerning the enhanced role of government.

The problems of the Wilson administration during World War I brought the Republicans back into power for a dozen years in the 1920s and early 1930s. In office, the GOP achieved some important goals, including the Budget Act of 1921, which gave the government greater control over its finances. Reductions in World War I tax rates helped fuel the economic boom of the 1920s. But the main thrust of the party was to assist business, limit immigration, and otherwise minimize intrusions into the economy. As prosperity remained in place, this approach helped elect Calvin Coolidge and Herbert Hoover to the White House.

But this Republican focus left a wide range of issues unaddressed. Unlike other industrialized countries in Western Europe, the United States in the 1920s had no system of old-age insurance, no provision for unemployment insurance during an economic downturn, no effective regulation of financial markets, no measures for insuring the safety of bank deposits, and no real limits on child labor. The Republicans might not have been able to implement all of these measures during their tenure of power, but realizing none of them left the GOP vulnerable when the Democrats took power in 1933.

The Republican view of the New Deal has always been an ambiguous one. So much of what Franklin D. Roosevelt did, especially the implementation of Social Security, has proved to be so popular and lasting that GOP members never felt politically comfortable making a straight-out intellectual case against Roosevelt's programs. Yet, as their skeptical view of Social Security and Medicare now reveals, neither have they seen New Deal programs as fully established and legitimate parts of the American political environment.

During the first quarter of the twentieth century, the Republicans found themselves the champions of a circumscribed role in foreign affairs for the nation. William McKinley and Theodore Roosevelt had launched the nation into imperialist adventures, with the Democrats opposing overseas expansion. By the time of World War I, however, Republicans split over whether the United States should intervene in the conflict. Republican reluctance to support Woodrow Wilson and the League of Nations was based on more credible considerations than Democratic critics realized in 1919–20, and the absence of firm public support for participation in the world organization was as much of a factor as the opposition of Henry Cabot Lodge and the Irreconcilables to Wilson's vision. So during the 1920s, Republicans followed American sentiment in not wanting to take a leadership role in world affairs.

In the 1940s, with the threat of the Fascist dictators looming, the Republicans again split into opposing camps of isolationists and interventionists on foreign policy. The extent to which the GOP leaders such as Robert Taft were willing to stay out of World War II even in the face of a German threat did not represent the finest hour for the party. In discussing the failures of the United States to intervene in World War II or the difficulties of the League of Nations in the 1930s, Republicans rarely point out how much their party did to sustain these now discredited policies.

Following World War II, with the arrival of Communism and the Cold War, the Republicans evidenced a better appreciation of the general nature of the Soviet threat than did the Democrats, and the GOP provided valuable support for the containment policies developed under Harry Truman in the late 1940s. By the time the Soviet Union collapsed, Republicans believed that they deserved primary credit for the nation's victory in the Cold War against Communism. That self-congratulation is not entirely justified, but the record of Republican presidents in opposing the Soviet Union was a very creditable part of the party's history. It established the party's reputation with the voters as more trustworthy than the Democrats on national defense.

But the Republicans also found the anti-Communism issue a tempting weapon to use against their political enemies. While espionage within the government was more prevalent than the Democrats admitted, there was less in the way of an internal Communist menace than Republicans such as Joseph R. McCarthy alleged. The Cold War saw the GOP fall back on stereotypes of Democratic disloyalty that originated first in the Civil War era.

In the 1950s and 1960s, the shape of American politics moved again as the Democrats became the party of civil rights and the Republicans rethought their heritage as the party of Abraham Lincoln. Within Congress, Republican votes were vital to the enactment of the civil rights acts of that period, but outside Washington the GOP moved away from its identification with black rights and toward a sympathy for the concerns of white voters in the South and West. This "southern strategy" did not elect Barry Goldwater in 1964, but it helped put Richard Nixon and Ronald Reagan into office.

The appeal to whites proved effective throughout the 1980s and 1990s, but it raised the same kind of questions that had long tormented the Democrats. Was Republican conservatism in the South largely a cover for racial attitudes that looked back fondly to the era of segregation? As the Republicans became more southern in tone and substance, their appeal outside that region showed signs of fraying. Balancing the racial views of a predominantly southern leadership with the changing demographics of a more ethnically and racially diverse nation did not prove easy as the twentieth century ended. A party that did not reach out to minorities could find itself at a permanent electoral disadvantage.

In the 1970s and 1980s, as the excesses of a large federal government turned Americans off, the Republicans won power with their criticism of bureaucracy, regulations, and intrusion from Washington. Yet while the American people wanted less government in principle, they showed little desire to see actual cuts in programs that benefited their interests. Republicans thus embraced tax rate reductions as their guiding economic principle but held back from reducing federal programs when such trimming might offend powerful interest groups or campaign contributors. Ronald Reagan's mantra that savings might be found from "fraud, waste, and abuse" proved illusory.

Ronald Reagan and George H. W. Bush sold their tax-cutting

programs to the American people with much skill. Where the Republicans fell short was in asking the voters to confront the intrinsic responsibilities of smaller government. If the nation was not going to fund government programs, the choice was deficits or a smaller role for Washington. But terminating programs and asking the voters to take less in the way of largesse required facing defeat at the polls in the short run for a longer term gain. That risk is one the Republicans in modern times have not been willing to take. Standing on principle even at the cost of losing power is a harsh demand to make on politicians, but the alternative is to allow problems to fester and the national interest to suffer.

The historical value of a conservative party is to act as a restraint on the reformist impulses of society and to provide a steadying hand for the ship of state. A conservatism that makes no demands and enforces no responsibilities is largely a rhetorical posture. Republicans denounce "root-canal policies" as dangerous at the polls, forgetting that for someone with dental problems such unpleasant surgery is often the necessary price for restored health.

Since its founding, the Republican Party has been willing to use national power in noneconomic areas to produce a more moral and upright society. Prohibition in the 1850s has a contemporary counterpart in the campaign against abortion, the war on drugs, pornography, and homosexual rights. The identification of the antiabortion campaign with the antislavery impulses of the 1850s attests to the continuity in Republican thinking in this area. Balancing the need to interfere with personal behavior in order to advance societal values is always difficult, but the Republican tendency in this direction has often been necessary and salutary. Some social restraint on personal desires, whether it be drugs, abortion, or pornography, is required for the American people to coexist with one another. Whatever its occasional excesses, the Republican Party has been a constructive participant in that national dialogue.

At the same time, the Republicans have at various periods in their history found that aggressive moralism can rebound against the party that espouses it. To the extent that the Grand Old Party becomes an instrument of those with intense religious agendas, it could find itself making more enemies in a diverse population than securing converts.

Many individuals have been leaders in the long history of the Republican Party. Any selection of the most important Republicans must be somewhat arbitrary. Four presidents stand out for the leadership they provided and the choices they offered to the GOP. Abraham Lincoln remains preeminent among all the people who have marched under the Republican banner. In his speeches, in his leadership of the nation during the Civil War, and in his ability to grow in office, he set a standard that few chief executives of either party have attained.

Theodore Roosevelt has now been overshadowed in Republican lore. Beyond his exciting personal characteristics and charismatic life story, Roosevelt is little remembered now for his positive view of government, belief in national power, and conviction that enlightened conservatism should embrace some amount of government regulation. As he said in 1912, "In the long run, this country will not be a good place for any of us to live in unless it is a reasonably good place for all of us to live in."[5] His posing of the regulatory issue represented a turning point in Republican history where the party might have taken up the cause of implementing moderate, gradual government programs for old-age insurance and medical care to improve the lot of the majority of Americans in an increasingly complex society. That Republicans chose not to do so in 1912 and afterward was a decisive moment in the history of the party.

Forty years later, Dwight D. Eisenhower, a very conservative man, concluded that some accommodation with the New Deal represented a wise social choice. He called this approach "Modern Republicanism," and it echoed the thinking, if not the charismatic allure, of Theodore Roosevelt. Restraint in defense spending, attention to social improvements, fiscal responsibility—all these were hallmarks of Eisenhower's thought as president. His most lasting achievement was the interstate highway system that facilitated national cohesion during the second half of the twentieth century. For a majority of Republicans, what Eisenhower meant by modern Republicanism was too much like a New Deal for their tastes, and the allure of Barry Goldwater and a rejection of intrusive government programs proved more compelling.

The last transcendent Republican figure was, of course, Ronald Reagan, who put forth a conservatism with a smiling face that asked little of his fellow citizens. Reduce taxes, spend more on defense, oppose Communism, and all would come out right in the end. But the Reagan Revolution proved to be mostly rhetoric. When hard choices loomed, Reagan and the people around him preferred a conservatism of gestures rather than one of substance. Believing from his own life that society imposed no limits, Reagan saw no reason to ask Americans to accept any boundaries on their own desires. If they wanted to preserve the New Deal, they could do so, without being asked to pay the costs of such a social commitment. The next generation or the one after that would pick up the tab. Republicanism under Reagan became palatable, easy, and painless. That is why the Reagan Revolution left so much of the American political landscape unchanged.

In the end, the Republican Party had waged a dogged, consistent rearguard action against the increasing power of the federal government throughout the twentieth century. At the same time, once they came into power, as they did in the 1990s, the Republicans simply accepted the existing size of government and reallocated monetary resources to the sectors of society they favored. That meant the party was an accessory after the fact to the existence of big government, not its sworn enemy.

With the challenge of terrorism lying ahead for the nation after 2000, the Republicans faced another serious choice as a party. Mobilizing the energies of the nation to fight a threat that could endure for generations would require a strong national government to allocate resources, protect society, and project American power around the world. How the creed of states' rights, small government, and low taxes would reconcile itself with demands for national action even more profound than those Abraham Lincoln faced in the 1860s was an issue that few Republicans had addressed in the early years of the twenty-first century.

In fact, the response to the terrorist attacks of September 11, 2001, found Republicans moving in two directions. Especially after their recapture of the Senate in the 2002 elections, they could proceed with their program of cutting taxes and reducing the size of government. President George W. Bush proposed changes in Social Security and Medicare that would transform them into voluntary programs and roll back much of what the New Deal had done. Deficit spending became a way of reducing the size of government by increasing debt and forcing a change in national priorities. Other initiatives envisioned a greater role for the states without the federal monies to implement the states' new responsibilities. With the baby boom generation approaching the time of collecting Social Security and drawing on Medicare benefits, a serious fiscal crisis waited for whichever party was in power. Yet neither Republicans nor Democrats took much heed of that impending disaster.

At the same time, the Republicans created a new Department of Homeland Security that consolidated hundreds of existing programs into an even bigger bureaucratic entity. The power of government over the daily lives of citizens mushroomed with significant restrictions on travel, dissent, and political activity. In foreign policy, some Republicans saw the terrorist challenge as an opportunity to go beyond Woodrow Wilson's attempt to make the world safe for democracy. These visionaries would make the world itself democratic. How a smaller government would achieve that monumental task has not yet been explained.

Finally, there was the nature of American politics itself and how the Republicans would fit into that process. Since the 1860s, the Grand Old Party has sometimes viewed the Democrats as a necessary evil and sometimes as just evil and traitorous. If a war or major domestic crisis gave the Republicans the opportunity to end the existence of the Democrats as a force in American politics, would they exercise it? If, as some Republicans believe, the proper end of political warfare is the unconditional surrender and eventual disappearance of their partisan rivals, then the Grand Old Party would have secured the complete national dominance it had so long sought. Would such a triumph be worth having for the citizens of a democratic republic, as well as any political party? It was not clear whether modern Republicans really believe in the two-party system as a core principle of politics.[6]

In all probability, the ebb and flow of American public life will continue, with Republicans and Democrats vying for power as they have done for so long. To that extended record of democratic government, the Republicans have added many noteworthy accomplishments and some false steps. While it is thinkable that national politics might reshape itself so that the two parties could splinter and then consolidate once again into new ideological coalitions, it seems more likely that the traditional alignments would persist. Betting against the tenacity and staying power of the Republican Party has often proven a bad wager, and so the Grand Old Party will likely remain one of the means by which the American people live together in the indefinite future.

NOTES

Preface and Acknowledgments

1. A good brief discussion of the origins of "GOP" is in Hans Sperber and Travis Trittschuh, *Dictionary of American Political Terms* (New York: McGraw-Hill, 1964), pp. 174–75. Some early examples of the use of the phrase "Grand Old Party" are "The Maine Election," *The Nation,* September 19, 1878, p. 172, line 16; and U.S. House of Representatives, *Congressional Record,* May 1, 1888, p. 3598, first column, last line. *The Wall Street Journal*'s decision about "GOP" is examined in "What Does 'GOP' Stand For?" CBSNews.com, December 4, 2002.

2. Sperber and Trittschuh, in *Dictionary of American Political Terms,* pp. 141–42, show that the association of elephants with the Republicans antedates Nash, but the cartoonist still deserves primary credit for making the symbol so popular. Morton Keller, *The Art and Politics of Thomas Nast* (New York: Oxford University Press, 1968), is a thorough introduction to Nast's life and impact as a cartoonist.

Chapter 1: THE PARTY OF LINCOLN, 1854–1865

1. Benjamin P. Thomas, *Abraham Lincoln* (New York: Alfred A. Knopf, 1952), p. 212. Thomas's book remains one of the very best single-volume biographies of Abraham Lincoln.

2. Julian is quoted in William E. Gienapp, *The Origins of the Republican Party* (New York: Oxford University Press, 1986), p. 103. Gienapp's encyclopedic treatment of the Republicans and their birth is a storehouse of information. I disagree with some of his conclusions about the party, but

every student of the Republicans is indebted to him for his impressive research. Robert F. Engs and Randall M. Miller, eds., *The Birth of the Grand Old Party: The Republicans' First Generation* (Philadelphia: University of Pennsylvania Press, 2002), is a collection of first-rate articles on the founding years of the party.

3. Michael F. Holt, *The Political Crisis of the 1850s* (New York: John Wiley and Sons, 1978), p. 113.

4. Gienapp, *Origins of the Republican Party*, p. 95.

5. Seward is quoted in Eric Foner, *Free Soil, Free Labor, Free Men: The Ideology of the Republican Party Before the Civil War* (New York: Oxford University Press, 1970), p. 41. Foner's work is a very important study of Republican ideology in this period.

6. Randolph B. Campbell, *An Empire for Slavery: The Peculiar Institution in Texas* (Baton Rouge: Louisiana State University Press, 1989), p. 212.

7. *Kennebec Journal,* April 28, 1854, quoted in Gienapp, *Origins of the Republican Party*, p. 5.

8. Gienapp, *Origins of the Republican Party*, pp. 5, 6.

9. Richard Jensen, *The Winning of the Midwest: Social and Political Conflict, 1888–1896* (Chicago: University of Chicago Press, 1971), quoting Joseph Baldwin, *Party Leaders* (New York, 1855), p. 3.

10. Kirk H. Porter and Donald Bruce Johnson, eds., *National Party Platforms, 1840–1968* (Urbana: University of Illinois Press, 1972), pp. 16, 17.

11. Holt, *Political Crisis*, p. 133.

12. *New York Tribune,* May 15, 1854, quoted in Gienapp, *Origins of the Republican Party*, p. 77.

13. Henry Steele Commager, ed., *Documents of American History*, 2 vols. (Englewood Cliffs, N.J.: Prentice-Hall, 1973), I, p. 321.

14. Ibid., p. 332.

15. Holt, *Political Crisis*, p. 154.

16. Gienapp, *Origins of the Republican Party*, pp. 104–05.

17. Michael P. Johnson, ed., *Abraham Lincoln, Slavery and the Civil War: Selected Writings and Speeches* (Boston: Bedford/St. Martin's Press, 2001), pp.

46, 49. This good brief introduction to Lincoln's political thought contains many of his key speeches and letters. For Lincoln's own writings in detail, see Roy P. Basler et al., eds., *The Collected Works of Abraham Lincoln*, 9 vols. (New Brunswick, N.J.: Rutgers University Press, 1953–55).

18. Holt, *Political Crisis*, p. 159.

19. Gienapp, *Origins of the Republican Party*, p. 95.

20. Ibid., p. 303.

21. Holt, *Political Crisis*, pp. 194–95; Gienapp, *Origins of the Republican Party*, p. 302 (quotation).

22. Beryl Frank, *Pictorial History of the Republican Party* (Secaucus, N.J.: Castle Books, 1980), p. 14, shows a Fremont banner. Porter and Johnson, *National Party Platforms*, p. 27.

23. Richard H. Sewell, *Ballots for Freedom: Antislavery Politics in the United States, 1837–1860* (New York: Oxford University Press, 1976), p. 291.

24. Foner, *Free Soil*, p. 291.

25. Ibid., pp. 266, 269; Johnson, ed., *Abraham Lincoln*, p. 73.

26. Gienapp, *Origins of the Republican Party*, p. 359.

27. Don E. Fehrenbacher, *Prelude to Greatness: Lincoln in the 1850s* (Stanford, Calif.: Stanford University Press, 1962), p. 106. This is one of the most important books about Abraham Lincoln and the Republican Party written in the past fifty years.

28. Johnson, ed., *Abraham Lincoln*, p. 90.

29. Fehrenbacher, *Prelude to Greatness*, p. 96.

30. David Donald, *Lincoln* (New York: Simon & Schuster, 1995), pp. 165–67, deals with Lincoln's attitude toward colonization. Fehrenbacher, *Prelude to Greatness*, p. 74.

31. Fehrenbacher, *Prelude to Greatness*, p. 74. Another significant interpretive study of the Lincoln-Douglas debates is Harry V. Jaffa, *Crisis of the House Divided: An Interpretation of the Issues in the Lincoln-Douglas Debates* (Garden City, N.Y.: Doubleday & Co., 1959), and Jaffa's elaboration of the points made in that book in *A New Birth of Freedom: Abraham Lincoln and the Coming of the Civil War* (Lanham, Md.: Rowman & Littlefield, 2000).

32. Johnson, ed., *Abraham Lincoln*, p. 72.

33. Holt, *Political Crisis*, p. 209.

34. Foner, *Free Soil*, p. 69.

35. Porter and Johnson, eds., *National Party Platforms,* pp. 32–33.

36. Heather Cox Richardson, *The Greatest Nation on Earth: Republican Economic Policies During the Civil War* (Cambridge, Mass.: Harvard University Press, 1997), p. 64. This is an important book for the governing philosophy of the Republicans.

37. William Frank Zornow, *Lincoln and the Party Divided* (Norman: University of Oklahoma Press, 1954), p. 153.

38. Ibid., p. 161. Joel H. Silbey, *A Respectable Minority: The Democratic Party in the Civil War Era* (New York: W. W. Norton, 1977), pp. 166–69. Mark E. Neely, *The Union Divided: Party Conflict in the Civil War North* (Cambridge, Mass.: Harvard University Press, 2002), pp. 158–72, discusses the Republican belief in the treasonous character of the Democrats in 1864.

39. Richardson, *Greatest Nation,* p. 90.

40. Ibid., p. 87.

41. Ibid., p. 54 (emphasis in original).

42. Ibid., p. 101.

43. Ibid., pp. 103 (third quotation), 120 (second quotation), 129 (first quotation).

44. Ibid., p. 143.

45. Brooks D. Simpson, *The Reconstruction Presidents* (Lawrence: University Press of Kansas, 1998), p. 62.

46. Richardson, *Greatest Nation,* p. 241.

47. Johnson, ed., *Abraham Lincoln*, p. 263.

Chapter 2: REPUBLICANS AND RECONSTRUCTION, 1865–1877

1. Kirk H. Porter and Donald Bruce Johnson, eds., *National Party Platforms, 1840–1968* (Urbana: University of Illinois Press, 1972), p. 53.

2. George Ticknor quoted in Morton Keller, *Affairs of State: Public Life in Late-Nineteenth-Century America* (Cambridge, Mass.: Belknap Press of Harvard University Press, 1977), p. 2.

3. Brooks D. Simpson, *The Reconstruction Presidents* (Lawrence: University Press of Kansas, 1998), p. 76.

4. Michael P. Johnson, ed., *Abraham Lincoln, Slavery and the Civil War: Selected Writings and Speeches* (Boston: Bedford/St. Martin's Press, 2001), p. 332.

5. An important introduction to Andrew Johnson's life is Eric L. McKitrick, *Andrew Johnson and Reconstruction* (Chicago: University of Chicago Press, 1960).

6. Marshall, Texas, *Texas Republican,* June 30, 1865.

7. *New York Times,* August 17, 1865, quoted in Michael Les Benedict, *A Compromise of Principle: Congressional Republicans and Reconstruction, 1863–1869* (New York: W. W. Norton, 1973), p. 122.

8. Keller, *Affairs of State,* p. 65.

9. Edward Ayers et al., *American Passages: A History of the United States* (Fort Worth, Tex.: Harcourt Publishers, 1999), p. A-11.

10. Albert Castel, *The Presidency of Andrew Johnson* (Lawrence: University Press of Kansas, 1979), p. 91.

11. Simpson, *Reconstruction Presidents,* p. 112.

12. Eric Foner, *Reconstruction: America's Unfinished Revolution, 1863–1877* (New York: Harper & Row, 1988), p. 236 (emphasis in original). This book is the best single account of all aspects of the Reconstruction process. In contrast, a popular history of the party largely slides over the issues of Reconstruction and the problems they presented for the Republicans: John Calvin Batchelor, *"Ain't You Glad You Joined the Republicans?" A Short History of the GOP* (New York: Henry Holt, 1996), pp. 55–56.

13. Jean Edward Smith, *Grant* (New York: Simon & Schuster, 2001), p. 456.

14. Ibid.

15. Foner, *Reconstruction: America's Unfinished Revolution,* pp. 313, 316.

16. Joel H. Silbey, *A Respectable Minority: The Democratic Party in the Civil War Era* (New York: W. W. Norton, 1977), p. 199.

17. Porter and Johnson, eds., *National Party Platforms*, pp. 37–38; Silbey, *A Respectable Minority*, p. 209.

18. Porter and Johnson, eds., *National Party Platforms*, p. 39.

19. William Dudley Foulke, *Life of Oliver P. Morton, Including His Important Speeches*, 2 vols. (Indianapolis, Ind.: Bowen-Merrill, 1899), I, pp. 474–75.

20. *Chicago Evening Journal*, November 10, 1868, quoted in Benedict, *Compromise of Principle*, p. 324.

21. *New York Tribune*, November 4, 1868, quoted in Benedict, *Compromise of Principle*, p. 336. Michael Zak, *Back to Basics for the Republican Party*, 2nd ed. (Washington, D.C.: Signature Books), 2001), p. 112.

22. Smith, *Grant*, p. 476, quoting Charles Francis Adams.

23. Porter and Johnson, eds., *National Party Platforms*, p. 44.

24. Roger Alan Cohen, "The Lost Jubilee: New York Republicans and the Politics of Reconstruction and Reform, 1867–1878" (Ph.D. diss., Columbia University, 1976), p. 35.

25. David M. Jordan, *Roscoe Conkling of New York: Voice in the Senate* (Ithaca, N.Y.: Cornell University Press, 1971), p. 80, gives Blaine's remark.

26. Foner, *Reconstruction: America's Unfinished Revolution*, p. 449.

27. Ibid., p. 427; Smith, *Grant*, p. 545.

28. Foner, *Reconstruction: America's Unfinished Revolution*, pp. 455, 456.

29. Ibid., p. 458.

30. *The Nation*, March 21, 1872, p. 181.

31. Smith, *Grant*, p. 548.

32. Porter and Johnson, eds., *National Party Platforms*, pp. 41, 44; Foner, *Reconstruction: America's Unfinished Revolution*, p. 503.

33. Smith, *Grant*, p. 550.

34. H. Wayne Morgan, *From Hayes to McKinley: National Party Politics, 1877–1896* (Syracuse, N.Y.: Syracuse University Press, 1969), p. 19.

35. Utica, New York, *Morning Herald*, November 26, 1872, quoted in Cohen, "The Lost Jubilee," p. 390.

36. Keller, *Affairs of State,* p. 189.

37. Porter and Johnson, eds., *National Party Platforms,* p. 49.

38. Jordan, *Roscoe Conkling,* p. 240.

39. Porter and Johnson, eds., *National Party Platforms,* pp. 53, 55.

40. Donald A. Ritchie, "1876," in Arthur M. Schlesinger, Jr., et al., eds., *Running for President: The Candidates and Their Images,* 2 vols. (New York: Simon & Schuster, 1994), I, p. 328. Michael E. McGerr, *The Decline of Popular Politics: The American North, 1865–1928* (New York: Oxford University Press, 1986), p. 27.

41. Cohen, "The Lost Jubilee," p. 669. The disputed election of 1876 has produced a large literature on how the sectional bargain was reached to settle the contest. The key works are C. Vann Woodward, *Reunion and Reaction: The Compromise of 1877 and the End of Reconstruction* (Garden City, N.Y.: Doubleday, 1951), and Keith Ian Polakoff, *The Politics of Inertia: The Election of 1876 and the End of Reconstruction* (Baton Rouge: Louisiana State University Press, 1973). Roy Morris, Jr., *Fraud of the Century: Rutherford B. Hayes, Samuel Tilden, and the Stolen Election of 1876* (New York: Simon & Schuster, 2003), is pro-Tilden in its theme.

42. Foner, *Reconstruction: America's Unfinished Revolution,* p. 574.

43. Ibid., p. 581.

Chapter 3: REPUBLICANS IN THE GILDED AGE, 1877–1893

1. The turbulence of the 1884 presidential election is well captured in Mark Wahlgren Summers, *Rum, Romanism, and Rebellion: The Making of a President, 1884* (Chapel Hill: University of North Carolina Press, 2000), p. xi. H. Wayne Morgan, *From Hayes to McKinley: National Party Politics, 1877–1896* (Syracuse, N.Y.: Syracuse University Press, 1969), p. 215 (first quotation).

2. James Bryce, *The American Commonwealth,* 2 vols. (New York: The Macmillan Company, 1894, 1909), II, p. 21.

3. Matthew Arnold, "Civilization in the United States," in Ray Ginger, ed., *The Nationalizing of American Life, 1877–1900* (New York: Free Press, 1965), p. 113.

4. Herbert Croly, *Progressive Democracy* (New York: The Macmillan Company, 1915), p. 87.

5. Thomas Richard Ross, *Jonathan Prentiss Dolliver: A Study in Political In-*

tegrity and Independence (Iowa City: Historical Society of Iowa, 1958), p. 59.

6. *New York Tribune*, October 25, 1890, quoted in R. Hal Williams, *Years of Decision: American Politics in the 1890s* (Prospect Heights, Ill.: Waveland Books, 1993), p. 7.

7. George W. Julian, "The Death Struggle of the Republican Party," *North American Review* 126 (1878): 292.

8. Samuel J. Tilden, quoted in R. Hal Williams, " 'Dry Bones and Dead Language': The Democratic Party," in H. Wayne Morgan, ed., *The Gilded Age*, rev. and enlarged ed. (Syracuse, N.Y.: Syracuse University Press, 1970), p. 134; Murat Halstead to Rutherford B. Hayes, February 22, 1877, Rutherford B. Hayes Papers, quoted in H. Wayne Morgan, *From Hayes to McKinley: National Party Politics, 1877–1896* (Syracuse, N.Y.: Syracuse University Press, 1969), p. 35.

9. Julia B. Foraker, *I Would Live It Again* (New York: Harper & Brothers, 1932), p. 140. Brand Whitlock, *Forty Years of It* (New York: D. Appleton, 1914), p. 27.

10. Edward McPherson, *A Hand-Book of Politics for 1876* (Washington: Solomon and Chapman, 1876), pp. 229, 230–31.

11. *New York Tribune*, July 6, 1882, quoted in Summers, *Rum, Romanism, and Rebellion*, p. 108.

12. George Frisbie Hoar, "Are the Republicans in to Stay?" *North American Review* 149 (1889): 621.

13. O. O. Stealey, *Twenty Years in the Press Gallery* (New York: Publishers Printing, 1906), p. 113.

14. James G. Blaine, *Political Discussions: Legislative, Diplomatic and Popular, 1856–1886* (Norwich, Conn.: Henry Bill, 1887), p. 452.

15. Henry L. West, "The Present Session of Congress," *The Forum* 32 (December 1901): 428. For a good discussion of the role of the tariff in Republican ideology at this time, see Charles W. Calhoun, "Political Economy in the Gilded Age: The Republican Party's Industrial Policy," *Journal of Policy History* 8 (1996): 292–309. Steven R. Weisman, *The Great Tax Wars* (New York: Simon & Schuster, 2002), is very old-fashioned about the role of the tariff in the politics of the Gilded Age.

16. *Speeches and Addresses of William McKinley* (New York: Appleton, 1893), p. 229.

17. Ibid., p. 194.

18. *New York Tribune,* June 15, 1899, quotes sugar magnate H. O. Havemeyer as saying, "The mother of all trusts is the customs tariff bill."

19. William E. Connelly, ed., *A Collection of the Writings of John James Ingalls* (Kansas City: Hudson-Kimberly, 1902), p. 43.

20. Thomas Wolfe, *From Death to Mourning* (New York: Charles Scribner's Sons, 1935), p. 121.

21. The standard biography of Blaine is David S. Muzzey, *James G. Blaine: A Political Idol of Other Days* (New York: Dodd, Mead, 1934), but R. Hal Williams of Southern Methodist University is completing a modern study.

22. James G. Blaine, *Twenty Years of Congress,* 2 vols. (Norwich, Conn.: Henry Bill, 1884), II, p. 160.

23. The letter that contains the famous words "Burn this letter" is from Blaine to Warren Fisher, April 16, 1876, Autograph File, Houghton Library, Harvard University. I am indebted to R. Hal Williams for this reference.

24. Morgan, *From Hayes to McKinley,* p. 56.

25. Ibid., p. 148.

26. Morton Keller, *Affairs of State: Public Life in Late-Nineteenth-Century America* (Cambridge, Mass.: Belknap Press of Harvard University Press, 1977), p. 267.

27. Summers, *Rum, Romanism, and Rebellion,* p. 175.

28. Matthew Josephson, *The Politicos* (New York: Harcourt, Brace, 1938), p. 336.

29. Morgan, *From Hayes to McKinley,* p. 226.

30. Ibid., p. 268.

31. Kirk H. Porter and Donald Bruce Johnson, eds., *National Party Platforms, 1840–1968* (Urbana: University of Illinois Press, 1972), p. 78.

32. Muzzey, *James G. Blaine,* p. 367.

33. Homer E. Socolofsky and Allan B. Spetter, *The Presidency of Benjamin Harrison* (Lawrence: University Press of Kansas, 1987), is the best intro-

duction to Harrison's career. For his marital problems, see Charles W. Calhoun, "Caroline Lavinia Scott Harrison," in Lewis L. Gould, ed., *American First Ladies: Their Lives and Their Legacy,* 2nd ed. (New York: Routledge, 2001), pp. 180–81.

34. Thomas B. Reed, "Rules of the House of Representatives," *Century Magazine* 15 (March 1889): 795.

35. Morgan, *From Hayes to McKinley,* p. 334; Williams, *Years of Decision,* p. 22.

36. Williams, *Years of Decision,* p. 31.

37. Ibid., p. 45.

38. Morgan, *From Hayes to McKinley,* pp. 354, 380–81. Mary Elizabeth Lease may not have actually uttered the famous quotation, but she endorsed its sentiments. Ironically, Lease became a Republican and supported McKinley in 1900. Mark Wahlgren Summers, *The Gilded Age or the Hazard of New Functions* (Upper Saddle River, N.J.: Prentice Hall, 1997), p. 223.

39. Morgan, *From Hayes to McKinley,* p. 355.

40. Ibid.

41. Williams, *Years of Decision,* p. 53.

42. Morgan, *From Hayes to McKinley,* p. 415.

43. Ibid., p. 437.

44. Woodrow Wilson, "Mr. Cleveland's Cabinet," *Review of Reviews* 7 (April 1893): 289.

Chapter 4: McKinley to Roosevelt, 1893–1904

1. Margaret Leech, *In the Days of McKinley* (New York: Harper & Brothers, 1959), p. 93. Canton during the 1896 election is described in Edward Thornton Heald, *The William McKinley Story* (Canton, Ohio: Stark County Historical Society, 1964), pp. 72–81. In preparing this chapter, I have drawn on research and writing I have done on the presidencies of William McKinley and Theodore Roosevelt.

2. H. Wayne Morgan, *From Hayes to McKinley: National Party Politics, 1877–1896* (Syracuse, N.Y.: Syracuse University Press, 1969), p. 447, quoting Hill.

3. R. Hal Williams, *Years of Decision: American Politics in the 1890s* (Prospect Heights, Ill.: Waveland Press, 1993), pp. 78–82.

4. B. F. Gilkeson to "My Dear Sir," October 30, 1893, Lewis L. Gould Political History Collection, Center for American History, University of Texas at Austin.

5. Morgan, *From Hayes to McKinley*, p. 477.

6. Samuel T. McSeveny, *The Politics of Depression: Political Behavior in the Northeast, 1893–1896* (New York: Oxford University Press, 1972), p. 88; Morgan, *From Hayes to McKinley*, p. 445.

7. Warren Hamill Wilson, "Grover Cleveland and the Wilson-Gorman Tariff" (master's thesis, University of Texas at Austin, 1977).

8. Henry Cabot Lodge to Charles A. Dana, May 21, 1894, Gould Collection. Nelson Dingley, Jr., "The Democratic Tariff Outcome," speech delivered in the House of Representatives, August 13, 1894 (Boston: Home Mark Club, 1896), p. 15; pamphlet in author's collection.

9. Williams, *Years of Decision*, pp. 87–89.

10. Robert W. Cherny, *American Politics in the Gilded Age, 1868–1900* (Wheeling, Ill.: Harlan Davidson, 1997), p. 117.

11. Theodore Roosevelt to Henry Cabot Lodge, September 2, 1894, in Elting E. Morison et al., eds., *The Letters of Theodore Roosevelt*, 8 vols. (Cambridge, Mass.: Harvard University Press, 1951–54), I, p. 398; Morgan, *From Hayes to McKinley*, p. 477.

12. William A. Robinson, *Thomas B. Reed, Parliamentarian* (New York: Dodd, Mead, 1930), p. 321.

13. On the significance of the 1894 elections, see Richard J. Jensen, *The Winning of the Midwest: Social and Political Conflict, 1888–1896* (Chicago: University of Chicago Press, 1971), p. 306; Williams, *Years of Decision*, p. 96.

14. Francis E. Warren to Henry L. West, April 4, 1896, Francis E. Warren Papers, American Heritage Center, University of Wyoming, Laramie.

15. On the situation of the Republicans as 1896 began, see Williams, *Years of Decision*, pp. 97–99. The best study of the 1896 election is Stanley L. Jones, *The Presidential Election of 1896* (Madison: University of Wisconsin Press, 1964).

16. The preeminent biography of William McKinley is H. Wayne Morgan, *William McKinley and His America* (Syracuse, N.Y.: Syracuse University

Press, 1963). The Kent State University Press published a revised and updated edition of Morgan's book in 2003.

17. On McKinley in 1896, see Lewis L. Gould, *The Presidency of William McKinley* (Lawrence: University Press of Kansas, 1981), pp. 6–7.

18. These quotations appear in Gould, *Presidency of William McKinley*, pp. 10, 242.

19. Ibid., p. 9.

20. Morgan, *From Hayes to McKinley*, p. 487.

21. Joseph P. Smith, comp., *McKinley's Speeches in September* (Canton, Ohio: Repository Press, 1896), p. 177.

22. Kirk H. Porter and Donald Bruce Johnson, eds., *National Party Platforms, 1840–1968* (Urbana: University of Illinois Press, 1972), p. 108.

23. Gould, *Presidency of William McKinley*, pp. 10–11; Morgan, *From Hayes to McKinley*, p. 502.

24. Louis W. Koenig, *Bryan: A Political Biography of William Jennings Bryan* (New York: G. P. Putnam's Sons, 1971), p. 197.

25. The issue of the campaign funds for McKinley in 1896 is still contentious in the modern debate over campaign finance reform. For historical discussions, see Morgan, *From Hayes to McKinley*, pp. 509–10; Williams, *Years of Decision*, pp. 121–22.

26. Jensen, *Winning of the Midwest*, p. 288; Morgan, *From Hayes to McKinley*, pp. 228–29.

27. For examples of McKinley's deft oratory, see Smith, comp., *McKinley's Speeches in September*, passim.

28. Morgan, *From Hayes to McKinley*, p. 524.

29. Roosevelt to Cecil Spring Rice, October 8, 1896, in Morison, *Letters of Theodore Roosevelt*, I, p. 562.

30. Jensen, *Winning of the Midwest*, pp. 49–57, deals with the coercion issue in 1896.

31. *Speeches and Addresses of William McKinley from March 1, 1897, to May 30, 1900* (New York: Doubleday & McClure, 1900), p. 114.

32. Gould, *Presidency of William McKinley,* pp. 37–39.

33. Ibid., pp. 40–48.

34. For a brief account of the war with Spain, see Lewis L. Gould, *The Spanish-American War and President McKinley* (Lawrence: University Press of Kansas, 1982, 1999).

35. Gould, *Presidency of William McKinley,* pp. 78–90.

36. Ibid., pp. 104, 130–31.

37. *Speeches and Addresses of William McKinley,* pp. 84–156.

38. Ibid., p. 98.

39. Gould, *Spanish-American War,* pp. 112–14.

40. William R. Day to McKinley, November 18, 1899, William McKinley Papers, Manuscript Division, Library of Congress.

41. *New York Tribune,* May 11, 1899.

42. Gould, *Presidency of William McKinley,* pp. 154–60.

43. Ibid., p. 162.

44. George Raywood Devitt, comp., *A Supplement to a Compilation of the Messages and Papers of the President, 1789–1902, by James D. Richardson* (Washington, D.C.: Bureau of National Literature and Art, 1903), p. 57.

45. Henry L. West, "The Republican and Democratic Platforms Compared," *The Forum* 30 (1900): 93.

46. Lewis L. Gould, ed., "Charles Warren Fairbanks and the Republican National Convention of 1900: A Memoir," *Indiana Magazine of History* 77 (1981): 370.

47. The two best books for understanding Roosevelt's life and his relationship with the Republican Party are John Morton Blum, *The Republican Roosevelt* (Cambridge, Mass.: Harvard University Press, 1954), and William H. Harbaugh, *The Life and Times of Theodore Roosevelt* (New York: Oxford University Press, 1975).

48. *Taft and Roosevelt: The Intimate Letters of Archie Butt, Military Aide,* 2 vols. (Garden City, N.Y.: Doubleday, Doran, 1930), II, p. 441.

49.   Gould, *Presidency of William McKinley,* pp. 216–17.

50.   Gould, "Charles Warren Fairbanks," p. 368; Leech, *In the Days of McKinley,* p. 537; Albert Shaw to W. T. Stead, June 25, 1900, Albert Shaw Papers, New York Public Library, Astor, Lenox, and Tilden Foundations.

51.   Charles S. Olcott, *Life of William McKinley,* 2 vols. (Boston: Houghton Mifflin, 1916), II, p. 296.

52.   Leech, *In the Days of McKinley,* p. 596.

53.   Gould, *Presidency of William McKinley,* p. 251.

54.   John Hay, *Addresses of John Hay* (New York: Century Company, 1906), p. 175.

55.   Archibald R. Colquhoun, *Greater America* (New York: Harper & Brothers, 1904), p. 34.

56.   *Theodore Roosevelt: An Autobiography. The Works of Theodore Roosevelt,* 20 vols. (New York: Charles Scribner's Sons, 1926), II, p. 417.

57.   Eugene Hale to William E. Chandler, September 29, 1901, William E. Chandler Papers, Manuscript Division, Library of Congress. Hale was a conservative Republican senator from Vermont.

58.   Nathan Miller, *The Roosevelt Chronicles* (Garden City, N.Y.: Doubleday, 1979), p. 260.

59.   Mark Sullivan, *Our Times: The United States.* Vol. III: *Pre-War America* (New York: Charles Scribner's Sons, 1930), p. 73 (calliope); Lyman Abbott, "A Review of President Roosevelt's Administration: Its Influence on Patriotism and Public Service," *Outlook* 91 (February 27, 1909): 430 (bully pulpit).

60.   Theodore Roosevelt, *Addresses and Presidential Messages of Theodore Roosevelt* (New York: Putnam, 1904), p. 15.

61.   Joseph Bucklin Bishop, *Theodore Roosevelt and His Time,* 2 vols. (New York: Charles Scribner's Sons, 1920), I, pp. 184–85.

62.   Arthur M. Johnson, "Theodore Roosevelt and the Bureau of Corporations," *Mississippi Valley Historical Review* 45 (March 1959): 571–90; Elizabeth Sanders, *Roots of Reform: Farmers, Workers, and the American State, 1877–1917* (Chicago: University of Chicago Press, 1999), pp. 273–77.

63.   John J. Jenkins to Theodore Roosevelt, October 6, 1902, Theodore Roosevelt Papers, Manuscript Division, Library of Congress. The Library of

Congress has microfilmed Roosevelt's papers, and they are available in an indexed collection that is very easy to use.

64. Roosevelt to William Emlen Roosevelt, November 6, 1902, in Morison, *Letters of Theodore Roosevelt,* III, p. 373.

65. Roosevelt to George O. Trevelyan, May 28, 1904, in Morison, *Letters of Theodore Roosevelt,* IV, p. 807.

66. On this point, see the argument in Lewis L. Gould, *Reform and Regulation: American Politics from Roosevelt to Wilson* (Prospect Heights, Ill.: Waveland Press, 1996), pp. 43–47.

67. Marcus A. Hanna to N. B. Scott, August 20, 1902, Hanna-McCormick Family Papers, Manuscript Division, Library of Congress.

68. Lewis L. Gould, *The Presidency of Theodore Roosevelt* (Lawrence: University Press of Kansas, 1991), p. 131.

69. Ibid., pp. 131–32.

70. *New York Tribune,* September 9, 1904.

71. Roosevelt, *Addresses and Presidential Messages,* p. 121.

72. M. W. Blumenberg, comp., *Official Proceedings of the Thirteenth Republican National Convention Held in the City of Chicago, June 21, 22, 23, 1904* (Minneapolis, Minn.: Harrison and Smith, 1904), p. 137.

73. Oswald Garrison Villard, *Fighting Years: Memoirs of a Liberal Editor* (New York: Harcourt, Brace, 1939), p. 181, quoting steel magnate Henry Clay Frick about Roosevelt.

74. Gould, *Reform and Regulation,* pp. 59, 62.

75. Roosevelt to Lodge, July 14, 1904, in Morison, *Letters of Theodore Roosevelt,* IV, p. 921.

76. Gould, *Reform and Regulation,* pp. 60, 61.

77. Albert Shaw to W. T. Stead, October 7, 1904, Shaw Papers; *New York Herald,* October 9, 1904.

78. *New York World,* October 26, 1904.

79. *Washington Post,* November 5, 1904.

80. *New York Tribune,* November 9, 1904.

81. Roosevelt to Philander Knox, November 10, 1904, in Morison, *Letters of Theodore Roosevelt,* IV, p. 1023.

Chapter 5: THE TAFT-ROOSEVELT SPLIT, 1905–1912

1. William Allen White, *The Autobiography of William Allen White* (New York: The Macmillan Co., 1946), p. 469; Daisy Borden Harriman, *From Pinafores to Politics* (New York: Henry Holt and Co., 1923), p. 99; *The Works of Theodore Roosevelt: Social Justice and Popular Rule,* 20 vols. (New York: Charles Scribner's Sons, 1926), XVII, p. 231.

2. Roosevelt to George Otto Trevelyan, November 24, 1904, in Elting E. Morison, *The Letters of Theodore Roosevelt,* 8 vols. (Cambridge, Mass.: Harvard University Press, 1951–54), IV, p. 1043.

3. Orville H. Platt to Nelson W. Aldrich, November 12, 1904, Orville H. Platt Papers, Connecticut Historical Society, Hartford.

4. Platt to Roosevelt, November 21, 1904, Platt Papers; *American Economist,* January 27, 1905, p. 41. For the origins of the "stand pat" term, see William Safire, *Safire's Political Dictionary* (New York: Ballantine Books, 1978), pp. 687–88.

5. The only biography of Aldrich is Nathaniel W. Stephenson, *Nelson W. Aldrich: A Leader in American Politics* (New York: Charles Scribner's Sons, 1930). Horace Samuel Merrill and Marion Galbraith Merrill, *The Republican Command, 1897–1913* (Lexington: University Press of Kentucky, 1971), is a critical account of the Republican congressional leadership.

6. Blair Bolles, *Tyrant from Illinois: Uncle Joe Cannon's Experiment with Personal Power* (New York: W. W. Norton, 1951), pp. 5–6, 11 (quotation). A modern treatment is Scott William Rager, "The Fall of the House of Cannon: Uncle Joe and His Enemies, 1903–1910" (Ph.D. diss., University of Illinois, 1994).

7. Albert B. Cummins to Albert J. Beveridge, November 12, 1906, Albert B. Cummins Papers, Iowa State Department of History and Archives, Des Moines.

8. Richard L. McCormick, "The Discovery That Business Corrupts Politics: A Reappraisal of the Origins of Progressivism," *American Historical Review* 86 (1981): 242–74.

9. Ibid., p. 264, quotes Cummins; *Washington Post,* January 31, 1905 (Roosevelt).

10. Lewis L. Gould, *Reform and Regulation: American Politics from Roosevelt to Wilson* (Prospect Heights, Ill.: Waveland Press, 1996), pp. 71–75.

11. Roosevelt to Kermit Roosevelt, June 13, 1906, Theodore Roosevelt Papers, Manuscript Division, Library of Congress.

12. James Harvey Young, *Pure Food: Securing the Federal Food and Drugs Act of 1906* (Princeton, N.J.: Princeton University Press, 1989). John Braeman, *Albert J. Beveridge: American Nationalist* (Chicago: University of Chicago Press, 1971), pp. 101–10, is good on the meat-inspection issue.

13. Roosevelt to Lyman Abbott, July 1, 1906, in Morison, *Letters of Theodore Roosevelt,* V, p. 328; *The Works of Theodore Roosevelt: American Problems,* 20 vols. (New York: Charles Scribner's Sons, 1926), XVI, p. 421.

14. *The Works of Theodore Roosevelt: State Papers as Governor and President, 1899–1909,* 20 vols. (New York: Charles Scribner's Sons, 1926), XVI, p. 416.

15. White, *Autobiography of William Allen White,* p. 428.

16. The best introduction to Robert M. La Follette is *La Follette's Autobiography: A Personal Narrative of Political Experiences* (Madison, Wisc.: La Follette Company, 1913). Nancy Unger, *Fighting Bob La Follette: The Righteous Reformer* (Chapel Hill: University of North Carolina Press, 2000), is a full, modern account of his life.

17. For examples of conservative reservations about Roosevelt's course on regulation in 1905, see the letter from Marshall Field to Jonathan P. Dolliver, February 15, 1905, Jonathan P. Dolliver Papers, Iowa Historical Society, Iowa City; and the letter from Joseph B. Foraker to D. M. Parry, November 27, 1905, Joseph B. Foraker Papers, Cincinnati Historical Society.

18. E. D. Crumpacker to Roosevelt, July 28, 1906, Roosevelt Papers; *Des Moines Register Leader,* August 17, 1906.

19. Gould, *Reform and Regulation,* pp. 83–85.

20. Roosevelt to William Allen White, July 30, 1907, in Morison, *Letters of Theodore Roosevelt,* V, p. 735.

21. E. L. Scharf to William Boyd Allison, July 25, 1907, Box 366, William Boyd Allison Papers, Iowa State Department of History and Archives, Des Moines; George F. Dominick to Herbert Parsons, November 9, 1907, Box 6, Herbert Parsons Papers, Columbia University Library.

22. Gould, *Reform and Regulation,* pp. 96–97.

23. The basic source for the historical reinterpretation of the Brownsville raid is John D. Weaver, *The Brownsville Raid* (College Station: Texas A&M University Press, 1970, 1992), which produced the belated exoneration of the accused soldiers during the early 1970s.

24. On the Foraker-Roosevelt encounter, see Lewis L. Gould, *The Presidency of Theodore Roosevelt* (Lawrence: University Press of Kansas, 1991), pp. 242–43.

25. Gould, *Reform and Regulation,* pp. 97–98.

26. William Loeb, Jr., to William Howard Taft, March 25, 1907, William Howard Taft Papers, Manuscript Division, Library of Congress, enclosing clipping from *Kansas City Times.*

27. Roosevelt to William Allen White, August 11, 1906, in Morison, *Letters of Theodore Roosevelt,* V, p. 354.

28. For Taft's reservations about Roosevelt's administrative style, see the letter from Taft to Helen Herron Taft, October 3, 1909, William Howard Taft Papers, Manuscript Division, Library of Congress.

29. Roosevelt to Albert Shaw, May 22, 1908, in Morison, *Letters of Theodore Roosevelt,* VI, p. 1033.

30. Judson Welliver to James C. Keely, August 21, 1908, Cummins Papers, Iowa State Department of History and Archives.

31. *Taft and Roosevelt: The Intimate Letters of Archie Butt,* 2 vols. (Garden City, N.Y.: Doubleday, Doran & Co., 1930), II, p. 551; Henry L. Stoddard, *As I Knew Them: Presidents and Politics from Grant to Coolidge* (New York: Harper & Brothers, 1927), p. 386.

32. Thomas H. Carter to Knute Nelson, July 30, 1908, Knute Nelson Papers, Minnesota Historical Society, St. Paul; Joseph L. Bristow to Samuel Judson Roberts, August 13, 1908, Joseph L. Bristow Papers, Kansas State Historical Society, Topeka.

33. *American Monthly Review of Reviews* 38 (1908): 517.

34. Roosevelt to Nicholas Longworth, September 21, 1908, in Morison, *Letters of Theodore Roosevelt,* VI, p. 1245.

35. Root to Roosevelt, September 12, 1908, Roosevelt Papers; Mark Sullivan to Roosevelt, September 11, 1908, Roosevelt Papers.

36. Roosevelt to Paul Morton, March 2, 1909, in Morison, *Letters of Theodore Roosevelt,* VI, p. 1541.

37. Taft to Roosevelt, November 7, 1908, William Howard Taft Papers, Manuscript Division, Library of Congress; Lucius B. Swift to Ella Swift, July 8, 1910, Lucius B. Swift Papers, Indiana State Library, Indianapolis.

38. Oscar Straus Diary, January 23, 1909, Oscar Straus Papers, Manuscript Division, Library of Congress; Lawrence F. Abbott, *The Letters of Archie Butt* (Garden City, N.Y.: Doubleday, Page & Co., 1924), p. 338.

39. Henry F. Pringle, *The Life and Times of William Howard Taft*, 2 vols. (New York: Farrar and Rinehart, 1939), I, p. 393; George von Lengerke Meyer Diary, January 4, 1909, Manuscript Division, Library of Congress.

40. Pringle, *Life and Times*, I, p. 394.

41. White, *Autobiography of William Allen White*, p. 424.

42. Pringle, *Life and Times*, I, p. 411.

43. William Howard Taft, *Our Chief Magistrate and His Powers* (New York: Columbia University Press, 1916), p. 144.

44. *Taft and Roosevelt*, I, p. 38; Oscar King Davis, *Released for Publication* (Boston: Houghton Mifflin, 1925), p. 99.

45. Lewis L. Gould, "Western Range Senators and the Payne-Aldrich Tariff," *Pacific Northwest Quarterly* 64 (1973): 49–56.

46. Alfred E. Eckes, *Opening America's Market: U.S. Foreign Trade Policy Since 1776* (Chapel Hill: University of North Carolina Press, 1995).

47. William Howard Taft, *Presidential Addresses and State Papers* (New York: Doubleday, Page & Co., 1910), p. 222.

48. Taft to Otto Bannard, June 11, 1910, William Howard Taft Papers.

49. Geoffrey F. Morrison, "A Political Biography of Champ Clark" (Ph.D. diss., St. Louis University, 1972), p. 203.

50. Roosevelt to Gifford Pinchot, January 17, 1910, and Roosevelt to Henry Cabot Lodge, May 5, 1910, in Morison, *Letters of Theodore Roosevelt*, VII, pp. 45, 80.

51. H. J. Haskell to William Allen White, July 21, 1910, William Allen White Papers, Manuscript Division, Library of Congress, quoting Taft's secretary.

52. *Taft and Roosevelt*, II, p. 434.

53. Roosevelt to Fremont Older, August 18, 1910, in Morison, *Letters of Theodore Roosevelt*, VII, pp. 118–19.

54. *The Works of Theodore Roosevelt: Social Justice and Popular Rule*, XVII, p. 10.

55. Ibid., p. 14.

56. Robert S. La Forte, "Theodore Roosevelt's Osawatomie Speech," *Kansas Historical Quarterly* 32 (1966): 199.

57. Henry L. Stimson, "Personal Recollections of the Convention and Campaign of 1910," Henry L. Stimson Papers, Yale University Library.

58. Mark Sullivan to George S. Loftus, December 27, 1911, James Manahan Papers, Minnesota Historical Society, St. Paul.

59. Roosevelt to William Allen White, January 24, 1911, in Morison, *Letters of Theodore Roosevelt*, VII, pp. 213–14.

60. *New York Times*, February 23, 1912.

61. Roosevelt to James R. Garfield, October 31, 1911, in Morison, *Letters of Theodore Roosevelt*, VII, p. 431.

62. Roosevelt to Benjamin B. Lindsey, December 5, 1911, in Morison, *Letters of Theodore Roosevelt*, VII, p. 451.

63. *The Works of Theodore Roosevelt: Social Justice and Popular Rule*, p. 231.

64. *New York Tribune*, April 18, 30, 1912.

65. Ibid., April 26, 30, 1912; Francis L. Broderick, *Progressivism at Risk: Electing a President in 1912* (Westport, Conn.: Greenwood Press, 1989), p. 50.

66. Nicholas Murray Butler, *The Supreme Issue of 1912* (New York: 1912), p. 7; Marjorie Phillips, *Duncan Phillips and His Collection* (Boston: Little, Brown, 1971), p. 45.

67. Pringle, *Life and Times*, II, p. 795.

68. Roosevelt to James Bronson Reynolds, June 11, 1912, in Morison, *Letters of Theodore Roosevelt*, VII, p. 561.

69. Broderick, *Progressivism at Risk*, p. 53; Victor Rosewater, *Back Stage in 1912: The Inside Story of the Split Republican Convention* (Philadelphia: Dorrance & Co., 1932), p. 165, 174.

70. *The Works of Theodore Roosevelt: Social Justice and Popular Rule,* pp. 204, 231.

71. Charles D. Hilles to Mrs. S. A. Willis, June 17, 1912, author's collection.

72. To the Republican National Convention, June 22, 1912, in Morison, *Letters of Theodore Roosevelt,* VII, p. 562; Kirk H. Porter and Donald Bruce Johnson, eds., *National Party Platforms, 1840–1968* (Urbana: University of Illinois Press, 1972), p. 183 (both quotations).

73. James S. Sherman to Frank S. Black, July 5, 1912, James S. Sherman Papers, New York Public Library, Astor, Lenox, and Tilden Foundations.

74. George W. Wickersham to Charles D. Nagel, September 19, 1912, Charles D. Nagel Papers, Yale University Library.

75. Winthrop Murray Crane to Taft, November 12, 1912, Charles D. Hilles Papers, Yale University Library.

Chapter 6: REPUBLICANS DURING THE WILSON YEARS, 1913–1921

1. Roosevelt to Henry Joseph Haskell, December 28, 1918, in Elting E. Morison et al., eds., *The Letters of Theodore Roosevelt,* 8 vols. (Cambridge, Mass.: Harvard University Press, 1951–54), VIII, p. 1418.

2. Roosevelt to William Allen White, April 4, 1918, in Morison, *Letters of Theodore Roosevelt,* VIII, p. 1306.

3. Memorandum, undated but identified as written on January 5, 1919, Morison, *Letters of Theodore Roosevelt,* VIII, p. 1422.

4. Hadley was then governor of Missouri and a Roosevelt progressive who stayed with the GOP. James Holt, *Congressional Insurgents and the Party System, 1909–1916* (Cambridge, Mass.: Harvard University Press, 1967), p. 101.

5. Alice Roosevelt Longworth, *Crowded Hours* (New York, 1931), p. 325.

6. Joseph G. Cannon to Mabel Boardman, November 18, 1912, Mabel Boardman Papers, Box 6, Manuscript Division, Library of Congress.

7. S. E. High to Claude Kitchin, September 21, 1916, Claude Kitchin Papers, Southern Historical Collection, University of North Carolina, Chapel Hill.

8. "President Wilson, the Democratic Party, and the 'New Competitive Tariff,' " *The Independent* 76 (October 9, 1913): 62.

9. Kirk H. Porter and Donald Bruce Johnson, eds. *National Party Platforms, 1840–1968* (Urbana: University of Illinois Press, 1972), p. 205.

10. Lewis L. Gould, *Reform and Regulation: American Politics from Roosevelt to Wilson* (Prospect Heights, Ill.: Waveland Press, 1996), pp. 171–73.

11. Herbert F. Margulies, *Reconciliation and Revival: James R. Mann and the House Republicans in the Wilson Era* (Westport, Conn.: Greenwood Press, 1991), p. 100.

12. A. Maurice Low, "The South in the Saddle," *Harper's Weekly* 57 (February 8, 1913): 20.

13. *New York Tribune*, July 28, 1914; Joseph L. Bristow to J. R. Harrison, October 12, 1914, Joseph L. Bristow Papers, Kansas State Historical Society, Topeka; Margulies, *Reconciliation*, pp. 102–03.

14. William Allen White to Norman Hapgood, March 24, 1916, in Walter Johnson, ed., *Selected Letters of William Allen White, 1899–1943* (New York: Henry Holt, 1947), p. 165.

15. Gould, *Reform and Regulation*, p. 176.

16. Ibid., p. 180.

17. For Roosevelt's reaction to the *Lusitania* sinking, see Roosevelt to Archibald Roosevelt, May 19, 1915, in Morison, *Letters of Theodore Roosevelt*, VIII, pp. 922–23. For Wilson's quotation, see Kendrick Clements, *Woodrow Wilson: World Statesman* (Boston: Twayne, 1987), p. 159.

18. Franklin K. Lane to Woodrow Wilson, June 8, 1916, Woodrow Wilson Papers, Manuscript Division, Library of Congress.

19. Roosevelt to Anna Roosevelt Cowles, February 3, 1916, and Roosevelt's statement of March 9, 1916, in Morison, *Letters of Theodore Roosevelt*, VIII, pp. 1011, 1024, n. 1.

20. Walter Prescott Webb and Terrell Webb, eds., *Washington Wife: Journal of Ellen Maury Slayden from 1897 to 1919* (New York: Harper & Row, 1962, 1963), p. 279. The only detailed biography of Hughes is Merlo Pusey, *Charles Evans Hughes*, 2 vols. (New York: Columbia University Press, 1963).

21. Roosevelt to Anna Roosevelt Cowles, June 16, 1916, in Morison, *Letters of Theodore Roosevelt*, VIII, p. 1063.

22. Porter and Johnson, eds., *National Party Platforms*, pp. 204, 205, 206.

23. Roosevelt to the Progressive National Committee, June 22, 1916, in Morison, *Letters of Theodore Roosevelt*, VIII, p. 1074.

24. Porter and Johnson, eds., *National Party Platforms*, p. 204.

25. *How Wilson Has Kept Faith with the Farmer* (n.p., 1916), p. 29, pamphlet in Perry-Castaneda Library, University of Texas at Austin.

26. Gould, *Reform and Regulation*, p. 185.

27. Arthur Willert to Geoffrey Robinson [Dawson], October 14, 1916, archives of *The Times*, London.

28. Gould, *Reform and Regulation*, p. 185. On "The Billionaires Special," see Molly M. Wood, "Mapping a National Campaign Strategy: Partisan Women in the Presidential Election of 1916," in Melanie Gustafson, Kristie Miller, and Elisabeth I. Perry, eds., *We Have Come to Stay: American Women and Political Parties* (Albuquerque: University of New Mexico Press, 1999), pp. 77–84.

29. *The Works of Theodore Roosevelt: America and the World War; Fear God and Take Your Own Part*, XVIII, pp. 451–52.

30. Ray Stannard Baker and William E. Dodd, eds., *The New Democracy: Presidential Messages, Addresses and Other Papers (1913–1917) by Woodrow Wilson*, 2 vols. (New York: Harper & Brothers, 1926), II, p. 371.

31. *New York Times*, September 5, 1916.

32. Gould, *Reform and Regulation*, p. 189.

33. Roosevelt to Quentin Roosevelt, November 7, 1916, in Morison, *Letters of Theodore Roosevelt*, VIII, p. 1124.

34. Edith Kermit Roosevelt to Ruth Lee, November 29, 1916, Papers of Lord Lee of Fareham, Courtauld Institute, London; William C. Widenor, *Henry Cabot Lodge and the Search for an American Foreign Policy* (Berkeley: University of California Press, 1980), p. 248.

35. Richard Barry, "Why We Need a Republican Congress: Interviews with Republican Leaders," *The Outlook* 120 (October 16, 1918): 263.

36. Widenor, *Henry Cabot Lodge*, p. 264; Theodore Roosevelt to Kermit Roosevelt, June 8, 1917, Kermit Roosevelt Papers, Manuscript Division, Library of Congress.

37. For the controversy over Wilson's partisanship, see Robert H. Ferrell, *Woodrow Wilson and World War I, 1917–1921* (New York: Harper & Row, 1985), pp. 50–51.

38. Melanie Susan Gustafson, *Women and the Republican Party, 1854–1924* (Urbana: University of Illinois Press, 2001), pp. 174–83.

39. Seward W. Livermore, *Politics Is Adjourned: Woodrow Wilson and the War Congress, 1916–1918* (Middletown, Conn.: Wesleyan University Press, 1966), p. 176.

40. Gould, *Reform and Regulation,* pp. 199–200.

41. Harold Ickes to James R. Garfield, February 18, 1918, Harold Ickes Papers, Manuscript Division, Library of Congress. On Hays, see John Milton Cooper, *Breaking the Heart of the World: Woodrow Wilson and the Fight for the League of Nations* (New York: Cambridge University Press, 2001), pp. 77–78, and Will H. Hays, *Memoirs* (Garden City: Doubleday, 1955).

42. Will H. Hays, "The Republican Position," *The Forum* 60 (August 1918): 136.

43. Gould, *Reform and Regulation,* p. 203; Herbert F. Margulies, *Senator Lenroot of Wisconsin: A Political Biography, 1900–1929* (Columbia: University of Missouri Press, 1977), p. 245.

44. "Start of the 1918 Political Drive," *Literary Digest,* April 13, 1918, p. 15; Hays, "The Republican Position," p. 152; Arthur Willert to Geoffrey Dawson, October 10, 1918, archives of *The Times,* London.

45. Livermore, *Politics Is Adjourned,* p. 216.

46. "An Appeal for a Democratic Congress," in Arthur S, Link, ed., *The Papers of Woodrow Wilson,* vol. 52: *1918* (Princeton, N.J.: Princeton University Press, 1985), p. 382; Charles D. Hilles to Taft, October 28, 1918, and Bernard Moses to Taft, October 28, 1918, William Howard Taft Papers.

47. John A. Garraty, *Henry Cabot Lodge: A Biography* (New York: Alfred A. Knopf, 1953), p. 356.

48. Cooper, *Breaking the Heart of the World,* pp. 33–37, examines Wilson's decision and does not believe it was fatal. Since some Republican votes would be required to approve the treaty, a serious attempt at bipartisanship was inescapable, no matter how repugnant Wilson deemed it. For Lodge's comment, see Lodge to William Allen White, November 16, 1918, William Allen White Papers, Manuscript Division, Library of Congress.

49. For the "round-robin," see Ralph Stone, *The Irreconcilables: The Fight Against the League of Nations* (Lexington: University Press of Kentucky, 1970), pp. 70–75.

50. Cooper, *Breaking the Heart of the World,* pp. 353–75.

51. On the ultimate defeat of the treaty, see Herbert F. Margulies, *The Mild Reservationists and the League of Nations Controversy in the Senate* (Columbia: University of Missouri Press, 1989), pp. 215–60.

52. Cooper, *Breaking the Heart of the World,* pp. 400–405.

53. James F. Vivian, *William Howard Taft: Collected Editorials, 1917–1921* (New York: Praeger, 1990), p. 425.

54. William E. Leuchtenburg, *The Perils of Prosperity, 1914–1932,* 2nd ed. (Chicago: University of Chicago Press, 1958, 1993), p. 66.

55. William Allen White, *Masks in a Pageant* (New York: The Macmillan Co., 1930), p. 390; Cooper, *Breaking the Heart of the World,* pp. 389, 390, n. 25.

56. White, *Masks in a Pageant,* p. 409. For a good discussion of Harding's marital difficulties, see Robert H. Ferrell, *The Strange Deaths of President Harding* (Columbia: University of Missouri Press, 1996), pp. 153–59. Ferrell also casts serious doubt on the long-standing tale that Harding had an affair and a child with Nan Britton.

57. Porter and Johnson, eds., *National Party Platforms,* pp. 229, 230, 231, 234, 237, 238.

58. Eugene P. Trani and David L. Wilson, *The Presidency of Warren G. Harding* (Lawrence: University Press of Kansas, 1977), pp. 22–23; Robert K. Murray, *The Harding Era: Warren G. Harding and His Administration* (Minneapolis: University of Minnesota Press, 1969), pp. 37–39.

59. Leuchtenburg, *Perils of Prosperity,* p. 86.

60. Margulies, *Senator Lenroot of Wisconsin,* pp. 328–31; Robert H. Ferrell, *The Presidency of Calvin Coolidge* (Lawrence: University Press of Kansas, 1998), pp. 15–16.

61. John A. Morello, *Selling the President, 1920: Albert D. Lasker, Advertising, and the Election of Warren G. Harding* (Westport, Conn.: Praeger, 2001), pp. 54–55.

62. Gustafson, *Women and the Republican Party,* pp. 187–93.

63. Richard B. Sherman, *The Republican Party and Black America from McKinley to Hoover, 1896–1933* (Charlottesville: University Press of Virginia, 1973), pp. 134–44.

64. Ibid., pp. 137, 140.

65. Murray, *The Harding Era,* p. 64.

66. Chester I. Long to Taft, October 11, 1920, William Howard Taft Papers.

67. Leuchtenburg, *Perils of Prosperity,* p. 88.

68. Gould, *Reform and Regulation,* p. 217.

Chapter 7: THE AGE OF REPUBLICAN DOMINANCE, 1921–1933

1. For descriptions of Harding's funeral train and the outpouring of public affection, see Robert K. Murray, *The Harding Era: Warren G. Harding and His Administration* (Minneapolis: University of Minnesota Press, 1969), pp. 451–55; Robert H. Ferrell, *The Strange Deaths of President Harding* (Columbia: University of Missouri Press, 1996), pp. 20–26.

2. "Mr. Harding for Simplicity," *The Nation* 112 (January 19, 1921): 72; "Tremendous Problems That Face Harding," *Literary Digest* 65 (March 5, 1921): 7; Carl Sferrazza Anthony, *Florence Harding: The First Lady, the Jazz Age, and the Death of America's Most Scandalous President* (New York: William Morrow, 1998), p. 263.

3. For Harding and Debs, see Murray, *Harding Era,* pp. 166–69, and for race relations, pp. 397–403.

4. *New York Times,* March 5, 1921. There are several on-line copies of Harding's inaugural; see bartleby.com, for example.

5. For the changes reshaping the United States in the 1920s, see William E. Leuchtenburg, *The Perils of Prosperity, 1915–1932,* 2nd ed. (Chicago: University of Chicago Press, 1958, 1993), pp. 178–86; Michael E. Parrish, *Anxious Decades: America in Prosperity and Depression, 1920–1941* (New York: W. W. Norton, 1992).

6. For the impact of the consumer culture on the 1920s, see James Mac-Gregor Burns, *The American Experiment,* vol. 2: *The Workshop of Democracy* (New York: Alfred A. Knopf, 1985), pp. 518–31.

7. The problems of the farm sector are discussed in Robert H. Ferrell, *The Presidency of Calvin Coolidge* (Lawrence: University Press of Kansas, 1998), pp. 81–94.

8. Robert H. Zieger, *Republicans and Labor, 1919–1929* (Lexington: University of Kentucky Press, 1969), looks at the GOP and its labor relations.

9. Roger Daniels, *Coming to America: A History of Immigration and Ethnicity in American Life* (New York: HarperCollins, 1990), pp. 282, 284 (quotation, p. 284).

10. There is a large literature on Prohibition during the 1920s. Norman H. Clark, *Deliver Us from Evil: An Interpretation of American Prohibition* (New York: Norton, 1976), is an excellent starting point on the problem.

11. The Klan had its greatest impact on the Democrats, but it affected Republican parties in states such as Indiana. Stanley Coben, *Rebellion Against Victorianism: The Impetus for Cultural Change in 1920s America* (New York: Oxford University Press, 1991), pp. 147–49.

12. Murray, *Harding Era*, p. 417.

13. Ibid., p. 93.

14. For Fall, see David H. Stratton, *Tempest over Teapot Dome: The Story of Albert B. Fall* (Norman: University of Oklahoma Press, 1998), and for Daugherty, see James N. Giglio, *H. M. Daugherty and the Politics of Expediency* (Kent, Ohio: Kent State University Press, 1991).

15. Murray, *Harding Era*, makes the best case for Harding's competence in office. For the president's efforts to reorganize the federal government, see Peri Arnold, *Making the Managerial Presidency: Comprehensive Reorganization Planning, 1905–1996* (Lawrence: University Press of Kansas, 1998), pp. 52–75.

16. The impact of the 1922 congressional elections is discussed in Murray, *Harding Era*, pp. 317–21.

17. Ibid., p. 418.

18. Ibid., p. 425; Ferrell, *Strange Deaths of President Harding*, pp. 5–9.

19. William Allen White, *The Autobiography of William Allen White* (New York: The Macmillan Co., 1946), p. 619.

20. Murray, *Harding Era*, p. 445.

21. Ferrell, *Strange Deaths*, pp. 30–49, disposes of the conspiracy theories. See also Eugene P. Trani and Donald L. Wilson, *The Presidency of Warren G. Harding* (Lawrence: University Press of Kansas, 1977), pp. 176–77.

22. For recent treatments of Teapot Dome, see Stratton, *Tempest over Teapot Dome*, pp. 229–300, and Martin R. Ansell, *Oil Baron of the Southwest: Ed-*

ward L. Doheny and the Development of the Petroleum Industry in California and Mexico (Columbus: Ohio State University Press, 1998), pp. 212–37.

23. Ferrell, *Presidency of Calvin Coolidge*, p. 24.

24. Ibid., p. 39. For the Republican interest in Coolidge during the 1980s, see Robert Sobel, *Coolidge: An American Enigma* (Washington, D.C.: Regnery, 1998), pp. 13–14.

25. John L. Blair, "Coolidge the Image-Maker: The President and the Press, 1923–1929," *New England Quarterly* 46 (December 1973): 499–522; Daniel J. Leab, "Coolidge, Hayes and 1920s Movies: Some Aspects of Image and Reality," in John Earl Haynes, ed., *Calvin Coolidge and the Coolidge Era* (Washington, D.C.: Library of Congress, 1998), pp. 97–131.

26. The best biography of Coolidge is Donald R. McCoy, *Calvin Coolidge: The Quiet President* (New York: The Macmillan Co., 1967). For the quotation about Mrs. Coolidge, see Ishbel Ross, *Grace Coolidge and Her Era: The Story of a President's Wife* (New York: Dodd, Mead, 1963), p. 9.

27. Sobel, *Coolidge: An American Enigma*, p. 191.

28. Ibid., p. 292; Ferrell, *Presidency of Calvin Coolidge*, pp. 167–75. Gene Smiley and Richard Keehn, "Federal Personal Income Tax Policy in the 1920s," *Journal of Economic History* 55 (June 1995): 285–303. The authors argue that the tax cuts of the 1920s were designed to counter tax avoidance that saw wealthy Americans rely on tax-exempt securities to lower their tax burden.

29. On Coolidge's campaign for the 1924 nomination and the role of Slemp, see Sobel, *Coolidge: An American Enigma*, pp. 240–41, and for how Coolidge locked up the Republican nod, see Ferrell, *Presidency of Calvin Coolidge*, pp. 51–55.

30. Ferrell, *Presidency of Calvin Coolidge*, pp. 45–46; David Burner, *The Politics of Provincialism: The Democratic Party in Transition, 1918–1932* (New York: Alfred A. Knopf, 1968), pp. 107–10.

31. Ferrell, *Presidency of Calvin Coolidge*, p. 56; Sobel, *Coolidge: An American Enigma*, p. 286; McCoy, *Calvin Coolidge*, p. 246 (quotation). The Borah anecdote probably gained something in the telling.

32. H. L. Mencken, *A Carnival of Buncombe* (Baltimore, Md.: Johns Hopkins Press, 1956), p. 97.

33. McCoy, *Calvin Coolidge*, p. 255.

34. Sobel, *Coolidge: An American Enigma*, p. 307.

35. Ibid., p. 313.

36. Ibid., pp. 311, 337; Ferrell, *Presidency of Calvin Coolidge*, pp. 169–72, discusses Coolidge and Andrew Mellon's tax policies.

37. For the McNary-Haugen plan and Coolidge's response to it, see Ferrell, *Presidency of Calvin Coolidge*, pp. 83–93 (quotation, p. 93).

38. Historians have long known that American involvement in world affairs in the 1920s was extensive, but the perception of isolation in the decade has persisted as one of the legacies attributed to Republican rule. John Milton Cooper, *Breaking the Heart of the World: Woodrow Wilson and the Fight for the League of Nations* (New York: Cambridge University Press, 2001), pp. 399–402, offers a good summary of the problem. See also William Appleman Williams, "The Legend of Isolationism in the 1920s," *Science and Society* 18 (1954): 1–20. Ferrell, *Presidency of Calvin Coolidge*, covers foreign policy in rich detail.

39. McCoy, *Calvin Coolidge*, p. 190, mentions the famous Coolidge quote.

40. McCoy, *Calvin Coolidge*, p. 313.

41. Paul Johnson, "Calvin Coolidge and the Lost Arcadia," in Haynes, ed., *Calvin Coolidge and the Coolidge Era*, pp. 11–12 (both quotations).

42. Coolidge's surprise announcement is discussed by all of his biographers. Ferrell, *Presidency of Calvin Coolidge*, pp. 192–94, analyzes the political reasoning behind the decision.

43. Alice Roosevelt Longworth, *Crowded Hours: Reminiscences* (New York: Charles Scribner's Sons, 1933), p. 327.

44. The presidential election of 1928 has been the subject of much historical writing. Richard Hofstadter, "Could a Protestant Have Beaten Hoover in 1928?" *The Reporter* 22 (1960): 31–33, was an early exploration of Hoover's appeal to voters in 1928. The best one-volume treatment of the contest is Allan J. Lichtman, *Prejudice and the Old Politics: The Presidential Election of 1928* (Chapel Hill: The University of North Carolina Press, 1979).

45. There are two insightful one-volume biographies of Hoover. Joan Hoff Wilson, *Herbert Hoover: Forgotten Progressive* (Boston: Little, Brown, 1975), and David Burner, *Herbert Hoover: A Public Life* (New York: Alfred A. Knopf, 1979), introduced historians to the analytic issues that Hoover raised as a politician and president. Mark M. Dodge, ed., *Herbert Hoover*

and the Historians (West Branch, Iowa: Herbert Hoover Presidential Library Association, 1989), is a good introduction to the huge body of writing about Hoover and his impact on American politics.

46. Wilson, *Herbert Hoover,* p. 122.

47. McCoy, *Calvin Coolidge,* pp. 386 (third quotation), 390 (first quotation); Louis Liebovich, *Bylines in Despair: Herbert Hoover, the Great Depression and the U.S. News Media* (Westport, Conn.: Praeger, 1994), p. 60 (second quotation); George H. Nash, "The 'Great Enigma' and the 'Great Engineer': The Political Relationship of Calvin Coolidge and Herbert Hoover," in Haynes, ed., *Calvin Coolidge and the Coolidge Era,* pp. 149–90.

48. Kirk H. Porter and Donald Bruce Johnson, eds., *National Party Platforms, 1840–1968* (Urbana: University of Illinois Press, 1972), pp. 280, 282, 291.

49. Herbert Hoover, *The New Day* (Stanford, Calif.: Stanford University Press, 1928), pp. 16, 150–51.

50. Ibid., p. 29.

51. Lichtman, *Prejudice and the Old Politics,* covers the various aspects of the 1928 campaign in detail.

52. Smith's limitations as a candidate are discussed in Burner, *Politics of Provincialism,* pp. 195 (quotation), 209–16.

53. On Hoover as a candidate, see Liebovich, *Bylines in Despair,* pp. 72–73; Wilson, *Herbert Hoover,* pp. 126–27; Martin L. Fausold, *The Presidency of Herbert C. Hoover* (Lawrence: University Press of Kansas, 1977), pp. 23–31.

54. Liebovich, *Bylines in Despair,* pp. 73–74.

55. Lichtman, *Prejudice and the Old Politics,* pp. 64–65.

56. Ibid., p. 154 (quotation). David James Ginzl, "Herbert Hoover and Republican Patronage Politics in the South, 1928–1932" (Ph.D. diss., Syracuse University, 1977), pp. 109–12, 118–19. See also Donald J. Lisio, *Hoover, Blacks and Lily-Whites: A Study of Southern Strategies* (Chapel Hill: University of North Carolina Press, 1985).

57. Hoover, *The New Day,* p. 217; Lichtman, *Prejudice and the Old Politics,* pp. 199–230, places the election results in the context of presidential politics from 1916 to 1940.

58. "Six Months of Hoover's Presidential Engineering," *Literary Digest* (September 21, 1929): 14.

59. Fausold, *Presidency of Herbert C. Hoover,* p. 142.

60. Michael E. Parrish, *Anxious Decades: America in Prosperity and Depression, 1920–1941* (New York: Norton, 1992), p. 232.

61. *Variety,* October 30, 1929, p. 1.

62. The notion that Hoover sat idly by while the Depression worsened has long been discredited. An early statement of the continuity in policy between Hoover and Franklin D. Roosevelt can be found in Walter Lippmann, "The Permanent New Deal," *Yale Review* 24 (June 1935): 649–67. It contends that in the fall of 1929 Hoover did "something utterly unprecedented in American history. The national government undertook to make the whole economic order operate prosperously" (p. 652).

63. There are good discussions of Hoover's active efforts to combat the Depression in Fausold, *Presidency of Herbert Hoover,* pp. 105–66, and in Wilson, *Herbert Hoover,* pp. 122–67. For an analysis of other treatments of his presidency, see Dodge, ed., *Herbert Hoover and the Historians,* pp. 39–85.

64. Alfred E. Eckes, Jr., *Opening America's Market: U.S. Foreign Trade Policy Since 1776* (Chapel Hill: University of North Carolina Press, 1995), pp. 100–139, argues that the Smoot-Hawley law did not have all the negative effects attributed to it. For Hoover's comment, see Fausold, *Presidency of Herbert C. Hoover,* p. 74.

65. William E. Leuchtenburg, *Franklin D. Roosevelt and the New Deal* (New York: Harper & Row, 1963), p. 13 (rose comment). Kennedy, *Freedom from Fear,* p. 91, has a variant on the Mellon story, which I first heard when I entered graduate school in the early 1960s.

66. Fausold, *Presidency of Herbert C. Hoover,* p. 111.

67. For the effects and results of the 1930 congressional elections, see Fausold, *Presidency of Herbert C. Hoover,* pp. 100–103, and Liebovich, *Bylines in Despair,* pp. 123–25.

68. For Michelson's activities and their impact, see Kennedy, *Freedom from Fear,* pp. 62, 91, and Liebovich, *Bylines in Despair,* p. 193.

69. Fausold, *Presidency of Herbert C. Hoover,* p. 142.

70. Wilson, *Herbert Hoover,* pp. 155–56; Fausold, *Presidency of Herbert C. Hoover,* pp. 154–55.

71. Wilson, *Herbert Hoover,* p. 157; Fausold, *Presidency of Herbert C. Hoover,* pp. 159–62.

72. On Republican presidential politics in 1932, see "G.O.P. Guesses About 1932," *Literary Digest* 108 (May 9, 1931): 8, and Fausold, *Presidency of Herbert C. Hoover,* pp. 193–96.

73. Porter and Johnson, eds., *National Party Platforms,* pp. 340, 350.

74. The Bonus March has been the subject of several studies. See Roger Daniels, *The Bonus March: An Episode of the Great Depression* (Westport, Conn.: Greenwood, 1971), and Donald J. Lisio, *The President and Protest: Hoover, Conspiracy and the Bonus Riot* (Columbia: University of Missouri Press, 1974). Liebovich, *Bylines in Despair,* pp. 155–77, argues that the administration's handling of the march did not hurt Hoover politically to the degree often assumed.

75. The Hoover campaign is analyzed in Liebovich, *Bylines in Despair,* pp. 194–97, and in Clyde P. Weed, *The Nemesis of Reform: The Republican Party During the New Deal* (New York: Columbia University Press, 1994), pp. 22–32; Robert S. McElvaine, *The Great Depression: America, 1929–1941* (New York: Times Books, 1984), pp. 131–32 (quotation).

Chapter 8: THE REPUBLICANS
IN THE AGE OF THE NEW DEAL, 1933–1945

1. Donald Bruce Johnson, *The Republican Party and Wendell Willkie* (Urbana: University of Illinois Press, 1960), p. 88.

2. Steve Neal, *Dark Horse: A Biography of Wendell Willkie* (Garden City, N.Y.: Doubleday & Co., 1984), pp. 89, 121.

3. Clyde P. Weed, *The Nemesis of Reform: The Republican Party During the New Deal* (New York: Columbia University Press, 1994), p. 37.

4. William E. Leuchtenburg, *Franklin D. Roosevelt and the New Deal, 1932–1940* (New York: Harper & Row, 1963), p. 39.

5. For Roosevelt's start as president, see David M. Kennedy, *Freedom from Fear: The American People in Depression and War, 1929–1945* (New York: Oxford University Press, 1999), pp. 133–59.

6. Leuchtenburg, *Franklin D. Roosevelt,* p. 60.

7. Weed, *Nemesis of Reform,* pp. 37–43, discusses the problems the GOP faced in responding to the New Deal.

8. Weed, *Nemesis of Reform,* pp. 37, 39.

9. James T. Patterson, *Mr. Republican: A Biography of Robert A. Taft* (Boston: Houghton Mifflin, 1972), pp. 151–52, quoting a 1934 Taft letter.

10. Leuchtenburg, *Franklin D. Roosevelt*, p. 117, n. 63. Weed, *Nemesis of Reform*, pp. 43–49, examines the impact of the 1934 elections on the party.

11. The New Deal programs of early 1935 are analyzed in Kennedy, *Freedom from Fear,* pp. 242–78. A representative Republican reaction to this surge of legislative activity can be seen in the speech of Arthur M. Hyde, Secretary of Agriculture under Hoover, delivered June 10, 1935, U.S. Senate, *Congressional Record,* June 19, 1935, pp. 9621–22, in which Hyde charged that "Government claims the right to plan, to order, to regiment the lives of 125,000,000 Americans."

12. Weed, *Nemesis of Reform*, p. 162; Sheryl R. Tynes, *Turning Points in Social Security: From "Cruel Hoax" to "Sacred Entitlement"* (Stanford, Calif.: Stanford University Press, 1996), p. 55.

13. Weed, *Nemesis of Reform*, p. 159.

14. Ibid., p. 60.

15. William Allen White to Carl Sandburg, February 20, 1936, in Walter Johnson, ed., *Selected Letters of William Allen White, 1899–1943* (New York: Henry Holt, 1947), p. 361.

16. White to E. Ben Johnson, August 19, 1935, in Johnson, ed., *Selected Letters of William Allen White*, p. 358. Donald R. McCoy, *Landon of Kansas* (Lincoln: University of Nebraska Press, 1966), is a comprehensive and sympathetic study of Landon's public career.

17. McCoy, *Landon of Kansas*, pp. 259–60; Kirk H. Porter and Donald Bruce Johnson, eds., *National Party Platforms, 1840–1968* (Urbana: University of Illinois Press, 1972), p. 365.

18. Porter and Johnson, eds., *National Party Platforms*, pp. 365–70. Republican National Committee, *Promise and Performance: The Administration of Franklin D. Roosevelt Reveals Itself* (Chicago, 1936), summarizes the GOP case.

19. McCoy, *Landon of Kansas*, p. 347 (*Chicago Tribune*); Leuchtenburg, *Franklin D. Roosevelt*, pp. 175–76, discusses the Landon campaign and its problems. Leuchtenburg goes into even more detail about the election contest in *The FDR Years: On Roosevelt and His Legacy* (New York: Columbia University Press, 1995), pp. 101–58, "The Election of 1936." See also Weed, *Nemesis of Reform*, pp. 98–116.

20. Peverill Squire, "Why the 1936 Literary Digest Poll Failed," *Public Opinion Quarterly* 52 (1988): 125–33; McCoy, *Landon of Kansas*, pp. 300–301; Leuchtenburg, *Franklin D. Roosevelt*, p. 196.

21. Leuchtenburg, *Franklin D. Roosevelt*, p. 184; McCoy, *Landon of Kansas*, p. 329.

22. Michael J. Webber, *New Deal Fat Cats: Business, Labor and Campaign Finance in the 1936 Presidential Election* (New York: Fordham University Press, 2000), pp. 17–28.

23. Leuchtenburg, *Franklin D. Roosevelt*, pp. 184–95, 189, n. 72 (quotation), is excellent on the aspects of the New Deal coalition. Webber, *New Deal Fat Cats*, pp. 127–34, discusses the class basis of the Republican defeat. Allan J. Lichtman, *Prejudice and the Old Politics: The Presidential Election of 1928* (Chapel Hill: University of North Carolina Press, 1979), pp. 225–26; the author believes it was World War II that enabled Roosevelt to be re-elected in 1940 and maintain the Democrats in power through the 1940s.

24. Steven F. Hayward, *The Age of Reagan: The Fall of the Old Liberal Order, 1964–1980* (Roseville, Calif.: Primus Publishing Co., 2001), pp. ix–xxxv; the author contends that liberalism dominated in the sphere of ideas, and he examines their decline leading to the emergence of Ronald Reagan. The first quotation is from the 1952 GOP platform. Porter and Johnson, eds., *National Party Platforms*, p. 497.

25. Patterson, *Mr. Republican*, p. 176, quoting a Taft speech from 1938.

26. The literature on the court-packing plan is vast and mostly focused on the Democrats and Roosevelt. A good source on the Republican strategy as the Democrats divided is Karl A. Lamb, "The Opposition Party as Secret Agent: Republicans and the Court Fight," *Papers of the Michigan Academy of Science, Arts, and Letters* 46 (1961): 539–50. A recent treatment of the episode that is critical of Roosevelt is Marian C. McKenna, *Franklin Roosevelt and the Great Constitutional War: The Court-Packing Crisis of 1937* (New York: Fordham University Press, 2002).

27. Leuchtenburg, *Franklin D. Roosevelt*, p. 243 (quotation). For the conservative reaction to labor's militance, see Kennedy, *Freedom from Fear*, pp. 308–15, 320–22.

28. The effects of the 1937–38 recession are discussed in Leuchtenburg, *Franklin D. Roosevelt*, pp. 243–51 (Roosevelt Depression quote, p. 250); Milton Plesur, "The Republican Congressional Comeback of 1938," *Review of Politics* 24 (1962): 540 (Roosevelt recession).

29. Plesur, "Republican Congressional Comeback," pp. 535–36, 543; Richard Norton Smith, *Thomas E. Dewey and His Times* (New York: Simon & Schuster, 1982), pp. 228–41.

30. James T. Patterson, *Mr. Republican*, pp. 174–79; Smith, *Thomas E. Dewey*, pp. 272–75. On the troubles of the New Deal after the 1938 elections, see Leuchtenburg, *Franklin D. Roosevelt*, pp. 277–79.

31. Justus D. Doenecke, *Storm on the Horizon: The Challenge to American Intervention, 1939–1941* (Lanham, Md.: Rowman & Littlefield, 2000), p. 31 (quotation).

32. For the internationalist wing of the GOP, see Neal, *Dark Horse*, pp. 74–79; George H. Mayer, *The Republican Party, 1854–1966*, 2nd ed. (New York: Oxford University Press, 1967), pp. 458–59; Smith, *Thomas E. Dewey*, pp. 304–305.

33. Neal, *Dark Horse*, p. 73.

34. Patterson, *Mr. Republican*, pp. 213–16; 213 (first quotation) summarizes Taft's problems as a candidate. Smith, *Thomas E. Dewey*, p. 311 (second quotation).

35. Smith, *Thomas E. Dewey*, pp. 289, 299, discusses Dewey's personality. Smith's book is an excellent, well-written, and perceptive biography.

36. On the predicament of the Republicans during the spring of 1940, see Smith, *Thomas E. Dewey*, pp. 302–309; Neal, *Dark Horse*, pp. 74–79; Mayer, *Republican Party*, pp. 456–57.

37. Willkie has been the subject of several biographies. Ellsworth Barnard, *Wendell Willkie: Fighter for Freedom* (Marquette: Northern Michigan University Press, 1966), and Joseph Barnes, *Willkie* (New York: Simon & Schuster, 1952), are both informative. Neal's book is the best modern study. James H. Madison, ed., *Wendell Willkie: Hoosier Internationalist* (Bloomington: Indiana University Press, 1992), is a collection of interesting essays about various phases of Willkie's public career.

38. Neal, *Dark Horse*, p. 38.

39. Ibid., p. 68.

40. On the appointment of the two Republicans to Roosevelt's Cabinet, see Johnson, *Republican Party and Wendell Willkie*, pp. 84–85.

41. Johnson, *Republican Party and Wendell Willkie*, pp. 65–70, and Neal, *Dark Horse*, pp. 66–92, are both good on the organization of the Willkie boom in 1940. Smith, *Thomas E. Dewey*, p. 306 (quotation).

42. Excellent accounts of the tumultuous 1940 convention are in the sources previously cited, including the Neal and Johnson volumes.

43. Porter and Johnson, eds., *National Party Platforms,* pp. 390, 392, 393.

44. Johnson, *Republican Party and Wendell Willkie,* p. 102 (first quotation); Smith, *Thomas E. Dewey,* p. 328 (second quotation). For a critique of Willkie's overall performance as a candidate, see Henry O. Evjen, "The Willkie Campaign: An Unfortunate Chapter in Republican Leadership," *Journal of Politics* 14 (May 1952): 241–56.

45. Neal, *Dark Horse,* p. 159.

46. On the passions that the campaign aroused, see the buttons displayed in Arthur M. Schlesinger, Jr., et al., eds., *Running for President: The Candidates and Their Images,* 2 vols. (New York: Simon & Schuster, 1994), II, p. 210. Leuchtenburg, *Franklin D. Roosevelt,* p. 319.

47. The backstage features of the 1940 presidential race were first brought to light in R.J.C. Butow, "The FDR Tapes," *American Heritage* (February/March 1982): 10–15, 20–22; William Doyle, *Inside the Oval Office: The White House Tapes from FDR to Clinton* (New York: Kodansha International, 1999), pp. 6–44. The impact on the presidential race of these events is discussed in Neal, *Dark Horse,* pp. 144–45.

48. Neal, *Dark Horse,* pp. 167–68.

49. The results of the 1940 election are discussed in Leuchtenburg, *Franklin D. Roosevelt,* pp. 321–22; Neal, *Dark Horse,* pp. 176–79; Johnson, *Republican Party and Wendell Willkie,* pp. 160–67.

50. Richard E. Darilek, *A Loyal Opposition in Time of War: The Republican Party and the Politics of Foreign Policy from Pearl Harbor to Yalta* (Westport, Conn.: Greenwood Press, 1976), p. 22.

51. Taft to Scandrett, January 29, 1941, in Clarence E. Wunderlin et al., eds., *The Papers of Robert A. Taft,* 2 vols. (Kent, Ohio: Kent State University Press, 1997), II, p. 218.

52. Neal, *Dark Horse,* p. 206.

53. Arthur H. Vandenberg, Jr., with Joe Alex Morris, eds., *The Private Papers of Senator Vandenberg* (Boston: Houghton Mifflin, 1952), p. 10; Patterson, *Mr. Republican,* p. 244.

54. Neal, *Dark Horse,* p. 217; "Statement After the Bombing of Pearl Harbor, December 8, 1941," in Wunderlin et al., eds., *Papers of Robert A. Taft,* II, p. 301.

55. Wes Pruden, "When All Else Fails, Find a Panic Button," *Washington Times,* May 17, 2002; Martin V. Melosi, *The Shadow of Pearl Harbor: Political Controversy over the Surprise Attack, 1941–1946* (College Station: Texas A&M University Press, 1977).

56. Taft made these remarks in a Chicago speech on December 19, 1941. See Wunderlin et al., eds., *Papers of Robert A. Taft,* II, p. 303.

57. Darilek, *A Loyal Opposition,* pp. 53–57.

58. Taft to Dwight Griswold, November 5, 1942, in Wunderlin et al., eds., *Papers of Robert A. Taft,* II, p. 385.

59. Smith, *Thomas E. Dewey,* pp. 343–51 ("fat friend" quotation, p. 346); Richard O. Davies, *Defender of the Old Guard: John Bricker and American Politics* (Columbus: Ohio State University Press, 1993), pp. 77–79; Taft to James H. Crummey, July 22, 1943, in Wunderlin et al., eds., *Papers of Robert A. Taft,* II, p. 468.

60. Darilek, *A Loyal Opposition,* pp. 106–12; Smith, *Thomas E. Dewey,* pp. 385, 387.

61. Vandenberg and Morris, eds., *Private Papers of Senator Vandenberg,* p. 58.

62. *New York Times,* April 28, 1944; Smith, *Thomas E. Dewey,* p. 397.

63. Davies, *Defender of the Old Guard,* p. 103.

64. Smith, *Thomas E. Dewey,* p. 48.

65. Davies, *Defender of the Old Guard,* pp. 82, 94.

66. Porter and Johnson, eds., *National Party Platforms,* pp. 408, 412.

67. Ibid., pp. 409, 411.

68. On the issue of Roosevelt's health in the 1944 presidential campaign, see Smith, *Thomas E. Dewey,* p. 421; Robert H. Ferrell, *Ill-Advised: Presidential Health and Public Trust* (Columbia: University of Missouri Press, 1992), pp. 28–46; Herbert Brownell, with John P. Burke, *Advising Ike: The Memoirs of Attorney General Herbert Brownell* (Lawrence: University Press of Kansas, 1993), pp. 58–59.

69. Smith, *Thomas E. Dewey,* pp. 409–10, 433–34; Schlesinger, ed., *Running for President,* II, p. 228. For Dewey's problems as a campaigner in 1944, see Richard L. Neuberger to Harold Ickes, October 3, 1944, Harold Ickes Papers, Manuscript Division, Box 238, Library of Congress.

70. Smith, *Thomas E. Dewey,* p. 416; Schlesinger, ed., *Running for President,* II, pp. 225–26.

71. Davies, *Defender of the Old Guard,* pp. 103–104; "24 Reasons Why It's Time for a Change," Dewey-Bricker campaign leaflet, author's copy.

72. Smith, *Thomas E. Dewey,* pp. 426–30; Melosi, *Shadow of Pearl Harbor,* pp. 82–88.

73. Smith, *Thomas E. Dewey,* p. 436.

74. Taft to David S. Ingalls, December 26, 1944, in Wunderlin et al., eds., *The Papers of Robert A. Taft,* II, p. 613.

75. Porter and Johnson, *National Party Platforms,* p. 499.

76. Morris and Vandenberg, eds., *Private Papers of Senator Vandenberg,* p. 165; Smith, *Thomas E. Dewey,* p. 449.

Chapter 9: FROM "HAD ENOUGH?"
TO MODERN REPUBLICANISM, 1945–1961

1. George L. Hart, reporter, *Official Report of the Proceedings of the Twenty-fifth Republican National Convention Held in Chicago, Illinois, July 7, 8, 9, 10, and 11, 1952* (Washington, D.C.: Judd & Detweiler, 1952), p. 178.

2. Byron C. Hulsey, *Everett Dirksen and His Presidents: How a Senate Giant Shaped American Politics* (Lawrence: University Press of Kansas, 2000), pp. 45–47, describes Dirksen's role in the convention. Richard Norton Smith, *Thomas E. Dewey and His Times* (New York: Simon & Schuster, 1982), p. 594.

3. Jack Gould, "Political Leaders Acclaim TV but Warn Against Its Misuse," *New York Times,* June 25, 1951.

4. For a recent treatment of the emergence of southern Republicanism after World War II, see Earl Black and Merle Black, *The Rise of Southern Republicans* (Cambridge, Mass.: The Belknap Press of Harvard University Press, 2002), pp. 57–71.

5. David M. Oshinsky, *A Conspiracy So Immense: The World of Joe McCarthy* (New York: Free Press, 1983), p. 102, quotes Velde, a Republican congressman from Illinois.

6. There has not been a thorough examination of the Republicans and the issue of anti-Communism in the post–World War II era. A recent biography favorable to Joseph McCarthy sheds some light on the question: See Arthur Herman, *Joseph McCarthy: Reexamining the Life and*

Legacy of America's Most Hated Senator (New York: Free Press, 2000). David W. Reinhard, *The Republican Right Since 1945* (Lexington: University Press of Kentucky, 1983), pp. 60–63, is useful, too.

7. The opening of the Soviet archives after the end of the Cold War, along with revelations about American code-breaking, has allowed evidence about Soviet penetration of the American government to be disclosed. For a recent treatment of these issues, see Derek Leebaert, *The Fifty-Year Wound: The True Price of America's Cold War Victory* (Boston: Little, Brown, 2002), pp. 106–21.

8. George Steven Roukis, *American Labor and the Conservative Republicans, 1946–1948* (New York: Garland, 1988), pp. 15–16.

9. James T. Patterson, *Mr. Republican: A Biography of Robert A. Taft* (Boston: Houghton Mifflin, 1972), p. 313.

10. Herman, *Joseph McCarthy*, pp. 30–32, 38–39, discusses McCarthy's war service and the 1946 election outcome. Irwin F. Gellman, *The Contender: Richard Nixon, the Congress Years, 1946–1952* (New York: Free Press, 1999), pp. 78–79; Reinhard, *Republican Right*, pp. 15–16.

11. Patterson, *Mr. Republican*, p. 313; Oshinsky, *A Conspiracy So Immense*, p. 49.

12. Reinhard, *Republican Right*, p. 15.

13. Roukis, *American Labor and the Conservative Republicans*, p. 46.

14. Reinhard, *Republican Right*, p. 36. Reed was a Republican congressman from New York.

15. Patterson, *Mr. Republican*, pp. 337, 339. Claude Pepper was a liberal Democratic senator from Florida.

16. For the enactment of the Taft-Hartley law, see Patterson, *Mr. Republican*, pp. 352–66, and Roukis, *American Labor*, pp. 95–118.

17. On Truman's credentials as a foe of Communism in 1947–48, see Alonzo Hamby, *Man of the People: A Life of Harry S. Truman* (New York: Oxford University Press, 1995), pp. 391–400, 427–29. Many historians argue that Truman's loyalty programs were as unfair to the civil liberties of accused Communists as the later tactics of Senator McCarthy. But Truman's actions made it more difficult to convince the public that the president was soft on Communism. After the 1948 election and the revelations about Communist espionage that took place, the Republicans would have more success with their campaign.

18. Gerald Johnson, a liberal columnist, is quoted in Zachary Karabell, *The Last Campaign: How Harry Truman Won the 1948 Election* (New York: Vintage Books, 2001), p. 203.

19. Gary A. Donaldson, *Truman Defeats Dewey* (Lexington: University Press of Kentucky, 1999), p. 173.

20. William B. Pickett, *Eisenhower Decides to Run: Presidential Politics and Cold War Strategy* (Chicago: Ivan R. Dee, 2000), p. 40, explores the general's actions in 1948 as a prelude to his candidacy in 1952.

21. State of New York, *Public Papers of Thomas E. Dewey, Fifty-first Governor of the State of New York 1948* (no publisher, 1949), p. 592.

22. Donaldson, *Truman Defeats Dewey*, p. 131.

23. *Public Papers of Thomas E. Dewey*, p. 636. Kirk H. Porter and Donald Bruce Johnson, eds., *National Party Platforms, 1840–1968* (Urbana: University of Illinois Press, 1972), pp. 451, 453.

24. Herbert Brownell, with John P. Burke, *Advising Ike: The Memoirs of Attorney General Herbert Brownell* (Lawrence: University Press of Kansas, 1993), p. 80.

25. On Truman's activities in 1948, see Smith, *Thomas E. Dewey*, pp. 504–505; Donaldson, *Truman Defeats Dewey*, pp. 167–69; Zachary Karabell, *The Last Campaign: How Harry Truman Won the 1948 Election*, pp. 191–94.

26. Smith, *Thomas E. Dewey*, pp. 512–13.

27. *Public Papers of Thomas E. Dewey*, pp. 649, 654, 690.

28. Smith, *Thomas E. Dewey*, pp. 535, 536.

29. Ibid., pp. 511–12; Karabell, *The Last Campaign*, pp. 207–11.

30. On polling in the 1948 election, see Donaldson, *Truman Defeats Dewey*, pp. 209–10; Karabell, *The Last Campaign*, pp. 255–57. Polling techniques improved in the aftermath of the 1948 embarrassment. See Susan Herbst, *Numbered Voices: How Opinion Polling Has Shaped American Politics* (Chicago: University of Chicago Press, 1993), pp. 109–11.

31. Smith, *Thomas E. Dewey*, pp. 47, 48.

32. Oshinsky, *A Conspiracy So Immense*, p. 163.

33. Clarence Budington Kelland, "Why the Republicans Lost," *American Mercury* 144 (February 1949): 181, 182. For a response from a less conservative Republican, see Henry Cabot Lodge, "Modernize the

GOP: Specifications for a Republican Program," *Atlantic* (March 1950): 23–28.

34. Smith, *Thomas E. Dewey*, p. 547.

35. Richard Nixon, *RN: The Memoirs of Richard Nixon* (New York: Grosset & Dunlap, 1978), p. 137.

36. A recording of McCarthy's speech at Wheeling did not survive, and so a precise record of what he said does not exist. A copy was printed in the *Congressional Record*, 81 Cong., 2 Sess. (January 26, 1950): 1002–08. These quotations are from Oshinsky, *A Conspiracy So Immense*, pp. 108–109. Herman, *Joseph McCarthy*, pp. 98–99, quotes other excerpts.

37. Oshinsky, *A Conspiracy So Immense*, p. 133.

38. Patterson, *Mr. Republican*, p. 453.

39. Ronald J. Caridi, *The Korean War and American Politics: The Republican Party as a Case Study* (Philadelphia: University of Pennsylvania Press, 1968), p. 95.

40. Ibid., p. 145.

41. Ibid., p. 174.

42. Reinhard, *The Republican Right Since 1945*, p. 80.

43. Patterson, *Mr. Republican*, pp. 499–516, traces the emergence of the Taft campaign.

44. Ibid., p. 514. Brownell, *Advising Ike*, p. 92. For Eisenhower's discussions with Taft about not running in 1952, see William B. Pickett, *Eisenhower Decides to Run*, p. 97.

45. The main source for "Eisenhower revisionism" is Fred I. Greenstein, *The Hidden-Hand Presidency: Eisenhower as Leader* (Baltimore, Md.: Johns Hopkins University Press, 1994). Greenstein's work was originally published in 1982. Also see Chester J. Pach, Jr., and Elmo Richardson, *The Presidency of Dwight D. Eisenhower* (Lawrence: University Press of Kansas, 1991).

46. The bitter struggle for delegates in 1952 can be followed in Patterson, *Mr. Republican*, pp. 535–36; Brownell, *Advising Ike*, pp. 105–21, 114 (quotation); Smith, *Thomas E. Dewey*, pp. 583–87.

47. Brownell, *Advising Ike*, pp. 114–18.

48. There is an extensive literature on the selection of Nixon to run with Eisenhower in 1952. Nixon, *RN: The Memoirs,* pp. 83–90, gives his personal perspective. Gellman, *The Contender,* pp. 440–49, is favorable to Nixon. Roger Morris, *Richard Milhous Nixon: The Rise of an American Politician* (New York: Henry Holt and Co., 1990), pp. 695–736, is strongly critical of Nixon's performance.

49. Patterson, *Mr. Republican,* pp. 569–78; Smith, *Thomas E. Dewey,* p. 598.

50. Oshinsky, *A Conspiracy So Immense,* pp. 242–43.

51. Andrew J. Dunar, *The Truman Scandals and the Politics of Morality* (Columbia: University of Missouri Press, 1984).

52. The furor over the Nixon fund has been the subject of much discussion among historians and Nixon biographers. Nixon gave his own account in *RN: The Memoirs of Richard Nixon,* pp. 92–110. Gellman, *The Contender,* pp. 346–47, discusses the origins of the fund. Morris, *Richard Milhous Nixon,* pp. 757–850, is the most detailed and critical account of these events.

53. Nixon, *RN: The Memoirs,* pp. 96, 98, 106 (quotations). Melvin Small, *The Presidency of Richard Nixon* (Lawrence: University Press of Kansas, 1999), p. 15, notes that Eisenhower was not pleased when Nixon said in the "Checkers speech" that all presidential and vice presidential candidates should make their finances public. Eisenhower had received a tax decision that made payment for his wartime memoirs subject only to capital gains taxes rather than be treated as ordinary income. See Tom Wicker, *One of Us: Richard Nixon and the American Dream* (New York: Random House, 1991), p. 101.

54. Pach and Richardson, *Presidency of Dwight D. Eisenhower,* pp. 26–27.

55. Nixon, *RN: The Memoirs,* p. 376.

56. Robert H. Ferrell, ed., *The Eisenhower Diaries* (New York: W. W. Norton, 1981), p. 291. For Eisenhower's views on spending and defense, see Pach and Richardson, *Presidency of Dwight D. Eisenhower,* pp. 76–81, and for the Bricker Amendment, see Duane Tananbaum, *The Bricker Amendment Controversy: A Test of Eisenhower's Political Leadership* (Ithaca, N.Y.: Cornell University Press, 1988).

57. Porter and Johnson, eds., *National Party Platforms,* p. 499.

58. For an extended discussion of Eisenhower's record on foreign policy, see Pach and Richardson, *Presidency of Dwight D. Eisenhower,* pp. 82–104, 131–32.

59. Greenstein, *Hidden-Hand Presidency,* p. 50.

60. Pach and Richardson, *Presidency of Dwight D. Eisenhower,* p. 67. The Eisenhower-McCarthy battle is dealt with in Greenstein, *Hidden-Hand Presidency,* pp. 155–226. Herman, *Joseph McCarthy,* pp. 213–17, discusses the Eisenhower administration's dislike for McCarthy and his tactics.

61. Reinhard, *Republican Right,* p. 132.

62. On the abortive effort to replace Nixon in 1956, see Nixon, *RN: The Memoirs,* pp. 169–75, which contains some adroit criticisms of Eisenhower, and Wicker, *One of Us,* pp. 191–200, which also raises doubts about Eisenhower's motives in the whole affair.

63. Porter and Johnson, eds., *National Party Platforms,* pp. 547, 550, 554, 555, 557. It was about this time that the Republicans, led by the chairman of the National Committee, Leonard Hall, started the practice of referring to their opposition as "the Democrat Party" on the grounds that there was nothing "democratic" about their appeal. The custom persists among Republicans but has never caught on with the press or the public at large. Hans Sperber and Travis Trittschuh, *Dictionary of American Political Terms* (New York: McGraw-Hill, 1962), p. 123.

64. Reinhard, *Republican Right,* p. 137.

65. See, for example, Richard Hofstadter, *The American Political Tradition and the Men Who Made It* (New York: Alfred A. Knopf, 1948), p. x: "Above and beyond temporary and local conflicts there has been a common ground, a unity of cultural and political tradition, upon which American civilization has stood."

66. There are several interesting recent accounts of the rise of conservatism in the 1950s and early 1960s: Mary C. Brennan, *Turning Right in the Sixties: The Conservative Capture of the GOP* (Chapel Hill: University of North Carolina Press, 1995), pp. 6–18; John A. Andrew III, *The Other Side of the Sixties: Young Americans for Freedom and the Rise of Conservative Politics* (New Brunswick, N.J.: Rutgers University Press, 1997), pp. 11–31; Rick Perlstein, *Before the Storm: Barry Goldwater and the Unmaking of the American Consensus* (New York: Hill and Wang, 2001), pp. 3–16.

67. In addition to the sources previously cited, see Reinhard, *The Republican Right Since 1945,* pp. 138–42, and Lee Edwards, *The Conservative Revolution: The Movement That Remade America* (New York: Free Press, 1999), a historical account by a participant in the movement.

68. Pach and Richardson, *Presidency of Dwight D. Eisenhower,* pp. 168–69; Reinhard, *Republican Right,* pp. 139–41.

69. Pach and Richardson, *Presidency of Dwight D. Eisenhower*, p. 167.

70. Lee Edwards, *Goldwater: The Man Who Made a Revolution* (Washington, D.C.: Regnery, 1995), and Robert Alan Goldberg, *Barry Goldwater* (New Haven: Yale University Press, 1995), are good introductions to Goldwater's life. For Goldwater's speech attacking the Eisenhower budget, see Barry Goldwater, "The Preservation of Our Basic Institutions: Effect of Governmental Spending and Taxation," *Vital Speeches of the Day*, May 15, 1957, pp. 457, 458.

71. Pach and Richardson, *Presidency of Dwight D. Eisenhower*, pp. 145–57, 170–74.

72. The impact of the disastrous 1958 election is discussed in Reinhard, *Republican Right*, pp. 145–47. Pach and Richardson, *Presidency of Dwight D. Eisenhower*, pp. 183–85; Edwards, *Goldwater: The Man*, pp. 105–106.

73. Cary Reich, *The Life of Nelson Rockefeller: Worlds to Conquer, 1908–1958* (New York: Doubleday, 1996–1997), looks at Rockefeller's rise to political prominence. Michael Kramer and Sam Roberts, *"I Never Wanted to Be Vice-President of Anything!" An Investigative Biography of Nelson Rockefeller* (New York: Basic Books, 1976), develops Rockefeller's limitation as a national Republican candidate.

74. For the events of the first half of 1960, see James T. Patterson, *Grand Expectations: The United States, 1945–1974* (New York: Oxford University Press, 1996), pp. 424–27, 433–35.

75. Reinhard, *Republican Right*, pp. 153–54; Kramer and Roberts, *I Never Wanted*, pp. 226–29.

76. Nixon does not discuss these events in his 1978 memoirs. Wicker, *One of Us*, pp. 221–24.

77. Perlstein, *Before the Storm*, pp. 83–87; Goldberg, *Barry Goldwater*, p. 144.

78. Perlstein, *Before the Storm*, p. 94.

79. Ibid., pp. 94–95; Edwards, *Barry Goldwater*, pp. 138–39.

80. Wicker, *One of Us*, p. 225; Nixon, *RN: The Memoirs*, p. 219.

81. Nixon chronicles some of the problems with his 1960 campaign in *RN: The Memoirs*, pp. 225–27. The quotation is from page 225.

82. For the debate over Nixon's actions in late 1960 that was triggered by the disputed presidential election of 2000, see David Greenberg, "Was Nixon Robbed? The Legend of the Stolen 1960 Presidential Election,"

October 16, 2000, *Slate.msn.com;* Gerald Posner, "The Fallacy of Nixon's Graceful Exit," November 10, 2000, *Salon.com;* and John H. Taylor, "Face It: Nixon Really Did Bow Out in '60," Letters from Yorba Linda #13, *www.nixonlibrary.org*. An important source that credits Nixon with not pushing a Republican recount in Illinois and Texas is Edmund F. Kallina, Jr., *Courthouse over White House: Chicago and the Presidential Election of 1960* (Orlando: University of Florida Press, 1988), pp. 102–105. Kallina notes, however (p. 105), that Nixon also "did little" to stop Republican efforts to overturn the results "by a public disavowal" lest he alienate party leaders. No doubt future Nixon biographers will explore this episode in greater detail.

Chapter 10: FROM GOLDWATER TO WATERGATE, 1961–1974

1. Barry Goldwater's acceptance speech in 1964 is widely available at *Washingtonpost.com/wp-srv/politics/daily/May98/goldwaterspeech.htm*. The scene in the Cow Palace and the events preceding the speech are described in Lee Edwards, *Goldwater: The Man Who Made a Revolution* (Washington, D.C.: Regnery, 1995), pp. 169–276, and Rick Perlstein, *Before the Storm: Barry Goldwater and the Unmaking of the American Consensus* (New York: Hill and Wang, 2001), pp. 389–93.

2. Frank S. Meyer, "Principles and Heresies: What Next for Conservatism?" *National Review,* December 1, 1964, p. 1057.

3. James T. Patterson, *Grand Expectations: The United States, 1945–1974* (New York: Oxford University Press, 1996), p. 457.

4. For Kennedy's inaugural address see *Public Papers of the Presidents of the United States: John F. Kennedy, 1961* (Washington, D.C.: Government Printing Office), 1962, pp. 1–2.

5. Until recently the protests of young people on the left received more attention than similar tremors on the right. The balance is now shifting. John A. Andrew III, *The Other Side of the Sixties: Young Americans for Freedom and the Rise of Conservative Politics* (New Brunswick, N.J.: Rutgers University Press, 1997).

6. Perlstein, *Before the Storm,* p. 215, quotes Evans and Novak.

7. Mary C. Brennan, *Turning Right in the Sixties: The Conservative Capture of the GOP* (Chapel Hill: University of North Carolina Press, 1995), pp. 41–43. Lisa McGirr, *Suburban Warriors: The Origins of the New American Right* (Princeton, N.J.: Princeton University Press, 2001) looks at the emergence of these forces in southern California. Jonathan M. Schoenwald, *A Time for Choosing: The Rise of Modern American Conservatism* (New York: Oxford University Press, 2001) looks at the relationship between conservatives and the party at large.

8. Barry Goldwater, *The Conscience of a Conservative* (New York: Manor Books, 1960, 1975), pp. 21, 23, 27, 43, 64. L. Brent Bozell, brother-in-law of William F. Buckley, ghosted the book for Goldwater.

9. Ibid., pp. 88–127.

10. Ibid., pp. 32–38. For Goldwater's civil rights record, see Robert Alan Goldberg, *Barry Goldwater* (New Haven, Conn.: Yale University Press, 1995), pp. 75, 88–90, 154–55.

11. For the problems that the John Birch Society posed for the right, see "The John Birch Society and the Conservative Movement," *National Review,* October 19, 1965, pp. 914–16; Perlstein, *Before the Storm,* pp. 154–56; Brennan, *Turning Right in the Sixties,* pp. 13–14, 54–55; Kevin J. Smant, *Principles and Heresies: Frank S. Meyer and the Shaping of the American Conservative Movement* (Wilmington, Del.: ISI Books, 2002), pp. 157–75.

12. Kennedy's record in the White House is examined in Patterson, *Grand Expectations,* pp. 458–517, and Hugh Brogan, *Kennedy* (New York: Longman, 1996).

13. The problems of the Republicans in the 1962 elections and the effects of the Cuban Missile Crisis can be followed in George H. Mayer, *The Republican Party, 1854–1966,* 2nd ed. (New York: Oxford University Press, 1967), pp. 517–18, and John Calvin Batchelor, *"Ain't You Glad You Joined the Republicans?" A Short History of the GOP* (New York: Henry Holt, 1996), pp. 301–305.

14. " 'Draft Goldwater' Move Starts—Its Meaning," *U.S. News & World Report,* April 29, 1963, pp. 42–45, looks at conservative hopes in the wake of the 1962 elections. For the effect of these contests on the GOP in the South, see Earl Black and Merle Black, *The Southern Republicans* (Cambridge, Mass.: The Belknap Press of Harvard University Press, 2002), pp. 90–91, 126–27. George N. Green and John J. Kushma, "John Tower," in Kenneth E. Hendrickson, Jr., and Michael L. Collins, eds., *Profiles in Power: Twentieth-Century Texans in Washington* (Arlington Heights, Ill.: Harlan Davidson, 1993), pp. 204–205, looks at the career of the first Republican senator from Texas since Reconstruction.

15. On the political impact of Rockefeller's divorce, see Perlstein, *Before the Storm,* pp. 195–97; Michael Kramer and Sam Roberts, *"I Never Wanted to Be Vice-President of Anything!" An Investigative Biography of Nelson Rockefeller* (New York: Basic Books, 1976), pp. 267–71.

16. The draft-Goldwater effort has often been chronicled: F. Clifton White, with William Gill, *Suite 3505: The Story of the Draft Goldwater Movement*

(New Rochelle, N.Y.: Arlington Books, 1967), is an account by the main architect of the effort. Perlstein, *Before the Storm*, p. 191 (quotation); Edwards, *Goldwater: The Man*, pp. 160–70, 195–215.

17. For Goldwater's announcement, see Goldberg, *Barry Goldwater*, pp. 179 (Johnson quotation), 181; Perlstein, *Before the Storm*, pp. 260–61; Edwards, *Goldwater: The Man*, p. 202.

18. Goldberg, *Barry Goldwater*, p. 177.

19. Edwards, *Goldwater: The Man*, p. 206.

20. On Goldwater and the issue of nuclear weapons, see Edwards, *Goldwater: The Man*, pp. 207–209; Goldberg, *Barry Goldwater*, pp. 184, 186.

21. David W. Reinhard, *The Republican Right Since 1945* (Lexington: University Press of Kentucky, 1983), p. 186.

22. On Margaret Chase Smith's campaign, see Janann Sherman, *No Place for a Woman: A Life of Senator Margaret Chase Smith* (New Brunswick, N.J.: Rutgers University Press, 2000), pp. 183–92.

23. Jeremy D. Mayer, *Running on Race: Racial Politics in Presidential Campaigns, 1960–2000* (New York: Random House, 2003), p. 55.

24. Background on the Johnson administration and the 1964 Civil Rights Act can be found in Irving Bernstein, *Guns or Butter: The Presidency of Lyndon Johnson* (New York: Oxford University Press, 1996), pp. 43–81.

25. Goldberg, *Barry Goldwater*, p. 197.

26. Ibid., pp. 154–55, 174, 197–98, discusses the political aspects of Goldwater's decision.

27. Robert Dallek, *Flawed Giant: Lyndon Johnson and His Times* (New York: Oxford University Press, 1998), p. 120.

28. The Goldwater forces and their dominance of the 1964 convention is discussed in Perlstein, *Before the Storm*, pp. 366–70, 380–85; Goldberg, *Barry Goldwater*, pp. 201–204.

29. Kirk H. Porter and Donald Bruce Johnson, eds., *National Party Platforms, 1840–1968* (Urbana: University of Illinois Press, 1972), pp. 683, 689.

30. Perlstein, *Before the Storm*, p. 389.

31. Harry V. Jaffa, "Goldwater's Famous 'Gaffe': Extremism Twenty Years Later," *National Review*, August 10, 1984, p. 36, makes an academic

rather than a political argument for the phrase he wrote. Edwards, *Barry Goldwater*, p. 267 (Goldwater quotation).

32. Richard Nixon, *RN: The Memoirs of Richard Nixon* (New York: Grosset & Dunlap, 1978), p. 260; Goldberg, *Barry Goldwater*, pp. 206 (reporter quotation), 208 (Buchanan's father).

33. The internal problems of the Goldwater campaign are discussed in Stephen Shadegg, *What Happened to Goldwater: The Inside Story of the 1964 Republican Campaign* (New York: Holt, Rinehart and Winston, 1965), pp. 171–75, 198–209. Perlstein, *Before the Storm*, pp. 415–48.

34. Reinhard, *The Republican Right*, p. 201.

35. On these episodes in the campaign, see Dallek, *Flawed Giant*, pp. 143–56, 179–82.

36. The story of the "daisy field" commercial is outlined in Edwin Diamond and Stephen Bates, *The Spot: The Rise of Political Advertising on Television*, 3rd ed. (Cambridge, Mass.: MIT Press, 1993), pp. 122–33, and Kathleen Hall Jamieson, *Packaging the Presidency: A History and Criticism of Presidential Campaign Advertising* (New York: Oxford University Press, 1984), pp. 198–203. The anger of the Goldwater campaign with Johnson's tactics can be followed in Edwards, *Goldwater: The Man*, pp. 305–12, and Goldberg, *Barry Goldwater*, pp. 225–27.

37. For Reagan's speech and its impact, see Perlstein, *Before the Storm*, p. 503.

38. Reston is quoted in Goldberg, *Goldwater: The Man*, p. 234. Edwards, *Barry Goldwater*, p. 344, gives a sampling of the negative press comments about the situation of the GOP after Goldwater's defeat.

39. Nixon, *RN: The Memoirs*, p. 271.

40. On this controversial subject, see Myra McPherson, *Long Time Passing: Vietnam and the Haunted Generation* (Garden City, N.Y.: Doubleday & Co., 1984), pp. 8–23 (Chuck Hagel), 163–64, 232–33 (David Stockman); John Gregory Dunne, *Crooning: A Collection* (New York: Simon & Schuster, 1999), pp. 141–57. For Republicans' Vietnam-era military service, see "The Chickenhawk Database," *www.nhgazette.com/chickenhawks.html*. For a defense of these Republicans in 2002, see Eliot A. Cohen, "Hunting 'Chicken Hawks,' " *Washington Post*, September 5, 2002, and for criticism, see James Bamford, "Untested Administration Hawks Clamor for War," *USA Today*, September 16, 2002.

41. Ronald Reagan, for example, called the Vietnam War a "noble cause"; Lou Cannon, *President Reagan: The Role of a Lifetime* (New York: Simon &

Schuster, 1991), p. 335. George H. W. Bush saw the Gulf War in 1991 as an opportunity to eliminate the "Vietnam syndrome" from American foreign policy: Herbert S. Parmet, *George Bush: The Life of a Lone Star Yankee* (New York: Scribner, 1997), pp. 477, 479.

42. For the enactment of the Voting Rights Act and Republican legislative support for the measure, see Byron C. Hulsey, *Everett Dirksen and His Presidents* (Lawrence: University Press of Kansas, 2000), pp. 210–13, 215–16.

43. Lewis L. Gould, "Never a Deep Partisan: Lyndon Johnson and the Democratic Party, 1963–1969," in Robert A. Divine, ed., *The Johnson Years;* vol. 3: *LBJ at Home and Abroad* (Lawrence: University Press of Kansas, 1994), p. 30.

44. Nixon, *RN: The Memoirs*, p. 273.

45. Alan L. Otten and Charles B. Seib, "The Minor Masterpiece of Ray C. Bliss," *Reporter*, February 10, 1966, pp. 35–38; "How Ray Bliss Plays the Cards for the GOP," *Business Week*, March 9, 1968, pp. 28–30; John F. Bibby and Robert J. Huckshorn, "Out-Party Strategy: Republican National Committee Rebuilding Politics, 1964–1966," in Bernard Cosman and Robert J. Huckshorn, eds., *Republican Politics: The 1964 Campaign and Its Aftermath for the Party* (New York: Praeger, 1968), pp. 205–33. Philip A. Klinker, *The Losing Parties: Out-Party National Committees, 1956–1993* (New Haven, Conn.: Yale University Press, 1994), pp. 71–87. The Ripon Society, a group of liberal Republicans, started in 1964 to be a voice for moderation within the GOP, but it never proved to be effective against the conservative tide within the party.

46. Lucas A. Powe, *The Warren Court and American Politics* (Cambridge, Mass.: Harvard University Press, 2000), pp. 408–10, looks at the law and order issue during the 1960s. The Nixon quotation is from Lewis L. Gould, *1968: The Election That Changed America* (Chicago: Ivan Dee, 1993), p. 93.

47. Carl Solberg, *Hubert Humphrey: A Biography* (New York: W. W. Norton, 1984), p. 297 (both quotations).

48. Tom Wicker, *One of Us: Richard Nixon and the American Dream* (New York: Random House, 1991), pp. 286–87. Stephen E. Ambrose, *Nixon*, vol. 2: *The Triumph of a Politician, 1962–1972* (New York: Simon & Schuster, 1989), p. 100 (Nixon quotation).

49. Matthew Dallek, *The Right Moment: Ronald Reagan's First Victory and the Decisive Turning Point in American Politics* (New York: Free Press, 2000) is a thorough look at Reagan's California victory. William E. Pemberton, *Exit with Honor: The Life and Presidency of Ronald Reagan* (Armonk, N.Y.: M. E. Sharpe, 1997), p. 69 (quotation).

50. Nixon, *RN: The Memoirs*, pp. 273–77, and Wicker, *One of Us*, pp. 282–87, cover the Johnson-Nixon encounter.

51. Theodore H. White, *The Making of the President, 1968* (New York: Atheneum, 1969), p. 59.

52. Gould, *1968: The Election*, p. 140.

53. Nixon, *RN: The Memoirs*, p. 298, denies that he had a secret plan for Vietnam. Gould, *1968: The Election*, p. 39.

54. Gould, *1968: The Election*, p. 40.

55. Ibid., p. 68.

56. Ibid., p. 98.

57. Nixon, *RN: The Memoirs*, p. 304.

58. Gould, *1968: The Election*, p. 102.

59. Wicker, *One of Us*, p. 343.

60. There is no good modern biography of Spiro Agnew. Richard N. Cohen and Jules Witcover, *A Heartbeat Away: The Investigation and Resignation of Vice President Spiro T. Agnew* (New York: Bantam Press, 1974), is a useful contemporary look at the Angew case. Stanley I. Kutler, *The Wars of Watergate: The Last Crisis of Richard Nixon* (New York: Alfred A. Knopf, 1990), pp. 393–97, covers the case briefly.

61. White, *The Making of the President, 1968*, pp. 254–55; Nixon, *RN: The Memoirs*, pp. 314–15.

62. Gould, *1968: The Election*, p. 112.

63. Ibid., p. 147.

64. For discussions of the climactic and complex events of the 1968 election, see Gould, *1968: The Election*, pp. 151–61; Wicker, *One of Us*, pp. 372–82; Jules Witcover, *The Year the Dream Died: Revisiting 1968 in America* (New York: Warner Books, 1997), pp. 404–406, 408–16, 418–19. Nixon, *RN: The Memoirs*, pp. 323–31, gives Nixon's account of these developments but does not mention some of the clandestine moves that his campaign was making to influence South Vietnam.

65. Joan Hoff Wilson, *Nixon Reconsidered* (New York: Basic Books, 1994), p. 341.

66. The best book on Nixon in the White House is Melvin Small, *The Presidency of Richard Nixon* (Lawrence: University Press of Kansas, 1999). Wilson, *Nixon Reconsidered,* takes a sympathetic look at Nixon's domestic policies but is critical of his record overseas. Richard Reeves, *President Nixon: Alone in the White House* (New York: Simon & Schuster, 2001), has many interesting insights and quotations from Nixon's papers.

67. Stanley I. Kutler, *Abuse of Power: The New Nixon Tapes* (New York: Free Press, 1997), p. 31.

68. Small, *Presidency of Richard Nixon,* p. 250.

69. Nixon, *RN: The Memoirs,* p. 770.

70. Small, *Presidency of Richard Nixon,* p. 154.

71. For a thorough and sympathetic treatment of Nixon's civil rights successes and failures, see Dean J. Kotlowski, *Nixon's Civil Rights: Politics, Principles, and Policy* (Cambridge, Mass.: Harvard University Press, 2001). More critical is the chapter in Kenneth O'Reilly, *Nixon's Piano: Presidents and Racial Politics from Washington to Clinton* (New York: Free Press, 1995), pp. 277–329.

72. Small, *Presidency of Richard Nixon,* p. 248.

73. The 1970 congressional elections can be followed in Small, *Presidency of Richard Nixon,* pp. 247–49, and Nixon, *RN: The Memoirs,* pp. 490–95.

74. Nixon, *RN: The Memoirs,* pp. 495, 496.

75. On the various aspects of Nixon's criminal activities in the White House, see John A. Andrew III, *Power to Destroy: The Political Uses of the IRS from Kennedy to Nixon* (Chicago: Ivan Dee, 2002), pp. 179–224; Kutler, *Wars of Watergate,* pp. 78–125; Small, *Presidency of Richard Nixon,* p. 254.

76. Reinhard, *Republican Right Since 1945,* pp. 223–25; Smant, *Principles and Heresies,* pp. 304–24.

77. Nixon, *RN: The Memoirs,* p. 669.

78. Ibid., pp. 761, 764.

79. Small, *Presidency of Richard Nixon,* p. 273.

80. Goldberg, *Barry Goldwater,* pp. 145, 274.

81. Parmet, *George Bush,* p. 161; Cannon, *President Reagan,* p. 76.

82. Kutler, *Wars of Watergate,* p. 361 (Baker), 451 (Buckley), 454 (Scott).

83. For the selection of Gerald Ford, see Small, *Presidency of Richard Nixon,* pp. 288–89; John Robert Greene, *The Presidency of Gerald R. Ford* (Lawrence: University Press of Kansas, 1995), pp. 11–13, 17 (quotation).

Chapter 11: REPUBLICANS IN THE REAGAN ERA, 1974–1988

1. Jack W. Germond and Jules Witcover, *Blue Smoke and Mirrors: How Reagan Won and Why Carter Lost the Election of 1980* (New York: The Viking Press, 1981), p. 280.

2. Lou Cannon, *President Reagan: The Role of a Lifetime* (New York: Simon & Schuster, 1991), p. 141.

3. David W. Reinhard, *The Republican Right Since 1945* (Lexington: University Press of Kentucky, 1983), p. 229.

4. Kirk H. Porter and Donald Bruce Johnson, eds., *National Party Platforms, 1840–1968* (Urbana: University of Illinois Press, 1972), pp. 393 (1940), 412 (1944), 453 (1948), 504 (1952), 554 (1956), 614 (1960); Fred Sperapani, comp., *Official Report of the Proceedings of the Thirtieth Republican National Convention Held in Miami Beach, Florida, August 21, 22, 23, 1972* (Washington, D.C.: Republican National Committee, 1972), p. 235.

5. For Schlafly's role, see Flora Davis, *Moving the Mountain: The Women's Movement in America Since 1960* (Urbana: University of Illinois Press, 1999), pp. 387–88; Reinhard, *Republican Right,* pp. 243–44; Robert Shogan, *War Without End: Cultural Conflict and the Struggle for America's Political Future* (Boulder, Colo.: Westview Press, 2002), pp. 166–68.

6. There is no good treatment of Republicans and the rise of the antiabortion movement since the *Roe v. Wade* decision of 1973. Shogan, *War Without End,* pp. 161–62, 175–83, has some useful information.

7. Irving Kristol, *Neo-Conservatism: The Autobiography of an Idea* (New York: Free Press, 1995), p. 32.

8. An insightful analysis of the rise of neoconservatism is Nina J. Easton, *Gang of Five: Leaders at the Center of the Conservative Ascendancy* (New York: Simon & Schuster, 2000), pp. 23–47, 177–79.

9. Steven F. Hayward, *The Age of Reagan: The Fall of the Old Liberal Order, 1964–1980* (Roseville, Calif.: Primus, 2001), pp. 524–29, 683–90, traces the emergence of supply-side policies within the GOP.

10. Eleanor Clift and Tom Brazaitis, *War Without Bloodshed: The Art of Politics* (New York: Simon & Schuster, 1996), pp. 112–16, provides good background on the changes in campaign finance practices.

11. On Viguerie, see Bruce J. Schulman, *The Seventies: The Great Shift in American Culture, Society, and Politics* (Boston: Da Capo, 2002), pp. 193–98.

12. John Robert Greene, *The Presidency of Gerald R. Ford* (Lawrence: University Press of Kansas, 1995), p. 73.

13. Allen J. Matusow, *Nixon's Economy: Booms, Busts, Dollars, and Votes* (Lawrence: University Press of Kansas, 1998), pp. 281–89.

14. Ibid., pp. 241–75.

15. Schulman, *Seventies: The Great Shift*, pp. 159–89.

16. Greene, *Presidency of Gerald R. Ford*, pp. 120–21.

17. Melvin Small, *The Presidency of Richard Nixon* (Lawrence: University Press of Kansas, 1999), p. 288.

18. Hayward, *Age of Reagan*, p. 399.

19. For the political impact of the Ford pardon of Nixon, see Greene, *Presidency of Gerald R. Ford*, pp. 53–66.

20. Hayward, *Age of Reagan*, p. 384.

21. Gerald R. Ford, *A Time to Heal: The Autobiography of Gerald R. Ford* (New York: Harper & Row, 1979), p. 333.

22. Robert Hartmann, *Palace Politics: An Insider's Account of the Ford Years* (New York: McGraw-Hill, 1980), p. 336.

23. Hayward, *Age of Reagan*, p. xix.

24. Pemberton, *Exit with Honor*, pp. 21–63, is good on Reagan's rise.

25. Reagan's view of government and civil rights is addressed in all of his biographies. A recent evaluation is Jeremy D. Mayer, *Running on Race: Racial Politics in Presidential Campaigns, 1960–2000* (New York: Random House, 2002), pp. 152–55. More critical of Reagan's stance is Kenneth O'Reilly, *Nixon's Piano: Presidents and Racial Politics from Washington to Clinton* (New York: Free Press, 1995). On the contrast between Reagan's view of the states in relation to the Union and that of Abraham Lincoln, see William Lee Miller, *Lincoln's Virtues: An Ethical Biography* (New York: Alfred A. Knopf, 2002), p. 444.

26. Ronald Reagan, "To Restore America," March 31, 1976, *www.conservative.org/rwr33176.htm.*

27. Ibid.

28. Hayward, *Age of Reagan,* p. 451.

29. Jerry R. Jones to Donald Rumsfeld and Dick Cheney, September 26, 1975, folder "Ronald Reagan (1)," Box 25, Jerry Jones File, Gerald R. Ford Library, *List of 1976 Campaign Documents, www.Ford.utexas.edu/Library/exhibits/2jones.htm.* Greene, *Presidency of Gerald R. Ford,* pp. 157–58.

30. Greene, *Presidency of Gerald R. Ford,* p. 160.

31. The early stages of the Ford-Reagan contest in 1976 can be followed in Greene, *Presidency of Gerald R. Ford,* pp. 162–64, and Hayward, *Age of Reagan,* pp. 455–65.

32. Hayward, *Age of Reagan,* p. 466.

33. Raleigh E. Milton, reporter, *Official Report of the Proceedings of the Thirty-first Republican National Convention Held in Kansas City, Missouri, August 16, 17, 18, 19, 1976* (Washington, D.C.: Republican National Committee, 1977), pp. 332–33, 347.

34. Ibid., p. 479.

35. Ibid., 479–80.

36. Greene, *Presidency of Gerald R. Ford,* pp. 178–79.

37. Max Frankel, *The Times of My Life and My Life with the Times* (New York: Random House, 1999), p. 229.

38. Raleigh E. Milton, reporter, *Official Report of the Proceedings of the Thirty-second Republican National Convention Held in Detroit, Michigan* (Washington, D.C.: Republican National Committee, 1981), p. 70.

39. Burton I. Kaufman, *The Presidency of James Earl Carter, Jr.* (Lawrence: University Press of Kansas, 1993), pp. 99, 100, 167–70.

40. Hayward, *Age of Reagan,* pp. 524–25.

41. John W. Sloan, *The Reagan Effect: Economics and Presidential Leadership* (Lawrence: University Press of Kansas, 1999), pp. 62–63; Michael Schaller and George Rising, *The Republican Ascendancy: American Politics, 1968–2001* (Wheeling, Ill.: Harlan Davidson, 2002), pp. 66–67.

42. Pemberton, *Exit with Honor,* p. 90 (emphasis in original).

43. For Reagan's road to the Republican nomination in 1980, see Germond and Witcover, *Blue Smoke and Mirrors,* pp. 93–140, which is thorough and informative.

44. Germond and Witcover, *Blue Smoke and Mirrors,* p. 170; Herbert S. Parmet, *George Bush: The Life of a Lone Star Yankee* (New York: Scribner, 1997), pp. 134, 246 (Reagan quotation).

45. Milton, *Thirty-second Republican National Convention,* pp. 245–46, 250 (blacks), 252 (Equal Rights Amendment), 255 (abortion), 270 (tariffs).

46. Ibid., pp. 294, 297.

47. Pemberton, *Exit with Honor,* p. 191.

48. Mayer, *Running on Race,* p. 168; Hayward, *Age of Reagan,* p. 696 (quotation).

49. Robert Shogan, *War Without End: Cultural Conflict and the Struggle for America's Political Future* (Cambridge, Mass.: Perseus Books, 2002), pp. 178–91.

50. Pemberton, *Exit with Honor,* p. 141.

51. "Inaugural Address," January 20, 1981, *www.reagan.utexas.edu/resource/speeches.1981.12081a.htm.*

52. For evaluations of Reagan's first term, see Pemberton, *Exit with Honor,* pp. 85–124; Schaller and Rising, *Republican Ascendancy,* pp. 84–93.

53. Cannon, *President Reagan,* pp. 232–79.

54. Asher & Associates, reporters, *Official Report of the Proceedings of the Thirty-fourth Republican National Convention Held in New Orleans, Louisiana, August 15, 16, 17, 18, 1988* (Washington, D.C.: Republican National Committee, 1989), p. 454.

55. Raleigh E. Milton, reporter, *Official Report of the Proceedings of the Thirty-third Republican National Convention Held in Dallas, Texas* (Washington, D.C.: Dulany-Vernay, 1984), pp. 416, 418.

56. Ibid., pp. 61 (Gramm), 424 (Reagan).

57. Ibid., pp. 271, 284.

58. Milton, *Thirty-second Republican National Convention,* p. 290. Cannon, *President Reagan,* pp. 528–34.

59. Milton, *Thirty-third Republican National Convention*, pp. 305 (pornography), 308 (abortion), 417 (Bush).

60. Ibid., p. 300.

61. O'Reilly, *Nixon's Piano*, p. 361.

62. Milton, *Thirty-third Republican National Convention*, p. 384.

63. Ibid., p. 429.

64. Lesley Stahl, *Reporting Live* (New York: Simon & Schuster, 1999), p. 213.

65. Richard Darman, *Who's in Control: Polar Politics and the Sensible Center* (New York: Simon & Schuster, 1996), p. 141.

66. Parmet, *George Bush*, p. 298.

67. Pemberton, *Exit with Honor*, p. 413.

68. Asher & Associates, *Thirty-fourth Republican National Convention*, p. 105.

69. Shogan, *War Without End*, pp. 188–91.

70. Ethan Bronner, *Battle for Justice* (New York: W. W. Norton, 1989) is a detailed look at the Bork episode.

71. Cannon, *President Reagan*, p. 807.

Chapter 12: BUSH TO GINGRICH TO BUSH, 1988–2000

1. Mel Steely, *The Gentleman from Georgia: A Biography of Newt Gingrich* (Macon, Ga.: Mercer University Press, 2000) is a friendly biography of the Speaker that discusses the 1994 campaign. Elizabeth Drew, *Showdown: The Struggle Between the Gingrich Congress and the Clinton White House* (New York: Simon & Schuster, 1996), pp. 25–35, 26 (quotation), gives the background for the September 27, 1994, event.

2. *Houston Chronicle*, October 13, 1987.

3. The best personal portrait of Dole emerges from Richard Ben Cramer, *What It Takes: The Way to the White House* (New York: Vintage Books, 1992, 1993), pp. 30–59, 97–111.

4. The most complete biography of the elder Bush is Herbert S. Parmet, *George Bush: The Life of a Lone Star Yankee* (New York: Scribner, 1997).

5. Jack W. Germond and Jules Witcover, *Blue Smoke and Mirrors: How Reagan Won and Why Carter Lost the Election of 1980* (New York: Viking Press, 1981), p. 170.

6. Parmet, *George Bush*, p. 309.

7. Ibid., pp. 310–20, 322–26, has the best discussion of the impact of the Iran-Contra issue on Bush's campaign in 1988.

8. John Brady, *Bad Boy: The Life and Politics of Lee Atwater* (Reading, Mass.: Addison Wesley, 1997), p. 162.

9. On the New Hampshire primary in 1988, see Parmet, *George Bush*, pp. 328–29.

10. Brady, *Bad Boy*, p. 84.

11. Parmet, *George Bush*, p. 344.

12. Ibid., pp. 345–47. For the computer dating comment, Ed Rollins, with Tom DeFrank, *Bare Knuckles and Back Rooms* (New York: Broadway Books, 1996), p. 191. See also Dan Quayle, *Standing Firm: A Vice-Presidential Memoir* (New York: HarperCollins, 1994), and David S. Broder and Bob Woodward, *The Man Who Would Be President: Dan Quayle* (New York: Simon & Schuster, 1992).

13. Parmet, *George Bush*, p. 342. Asher & Associates, reporters, *Official Report of the Proceedings of the Thirty-fourth Republican National Convention Held in New Orleans, Louisiana, August 15, 16, 17, 18, 1988* (Washington, D.C.: Republican National Committee, 1989), pp. 553–54, 558.

14. Ibid., p. 554.

15. Overviews of the 1988 campaign are available in Parmet, *George Bush*, pp. 349–55; Cramer, *What It Takes*, pp. 997–1011; Brady, *Bad Boy*, pp. 179–80, 183–86, 187–94.

16. In addition to the sources previously cited, for the Horton issue see Jeremy D. Mayer, *Running on Race: Racial Politics in Presidential Campaigns, 1960–2000* (New York: Random House, 2002), pp. 201–28, and Kathleen Hall Jamieson, "The Subversive Effects of a Focus on Strategy in News Coverage of Presidential Campaigns," in Twentieth Century Fund, *1-800 President* (New York: Twentieth Century Fund Press, 1993).

17. Parmet, *George Bush*, pp. 336–37; Brady, *Bad Boy*, p. 176.

18. Brady, *Bad Boy*, pp. 210–18, is very good on the implications of the issue for the election.

19. Parmet, *George Bush*, p. 354, has the Bentsen-Quayle exchange. When I interviewd Lloyd Bentsen for an oral history in 1989–90, he said that the possibility of Quayle comparing himself to Jack Kennedy had arisen in a debate practice session. He was thus ready with a devastating response.

20. John B. Judis and Ruy Teixeira, *The Emerging Democratic Majority* (New York: Scribner, 2002), pp. 26–27, 127–28.

21. David Mervin, *George Bush and the Guardianship Presidency* (New York: St. Martin's, 1998), p. 21.

22. Parmet, *George Bush*, pp. 348, 361.

23. Richard Darman, *Who's in Control: Polar Politics and the Sensible Center* (New York: Simon & Schuster, 1996), pp. 230–48.

24. Ibid., pp. 251, 263.

25. Steely, *Gentleman from Georgia*, pp. 222–23.

26. John Robert Greene, *The Presidency of George Bush* (Lawrence: University Press of Kansas, 2000), pp. 87–88.

27. The Clarence Thomas confirmation fight still arouses hard feelings. Kevin Merida and Michael A. Fletcher, "Supreme Discomfort: More Than a Decade After His Bitter Confirmation Battle, African Americans Are Still Judging Clarence Thomas Guilty. Is That Justice?" *Washington Post*, August 4, 2002. Greene, *Presidency of George Bush*, pp. 156–59.

28. Mervin, *George Bush and the Guardianship Presidency*, p. 224.

29. Peter Goldman et al., *Quest for the Presidency, 1992* (College Station: Texas A&M University Press, 1994), pp. 14–16.

30. Ibid., pp. 16–17, 617 (quotation); Greene, *Presidency of George Bush*, pp. 161–62.

31. Goldman, *Quest for the Presidency*, p. 301.

32. Ibid., p. 9.

33. Ibid., p. 358.

34. Greene, *Presidency of George Bush*, p. 168; Goldman, *Quest for the Presidency*, p. 324.

35. Goldman, *Quest for the Presidency*, pp. 340–49.

36. Ibid., p. 675.

37. Ibid.

38. Greene, *Presidency of George Bush*, pp. 167, 174–76.

39. Goldman, *Quest for the Presidency*, p. 404. Parmet, *George Bush*, p. 503.

40. On the Walsh-Weinberger episode, see Goldman, *Quest for the Presidency*, pp. 608–609; Parmet, *George Bush*, p. 505.

41. Eleanor Clift and Tom Brazaitis, *War Without Bloodshed: The Art of Politics* (New York: Scribner, 1996; Touchstone, 1997), p. 72.

42. Elizabeth Drew, *The Corruption of American Politics: What Went Wrong and Why* (Woodstock, N.Y.: Overlook Press, 1999, 2000), pp. 61–85.

43. David Maraniss and Michael Weiskopff, *"Tell Newt to Shut Up"* (New York: Simon & Schuster, 1996), pp. 36–71.

44. Nina J. Easton, *Gang of Five: Leaders at the Center of the Conservative Ascendancy* (New York: Simon & Schuster, 2000), pp. 359–82, is even-handed on the tensions among conservative Republicans on social issues.

45. Michael Schaller and George Rising, *The Republican Ascendancy: American Politics, 1968–2001* (Wheeling, Ill.: Harlan Davidson, 2002), pp. 145–46.

46. The Republican attitude toward these issues can be seen in the 2000 party platform. See Alderson Reporting Co., *Official Report of the Proceedings of the Thirty-seventh Republican National Convention Held in Philadelphia, Pennsylvania, July 31, 2000, August 1, 2, 3, 2000* (Washington, D.C.: Republican National Committee, n.d.), pp. 404–30.

47. Judis and Teixiera, *Emerging Democratic Majority*, pp. 57–62, see immigrants as fertile ground for that party because of Republican policies.

48. E. J. Dionne, "Confederate Nostalgia," *Washington Post*, January 16, 2001, and David W. Blight, "A Confederacy of Denial," *Washington Post*, January 29, 2001.

49. John T. Noonan, Jr., *Narrowing the Nation's Power: The Supreme Court Sides with the States* (Berkeley: University of California Press, 2002).

50. Peter Baker, *The Breach: Inside the Impeachment and Trial of William Jefferson Clinton* (New York: Scribner, 2000), p. 258.

51. Joe Klein, *The Natural: The Misunderstood Presidency of Bill Clinton* (New York: Doubleday, 2002), p. 54; Schaller and Rising, *Republican Ascendancy*, pp. 122–23.

52. For examples of the polemical literature against Clinton that flourished during the 1990s and beyond, see Gary Aldrich, *Unlimited Access: An FBI Agent Inside the Clinton White House* (Washington, D.C.: Regnery, 1996); Ann Coulter, *High Crimes and Misdemeanors: The Case Against Bill Clinton* (Washington, D.C.: Regnery, 1998); R. Emmett Tyrell, *Boy Clinton: The Political Biography* (Washington, D.C.: Regnery, 1996).

53. Eaton, *Gang of Five*, p. 275.

54. *Congressional Quarterly Almanac, 103rd Congress, 1st Session, 1993* (Washington, D.C.: Congressional Quarterly, 1994), p. 122 (Armey and Gingrich); *New York Times*, June 24, 1993 (Gramm).

55. Limbaugh's views are outlined in *The Way Things Ought to Be* (New York: Pocket Star Books, 1993). No careful assessment of his influence on the party, or indeed the role of talk radio on the Republicans, has yet been made, but there is little doubt of Limbaugh's importance.

56. Steely, *Gentleman from Georgia*, pp. 32–129, offers a sympathetic account of Gingrich's rise to prominence. Newt Gingrich, *To Renew America* (New York: HarperCollins, 1995), conveys the broad themes of his political thought.

57. Steely, *Gentleman from Georgia*, pp. 114–15, 395.

58. Ibid., p. 266.

59. Elizabeth Drew, *Showdown: The Struggle Between the Gingrich Congress and the Clinton White House* (New York: Simon & Schuster, 1996), pp. 27–33.

60. Steely, *Gentleman from Georgia*, p. 249.

61. On the 1994 election results, see Jeffrey M. Stonecash and Mack D. Mariani, "Republican Gains in the House in the 1994 Elections: Class Polarization in American Politics," *Political Science Quarterly* 115 (2000): 93–113. Linda Killian, *The Freshmen: What Happened to the Republican Revolution* (Boulder, Colo.: Westview Press, 1998), offers an in-depth look at some of the Republican winners in 1994. David Pace, "AP: Government Changed Spending of Billions," Yahoo! News, August 6, 2002, quotes Armey.

62. Drew, *Showdown: The Struggle*, p. 56; Schaller and Rising, *Republican Ascendancy*, pp. 132–33; Maraniss and Weiskopff, *"Tell Newt to Shut Up!"*, p. 13.

63. Easton, *Gang of Five*, p. 303. Drew, *Showdown: The Struggle*, pp. 316–19.

64. The events of the budget fight in 1995–96 are covered in Drew, *Showdown: The Struggle*, pp. 321–75.

65. Alderson Reporting Co., *Official Report of the Thirty-sixth Republican National Convention, Held in San Diego, California* (Washington, D.C.: Republican National Committee, 1996), p. 491.

66. Easton, *Gang of Five*, pp. 274–75; Schaller and Rising, *Republican Ascendancy*, pp. 119, 136.

67. William C. Berman, *From the Center to the Edge: The Politics and Policies of the Clinton Presidency* (Lanham, Md.: Rowman & Littlefield, 2001), p. 66; Dick Morris, *Behind the Oval Office: Winning the Presidency in the Nineties* (New York: Random House, 1997), pp. 311–12.

68. Drew, *Corruption of American Politics*, pp. 86–100, is good on the fundraising scandals.

69. Schaller and Rising, *Republican Ascendancy*, pp. 137–38.

70. Baker, *Breach: Inside the Impeachment*, p. 17.

71. Steely, *Gentleman from Georgia*, pp. 347–53.

72. The literature on the politics of the Clinton impeachment is extensive and controversial. Baker, *Breach: Inside the Impeachment*, pp. 15–42, passim, is good on the legislative battles. Jeffrey Toobin, *A Vast Conspiracy: The Real Story of the Sex Scandal That Nearly Brought Down a President* (New York: Random House, 1999), and Joe Conason and Gene Lyons, *The Hunting of the President: The Ten-Year Campaign to Destroy Bill and Hillary Clinton* (New York: St. Martin's Press, 2000), are useful for the development of the issue. Few of the legislative participants in the events of 1998–99 have provided personal accounts. The counsel for the House Judiciary Committee's Republican majority provided his interpretation. See David Schippers and Alan P. Henry, *Shut Out: The Inside Story of President Clinton's Impeachment* (Washington, D.C.: Regnery, 2000).

73. Schaller and Rising, *Republican Ascendancy*, pp. 143–45.

74. Steely, *Gentleman from Georgia*, pp. 389–94.

75. The conclusions about Republican strategy are based on the works previously cited and my own observations of the impeachment process.

76. Alderson Reporting Co., *Thirty-seventh Republican National Convention*, p. 626.

77. In the interest of full disclosure, I should say that Karl Rove took an individual undergraduate conference course with me during the spring
semester of 1998 at the University of Texas at Austin on the role of
Theodore Roosevelt in the 1896 election. The comparison of George W.
Bush's candidacy in 2000 with William McKinley's role in 1896 arose
from Rove's research for the paper he prepared. By 2002, McKinley had
given way to Andrew Jackson as a historical precedent for President
Bush's executive style.

78. Drew, *Corruption of American Politics*, pp. 172–73.

79. Alderson Reporting Co., *Thirty-seventh Republican National Convention*, p.
633 (both quotations).

80. Terry M. Neal, "Bush Backs into Nation Building," *Washington Post*, February 26, 2003.

81. The events of election night 2000 are covered in Jake Tapper, *Down and
Dirty: The Plot to Steal the Presidency* (Boston: Little, Brown, 2001), pp.
3–53; Jeffrey Toobin, *Too Close to Call: The Thirty-six-Day Battle to Decide the
2000 Election* (New York: Random House, 2001), pp. 3–25.

82. Tapper, *Down and Dirty*, pp. 259–75.

83. Toobin, *Too Close to Call*, pp. 248–70.

84. Judis and Teixeira, *Emerging Democratic Majority*, pp. 145–61, assess the
competing arguments about the future of both parties. Their references
will take the reader to proponents of the case for the Republicans.

85. James S. Clarkson, "The Policies of the Republican Party," pamphlet in
author's possession, based on Clarkson's article in *The Independent*, September 29, 1892.

86. James Bryce, *The American Commonwealth*, 2 vols. (London: Macmillan,
1894, 1909), II, pp. 28–29; *Speeches and Addresses of William McKinley from
His Election to Congress to the Present Time* (New York: D. Appleton, 1893),
p. 557.

Conclusion: THE HISTORICAL LEGACY OF THE REPUBLICAN PARTY

1. Randy Ridgel, "An Open Letter to Bill Back," January 9, 2003, at
http://talkingpointsmemo.com/docs.ridgel1.html. For background on Ridgel
and the larger context in which this letter was written, see Michael
Finnegan, "Racially Charged GOP Feud Escalates," at *latimes.com*, January, 17, 2003. For the purposes of this essay, Ridgel's statement is separate and distinct from the controversy in which the letter was written.

2. Patricia Beard, *Growing Up Republican: Christie Whitman: The Politics of Character* (New York: HarperCollins, 1996); Ed Rollins, with Tom De-Frank, *Bare Knuckles and Back Rooms: My Life in American Politics* (New York: Broadway Books, 1996), pp. 40–41. Sheldon Buck came to my attention when I purchased some political memorabilia on eBay, from his son, Richard Buck. He let me see some of his father's papers that detailed his activities within the Michigan GOP. Through the courtesy of Richard Buck, I can cite these examples of his father's work as a loyal Republican on the local level: Carl A. Gerstacker to Sheldon Buck, March 6, 1952, "How You Can Help Eisenhower"; Sheldon S. Buck to Elford Cederberg, September 12, 1952; Henry Charles Barnes to "Fellow Republicans," June 15, 1955; Robert Richardson to Sheldon S. Buck, December 29, 1966; and Yvonne C. Ostrander to "Dear Fellow Republican," November 27, 1972; copies in author's possession.

3. Don E. Fehrenbacher, *Prelude to Greatness: Lincoln in the 1850s* (Stanford, Calif.: Stanford University Press, 1962), p. 74.

4. David Donald, *Lincoln* (New York: Simon & Schuster, 1995), p. 398.

5. *New York Tribune*, April 11, 1912.

6. Ann Coulter, *Treason: Liberal Treachery from the Cold War to the War on Terrorism* (New York: Crown Forum, 2003), is the most explicit statement of the Republican view that Democrats are opposed to American patriotism.

SUGGESTIONS FOR FURTHER READING

General Works

A full bibliography of the writing on the Republicans would be impossible to include in a single volume. The following titles are meant as a guide and also reflect my own preferences about which historians have the most to offer. Anyone who delves into these works will soon find leads to other authors that will provide further perspectives.

The general histories of the Republican Party are either written by partisans of the Grand Old Party or are somewhat dated in their coverage. John Calvin Batchelor, *"Ain't You Glad You Joined the Republicans?" A Short History of the GOP* (New York: Henry Holt, 1996) is anecdotal and lacks an organizing theme. Michael Zak, *Back to Basics for the Republican Party* (Chicago: Thiessen Printing, 2001) is critical of the party's current emphasis on social issues and evokes the reformist past of the early years of the Republicans. Robert Allen Rutland, *The Republicans: From Lincoln to Bush* (Columbia, Mo.: University of Missouri Press, 1966) is a brief, popular account. Matthew Rees, *From the Deck to the Sea: Blacks and the Republican Party* (Wakefield, Mass.: Longwood Academic, 1991) looks at the party's troubled history with African Americans. Melanie Susan Gustafson, *Women and the Republican Party, 1854–1924* (Urbana: University of Illinois Press, 2001) traces the role of women in the GOP during its formative years. George H. Mayer, *The Republican Party, 1854–1966* (New York: Oxford University Press, 1967) is an older study that contains much useful information. Beryl Frank, *The Pictorial History of the Republican Party* (Secaucus, N.J.: Castle Books, 1980) has images of the party's history.

Chapter 1: THE PARTY OF LINCOLN, 1854–1865

The literature on the foundation of the Republican Party and its first decade of existence is vast and controversial. Three excellent books provide a fine starting point: Eric Foner, *Free Soil, Free Labor, Free Men: The Ideology of the Republican Party Before the Civil War* (New York: Oxford University Press, 1970, 1995) offers an insightful survey of the party's ideology. Michael F. Holt, *The Political Crisis of the 1850s* (New York: W. W. Norton, 1978, 1983) is a thoughtful analytical narrative of the period in which the Republicans came into being. Holt is generally critical of the new party for its militant stand against slavery and the South. A similar conclusion is evident in William E. Gienapp, *The Origins of the Republican Party, 1852–1856* (New York: Oxford University Press, 1987). Gienapp's thorough research and mastery of the sources make his book a storehouse of information on Republican origins. Robert F. Engs and Randall M. Miller, eds., *The Birth of the Grand Old Party: The Republicans' First Generation* (Philadelphia: University of Pennsylvania Press, 2002) is a collection of essays that will bring the interested reader up to date on how historians view the GOP's early years.

For Abraham Lincoln and the Republicans in the Civil War, any selection must be arbitrary. Don E. Fehrenbacher, *Prelude to Greatness: Lincoln in the 1850s* (Stanford, Calif.: Stanford University Press, 1962) sheds much light on Lincoln's political style and his moral philosophy. Heather Cox Richardson, *The Greatest Nation of the Earth: Republican Economic Policies During the Civil War* (Cambridge, Mass.: Harvard University Press, 1997), is enlightening on the Republican willingness to use the power of government during the Civil War. David Herbert Donald, *Lincoln* (New York: Touchstone Books, 1995) is a good one-volume introduction to the immense complexities of Lincoln as president and war leader.

Chapter 2: REPUBLICANS AND RECONSTRUCTION, 1865–1877

Reconstruction is one of those areas where popular impressions about the Republicans and scholarly work on the party have seriously diverged. The notion lingers that the Republicans did too much to change the defeated South while historians now contend that the party did too little to help the freed slaves gain political and economic power. Eric Foner, *Reconstruction: America's Unfinished Revolution, 1863–1877* (New York: Harper & Row, 1988) is the indispensable starting place for understanding the debate. Foner's research is encyclopedic and his insights striking. Critical of Republican performance is Heather Cox Richardson, *The Death of Reconstruction: Race, Labor, and Politics in the Post–Civil War North, 1865–1901* (Cambridge, Mass.: Harvard University Press, 2001). Brooks D. Simpson, *The Reconstruction Presidents* (Lawrence: University Press of Kansas, 1998) gives the perspective from Washington on the political problems of this period of Republican history. An older study by Eric McKitrick, *Andrew Johnson and Reconstruction* (Chicago: University of Chicago Press, 1960) began the reappraisal of that president. Joel H. Silbey, *A Respectable Minority: The Democratic Party in the Civil War Era* (New York: W. W. Norton, 1977) is important for providing the partisan context in which the Republicans operated.

Chapter 3: Republicans in the Gilded Age, 1877–1893

The best book on the politics of the late nineteenth century remains H. Wayne Morgan, *From Hayes to McKinley: National Party Politics, 1877–1896* (Syracuse, N.Y.: Syracuse University Press, 1969). An excellent brief synthesis is Robert W. Cherny, *American Politics in the Gilded Age, 1868–1900* (Wheeling, Ill.: Harlan Davidson, 1997). Morton Keller, *Affairs of State: Public Life in Late Nineteenth-Century America* (Cambridge, Mass.: Harvard University Press, 1977) is thorough on the public issues. R. Hal Williams, *Years of Decision: American Politics in the 1890s* (Prospect Heights, Ill.: Waveland Press, 1978, 1993) is a lively narrative that puts the major parties in a persuasive context. Williams is writing what promises to be the definitive biography of James G. Blaine, the most important Republican of this period.

Chapter 4: McKinley to Roosevelt, 1893–1904

In *The Presidency of William McKinley* (Lawrence: University Press of Kansas, 1980) and *The Presidency of Theodore Roosevelt* (Lawrence: University Press of Kansas, 1991), I outline my interpretation of how these two presidents interacted with their party. H. Wayne Morgan, *William McKinley and His America* (Syracuse, N.Y.: Syracuse University Press, 1963) is a good interpretive biography of this important president. An updated version will be published soon. For Roosevelt, John Morton Blum, *The Republican Roosevelt* (Cambridge, Mass.: Harvard University Press, 1954) began the rethinking about Roosevelt as a politician. William H. Harbaugh, *The Life and Times of Theodore Roosevelt* (New York: Oxford University Press, 1975) is a good synthesis about Roosevelt as a politician. Edmund Morris, *The Rise of Theodore Roosevelt* (New York: Coward, McCann & Geoghegan, 1979) and *Theodore Rex* (New York: Random House, 2001) are stronger on Roosevelt's personality than on his role as a Republican. The same can be said for H. W. Brands, *TR: The Last Romantic* (New York: Basic Books, 1997), and Kathleen Dalton, *Theodore Roosevelt: A Strenuous Life* (New York: Alfred A. Knopf, 2002). Stacy A. Cordery, *Theodore Roosevelt: In the Vanguard of the Modern* (Belmont, Calif.: Thomson/Wadsworth, 2003) is a good brief introduction to Roosevelt.

Chapter 5: The Taft-Roosevelt Split, 1905–1912

For the Taft-Roosevelt split and its consequences, there is not as yet a thorough, well-researched treatment. Henry F. Pringle, *The Life and Times of William Howard Taft*, 2 vols. (New York: Farrar and Rinehart, 1939) is still the best book on this president. Lewis L. Gould, *Reform and Regulation: American Politics from Roosevelt to Wilson* (Prospect Heights, Ill.: Waveland Press, 1996) provides a narrative interpretation of these events. Francis L. Broderick, *Progressivism at Risk: Electing a President in 1912* (Westport, Conn.: Greenwood Press, 1989) discusses that crucial election. Elizabeth Sanders, *Roots of Reform: Farmers, Workers, and the American State, 1877–1917* (Chicago: University of Chicago Press, 1999) looks at this period of Republican legislative dominance from the perspective of those who were critical of the GOP's record. For Joseph G. Cannon, a key Republican player, see the essay by Scott William Rager in Roger H. Davidson et al., eds., *Masters of the House: Congressional Leaders over Two Centuries* (Boulder, Colo.: Westview Press, 1998), pp. 63–89. A good state study is Paul E. Isaac, *Tennessee Republicans in the Era of William McKinley, Theodore Roosevelt, and William Howard Taft: Factions, Leaders, and Patronage* (Lewiston, N.Y.: Eric Mellen Press, 1998).

Chapter 6: REPUBLICANS DURING THE WILSON YEARS, 1913–1921

For the period when Woodrow Wilson was president, the best examination of Republicans in Congress is Herbert F. Margulies, *Reconciliation and Revival: James R. Mann and the House Republicans in the Wilson Era* (Westport, Conn.: Greenwood Press, 1996). Henry Cabot Lodge's impact on the party's thinking about foreign policy is well analyzed in William C. Widenor, *Henry Cabot Lodge and the Search for an American Foreign Policy* (Berkeley: University of California Press, 1980). Richard B. Sherman, *The Republican Party and Black America: From McKinley to Hoover, 1896–1933* (Charlottesville: University Press of Virginia, 1973) examines the party's shifting attitude toward African Americans. John Milton Cooper, *Breaking the Heart of the World: Woodrow Wilson and the Fight for the League of Nations* (New York: Cambridge University Press, 2001) sheds much fresh light on this episode in a way that fairly assesses the role of both the Democrats and the Republicans.

Chapter 7: THE AGE OF REPUBLICAN DOMINANCE, 1921–1933

Warren G. Harding's brief presidency is examined in Eugene P. Trani and David L. Wilson, *The Presidency of Warren G. Harding* (Lawrence: University Press of Kansas, 1977). Many of the more sensational legends about Harding are debunked in Robert H. Ferrell, *The Strange Deaths of President Harding* (Columbia: University of Missouri Press, 1996). The book shows, for example, that Harding did not have an affair with Nan Britton.

Robert H. Ferrell, *The Presidency of Calvin Coolidge* (Lawrence: University Press of Kansas, 1998) is a thoughtful reexamination of Coolidge's performance in office. John Earl Haynes, ed., *Calvin Coolidge and the Coolidge Era* (Washington, D.C.: Library of Congress, 1998) has some revealing and informative essays about Coolidge's impact on the 1920s and the place of the Republicans in that period as well.

The life and career of Herbert Hoover has spawned a cottage industry of books about this important president, but efforts to complete a full modern biography have run up against the abundance of source material and the complexity of Hoover's record. Martin L. Fausold, *The Presidency of Herbert C. Hoover* (Lawrence: University Press of Kansas, 1985) is a good synthesis about Hoover in office. Important for revising the historical impression of Hoover are Joan Hoff-Wilson, *Herbert Hoover: Forgotten Progressive* (Boston: Little, Brown, 1975), and David Burner, *Herbert Hoover: The Public Life* (New York: Alfred A. Knopf, 1979).

Chapter 8: THE REPUBLICANS IN THE AGE OF THE NEW DEAL, 1933–1945

For the period of the New Deal, there are several interesting studies of the Republican response to the Democratic political resurgence. Clyde P. Weed, *The Nemesis of Reform: The Republican Party During the New Deal* (New York: Columbia University Press, 1994) is a good analysis that is focused more on the mid-1930s than its title suggests. Richard Norton Smith, *Thomas E. Dewey and His Times* (New York: Simon & Schuster, 1982) is one of the best biographies of any major Republican figure. Another outstanding life of a significant GOP leader is James T. Patterson, *Mr. Republican: A Biography of Robert A. Taft* (Boston: Houghton Mifflin, 1972). Donald Bruce Johnson, *The Republican Party and Wendell Willkie* (Urbana: University of Illinois Press, 1960) is an older account but one that contains much useful information.

Chapter 9: FROM "HAD ENOUGH?"
TO MODERN REPUBLICANISM, 1945–1961

For the 1940s and 1950s, the books by James T. Patterson on Robert Taft and Richard Norton Smith on Thomas E. Dewey remain relevant. The newer historical view of Dwight D. Eisenhower is advanced in Fred I. Greenstein, *The Hidden-Hand Presidency: Eisenhower as Leader* (Baltimore, Md.: Johns Hopkins Press, 1982, 1994) and developed for the presidential administration in Chester J. Pach, Jr., and Elmo Richardson, *The Presidency of Dwight D. Eisenhower* (Lawrence: University Press of Kansas, 1991).

The other central player for this period is Joseph R. McCarthy. A balanced, critical treatment is David M. Oshinsky, *A Conspiracy So Immense: The World of Joe McCarthy* (New York: Free Press, 1983). Arthur Herman, *Joseph McCarthy: Reexamining the Life and Legacy of America's Most Hated Senator* (New York: Free Press, 2000) seeks to rehabilitate McCarthy's reputation.

For Richard Nixon, a new sympathetic assessment is Irwin F. Gellman, *The Contender: Richard Nixon, The Congress Years, 1946–1952* (New York: Free Press, 1999). David W. Reinhard, *The Republican Right Since 1945* (Lexington: University Press of Kentucky, 1983) is illuminating on the ideological strains within the GOP.

Chapter 10: FROM GOLDWATER TO WATERGATE, 1961–1974

A surge of interest in the emergence of conservatism during the 1960s has produced a recent flurry of informative books on this period. For Barry Goldwater, Robert Alan Goldberg, *Barry Goldwater* (New Haven, Conn.: Yale University Press, 1995) is lively and comprehensive. Mary Brennan, *Turning Right in the Sixties: The Conservative Capture of the GOP* (Chapel Hill: University of North Carolina Press, 1995) is a brief, interesting account of the rise of conservatives within the party. Rick Perlstein, *Before the Storm: Barry Goldwater and the Unmaking of the American Consensus* (New York: Hill and Wang, 2001) is a richly detailed account of the 1964 campaign. The evolution of the Republicans after Goldwater's defeat remains a good subject for analysis. Byron C.

Hulsey, *Everett Dirksen and His Presidents: How a Senate Giant Shaped American Politics* (Lawrence: University Press of Kansas, 2000) is a model of congressional biography and a fascinating look at one of the most intriguing Republicans of this era.

For Richard Nixon, Lewis L. Gould, *1968: The Election That Changed America* (Chicago: Ivan Dee, 1993) considers how he won the presidency. Melvin Small, *The Presidency of Richard Nixon* (Lawrence: University Press of Kansas, 1999) is a perceptive, measured appraisal of Nixon's record in office. In the sea of Watergate titles, Stanley Kutler, *The Wars of Watergate: The Last Crisis of Richard Nixon* (New York: Alfred A. Knopf, 1990) is a good place to begin for the facts and historical significance of this scandal.

Chapter 11: REPUBLICANS IN THE REAGAN ERA, 1974–1988

John Robert Greene, *The Presidency of Gerald R. Ford* (Lawrence: University Press of Kansas, 1995) supplies a sound narrative of Ford's brief presidency. Steven F. Hayward, *The Age of Reagan: The Fall of the Old Liberal Order, 1964–1980* (Roseville, Calif.: Forum, 2001) seeks to do for Ronald Reagan what Arthur M. Schlesinger, Jr., did for Franklin D. Roosevelt in the 1950s. The literature on Ronald Reagan tends to be overly critical or adulatory. William E. Pemberton, *Exit with Honor: The Life and Presidency of Ronald Reagan* (Armonk, N.Y.: M. E. Sharpe, 1997) is balanced and incisive. Lou Cannon, *President Reagan: The Role of a Lifetime* (New York: Simon & Schuster, 1991) provides a storehouse of information about the presidency. Derek Leebaert, *The Fifty-Year Wound: The True Price of America's Cold War Victory* (Boston: Little, Brown, 2002) places Reagan at the center of American foreign policy during the 1980s. A brief, thorough narrative of the Republicans in this period is Michael Schaller and George Rising, *The Republican Ascendancy: American Politics, 1968–2001* (Wheeling, Ill.: Harlan Davidson, 2002) which contains a good bibliographical essay. An examination of Reagan's relations with the Republican Party is an important next step in the history of the GOP.

Chapter 12: BUSH TO GINGRICH TO BUSH, 1988–2000

For George H. W. Bush and his presidency, John R. Greene, *The Presidency of George Bush* (Lawrence: University Press of Kansas, 2000) is a good summary that will no doubt be modified as the papers of the elder Bush are opened. Herbert S. Parmet, *George Bush: The Life of a Lone Star Yankee* (New York: Scribner, 1997) is a biography based on access to Bush's papers and diaries. It has much information and many shrewd insights. Peter Goldman et al., *Quest for the Presidency, 1992* (College Station: Texas A&M University Press, 1994) is a large survey of that crucial presidential contest which is valuable as well for the documents from the Republican campaign that are included.

The Republican takeover of Congress during the 1990s under Newt Gingrich spawned an abundance of journalistic appraisals. Mel Steely, *The Gentleman from Georgia: The Biography of Newt Gingrich* (Macon, Ga.: Mercer University Press, 2000) is a friendly account by a former aide. More critical is

David Maraniss and Michael Weisskopf, *"Tell Newt to Shut Up!"* (New York: Simon & Schuster, 1996). Elizabeth Drew, *Showdown: The Struggle Between the Gingrich Congress and the Clinton White House* (New York: Simon & Schuster, 1996) is informative on the presidential-congressional confrontation. A balanced and fair-minded evaluation of the intellectuals who drove the GOP's agenda during the 1990s is Nina J. Easton, *Gang of Five: Leaders at the Center of the Conservative Ascendancy* (New York: Simon & Schuster, 2000). Robert Shogan, *War Without End: Cultural Conflict and the Struggle for America's Political Future* (Boulder, Colo.: Westview Press, 2002) looks at the contemporary cultural context in which the Republicans are operating. Sheldon Pollack, *Refinancing America: The Republican Antitax Agenda* (Albany: State University of New York Press, 2003) looks at the party's main policy goal of the last two decades. The election of 2000, the war on terrorism, and the Republican victory in the 2002 congressional elections are as yet too recent to have produced historical works of lasting value that can be recommended to those interested in the history of the Republican Party.

INDEX

Page numbers in *italics* refer to illustrations.

LEWIS L. GOULD is the Eugene C. Barker Centennial Professor Emeritus in American History at the University of Texas at Austin. A winner of awards for outstanding teaching and writing, he is the author of numerous works of political history. He lives with his wife in Austin, Texas.

ABOUT THE TYPE

This book was set in Baskerville, a typeface which was designed by John Baskerville, an amateur printer and typefounder, and cut for him by John Handy in 1750. The type became popular again when the Lanston Monotype Corporation of London revived the classic Roman face in 1923. The Mergenthaler Linotype Company in England and the United States cut a version of Baskerville in 1931, making it one of the most widely used typefaces today.